D1177559

A SOURCE BOOK FOR

MEDIÆVAL HISTORY

A SOURCE BOOK FOR
MEDIÆVAL HISTORY

SELECTED DOCUMENTS ILLUSTRATING
THE HISTORY OF EUROPE IN
THE MIDDLE AGE

BY

OLIVER J. THATCHER, Ph.D.

AND

EDGAR HOLMES McNEAL, Ph.D.

PROFESSOR OF EUROPEAN HISTORY IN THE OHIO STATE UNIVERSITY

CHARLES SCRIBNER'S SONS
NEW YORK   CHICAGO   BOSTON

PREFACE

THE use of original sources in the teaching of mediæval history is still hampered by the scarcity of material adapted to the needs of the student. This situation is sufficient excuse for the publication of a new book of translations of important mediæval documents, if such a book does more than reëdit old material—if it presents, along with the usual and familiar sources, documents not elsewhere translated or brings together documents not otherwise easily accessible. We believe the present work does that, and that it also makes the use of this material more practicable by giving fuller notes and explanations than has usually been attempted.

Our purpose in general has been to present material touching only what may be called the most important matters (persons, events, movements, institutions, and conditions) of the whole mediæval period. We have not tried to make a complete source-book for the period, but only to offer in usable form illustrative material which may be of service to both teacher and student in general or information courses. Each document is meant to illustrate or illumine one particular thing. While it may throw light on many other things, the teacher should be warned not to attempt to deduce from these few documents the whole history and life of the Middle Age.

We are fully aware that in the choice of documents we shall not please all. Many of the documents here given are clearly essential and must be found in such a book as we have tried to make. Concerning all such there can be no question. As to the others, there are hundreds of documents which would serve our purpose quite as well as those we have used, perhaps even better. In making our selections we have been guided by a great variety of considerations which it would be useless to enumerate. While another would have made a different selection, we believe that the documents which we present really illustrate the matter in question, and therefore will be found satisfactory. With this we shall be quite content. The necessity of selection has also led us to omit the political history of France and England. We felt that we could properly leave out English documents, because there are already several excellent collections of English sources, such as those of Lee, Colby, Adams, and Stephens, etc. In regard to France we were in doubt for some time, but the desire to keep the size of the book within certain limits at length prevailed. We hope, however, to atone for this omission by publishing soon a small collection of documents relating exclusively to France.

It will be observed that we have made use chiefly of documents, quoting from chronicles only when it seemed absolutely necessary. An exception to this general principle is found in section I, where a larger use of chronicles was rendered necessary by the lack of documentary sources for much of the period covered; but it is perhaps unnecessary to apologize for presenting selections from the important histories of Tacitus, Gregory, Einhard, and Widukind. In the matter of form (translation, omissions, arrangements, notes, etc.), we were guided by considerations of the purpose of the book. The style of most of the documents in the original is involved, obscure, bombastic, and repetitious. A faithful rendition into English would often be quite unintelligible. We have endeavored to make a clear and readable translation, but always to give the correct meaning. If we have failed in the latter it is not for want of constant effort. We have not hesitated to omit phrases and clauses, often of a parenthetical nature, the presence of which in the translation would only render the passage obscure and obstruct the thought. As a rule we have given the full text of the body of the document, but we have generally omitted the first and last paragraphs, the former containing usually titles and pious generalities, and the latter being composed of lists of witnesses, etc. We have given a sufficient number of the documents in full to illustrate these features of mediæval diplomatics. All but the most trivial omissions in the text (which are matters rather of form of translation) are indicated thus: . . . Insertions in the text to explain the meaning of phrases are inclosed in brackets [ ]. Quotations from the Bible are regularly given in the words of the Authorized Version, but where the Latin (taken from the Vulgate) differs in any essential manner, we have sometimes translated the passage literally.

Within each section the documents are arranged in chronological order, except in a few cases where the topical arrangement seemed necessary. We believe that the explanatory notes in the form of introductions and foot-notes will be found of service; they are by no means exhaustive, but are intended to explain the setting and importance of the document and the difficult or obscure passages it may contain. The reference to the work or the collection in which the original is found is given after the title of practically every document; the meaning of the references will be plain from the accompanying bibliography. The original of nearly all the documents is in Latin; some few are in Greek, Old French, or German, and in such cases the language of the original is indicated.

It is impossible, of course, to give explicit directions as to the use of the book, other than the very obvious methods of requiring the student to read and analyze the documents assigned in connection with the lesson in the text-book, and of making clear to him the relation of the document to the event. It may be possible also for the teacher to give the student some notion of the meaning of "historical method"; *e.g.*, the necessity of making allowance for the ignorance or the bias of the author in chronicles, or the way in which a knowledge of institutions is deduced from incidental references in documents. Suggestions of both sorts will be found in the introduction and notes. The teacher should insist on the use of such helps as are found in the book: notes, cross-references, glossary, etc. Groups of documents can be used to advantage in topical work: assigned topics worked up from authorities can be illustrated by documents selected from the book; *e.g.*, imperial elections, papal elections, the Normans in Sicily, history of the Austrian dominions, Germans and Slavs on the eastern frontier, relations of the emperors and the popes before the investiture strife, etc.

TABLE OF CONTENTS

CONTENTS   XI

CONTENTS xiii

CONTENTS

XV

CONTENTS

CONTENTS

CONTENTS

PAGE

A SOURCE BOOK FOR MEDIÆVAL HISTORY

I. THE GERMANS AND THE EMPIRE TO 1073

THE documents in this section are intended to illustrate the history of the Germans from the period before the migrations to the beginning of the struggle between the empire and the papacy, 1073. The historical development of this period resulted in the formation of the Holy Roman Empire, as the form of government for western Europe. The civilization of the Middle Age was in the main the result of the union of Roman and German elements. This union was brought about by the invasion of the Roman empire by the tribes of German blood that lay along and back of the frontier of the empire. It is important, therefore, to understand the character of the German race and institutions, which are illustrated by nos. 1 to 4. The leaders and organizers of the Germans after the settlement were the Franks, who under the Merovingian and Carolingian lines of rulers united the German tribes and bound them together in one great state. This movement is shown in nos. 5 to 14. In this development the life of Karl the Great (nos. 7 to 14) is of especial importance, because of the permanent result of much of his work, particularly his organization of the government (nos. 7 to 9), and his founding of the empire by the union of Italy and Germany (nos. 8, 13, and 14). The dissolution of his vast empire, resulting in the formation of France as a separate state, and in the appearance of the feudal states, is shown in nos. 15 to 22. In the rest of the documents the history of Germany and Italy, the real members of the empire, is followed. Of this the important features are: the continued connection of Germany with Italy (nos. 23 and 29), resulting in the restoration of the empire by Otto I; the feudal organization of Germany (nos. 24, 25, and 27); and the increase of the German territory toward the east (nos. 26, 28, 32). This brings the history down to the accession of Henry IV, with whom begins the long conflict between the empire and papacy which is treated in section III.

1. SELECTIONS FROM THE GERMANIA OF TACITUS, *ca.* 100 A.D.

The *Germania* of the Roman historian Tacitus (54-119 A.D.) is a treatise on the manners, customs, and institutions of the Germans of his time. It is one of the most valuable sources of knowledge of the condition of the Germans before the migrations. These sources are mainly of two kinds: the accounts of contemporary writers, chiefly Roman authors; and the documentary sources of the period of the tribal kingdoms, particularly the tribal laws, such as the laws of the Salic Franks (see no. 4), Burgundians, Anglo-Saxons, etc. It will be evident to the student that the sources of both kinds fall short of realizing the needs of historical trustworthiness: the first kind, because the Roman authors were describing institutions and customs which they knew only superficially or from a prejudiced point of view; the second, because the laws and documents of the tribal period reflect a stage of development which had changed considerably from the primitive stage. Conclusions in regard to the conditions of the Germans in the early period are based on the careful criticism of each single document and on a comparison of each with all the others. Some indication of this method is suggested in the notes to nos. 1 and 4. Even at best the results are subject to uncertainty. The *Germania* of Tacitus is the clearest and most complete of the sources of the first type, but it is not free from obscurity. Since there are numerous editions of it, we have not thought it necessary to refer to any particular one.

5. The land [inhabited by the Germans] varies somewhat in character from one part to another, but in general it is covered with forests and swamps, and is more rainy on the side toward Gaul and bleaker toward Noricum and Pannonia. It is moderately fertile, but not suited to the growing of fruit trees; it supports great numbers of cattle, of small size, however.

6. Iron is not abundant, as appears from the character of the weapons of the inhabitants; for they rarely use swords or the larger spears; instead they carry darts with

small, narrow heads, which they call *frameæ*. But these are so sharp and so easily handled that they are used in fighting equally well at a distance and at close quarters. . . . The number of warriors is definitely fixed, one hundred coming from each district, and the warriors are known by that name [*i.e.*, hundred]; so that what was originally a number has come to be a name and a title.[1]

7. Kings are chosen for their noble birth;[2] military leaders for their valor. But the authority of the king is not absolute, and the war-leaders command rather by example than by orders, winning the respect and the obedience of their troops by being always in the front of the battle. . . . These troops are not made up of bodies of men chosen indiscriminately, but are arranged by families and kindreds, which is an added incentive for bravery in battle. So, also, the cries of the women and the wailing of children, who are taken along to battle, encourage the men to resistance.

8. It is said that on more than one occasion broken and fleeing ranks have been turned back to the fight by the prayers of the women, who fear captivity above everything else. . . . They believe that women are specially gifted by the gods, and do not disdain to take council with them and heed their advice.

11. [In the assemblies of the tribe,] minor affairs are discussed by the chiefs, but the whole tribe decides questions of general importance. These things, however, are generally first discussed by the chiefs before being referred to the tribe. They meet, except in the case of a sudden emergency, at certain fixed times, at the new or the full moon, for they regard these as auspicious days for undertakings. They reckon the time by nights, instead of by days, as we do. . . . One evil result arising from their liberty is the fact that they never all come together at the time set, but consume two or three days in assembling. When the assembly

is ready, they sit down, all under arms. Silence is proclaimed by the priest, who has here the authority to enforce it. The king or the leader speaks first, and then others in order, as age, or rank, or reputation in war, or eloquence may give them the right. The speakers depend rather upon persuasion than upon commands. If the speech is displeasing to the multitude, they reject it with murmurs; if it is pleasing, they applaud by clashing their weapons together, which is the kind of applause most highly esteemed.[3]

12.   Criminals are also tried at these assemblies, and the sentence of death may be decreed. They have different kinds of punishments for different crimes; traitors and deserters are hanged on trees, cowards and base criminals are sunk in the swamps or bogs, under wicker hurdles.   .   .   .   There are penalties also for the lighter crimes, for which the offenders are fined in horses or cattle. Part of the fine goes to the king or the state, and part to the person injured or to his relatives. In this assembly they also choose leaders to administer the law in the districts and villages of the tribe, each of them being assigned a hundred companions from the tribe to act as counsellors and supporters.[4]

13.   They go armed all the time, but no one is permitted to wear arms until he has satisfied the tribe of his fitness to do so. Then, at the general assembly, the youth is given a shield and a sword by his chief or his father or one of his relatives. This is the token of manhood, as the receiving of the toga is with us. Youths are sometimes given the position of chiefs because of their noble rank or the merits of their ancestors; they are attached to more mature and experienced chiefs, and think it no shame to be ranked as companions. The companions have different ranks in the company, according to the opinion of the chief; there is a great rivalry among the companions for first place with the chief, as there is among the chiefs for the possession of the largest and bravest band of followers. It is a source of

dignity and of power to be surrounded by a large body of young warriors, who sustain the rank of the chief in peace and defend him in war. The fame of such a chief and his band is not confined to their own tribe, but is known among foreign peoples; they are sought out and honored with gifts in order to secure their alliance, for the reputation of such a band may decide a whole war.

14. In battle it is shameful for the chief to allow any one of his followers to excel him in courage, and for the followers not to equal their chief in deeds of valor. But the greatest shame of all, and one that renders a man forever infamous, is to return alive from the fight in which his chief has fallen. It is a sacred obligation of the followers to defend and protect their chief and add to his fame by their bravery, for the chief fights for victory and the companions for the chief. If their own tribe is at peace, young noble chiefs take part in the wars of other tribes, because they despise the peaceful life. Moreover, glory is to be gained only among perils, and a chief can maintain a band only by war, for the companions expect to receive their warhorse and arms from the leader, . . . and the means of liberality are best obtained from the booty of war.[5]

16. The Germans do not dwell in cities, and do not build their houses close together. They dwell apart and separate, where a spring or patch of level ground or a grove may attract them. Their villages are not built compactly, as ours are, but each house is surrounded by a clear space.

21. It is a matter of duty with them to take up the enmities of their parents or kinsmen, as well as the friendships, but these feuds are not irreconcilable; the slaying of a man may be atoned for by the payment of a fixed number of cattle, and the kindred of the slain man all share in the price of atonement. This practice of compounding manslaughter is of advantage to the public weal, for such feuds may become very dangerous among a free people.[6]

26. The arable lands, according to the number of cultivators, are occupied in turn by all the members of the community, and are divided among them according to the quality [of the lands].[7] The extent of the land gives ample opportunity for division; the arable fields are changed every year, and there is plenty of land left over.[8]

The following section is condensed from chapters 27 to 46.

27–46.[9] Such is the account I have received of the origin and the customs of the Germans as a whole; we must now undertake a discussion of the separate tribes. The divine Julius [Cæsar] says in his book that the Gauls had once been a more powerful and prosperous people than the Germans. So it is not impossible that they may have at some time even invaded Germany. For the Helvetians once dwelt in Germany between the Hercynian forest and the Rhine and Main rivers, while the Boii inhabited lands still farther within Germany, as is shown by the name Boihaem [Bohemia] which still clings to their former place, now inhabited by another people. The Treveri and the Nervii lay claim to German origin, as if to repudiate connection with the indolent Gauls. The inhabitants of the Rhine bank, the Vangiones, Treboci, and Nemetes, are undoubtedly of German blood; and the Ubii also, although they have become a Roman colony and have taken the name of Agrippenses from their founder. Of all the tribes along the lower Rhine the chief are the Batavi, who dwell mainly on an island in the mouth of the Rhine. They were a portion of the Chatti, but left their homes as the result of a domestic quarrel and entered the Roman empire. They still retain, however, their old honor and dignity as allies, not being subject to taxation or to any public duties except that of war. Beyond the Agri Decumates are the Chatti, whose territory borders on the Hercynian forest. Next to the Chatti, descending the Rhine, are the Usipii and Tencteri; their neighbors, it is said, were formerly the Bructeri, who have been driven out and their place taken by the Angrivarii and Chamavi. Back of the Angrivarii and the Chamavi [to the south] are the Dulgubnii and Chasuarii; in front [to the north] are the Frisii, who are divided into two parts, the greater and lesser Frisii. They dwell along the shores of the ocean north of the Rhine. Next are the Chauci, and on the boundaries of the Chauci and the Chatti [to the east], the Cherusci. The Cimbri dwell in the same region, on the shores of the ocean.

We come next to the Suebi. They are not a single tribe, as the Chauci or Tencteri, for example; they include a great many tribes, each one with its own name, but all called in common Suebi. The Semnones claim to be the most ancient and the noblest of the Suebi. They inhabit a hundred districts and consider themselves, because of their number, the most important tribe of the Suebi. On the other hand, the Lombards are known for the small number of their members, but they are secure from conquest by their more powerful neighbors by reason of their courage and their experience in war. Then come the Reudigni, Aviones, Angli, Warini, Eudoses, Suardones, and Nuitones. Then, following along the Danube, the Hermunduri; then the Naristi, Marcomanni, and Quadi. The Marcomanni drove the Boii out of their land, which they now inhabit. Back of these tribes lie the Marsigni, Cotini, Osi, and Buri. The Marsigni and the Buri have the same language and worship as the Suebi; but the fact that the Cotini speak a Gallic language and the Osi a Pannonian would indicate that they are not German tribes. A continuous mountain range divides Suebia in this region; beyond it lie many races, of whom the greatest is that of the Lugii, a name applied to several tribes, the Harii, Helveconæ, Manimi, Elisii, Nahanarvali. Beyond the Lugii are the Gutones. The tribes of the Suiones inhabit a land situated in the midst of the ocean [Scandinavia], and are famous for their fleets. Beyond the

Suiones is that dreary ocean which is believed to encircle the whole world. On the right [east] shore of the Suebian Sea [the Baltic] dwell the Aestii, a people that have the same customs and manners as the Suebi, but speak a language more like that of the inhabitants of Britain. The land of the Suiones is continued by that of the Sithones. This is the end of Suebia. I am uncertain whether to assign the Peucini, Veneti, and Fenni to the German or Sarmatian race, although the Peucini, called by some Bastarnæ, have the same language, worship, and sort of houses as the Germans.

[1] In the tribal laws and other documents of the tribal period a district called the "hundred" actually appears as the division of the county (see no. 4, introductory note). Tacitus uses the term here as a division of the tribe, but the original tribe in several instances appears as a county of the larger tribal kingdom, among the Franks and Anglo-Saxons, at least. The origin of the hundred as a territorial district suggested in this passage by Tacitus is probably the correct one: the whole tribe was divided for military purposes into companies of about one hundred men; then when the tribe settled on the land which had been conquered, the lands were distributed to the hundreds, and the districts thus formed came to bear that name.

[2] The existence of a noble class, i.e., a number of families having higher social rank and special consideration and privileges, is vouched for by all the sources. The origin of the class and the extent of the privileges which they enjoyed in this primitive time are uncertain. The king was chosen usually from one noble family, but not by strict heredity.

[3] The general assembly was composed of all the freemen of the tribe. All public business, that is, affairs in which the whole tribe was concerned, was conducted here, including the making of war and peace, the election of the king and chief officials, etc. It would appear from what Tacitus says that the assembly had jurisdiction in the graver offenses and in cases of appeal from the hundred-court.

[4] These leaders were probably the officials who presided over the hundred-court, the assembly of the freemen of the hundred, which was the regular court of justice. We find such an official mentioned

in several of the tribal laws; in the Salic and the Alamannian law
he is called the "centenarius," and in the Anglo-Saxon laws the
"hundredes-ealdor." The hundred companions of the official mentioned by Tacitus were probably the whole body of the freemen of
the hundred. They attended the hundred-court and had a share in
rendering the decision.

5 The chief with his band of followers is found in many primitive warlike societies. The various traditions of the German tribes
are full of references to this institution. Famous warriors would
gather about them a band of young men eager for reputation and
experience. These bands would form the élite of the army when
the whole tribe went to war, but would also conduct warlike enterprises on their own account. The viking raids of the Northmen
were instances of this practice. It not infrequently happened that
the success of private bands would lead the whole tribe to follow
and settle on the land which they had begun to conquer, as in the
traditional account of the conquest of Britain by the Angles and
Saxons.

6 The obligation of following up the blood-feud is a common
feature of primitive society. It forms the basis of many of the
popular tales and traditions of the German people. The law
attempted to make the kindred of the slain man give up the feud
in return for the payment of a fixed sum by the slayer of his kin,
but the attempt was not always successful. The sum paid is known
as the *wergeld* and is mentioned in all the tribal laws (see no. 4,
title XLI and note).

7 The form of land-holding among the early Germans has been
the subject of much study and investigation. Chapters 16 and 26
of Tacitus have been discussed and commented on at great length
by many scholars and no absolute agreement has been reached in
regard to the interpretation of them. The above translation is as
literal and untechnical as we could make it, but it is not free from
objection. It would seem to mean that the land of the tribe was
held by small groups or communities dwelling in little farming villages and cultivating the land assigned them. The land in the time
of Tacitus was probably owned in common by the community and
apportioned equally among the householders for the purpose of cultivation, and then redistributed at regular periods, once a year according to Tacitus.

8 In order to understand the conditions of German life as
described by Tacitus, the student would do well to pick out, bring
together, and classify all that he says in different places about the

important features of their life: (1) the king, his election, powers, etc.; (2) the assemblies, their composition, procedure, authority; (3) the officials; (4) manners and customs.

9 The chapters devoted to the enumeration and description of the separate tribes have been summarized, the purpose being to show the location and the names of the tribes in the time of Tacitus; the student should compare these with the situation as shown by a map of Europe at the time of the migrations. Note that very few of these names appear at the time of the migrations; this is because most of the tribes had lost their identity before that time, being united into larger groups, or absorbed by other peoples, as by the Huns, Romans, etc. Of the tribes mentioned before the Suebi, most were later united into the confederations of the Franks, Alamanni, and Saxons; thus the Chatti, Chamavi, Chasuarii, etc., are found among the Franks; the Tencteri, Usipii among the Alamanni; the Chauci, Cherusci, Angrivarii among the Saxons. The Frisii remained in the same region and were finally added to the Frankish kingdom by Karl Martel; their name still exists in the Friesland of modern Holland. The Ubii were settled by M. Agrippa on land near Cologne, the Roman town Colonia Agrippina. The Agri Decumates or "tithe lands" were the territory contained within the triangle formed by the upper Rhine, the upper Danube, and a line of fortifications, called the *Limes*. This advanced frontier was established by Trajan (98–117). The territory received its name from the fact that the colonists who settled there paid a tithe or tenth of the produce to the state as rent. Under the name Suebi, Tacitus classes a great many tribes, some of whom are not even of German race. The real nature of the Suevic Confederation is a matter of great uncertainty. Some of the tribes mentioned by Tacitus under this head appear later; the Semnones are conjectured to be the tribe later known as the Suevi, who joined the Vandals in their raid and remained in northern Spain until conquered by the West Goths; the Lombards remained a separate tribe and moved south into Pannonia and then into Italy; a portion of the Angli joined the Saxons in their invasion of England; the rest were apparently united with the Warini in the Thuringian kingdom, the principal tribe of which was the Hermunduri; the Marcomanni and the Quadi, perhaps with some other tribes, composed the later Bavarians; the Lugii, or Lygians, are mentioned by later Roman writers as among the Germans who threatened the Danube frontier, but the name disappeared after that; the Gutones are the Goths; the Suiones and Sithones are Scandinavian Germans; the Peucini are the same as the Bas-

tarnæ, who were given lands on the Danube by Emperor Probus (276–282); the Veneti are the Wends, a Slavic tribe; the Fenni, the modern Finns.

2. PROCOPIUS, VANDAL WAR. (GREEK.)

Procopius, in Corpus Scriptorum Historiæ Byzantinæ.

This and the following number are taken from the writings of Procopius, a Roman official and historian who lived about 500 to 560 A.D., and had a personal share in the wars of Justinian against the East Goths and Vandals. The earlier parts of his histories are drawn largely from tradition.

I, 2. During the reign of Honorius [395–423] in the west the barbarians began to overrun the empire. . . . The invaders were mainly of the Gothic race, the greatest and most important tribes being the East Goths, the Vandals, the West Goths, and the Gepidæ. . . . These tribes have different names, but in all other respects they resemble one another very closely; they all have light complexions, yellow hair, large bodies, and handsome faces; they obey the same laws and have the same religion, the Arian; and they all speak the same language, Gothic. I am of the opinion, therefore, that they were originally one people and have separated into tribes under different leaders. They formerly dwelt beyond the Danube; then the Gepidæ occupied the land about Sirmium on both sides of that river, where they still dwell.

The first to move were the West Goths. This tribe entered into an alliance with the Romans, but later, since such an alliance could not be permanent, they revolted under Alaric. Starting from Thrace, they made a raid through all of Europe, attacking both emperors.

[Alaric sacks Rome.] Soon after, Alaric died, and the West Goths, under Athaulf, passed on into Gaul.

3. Under the pressure of famine, the Vandals, who formerly dwelt on the shores of the Mæotic Gulf [Sea of Azof],

moved on toward the Rhine, attacking the Franks. With them went the Alani. . . . [Crossing the Rhine into Gaul] they proceeded down into Spain, the most western province of the Roman empire, and settled there under their king, Godegisel, Honorius having made an agreement with him by which the Vandals were to be allowed to settle in Spain on condition that they should not plunder the land.

At that time the greatest Roman generals were Boniface and Aëtius, who were political rivals. . . . Boniface sent secretly to Spain and made an agreement with Gunderich and Geiserich, the sons and successors of Godegisel, whereby they were to bring the Vandals into Africa, and the three were to divide the rule of Africa among themselves, mutually supporting one another in case of attacks from outside. Accordingly the Vandals crossed the strait at Gades and entered Africa, while the West Goths moved forward from Gaul into Spain after them. [Gunderich dies, leaving Geiserich sole ruler of the Vandals; Geiserich quarrels with Boniface and drives him out of Africa, ruling the whole territory with his Vandals.]

5. Geiserich now got together a large fleet and attacked Italy, capturing Rome and the palace of the emperor. The usurper Maximus was slain by the populace and his body torn to pieces. Geiserich took back to Carthage Eudoxia, the empress, and her two daughters, Eudocia and Placidia, carrying off also an immense booty in gold and silver. The imperial palace was plundered of all its treasures, as was also the temple of Jupiter Capitolinus, including a large part of the roof, which was made of bronze, heavily plated with gold. . . .

3. PROCOPIUS, GOTHIC WAR. (GREEK.)

Procopius, in Corpus Script. Hist. Byz.; Muratori, Scriptores, I, i, 247 f.

I, 1. While Zeno [474–491] was emperor in Byzantium, the west was ruled by Augustus, whom the Romans called

Augustulus, because of his youth. The actual government was in the hands of his father Orestes, a most able man. Some time before this, as a result of the reverses which they had suffered at the hands of Attila and Alaric, the Romans had taken the Sciri, Alani, and other German tribes into the empire as allies. The renown of Roman arms had long since vanished, and the barbarians were coming into Italy in ever-increasing numbers, where they were actual masters under the false name of allies (*federati*). They continually seized more and more power, until finally they demanded a third of all the lands of Italy. When Orestes refused to grant this they slew him. Then one of the imperial officers, Odovaker, also a barbarian, promised to secure this for them if they would recognize him as ruler. In spite of the power which he thus acquired, Odovaker did not attack the emperor [Romulus Augustulus], but only forced him to retire to private life. He then gave the barbarians the third of the lands which they had demanded, thus binding them more closely to him, and ruled over Italy unopposed for ten years.

About this time the East Goths, who had been allowed to settle in Thrace, rose against the emperor under their king, Theoderich. He had been brought up at Byzantium, where he had been given the rank of a patrician, and had even held the title of consul. The emperor Zeno, a master in diplomacy, persuaded Theoderich to invade Italy and attack Odovaker, with the chance of winning the whole west for himself and the East Goths. . . . Theoderich seized on this opportunity eagerly, and the whole tribe set out for Italy, taking along with them in wagons their women and children and all their movables. . . . Odovaker hastened with an army to oppose this invasion, but was defeated in several battles, and finally shut up in Ravenna. . . . After the siege had lasted for about three years both parties were willing to come to terms, the Goths being weary of the long siege and the soldiers of Odovaker being on the verge of starvation. So, through the efforts of the bishop of Ravenna, a treaty was made according to which Theoderich and Odovaker were to rule the city jointly. This treaty was kept for a short time, but finally Theoderich treacherously seized Odovaker at a banquet to which he had invited him, and had him put to death. He then won over to him all his enemies, and from that time on ruled over Goths and Italians unopposed. Theoderich never assumed the name or dignity of emperor, being content to be known as king, as the barbarians call their rulers. In fact, however, the subjects bore the same relation to him as to an emperor. He dispensed justice with a strong hand, and rigidly enforced the law and kept peace. In his time the land was protected from the attacks of neighboring barbarians, and his might and his wisdom were famous far and wide. He allowed his subjects neither to suffer nor to commit wrongs; his own followers were given only the lands which Odovaker had taken for his supporters. Thus Theoderich, although he bore the title of a tyrant, was in fact a righteous emperor. . . . He loved the Goths and the Italians equally, recognizing no difference between them, contrary as this may seem to human nature. . . . After a reign of thirty-seven years, he died lamented by all his people.

4. The Salic Law.

In the period before the migrations, each of the German tribes had its primitive code of laws. This law was not put in writing, but was held in memory; it was not based on abstract reasons of right and justice, but grew up out of practice and custom. The migrations and the development of tribal kingdoms on Roman soil brought about important changes in the public and private life of the Germans, partly the result of changed conditions, partly the direct influence of Roman manners and institutions. One result was that the old unwritten customary laws were codified and published in written form. These codes, called the *Leges Barbarorum*, or laws of the barbarians, form an important historical source, for of course they reflect the new conditions in which the Germans found themselves after their settlement. Some of them show the influence of Roman law and institutions in a marked degree; others are more purely Germaniç. They were in most cases written in Latin, although the Angles and Saxons in England published their early codes in Old English or Anglo-Saxon. One of the oldest and at the same time one of the most purely German in character is the law of the Salic Franks, called in Latin, *Lex Salica;* it was probably written about the year 500, in the reign of Chlodovech (481–511). In the most authentic form it contains sixty-five chapters, or "titles," most of which are composed of several sections. The title usually has a heading, as: XVII. *De vulneribus* (Concerning wounds).

The parts translated are intended to illustrate: (1) the character of the tribal laws in general, and (2) certain important institutions and customs of the Franks. Certain features of the Salic law are common to nearly all of the German laws; these are suggested here for the convenience of the reader.

1. The code contains mainly private law. Most of the law is taken up with a scale of fines and compensations for injury, damage, and theft, as in the case of injuries, titles XVII and XXII. This is characteristic of most of the German codes; they are concerned with private and not with public or administrative law.

2. The law makes minute specification of injuries. Note that the different injuries are carefully described and particular fines given for each, as in titles XVII and XXIX. This feature is found in most of the codes and is characteristic of a primitive stage of legal conception and a barbarous state of society. The important function of primitive law is the settlement of differences between individuals to prevent personal reprisals, so the various injuries that are apt to occur are specified and provided with special fines.

3. A large part of the procedure takes place out of court, and is conducted by the individuals concerned. So in title I, 3, the plaintiff summons the defendant in person; in title L, 2, the creditor tries to collect the amount fixed by the court; in title XLVII the whole process of tracing and recovering stolen property, except the last stage, is conducted out of court. This also is a common feature of Germanic law; the objection, common among uncivilized peoples, to the state's interference with private affairs of the individual operates here to restrict the function of the law to the simple decision of the case.

4. All the German laws provide for the payment of the *wergeld*. The origin of this is doubtless to be found in the underlying conception of primitive law referred to in paragraph 2. The purpose be-

ing to put an end to private revenge, which would mean continual private war, the law prescribes the amount to be paid to the kindred of the slain man, and they must on receipt of that give up the blood-feud. (See no. 1, ch. 21, and note.) In many of the codes different values are assigned to different classes of people, as here in title XLI.

The public institutions of the Franks are referred to in the law only incidentally, the law being concerned, as has been said, mainly with private matters, and taking for granted a knowledge of public law. Following is a brief statement of the form of government, administration of justice, etc. The state ruled by the king of the Salic Franks was composed of several small tribes, originally independent (see no. 1, notes 1 and 9), but now incorporated into a single state. The kingdom was divided into counties, some of which correspond to the former independent tribes, and some to old Roman political divisions. The county was governed by a representative of the king, an official who is called in the Salic law by the German title *grafio* (modern German "Graf"), and in later documents by the Latin title *comes* (count). The judicial system was based on the division of the county known as the hundred (see no. 1, note 1), the assembly of the freemen of the hundred being the regular public court. It was presided over by the "hundred-man," in the Salic law called either *centenarius*, which means simply hundred-man, or *thunginus*, a word of uncertain meaning. The function of the *grafio*, the representative of the king in the county, was mainly executive; he was appealed to only when every other means of forcing the delinquent to obey the law or the decision of the court had failed, but he has no part in the trial of cases. See title L, 3, for an instance of the function of the *grafio*.

I.   LEGAL SUMMONS.[1]

1. If anyone is summoned to the court and does not come, he shall pay 600 denarii, which make 15 solidi.[2]

3. When anyone summons another to court, he shall go with witnesses to the house of that person, and if he is not present the summoner shall serve notice on his wife or his family that he is legally summoned.

[1] This title illustrates what is said in the introduction about the process out of court. The person who has a cause for legal action against another, goes himself to the house of his antagonist

and summons him before witnesses. The law steps in, however, and forces the one who is summoned to come to court under penalty. See also title LVI.

2 The monetary system of the Salic law was taken from the Romans. The basis was the gold solidus of Constantine, $\frac{1}{72}$ of a pound of gold. The small coin was the silver denarius, forty of which made a solidus. This system was adopted as a monetary reform by Chlodovech, and the statement of the sum in terms of both coins is probably due to the newness of the system at the time of the appearance of the law.

XVII. Wounds.

1. If anyone is convicted of trying to kill another, even though he fails, he shall pay 2,500 denarii, which make 63 (62½) solidi.

2. If anyone is convicted of shooting a poisoned arrow at another, even though he misses him, he shall pay 2,500 denarii, which make 63 solidi.

3. If anyone wounds another in the head, so that the brain appears and the three bones which lie above the brain are uncovered, he shall pay 1,200 denarii, which make 30 solidi.

4. If anyone wounds another between the ribs or in the abdomen, so that the wound can be seen and extends to the vitals, he shall pay 1,200 denarii, which make 30 solidi, besides 5 solidi for the healing.

5. If anyone wounds another so that the blood falls to the ground, he shall pay 600 denarii, which make 15 solidi.

6. If a freeman strikes another freeman with a club, so that the blood does not flow, he shall pay 120 denarii, which make 3 solidi, for each blow, up to three.

7. If the blood does flow, he shall pay as much for each blow as if he had wounded him with a sword.

8. If anyone strikes another with the closed fist, he shall pay 360 denarii, which make 9 solidi; that is, 3 solidi for each blow up to three.

9. If anyone is convicted of trying to rob another on the highroad, even though he fails, he shall pay 2,500 denarii, which make 63 solidi.

XXIX. Injuries.

1. If anyone destroys the hand or the foot of another, or cuts out his eye, or cuts off his nose, he shall pay 4,000 denarii, which make 100 solidi.

2. If the injured hand hangs loose and useless, he shall pay 2,500 denarii, which make 63 (62½) solidi.

3. If anyone cuts off the thumb or the great toe of another, he shall pay 2,000 denarii, which make 50 solidi.

4. If the thumb or the toe hangs useless, he shall pay 1,200 denarii, which make 30 solidi.

5. If he cuts off the second finger, by which the bowstring is drawn, he shall pay 1,400 denarii, which make 35 solidi.

6. If he cuts off the rest of the fingers (that is, the other three) at one blow, he shall pay 50 solidi.

7. If he cuts off two of them, he shall pay 35 solidi.

8. If he cuts off one of them, he shall pay 30 solidi.

XLI. Manslaughter.[1]

1. If anyone is convicted of killing a free Frank or a barbarian living by the Salic law, he shall pay 8,000 denarii, which make 200 solidi.

2. If he has put the body in a well, or under water, or has covered it with branches or other things for the purpose of hiding it, he shall pay 24,000 denarii, which make 600 solidi.[2]

3. If anyone kills a man in the king's trust, or a free woman, he shall pay 24,000 denarii, which make 600 solidi.

4. If he kills a Roman who was a table-companion of the king, he shall pay 12,000 denarii, which make 300 solidi.

6. If the slain man was a Roman landowner, and not

a table-companion of the king, he who slew him shall pay 4,000 denarii, which make 100 solidi.

7.   If anyone kills a Roman *tributarius*, he shall pay 63 solidi.

1 The fine for slaying a man is the *wergeld* referred to in the introduction. It was paid to the kin of the slain man by the slayer or his kin. The *wergeld* has different values for different classes; note the classes in the Salic law, particularly the position of the persons in the royal service, the importance of which must have been of comparatively recent origin, and the position of the Roman population. The freeman of the Frankish tribe has a *wergeld* of 200 solidi, the free woman three times that, 600 solidi; the Roman *possessor*, or free landowner, 100 solidi; the Roman *tributarius*, who cultivated the land of another at a fixed rent, and was regarded as less than a freeman, 62½ solidi. If the freeman was in the king's trust, that is, in the service of the king and probably bound to him by a special oath (these men are also called *antrustiones;* see nos. 180 and 189), his *wergeld* was three times that of the ordinary freeman, 600 solidi; that of the Roman who was a table-companion of the king, a relation similar to that of the man in the king's trust, was also tripled, 300 solidi.

2 The fact of concealment is the distinguishing mark between murder and manslaughter.

XLV.   THE MAN WHO REMOVES FROM ONE VILLAGE TO ANOTHER.[1]

1.   If anyone desires to enter a village, with the consent of one or more of the inhabitants of that village, and a single one objects, he shall not be allowed to settle there.

3.   But if anyone settles in another village and remains there twelve months without any one of the inhabitants objecting, he shall be allowed to remain in peace like his neighbors.

1 This title throws some light on the original character of the village community. The village was in origin probably a group of kindred, and new-comers were admitted only by the consent of all the householders. Moreover, as much of the land was still held in common by the village—the wood, pasture, and meadow—the admission of a new member concerned all the householders.

XLVII. The Tracing of Stolen Goods.

If one has recognized a slave, or a horse, or an ox, or anything of his own in the possession of another, he is to "send him to the third hand." [1] And he in whose hands the thing was recognized is to swear [to his own innocence]; and if both parties [i.e., the rightful owner and the man in whose possession it was found] dwell on this side of the Loire and the Carbonaria,[2] a term of forty days shall be set within which all are to be summoned who have had any part in the affair, who have sold or exchanged or perhaps given in payment the article. That is, each one is to summon the man from whom he got it. And if anyone of these has been summoned and legal hindrance has not kept him away, and he does not come within the appointed term, then the one who had dealings with this delinquent is to bring three witnesses to the fact that he had summoned him and three more to the fact that he had obtained the property from him legally and in good faith; if he does this he is clear of suspicion of theft. But he who would not come and against whom the witnesses have borne testimony, shall be held to be the thief of the man who recognized his own, and he [the thief] shall return the price to the man who dealt with him and shall pay the lawful compensation to the man who recognized his own.[3] All these things are to be done in that court to which he is answerable in whose hands the stolen thing was first recognized and with whom the process started. But if he in whose hands it was recognized dwells beyond the Loire or the Carbonaria the time allowed shall be eighty days.

[1] The expression *mittat eum in tertia manu* has been interpreted in various ways; it means apparently either that the possessor is to place the article in question in the hands of a third disinterested party who is to hold it until the case has been tried, or that he is to refer the claimant to the "third party"; that is, the man from whom he obtained it.

2 A much-discussed phrase, which has been used to show that the Salic law belongs to a period after the Frankish control had extended beyond the Loire. The word in the text (*ligere*) has also been taken to mean the river Leye, but this is not generally accepted. The Carbonaria (German, *Kohlenwald*) was a large forest in what is now Belgium.

3 The form of statement is rather confusing, but the process is fairly clear. The burden of proof lies on the man in whose possession the stolen article is found, and he must clear himself by producing the man from whom he got it. This shifts the responsibility to the latter, who in turn must produce the man from whom he obtained it, and so on back until the person is reached who obtained the article illegally, and so is not likely to obey the summons to appear in court. Then the last man in the chain before the thief proves his innocence of bad faith by showing that he bought the article publicly and so obtained it in good faith, and that he had served notice on the delinquent in the present process. Inasmuch as legal sales were held publicly before witnesses, it is fairly certain in this way that the guilt will be located. The man in whose possession it was found then restores the article to its owner, and receives back the price he paid for it from the man from whom he got it; and this repayment is repeated in each case until the thief is reached; the man who dealt with him has a legal action for recovery of the price against the thief, while the owner has also an action for the recovery of damages.

L. The Given Pledge.

1. If a free man or a letus [1] has given pledge [that is, made a solemn promise at the court] to another, then he to whom the pledge was given shall go to the house of the other within forty nights,[2] or whatever period was set, with witnesses or with such as can estimate the price.[3] And if the delinquent will not redeem the pledge given, he shall be held liable for 15 solidi above the amount for which he had given pledge.

2. If still he will not pay, the complainant shall summon him to the *mallus*, and thus he shall proceed to have him constrained by law: "I ask thee, *thunginus*, to constrain by law this my debtor who has given me a pledge and is in my

debt." And he shall state how much the debt is. Then the *thunginus* shall say: "I constrain this man by law, in accordance with the Salic law." Then he to whom the pledge was given shall give notice that the delinquent can neither pay nor give pledge of payment to any other until he has fulfilled what he promised him [the creditor].[2] And straightway on that day before the sun sets he shall go with witnesses to the house of the debtor and ask him to pay the debt. If he will not, let the sun set upon him.[4] Then when the sun has set, 120 denarii, which make 3 solidi, are added to the amount owed. And this thing is to be done three times in three weeks, and if on the third summons he will not pay all this, then 360 denarii, which make 9 solidi, are to be added to the debt, that is, 3 solidi for every summons and setting of the sun.

The next two sections are now generally regarded as a later addition—*i.e.*, the first two are supposed to belong to an early period, while the last two belong to the period when the *grafio*, the royal representative, had acquired executive functions within the county. If this is so, then sections 3 and 4 have replaced certain older sections which must have completed the process described in sections 1 and 2; there must have been a further stage in which the delinquent was finally forced to pay, perhaps the process described in title LVI, by which a delinquent can be outlawed if he is still contumacious.

3. If anyone refuses to redeem his promise within the lawful term, then he to whom he gave the pledge shall go to the *grafio* of the county within which the debtor lives, and shall lay hold on the staff and say: "*Grafio*, this man has given pledge to me and I have given lawful notice of his indebtedness and have sued him before the *mallus* in accordance with the Salic law. I pledge myself and my fortune that you may safely and lawfully lay hands on his property." And he declares for what cause and to what amount the pledge had been given. Then the *grafio* shall take with him

seven suitable *rachinburgii*,[5] and go to the house of him who gave the pledge and say: "You, who are here present, pay this man of your own free will that for which you gave him pledge. Choose two men, whomsoever you will, who together with these *rachinburgii* shall assess from your goods the amount you ought to pay. And so shall you make good what you owe according to legal value." But if he, being present, will not heed, or if he is absent, then the *rachinburgii* shall take from his goods a value equal to the amount which he owes, and of that amount two parts shall go to him who brought suit, and the third part the *grafio* shall take for himself as *fredus*,[6] if the *fredus* for this case has not already been paid.

4. If the *grafio* has been appealed to and legal hindrance or his master's [the king's] business has not detained him, and he neither goes himself nor sends a representative, he shall be punished with death or he may redeem himself with his possessions.

[1] The term *letus* is used of a class of population whose position was between that of the free man and that of the slave; a similar class is found among nearly all the Germanic tribes. They were perhaps descendants of conquered peoples that had been incorporated into the tribe; they did not own land, but cultivated the land of others on terms of a fixed rental in produce and services. Thus while not free, their position was above that of the slaves, since they might acquire possessions and profits above the rent paid, while the earnings of the slave belonged in theory entirely to the master.

[2] The regular interval between the meetings of the hundred-court or *mallus*.

[3] The use of appraisers, referred to here and elsewhere, indicates that fines and debts were paid regularly in kind, and that money was still an unfamiliar convenience.

[4] That is, the delinquent is to be given the full legal day, and when that has passed with the setting of the sun, the penalty is incurred. It is interesting to notice the same feature in the law of the XII Tables, which was apparently merely the primitive tribal law of the early Romans reduced to written form. There, in the first table, the description of a public court process ends with the

sentence: "Sol occasus suprema tempestas esto"—sunset is to be the latest hour [of the legal day].

5 *Rachinburgii* is the name generally used in the law for the board of judges, seven in number, who are chosen at every hundred-court to render the judgment (see title LVI). Here, however, the term is used for appraisers who apparently are not connected with the *rachinburgii* of the hundred-court.

6 The *fredus* is that portion of the fine which goes to the state, apparently as compensation for executing the sentence. It furnished a part at once of the royal revenues and of the salary of the *grafio*, since half went to him and half to the royal treasury.

LII. PROPERTY THAT HAS BEEN LOANED.

If one has loaned anything of his goods to another, and that person will not restore it to him, he shall sue for it in this way: He shall go with witnesses to the house of him to whom he loaned his property and serve this notice on him: "Since you will not restore to me my goods which I have loaned to you, you may keep them until the following night, in accordance with the Salic law."[1] And if still he will not restore them, let the sun set on him.[2] If he still will not restore them, the owner is to give him a space of seven nights, and at the end of these seven nights he shall serve notice as before that he may keep them till the following night, in accordance with the Salic law. If then he will not restore them, at the end of another seven nights he is to go with witnesses again and ask him to pay what he owes. If he will not pay, let the sun set on him. But when the sun has set on him three times, for each time 120 denarii (which make 3 solidi) are to be added to the original amount of the debt. And if still he will neither pay nor give pledge of payment, he is to be held liable to him who loaned him the goods for 600 denarii (which make 15 solidi) above the original debt and above the 9 solidi which accrued through the three summons.

1 This is to give the man legal and public notice and to allow

him a full day's time in which to obey. The guilt is incurred, therefore, at sunset of the following day.

2 See title L, note 4.

LIV. THE SLAIN GRAFIO.

1. If anyone kills a *grafio* [1] he shall pay 24,000 denarii, which make 600 solidi.

2. If anyone kills a *sacebaro*, [2] or an *obgrafio* who is a king's slave, he shall pay 12,000 denarii, which make 300 solidi.

1 For the position of the *grafio*, see introduction. His *wergeld* is seen to be the same as that of the freeman in the king's service, and may indeed be regarded as a special instance of the general case of a man employed in the royal service.

2 The *sacebaro* and the *obgrafio* are apparently subordinate officials of the *grafio*. They were probably not infrequently unfree persons, as they are here.

LVI. HE WHO REFUSES TO COME TO COURT.

If anyone refuses to come to court or to do what the *rachinburgii* have commanded, that is, to give pledge for payment, or for the ordeal, or for anything which the law requires, then the complainant is to summon him to the presence of the king. And twelve witnesses, being sworn in turn by threes, shall say: [the first three] that they were present when the *rachinburgius* condemned him to undergo ordeal or to give pledge for payment, and that he had not obeyed. The second three are to swear that they were present on the day when the *rachinburgii* [again] condemned him to clear himself by ordeal or by paying the fine; that is, that, forty nights from the first day, the sun set on him in the *mallberg* [1] again, and that he would in no way obey the law. Then the complainant is to summon him before the king, in fourteen nights [after the last *mallus*], and three witnesses are to swear that they were present when he summoned him and the sun set on him. If he will not come, then these nine witnesses, having sworn, are to say what we have said above. Likewise, if he will not come [to the king's court] on that day, let the sun set on him, and there shall be three witnesses who were present when the sun set.[2] If the complainant has done all these things, and he who was summoned refuses to come to any court, the king shall put him outside of his protection [i.e., outlaw him]. Then the criminal and all his goods are liable. And whoever shall feed him or give him hospitality, even if it be his own wife, shall be held liable for 600 denarii, which make 15 solidi, until he shall have paid all that has been imposed on him.

[1] *Mallberg* or *malloberg* is the place where the *mallus* or public court is held, and is here used as equivalent to the court.

[2] The process described from the end of the first sentence to this point is supposed to have taken place before the summons to the king's court mentioned in that first sentence; this is shown by the statement that there are to be twelve witnesses at the king's court, these twelve witnesses appearing in the passage as follows: three each for the two public trials in the *mallus*, three for the summons to the king's court fourteen days after the second trial, and three for the first session of the king's court; these delays having been granted and the delinquent not appearing at the second session of the royal court, he is there finally outlawed.

5. SELECTIONS FROM THE HISTORY OF THE FRANKS, BY GREGORY OF TOURS.

M. G. S. S. 4to, rerum mer., I.

By the end of the fifth century, the Roman government in the west had practically come to an end and most of the territory was occupied by German tribes. The confederated tribes living along the middle and lower Rhine began to be called Franks about 200 A.D. For the next two centuries, the Roman garrisons had great difficulty in keeping them out of northern Gaul. With the weakening and final withdrawal of these garrisons in the beginning of the fifth century, the Franks spread over northern Gaul and by about 450 had occupied the land as far south as the river Somme. Under Chlodovech the confederated tribes, which still had their own kings, were united under his single rule, and the other inhabitants of Gaul —Romans, Alamanni, West Goths, and Burgundians—were absorbed or reduced to dependence. The work of Chlodovech was carried on by his sons and grandsons with the conquest of the Burgundians, Thuringians, Bavarians, etc. Then came the civil wars among the descendants of Chlodovech which prevented further advance until the rise of the house of Karl the Great.

There are few documents or chronicles for the history of the Franks during the fifth to the seventh centuries. The only connected account is that of Gregory, bishop of Tours from 573 to 594. His position made him one of the most influential men of his time and he was well acquainted with the contemporary events which he narrates. The earlier part of his work is, of course, less reliable, because he depended upon tradition.

II, 9. It is not known who was the first king of the Franks. . . . We read in the lists of consuls that Theodomer, king of the Franks, son of a certain Richemer, and his mother Ascyla were. slain by the sword. They say also that afterward Chlogio, a brave and illustrious man of that race, was king of the Franks and had his seat at Dispargum, on the boundary of the Thuringians. In the region [about Tours], as far south as the Loire, dwelt the Romans; beyond the Loire the Goths held sway, while the Burgundians, who followed the heresy of Arius, dwelt across the Rhône, on which is situated the city of Lyon. Chlogio sent spies to the city of Cambrai[1] to spy out the situation and report to him. Then he seized the city and dwelt there a short time, occupying the land as far as the Somme. Some assert that king Merovech, whose son was Childerich,[2] belonged to the line of Chlogio. . . .

27. After the death of Childerich his son Chlodovech ruled in his stead [481]. In the fifth year of his reign, Syagrius, son of Ægidius, was ruling in Soissons as king of the Romans,[3] where the said Ægidius had held sway. Now Chlodovech and his relative Ragnachar advanced against Syagrius and challenged him to battle; and the latter eagerly accepted the challenge. But in the course of the conflict Syagrius, seeing that his army was defeated, turned and fled

from the field, seeking safety with king Alaric at Toulouse.[4]
Then Chlodovech sent to Alaric, ordering him to surrender
Syagrius, on pain of being himself attacked; and Alaric,
fearing to incur the wrath of the Franks, as is the habit of
the Goths, gave over Syagrius bound to the messengers of
Chlodovech. Then Chlodovech had him thrown into prison,
and, after seizing his kingdom, had him secretly slain. . . .

28. Now Gundevech, of the line of the persecuting king,
Athanaric, was king of the Burgundians.[5] He had four
sons, Gundobad, Godegisel, Chilperic, and Godomar. Gundobad slew his brother Chilperic, and drowned Chilperic's
wife by tying a stone about her neck and throwing her into
the water. He also condemned Chilperic's two daughters to
exile; of these the older was Chrona, who became a nun,
and the younger was Chlothilde.. . . . Chlodovech sent an
embassy to Gundobad demanding the hand of Chlothilde in
marriage, and Gundobad, fearing to refuse him, surrendered
her to the messengers of Chlodovech, who bore her straightway to the king. . . .

30. The queen [Chlothilde] continually urged Chlodovech to abandon his idols and accept the true God. She was
not successful, however, until finally, when he was waging
war on the Alamanni,[6] he was compelled by necessity to
accept that which he had formerly refused. For in the
course of the battle, when the two armies were engaged in
fierce struggle, it happened that the army of Chlodovech was
on the verge of utter rout, and seeing this the king raised
his eyes to heaven, and cried: "Jesus Christ, thou whom
Chlothilde doth call the son of the living God, who dost
comfort those in travail and give victory to those that believe
in thee, I now devoutly beseech thy aid, and I promise if
thou dost give me victory over these mine enemies and if
I find thou hast the power which thy believers say thou
hast shown, that I will believe in thee and be baptized in
thy name. For I have called on my own gods and they have

failed to help me; therefore I believe they have no power, since they do not come to the aid of their worshippers. I call now upon thee; I desire to believe in thee, that I be not destroyed by mine enemies." And as soon as he had cried thus, the Alamanni turned and fled. And when they saw that their king was slain they surrendered to Chlodovech, saying: "Let not thy people perish further, we beseech thee, for we are thine."

31. . . . Then the king demanded that he should be the first to be baptized by the bishop. So the new Constantine advanced to the font, to be cleansed from the old leprosy of his sin, and from the sordid stains of his past life, in the water of baptism. As he approached the font, the saint of God addressed him in these fitting words: "Bow thy head, Sigambrian;[7] adore what thou hast burned, burn what thou hast adored." . . . Then the king having professed his belief in omnipotent God the Trinity, was baptized in the name of the Father, Son, and Holy Spirit, and was anointed with the holy oil with the sign of the cross of Christ. And more than 3,000 of his army were baptized also. . . .

32. The brothers Gundobad and Godegisel were at this time ruling the land about the Rhône and the Saône and the province of Marseilles. They, as well as their people, were Arian. And when war was on the point of breaking out between them, Godegisel, who had heard of the conquests of Chlodovech, sent to him secretly, saying: "If you will give me aid in overthrowing my brother, so that I may kill him in battle or drive him from the kingdom, I will pay you such yearly tribute as you shall demand." Chlodovech accepted the conditions gladly and promised to send aid to Godegisel whenever he should require it. At the time appointed, Chiodovech advanced with his army against Gundobad. When Gundobad, ignorant of the treachery of Godegisel, learned of the approach of Chlodovech, he sent to his brother, saying:

"Come to my aid, for the Franks are coming against me to seize my kingdom. Let us unite to withstand this enemy, lest if we remain divided, each of us should suffer the fate of the other nations." And Godegisel replied that he would bring his army to the aid of his brother. Thus the three armies advancing at the same time, came together at Dijon, and Godegisel and Chlodovech joined forces and defeated Gundobad. Gundobad, seeing the treachery of his brother, which he had not before suspected, turned and fled along the bank of the Rhône until he came to Avignon. . . .

35. Now when Alaric, king of the Goths, saw. that Chlodovech was conquering many nations, he sent to him and said: "If it please my brother, let us unite our interests under the protection of God." And Chlodovech, agreeing, came to him, and they met on an island in the Loire, near the town of Amboise in the vicinity of Tours. There they held a conference, and ate and drank together, and separated in peace, having exchanged vows of friendship. But already many of the Gauls [under Alaric] were greatly desirous of being under Frankish rule.

37. Then Chlodovech said to his followers: "It causes me great grief that these Arians [8] should hold a part of Gaul. Let us go with the aid of God and reduce them to subjection." And since this was pleasing to all his followers, he advanced with his army toward Poitiers. . . . . And Chlodovech came up with Alaric, king of the Goths, at Vouillé, about ten miles from Poitiers. . . . There the Goths fled, according to their custom, and Chlodovech gained a great victory with the aid of God. And Chloderic, the son of Sigibert the Lame, aided him in this battle.

40. Now while Chlodovech was staying at Paris, he sent secretly to the son of Sigibert, saying: "Behold now your father is old and lame. If he should die his kingdom would come to you and my friendship with it." So the son of Sigibert, impelled by his cupidity, planned to slay his father,

And when Sigibert set out from Cologne and crossed the Rhine to go through the Buchonian forest [in Hesse, near Fulda], his son had him slain by assassins while he was sleeping in his tent, in order that he might gain the kingdom for himself. But by the judgment of God he fell into the pit which he had digged for his father. He sent messengers to Chlodovech to announce the death of his father and to say: "My father is dead, and I have his treasures, and the kingdom as well. Now send messengers to me, that I may send to you whatever you would like from his hoard." Chlodovech replied: "I thank you for your kindness, and beg you merely to show my messengers all your possessions, after which you may keep them yourself." And when the messengers of Chlodovech came, the son of Sigibert showed them the treasures which his father had collected. And while they were looking at the various things, he said: "My father used to keep his gold coins in this little chest." And they said: "Put your hand down to the bottom, that you may show us everything." But when he stooped to do this, one of the messengers struck him on the head with his battle-axe, and thus he met the fate which he had visited upon his father. Now when Chlodovech heard that both Sigibert and his son were slain, he came to that place and called the people together and said to them: "Hear what has happened. While I was sailing on the Scheldt river, Chloderic, son of Sigibert, my relative, attacked his father, pretending that I had wished him to slay him. And so when his father fled through the Buchonian forest, the assassins of Chloderic set upon him and slew him. But while Chloderic was opening his father's treasure chest, some man unknown to me struck him down. I am in no way guilty of these things, for I could not shed the blood of my relatives, which is very wrong. But since these things have happened, if it seems best to you, I advise you to unite with me and come under my protection." And those who heard him applauded his speech, and, raising him on a shield, made him king over them. Thus Chlodovech gained the kingdom of Sigibert and his treasures and won over his subjects to his own rule. For God daily overwhelmed his enemies and increased his kingdom because he walked uprightly before him and did that which was pleasing in his sight.

41. Then Chlodovech turned against Chararic. For when he was waging war against Syagrius, this Chararic, although Chlodovech had asked him for aid, had kept out of the struggle and had given him no help, waiting to see the issue, that he might then make friends with the victor. On this account, Chlodovech was angry with him and attacked him. When he had succeeded in seizing Chararic and his son by treachery, he caused their heads to be shaved and ordered Chararic to be ordained a priest and his son a deacon. It is said that when Chararic was lamenting his humiliation, his son replied: " These twigs were cut from a green tree, which is not all dead; they will come out again rapidly when they begin to grow. Would that he who did this thing might as quickly perish." But when it was reported to Chlodovech that they planned to let their hair grow again and slay him, he ordered their heads to be cut off, and thus by their death acquired their realm and treasures and subjects.

42. . . . Then Chlodovech made war upon his relative, Ragnachar [king of the region about Cambrai]. And when Ragnachar saw that his army was defeated, he attempted to flee, but his own men seized him and his brother Richar and brought them bound before Chlodovech. Then Chlodovech said: "Why have you disgraced our family, by allowing yourself to be taken? It would have been better for you to have been slain." And raising his battle-axe he slew him. Then turning to the brother of Ragnachar, he said: " If you had aided your brother he would not have been taken;" and he slew him with the axe also. . . . Thus by their death Chlodovech took the kingdom and treasures. And

many other kings and relatives of his, who he feared might take his kingdom from him, were slain, and his kingdom was extended over all Gaul.[9] . . .

43. And after this he died at Paris and was buried in the basilica of the holy saints which he and his queen, Chlothilde, had built. He passed away in the fifth year after the battle of Vouillé, and all the days of his reign were thirty years.

III, 1. Now Chlodovech being dead, his four sons, Theodoric, Chlodomer, Childebert, and Chlothar, received his kingdom and divided it equally.[10] . . .

[Chlodomer was slain in an attack on the Burgundians, and his mother, Chlothilde, took his sons, Theodoald, Gunther, and Chlodoald, under her protection.]

18. But while Chlothar was staying at Paris, Childebert, perceiving that his mother Chlothilde loved the sons of Chlodomer greatly, was stirred with envy and with the fear that they might be restored to the kingdom of their dead father by aid of the queen-mother. So he sent secretly to his brother, king Chlothar, saying: "Our mother is keeping the sons of our dead brother Chlodomer, and intends to restore them to his kingdom; come now to Paris and advise with me as to what shall be done; whether their hair shall be cut off and they shall thus be made like the common people, or whether we shall slay them and divide the kingdom of our brother between us." Chlothar was delighted with these words and hastened to Paris. Now Childebert had caused the rumor to be spread among the people that the two kings were coming together to consider the establishing of the children on the throne of their father. And after they had met they sent word to the queen, who was dwelling in the same city, saying: " Send the children to us that we may place them on the throne." And she, rejoicing and thinking no evil, sent them the children. . . . But when the children had left her they were immediately seized and

separated from their servants and imprisoned by themselves. Then Childebert and Chlothar sent a certain Arcadius, their messenger, to the queen with a pair of shears and a naked sword. And when he came he showed both to the queen and said: " Your sons wish to know your will in regard to the boys; whether they should be shorn of their locks and live, or be slain." The queen, terrified and distracted at the message and especially at the sight of the shears and the sword, said in the bitterness of her heart and not knowing what she was saying: " If they are not to reign, I would rather see them dead than shorn of their locks." . . . And when the messenger brought back this reply, Chlothar immediately seized the oldest boy by the arm and throwing him on the floor slew him with his dagger. But when he shrieked, his young brother threw himself at the feet of Childebert and clinging to his knees cried: " Save me, dearest uncle, that I be not slain like my brother." And Childebert, the tears raining down his face, said to his brother: " Brother, I pray you grant me the life of the boy; I will give you anything you ask in exchange for his life, only do not slay him." But Chlothar, reviling him, said: " Cast him from you, or you shall die for him. You are the instigator of this business, and do you so soon repent?" At this Childebert cast the boy from him, and Chlothar thrust the dagger into his side and slew him as he had slain his brother. . . . Of the boys one was ten and the other seven years old. But the third boy, Chlodoald, escaped by the aid of certain powerful persons; rejecting a worldly kingdom, he turned to God, and became a priest, cutting off his hair with his own hands. And Childebert and Chlothar divided the kingdom of Chlodomer between them.

[After the death of his brothers, Chlothar united the whole Frankish kingdom under his single rule (558–61). He left four sons, Charibert, Gunthram, Chilperic, and Sigbert, who divided the kingdom among themselves.]

IV, 27. Now when Sigbert saw that his brothers had

taken wives of lowly rank, he sent an embassy to Spain and sought the hand of Brunhilda, daughter of king Athanagild [king of the West Goths]. . . .

28. When. Chilperic heard of this, although he already had several wives, he sought the hand of Galeswintha, sister of Brunhilda, promising that he would leave his other wives, if he should be given a wife of royal rank. Athanagild, believing the promise of Chilperic, sent him his daughter Galeswintha with rich gifts, as he had already sent Brunhilda. And when she came to king Chilperic, he received her with great honor and was married to her; and he loved her greatly, for she brought rich treasures with her. But great strife was caused by the love of Chilperic for Fredegonda, with whom he had formerly lived. Galeswintha complained to the king of the indignity offered to her and said that she had no honor in his house, and she begged him to keep the treasures which she had brought with her and let her depart alone to her own land. But the king attempted to placate her with soft and deceitful words. Finally he ordered her to be slain by a servant, and she was found dead in her bed. . . . And Chilperic, having mourned her death, after a few days married Fredegonda.[11]

1 Chlogio died in 457. The advance of the Franks to the Somme was made easy by the depopulation of the land through two centuries of border raids and by the withdrawal of the garrisons.

2 The tomb of Childerich, father of Chlodovech, was discovered at Tournai in 1653. In it were found along with the body, coins, a seal, remnants of a purple mantle, covered with the famous golden bees which Napoleon appropriated and wore, etc.

3 Ægidius and Syagrius, whom Gregory calls kings of the Romans, were probably Roman military commanders who still held out in Gaul in the name of the emperor. Syagrius held the territory between the Somme and the Loire.

4 Alaric II, king of the West Goths, 485–507. At this time the strength of the West Gothic kingdom was apparently in southern Gaul with the capital at Toulouse. After the defeat of Alaric and the acquisition by the Franks of most of the land north of the

Pyrenees, the kingdom of the West Goths was practically confined to Spain.

[5] The Burgundians were an East German people related to the Goths. They had moved south and west from near the Vistula and had settled on the Main and Rhine about Worms somewhere about 400. At the time of the invasion of Attila they fought with the Romans against him and suffered severely. They were then allowed by the Romans to settle just within the boundaries of the empire in modern Savoy. From here they later overran and occupied the valleys of the Rhône and Saône. Like all the German tribes except the Franks, the Burgundians had been converted to the Arian form of Christianity, which was regarded by the west as a heresy. Owing to the efforts of the popes and the catholic clergy some of the Burgundians had been converted to the orthodox faith, among them the princess Chlothilde, the wife of Chlodovech. Chlodovech's conversion to Catholic Christianity was of great assistance to him in his conquest of the heretical German kingdoms, since the sympathies of the Roman population were with him.

[6] The Alamanni were a confederation of tribes who had occupied the Agri Decumates (see no. 1, Tacitus, note 9) during the century 300–400, and had then spread over the Rhine into the territory of modern Elsass.

[7] Sigambrian—the Sigambri or Sycambri were one of the early tribes that made up the Frankish confederation. It is used here as synonymous with Frank.

[8] The hostility between the West Goths and the conquered Roman provincials, among whom they settled, was kept alive by religious differences. The dissatisfaction of the Roman population and their leaning to the Franks after the conversion of this tribe were of great aid to Chlodovech in his wars with the West Goths and Burgundians. The same religious differences explain also to some extent the failure of the East Goths and the Vandals to build permanent states in the territory which they occupied. On the other hand, the West Goths in Spain did later become Roman Catholics and enjoyed a longer existence.

[9] Chlodovech was originally king of only one of the numerous tribes of the Frankish confederation, but was the natural leader in war of the whole body. We have three kings mentioned by name by Gregory, Sigebert, Chararic, and Ragnachar, but he speaks also of "many other kings and relatives of Chlodovech." The result of these assassinations was the union of all the Franks under the rule of the house of Chlodovech.

10 The division of the kingdom of Chlodovech among his sons was fatal to the peace of the land and to the development of a permanent government. The strife broke out almost immediately, as appears from the account in ch. 18, and was continued in the later generations, among the sons and grandsons of Chlothar.

11 The murder of Galeswintha was the immediate occasion for the outbreak of the long civil war between the two queens, Fredegonda and Brunhilda, and their husbands and descendants. The incidents need not be followed; the war involved numerous murders and assassinations and resulted in the weakening of the monarchy, the rise of the mayors of the palace, and the independence of the outlying portions of the empire, such as Aquitaine, Bavaria, Alamannia, etc., under native rulers.

6. THE CORONATION OF PIPPIN, 751.

Einhard's Annals, M. G. SS. folio, I, pp. 137 f.

One of the most important results of the civil wars and weakening of the monarchy in the later Merovingian period was the rise to power of the mayor of the palace. The mayor of the palace was originally the chief servant of the king's household. As the king used his private servants in the administration of public affairs the chief servant became eventually the chief public official. In the eastern Frankish kingdom (Austrasia) this office, like many other offices in this period, had become hereditary in the hands of one of the great families. The last stage of the civil war (see no. 5, note 11) was fought out really between the mayors of the palaces of Austrasia and Neustria, and resulted in the permanent triumph of the Austrasian house. The actual power and the wise administration of the mayors of this house were in striking contrast to the weakness and the inefficiency of the last Merovingian kings, and this was the chief reason for the change in succession related in this passage. The appeal to the pope and his favorable report on the contemplated change, and the later attack upon the Lombards by Pippin at the pope's instance, are the first steps in the formation of a connection between the kings of the Franks and the popes.

Anno 749. Burchard, bishop of Würzburg, and Fulrad, priest and chaplain, were sent [by Pippin] to pope Zacharias to ask his advice in regard to the kings who were then ruling in France, who had the title of king but no real royal authority. The pope replied by these ambassadors that it would be better that he who actually had the power should be called king.

750 [751]. In this year Pippin was named king of the Franks with the sanction of the pope, and in the city of Soissons he was anointed with the holy oil by the hands of Boniface, archbishop and martyr of blessed memory, and was raised to the throne after the custom of the Franks. But Childerich, who had the name of king, was shorn of his locks and sent into a monastery.

753. . . . In this year pope Stephen came to Pippin at Kiersy, to urge him to defend the Roman church from the attacks of the Lombards.[1]

754. And after pope Stephen had received a promise from king Pippin that he would defend the Roman church, he anointed the king and his two sons, Karl and Karlmann, with the holy oil. And the pope remained that winter in France.

[1] For the papal account of this, see no. 44.

7. EINHARD'S LIFE OF KARL THE GREAT.

Einhard, Vita Karoli Magni; M. G. SS. folio, II, pp. 443 ff.

Einhard, who lived about 770 to 840, was a scholar, and a member of the court and the circle of Karl the Great. His biography of Karl is the most reliable and intimate account of the life and the character of the emperor that we possess.

3. After ruling as king of the Franks for fifteen years, Pippin died at Paris, leaving two sons to succeed him, Karl and Karlmann. . . . Karlmann, however, died after two years of joint rule, and Karl became king of all the Franks.

5. The first of his wars was that against the duke of Aquitaine,[1] which was begun but not completed by his father. Karl had asked his brother to aid him in this undertaking, but Karlmann had failed to send the help which he had promised. Karl, however, undertook the war alone and carried it through successfully. Hunold, who had tried to

recover the duchy of Aquitaine after the death of Waifer, was driven out of the province and forced to take refuge in Gascony. But Karl advanced across the Garonne, threatening Lupus, the duke of Gascony, with war unless he should surrender the fugitive. Thereupon Lupus not only gave up Hunold, but acknowledged the authority of Karl over his own duchy as well.

6. After the pacification of Aquitaine and the death of his brother, Karl made war on the Lombards in response to the prayer of Adrian, bishop of Rome. His father Pippin had also attacked the Lombards in the time of king Aistulf, at the request of pope Stephen, . . . but had been content with besieging Aistulf in Ticino and securing pledges that he would restore the places which he had taken and would never renew his attack upon Rome. Karl went further: he overthrew Desiderius, king of the Lombards, and drove his son Adalgisus out of Italy; restored to the Romans their possessions; defeated a new rising under Radegaisus, duke of Friuli; and subjugated all of Italy, making his son Pippin king.[2]

7. Then Karl returned to the attack which he had been making upon the Saxons [3] and which had been interrupted by the Lombard invasion. This was the longest and most severe of all his wars, for the Saxons, being barbarians and pagans like most of the tribes in Germany, were bound by the laws neither of humanity nor of religion. For a long time there had been continual disturbances along the border, since there was no natural barrier marking the boundary between the two races, except in a few places where there were heavier forests or mountains. So the Franks and the Saxons were accustomed to make almost daily raids on the territory of each other, burning, devastating, and slaying. Finally the Franks determined to put an end to this condition of affairs by conquering the Saxons. In this way that war was begun which was waged continually for thirty-three

years, and which was characterized by the most violent animosity on both sides, although the Saxons suffered the greater damage. The final conquest of the Saxons would have been accomplished sooner but for their treachery. It is hard to tell how often they broke faith; surrendering to the king and accepting his terms, giving hostages and promising to accept the Christian faith and abandon their idols, and then breaking out into revolt again. This happened in almost every year of that war, but the determination of the king could not be overcome by the difficulties of the undertaking nor by the treachery of the Saxons. He never allowed a revolt to go unpunished, but immediately led or sent an army into their territory to avenge it. Finally after all the warriors had been overthrown or forced to surrender to the king, he transplanted some ten thousand men with their wives and children, from their home on the Elbe, to Gaul and Germany, distributing them through these provinces. Thus they were brought to accept the terms of the king, agreeing to abandon their pagan faith and accept Christianity, and to be united to the Franks; and this war which had dragged on through so many years was brought to an end.

9. While this long war was going on, the king also made an expedition into Spain, leaving garrisons behind to hold the Saxons in check. Crossing the Pyrenees with a large army he conquered all the cities and fortresses in the region and returned safely with his whole army, except for those that were slain by the treachery of the Basques. For when the army was coming back through the passes of the Pyrenees, strung out in a long line of march because of the narrowness of the defiles, the Basques made a sudden attack upon the rear-guard, which was protecting the wagons and baggage of the army. The place was well suited to an ambuscade, being thickly wooded and very steep; the Basques suddenly rushed down from the heights where they had been hiding and fell upon the rear-guard and destroyed it to the

last man, seizing the baggage and escaping under cover of the approaching night. . . . In this attack were slain Eggihard, the king's seneschal, Anselm, count of the palace, and Hrotland, the warden of the marches of Brittany, along with many others. Up to the present time this attack has not been avenged, for the enemy dispersed so quickly that it was impossible to find them or to discover who were guilty.[4]

10. Karl also conquered the Bretons, a people dwelling in the remote western part of Gaul, along the shores of the ocean. . . . Then he again invaded Italy, this time marching through Rome to Capua, a city of Campania, and forcing the submission of Aragaisus, duke of Beneventum.

11. His next expedition was against Bavaria, which was soon reduced to subjection. This war was caused by the insubordination of duke Tassilo, whose wife, a daughter of Desiderius, urged him on to avenge the overthrow of her father. Tassilo made an alliance with the Huns, his neighbors, and prepared to attack the king. Karl, incensed at such presumption, immediately led an army in person to Bavaria, encamping on the river Lech, which separates Alamannia and Bavaria. Before invading the province he sent an embassy to the duke, who, seeing the hopelessness of attempting to oppose the king, immediately made his submission, offering hostages (among them his son Theodo) and swearing never again to revolt. Thus this war, which in the beginning threatened to be a serious affair, was brought to a rapid and successful conclusion.[5] But the king later summoned Tassilo to his presence and kept him a prisoner, not permitting him to return to his duchy; and from that time on the province was not ruled by a duke, but was divided into counties over which Karl placed counts of his own choosing.

12. This rebellion having been put down, the king next made an attack upon a tribe of the Slavs, whom we call the Wiltzi, in their own tongue, Welatabi. . . . The cause

of this war was the attacks which the Welatabi were making upon the Abodriti, who were formerly allies of the Franks, and their refusal to desist from these attacks at the command of the king. There is a great gulf [Baltic Sea] extending east from the western ocean [Atlantic], whose length is unknown, but whose width nowhere exceeds one hundréd miles, and is in many places narrower. Many tribes dwell along its shores: on the northern shore and in the islands, the Danes and the Swedes, whom we call Northmen; on the southern shore, the Slavs and the Aisti, and other tribes, among whom are these Welatabi. These latter were defeated in a single campaign and have never dared to revolt again.

13. The greatest of all the wars of Karl except the Saxon war, was that against the Avars and the Huns. . . . The king himself led one expedition against them into Pannonia, where they dwelt, but intrusted the later ones to his son Pippin and to the dukes and counts of the neighboring regions. The war lasted for eight years, and the bloody character of it is shown by the fact that to-day Pannonia is uninhabited and the site of the Khan's palace is a desert, containing no trace of former human habitation. The whole nobility of the Huns was destroyed in the course of this war, and all the treasure of the Avars carried away by the Franks.[6] . . .

14. . . . His last war was waged against the Danes or Northmen. Beginning with small piratical raids, they had grown so bold that they attacked the shores of Gaul and Germany with large fleets, and their king, Godfrid, planned the conquest of Germany itself. He already claimed the Frisians and Saxons as his subjects, and had subjected the Abodriti and made them tributary. He even boasted that he would shortly proceed to Aachen and attack Karl himself. And indeed there was real danger that he might undertake this, but he was slain by one of his own followers and the danger passed.

15. These are the wars waged by this mighty king during the forty-seven years of his reign. Through his conquests the kingdom of the Franks as he had received it from his father Pippin was almost doubled in area. When he came to the throne it included only a part of Gaul and of Germany; in Gaul, that part bounded by the ocean [Atlantic], the Rhine, the Loire, and the Balearic Sea [Mediterranean]; in Germany, that part bounded by the Rhine, the Danube, the land of the Saxons, and the Saale, . . . with the overlordship of Bavaria and Alamannia. Karl added by his wars Aquitaine and Gascony; the Pyrenees and the land south to the Ebro; . . . all of Italy as far south as lower Calabria; . . . Saxony, which forms a considerable part of Germany; . . . Pannonia and Dacia; Istria, Liburnia, and Dalmatia, except the maritime cities which were allied with the emperor of Constantinople; and, finally, all the barbarous tribes inhabiting Germany, between the Rhine, the Danube, the Vistula, and the ocean [Baltic], . . . of whom the most important are the Welatabi, the Sorabi, the Abodriti, and the Bohemians.

16. The glory of his reign was also greatly enhanced by his alliances and friendships with foreign kings and peoples. Thus Aldefonso, king of Gallicia and Asturia,[7] was his ally, and spoke of himself by letters and ambassadors as the man of Karl. The kings of the Scots also were wont to address him as master, calling themselves his subjects and servants, of which expressions there are evidences in letters still existing which they have written to him. He was also in close relations with Aaron [Haroun-al-Raschid],[8] king of the Persians, who ruled almost all of the east outside of India, and who always expressed the greatest friendship and admiration for Karl. On one occasion, when Karl sent an embassy with gifts for the holy sepulchre of our Lord and Saviour, he not only permitted them to fulfil their mission, but even made a present of that holy spot to Karl, to rule as his own. And

when the embassy of Karl returned, it was accompanied by ambassadors from Aaron, bearing presents of fine robes, spices, and other eastern treasures. A few years before he sent to Karl at his request an elephant which was the only one he at that time possessed. The emperors of Constantinople, Nicephorus, Michael, and Leo, were his friends and allies and sent many embassies to him. Even when they suspected him of desiring to seize their empire, because he took the title of emperor, they nevertheless entered into alliance with him, to avoid a rupture.

25. He was very eloquent and could express himself clearly on any subject. He spoke foreign languages besides his own tongue, and was so proficient in Latin that he used it as easily as his own language. Greek he could understand better than he could speak. . . . He was devoted to the study of the liberal arts and was a munificent patron of learned men. Grammar he learned from Peter, an aged deacon of Pisa; in the other studies his chief instructor was Alcuin, a Saxon from England, also a deacon, and the most learned man of his time. With him he studied rhetoric, dialectic, and especially astronomy. . . . He tried also to learn to write, keeping tablets under the pillow of his couch to practise on in his leisure hours. But he never succeeded very well, because he began too late in life.[9]

28. His last visit to Rome was made because the Romans had attacked and injured pope Leo, tearing out his eyes and tongue, and had thus forced the pope to call on the king for aid. And having come to Rome to restore the church which had greatly suffered during the strife, he remained there all winter. It was during this time that he received the title of emperor and Augustus, to which he was at first so averse, that he was wont to say that he would never have entered the church on that day, although it was a great feast day [Christmas], if he had foreseen the plan of the pope. But his great patience and magnanimity finally overcame

the envy and hatred of the Roman emperors [of the east],
who were indignant at his receiving the title. This he did
by sending them frequent embassies and addressing them in
his letters as brothers.[10]

29. After he became emperor he undertook a revision of
the laws of his empire, which were very defective, for the
Franks had two laws [Salic and Ripuarian] differing in
many points from one another. But he was never able to do
more than to complete the various laws with a few additional
sections and cause all the unwritten laws to be put into writing. He also wrote down for preservation the ancient German
songs, in which the wars and adventures of old heroes are
celebrated. He began also to make a grammar of his native
tongue. . . .

30. . . . While he was spending the winter in Aachen,
he was taken with a severe fever, which the Greeks call pleu-
risy, and died there on Tuesday, the fifth of the Kalends of
February [January 28], in the seventy-second year of his
age and the forty-seventh of his reign.

31. On the same day his body was prepared for burial
and borne to the church of the Virgin Mary, which he had
founded, in the midst of the lamentation of all his people,
and there laid to rest. Over his tomb was erected an arch,
covered with gold, and having his image and this inscription
on it: " Under this tomb lies the body of Karl, the great
and orthodox emperor, who greatly increased the kingdom
of the Franks and ruled gloriously for forty-seven years.
He died when over seventy years of age, in the year of our
Lord 814, the 7th indiction, on the fifth of the Kalends
of February."

---

[1] In the late Merovingian period the outlying parts of the kingdom had become practically independent under native rulers, called
dukes. One of the first things undertaken by the rulers of the new
line was the reduction of these great provinces to subjection as a
necessary step in the restoration of the central authority. Much

was accomplished in this direction by the mayors, Pippin the Younger (688–714) and Karl Martel (714–741), who attacked the Frisians, the dukes of Aquitaine, Bavaria, and Alamannia. But the work had to be done over and over, and indeed was never permanently accomplished. In Aquitaine Pippin the Short, king from 751 to 768, had several conflicts with the dukes of Aquitaine, Hunold and his son Waifer. This is the struggle which Karl brought to an end as here related.

2 Pippin had begun his war upon the Lombards for the purpose of freeing the papal domains from their attacks. The Lombards had conceived the ambitious plan of possessing all Italy, and under their kings Liutprand, Aistulf, and Desiderius had begun to carry it out by attacking the exarchate of Ravenna and the lands held by the pope. Pippin had forced Aistulf to give up his conquests (chiefly the exarchate) and had given that territory to the pope (see no. 45). Karl was called into Italy to defend the pope against a new attack by Desiderius, and put a definite end to this danger by conquering the Lombard kingdom and adding it to his own rule. This is a further stage in the connection between the popes and the emperor, between Germany and Italy.

3 The war against the Saxons and their conquest practically completed the unification of the German tribes on the continent, there remaining outside of the empire of Karl only the Scandinavian peoples in the north and the Angles and Saxons in England. By the conquest of the Saxons a vigorous race of pure German blood was added to the empire; their addition tended to increase the differences between the German and the Gallic portions of the empire, which was the natural basis of the division between France and Germany. The Saxons in the tenth and eleventh centuries were perhaps the chief race of the German kingdom, furnishing the rulers from the accession of Henry I in 919 to the death of Henry II in 1024. Karl's insistence upon the conversion of the Saxons to Christianity is in line with the policy of his predecessors to Christianize all the Germans.

4 The chief interest of this passage lies in the fact that it is the historical basis of the great French epic, the *Chanson de Roland*. Einhard mentions the death of three men in this attack as of special note; one of them was Hrotland, count of the mark of Brittany, the Roland of the poem.

5 The overthrow of Tassilo, duke of Bavaria, is a part of the policy of Karl to reduce the great duchies to control. In order to keep these outlying provinces in subjection and to govern them efficiently Karl divided them into counties over which he placed officials de-

pendent directly upon himself and not upon a duke. This policy was carried out in Alamannia, Aquitaine, and Saxony as well, the purpose being to prevent the formation of independent power in the large divisions of the empire. It was successful under Karl, but later the civil wars among his descendants gave opportunity for the rise of similar great rulers in the same provinces (see nos. 24 and 25).

6 The Avars had come into Europe in the middle of the sixth century, along the Danube. After the Lombards moved into Italy the Avars occupied the whole Danube valley from Vienna to the mouth of the river. The kingdom of the Khan of the Avars probably included the remnants of the Hunnish empire and of the German tribes that had been subject to the Huns.

7 The kingdom of Gallicia and Asturia was one of the small Christian states in Spain composed of the former inhabitants that had retreated in large numbers to the mountains in the north and west at the time of the Mohammedan invasion (711–720). From these regions they later slowly won back the land from the Mohammedans.

8 Haroun-al-Raschid was Caliph of the Mohammedan world from 786–809, with his capital at Bagdad. His caliphate is the golden age of the Mohammedans reflected in the "Arabian Nights." The connection of Karl with Haroun and especially the negotiations mentioned here in regard to Jerusalem gave rise to the later legends concerning the crusades of Karl.

9 The reign of Karl is sometimes spoken of as the Carolingian Renaissance, because of the revived interest in letters and learning that took its impulse from the court of Karl. Here was the famous "palace school" that included such persons as Alcuin, Angilbert, Einhard, Peter of Pisa, Paul the Lombard, etc. The results of the movement were seen in the writings of the time: Einhard's Annals and Vita; the History of the Lombards, by Paul; the poems and letters of Angilbert, etc.; in the formation of the monastery and cathedral schools, and the better learning of the monks and clergy; in the attempts of Karl to revise the texts of the Scriptures and to make new text-books; and in the theological discussions of the ninth century. Evidences of this movement are seen also in some of the letters of Karl that are translated below.

10 See the note on the coronation of Karl, no. 8. The statement of Einhard that Karl was displeased at this action of the pope has caused considerable discussion; the reason probably was that he was unwilling to arouse the ill-will of the eastern emperors, who

would undoubtedly regard the assumption of the imperial crown by Karl as an infringement of their authority and position. See also nos. 13 and 14.

8. The Imperial Coronation of Karl the Great, 800.

Duchesne, Liber Pontificalis, II, 7.

Since 476 there had been no emperor in the west, and the emperor at Constantinople had lost control of that part of the Roman empire. The west, however, still regarded itself as a part of the one great empire. The coronation of Karl the Great in 800 is the famous *translatio imperii*, the transfer of the empire, by which according to the papal theory the crown of the Roman empire was taken by the pope from the emperors at Constantinople, and conferred upon the king of the Franks. From this point of view it was the final act in the rebellion of the popes from the control of the emperors of the east. From the point of view of Frankish history, it was the culmination of the connection between the popes and the king of the Franks begun with the coronation of Pippin (see no. 6 and note).

After this, on Christmas day, all gathered together in the aforesaid church of St. Peter and the venerable pope crowned Karl with his own hands with a magnificent crown. Then all the Romans, inspired by God and by St. Peter, keeper of the keys of heaven, and recognizing the value of Karl's protection and the love which he bore the holy Roman church and the pope, shouted in a loud voice: " Long life and victory to Karl, the pious Augustus crowned of God, the great and peace-bringing emperor." The people, calling on the names of all the saints, shouted this three times, before the holy confession of St. Peter, and thus he was made emperor of the Romans by all. Then the pope anointed Karl and his son with the holy oil.

9. General Capitulary about the Missi, 802.

M. G. LL. 4to, II, 1, no. 33; Altmann und Bernheim, no. 2.

The attempts of Karl to create a permanent central government are reflected in the great amount of legislation which has come down to us from his reign. This legislation is mainly in the form of capitularies, *i.e.*, edicts or instructions, covering a wide range of subjects and interests. The general capitulary of the year 802, a portion of which is translated here, was issued by Karl after his imperial coronation and his return from Italy. It embodied a great number of instructions to his officials and subjects in regard to their relation to him in his new capacity as emperor. The publication and the enforcement of these instructions were intrusted to the *missi*, who appear now for the first time as regular officials of the empire. These officials were chosen from the counsellors, officials, and great men of the court, both ecclesiastic and secular, and were assigned to definite districts, two *missi* to each district. The districts were large administrative divisions of the empire including many counties (the regular divisions), and the two *missi* were to travel through the district assigned to them, looking into the general condition of the people, the administration of local officials, the condition of the royal lands, etc. They held four public courts a year in their district, at which they heard complaints, tried cases, etc. They had authority to control the regular officials and to depose them if necessary. They were supposed to report to the emperor the condition of the empire and to refer to him such cases as they were not able to decide. By means of these officials Karl kept in closer touch with, and maintained a firmer hold upon, the various parts of his empire than was possible merely by his own oversight over the counts, and at the same time avoided the other danger of creating independent rulers in the large districts, by changing the *missi* every year.

1. Concerning the representatives sent out by the emperor. The most serene and Christian emperor, Karl, chose certain of the ablest and wises men among his nobles, archbishops, bishops, abbots, and pious laymen, and sent them out through his realm, and through these, his representatives, he gave his people rules to guide them in living justly. He ordered these men to investigate and to report to him any inequality or injustice that might appear in the law as then constituted, that he might undertake its correction. He ordered that no one should dare to change the prescribed law by any trickery or fraud, or to pervert the course of justice for his own ends, as many were wont to do, or to deal unjustly with the churches of God, with the poor or

the widows and orphans, or with any Christian man. But he commanded all men to live righteously according to the precepts of God, and to remain each in his own station and calling; the regular clergy to observe the rules of monastic life without thought of gain, nuns to keep diligent watch over their lives, laymen to keep the law justly without fraud, and all, finally, to live together in perfect peace and charity. And he ordered his *missi*, as they desired to win the favor of Almighty God and keep the faith which they had promised him, to inquire diligently into every case where any man complained that he had been dealt with unjustly by anyone, and in the fear of God to render justice to all, to the holy churches of God, to the poor, to widows and orphans, and to the whole people. And if any case arises which they can not correct and bring to justice with the aid of the local counts, they are to make a clear report of it to the emperor. They are not to be hindered in the doing of justice by the flattery or bribery of anyone, by their partiality for their own friends, or by the fear of powerful men.

2. The oath of fidelity to the emperor. He has also commanded that every man in his kingdom, clergyman or layman, who has already taken the oath of fidelity to him as king, shall now renew it to him as emperor; and that all persons over twelve years of age who have not yet taken the oath shall do so now. The nature and extent of the promise should be made known to all, for it includes not only, as some think, a promise of fidelity to the emperor for this life, and an engagement not to bring any enemy into the kingdom nor to take part in or conceal any infidelity to him, but includes all the following:

3. First, that each one shall strive with all his mind and strength on his own account to serve God according to the commandments and according to his own promise, for the emperor is not able to give the necessary care and oversight to all his people.

4. Second, that no one shall ever wrongfully claim, take, or conceal anything that belongs to the emperor, such as lands or slaves, by perjury or fraud, or through partiality or bribery; and that no one shall take or conceal fugitive serfs from the royal lands, by perjury or fraud. . . .

5. That no one shall do any violence or harm to the holy churches of God, to widows and orphans, or to strangers; for the emperor, after God and his saints, is constituted their special protector. . . .

10. SELECTIONS FROM THE MONK OF ST. GALL.

Monachus Sangallensis, M. G. SS. folio, II, pp. 731 ff.

The following documents, nos. 10–12, are intended to illustrate the interest and activity of Karl in the revival of learning in his realm. See also no. 7, Einhard's Life of Karl, ch. 25. The disappearance of classical culture in the west through the disorders incident upon the decline of the Roman empire, the migrations, and the civil wars of the Merovingian period, was shown not only in the general ignorance among the common people, but also in the decline of learning and culture in the church. The selection from the Monk of St. Gall throws light upon the palace school of Karl and his court, the other numbers illustrate the interest of Karl in the education of the clergy and the reformation of the church services. The Monk of St. Gall is the unknown author of a chronicle account of the life and times of Karl, written in the latter part of the ninth century. It contains many tales and stories which are popular and in part legendary, showing how the figure of Karl was being magnified in the imagination of posterity.

I, 2. When Albinus (Alcuin), who was an Englishman, learned of the great favor with which Karl received wise men, he took ship and came over to him. This man was the most learned of all men of recent times in the holy writ, being the pupil of the learned priest Beda, who was the greatest commentator on the scriptures since St. Gregory [I]. Karl kept him at his side continually until his death, save for occasions when the emperor was at war. The emperor was always desirous of being known as the pupil of

Alcuin. He also gave him the monastery of Tours to serve
as a source of revenue during his own absence and as a place
where Alcuin might live and instruct the scholars who sought
him. His teaching bore such fruit among the Gauls and
Franks that they approached the ancient Romans and Athe-
nians in learning.

3. Now when the most victorious Karl after a long absence returned to Gaul he ordered the boys whom he had
intrusted to Clement to come to him and show him their
letters and verses. And the youths of lowly birth showed
him writings adorned with all the graces of learning, beyond
what had been expected, but the youths of noble rank presented trivial and worthless specimens. Then the wise
Karl, imitating the justice of the eternal judge, separated
the youths into two divisions and placed those who had done
well on his right hand and addressed them thus: " Receive
my thanks, children, for you have been zealous in obeying
my orders and in improving yourselves. Strive now to perfect yourselves, and I will give you the best bishoprics and
monasteries, and will ever hold you in my favor." Then
turning a severe countenance upon those on his left hand,
and striking terror into their hearts with his piercing eye,
he hurled these ironical words at them in a voice of thun-
der: " You nobles, you sons of prominent men, you delicate
and handsome youths! Relying on your birth and wealth,
and caring nothing for our commands or for your own improvement, you have neglected the study of letters, and have
indulged yourselves in pleasures and idleness and empty
games." Then, lifting up his august head and raising his
unconquered right hand to heaven, he thundered forth at them
with his usual oath: "By the King of heaven, I care little
for your noble birth and your beauty, though others may
admire you for them; know this, that unless you straightway
make up for your former negligence by earnest study, you
need never expect any favor from the hand of Karl."

28. Such peace as the mighty emperor Karl was able to secure, he was not content to spend in idleness, but devoted it to the service of God. Thus he undertook to build, in Germany, a church after his own plan, which should surpass the ancient buildings of the Romans. . . . The oversight he intrusted to a certain abbot, not knowing his cunning. But whenever the emperor was absent, the abbot would allow some of the laborers to purchase their release for money, but those who were unable to pay for this, or who were not permitted to leave by their masters, he oppressed with continual tasks, as the Egyptians once oppressed the people of God, so that they had scarcely any rest. By this means he gathered together an immense treasure of gold and silver and silken hangings. . . . Suddenly he was informed that his house was on fire. Hastening home he broke through the flames into the chamber where he kept the chests of gold. Seizing two of these, one on each shoulder (for he was not satisfied with saving just one), he tried to escape by the door. But a great beam, burned in two by the fire, fell upon him and killed him, his body being destroyed by terrestrial flames, but his soul despatched to that fire which was not kindled by mortal hands [the flames of hell]. Thus the judgment of God watched over the interests of Karl, whenever the cares of the empire prevented him from looking after them himself.

II, 1. Adalbert told me about the defenses of the Huns [Avars]. "The land of the Huns," he said, "was surrounded with nine rings. . . . The distance from the first to the second ring was as far as from Zürich to Constance; the outer ring was composed of oak, beech, and pine trees, and was twenty feet across and twenty feet high, the space in between the trees being filled with stones and clay, and the outer surface covered with thick sod. . . . Within these [the first and second] rings the villages were so arranged that the voice of a man could be heard from one to another. . . . The distance from the second to the third ring was ten German miles, which equal forty Italian miles, and so on to the ninth, although, of course, each succeeding ring was narrower [contained less land] than the one preceding it. The fortifications and dwellings within each ring were so situated that a signal from a horn could be heard from any one of them. In this defense the riches of the west had been gathered together for more than two hundred years . . . but the victorious Karl was able in eight years so completely to conquer the Huns, that not a trace of them is left."

9. Aaron [Haroun] recognized by this incident the might of Karl, and spoke [to Karl's ambassadors] these words of praise: "Now I understand, how true are the things which I have heard about my brother Karl; how he is accustomed by his ceaseless efforts and unwearied striving to make everything under the sun serve as a means of discipline for his body and his mind. What can I send back that will be worthy of him who has so honored me? If I should give him the land of Abraham which was given to Joshua, he would not be able to defend it, because of its distance from him; or if he determined in his magnanimity to defend it, I fear that the neighboring provinces would revolt in his absence from the Frankish rule. Nevertheless I will try to equal him in generosity by this means: I will give him authority over that land, and I will act as his representative in it; he may send ambassadors to me when it pleases him or is convenient for him, and he will find that I am the most faithful defender of the incomes of that land."[1]

[1] Notice the popular or legendary character of these stories. They are just such tales as would grow up among the people around a figure like that of Karl. Compare the stories of the conquest of the Avars and the embassy to Haroun in Einhard (no. 7, chs. 13 and 16), with the same stories here. The circumstantial details are in all probability added by popular tradition.

11. LETTER OF KARL THE GREAT TO BAUGULF, ABBOT OF FULDA, 787.

Jaffé, IV, pp. 343 ff.

Karl, by the grace of God king of the Franks and the Lombards and patricius of the Romans, sends loving greeting in the name of omnipotent God to abbot Baugulf, and to the household of monks committed to his charge. Know that we, with the advice of our faithful subjects, have regarded it as important that in the bishoprics and monasteries of our realm those who show themselves apt in learning should devote themselves to study, in addition to their regular duties as monks. For as the observance of monastic rules promotes good morals and character, so also the practice of teaching and learning develops a pure and agreeable style. Let those who seek to please God by living uprightly, seek to please Him also by speaking correctly. For it is written: " By thy words thou shalt be justified, and by thy words thou shalt be condemned " [Matt. 12:37]. For although well-doing is more important than knowledge, nevertheless knowledge must precede action. . . . We have been led to write of this, because we have frequently received letters from monks in which they make known to us what they are praying for, and in these letters we have recognized correct sentiments, but an uncouth style and language. The sentiments inspired in them by their devotion to us they could not express correctly, because they had neglected the study of language. Therefore we have begun to fear lest, just as the monks appear to have lost the art of writing, so also they may have lost the ability to understand the Holy Scriptures; and we all know that, though mistakes in words are dangerous, mistakes in understanding are still more so. Therefore we urge you to be diligent in the pursuit of learning, and to strive with humble and devout minds to understand more fully the mysteries of the Holy Scriptures. For it is well known that the sacred writings contain many rhetorical figures, the spiritual meaning of which will be readily apprehended only by those who have been instructed in the study of letters. And let those men be chosen for this work who are able and willing to learn and who have the desire to teach others. And let this be done in the spirit in which we have recommended it. For we desire that you, as becomes your station, shall be both devout and learned, both chaste in life and correct in speech. Thus when anyone shall be moved by your reputation for devotion and holiness, and shall desire to see you, he may be both edified by your appearance and instructed by your learning, which shall appear in your reading and singing; and so he may go away rejoicing and giving thanks to God. Do not fail to send copies of this letter to all your suffragans and fellow-bishops and all the monasteries, if you desire our favor.

12. Letter of Karl the Great in Regard to the Two Books of Sermons Prepared by Paul the Deacon, ca. 790.

Jaffé, IV, pp. 372 f.

Karl, by the aid of God king of the Franks and Lombards and patricius of the Romans, to the clergy of his realm. . . . Now since we are very desirous that the condition of our churches should constantly improve, we are endeavoring by diligent study to restore the knowledge of letters which has been almost lost through the negligence of our ancestors, and by our example we are encouraging those who are able to do so to engage in the study of the liberal arts. In this undertaking we have already, with the aid of God, corrected all the books of the Old and New Testament, whose texts had been corrupted through the ignorance of copyists. Moreover, inspired by the example of our father, Pippin, of blessed memory, who introduced the

Roman chants into the churches of his realm, we are now trying to supply the churches with good reading lessons. Finally, since we have found that many of the lessons to be read in the nightly service have been badly compiled and that the texts of these readings are full of mistakes, and the names of their authors omitted, and since we could not bear to listen to such gross errors in the sacred lessons, we have diligently studied how the character of these readings might be improved. Accordingly we have commanded Paul the Deacon,[1] our beloved subject, to undertake this work; that is, to go through the writings of the fathers carefully, and to make selections of the most helpful things from them and put them together into a book, as one gathers occasional flowers from a broad meadow to make a bouquet. And he, wishing to obey us, has read through the treatises and sermons of the various catholic fathers and has picked out the best things. These selections he has copied clearly without mistakes and has arranged in two volumes, providing readings suitable for every feast day throughout the whole year. We have tested the texts of all these readings by our own knowledge, and now authorize these volumes and commend them to all of you to be read in the churches of Christ.

[1] Paul the Deacon was a Lombard scholar and clergyman who after the fall of the Lombard kingdom was invited to the court of Karl and became one of his circle. Paul is the author of the only detailed history of the Lombards.

13. RECOGNITION OF KARL BY THE EMPERORS AT CONSTANTINOPLE, 812.

Annales Laurissenses et Einhardi, M. G. SS. folio, I, p. 199.

The following passages throw light upon the statement of Einhard (no. 7, ch. 28) in regard to the relation of Karl with the eastern emperors after his imperial coronation. We know from other sources that Karl wished to acquire the title of emperor and that he had already entered into negotiations with the empress Irene looking to a peaceful acquisition of it, before the pope gave him the crown.

He was apparently not satisfied with his position until he obtained recognition from the emperors in the east, whom he still regarded as the legal successors of the Roman emperors.

The emperor, Nicephorus, after winning many notable victories in Mœsia, fell in battle against the Bulgarians, and his son-in-law Michael was made emperor. He received the ambassadors in Constantinople whom Karl had sent to Nicephorus and dismissed them, sending back to Karl with them his own ambassadors, Michael, a bishop, and Arsaphius and Theognostus, commanders of the imperial body-guard, to confirm the treaty which had been proposed in the time of Nicephorus. They came to the emperor at Aachen and received a copy of the treaty from him in the church of Aachen. In their address to him on this occasion, which they delivered in Greek, they called him emperor and *basileus*. They then proceeded to Rome on their way back, and received a copy of the treaty from the pope in the church of St. Peter, the apostle.

14. LETTER OF KARL TO EMPEROR MICHAEL I, 813.

Jaffé, IV, pp. 415 f.

In the name of the Father, Son, and Holy Spirit. Karl, by the grace of God emperor and Augustus, king of the Franks and the Lombards, to his dear and honorable brother, Michael, glorious emperor and Augustus, eternal greeting in our Lord Jesus Christ. We bless and praise our Lord Jesus Christ with all our heart and strength for the ineffable gift of his kindness, with which he has enriched us. For he has deigned in our day to establish that peace between the east and the west, which we have long sought for and have always desired, and, in answer to the daily prayers which we have offered to him, has unified the holy immaculate catholic church throughout the whole world and given it peace. We speak of this peace as if it had been already brought about, for we have done our part, and we are sure you are willing to do yours. We put our trust in God who has ordained that this matter, the making of peace between us, should be carried out; for he is faithful and true, giving his aid to all who are engaged in good works, and he will bring to perfection this work which we have begun. Desiring now to bring about this consummation, we have sent you our legates, Amalhar, venerable bishop of Trier, and Peter, abbot of the monastery of Nonantula, to receive from the holy altar by your hands a copy of the treaty of peace, bearing the signatures of your priests, patriarchs, and nobles, just as your legates, Michael, venerable metropolitan, and Arsaphius and Theognostus, commanders of the royal body-guard, received the copy from us, with our signature and the signatures of our priests and nobles. . . .

15. LETTER TO LUDWIG THE PIOUS CONCERNING THE APPEARANCE OF A COMET, 837.

Jaffé, IV, pp. 459 f.

The dissolution of the empire of Karl the Great began in the reign of his son and successor, Ludwig, with the disintegration of the public service and the attacks of Northmen and Slavs on the frontier. The invasions of the Northmen are mentioned by Einhard as occurring in the last days of Karl (no. 7, chapter 14). In the reigns of Ludwig and his successors the invaders continually ravaged the shores of Gaul and northern Germany and added materially to the distress of the period. This letter refers in its last part to one of these raids, but it is interesting chiefly as an illustration of the mental attitude of the men of its age.

It is believed by almost all the ancient authorities that the appearance of new and unknown heavenly bodies portends to wretched mortals direful and disastrous events, rather than pleasant and propitious ones. The sacred scriptures alone tell of the propitious appearance of a new star; that is, that star which the wise men of the Chaldæans are said to have seen when, conjecturing from its most brilliant light the recent birth of the eternal king, they brought with veneration gifts worthy the acceptance of so great a lord. But the appearance of this star which has lately arisen is reported by all who have seen it to be terrible and malignant. And indeed I believe it presages evils which we have deserved, and foretells a coming destruction of which we are worthy. For what difference does it make whether this coming danger is foretold to the human race by man or angel or star? The important thing is to understand that this appearance of a new body in the heavens is not without significance, but that it is meant to forewarn mortals that they may avert the future evil by repentance and prayers. Thus by the preaching of the prophet Jonah the destruction of the city, which had been threatened by him, was deferred because the inhabitants turned from their iniquities and evil lives. . . . So we trust that merciful God will turn this threatened evil from us also, if we like them repent with our whole hearts. Would that the destruction which the fleet of the Northmen is said to have inflicted upon this realm recently might be regarded as the sufficient occasion for the appearance of this comet, but I fear that it is rather some new distress still to come that is foretold by this terrible omen.

16. THE STRASSBURG OATHS, 842.

Nithard, III, 5; M. G. SS. folio, II, pp. 665 ff.

The occasion of these oaths was the alliance between the two brothers, Ludwig the German and Charles the Bald, against their brother Lothar. Lothar had been defeated at the battle of Fontenay, 841, by his brothers, who then made this league. The oaths are given in this form by Nithard, the historian of the later Carolingians, who was the son of Angilbert and Bertha, the daughter of Karl the Great. The *lingua romana* and the *lingua teudisca* are the vulgar languages respectively of the followers of Charles the Bald and Ludwig the German, that is, of the inhabitants of France and of Germany. The appearance of a Latin dialect as the language of the inhabitants of the western kingdom indicates that the Roman elements had after all survived in Gaul and were absorbing the

German elements; the formation of two languages mutually exclusive in the two portions of the empire suggests a fairly advanced stage of differentiation between the German and the French parts. But the chief interest of this document is in the field of language study. The *lingua romana* shows an early stage in the development of French from Latin, while the *lingua teudisca* is one of the earliest forms of Old High German. The *lingua romana* shows the process by which the French language grew out of Latin; note that inflectional endings have largely disappeared, and case is shown by the use of prepositions, and that phonetic changes (changes of vowels and consonants) have also taken place. Some of the words are good Latin, others are very nearly modern French, and still others stand midway between Latin and French. Most of the words in the *lingua teudisca* can be identified with modern German words. Note that each leader took the oath in the language of the followers of the other, in order that his brother's followers might understand him. So Ludwig the German speaks in the *lingua romana* and Charles the Bald in the *lingua teudisca*.

So Ludwig and Charles came together at Argentaria, which is called Strassburg in the common tongue, and there took the oaths which are given below, Ludwig speaking in the *lingua romana* and Charles in the *lingua teudisca*. . . . . Ludwig, being the elder, took the oath first, as follows:

Pro deo amur et pro christian poblo et nostro commun salvament, d'ist di in avant, in quant deus savir et podir me dunat, si salvaraeio cist meon fradre Karlo et in aiudha et in cadhuna cosa, si cum om per dreit son fradra salvar dist, in o quid il mi altresi fazet, et ab Ludher nul plaid numquam prindrai, qui meon vol cist meon fradre Karle in damno sit.

When Ludwig had finished, Charles took the oath in the *lingua teudisca*:

In godes minna ind in thes christânes folches ind unsêr bêdhero gehaltnissî, fon thesemo dage frammordes, sô fram sô mir got geuuizci indi mahd furgibit, sô haldih thesan minan bruodher, sôso man mit rchtu sînan bruodher scal, in

thiu thaz er mig sô sama duo, indi mit Ludheren in noh-
heiniu thing ne gegango, the mînan uuilon imo ce scadhen
uuerdhên.

Literal translation of the *lingua romana*, the *lingua teudisca* being the same with the names changed:

" By God's love and by this Christian people and our common salvation, from this day forth, as far as God gives me to know and to
have power, I will so aid this my brother Charles in each and every
thing as a man ought to aid his brother, in so far as he shall do the
same for me; and I will never have any dealings with Lothar that
may by my wish injure this my brother Charles."

And this is the oath which the followers of each took in
their own tongues:

Lingua romana:

Si Lodhuuigs sagrament, que son fradre Karlo iurat, con-
servat, et Karlus meos sendra de suo part non los tanit, si
io returnar non l'int pois: ne io ne neuls, cui eo returnar
int pois, in nulla aiudha contra Lodhuuuig nun li iv er.

Lingua teudisca:

Oba Karl then eid, then er sînemo bruodher Ludhuuuîge
gesuor, geleistit, indi Ludhuuuîg mîn hêrro then er imo
gesuor forbrihchit, ob ih inan es iruuenden ne mag: noh ih
noh thero nohhein, then ih es iruuenden mag, uuidhar Karle
imo ce follusti ne uuirdhit.

Literal translation of the *lingua romana*, the same as the other
with names changed:

" If Ludwig keeps the oath which he swore to his brother Charles,
and Charles, my lord, on his part does not keep it, if I cannot prevent
it, then neither I nor anyone whom I can prevent shall ever defend
him against Ludwig."

17–18. THE TREATY OF VERDUN, 843.

17. ANNALES BERTINIANI.

M. G. SS. folio, I, p. 440.

The treaty of Verdun is the division of the empire among the three
sons of Ludwig the Pious, Lothar, Ludwig the German, and Charles

the Bald. It recognized the failure of the attempt of Karl to weld
western Europe and the German tribes into one state and marks the
beginning of the states of Germany and France. The student should
follow on a map the line described in the treaty. The long narrow
strip which composed the northern portion of the kingdom of Lothar
had no elements of cohesion, geographically, racially, or politically.
So it became the debatable land over which the two neighboring
states of Germany and France have ever since fought. The fate of
this middle territory may be glanced at in anticipation: The extreme
northern portion came to the empire in 870 and formed the duchy
of Lotharingia, but it fell apart into little feudal territories practically independent of the empire and finally became separate as the
Netherlands; the central portion also broke up into small territories,
part of which remained in the empire, as the Palatinate of the Rhine,
and the great Rhine bishoprics; part, like Elsass and Lorraine,
vacillated between France and Germany; the southern portion became the kingdoms of upper and lower Burgundy, then the united
kingdom of Burgundy or Arles, and then after the acquisition of that
kingdom by the empire, broke up into small territories, part going
to Germany, part to France, and part becoming independent.

Charles met his brothers at Verdun and there the portions of the empire were assigned. Ludwig received all
beyond the Rhine, including also Speier, Worms, and Mainz
on this side of the Rhine; Lothar received the land bounded
[by that of Ludwig on the west, and] by a line following along
the lower Rhine, the Scheldt, and the Meuse, then through
Cambrai, Hainault, Lomme, including the counties east of
the Meuse, to where the Saône flows into the Rhône, then
along the Rhône to the sea, including the counties on both
sides of the Rhône; the rest as far as Spain, went to Charles.

18. Regino.

M. G. SS. folio, I, p. 568.

Anno 842 (843). The three brothers divided the kingdom
of the Franks among themselves; to Charles fell the western
portion from the British ocean to the Meuse; to Ludwig,
the eastern portion, that is, Germany as far west as the
Rhine, including certain cities and their counties east of

the Rhine to furnish him with wine; to Lothar, who, as the oldest, bore the title of emperor, the part in between, which still bears the name of Lotharingia, and all of Provence and the land of Italy with the city of Rome.

19. THE TREATY OF MEERSEN, 870.

M. G. LL. folio, I, p. 516; Altmann und Bernheim, no. 4.

The northern portion of the kingdom of Lothar was divided on his death (855) between two of his sons, Lothar and Charles, the other, Louis, taking Italy. Charles died in 863 and Lothar in 869; thereupon their uncles, Charles the Bald and Ludwig the German, divided that territory between them by the treaty of Meersen, the preliminaries of which are given here. See a map for the line of the division.

In the year of the incarnation of our Lord 870, the third indiction, the day before the nones of March [March 6], in the 32d year of the reign of the glorious king Charles [the Bald], in the palace of the king at Aachen, this agreement was made between him and his brother Ludwig.

Count Ingelram, for king Charles.

I promise for my lord that my lord, king Charles, will permit his brother, king Ludwig, to have such portion of the kingdom of Lothar as they two or their representatives may decide upon as just and equitable. Charles will never molest him in his possession of that portion or of the kingdom which he held before, if Ludwig on his side will keep the same faith and fidelity toward him, which I have promised for my lord.

Count Leutfrid, for king Ludwig.

I promise for my lord that my lord, king Ludwig, will permit his brother, king Charles, to have such portion of the kingdom of Lothar as they two or their representatives may decide upon as just and equitable. Ludwig will never molest him in his possession of that portion or of the kingdom which he held before, if Charles on his side will keep the same faith and fidelity toward him, which I have promised for my lord.

20. INVASIONS OF NORTHMEN AT THE END OF THE NINTH CENTURY.

Annals of Fulda, M. G. SS. folio, I, pp. 398 ff.

See introductory note to no. 15 for the nature of these invasions. The chronicle accounts in this and the next document illustrate very well the necessity which lay upon the local officials of defending the country against invaders. The particular feature of the events narrated here is the participation of the ecclesiastical lords, archbishops and bishops, in these warlike enterprises. This was due to the fact that the ecclesiastical lords were great landholders and exercised all the functions of secular officials.

Ad annum 883. The Northmen, ascending the Rhine, plundered and burnt many villages. Liutbert, archbishop of Mainz, with a small band of troops, attacked them and, after killing many of them, recovered much of the booty which they had taken. Cologne [which had been burnt by the Northmen, 881] was rebuilt, except its churches and monasteries, and its walls with their gates and towers were restored.

Ad annum 885. The Northmen entered the territory about Liège, collected all kinds of provisions, and prepared to spend the winter there. But Liutbert, archbishop of Mainz, and count Heimrih, with others, fell upon them suddenly, killed many of them, and drove the others into a small stronghold. They then seized the provisions which the Northmen had collected. The Northmen, after enduring a long siege, during which they suffered from hunger, finally fled from the stronghold by night.

21. INVASION OF THE HUNGARIANS, ca. 950.

Thietmar of Merseburg, II, 27; M. G. SS. folio, III, pp. 752 f.

Michael, bishop of Regensburg, after governing his diocese well for some years, gathered his troops and joined the other

Bavarian nobles in resisting an invasion of the Hungarians. In the battle which followed, our troops were defeated. One of the bishop's ears was cut off, and after receiving many other wounds he was left for dead on the field. One of his personal enemies had fallen at his side, and, by feigning death when the Hungarians searched the battle-field, he escaped with his life. When he saw that he was alone with the bishop whom he hated, he seized a lance and tried to kill him. But the bishop, having recovered consciousness, was able to defend himself, and, after a fierce struggle with his enemy, succeeded in striking him down. After a long and perilous journey the bishop found his way back to Regensburg, greatly to the joy of his flock. All his clergy welcomed him as a bold warrior, his flock honored and cherished him as an excellent pastor, and his wounds and maiming redounded to his honor.

22. Dissolution of the Empire.

Regino, M. G. SS. folio, I, pp. 590 ff.

The empire divided in 843 was for a brief period reunited under Karl the Fat from 884-887. But the failure of Karl either to enforce his authority in the empire or to protect its boundaries led to his deposition and to the definite division of the empire into small kingdoms under local rulers. Arnulf, an illegitimate son of Karlmann, the brother of Karl the Fat, became king of Germany; in France, as early as 879, Provence or lower Burgundy had elected a local count, Boso, as king; in 888, after the deposition of Karl the Fat, most of the French nobles elected Odo, duke of Francia, who belonged to the family of the counts of Paris, as their king, while upper Burgundy chose its own ruler in count Rudolf, and Aquitaine still held out under its duke for the young Charles the Simple, grandson of Charles the Bald. In Italy Charles the Bald, Ludwig, and Karl the Fat had attempted in vain to assert the authority of the emperor there, and Italy went its own way and became the field of battle between rival claimants for the crown, both of them local Italian nobles. Thus by 888 there were, including Aquitaine, six separate kingdoms, Germany, Italy, France, Aquitaine, Provence, and Burgundy.

Anno 879. Boso, on hearing of the death of Louis [the Stammerer], set out from Provence and undertook to seize the whole of Burgundy. And after he had won over several bishops to his cause by threats and persuasion, he proceeded to Lyon and there was anointed king over the Burgundian realm by Aurelian, the metropolitan of Lyon, and the other bishops. He ignored the young sons of Louis, treating them as illegitimate because their mother had been disgraced and put away at the order of Charles [the Bald]. But these youths, Louis and Carlman, were raised to the throne by abbot Hugo and the other nobles, and warred against Boso all their lives. Not only they but also the other kings of the Franks hated him for his usurpation, and made their dukes and vassals promise that they would try to overthrow and slay him.

Anno 887. In this year there died at Orleans abbot Hugo, who had held and ruled manfully the duchy [of Robert the Strong, *i.e.*, Francia], and the duchy was given by the emperor to Robert's son, Odo, who had been up to that time count of Paris, and who, together with Gozlinus, bishop of Paris, had protected that city with all his might against the terrible onslaughts of the Northmen. . . .

In the month of November on St. Martin's day [November 11, 887], Karl [the Fat] came to Tribur and held a general diet. Now when the nobles of the kingdom saw that the emperor was failing not only in bodily strength, but in mind also, they joined in a conspiracy with Arnulf, son of Karlmann, to raise him to the throne, and they fell away from the emperor to Arnulf in such numbers that after three days scarcely anyone was left to do the emperor even the services demanded by common humanity. . . .
King Arnulf, however, gave Karl certain imperial lands in Alamannia for his sustenance, and then, after he had settled affairs in Franconia, he himself returned to Bavaria.

Anno 888. After the death of Karl the kingdoms which

had obeyed his rule fell apart and obeyed no longer their natural lord [*i.e.*, Arnulf], but each elected a king from among its own inhabitants. This was the cause of many wars, not because there were no longer any princes among the Franks fitted by birth, courage, and wisdom to rule, but because of the equality of those very traits among so many princes, since no one of them so excelled the others that they would be willing to obey him. For there were still many princes able to hold together the Frankish empire, if they had not been fated to oppose one another instead of uniting.

In Italy one portion of the people made Berengar, son of Everhard, markgraf of Friuli, king, while another portion chose as king Guido, son of Lambert, duke of Spoleto. Out of this division came so great a strife and so much bloodshed that, as our Lord said, the kingdom, divided against itself, was almost brought to desolation [Matt. 12:25]. Finally Guido was victorious and Berengar was driven from the kingdom. . . .

Then the people of Gaul came together, and with the consent of Arnulf, chose duke Odo, son of Robert, a mighty man, to be their king. . . . He ruled manfully and defended the kingdom against the continual attacks of the Northmen.

About the same time, Rudolf, son of Conrad, the nephew of abbot Hugo, seized that part of Provence between the Jura and the Pennine Alps [Upper Burgundy], and in the presence of the nobles and bishops, crowned himself king. . . . But when Arnulf heard of this he advanced against Rudolf, who betook himself to the most inaccessible heights and held out there. All his life Arnulf, with his son Zwentibold, made war on Rudolf, but could not overcome him, because he held out in places where only the chamois could go and where the troops of the invaders could not reach him.

23. THE CORONATION OF ARNULF, 896.

Regino, M. G. SS. folio, I, p. 607.

Arnulf regarded himself as the successor to Karl the Great and attempted to exercise some real authority over the whole empire. This appears in his relations to Odo of France, to the kings of the Burgundies, and to the claimants in Italy. The expedition which he undertook to Italy in order to end the disorders there resulted in his receiving the imperial crown.

Anno 896. A second time Arnulf went down into Italy and came to Rome, and with the consent of the pope stormed the city. This was an unheard-of thing, not having happened since Brenno and the Gauls captured Rome many years before the birth of Christ.[1] The mother of Lambert, whom he had left to defend the city, fled with her troops. Arnulf was received into the city with the greatest reverence by pope Formosus and was crowned emperor by him before the altar of St. Peter. But as he returned from Rome he was seized with an illness that troubled him for a long time.

[1] Not true; see no. 2, for the sack of Rome by Alaric, 410, and by Geiseric, 455.

24, 25. RISE OF THE TRIBAL DUCHIES IN GERMANY, ca. 900.

24. SAXONY.

Widukind, History of the Saxons, I, c. 16; M. G. SS. folio, III, p. 425.

In the beginning of the tenth century we find Germany divided into five great duchies, Lotharingia, Franconia, Saxony, Bavaria, and Suabia. The boundaries of the last four corresponded pretty closely to the boundaries of old German tribes: Franks, Saxons, Bavarians, and Alamanni. The attempt of Karl to weld the various German tribes into one state was successful during his reign, but that period was too brief to extinguish the tribal feeling, and his weak successors, occupied with schemes of selfish aggrandizement, abandoned his larger policy. During the later Carolingian period the impotence of the central government put the burden of ruling upon the local officials, who under the weak rule of Ludwig the

Child usurped the title of duke in each of the large divisions. This usurpation was successful largely because the people in each duchy regarded their new duke as the representative of tribal unity. In Saxony and Bavaria the counts of the marks took the position of leaders of the nobles and people of the whole provinces against the invasions of Slavs and Hungarians, and were rewarded by the fidelity and allegiance of the duchy. In Franconia and Suabia the same position was won by local officials, but in these cases it was as the result of struggles between rival families for supreme position in the duchy. The references in documents to these events are very meager, but it will be observed that dukes of Saxony, Bavaria, Franconia, Suabia are mentioned in these passages.

The last of the Carolingian emperors of the East Franks was Ludwig [the Child], son of Arnulf. . . . This Ludwig married Liudgard, sister of Bruno and the great duke Otto, and soon after died. These men, Bruno and Otto, were the sons of Liudolf. . . . Bruno ruled the duchy of all Saxony, but perished with his army in resisting an incursion of the Danes, thus leaving the duchy to his younger and far abler brother Otto. Ludwig the Child left no son, and all the people of Franconia and Saxony tried to give Otto the crown. But he refused to undertake the burden of ruling, on the ground that he was too old, and by his advice Conrad, duke of Franconia, was anointed king.

25. SUABIA.

Annales Alamannici, M. G. SS. folio, I, pp. 55 f.

Anno 911. Burchart, count and prince of the Alamanni, was unjustly slain by the judgment of Anselm, and his sons Burchart and Udalrich were driven out and his possessions and fiefs divided among his enemies. . . .

Anno 913. In this year Conrad the king attacked the king of Lotharingia. A conflict arose between Conrad and Erchanger [a count palatine in Suabia]. The Hungarians break into Alamannia; on their return Arnulf [duke of Bavaria] and Erchanger, with Berthold and Udalrich, attack and defeat the Hungarians. In this year peace is made between the king and Erchanger, and the king marries the sister of Erchanger.

Anno 914. Conrad again comes into Alamannia. Erchanger attacks bishop Salomon and captures him. In the same year Erchanger is captured by the king and exiled. Immediately the young Burchart [son of Burchart] rebels against the king and devastates his own fatherland.

Anno 915. . . . Erchanger returns from exile and attacks Burchart and Berthold and conquers them at Wallwis, and is made duke of the Alamanni [duke of Suabia].

26. HENRY I AND THE SAXON CITIES, 919–36.

Widukind, I, 35; M. G. SS. folio, III, p. 432.

Henry, duke of Saxony, king of the Germans, 919–936, was the first king of the Saxon house. He was also the first king of the Germans to accept the feudal state and to attempt to build up a government on that basis. He did not revive the imperial claims on Italy, but devoted himself to strengthening his own authority in Saxony, to defending the frontiers of the kingdom, and to creating a German state. This selection is from the history of the Saxons written by Widukind, a monk in the monastery of New Corvey, who wrote in the latter part of the tenth century. The passage illustrates the relations of the Germans to the Slavs on the east and the origin of the Saxon cities. The Slavs had moved as far west as the Elbe, occupying the lands left vacant by the Germans after the migrations. Much of this territory was gradually recovered by the Germans from the time of Henry. Here we see the capture of the city of Brandenburg and the reduction of Bohemia. Following the conquest came the establishment of the marks and the colonization and Germanizing of the land.

It lies beyond my power to relate in detail how king Henry, after he had made a nine years' truce with the Hungarians, undertook to develop the defenses of his own land [Saxony] and to subdue the barbarians; and yet this must not be passed over in silence. From the free peasants subject to military service he chose one out of every nine, and

ordered these selected persons to move into the fortified
places and build dwellings for the others. One-third of all
the produce was to be stored up in these fortified places,
and the other peasants were to sow and reap and gather the
crops and take them there. The king also commanded all
courts and meetings and celebrations to be held in these
places, that during a time of peace the inhabitants might
accustom themselves to meeting together in them, as he
wished them to do in case of an invasion. The work on
these strongholds was pushed night and day. Outside of
these fortified places there were no walled towns. While
the inhabitants of his new cities were being trained in this
way, the king suddenly fell upon the Heveldi [the Slavs
who dwell on the Havel], defeated them in several engage-
ments, and finally captured the city of Brandenburg. This
was in the dead of winter, the besieging army encamping
on the ice and storming the city after the garrison had been
exhausted by hunger and cold. Having thus won with the
capture of Brandenburg the whole territory of the Heveldi,
he proceeded against Dalamantia, which his father had attacked on a former occasion, and then besieged Jahna and
took it after twenty days. . . . Then he made an attack
in force upon Prague, the fortress of the Bohemians, and
reduced the king of Bohemia to subjection.

27. THE ELECTION OF OTTO I, 936.

Widukind, II, 1, 2; M. G. SS. folio, III, pp. 437 ff.

This passage is also taken from Widukind. It shows the ceremony of election and coronation in the tenth century. Note the steps
in the process: (1) designation by his father, at which time the son
was probably accepted by an assembly of the nobles; (2) election
by the general assembly after the death of the father; the general
assembly at this period probably consisted only of nobles and high
ecclesiastics; (3) elevation to the throne by the feudal nobles, a
survival of the ancient ceremony of raising the king on the shield

by the warriors of the tribe; (4) presentation to the people by the bishops, and acceptance; (5) solemn coronation and anointing by the archbishops.

1. After Henry, the father of his country and the greatest and best of kings, had died, all the people of the Franks and the Saxons chose for their king his son Otto, whom Henry had already designated as his successor, and they sent out notices of the coronation, which was to take place at Aachen. . . . And when all were assembled there, the dukes and the commanders of the soldiers and other military leaders raised Otto upon the throne, which was erected in the portico adjoining the church of Karl the Great, and giving him their hands and promising him their fidelity and aid against all his enemies, they made him king according to their custom. Meanwhile the archbishop of Mainz and the clergy and people awaited him within the church. And when he approached the archbishop met him, . . . and went with him to the centre of the church; . . . then turning to the people . . . he said: "I bring you Otto, chosen by God, designated by our lord Henry, and now made king by all the princes; if this choice pleases you, raise your right hands." At this, the whole people raised their right hands to heaven and hailed the new ruler with a mighty shout. Then the archbishop advanced with the king, who was clothed with a short tunic after the Frankish custom, to the altar, on which lay the royal insignia, the sword and belt, the cloak and armlets, the staff with the sceptre and diadem. The primate at this time was Hildibert, a Frank by birth and a monk by training. He had been brought up and educated at the monastery of Fulda, and finally was made archbishop of Mainz. . . . Now when there had arisen a dispute as to who should consecrate the king (for the honor was claimed by the archbishops both of Trier and of Cologne, the former because his see was the oldest and had been founded, as it

were, by St. Peter, and the latter because Aachen was in his diocese),[1] the difficulty was settled by both of them yielding with all good will to Hildibert.

The archbishop, going up to the altar, took up the sword and belt and, turning to the king, said: " Receive this sword with which you shall cast out all the enemies of Christ, both pagans and wicked Christians, and receive with it the authority and power given to you by God to rule over all the Franks for the security of all Christian people." Then taking up the cloak and armlets he put them on the king and said: " The borders of this cloak trailing on the ground shall remind you that you are to be zealous in the faith and to keep peace." Finally, taking up the sceptre and staff, he said: " By these symbols you shall correct your subjects with fatherly discipline and foster the servants of God and the widows and orphans. May the oil of mercy never be lacking to your head, that you may be crowned here and in the future life with an eternal reward." Then the archbishops Hildibert of Mainz and Wicfrid of Cologne anointed him with the sacred oil and crowned him with the golden crown, and now that the whole coronation ceremony was completed they led him to the throne, which he ascended. The throne was built between two marble columns of great beauty and was so placed that he could see all and be seen by all.

2. Then after the Te Deum and the mass, the king descended from his throne and proceeded to the palace, where he sat down with his bishops and people at a marble table which was adorned with royal lavishness; and the dukes served him. Gilbert, duke of Lotharingia, who held the office by right, superintended the preparations [*i.e.,* acted as chamberlain], Eberhard, duke of Franconia, presided over the arrangements for the king's table [acted as seneschal], Herman, duke of Suabia, acted as cupbearer, Arnulf, duke of Bavaria, commanded the knights and chose the place of encampment [acted as marshal].[2] Siegfrid, chief of

the Saxons, second only to the king, and son-in-law of the former king, ruled Saxony for Otto, providing against attacks of the enemy and caring for the young Henry, Otto's brother.

1 In the time of Leo IX (1048–1054) this quarrel was settled in favor of the archbishop of Cologne because Aachen was in his diocese.

2 The famous banquet of Otto has been made much of by many authors to show the power of Otto over the great dukes. It is doubtful, however, if much importance should be attached to this. The great offices of the court in Germany were ceremonial and titular, and since they did not become important departments of the public service, as they did in France and England, they were allowed to remain in the hands of the great dukes. The serving of the dukes at the banquet cannot be made to prove their subservience to Otto; Otto's method of controlling the dukes was to put his own relatives in those positions. The four offices of the seneschal, cupbearer, chamberlain, and marshal are the court positions of the later secular electoral princes (see no. 16C), the count palatine of the Rhine, the king of Bohemia, the elector of Saxony, and the margrave of Brandenburg. These princes on the breaking up of the tribal duchies succeeded to the position of first rank among the nobles, which had been held by the tribal dukes.

28. OTTO I AND THE HUNGARIANS.

Widukind, III, chs. 44 ff; M. G. SS. folio, III, pp. 457 f.

The Hungarians appear on the borders of the empire about the end of the ninth century. From that time they are a continual source of trouble to the kings of Germany. Arnulf had made an alliance with them against the Slavs; the reigns of Ludwig the Child and Conrad I had suffered from their attacks, and Henry I had succeeded in forcing them to make a truce. Otto then defeated them in the battle of the Lechfeld (955), which is narrated here, after which they settled in the region where they are found to-day.

44. While Otto was in Saxony, ambassadors of the Hungarians came to him, under the pretext of the old alliance and friendship, but in reality, it was supposed, in order to discover the outcome of the civil war in which Otto had been engaged. After he had entertained them and sent them away with gifts, he received a message from his brother, the

duke of Bavaria, saying: "Lo, the Hungarians are over-
running your land, and are preparing to make war upon
you." As soon as the king heard this, he immediately
marched against this enemy, taking with him only a few
Saxons, since the rest were occupied at that time with a
conflict against the Slavs. He pitched his camp in the territory of the city of Augsburg and was joined there by the
army of the Franconians and Bavarians and by duke Conrad with a large following of knights. Conrad's arrival so
encouraged the warriors that they wished to attack the enemy
immediately. Conrad was by nature very bold, and at the
same time very wise in council, two things which are not
usually found in the same man. He was irresistible in war,
whether on foot or on horseback; and was dear to his friends
in peace as well as in war. It now became apparent
through the skirmishes of the advance posts that the two
armies were not far apart. A fast was proclaimed in the
camp, and all were commanded to be ready for battle on
the next morning. At the first gleam of dawn they all
arose, made peace with one another, and promised to aid
first their own leaders and then each other. Then they
marched out of the camp with standards raised, some eight
legions in all. The army was led by a steep and difficult
way in order to avoid the darts of the enemy, which they
use with great effect if they can find any bushes to hide
behind. The first, second, and third lines were composed of
Bavarians led by the officers of duke Henry, who himself
was lying sick some distance from the field of battle—a sick-
ness from which he died not long after. The fourth legion
was composed of Franconians, under the command of duke
Conrad. The king commanded the fifth line. This was
called the royal legion and was made up of selected warriors, brave youths, who guarded the standard of the angel,
the emblem of victory. The sixth and seventh lines were
composed of Suabians, commanded by duke Burchard, who

had married the daughter of the brother of Otto [Hedwig, daughter of Henry]. The eighth was made up of a thousand chosen warriors of the Bohemians, whose equipment was better than their fortune; here was the baggage and the impedimenta, because the rear was thought to be the safest place. But it did not prove to be so in the outcome, for the Hungarians crossed the Lech unexpectedly, and turned the flank of the army and fell upon the rear line, first with darts and then at close quarters. Many were slain or captured, the whole of the baggage seized, and the line put to rout. In like manner the Hungarians fell upon the seventh and sixth lines, slew a great many and put the rest to flight. But when the king perceived that there was a conflict going on in front and that the lines behind him were also being attacked, he sent duke Conrad with the fourth line against those in the rear. Conrad freed the captives, recovered the booty, and drove off the enemy. Then he returned to the king, victorious, having defeated with youthful and untried warriors an enemy that had put to flight experienced and renowned soldiers.

46. . . . When the king saw that the whole brunt of the attack was now in front . . . he seized his shield and lance, and rode out against the enemy at the head of his followers. The braver warriors among the enemy withstood the attack at first, but when they saw that their companions had fled, they were overcome with dismay and were slain. Some of the enemy sought refuge in near-by villages, their horses being worn out; these were surrounded and burnt to death within the walls. Others swam the river, but were drowned by the caving in of the bank as they attempted to climb out on the other side. The strongholds were taken and the captives released on the day of the battle; during the next two days the remnants of the enemy were captured in the neighboring towns, so that scarcely any escaped. Never was so bloody a victory gained over so savage a people.

29. THE IMPERIAL CORONATION OF OTTO I, 962.

Continuation of Regino; M. G. SS. folio, I, p. 625.

The coronation of Otto is regarded as the restoration of the Holy Roman Empire. From the time of the coronation of Arnulf (896) (see no. 23) to Otto's first expedition, 951, the German kings had been too much occupied at home to interfere in Italy. During these years Italy had been the scene of a long struggle for the crown, in which the papacy had taken part as a secular power. The result was feudal anarchy in Italy and the degradation of the papacy. The desire to restore order in Italy, to revive the old imperial claims, and to reform the papacy, led Otto to accept the invitation of the pope and to make a second expedition which ended in the coronation. Otto thus revived the Carolingian policy which had been handed on by Arnulf. The union of Germany and Italy to form the mediæval empire was made certain by this coronation. The kings of Germany were pledged to the maintenance of their authority in Italy, a policy which caused them to waste in Italy the strength and the opportunity which they should have used to build up a German state.

Anno 962. King Otto celebrated Christmas at Pavia in this year [961], and went thence to Rome, where he was made emperor by pope John XII with the acclamation of all the Roman people and clergy. The pope entertained him with great cordiality and promised never to be untrue to him all the days of his life. But this promise had a very different outcome from what was anticipated by them.

(Otto leaves Rome to attack Berengar, who claimed to be king of Italy, and his sons Adalbert and Guido.)

963. . . . In the meantime pope John, forgetting his promise, fell away from the emperor and joined the party of Berengar, and allowed Adalbert to enter Rome. When Otto heard of this he abandoned the siege [of San Leo] and hastened with his army to Rome. But pope John and Adalbert, fearing to await his arrival, seized most of the treasures of St. Peter and sought safety in flight. Now the Romans were divided in sympathy, part favoring the emperor because of the oppressions of the pope, and part favoring the

papal cause; nevertheless, they received him in the city with the proper respect, and gave hostages for their complete obedience to his commands. The emperor having entered Rome, called together there a large number of bishops and held a synod; it was decided at this synod that he should send an embassy after the pope to recall him to the apostolic seat. But when John refused to come, the Roman people unanimously elected the papal secretary Leo [VIII] to fill his place.

30–31. THE ACQUISITION OF BURGUNDY BY THE EMPIRE, 1018–1032.

30. THIETMAR OF MERSEBURG.

M. G. SS. folio, III, p. 863.

The kingdom of Burgundy or Arles was formed by the union of the two small kingdoms of Provence and Upper Burgundy, the beginning of which is told in Regino (see no. 22). The result of the acquisition of Burgundy was not to increase the territory of Germany, but to add another kingdom to the empire, which now included Germany, Italy, and Burgundy.

VIII, 5. Now I shall break off the relation of these negotiations in order to tell of the good fortune which lately befell our emperor, Henry [II]. For his mother's brother, Rudolf, king of Burgundy, had promised him his crown and sceptre in the presence and with the consent of his wife and his step-sons and all his nobles, and now this promise was repeated with an oath. This happened at Mainz in the same year [February, 1018].

31. WIPO, LIFE OF CONRAD II.

M. G. SS. folio, XI, pp. 263 ff.

8. Rudolf, king of Burgundy, in his old age ruled his realm in a careless fashion and thereby aroused great dissatisfaction among his nobles. So he invited his sister's son, the emperor Henry II, to come to him, and he desig-

nated him as his successor and caused all the nobles of his realm to swear fealty to him. . . . Now after the death of Henry [1024], king Rudolf wished to withdraw his promise, but Conrad [II], desiring to increase rather than to diminish the empire and to reap the fruits of his predecessor's efforts, seized Basel in order to force Rudolf to keep his promise. But queen Gisela, the daughter of Rudolf's sister, brought about reconciliation between them.

29. In the year of our Lord 1032, Rudolf, king of Burgundy, died, and count Odo of Champagne, his sister's son, invaded the kingdom and had already seized many castles and towns, partly by treachery and partly by force. . . . In this way he gained a large part of Burgundy, although the kingdom had been promised under oath a long time before by Rudolf to Conrad and his son, king Henry. But while Odo was doing this in Burgundy, emperor Conrad was engaged in a campaign against the Slavs. . . .

30. In the year of our Lord 1033, emperor Conrad, with his son, king Henry, celebrated Christmas at Strassburg. From there he invaded Burgundy by way of Solothurn, and at the monastery of Peterlingen on the day of the purification of the Virgin Mary [February 2] he was elected king of Burgundy by the higher and lower nobility, and was crowned on the same day.

32. HENRY III AND THE EASTERN FRONTIER, 1040 TO 1043.

Lambert of Hersfeld, Annals, M. G. SS. folio, V, pp. 152 f.

The expansion of Germany to the east was slow and unstable. Poles, Bohemians, and Hungarians refused to remain tributary, but took every opportunity to rebel against the Germans. We give a few passages from Lambert's Annals to show that Henry III was aware of the policy bequeathed him by his predecessors, although he was not very successful in his efforts to carry it into effect.

Anno 1040. King Henry [III] led an army into Bohemia, but suffered heavy losses. Among others, count Werner and the standard bearer of the monastery of Fulda were slain.

Peter, king of Hungary, was expelled by his people. He fled to Henry and asked his aid.

1041. King Henry entered Bohemia a second time and compelled their duke, Bretislaw, to surrender. He made his territory tributary to Henry.

Ouban, who had usurped the crown of Hungary, invaded Bavaria and Carinthia (Kaernthen) and took much booty. But the Bavarians united all their forces, followed them, retook the booty, killed a great many of them, and put the rest to flight.

1042. King Henry made his first campaign against Hungary, and put Ouban to flight. He went into Hungary as far as the Raab river, took three great fortresses, and received the oath of fidelity from the inhabitants of the land.

1043. The king celebrated Christmas at Goslar, where the duke of Bohemia came to see him. He was kindly received by the king, honorably entertained for some time, and at length sent away in peace. Ambassadors came to him there from many peoples, and among them those of the Rusci, who went away sad because Henry refused to marry the daughter of their king. Ambassadors also came from the king of Hungary and humbly sued for peace. But they did not obtain it, because king Peter, who had been deposed and driven out by Ouban, was there and was begging for the help of Henry against Ouban.

II. THE PAPACY TO THE ACCESSION OF GREGORY VII, 1073

The chief purpose of the documents offered in this section is to illustrate the growth of the papal power and the development of the conflicting claims of the empire and the papacy. The organization of the church was a matter of slow growth, and at first the bishop of Rome actually exercised ecclesiastical authority in a decisive way only in his own diocese. But by 1073 the organization of the church was so developed that the supremacy of the pope over the church and ecclesiastical affairs in the west was in a fair way of becoming an accomplished fact. He had secured the sole right to be called pope, universal, and apostolic.

The growth of his temporal power is even more clearly marked. At the time of Constantine the bishop of Rome had no temporal authority. But gradually he acquired power over temporal matters and exercised various secular and even imperial prerogatives, until Gregory VII found it easy to formulate and put forth the claim that the pope was master of the emperor and the real ruler of the world even in temporal things. Before 1073 there was occasional friction between the empire and the papacy, but this did not develop into a real and definite struggle for world supremacy until Gregory VII became pope.

Selections are here given to illustrate (1) the election of bishops, and especially the early election of the bishop of Rome, nos. 33, 34, 37, 38; (2) the chief means by which the pope acquired recognition of his ecclesiastical headship in the west, that is, his missionary work, nos. 35, 39, 40; (3) the rebellion of the pope against the rule of the Greek emperors, nos. 41, 42; (4) the acquisition of land and of temporal authority by the pope, nos. 36, 43-46, 54; (5) the development of specific conflicting claims of pope and emperor regarding the election and consecration of the pope, the creation and coronation of the emperor, and the exercise of functions which had been regarded as imperial, nos. 47-53, 55-59.

33. LEGISLATION CONCERNING THE ELECTION OF BISHOPS, FOURTH TO THE NINTH CENTURY.

Corpus Juris Canonici, Dist. LXIII, c. vi, vii, and i.

In the election of the clergy, especially of the bishops, it was some centuries before the theory and the practice of the church entirely agreed. In theory the laity should have nothing to do with the election of the clergy, but in fact, they have, at various times and in different degrees, exercised authority over such matters. Thus, for instance, the people of Rome had a part in the election of their bishop; the emperors at Constantinople, at first in person, later through the exarch at Ravenna, confirmed his election; Karl the Great and his successors named the bishops of Germany; Otto I and Henry III made and unmade bishops of Rome. This state of affairs lasted well into the eleventh century. The church strove more and more to free itself from all outside influence, while the emperors struggled to retain their control of it.

The Corpus Juris Canonici (Body of Canon Law), which consists chiefly of decisions of church councils and of papal decrees and bulls, is the code of laws by which the church is governed. Frequent additions were made to it until Gregory XIII (1572–85) prepared a standard edition of it. It has been republished a great many times. For the sake of brevity we have made use of a few of its chapters here instead of the longer originals from which they are taken.

C. vi. Laymen have not the right to choose those who are to be made bishops.

(From the Council of Laodicæa, fourth century.)

C. vii. Every election of a bishop, priest, or deacon, which is made by the nobility [that is, emperor, or others in authority], is void, according to the rule which says: " If a bishop makes use of the secular powers to obtain a diocese, he shall be deposed and those who supported him shall be cast out of the church."

(From the third canon of the second council at Nicæa, 787, quoting the 30th canon of the Apostolic Constitutions; Mansi, XVI, 748.)

C. i. No layman, whether emperor or noble, shall interfere with the election or promotion of a patriarch, metropolitan, or bishop, lest there should arise some unseemly disturbance or contention; especially since it is not fitting that any layman or person in secular authority should have any authority in such matters. . . . If any emperor or nobleman, or layman of any other rank, opposes the canonical election of any member of the clergy, let him be anathema until he yields and accepts the clear will of the church in the election and ordination of the bishop.

(From the twenty-second canon of the eighth synod of Constantinople, 869; Mansi, XVI, 174 f.)

34. THE POPE MUST BE CHOSEN FROM THE CARDINAL CLERGY OF ROME, 769.

Enactment of a Latin council held by Stephen III, 769, Cor. Jur. Can., Dist. LXXIX. (See also Mansi, XII, 719.)

C. iii. It is necessary that our mistress the holy Roman Catholic church be governed properly, and in accordance with the precedents established by St. Peter and his successors, and that the pope be chosen from the cardinal priests or cardinal deacons. C. iv. No one, whether layman or clergyman, shall presume to be made pope unless he has risen through the regular grades [1] at least to the rank of cardinal deacon or has been made a cardinal priest.

[1] The grades are given as follows in the Cor. Jur. Can., Dist. LXXVII, c. i. The candidate for the office of bishop must first have been doorkeeper (*ostiarius*), then reader (*lector*), then exorcist (*exorcista*), then consecrated as an acolyte (*acolythus*), then subdeacon (*subdiaconus*), then deacon (*diaconus*), then priest (*presbyter*), and then if he is elected he may be ordained bishop. The law expressed in chap. iii, so thoroughly in the interests of the ambitious clergy of Rome, was not long observed, for it frequently happened that the bishop of some other city was chosen pope. But it was in accord with previous legislation. The church had early declared against the removal of a clergyman from one congregation to another. Thus the council of Nicæa, 325, in its fifteenth canon (cf. Hefele, Conciliengeschichte, I, pp. 418 f), "forbids bishops, priests, and deacons to move from one town (congregation) to another, because such a practice is against the rule of the church and has often caused disturbances and divisions between congregations. If any bishop, priest, or deacon disobeys this command and removes

to another congregation, his action shall be illegal, and he shall be
sent back to the congregation which he was serving."

35. THE PETRINE THEORY AS STATED BY LEO I, 440–61.

Migne, 64.

Leo I (440–61) made frequent use of the Petrine theory. In brief
this theory is that to Peter as the prince of the apostles was committed the supreme power over the church. To him the keys were
intrusted in a special manner. In this consisted his primacy, his
superiority over the other apostles. This primacy or first rank he
communicated to his successors, the bishops of Rome, who, by virtue
of being his successors, held the same primacy over the church and
over all other bishops as Peter held over the other apostles. The passage on which this theory is based is found in Matt. 16:18 f: " And
I say unto thee, That thou art Peter, and upon this rock I will build
my church; and the gates of hell shall not prevail against it. And I
will give unto thee the keys of the kingdom of heaven: and whatsoever thou shalt bind on earth shall be bound in heaven: and whatsoever thou shalt loose on earth shall be loosed in heaven."

We offer the following detached passages from the works of Leo I
to illustrate his conception of the theory.

Col. 628. Our Lord Jesus Christ, the Saviour of the
world, caused his truth to be promulgated through the apostles. And while this duty was placed on all the apostles, the
Lord made St. Peter the head of them all, that from him
as from their head his gifts should flow out into all the
body. So that if anyone separates himself from St. Peter
he should know that he has no share in the divine blessing.

Col. 656. If any dissensions in regard to church matters
and the clergy should arise among you, we wish you to settle
them and report to us all the terms of the settlement, so
that we may confirm all your just and reasonable decisions.

Col. 995. Constantinople has its own glory and by the
mercy of God has become the seat of the empire. But secular matters are based on one thing, ecclesiastical matters on
another. For nothing will stand which is not built on the
rock [Peter] which the Lord laid in the foundation [Matt.
16:18]. . . . Your city is royal, but you cannot make it

apostolic [as Rome is, because its church was founded by St. Peter].

Col. 1031.   You will learn with what reverence the bishop of Rome treats the rules and canons of the church if you read my letters by which I resisted the ambition of the patriarch of Constantinople, and you will see also that I am the guardian of the catholic faith and of the decrees of the church fathers.

Col. 991.   On this account the holy and most blessed pope, Leo, the head of the universal church, with the consent of the holy synod, endowed with the dignity of St. Peter, who is the foundation of the church, the rock of the faith, and the door-keeper of heaven, through us, his vicars, deprived him of his rank as bishop, etc.   [From a letter of his legates.]

Col. 615.   And because we have the care of all the churches, and the Lord, who made Peter the prince of the apostles, holds us responsible for it, etc.

Col. 881.   Believing that it is reasonable and just that as the holy Roman church, through St. Peter, the prince of the apostles, is the head of all the churches of the whole world, etc.

Col. 147.   This festival should be so celebrated that in my humble person he [Peter] should be seen and honored who has the care over all the shepherds and the sheep committed to him, and whose dignity is not lacking in me, his heir, although I am unworthy.

36.   THE EMPEROR GIVES THE POPE AUTHORITY IN CERTAIN SECULAR MATTERS.

The Pragmatic Sanction of Justinian, 554; M. G. LL. folio, V, p. 175.

One of the chief effects of the invasions of the barbarians was an increased lawlessness and disorder throughout the territory in which they settled. The administration of justice was seriously disturbed by their presence in the country, and the machinery of government was, to a certain extent, destroyed by them. Under

these circumstances the clergy, by virtue of their office and character, were looked on as representatives of law, order, and justice,
and they were quite naturally given a voice in the administration
of justice and in the general management of affairs. The selections
from the pragmatic sanction, which Justinian issued in 554, show
in part the use which he made of the bishop of Rome to restore and
secure order and good government in Italy after the long, destructive,
and demoralizing wars which he waged with the East Goths.

§ 12. The bishops and chief men shall elect officials for
each province who shall be qualified and able to administer
its government, etc.

§ 19. That there may be no opportunity for fraud or
loss to the provinces, we order that, in the purchase and sale
of all kinds of produce [grain, wine, oil, etc.] and in the
payment and receipt of money, only those weights and measures shall be used which we have established and put under
the control of the pope and of the senate.

37. THE EMPEROR HAS THE RIGHT TO CONFIRM THE
ELECTION OF THE BISHOP OF ROME, *ca.* 650. A LETTER
FROM THE CHURCH AT ROME TO THE EMPEROR AT CON-
STANTINOPLE, ASKING HIM TO CONFIRM THE ELECTION OF
THEIR BISHOP.

Liber Diurnus, no. 58, Rozière's edition, pp. 103 ff; Von Sickel's edition. pp.
47 ff.

For a long time the emperor at Constantinople had exercised the
right of confirming the election of the bishop of Rome. No one
could be ordained and consecrated pope until his election had been
confirmed by the emperor.

The *Liber Diurnus* is a collection of letters or formulas which
were used by the papal secretaries as models in drawing up the
pope's letters. This particular collection was in use at the papal
court from about 600 to 900 A.D. When it became necessary to
write to the emperor at Constantinople to secure his confirmation
of the election of a bishop of Rome, a secretary would copy this
letter, inserting the proper names in the appropriate places and
making such other changes in its wording as might be necessary to
fit the particular case.

Although God himself has brought about such harmony and unity in the election of a successor to the pope who has just died that there is scarcely one that opposes it, it is necessary that we humbly pour out the prayers of our petition to our most serene and pious lord who is known to rejoice in the harmony of his subjects and graciously to grant what they unite in asking. Now, when our pope (name), of blessed memory, died, we all agreed in the election of (name), venerable archdeacon of the apostolic see, because from his early youth he had served in this church and had shown himself so able in all things that on the score of his merits he deserved to be put at the head of the government of the church; especially since he was of such a character that with the help of Christ and by constant association with the aforesaid most blessed pope (name), he has attained to the same high merits with which his predecessor (name), of blessed memory, was graced; with his eloquence, he stirred within us a desire for the holy joys of heaven; so we confidently believe that what we have lost in his predecessor we have found again in him. Therefore, with tears, all your servants beg that you, our lord, may deign to grant our petition and accede to our wishes concerning the ordination of him whom we have elected, and, to the glory of the realm, authorize his ordination; that thus, after you have established him over us as our pastor, we may constantly pray for the life and government of our lord the emperor to the omnipotent Lord and to St. Peter, over whose church, with your permission, a worthy governor is now to be ordained.

Signatures of the clergy:

I, (name), by the mercy of God, priest of the holy Roman Church, have signed this our action regarding (name), venerable archdeacon of the holy apostolic see, our pope elect.

Signatures of the laity:

I, (name), your servant, have with full consent signed

this our action regarding (name), venerable archdeacon of
the holy apostolic see, our pope elect.

38. A Letter from the Church at Rome to the
Exarch at Ravenna, Asking him to Confirm the Election of their Bishop, *ca.* 600.

Liber Diurnus, no. 60, Roziere's edition, pp. 110 ff; Von Sickel, pp. 50 ff.

As is clear from the preceding number, the confirmation of the
election of the bishop of Rome was in the hands of the emperor.
His residence was at Constantinople, but he was, of course, not
always to be found there. Because of his distance from Rome it
might take several months to secure his confirmation. Such delays
interfered with the administration of the office and were very bur-
densome to the Romans because the pope had a large share in the
government of the city. Until their new bishop was confirmed the
government of the city was almost at a standstill. So, in the seventh century, the emperor, at the request of the Romans, commissioned his exarch at Ravenna to act for him in this matter.

To the most excellent and exalted lord (may God graciously preserve him to us for a long life in his high office),
(name), exarch of Italy, the priests, deacons, and all the
clergy of Rome, the magistrates, the army, and the people
of Rome, as suppliants, send greeting.

Providence is able to give aid and to change the weeping
and groaning of the sorrowing into rejoicing, that those who
were recently smitten down with affliction may afterward be
fully consoled. For the poet king, from whose prophetic
heart the Holy Spirit spoke, has said: "Weeping may endure for a night, but joy cometh in the morning" [Ps.
30:5]. And again, giving thanks to God, he sings of the
greatness of his mercies, and says: "Thou hast turned for
me my mourning into dancing: thou hast put off my sack-
cloth, and girded me with gladness: to the end that my
glory may sing praise to thee, and not be silent" [Ps. 30:
11–12]. For he careth for us [1 Peter, 5:7] as that
chosen vessel [Peter] and our confession of faith declare.

For the things which were causing sadness He has changed to rejoicing and has mercifully given aid to us, unworthy sinners. Now, our pope (name) having been called from present cares to eternal rest, as is the lot of mortals, a great load of sorrow oppressed us, deprived, as we were, of our guardian. But because we hoped in God, He did not permit us long to remain in this affliction. For after we had spent three days in prayer that He would deign to make known to all who was worthy and should be elected pope, with the aid of his grace which inspired our minds, we all came together in the accustomed manner; that is, the clergy and the people of Rome, the nobility and the army, as we say, from the least to the greatest; and the election, with the help of God and the aid of the holy apostles, fell upon the person of (name), most holy archdeacon of this holy apostolic see of the church of Rome. The holy and chaste life of this good man, beloved of God, was so pleasing to all that no one opposed his election, and no one dissented from it. Why should not men unanimously agree upon him whom the incomparable and never failing providence of God had foreordained to this office? For without doubt this had been determined on in the presence of God. So, solemnly fulfilling God's decrees and confirming the desires of our hearts with our signatures, we have sent you our fellow-servants as the bearers of this writing, (name), most holy bishop, (name), venerable priest, (name), regionary notary, (name), regionary subdeacon, (names), honorable citizens, and from the most flourishing and successful army of Rome, (name), most eminent consul, and (names), chief men, tribunes of the army, together most earnestly begging and praying that you may approve our choice. For he who has been unanimously elected by us, is, so far as man can discern, above reproach. And therefore we beg and beseech you to grant our petition quickly, because there are many matters arising daily which require the solicitous care and

attention of a pope. And the affairs of the province and all
things connected therewith also need and are awaiting some
one to control them. Besides we need some one to keep the
neighboring enemy in check, a thing which can be done only
by the power of God and of the prince of the apostles,
through his vicar, the bishop of Rome. For it is well known
that at various times the bishop of Rome has driven off our
enemies by his warnings, and at others he has turned them
aside and restrained them with his prayers; so that by his
words alone, on account of their reverence for the prince of
the apostles, they have offered voluntary obedience; and thus
they whom the force of arms had not overcome have yielded
to papal threats and prayers.

Since these things are so, again and again we beseech you,
our exalted lord, with the aid and inspiration of God, to
perform the duty of your imperial office by granting our
request. And we, your humble servants, on seeing our desires fulfilled, may then give unceasing thanks to God and
to you, and with our spiritual pastor, our bishop, enthroned
on the apostolic seat, we may pour out prayers for the life,
health, and complete victories of our most exalted and Christian lords, (names), the great and victorious emperors, that
the merciful God may grant manifold victories to their royal
courage, and cause them to triumph over all peoples; and
that God may give them joy of heart because the ancient
rule of Rome has been restored. For we know that he whom
we have elected pope can, with his prayers, influence the
divine Omnipotence; and he has prepared a joyful increase
for the Roman empire, and he will aid you in the government of this province of Italy which is subject to you, and
he will aid and protect all of us, your servants, through
many years.

Signatures of the clergy:

I, (name), humble archpriest of the holy Roman church,
have with full consent subscribed to this document which we

have made concerning (name), most holy archdeacon, our bishop elect.

And the signatures of the laity:

I, (name), in the name of God, consul, have with full consent subscribed to this document which we have made concerning (name), most holy archdeacon, our bishop elect.

39. GREGORY I SENDS MISSIONARIES TO THE ENGLISH, 596.

Bede's Ecclesiastical History of the English, Bk. I, chs. 23 and 25.

The pope secured recognition of his supremacy largely because much of the west was Christianized through his efforts. The mission established by Augustine in England was one of the most important missionary undertakings of the pope because it succeeded in making England Roman Catholic. And not only that, but after the conversion of England, Englishmen were largely instrumental in Christianizing many parts of Europe and in subjecting them to the bishop of Rome. Thus it was an Englishman, Boniface, who organized the church in Germany and put it under papal control. By English and German missionaries the barbarians to the north and east of Germany, that is, the Danes, Norwegians, Swedes, Poles, Bohemians, and Hungarians, were Christianized and made tributary to the pope.

23. . . . Gregory was divinely led to send Augustine, the servant of God, and with him several other pious monks to preach the word of God to the English. . . .

25. . . . So Augustine and the servants of Christ who were with him came into Britain. At that time Ethelbert was king in Kent. He was a powerful king and had extended the boundaries of his realm to the Humber river, which separates the English of the north from those of the south. On the east shore of Kent there is a small island called Thanet, about large enough for 600 families, according to the English way of reckoning. . . . Here Augustine, the servant of the Lord, landed with his companions, who, it is said, numbered about forty. At the suggestion of the pope, they brought with them some Franks

as interpreters. They sent word to Ethelbert that they had come from Rome, bearing good tidings which would surely bring to all who obeyed them eternal joy in heaven and a kingdom without end with the true and living God. The king ordered them to remain where they were and to be supplied with food until he should make up his mind what to do with regard to them. For he already knew about Christianity. Indeed his wife, Bertha, of the royal family of the Franks, was a Christian. Her family had consented to her marriage with Ethelbert only on the condition that she should be permitted to remain faithful to her religion, and, to aid her in this, they had sent with her a bishop named Liudhard.

After some days the king came to Thanet and ordered Augustine and his companions to come to him. . . . At the command of the king they sat down, and after they had preached the word of God to the king and his companions, he responded as follows: "Beautiful indeed are your words and the promises which you make. But because they are new and untried I cannot accept them and desert those things which I and all the English have held for so long. However, since you are strangers and have come so far, and since I see that you desire to share with us those things which you think are true and best, we do not wish to offend you. On the contrary, we extend to you our gracious hospitality and will supply you with the necessities of life. And you may also preach, and convert to your faith as many as you can." And he gave them a dwelling-place in Canterbury, which is the chief city of his kingdom.

40. THE OATH OF BONIFACE TO POPE GREGORY II, 723.
Migne, 89, cols. 803 ff.

Although the Franks accepted Christianity in 496, they had made little progress in ecclesiastical discipline and in the knowledge of Christian doctrine. Heathen beliefs and practices were mixed with their Christianity, and the clergy were ignorant and undisciplined.

The influence and authority of the pope did not extend to them. Boniface was an Englishman, a monk, and a devoted supporter of the doctrine of papal supremacy. He spent his life as a missionary among the Germans and gained the title of the "apostle of Germany." From 715 to his death in 754 he labored with untiring zeal to convert them and to attach them to Rome. He visited Rome several times to secure the pope's consent and blessing on his work, and bound himself by an oath to labor for the advancement of papal interests. He established bishoprics which became famous, such as Würzburg, Eichstädt, and Erfurt, and monasteries, such as Fritzlar, and Fulda. By his efforts the German church was bound firmly to Rome and the pope's authority established over the church in Germany.

The pope required the newly elected bishops of his diocese to take an oath to be obedient and true to him. The unity of the church was to be secured by the obedience of all to one head, that is, the pope. So when the Lombards were converted to the orthodox faith the pope required their bishops to take the same oath to him as did the bishops of his diocese. Their oath is, with the exception of a few phrases, identical with this oath of Boniface. That is, the pope regarded Lombardy and Germany as having the same relation to him as did his own diocese about Rome.

I, Boniface, by the grace of God bishop, promise thee, St. Peter, prince of the apostles, and thy vicar, blessed pope Gregory, and his successors, through the Father, Son, and Holy Spirit, the inseparable Trinity, and on this thy most holy body, that I will hold the holy Catholic faith in all its purity, and by the help of God I will remain in unity with it, without which there is no salvation. I will in no way consent to anyone who acts against the unity of the church, but, as I have said, I will preserve the purity of my faith and give my support to thee [St. Peter] and to thy church, to which God has given the power of binding and loosing, and to thy vicar, and to his successors. And if I find out that any bishops are acting contrary to the ancient rules of the holy fathers, I will have no communion or association with them, but I will restrain them as far as I can. But if I cannot restrain them I will report it at once to my lord the pope. And if I shall ever in any way, by any deceit, or under any pretext, act contrary to this my promise, I shall be found guilty in the day of judgment, and shall suffer the punishment of Ananias and Sapphira, who presumed to try to deceive thee about their possessions and to lie to thee. This text of my oath, I, Boniface, unworthy bishop, have written with my own hand, and have placed it over the most holy body of St. Peter; before God as my witness and judge, I have taken this oath, which also I promise to keep.

41–42. The Rebellion of the Popes against the Emperor.

41. Letter of Pope Gregory II to the Emperor, Leo III, 726 or 727.

Migne, 89, cols. 521 ff

From the days of Constantine the Great the emperors assumed and actually exercised extensive authority over the church, presuming even to dictate in matters which concerned the doctrine and practice of the church. Since the emperor often supported doctrines which the bishop of Rome held to be heretical, the relations between him and the pope became more and more strained. The harsh way in which the emperors treated the popes who resisted them angered the papal adherents. There were other reasons also why the rule of the emperor was disliked in Rome, and so it soon came about that the people of Rome, and even of central Italy, looked upon the pope as the head of the opposition to the emperor and heartily supported him when he rebelled against the Greek rule.

The emperors met with increasing resistance when they interfered with the bishop of Rome. Pope Vigilius (547–554) was humiliated and deposed by Justinian and died in exile. Because Martin I (649–655) resisted the emperor in a doctrinal matter, Constans II (642–668) had him brought as a prisoner to Constantinople (653) and afterward exiled him to the Crimea. But Sergius I (687–701) successfully resisted the emperor and escaped arrest and deposition because the people of central Italy supported him and threatened to revolt if the emperor should seize and carry away their pope.

The struggle about the use of images gave the popes an opportunity to rebel and assert their complete independence of the emperor. In 726 the emperor, Leo III, began to condemn the presence and use of images in the churches. He met with great resistance, especially in the west, where pope Gregory II vigorously defended the images. There followed a heated controversy, in the course of which the pope laid down the principle that the emperor has no authority in ecclesiastical matters. In the letter here given Gregory II asserts his independence and practically excommunicates the emperor. And Gregory III published a general excommunication of all iconoclasts, as those who destroyed images were called. The emperor was of course included in this excommunication. Peace was never again established between the pope and emperor, and the rebellion of the west was consummated in 800 when pope Leo III crowned Karl the Great emperor.

We have received the letter which you sent us by your ambassador Rufinus. We are deeply grieved that you should persist in your error, that you should refuse to recognize the things which are Christ's, and to accept the teaching and follow the example of the holy fathers, the saintly miracle-workers and learned doctors. I refer not only to foreign doctors, but also to those of your own country. For what men are more learned than Gregory the worker of miracles, Gregory of Nyssa, Gregory the theologian, Basil of Cappadocia, or John Chrysostom—not to mention thousands of others of our holy fathers and doctors, who, like these, were filled with the spirit of God? But you have followed the guidance of your own wayward spirit and have allowed the exigencies of the political situation at your own court to lead you astray. You say: "I am both emperor and bishop." But the emperors who were before you, Constantine the Great, Theodosius the Great, Valentinian the Great, and Constantine the father of Justinian, who attended the sixth synod, proved themselves to be both emperors and bishops by following the true faith, by founding and fostering churches, and by displaying the same zeal for the faith as the popes. These emperors ruled righteously; they held synods in harmony with the popes, they tried to establish true doctrines, they founded and adorned churches. Those who claim to be both emperors and priests should demonstrate it by their works; you, since the beginning of your rule, have constantly failed to observe the decrees of the fathers. Wherever you found churches adorned and enriched with hangings you despoiled them. For what are our churches? Are they not made by hand of stones, timbers, straw, plaster, and lime? But they are also adorned with pictures and representations of the miracles of the saints, of the sufferings of Christ, of the holy mother herself, and of the saints and apostles; and men expend their wealth on such images. Moreover, men and women make use of these pictures to instruct in the faith their little children and young men and maidens in the bloom of youth and those from heathen nations; by means of these pictures the hearts and minds of men are directed to God. But you have ordered the people to abstain from the pictures, and have attempted to satisfy them with idle sermons, trivialities, music of pipe and zither, rattles and toys, turning them from the giving of thanks to the hearing of idle tales. You shall have your part with them, and with those who invent useless fables and babble of their ignorance. Hearken to us, emperor: abandon your present course and accept the holy church as you found her, for matters of faith and practice concern not the emperor, but the pope,[1] since we have the mind of Christ [1 Cor. 2:16]. The making of laws for the church is one thing and the governing of the empire another; the ordinary intelligence which is used in administering worldly affairs is not adequate to the settlement of spiritual matters. Behold, I will show you now the difference between the palace and the church, between the emperor and the pope; learn this and be saved; be no longer contentious. If anyone should take from you the adornments of royalty, your purple robes, diadem, sceptre, and your ranks of servants, you would be regarded by men as base, hateful, and abject; but to this condition you have reduced the churches, for you have deprived them of their ornaments and made them unsightly. Just as the pope has not the right to interfere in the palace or to infringe upon the royal prerogatives, so the emperor has not the right to interfere in the churches, or to conduct elections among the clergy, or to consecrate, or to administer the sacraments, or even to participate in the sacraments without the aid of a priest; let each one of us abide in the same calling wherein he is called of God [1 Cor. 7:20]. Do you see, emperor, the difference between popes and emperors? If anyone has offended you, you confiscate his house and take everything from him but his life, or you hang him or cut off his head, or you banish him, sending him far from his children and from all his relatives and friends. But popes do not so; when anyone has sinned and has confessed, in place of hanging him or cutting off his head, they put the gospel and the cross about his neck, and imprison him, as it were, in the sacristy or the treasure chamber of the sacred vessels; they put him into the part of the church reserved for the deacons and the catechumens; they prescribe for him fasting, vigils, and praise. And after they have chastened and punished him with fasting, then they give him of the precious body of the Lord and of the holy blood. And when they have restored him as a chosen vessel, free from sin, they hand him over to the Lord pure and unspotted. Do you see now, emperor, the difference between the church and the empire? Those emperors who have lived piously in Christ have obeyed the popes, and not vexed them. But you, emperor, since you have transgressed and gone astray, and since you have written with your own hand and confessed that he who attacks the fathers is to be execrated, have thereby condemned yourself by your own sentence and have driven from you the Holy Spirit. You persecute us and vex us tyrannically with violent and carnal hand. We, unarmed and defenseless, possessing no earthly armies, call now upon the prince of all the armies of creation, Christ

seated in the heavens, commanding all the hosts of celestial
beings, to send a demon upon you;[2] as the apostle says:
" To deliver such an one unto Satan for the destruction of
the flesh, that the spirit may be saved " [1 Cor. 5:5].   Do
you see now, emperor, to what a pitch of impudence and
inhumanity you have gone?   You have driven your soul
headlong into the abyss, because you would not humble yourself and bend your stubborn neck.   When a pope is able by
his teaching and admonition to bring the emperor of his
time before God, guiltless and cleansed from all sin, he gains
great glory from Him on the holy day of resurrection, when
all our secrets and all our works are brought to light to our
confusion in the presence of his angels.   But we shall blush
for shame, because you will have lost your soul by your disobedience, while the popes that preceded us have won over
to God the emperors of their times.   How ashamed we will
be on that day, that the emperor of our time is false and
ignominious, instead of great and glorious.   Now, therefore,
we exhort you to do penance; be converted and turn to the
truth; obey the truth as you found and received it.   Honor
and glorify our holy and glorious fathers and doctors who
dispelled the blindness from our eyes and restored us to
sight.   You ask: " How was it that nothing was said about
images in six councils? "[3]   What then?   Nothing was said
about bread or water, whether that should be eaten or not;
whether this should be drunk or not; yet these things have
been accepted from the beginning for the preservation of
human life.   So also images have been accepted; the popes
themselves brought them to councils, and no Christian would
set out on a journey without images, because they were possessed of virtue and approved of God.   We exhort you to be
both emperor and bishop, as you have called yourself in your
letter.   But if you are ashamed to take this upon yourself
as emperor, then write to all the regions to which you have
given offence, that Gregory the pope and Germanus the patri-

arch of Constantinople are at fault in the matter of the images [that is, are responsible for the destruction of the images],[4] and we will take upon ourselves the responsibility for the sin, as we have authority from God to loose and to bind all things, earthly and celestial; and we will free you from responsibility in this matter. But no, you will not do this! Knowing that we would have to render account to Christ the Lord for our office, we have done our best to convert you from your error, by admonition and warning, but you have drawn back, you have refused to obey us or Germanus or our fathers, the holy and glorious miracle-workers and doctors, and you have followed the teaching of perverse and wicked men who wander from the truth. You shall have your lot with them. As we have already informed you, we shall proceed on our way to the extreme western regions, where those who are earnestly seeking to be baptized are awaiting us. For although we have sent them bishops and clergymen from our church, their princes have not yet been induced to bow their heads and be baptized, because they hope to be received into the church by us in person. Therefore we gird ourselves for the journey in the goodness of God, lest perchance we should have to render account for their condemnation and for our faithlessness. May God give you prudence and patience, that you may be turned to the truth from which you have departed; may he again restore the people to their one shepherd, Christ, and to the one fold of the orthodox churches and prelates, and may the Lord our God give peace to all the earth now and forever to all generations. Amen.

1 Note the plain statement that the emperor has no authority in ecclesiastical matters. Observe also the general tone of the whole letter.

2 This is equivalent to the excommunication of the emperor. But as Gregory's authority was not recognized in Constantinople, his excommunication of the emperor would not be observed.

3 The first six general councils of the church here referred to

were (1) Nicæa, 325; (2) Constantinople, 381; (3) Ephesus, 431;
(4) Chalcedon, 451; (5) Constantinople, 553; (6) Constantinople,
681.

⁴ The text of this passage, as Migne has it, is perhaps corrupt;
its meaning, at any rate, is obscure. We have given the only reasonable interpretation that seemed possible. Apparently the pope
agrees to assume the responsibility for the destruction of images
in the past, if only the emperor will accept the papal view and
cease from his opposition to images in the future.

42. GREGORY III EXCOMMUNICATES ALL ICONOCLASTS, 731 A.D.

Mansi, XII, cols. 272 f; Duchesne, Liber Pontificalis, I, p. 416.

See introductory note to no. 41.

The pope [Gregory III] made a decree in the council
that if anyone, in the future, should condemn those who
hold to the old custom of the apostolic church and should
oppose the veneration of the holy images, and should remove,
destroy, profane, or blaspheme against the holy images of
God, or of our Lord Jesus Christ, or of his mother, the
immaculate and glorious Virgin Mary, or of the apostles,
or of any of the saints, he should be cut off from the body
and blood of our Lord Jesus Christ. And all the clergy
present solemnly signed this decree.

43. THE POPE, GREGORY III, ASKS AID OF THE FRANKS AGAINST THE LOMBARDS, 739. A LETTER OF GREGORY III TO KARL MARTEL.

Jaffé, IV, p. 14.

When the pope was attacked by the Lombards he found himself
without protection. Aside from the fact that the Greek emperor
was wholly occupied in the east, the pope was in rebellion against
him and so could not expect aid from him. Under these circumstances there was nothing to do but seek help from the Franks.
But Karl Martel was a friend of the Lombards and so, although
the pope appealed to him more than once, Karl declined to give him
aid and to interfere in the affairs of Italy.

Pope Gregory to his most excellent son, Karl, sub-king.

In our great affliction we have thought it necessary to write to you a second time, believing that you are a loving son of St. Peter, the prince of apostles, and of ourselves, and that out of reverence for him you would obey our commands to defend the church of God and his chosen people. We can now no longer endure the persecution of the Lombards, for they have taken from St. Peter all his possessions, even those which were given him by you and your fathers. These Lombards hate and oppress us because we sought protection from you; for the same reason also the church of St. Peter is despoiled and desolated by them. But we have intrusted a more complete account of all our woes to your faithful subject, our present messenger, and he will relate them to you. You, oh son, will receive favor from the same prince of apostles here and in the future life in the presence of God, according as you render speedy aid to his church and to us, that all peoples may recognize the faith and love and singleness of purpose which you display in defending St. Peter and us and his chosen people. For by doing this you will attain lasting fame on earth and eternal life in heaven.

44–46.   THE ACQUISITION OF LAND BY THE POPE.
44.   PROMISE OF PIPPIN TO POPE STEPHEN II, 753–54.
Duchesne, Liber Pontificalis, I, pp. 447 ff.

The Lombards entered Italy in 568 and soon established themselves in the valley of the Po. For some years the boundary line between them and the Byzantine possessions, that is, the lands still held by the emperor, ran, roughly speaking, from Monselice (near Padua) west to Mantua, then southwest to Reggio, then northwest to Parma, then southwest to Berceto in the Apennines. But after Authari (583–90) became king of the Lombards he renewed the war of conquest which had been interrupted for a few years. He and his successors conquered the Byzantine possessions bit by bit and added them to the Lombard kingdom. In this way Lombardy was slowly enlarged and the Byzantine land, which was called the

"province Italy" (Italia provincia), was correspondingly reduced
in size. Success made the Lombard kings more ambitious and led
them to plan the conquest of all Italy. A great step forward was
taken in 749 when Aistulf took Ravenna, drove out the exarch, and
put an end to the Byzantine rule in central Italy. Tuscany, which
was separated from Liguria by a line from Luna to Berceto, was
already in their hands, and Corsica, after suffering several invasions,
had finally been occupied by them in the eighth century. Venice,
Istria, and the duchies of Rome, Spoleto, and Benevento were next
attacked, but they united to resist their common enemy, and put
themselves under the protection of the pope. Under these circumstances Stephen II (752–757) saw an opportunity to unite all these
provinces and to make himself their political head. He determined
to try to succeed to the power of the emperor in Italy. He accordingly went to France and secured the promise from Pippin to give
him all the above-named territories and to force the Lombards to
withdraw from them into the territory which they had first occupied.
See no. 6. It was an ambitious plan which Stephen II formed, but
he could not carry it into effect. Pippin fulfilled his promise only
in part, and the pope was content with a few cities and the promise
of Aistulf that he would never again attack any of the territories
named in Pippin's promise. Desiderius (756–774), however, did not
keep the promise which Aistulf, his predecessor, had given, but
made war on the duchy of Rome. Adrian I (772–795) called on Karl
the Great to come to his aid. Karl came, and, while spending
Easter (774) at Rome, at the earnest request of Adrian, renewed
the promise of his father. But Karl did not keep this promise
which had been so solemnly made. Contrary to the wishes of the
pope he made himself king of the Lombards and thereby inherited
the ambitions, pretensions, policy, and interests of the Lombard
kings. The situation was changed. To Karl, as well as to the
dukes of Benevento and Spoleto, and to the people of Istria, an
increase in the power of the pope was no longer a desirable thing.
So Karl refused to keep his promise. Adrian angrily protested.
But Karl was deaf to protests and threats. Their relations were
consequently strained for some time, but eventually they made a
compromise. Karl gave him certain Tuscan cities and some taxes
from the rest of Tuscany and from Spoleto. For nearly 200 years
the promise of Pippin lost all importance, until it was renewed in
962 by Otto I, who incorporated it in his famous gift to John XII.
See no. 54.

When the king learned of the approach of the blessed pope,

he hastened to meet him, accompanied by his wife and sons and nobles, and sent his son Charles and certain of the nobles nearly one hundred miles in advance to meet the pope. He himself, however, received the pope about three miles from his palace of Pontico, dismounting and prostrating himself with his wife and sons and nobles, and accompanying the pope a little distance on foot by his saddle as if he were his esquire. Thus the pope proceeded to the palace with the king, giving glory and praise to God in a loud voice, with hymns and spiritual songs. This was on the sixth day of the month of January, on the most holy festival of the Epiphany of our Lord Jesus Christ. And when they were seated in the palace the pope began to beseech the king with tears to make a treaty with St. Peter and the Roman state [1] and to assume the protection of their interests. And the king assured the pope on his oath that he would strive with all his powers to obey his prayers and admonitions and to restore the exarchate of Ravenna and the rights and territories of the Roman state, as the pope wished. . . .

The aforesaid king Pippin, after receiving the admonitions and the prayers of the pope, took leave of him and proceeded to the place called Kiersy,[2] and called together there all the lords of his kingdom, and by repeating to them the holy admonitions of the pope he persuaded them to agree to fulfil his promise to the pope.

[1] Rome is evidently regarded as the possession of St. Peter. In that case the administration of its government is in the hands of the pope, who is the vicar of St. Peter on earth.

[2] The meeting at Kiersy took place April 14, 754.

45. DONATION OF PIPPIN, 756.

Duchesne, Liber Pont., I, p. 454.

See introductory note to no. 44.

The most Christian king of the Franks [Pippin] despatched his counsellor Fulrad, venerable abbot and priest, to receive these cities, and then he himself straightway returned to France with his army.   The aforesaid Fulrad met the representatives of King Aistulf at Ravenna, and went with them through the various cities of the Pentapolis and of Emilia, receiving their submission and taking hostages from each and bearing away with him their chief men and the keys of their gates.   Then he went to Rome, and placed the keys of Ravenna and of the other cities of the exarchate along with the grant of them which the king had made, in the confession of St. Peter,[1] thus handing them over to the apostle of God [Peter] and to his vicar the holy pope and to all his successors to be held and controlled forever. These are the cities: Ravenna, Rimini, Pesaro, Conca, Fano, Cesena, Sinigaglia, Forlimpopoli, Forli with the fortress of Sussubium, Montefeltre, Acerreagium, Monte Lucati, Serra, San Marino, Bobbio, Urbino, Cagli, Lucioli, Gubbio, Comacle; and also the city of Narni, which in former years had been taken from the duchy of Spoleto by the Romans.

[1] The grave of St. Peter is under the high altar of St. Peter's in Rome.   In front of the grave and on the same level with it is a large open space to which one descends by a flight of steps.   This open space in front of the tomb is called the " confession of St. Peter."

46.   Promise of Charles to Adrian I, 774.

Duchesne, Liber Pont., I. p. 498.

See introductory note to no. 44.

Now on Wednesday the aforesaid pope [Adrian] came to the church of St. Peter the apostle, with all his officials, both ecclesiastical and military, and held a conference with the king and earnestly besought, admonished, and exhorted him by his paternal love to fulfil the promise which his father, Pippin, the former king, and he himself [that is, Karl], along with his brother Karlmann and all the officials of the Franks, had made to St. Peter and to his vicar the holy pope, Stephen II, of blessed memory, when he went to France; that is, to give to St. Peter and to all his vicars certain cities and their territories in the province of Italy to be held forever. And when the king had caused them to read to him that promise which had been made at Kiersy in France, he and his officials ratified all its provisions. And of his own will and gladly the aforesaid Karl, the most excellent and truly Christian king of the Franks, ordered another promise of the gift, an exact copy of the former, to be drawn up by Etherius, his chaplain and notary, in which he granted to St. Peter the same cities and their territories, and promised that they would be handed over to the pope according to the designated boundaries as they were contained in that gift; that is, Corsica, and from Luna to Suriano, thence over the Apennines to Berceto, thence to Parma, thence to Reggio, and thence to Mantua and Monselice; and besides the whole exarchate of Ravenna as it was of old, and the provinces of Venetia and Istria, as well as the duchies of Spoleto and Benevento. And when the grant had been drawn up and signed with his own hand, Karl caused all the bishops, abbots, dukes, and counts to sign it also. And placing it first on the altar of St. Peter, and then within his holy confession, the king of the Franks and his officials gave it thus to St. Peter and to his vicar the holy pope Adrian, promising with a solemn oath that they would observe everything contained in that grant. And this most Christian king of the Franks caused Etherius to draw up a copy of this grant and placed it himself upon the body of St. Peter, under the gospels which are kissed there, that it might be a perpetual testimonial of the gift and an eternal memorial of his name and of the Frankish kingdom. And the king took with him other copies of the same grant that were made by the notary of the holy Roman church.

47. KARL THE GREAT DECLARES THE POPE HAS ONLY SPIRITUAL DUTIES, 796. LETTER OF KARL TO LEO III.

Jaffé, IV, pp. 354 ff.

Karl the Great had a keen sense of his authority and position, and resented any action which seemed to him an infringement of his prerogatives. Adrian I had offended him by presuming to approve and publish the acts of the council of Nicæa, 787, without waiting for Karl's authorization. By this letter to the pope, Leo III, Karl made it plain to him that his duties were only spiritual.

Karl, by the grace of God king of the Franks and Lombards, and patricius of the Romans, to his holiness, pope Leo, greeting. . . . Just as I entered into an agreement with the most holy father, your predecessor, so also I desire to make with you an inviolable treaty of mutual fidelity and love; that, on the one hand, you shall pray for me and give me the apostolic benediction, and that, on the other, with the aid of God I will ever defend the most holy seat of the holy Roman church. For it is our part to defend the holy church of Christ from the attacks of pagans and infidels from without, and within to enforce the acceptance of the catholic faith. It is your part, most holy father, to aid us in the good fight by raising your hands to God as Moses did [Ex. 17:11], so that by your intercession the Christian people under the leadership of God may always and everywhere have the victory over the enemies of His holy name, and the name of our Lord Jesus Christ may be glorified throughout the world. Abide by the canonical law in all things and obey the precepts of the holy fathers always, that your life may be an example of sanctity to all, and your holy admonitions be observed by the whole world, and that your light may so shine before men that they may see your good works and glorify your father which is in heaven [Matt. 5:16]. May omnipotent God preserve your holiness unharmed through many years for the exalting of his holy church.

48. KARL THE GREAT EXERCISES AUTHORITY IN ROME, 800.

Einhard's Annals, M. G. SS. folio, I, p. 188.

The title of patricius of Rome was somewhat vague and it is impossible to say exactly how much actual authority attached to it. But it is evident from Karl's conduct that he regarded himself as responsible for the government of Rome. The passage from Einhard's Annals shows that Karl was the supreme authority in legal matters there. He acted as judge even in the case of the pope. There was no one willing to make a formal charge against Leo, and hence he might have been declared innocent. But he was not willing to receive that sort of acquittal. So of his own accord he took an oath to his innocence.

Anno 800. The day before Karl reached Rome pope Leo came to Nomentum to meet him. Karl received him with great honor and they dined together. The pope preceded Karl to Rome, and the next morning took his stand, with the bishops and all the clergy of the city, on the steps of St. Peter's to receive Karl when he should come. . . . Seven days later Karl called a public meeting, in which he made known the reasons why he had come to Rome. He then devoted himself every day to the accomplishment of the things which had called him to the city. Of these he began with the most important as well as the most difficult, namely, the investigation of the crimes with which the pope was charged. As there was no one who was willing to prove the truth of those charges, Leo took the gospels in his hand, and, in the presence of all the people, mounted the pulpit in St. Peter's, and took an oath that he was innocent of the crimes laid to his charge.

49. THE OATH OF POPE LEO III BEFORE KARL THE GREAT, 800.

Jaffé, IV, pp. 378 ff.

See introductory note to no. 48.

Most beloved brethren, it is well known that evil men rose up against me and wished to do me harm and accused

me of grave crimes. And now the most clement and serene
king, Karl, has come with his priests and nobles to this city
to try the case. Therefore, I, Leo, bishop of the holy Roman church, neither judged nor coerced by anyone, do clear
and purge myself from these charges before you in the sight
of God, who knows my secret thoughts, and of his holy
angels, and of St. Peter, in whose church we now stand. I
swear that I neither did these wicked and criminal things
of which my enemies accuse me, nor ordered them to be
done, and of this God is my witness, in whose presence we
now stand and into whose judgment we shall come. And
I do this in order to clear myself of these suspicions, and
not because it is commanded in the canons, or because I
desire to impose this practice as a precedent upon my successors or brothers and fellow-bishops.

50. The Oath of the Romans to Ludwig the Pious and Lothar, 824.

Altmann und Bernheim, no. 35.

The emperor, Ludwig the Pious, intrusted the government of Italy
to his oldest son, Lothar. In order to keep control of the papal
elections, Lothar compelled the Romans to take the following oath:

I, (name), promise in the name of the omnipotent God
and on the four holy gospels and on this cross of our Lord
Jesus Christ and on the body of most blessed Peter, prince
of the apostles, that from this day I will be faithful to our
lords, the emperors, Ludwig [the Pious] and Lothar, all
my life, according to my strength and understanding, without any fraud or deceit, in so far as this shall not violate
the oath of fidelity which I have sworn to the pope. And
I promise that according to my strength and understanding
I will not permit a papal election to take place in any way
except canonically and legally, and that he who may be elected
pope shall not with my consent be consecrated until, in the
presence of the emperor's ambassadors and of the people,

he takes such an oath as pope Eugene [1] did that he will rule
without any change.

[1] Eugene II (824–827) was then pope. The text of the oath which
he had sworn to Lothar is not preserved. But we may infer its
contents from the expression "that he will rule without any change."

**51.   The Emperor Admits the Right of the Pope to
Confer the Imperial Title.   Passages from a Letter of
Ludwig II, Emperor, to Basil, Emperor at Constanti-
nople, 871.**

Bouquet, VII, pp. 572 ff.

Although the Greek emperor, Michael, recognized Karl the Great
as emperor in the west (see nos. 13–14), some of his successors took
a different view of the matter and declared the emperors in the
west usurpers.   Basil had written to Ludwig II saying that the
latter was not emperor and therefore should not assume the title.
Ludwig replied with some vigor, advancing various arguments in
his own favor.   The student should examine this letter to discover
(1) the objections which Basil had made, and (2) the arguments
by which Ludwig II refuted them.

Among other things, Ludwig said he had a right to the title of
emperor:

Because all the patriarchs and all men of every rank, except you alone, have, of their own accord, addressed us as
such whenever they have written to us.   And besides, our
uncles [Charles the Bald and Ludwig the German], glorious kings, willingly call us emperor.   And they do so, not
out of regard for our age, for they are older than we, but
because of the anointing and consecration by which, with
God's will, we were advanced to this high office through
the laying on of the hands of the pope, and because, at
God's command, we have the government of the Roman
empire. . . .

We are much surprised that you should say we are laying claim to a title which is new to our family.   For that
cannot be a new title which was held by our grandfather.
And he did not usurp it, as you say he did, but he received

it at the command of God, by the decision of the church, and through the anointing and laying on of the hands of the pope. . . .

It is absurd that you should say I have not inherited the imperial name, and that my race is not worthy to have such a dignity. Even my grandfather inherited it from his father. Why is not my race worthy of producing an emperor, since emperors have been chosen from among the Spaniards and Isaurians and Khazars? For surely you cannot say that those nations are more renowned than the Franks either in religion or in courage. . . . To your statement that we do not rule over even all of France, here is a brief answer: We surely do rule over all France, since we certainly have what they have, with whom we are one in flesh and blood and one spirit through the Lord.

You wonder that we are called emperor of the Romans instead of emperor of the Franks. But you ought to know that if we were not emperor of the Romans we could not be emperor of the Franks. For we have received this name and dignity from the Romans, whose people and city, the mother of all the churches of God, we have received, in accordance with God's will, to govern, to defend, and to exalt, and from her our family received the authority, first, to rule as kings, and, afterward, as emperors. For the rulers of the Franks were first called kings and afterward those who were anointed with holy oil by the popes to this office were called emperors. Karl the Great, our grand-grandfather, having been anointed in this way, because of his great piety, was the first of our race and family to be called emperor and to be the anointed of the Lord. How much greater right have we to the imperial title, therefore, than the many who have been made emperor without any religious ceremony or holy rite being performed by a pope, being elected only by the senate and people of Rome, who had no regard for such holy rites? And some have been made emperor by even less authority, being proclaimed by the army, and others by women, and others in still other ways.

Now, if you blame the Roman bishop for what he did [in crowning Karl the Great], you must also blame Samuel, because, after anointing Saul, he rejected him and anointed David to be king. But it will be easy to answer anyone who shall make even one complaint against the pope [for having anointed Karl the Great as emperor]. If you will search the pages of the Greek annals and see what the bishops of Rome had to endure from their enemies, and yet received no protection from you, and even what they had to endure from you and your people, you will find many things which will prevent you from blaming them. But these external matters were of little importance compared with the efforts of the Greeks to destroy the church by their many heresies. So, very properly, the bishops of Rome deserted the apostate Greeks—for what concord hath Christ with Belial? [2 Cor. 6:15]—and joined a people which clung to God and brought forth the fruits of his kingdom. For "God is no respecter of persons," as the great apostle said, " but in every nation he that feareth him is accepted with him " [Acts 10:34, 35]. Therefore, since this is so, why do you make it a reproach to us who have the imperial crown that we are born of the Franks, when in every nation he that feareth God is accepted with him? Theodosius the elder [379–395] and his sons, Arcadius and Honorius, and Theodosius the younger, son of Arcadius, were Spaniards, and yet we do not find that anyone blamed Theodosius or objected to him because he was a Spaniard, and not a Roman, or tried to prevent his sons from succeeding to the position and honor of their father, as you now try to do,.as if the race of the Franks did not belong to that inheritance concerning which the Father speaks to the Son, saying: " Ask of me and I shall give thee the heathen for thine inheritance, and the uttermost parts of the earth for thy possession " [Ps. 2:8].

And in another place: "For them that honor me I will honor" [1 Sam. 2:30]. And there are many other such sayings.

Therefore, my dearest brother, cease to be contentious in this matter and to listen to flatterers. For the race of the Franks has brought forth the most abundant fruits to the Lord, not only in believing quickly, but also in converting others to the faith. But the Lord spoke of you when he said: "The kingdom shall be taken from you and given to a nation bringing forth the fruits thereof" [Matt. 21:43]. For as God was able of stones to raise up children unto Abraham [Matt. 3:9], so from the hardness of the Franks he was able to raise up successors to the Roman emperors. . . . And as Christians, through faith in Christ, are the seed of Abraham, and the Jews, through lack of faith, ceased to be sons of Abraham, so also we, through our correct belief, that is, through our orthodoxy, received the government of the Roman empire, and the Greeks, because of their heresy, ceased to be emperors. They deserted not only the city which was the seat of the empire, but even the Roman people, and moved to other parts [that is, Constantinople], and have even lost the Latin tongue.

52. THE POPE ENACTS THAT PAPAL ELECTIONS MUST TAKE PLACE IN THE PRESENCE OF THE EMPEROR'S REPRESENTATIVES. ENACTMENT OF A ROMAN SYNOD HELD BY JOHN IX, 898.

Cor. Jur. Can., Dist. LXIII, c. xxviii; M. G. LL. folio, II, parte sec., p. 158.

The election of a pope was often attended with violence on the part of Roman factions, which, under the leadership of various noble families, sought to elect one of their own party. John IX recognized that the emperor was the only one who could prevent these abuses and so enacted that all papal elections should take place in the presence of the emperor's representatives.

Since the holy Roman church, over which in accordance

with God's will we preside, on the death of a pope often suffers violence from many persons, because the pope is elected without the knowledge of the emperor, and hence the emperor does not send messengers, as canonical custom and practice require that he should, who may be present and prevent all disturbances during the election, we decree that when a pope is to be elected, the bishops [1] and all the clergy shall come together and the election shall take place in the presence of the senate and people. And the one thus chosen shall be consecrated in the presence of the emperor's messengers.

[1] More than thirty bishops took part in the election of Stephen VI, 896, although there were but seven cardinal bishops. Hence this probably means all the bishops of the whole diocese of Rome, not simply the seven cardinal bishops. It is apparent therefore that in the ninth century the cardinal clergy had not yet secured any special prerogative in the election of a pope. Many think that this enactment was made in 816 instead of 898.

53. THE OATH OF OTTO I TO JOHN XII, 961.
M. G. LL. 4to, IV, 1, no. 10.

Although the pope needed the help of the king of the Germans, and was willing to confer upon him the title of emperor, yet he was afraid that Otto might assume too much authority and deprive the papal office of much of its power. He accordingly attempted to secure his position by demanding the following oath of Otto. It will be observed that Otto did not take the oath in person but sent his representative to take it for him. It was, nevertheless, binding on Otto. However, it did not prevent him from afterward deposing John and putting another pope in his place.

I, Otto, king, cause my representative to promise and swear to you, pope John, in my name, by the Father, Son, and Holy Spirit, and by this piece of the life-giving cross and by these relics of the saints, that, if I shall come to Rome with the consent of God, I will exalt the holy Roman church and you, her ruler, to the best of my ability. And you shall never by my wish, advice, consent, or instigation,

suffer any loss in life or in limb, or in the honor which you
now have or which you shall have obtained from me. I
will never make laws or rules in regard to the things which
are under your jurisdiction or the jurisdiction of the Romans without your consent. I will restore to you all of the
lands of St. Peter that shall have come into my hands; and
I will cause the one to whom I shall have committed Italy
to rule in my absence [2] to swear to you that he will always
aid you according to his ability in defending the lands of
St. Peter.

[2] In accordance with imperial theory, Otto, as emperor, would rule
over Italy. He agrees to protect the pope " in the things which are
under his jurisdiction," but that does not mean that the pope had
jurisdiction in all things. The supreme authority is the emperor,
to whom the pope, as well as all other bishops and princes of Italy,
are subject.

54. Otto I Confirms the Pope in the Possession of his Lands, 962.

M. G. LL. 4to, IV, 1, no. 12; Altmann und Bernheim, no. 36.

In order to secure his possessions, John XII persuaded Otto I to
confirm his rights to them. In section 15 Otto reserves his imperial
rights, thus furnishing another proof that he was sovereign over
the lands which the pope held. By comparing this document with
the donations of Pippin and of Karl the Great (nos. 45 and 46), the
growth of the papal land claims will be apparent.

In the name of omnipotent God, the Father, Son, and
Holy Ghost. We, Otto, by the grace of God emperor and
Augustus, together with our glorious son, king Otto, promise
and pledge to thee, St. Peter, prince of apostles and keeper
of the keys of heaven, and through thee to thy vicar,
pope John XII, the following possessions, as his predecessors have held and possessed them up to the present
time; namely, (1) the city of Rome with its duchy, and
its neighboring villages and territories, highland and low-
land, shores and ports; (2) all the cities, towns, fortresses,

and villages of Tuscany; that is, Porto, Civita Vecchia, Ceri, Bieda, Marturianum, Sutri, Nepi, Gallese, Orte, Polimartium, Ameria, Todi, Perugia, with its three islands, the larger and the smaller, and Pulvensis, Narni, and Otricoli, with all the territories belonging to the aforesaid cities; (3) the whole exarchate of Ravenna with all the cities, towns, and fortresses which our predecessors the most excellent emperors, Pippin and Karl, conferred on St. Peter and your predecessors by a deed of gift; namely, the city of Ravenna and the district of Emilia, including the following towns: Bobbio, Cesena, Forlimpopoli, Forli, Faenza, Imola, Bologna, Ferrara, Comacle, Adria, and Gabello, with all the territories and islands by land and sea which belong to the aforesaid cities; (4) likewise also the Pentapolis; that is, Rimini, Pesaro, Fano, Sinigaglia, Ancona, Osimo, Humana, Iesi, Forum Sempronii, Montefeltre, Urbino, and the territory of Balneum, Cagli, Lucioli, and Gubbio, with all the territories belonging to the aforesaid cities; (5) likewise the whole Sabine territory as it was granted to St. Peter by our predecessor, emperor Karl, by a deed of gift; (6) likewise in Lombard Tuscany the fortress of Felicitas, and the towns of Orvieto, Bagnorea, Ferento, Viterbo, Orcle, Marca, Toscanella, Soana, Populonia, and Roselle, with all their suburbs and villages and all their territories, towns, and boundaries; (7) and likewise from Luna, with the island of Corsica, to Suriano, thence over the Apennines to Berceto, thence to Parma, thence to Reggio, thence to Mantua and Monselice, together with the provinces of Venetia and Istria and all the duchies of Spoleto and Benevento, and the church of St. Christina which is situated on the Po about four miles from Pavia; (8) and likewise in Campania, Sora, Arce, Aquino, Arpino, Teano, Capua; (9) likewise the patrimonies under your power and sway, such as the patrimonies of Benevento, Naples, and upper and lower Calabria, and also of the island of Sicily, if God shall give it unto our hand; (10) likewise the cities of Gaeta and Fondi with all their belongings; (11) moreover we offer to thee, St. Peter, the apostle, and to thy vicar, pope John and his successors, for the salvation of our own soul and the souls of our son and our parents, the following cities and towns from our own lands; namely, Rieti, San Vittorino [on the Aterno], Furco, Norcia, Balua, Marsi, and besides the city of Teramne. (12) All the aforesaid provinces, cities, towns, fortresses, villages, territories, and patrimonies, we now grant to thee, St. Peter, and through thee to thy vicar, our spiritual father, pope John, and his successors to the end of the world, for the salvation of our own soul and the souls of our son, our parents, and our successors, and for the preservation of the whole Frankish people; and we grant them in such a way that the popes shall possess them in their own right and government and control. (13) Likewise, by this agreement we confirm all the gifts which king Pippin and emperor Karl voluntarily gave to St. Peter, the apostle, and also the rents and payments and taxes which were paid annually to the king of the Lombards from Tuscany and the duchy of Spoleto, as is contained in the aforesaid donation and as was agreed upon between pope Adrian of blessed memory and the emperor Karl, when the same pope surrendered to the emperor his claims on the provinces of Tuscany and Spoleto on condition that the aforesaid taxes should be paid each year to the church of St. Peter, the apostle. But in all this our authority over these provinces and their subjection to us and to our son are not in any way diminished. (14) We therefore confirm your possession of all the things mentioned above in this document; they shall remain in your right and ownership and control, and no one of our successors shall on any pretext take from you any part of the aforesaid provinces, cities, towns, fortresses, villages, dependencies, territories, patrimonies, or taxes, or lessen your authority over them. We will never do so, nor allow others to do so, but we will always defend the church of St. Peter and the popes who rule over that church in their possession of all these things, as far as in us lies, that the popes may be able to keep these things in their control to use, enjoy, and dispose of. (15) In all this there shall be no derogation of our power or of the power of our son and our successors.

55. Leo VIII Grants the Emperor the Right to Choose the Pope and Invest all Bishops, 963.

Cor. Jur. Can., Dist. LXIII, c. xxiii; Migne, 134, cols. 992 ff.

Otto I, after the rebellion of John XII, deposed him and caused a layman to be made pope, who took the title Leo VIII. The new pope then issued a decree, the essence of which is contained in the following document. It shows how determined Otto was to assert his imperial authority and is important as a statement of the imperial theory. Leo VIII is regarded as an anti-pope by the Roman church, because, according to the papal theory, Otto had no power to depose a pope. John XII was the legal pope and there could be no other until he died.

In the synod held at Rome in the Church of the Holy Saviour. Following the example of blessed pope Adrian, who granted to Karl, victorious king of the Franks and Lombards, the dignity of the patriciate and the right to ordain the pope and to invest bishops, we, Leo, bishop, servant of the servants of God, with all the clergy and people of Rome, by our apostolic authority bestow upon lord Otto I, king of the Germans, and upon his successors in the kingdom of Italy forever, the right of choosing the successor of the pope, and of ordaining the pope and the archbishops and bishops, so that they shall receive their investiture and consecration from him, with the exception of those prelates whose investiture and consecration the emperor has conceded to the pope or the archbishops. No one, no matter what his dignity or ecclesiastical rank, shall have the authority to choose

the patricius or to ordain the pope or any bishop without
the consent of the emperor, and that without bribery; and
the emperor shall be by right both king [of Italy] and patricius [of Rome]. But if anyone has been chosen bishop
by the clergy and people, he shall not be consecrated unless
he has been approved by the aforesaid king and has received
his investiture from him. . . .

56. THE POPE CONFERS THE ROYAL TITLE. A LETTER OF POPE SYLVESTER II TO STEPHEN OF HUNGARY, 1000.

Migne, 139, cols. 274 ff.

Previous to this time, it was considered the emperor's right to
confer the royal title and to elevate a person to the rank of king.
Here, for the first time in the history of the papacy, a pope confers
the royal title, thereby intrenching on the imperial prerogative.
Otto III, who was then emperor, did not resist this papal infringement of his rights. Later popes were not slow to see the value of
this act as a precedent (see nos. 69, 72, 128), and exercised the right
to confer titles and dignities as they pleased. This act of Sylvester
II is, therefore, an important milestone in the history of the development of the papal prerogatives.

Sylvester, bishop, servant of the servants of God, to Stephen, king of the Hungarians, greeting and apostolic benediction. Your ambassadors, especially our dear brother,
Astricus, bishop of Colocza, were received by us with the
greater joy and accomplished their mission with the greater
ease, because we had been divinely forewarned to expect an
embassy from a nation still unknown to us. . . . Surely,
according to the apostle: " It is not of him that willeth nor
of him that runneth, but of God that showeth mercy" [Rom.
9:16]; and according to the testimony of Daniel: " He
changeth the times and the seasons; he removeth kings and
setteth up kings; he revealeth the deep and secret things;
he knoweth what is in the darkness" [Dan. 2:21, 22];
for in him is that light which, as John teaches, "lighteth
every man that cometh into the world" [John 1:9]. There-

fore we first give thanks to God the Father, and to our Lord Jesus Christ, because he has found in our time another David, and has again raised up a man after his own heart to feed his people Israel, that is, the chosen race of the Hungarians. Secondly, we praise you for your piety toward God and for your reverence for this apostolic see, over which, not by our own merits, but by the mercy of God, we now preside. Finally, we commend the liberality you have shown in offering to St. Peter yourself and your people and your kingdom and possessions by the same ambassadors and letters. For by this deed you have clearly demonstrated that you already are what you have asked us to declare you [i.e., a king]. But enough of this; it is not necessary to commend him whom God himself has commended and whose deeds openly proclaim to be worthy of all commendation. Now therefore, glorious son, by the authority of omnipotent God and of St. Peter, the prince of apostles, we freely grant, concede, and bestow with our apostolic benediction all that you have sought from us and from the apostolic see; namely, the royal crown and name, the creation of the metropolitanate of Gran, and of the other bishoprics. Moreover, we receive under the protection of the holy church the kingdom which you have surrendered to St. Peter, together with yourself and your people, the Hungarian nation; and we now give it back to you and to your heirs and successors to be held, possessed, ruled, and governed. And your heirs and successors, who shall have been legally elected by the nobles, shall duly offer obedience and reverence to us and to our successors in their own persons or by ambassadors, and shall confess themselves the subjects of the Roman church, who does not hold her subjects as slaves, but receives them all as children. They shall persevere in the catholic faith and the religion of our Lord and Saviour Jesus Christ, and strive always to promote it. And because you have fulfilled the office of the apostles in

preaching Christ and propagating his faith, and have tried
to do in your realm the work of us and of our clergy, and
because you have honored the same prince of apostles above
all others, therefore by this privilege we grant you and your
successors, who shall have been legally elected and approved
by the apostolic see, the right to have the cross borne before
you as a sign of apostleship,[1] after you have been crowned
with the crown which we send and according to the ceremony which we have committed to your ambassadors. And
we likewise give you full power by our apostolic authority
to control and manage all the churches of your realm, both
present and future, as divine grace may guide you, as representing us and our successors. All these things are contained more fully and explicitly in that general letter which
we have sent by our messenger to you and to your nobles
and faithful subjects. And we pray that omnipotent God,
who called you even from your mother's womb to the kingdom and crown, and who has commanded us to give you the
crown which we had prepared for the duke of Poland, may
increase continually the fruits of your good works, and
sprinkle with the dew of his benediction this young plant
of your kingdom, and preserve you and your realm and protect you from all enemies, visible and invisible, and, after
the trials of the earthly kingship are past, crown you with
an eternal crown in the kingdom of heaven. Given at Rome,
March 27, in the thirteenth indiction [the year 1000].

[1] The title "apostolic king of Hungary" is still used by the
emperor of the Austro-Hungarian Empire.

57. The Emperor, Henry III, Deposes and Creates Popes, 1048.

Annales Romani; in Watterich, Pontificum Romanorum Vitae, I, pp. 73 ff.

The papacy having again fallen under the control of Roman factions, there were three men claiming to be pope. The emperor
regarded it as his duty as well as his right to decide who was the
true pope, and came to Italy for that purpose. He not only deposed

the three contesting popes and named another, but so long as he lived he controlled the papal elections.

Now when the report of this incredible controversy had reached the ears of Henry, by the grace of God most invincible emperor, he set out for Italy with a great force and an immense army. And when he came to the city called Sutri, he called to him pope Gregory and the clergy of Rome and decreed that a great synod should be held in the holy church of Sutri. And after he had tried the case canonically and justly and had made the rights of the matter plain to the holy and religious bishops according to the canons, he condemned with perpetual anathema John, bishop of Sabina, to whom they had given the name Silvester, John the archpresbyter, whom they called Gregory, and the aforesaid pope Benedict. Then he proceeded to Rome with so great a following that the city could not hold it. Henry, by the grace of God pious and benign king, called together the multitude of the Roman people and the bishops and abbots and the whole Roman clergy in the basilica of St. Peter, and held there a holy and glorious synod; and on the day before Christmas he appointed an excellent, holy, and benign pope, who took the name of Clement. And on Christmas day the aforesaid king was crowned by the holy and benign pope, and the whole city of Rome rejoiced and the holy Roman church was exalted and glorified because so dangerous a schism had at length by the mercy of God been ended. And then the most serene emperor, perceiving the desire of the whole Roman people, as they had expressed it to him, placed on his own head the band with which the Romans from of old had been wont to crown their *patricii*. And the pope and the clergy and the Romans granted him the right to create popes and such bishops as have regalian rights; and it was further agreed that no bishop should be consecrated until he had received his investiture from the hand of the king. And just as pope Adrian had confirmed these things by a charter, so also they, by a charter, gave, confirmed, and put in the power of Henry and his successors the patriciate and the other rights as stated above.[1]

Now after the king had returned to his own realm, pope Clement sat upon the apostolic throne nine months and sixteen days, and then left the terrestrial for the celestial kingdom.

Then the Roman people, assembled together, sent messengers to king Henry with a letter beseeching him, as servants beseech their lord, or children their father, to appoint for them a chaste and benign man of godly life as shepherd of the holy Roman church and of the whole world. Now when Benedict, the former pope, learned of the death of Clement (for he was staying at Tusculum), he succeeded in winning over a part of the Roman people by bribery and again usurped the pontificate. But when the ambassadors of the Romans came to the king, he received them in his palace with great honor and gave them many gifts; then, calling together a great assembly of bishops, abbots, counts, margraves, and other princes, according to the decrees of the holy fathers, he chose a pope who should be pleasing to God and the whole people.

The ambassadors of the Romans returned to Rome, preceding the new pope, Damasus. But the good pope himself changed his route and betook himself to Italy. Now when he had come to the margrave Boniface, who had assisted the aforesaid pope Benedict to seize the papal throne, the margrave addressed him in these cunning words: " I cannot go on to Rome with you, because the Romans have restored the former pope, and he has regained the power which he had formerly, and has made peace with them. Therefore I cannot go to Rome, especially as I am now an old man." When the holy pope heard this, he returned and told all these things to the emperor. When the king heard it, he recognized the shrewdness and cunning of the margrave, and addressed him by letter, as follows: "Since you have restored to the pontificate a pope who was canonically deposed, and have been led by your love of gain to hold our empire in contempt, understand now that, unless you mend your ways, I will come quickly and make you mend against your will, and I will give the Roman people a pope worthy in the sight of God." Then Boniface, seeing that his rebellion would profit him nothing, drove Benedict from the papal throne by his ambassador and went to Rome with pope Damasus. . . . And Damasus held the pontificate twenty-three days and then died, and Leo was enthroned in the Roman see by the emperor and his nobles.

[1] Apparently this was a reënactment of the grant of Leo VIII to Otto I, 963. See no. 55.

58. The Pope Becomes the Feudal Lord of Southern Italy and Sicily, 1059. The Oaths of Robert Guiscard to Pope Nicholas II, 1059.

Baronius, Annales, anno 1059, §§ 70 and 71.

Southern Italy and Sicily had been allowed to take care of themselves. The Greek emperor had not been able to retain his hold on them, and the German emperor, while claiming them, had never succeeded in extending his power over them. A handful of adventurous Normans had established themselves on the mainland and had assumed the title of counts. Their ambition grew with their fortune; they desired a higher title than count and wished to increase their possessions. So they turned to the pope and asked him to confer upon them the title of duke, and to give them his blessing in their proposed conquest of Sicily, which was in the hands of the Mohammedans. In granting the request of these Normans, the pope assumed the lordship over southern Italy and Sicily, to which he had no right, and thereby put forth claims which conflicted with those of both emperors. For more than two centuries the possession of southern Italy and Sicily was the ground for a bitter struggle between the popes and the German emperors.

The importance of this event is seen when we consider that the long struggle between the papacy and the empire was about to begin. The pope had little besides his spiritual weapons (excommunication, ,nterdict) with which to oppose the emperor. But in Robert Guiscard he secured a powerful vassal who was to render him great military aid against the emperor.

§ 70. I, Robert, by the grace of God and of St. Peter duke of Apulia and Calabria, and with their aid to be duke of Sicily [that is, when I shall have conquered it], in confirmation of the gift and in recognition of my oath of fidelity, promise that from all the lands which I hold under my own sway, and which I have never conceded that anyone from beyond the mountains [1] [Alps, that is, Germany] holds, I will pay annually for each yoke of oxen. 12 denarii of the mint of Pavia to you, my lord, Nicholas, pope, and to all your successors, or to your or their legates. And this payment shall be made at the end of the year on easter day. I bind myself and my heirs and my successors to pay this sum to my lord, Nicholas, pope, and to your successors. So help me God and these holy gospels.

§ 71. I, Robert, by the grace of God and St. Peter duke of Apulia and Calabria, and by the aid of both to be duke of Sicily, from this hour forth will be faithful to the holy Roman church and to you, my lord, Nicholas, pope. I will have no share in any counsel or act intended to deprive you of life or limb, or to capture you by any fraud. Any secret plan which you may reveal to me with the command not to tell it I will not wittingly publish to your hurt. I will always aid with all my might the holy Roman church to acquire the regalia and possessions of St. Peter, and to hold them against all men. I will aid you to hold in security and honor the papal office, the land of St. Peter, and the government. I will not try either to usurp or to seize it, nor will I devastate it without your permission or that of your successors, except only that land which you or your successors may give me. I will earnestly strive to pay at the appointed time the sum agreed on from the land of St. Peter which I may hold. I put all the churches, with their possessions, which are in my lands, under your authority, and I will defend them according to my oath of fidelity to the holy Roman church. And if you or your successors shall die before I do, according as I shall have been advised by the better cardinals, the clergy of Rome, and the laity, I will do all that I can that a pope may be elected and ordained to the honor of St. Peter. All the above written things I will observe with true faithfulness to the holy Roman church and to you. And this oath of fidelity I will observe to those of your successors who may confirm to me the investiture which you have granted me. So help me God and these holy gospels.

1 Robert here denies that the German emperor has any right to Sicily and southern Italy. He had never held them, and hence they were not a part of his empire.

59. THE PAPAL ELECTION DECREE OF NICHOLAS II, 1059.

Scheffer-Boichorst, Die Neuordnung der Papstwahl durch Nicholas II, pp. 14 ff; Doeberl, III, no. 4 a.

Henry III (1039-56) deposed and appointed popes as he pleased (see no. 57). But with the spread of Cluniac ideas, there grew up a party in the church which strove with increasing energy and clearness of purpose to make the church self-governing and independent of all lay influence. Its aim was to unify and organize the government of the church by putting all ecclesiastical power in the hands of the pope, who should rule the church through a hierarchy of archbishops and bishops. Of this party, which was called hierarchical, the archdeacon, Hildebrand, was the head. It took advantage of the opportunity offered by the youth of Henry IV and the weak rule of the regent, his mother Agnes, to establish a way by which the pope might be elected by the clergy instead of being appointed by the emperor. The document by which this was done is know as the election decree of Nicholas II (1059-61) and was enacted in a council at Rome in 1059. Since 1048 Hildebrand had been the power behind the papal throne, and with rare skill he had directed the policy of each successive pope. He had been able to do much toward accomplishing the purpose of this party. But at the death of Stephen IX in 1058 a faction of the Roman nobility, known as the Tusculan party, threatened to overturn all that the hierarchical party had accomplished. While Hildebrand was absent from Rome on a mission to Germany, Stephen IX died and the Tusculan party set up one of its own members as pope, who called himself Benedict X. The cardinals who attempted to resist this election were persecuted and compelled to flee. When Hildebrand heard of this he hastened to call a council at Siena. This council, which was composed chiefly of five cardinal bishops, deposed Benedict X and elected Gerhard, bishop of Florence, pope, who assumed the name of Nicholas II.

According to this decree the election of a pope consisted of the five following parts: (1) The seven cardinal bishops chose the pope. Although their choice was supposed to be final it must (2) be confirmed by the other cardinal clergy. (3) Then the rest of the clergy and the people of Rome must express their consent. (4) The election was then reported to the emperor, who was expected to confirm it, and then (5) the pope elect was consecrated as pope and enthroned in the chair of St. Peter by the cardinal bishops. This latter part of the ceremony must, of course, take place at Rome. The decree does not say what shall be done if the other clergy or the emperor should refuse to confirm the choice of the cardinal bishops.

There were those who demanded that the emperor be permitted to approve or reject the candidate before the election took place. As precedents in favor of this they referred to the long list of popes who had been either nominated or appointed by various emperors. The part which the emperor was to have in the election of a pope is not stated in the decree, but section 4 shows plainly that Nicholas and Henry had come to an agreement on that subject, and from other sources we know what its terms were. This agreement was limited to Henry alone, for each of his successors must secure his share in the papal election by demanding it of the pope.

This decree seems to justify certain irregularities or peculiarities in the election of Nicholas himself and hence may be said to have an apologetic character. (1) His election took place not in Rome, but in Siena. (2) He was not a member of the church in Rome, but was bishop of Florence. (3) It was chiefly the cardinal bishops who elected him. (4) Since the Tusculan party held Rome it was some time before he could be consecrated and enthroned, but in the meanwhile he exercised papal authority.

The cardinal bishops had already acquired certain prerogatives over the other cardinal clergy. They alone, besides the pope, could say mass at the high altar in St. John's in Lateran; they represented the pope during his absence from Rome; they consecrated and enthroned the pope; they assisted the pope in anointing and crowning the emperor; and without their consent the pope could not bestow the pallium upon an archbishop. By this decree they now acquire the new and important right of nominating the pope. But this high prerogative they were not able to retain permanently. From 1050 to 1100 they succeeded in depriving the other cardinal clergy of much of their power and influence. They were the chief advisers of the popes. In accordance with the terms of this decree they elected Alexander II (1061-73) (the election of Gregory VII (1073-85) was somewhat irregular), Victor III (1086-87), and Urban II (1087-99). But the other cardinal clergy were not content to be thus thrust down; they struggled successfully against the growing power of the cardinal bishops and finally regained the right which had once been theirs. The election of Paschal II (1099-1118) was made by all the cardinal clergy, not by the cardinal bishops alone, and afterward the election of a pope was the concern of all the cardinal clergy.

The original of this decree is lost and the copy which has come down to us is slightly imperfect, as there are omissions in it. Some one representing the imperial party, not satisfied with the share which it gave the emperor in the papal election, changed it to suit the demands of his party. It is now known that this imperial form of the decree is a forgery.

In section 2 the quotation from Leo I (440-461) is meant in a general way to justify the prerogative here attributed to the cardinal bishops, and especially their right to consecrate and enthrone the pope.

In the name of the Lord God, our Saviour Jesus Christ, in the 1059th year from his incarnation, in the month of April, in the 12th indiction, in the presence of the holy gospels, the most reverend and blessed apostolic pope Nicholas presiding in the Lateran patriarchal basilica which is called the church of Constantine, the most reverend archbishops, bishops, and abbots, and the venerable presbyters and deacons also being present, the same venerable pontiff by his apostolic authority decreed thus concerning the election of the pope: "Most beloved brothers and fellow-bishops, you know, since it is not hidden even from the humbler members, how after the death of our predecessor, Stephen of blessed memory, this apostolic seat, which by the will of God I now serve, suffered many evils, how indeed it was subjected to many serious attacks from the simoniacal money-changers, so that the column of the living God seemed about to topple, and the skiff of the supreme fisherman [Peter] was nearly wrecked by the tumultuous storms. Therefore, if it pleases you, we ought now, with the aid of God, prudently to take measures to prevent future misfortunes, and to provide for the state of the church in the future, lest those evils, again appearing, which God forbid, should prevail against it. Therefore, fortified by the authority of our predecessors and the other holy fathers, we decide and declare:

"1. On the death of a pontiff of the universal Roman church, first, the cardinal bishops,[1] with the most diligent consideration, shall elect a successor; then they shall call in the other cardinal clergy [to ratify their choice], and finally the rest of the clergy and the people shall express their consent to the new election.

"2. In order that the disease of venality may not have any opportunity to spread, the devout clergy shall be the leaders in electing the pontiff, and the others shall acquiesce. And surely this order of election is right and lawful, if we consider either the rules or the practice of various fathers, or if we recall that decree of our predecessor, St. Leo, for he says: 'By no means can it be allowed that those should be ranked as bishops who have not been elected by the clergy, and demanded by the people, and consecrated by their fellow-bishops of the province with the consent of the metropolitan.' But since the apostolic seat is above all the churches in the earth, and therefore can have no metropolitan over it, without doubt the cardinal bishops perform in it the office of the metropolitan, in that they advance the elected prelate to the apostolic dignity [that is, choose, consecrate, and enthrone him].

"3. The pope shall be elected from the church in Rome, if a suitable person can be found in it, but if not, he is to be taken from another church.

"4. In the papal election—in accordance with the right which we have already conceded to Henry and to those of his successors who may obtain the same right from the apostolic see—due honor and reverence shall be shown our beloved son, Henry, king and emperor elect [that is, the rights of Henry shall be respected].

"5. But if the wickedness of depraved and iniquitous men shall so prevail that a pure, genuine, and free election cannot be held in this city, the cardinal bishops with the clergy and a few laymen shall have the right to elect the pontiff wherever they shall deem most fitting.

"6. But if after an election any disturbance of war or any malicious attempt of men shall prevail so that he who is elected cannot be enthroned according to custom in the papal chair, the pope elect shall nevertheless exercise the right of ruling the holy Roman church, and of disposing of all its revenues, as we know St. Gregory did before his consecration.

"But if anyone, actuated by rebellion or presumption or any other motive, shall be elected or ordained or enthroned in a manner contrary to this our decree, promulgated by the authority of the synod, he with his counsellors, supporters, and followers shall be expelled from the holy church of God by the authority of God and the holy apostles Peter and Paul, and shall be subjected to perpetual anathema as Antichrist and the enemy and destroyer of all Christianity; nor shall he ever be granted a further hearing in the case, but he shall be deposed without appeal from every ecclesiastical rank which he may have held formerly. Whoever shall adhere to him or shall show him any reverence as if he were pope, or shall aid him in any way, shall be subject to like sentence. Moreover, if any rash person shall oppose this our decree and shall try to confound and disturb the Roman church by his presumption contrary to this decree, let him be cursed with perpetual anathema and excommunication, and let him be numbered with the wicked who shall not arise on the day of judgment. Let him feel upon him the weight of the wrath of God the Father, the Son, and the Holy Spirit, and let him experience in this life and the next the anger of the holy apostles, Peter and Paul, whose church he has presumed to confound. Let his habitation be desolate and let none dwell in his tents [Ps. 69:25]. Let his children be orphans and his wife a widow. Let him be driven forth and let his sons beg and be cast out from their habitations. Let the usurer take all his substance and let others reap the fruit of his labors. Let the whole earth fight against him and let all the elements be hostile to him, and let the powers of all the saints in heaven confound him and show upon him in this life their evident vengeance. But may the grace of omnipotent God protect those who observe this decree and free them from the bonds of all their sins by the authority of the holy apostles Peter and Paul."

I, Nicholas, bishop of the holy Catholic and apostolic church, have subscribed this decree which has been promulgated by us, as said above. I, Boniface, by the grace of God bishop of Albano, have subscribed. I, Humbert, bishop of the holy church of Silva Candida, have subscribed. I, Peter, bishop of the church of Ostia, have subscribed. And other bishops to the number of seventy-six, with priests and deacons.

¹ The seven cardinal bishops were those of Palæstrina, Porto, Ostia, Tusculum, Silva Candida, Albano, and Sabina.

III. THE STRUGGLE BETWEEN THE EMPIRE AND THE PAPACY, 1073-1250

60–64. PROHIBITION OF SIMONY, MARRIAGE OF THE CLERGY, AND LAY INVESTITURE, 1074–1123.

According to Roman ideas religion and its ministers were a part of the state and hence under the control of the government. When Constantine made Christianity a legal religion the state took the same attitude toward the new religion that it had toward the old. The emperor assumed control over the Christian clergy, and the view soon prevailed that they were officials of the state. Their duties, which were at first purely spiritual, were soon extended to secular matters. For obvious reasons the bishops were given an oversight over the administration of justice. During the invasions of the barbarians the secular functions of the bishops were greatly increased. Karl the Great made constant use of the bishops in the administration of his realm. By the tenth century many bishops were intrusted to a large extent with the secular government of their dioceses and so were full-fledged officials of the state. Attendance on diets was required of all officials, and eventually it was required only of officials. So it came about that the bishops especially formed an important part of the diet. Because of their learning they were indispensable to the emperor in conducting the affairs of his court and government; they naturally became his chief advisers. The bishops, then, have two sets of functions, the one spiritual, the other secular.

Through bequests and gifts from various sources the clergy, and especially the bishops and chief abbots, became great landholders. Many gave to the clergy for religious reasons, such as the salvation of their souls. But the emperors had still other motives: because of their office as emperor they were bound to build up the church; they felt it to be their duty to reward and to strengthen the clergy who were their faithful officials; and, furthermore, since they frequently met with opposition from the lay nobility, they thought it advisable to build up a strong ecclesiastical nobility to serve as a check upon the former.

As all other offices and relations became feudalized, so all the clergy underwent the same process. The bishops became the vassals of the emperor, and sustained the same feudal relations to him as did the lay nobility.

Since the bishops were both the officials and vassals of the emperor, it is certain that he would insist on having a voice in their election. Although the laws of the church did not permit this, nevertheless we find that from Karl the Great to Henry III all the emperors exercised the right of naming or appointing the bishops. Although at the time no objection was made to this action of the emperors, a new party had now arisen in the church which condemned it as simoniacal. This new party had its origin in the monastery of Cluny, from which it took its name. It was famous for the great reforms which it was trying to bring about. Now it was a part of the Cluniac programme that the church should be freed from all lay influence and that all ecclesiastical offices should be filled not by lay appointment but by election by the clergy (canonical election). Thus they gave simony a new meaning by declaring that every election which was not canonical was simoniacal. For simony was originally only the purchase or sale of any ecclesiastical office, but as the church, under the influence of this Cluniac party, developed her laws regarding canonical election and investiture, it came to be applied to every form of election and investiture other than canonical. The emperors had not only appointed the bishops, but they had also inducted them into their office. The induction into office was called investiture. Without it no one could fill the office to which he had been elected. To symbolize the power of the office the emperor presented the bishop with certain objects, such as a ring and a staff, which represented his spiritual authority over his diocese, and with a sceptre, which represented his temporal authority. The Cluniac party opposed all lay investiture and insisted that all the clergy should receive the symbols of their power from the church. But since the emperor's temporal interests were so largely involved, he could not yield to the Cluniac demands without great loss of power. He could not tamely surrender to the pope the control of the bishops and their broad lands. Nor was it probable that the nobility would give up their rights (as patrons, etc.) to appoint the local clergy and to invest them with their office. So the struggle over investiture was long and bitter.

Lay investiture had already been prohibited by Nicholas II in the Lateran synod of 1059 but no steps had been taken to enforce the prohibition. Gregory VII renewed the prohibition and made it one of the prominent parts of his programme.

Although the opinion had long prevailed in the church that the celibate life, or chastity, was more holy than the married life, and therefore more becoming in the clergy, yet it was not uncommon for clergymen to marry. The Cluniac party regarded this state of affairs as especially blameworthy, and demanded that all the clergy be required to take the vow of perpetual chastity. In this, as in other respects, Gregory VII endeavored to carry out the Cluniac programme and so exerted himself to suppress clerical marriage, or, as the Cluniac party called it, clerical concubinage.

The following documents, nos. 60–64, illustrate the legislation of the church in regard to simony, celibacy, and investiture.

60. Prohibition of Simony and of the Marriage of the Clergy, 1074 a.d.

Sigebert of Gembloux, ad annum 1074; M. G. SS. folio, VI, p. 362.

Pope Gregory [VII] held a synod in which he anathematized all who were guilty of simony. He also forbade all clergy who were married to say mass, and all laymen were forbidden to be present when such a married priest should officiate. In this he seemed to many to act contrary to the decisions of the holy fathers who have declared that the sacraments of the church are neither made more effective by the good qualities, nor less effective by the sins, of the officiating priest, because it is the Holy Spirit who makes them effective.

61. Simony and Celibacy. The Roman Council, 1074.

Mansi, XX, p. 404.

Those who have been advanced to any grade of holy orders, or to any office, through simony, that is, by the payment of money, shall hereafter have no right to officiate in the holy church. Those also who have secured churches by giving money shall certainly be deprived of them. And in the future it shall be illegal for anyone to buy or to sell [any ecclesiastical office, position, etc.].

Nor shall clergymen who are married say mass or serve the altar in any way. We decree also that if they refuse to obey our orders, or rather those of the holy fathers, the people shall refuse to receive their ministrations, in order that those who disregard the love of God and the dignity of their office may be brought to their senses through feeling the shame of the world and the reproof of the people.

62. Celibacy of the Clergy. Gregory VII, 1074.

Mansi, XX, p. 433; Corpus Juris Can., Dist. LXXXI, c. xv.

If there are any priests, deacons, or subdeacons who are married, by the power of omnipotent God and the authority of St. Peter we forbid them to enter a church until they repent and mend their ways. But if any remain with their wives, no one shall dare hear them [when they officiate in the church], because their benediction is turned into a curse, and their prayer into a sin. For the Lord says through the prophet, "I will curse your blessings" [Mal. 2:2]. Whoever shall refuse to obey this most salutary command shall be guilty of the sin of idolatry. For Samuel says: "For rebellion is as the sin of witchcraft, and stubbornness is as iniquity and idolatry" [1 Sam. 15:23]. Whoever therefore asserts that he is a Christian but refuses to obey the apostolic see, is guilty of paganism.

63. Action of the Ninth General Council in the Lateran Against the Marriage of the Clergy, 1123 a.d.

Denzinger, p. 106; Hefele, V, p. 194.

We forbid priests, deacons, and subdeacons to live with wives or concubines, and no woman shall live with a clergyman except those who are permitted by the council of Nicæa, viz.: mother, sister, aunt, or others of such sort that no suspicion may justly arise concerning them.

64. PROHIBITION OF LAY INVESTITURE, NOVEMBER 19, 1078.

Jaffé, II, p. 332; Doeberl, III, no. 5 a.

Since we know that investitures have been made by laymen in many places, contrary to the decrees of the holy fathers, and that very many disturbances injurious to the Christian religion have thereby arisen in the church, we therefore decree: that no clergyman shall receive investiture of a bishopric, monastery, or church from the hand of the emperor, or the king, or any lay person, man or woman. And if anyone has ventured to receive such investiture, let him know that it is annulled by apostolic authority, and that he is subject to excommunication until he has made due reparation.

65. DICTATUS PAPÆ, *ca.* 1090.

Jaffé, II, p. 174; Doeberl, III, no. 6.

Until recently the *Dictatus Papæ* was supposed to have been written by Gregory VII, but it is now known to have had a different origin. In 1087 cardinal Deusdedit published a collection of the laws of the church, which he drew from many sources, such as the actions of councils and the writings of the popes. The *Dictatus* agrees so clearly and closely with this collection, that it must have been based on it; and so must be later than the date of its compilation, 1087. It seems evident that some one, while reading the collection of Deusdedit, wishing to formulate the papal rights and prerogatives, expressed them in these twenty-seven theses. Although they were not formulated by Gregory himself, there is no doubt that they express his chief principles.

1. That the Roman church was established by God alone.

2. That the Roman pontiff alone is rightly called universal.

3. That he alone has the power to depose and reinstate bishops.

4. That his legate, even if he be of lower ecclesiastical

rank, presides over bishops in council, and has the power to give sentence of deposition against them.

5. That the pope has the power to depose those who are absent [*i.e.*, without giving them a hearing].

6. That, among other things, we ought not to remain in the same house with those whom he has excommunicated.

7. That he alone has the right, according to the necessity of the occasion, to make new laws, to create new bishoprics, to make a monastery of a chapter of canons, and *vice versa*, and either to divide a rich bishopric or to unite several poor ones.

8. That he alone may use the imperial insignia.

9. That all princes shall kiss the foot of the pope alone.

10. That his name alone is to be recited in the churches.

11. That the name applied to him belongs to him alone.

12. That he has the power to depose emperors.

13. That he has the right to transfer bishops from one see to another when it becomes necessary.

14. That he has the right to ordain as a cleric anyone from any part of the church whatsoever.

15. That anyone ordained by him may rule [as bishop] over another church, but cannot serve [as priest] in it, and that such a cleric may not receive a higher rank from any other bishop.

16. That no general synod may be called without his order.

17. That no action of a synod and no book shall be regarded as canonical without his authority.

18. That his decree can be annulled by no one, and that he can annul the decrees of anyone.

19. That he can be judged by no one.

20. That no one shall dare to condemn a person who has appealed to the apostolic seat.

21. That the important cases of any church whatsoever shall be referred to the Roman church [that is, to the pope].

22. That the Roman church has never erred and will never err to all eternity, according to the testimony of the holy scriptures.

23. That the Roman pontiff who has been canonically ordained is made holy by the merits of St. Peter, according to the testimony of St. Ennodius, bishop of Pavia, which is confirmed by many of the holy fathers, as is shown by the decrees of the blessed pope Symmachus.

24. That by his command or permission subjects may accuse their rulers.

25. That he can depose and reinstate bishops without the calling of a synod.

26. That no one can be regarded as catholic who does not agree with the Roman church.

27. That he has the power to absolve subjects from their oath of fidelity to wicked rulers.

Section 1 means that the Roman church received the primacy over the whole church directly from Christ. Section 8 is based on the forged Donation of Constantine, according to which the emperor gave the pope the right to use the imperial insignia. In section 11 it is not clear what name is meant. It may be " universal " as in section 2. The bishop of Rome claimed the exclusive right to call himself pope, apostolic, and universal. Papa or pope was at first the common title of all priests, and is still so in the Greek church. But in the course of time it was limited in the west to the bishop of Rome. " Apostolic " was at first applied to all bishops, but eventually the bishop of Rome claimed the exclusive right to it and forbade all other bishops to use it. Since the bishop of Rome was the head of the whole church he was the only one who could call himself " universal." The right of ordaining, section 14, that is, of raising to the clerical rank, belonged to each bishop, but he could exercise it only in his own diocese. But the bishop of Rome had the whole world for his diocese, and hence he could ordain any one, no matter to what bishopric he belonged. In explanation of section 23 the following passage from pope Symmachus (498–514) is offered (Hinschius, " Decretales," p. 666). " We do not judge that St. Peter received from the Lord with the prerogative of his chair [that is, with his primacy] the right to sin. But he passed

on to his successors the perennial dower of his merits with his
heritage of innocence. Who can doubt that he who is exalted to the
height of apostolic dignity is holy? "

66. Letter of Gregory VII to all the Faithful, Commending his Legates, 1074.

Migne, 148, col. 392.

It had not been uncommon for the popes to send their legates on
missions to various parts of the world, but Gregory VII made a far
more frequent use of them than any of his predecessors. He practically ruled the church through them and demanded that they be
received and obeyed by all. This letter shows his general attitude
on the matter, the authority he gave them, and the reception which
he expected them to have.

Gregory, bishop, servant of the servants of God, to all the
faithful subjects of St. Peter, to whom these presents come,
greeting and apostolic benediction.

You see that wickedness is increasing and that the wiles
of the devil are prevailing in the earth, that Christian charity has grown cold and religious zeal has almost disappeared
within the church. But since we cannot be everywhere present in person to attend to all these matters, we have sent
to you two beloved sons of the holy Roman church, Geizo,
abbot of St. Boniface, and Maurus, abbot of St. Sabba, who
shall represent us to you and have authority to do in our
name whatever may be to the advantage of the church. Remember therefore that saying of the gospel: "He that heareth you heareth me; and he that despiseth you despiseth
me" [Luke 10:16]. As you care for the friendship and for
the favor of St. Peter, whose messengers they are, receive
them with the proper reverence and kindness, and obey them
in all matters which may arise as part of their mission or
through the exigencies of the situation among you. If it
becomes necessary or expedient for the legates to separate
and go to different regions, each one of them shall be received and obeyed as our representative.

67. OATH OF THE PATRIARCH OF AQUILEIA TO GREGORY VII, 1079 A.D.

Mansi, XX, p 525.

Gregory VII required an oath of fidelity from all bishops. By comparing the oath of Boniface to Gregory II (no. 40) and the oath of Richard of Capua (no. 68) with this oath of the patriarch of Aquileia, interesting light will be thrown on the theory and practice of Gregory VII.

From now henceforth I will be faithful to St. Peter and to pope Gregory [VII] and to his successors who shall be elected by the better cardinals. Neither in counsel nor in deed will I do anything to cause them to lose their life, or limb, or the papacy, or that they be taken prisoner through any treacherous trick. To whatsoever synod they, either in person or by messenger or by letter, may call me, I will come and I will obey them according to the law; or if I shall not be able to come, I will send my representative. I will aid and defend them in holding and defending the papacy and the regalia of St. Peter, saving the duties of my position. If they, either in person or by messenger or by letter, shall intrust me with a secret, I will not knowingly reveal it to anyone to their harm. I will treat with honor a papal legate, whether coming [from Rome] or going [back to Rome], and I will give him my aid whenever he needs it. I will not wittingly associate with any whom the pope has excommunicated. Whenever I shall have been called on I will aid the Roman church with my military forces. All these duties I will perform unless I shall have been excused from them.

68-73. GREGORY VII EXERCISES SECULAR AUTHORITY.

68. THE OATH OF FIDELITY WHICH RICHARD, PRINCE OF CAPUA, SWORE TO GREGORY VII, 1073.

Migne, 148, col. 304.

Gregory VII, in accordance with his political pretensions, endeavored to compel all rulers of the Christian world to acknowledge his supremacy over them. He made the broadest claims to the proprietorship of all kingdoms, duchies, counties, etc., and tried to compel all rulers of every rank to take an oath of vassalage to him and to receive their lands from him as fiefs. Nos. 68-73 illustrate this feature of his policy.

I, Richard, by the grace of God and St. Peter prince of Capua, from this time forth will be faithful to the holy Roman church, to the apostolic see, and to you, pope Gregory. I will have no share in any plan or any deed to injure you in life or limb or to make you captive. Any plan which you may confide to me, wishing it to be kept secret, I will never divulge consciously to your injury. I will faithfully aid you and the holy Roman church to keep, acquire, and defend the regalia and the possessions of St. Peter against all men and I will assist you to hold the papacy and the lands of St. Peter in peace and honor. I will never attempt to attack, seize, or devastate any lands without the express permission of you or your successors, except such lands as you or your successors may have given to me. I promise to pay to the Roman church the legal tribute from the lands of St. Peter, which I hold or shall hold. I will surrender to your authority all the churches which are in my lands, with all their goods, and I will defend them in their fidelity to the holy Roman church. I will swear fidelity to king Henry whenever I shall be commanded to do so by you or your successors, always saving my fidelity to the holy Roman church. If you or any of your successors shall die before I do, I will support the better part of the cardinals and the clergy and the people of Rome in the election and establishment of a new pope to the honor of St. Peter. I will keep all the above promises to you and to the holy Roman church in good faith, and I will keep my oath of fidelity to your successors who shall be ordained popes, if they are willing to confirm the investiture which you have conferred upon me.

69. LETTER OF GREGORY VII TO THE PRINCES WISHING
TO RECONQUER SPAIN, 1073.

Migne, 148, cols. 289 f.

See introductory note to no. 68.

Gregory, pope elect, to all the princes desiring to go into
Spain, perpetual greeting in the Lord Jesus Christ.

We suppose you know that the kingdom of Spain belonged
of old to St. Peter, and that this right has never been lost,
although the land has long been occupied by pagans. Therefore the ownership of this land inheres in the apostolic see
alone, for whatever has come into the possession of the
churches by the will of God, while it may be alienated from
their use, may not by any lapse of time be separated from
their ownership except by lawful grant. Count Evolus of
Roceio, whose fame you must know, wishes to attack that
land and rescue it from the heathen. Therefore we have
granted him the possession of such territory as he may win
from the pagans by his own efforts or with the aid of allies,
on conditions agreed upon by us as the representative of
St. Peter. You who join him in this undertaking should
do so to the honor of St. Peter, that St. Peter may protect
you from danger and reward your fidelity to him. But if
any of you plan to attack that land independently with your
own forces, you should do so in a spirit of devotion and
with righteous motives. Beware lest after you have conquered the land you wrong St. Peter in the same way as
the infidels do who now hold it. Unless you are prepared
to recognize the rights of St. Peter by making an equitable
agreement with us, we will forbid you by our apostolic authority to go thither, that your holy and universal mother,
the church, may not suffer from her sons the same injuries
which she now suffers from her enemies, to the loss not only
of her property, but also of the devotion of her children.
To this end we have sent to Spain our beloved son, Hugo,

cardinal priest of the holy Roman church, and he will inform you more fully of our terms and conditions.

70. LETTER OF GREGORY VII TO WRATISLAV, DUKE OF BOHEMIA, 1073.

Migne, 148, cols. 299 f.

See introductory note to no. 68.

Gregory, etc., to Wratislav, etc. We give thanks to omnipotent God that you have been led by your devotion and
reverence for the apostles Peter and Paul, princes of the
apostles, to receive our legates with kindness and treat them
with the graciousness which is becoming to your majesty.
Receive the assurance of our good-will in return for this
evidence of your fidelity. It has not been usual for papal
legates to visit your land; this, however, is partly the fault
of your forefathers, as well as of our predecessors, for the
dukes of Bohemia should have requested the pope to send
them legates. But some of your subjects have regarded our
sending of legates as an innovation, and have treated them
with contempt, forgetting the word of God: "He that receiveth you receiveth me" [Matt. 10:40]; "and he that
despiseth you despiseth me" [Luke 10:16]. So in failing
to show due reverence to our legates, they have not so much
despised them, as they have despised the word of truth. . . .

71. LETTER OF GREGORY VII TO SANCHO, KING OF ARAGON, 1074.

Migne, 148, col. 339.

See introductory note to no. 68.

Gregory, bishop, servant of the servants of God, to Sancho,
king of Aragon, greeting and apostolic benediction.

We received your gracious letter with great joy, because
of the evidence which it contained of your fidelity to the

princes of the apostles, Peter and Paul, and to the holy Roman church. But indeed even if we had not received your letter we should have been well aware of your fidelity through the report of our legates. By enforcing the observances of the Roman form of service in the churches of your kingdom you have shown that you are a true son of the Roman church and that you bear the same friendship to us that former kings of Spain have borne to the Roman pope. Be firm and constant in the faith and complete the good work which you have begun; then the blessed St. Peter, whom our Lord Jesus Christ has made ruler over the kingdoms of this world, will bring to pass the desires of your heart and will make you victorious over your enemies, because of the trust which you have placed in him. . . .

72. LETTER OF GREGORY VII TO SOLOMON, KING OF HUNGARY, 1074.

Migne, 148, col. 373.

See introductory note to no. 68.

Gregory, bishop, servant of the servants of God, to Solomon, king of Hungary, greeting and apostolic benediction.

Your letter was late in reaching us because of the delay of the messenger, but when it did come we were displeased with it because its terms were offensive to St. Peter. For the kingdom of Hungary, as you can learn from your own princes, belongs of right to the holy Roman church, having been offered and surrendered to St. Peter with all its rights and powers by the former king Stephen. And when the emperor Henry [II] of blessed memory, attacked the kingdom in the defense of the honor of St. Peter and captured the king, he forwarded to the grave of St. Peter the lance and crown, the insignia of kingship. But we hear that you have accepted the kingdom as a fief from the king of the Germans, thereby infringing the rights and the honor of St. Peter and acting in a manner incompatible with the virtue and character of a king. If you wish to have the favor of St. Peter and our good will, you must correct your faults; you know yourself that you cannot hope for justice, that, indeed, you cannot reign any length of time, unless you admit that you hold the sceptre of your kingdom from the pope and not from the king. As far as God shall give us strength, we will never through fear or affection or any personal consideration consent to the diminishing of the honor of him whom we serve. But if you are willing to mend your ways and act as a king should, you may easily win the love of your mother, the holy Roman church, and our friendship in Christ.

73. Letter of Gregory VII to Demetrius, King of the Russians, 1075.

Migne, 148, col. 425.

See introductory note to no. 68.

Gregory, bishop, servant of the servants of God, to Demetrius, king of the Russians, and to his wife, the queen, greeting and apostolic benediction.

Your son has visited us at Rome, and has asked that we invest him with the kingdom of the Russians in the name of St. Peter. He has given sufficient evidence of his fidelity to St. Peter, and has assured us that he is acting with your consent in making the petition. We have felt justified in granting his petition because of your consent and of the devotion which he has evidenced; therefore we have conferred upon him in the name of St. Peter the government of your kingdom. We pray that St. Peter may protect you and your kingdom and all your possessions by his intercession with God, that he may cause you to hold your kingdom in peace, glory, and honor, all your days, and that at the end of this life he may obtain for you an eternal glory with the King of Heaven. We shall always be ready to grant your request whenever you call upon us in any righteous

cause. In regard to this matter of the investiture and other
affairs not mentioned in this letter, we have sent you these
legates, one of whom is a well-known and faithful friend of
yours. Treat them kindly out of reverence for St. Peter,
whose legates they are; listen to them and believe without
hesitation whatever they may say on our behalf. Do not
allow them to be hindered in the discharge of any of the
duties with which we have intrusted them, but give them
your faithful assistance. May omnipotent God illumine your
soul and lead you through this temporal life to his eternal
glory.

74-81. Conflict between Henry IV and Gregory VII.

74. Letter of Gregory VII to Henry IV, December, 1075.

Jaffé, II, pp. 218 ff; Doeberl, III, no. 7.

Gregory VII met with vigorous opposition from the German clergy
as well as from the king when he attempted to enforce his laws
against simony and the marriage of the clergy. In a synod at Rome,
1075, Feb. 24-28, Gregory excommunicated five of Henry's intimate
advisers for the sin of simony. Henry refused to recognize the
validity of this excommunication, and, regardless of papal protests,
persisted in his policy of disposing of bishoprics (Milan, Fermo,
Spoleto, for example) as he chose. Gregory determined to proceed
to extreme measures. He sent messengers to Henry, bearing this
letter (no. 74) in which he defended his decrees against simony
and the marriage of the clergy, and announced his determination
to hold fast to them and to compel the whole world to accept them.
He also intrusted an oral message to the bearers of the letter to the
effect that if Henry did not mend his evil life, and drive his
excommunicated counsellors from his court, Gregory would not only
excommunicate him but also depose him.

Henry's answer to this message and letter was given at a national
synod at Worms, Jan. 24, 1076. This synod deposed Gregory and
informed him of their action by two letters, one by Henry (no. 75),
and the other by the German bishops (no. 76). Gregory replied by
excommunicating and deposing the king (no. 77).

Gregory, bishop, servant of the servants of God, to Henry, the king, greeting and apostolic benediction—that is, if he shall prove obedient to the apostolic see as a Christian king should.

We have sent you our apostolic benediction with some hesitation, knowing that we must render account to God, the severe judge, for all our acts as pope. Now it is reported that you have knowingly associated with men who have been excommunicated by the pope and the synod. If this is true, you know that you cannot receive the blessing either of God or of the pope until you have driven them from you and have compelled them to do penance, and have yourself sought absolution and forgiveness for your transgressions with due penance and reparation. Therefore, if you realize your guilt in this matter, we counsel you to confess straightway to some pious bishop, who shall absolve you with our permission, enjoining upon you suitable penance for this fault, and who shall faithfully report to us by letter, with your permission, the character of the penance prescribed.

We wonder, moreover, that you should continue to assure us by letter and messengers of your devotion and humility; that you should call yourself our son and the son of the holy mother church, obedient in the faith, sincere in love, diligent in devotion, and that you should commend yourself to us with all zeal of love and reverence—whereas in fact you are constantly disobeying the canonical and apostolic decrees in important matters of the faith. For, to say nothing of the rest, in the case of Milan, concerning which you gave us your promise through your mother and through our fellow-bishops whom we sent to you, the event has shown how far you intended to carry out your promise [that is, not at all] and with what purpose you made it. And now, to inflict wound upon wound, contrary to the apostolic decrees you have bestowed the churches of Fermo and Spoleto—if indeed a church can be bestowed by a layman—upon certain persons quite unknown to us; for it is not lawful to ordain men before they have been known and proved.

Since you confess yourself a son of the church, you should treat with more honor the head of the church, that is, St. Peter, the prince of the apostles. If you are one of the sheep of the Lord, you have been intrusted to him by divine authority, for Christ said to him: "Peter, feed my sheep" [John 21:16]; and again: "And I will give unto thee the keys of the kingdom of Heaven; and whatsoever thou shalt bind on earth shall be bound in heaven; and whatsoever thou shalt loose on earth shall be loosed in heaven" [Matt. 16:19]. And since we, although an unworthy sinner, exercise his authority by divine will, the words which you address to us are in reality addressed directly to him. And although we only read or hear the words, he sees the heart from which the words proceed. Therefore your highness should be very careful that no insincerity be found in your words and messages to us; and that you show due reverence, not to us indeed, but to omnipotent God, in those things which especially make for the advance of the Christian faith and the well-being of the church. For our Lord said to the apostles and to their successors: "He that heareth you heareth me; and he that despiseth you despiseth me" [Luke 10:16]. For no one will disregard our admonitions if he believes that the decrees of the pope have the same authority as the words of the apostle himself. For if our Lord commanded the apostles out of reverence for the seat of Moses to observe the sayings of the scribes and Pharisees who occupied that seat, then surely the faithful ought to receive with all reverence the apostolic and evangelical doctrine through those who are chosen to the ministry of preaching.

Now in the synod held at the apostolic seat to which the divine will has called us (at which some of your subjects also were present) we, seeing that the Christian religion

had been weakened by many attacks and that the chief and
proper motive, that of saving souls, had for a long time been
neglected and slighted, were alarmed at the evident danger
of the destruction of the flock of the Lord, and had recourse
to the decrees and the doctrine of the holy fathers; we
decreed nothing new, nothing of our invention [that is,
against simony and the marriage of the clergy]; but we
decided that the error should be abandoned and the single
primitive rule of ecclesiastical discipline and the familiar
way of the saints should be again sought out and followed.
For we know that no other door to salvation and eternal
life lies open to the sheep of Christ than that which was
pointed out by him who said: "I am the door, by me if
any man enter in he shall be saved, and find pasture" [John
10:9]; and this, we learn from the gospels and from the
sacred writings, was preached by the apostles and observed by
the holy fathers. And we have decided that this decree—
which some, placing human above divine honor, have called an
unendurable weight and an immense burden, but which we
call by its proper name, that is, the truth and light necessary to salvation—is to be received and observed not only
by you and your subjects, but also by all princes and peoples of the earth who confess and worship Christ; for it is
greatly desired by us, and would be most fitting for you,
that, as you are greater than others in glory, in honor, and
in virtue, so you should be more distinguished in devotion
to Christ.

Nevertheless, that this decree may not seem to you beyond
measure grievous and unjust, we have commanded you by
your faithful ambassadors to send to us the wisest and most
pious men whom you can find in your kingdom, so that if
they can show or instruct us in any way how we can temper
the sentence promulgated by the holy fathers without offence
to the eternal King or danger to our souls, we may consider
their advice. But, even if we had not warned you in so

friendly a manner, it would have been only right on your part, before you violated the apostolic decrees, to have asked justice of us in a reasonable manner in any matter in which we had injured or affected your honor. But it is evident in what you have since done and decreed how little you care for our warnings or for the observance of justice.

But since we hope that, while the long-suffering patience of God still invites you to repent, you may become wiser and your heart may be turned to obey the commands of God, we warn you with fatherly love that, knowing the rule of Christ to be over you, you should consider how dangerous it is to place your honor above his, and that you should not interfere with the liberty of the church which he has deigned to join to himself by heavenly union, but rather with faithful devotion you should offer your assistance to the increasing of this liberty to omnipotent God and St. Peter, through whom also your glory may be amplified. You ought to recognize what you undoubtedly owe to them for giving you victory over your enemies, that as they have gladdened you with great prosperity, so they should see that you are thereby rendered more devout. And in order that the fear of God, in whose hands is all power and all rule, may affect your heart more than these our warnings, you should recall what happened to Saul when, after winning the victory which he gained by the will of the prophet, he glorified himself in his triumph and did not obey the warnings of the prophet, and how God reproved him; and, on the other hand, what grace king David acquired by reason of his humility, as well as his other virtues.

Finally, in regard to those matters in your letter which we have not yet touched upon, we will not give a definite answer until your ambassadors, Rapoto, Adelbert, and Wodescalc, and those whom we have sent with them, shall return to us and shall make known more fully your intention in regard to the matters which we committed to them to be

discussed with you.   Given at Rome, the 6th of the Ides of
January, the 14th indiction.

75.   THE DEPOSITION OF GREGORY VII BY HENRY IV,
JANUARY 24, 1076.

M. G. LL. folio, II, pp. 47 ff; Doeberl, III, no. 8 b.

See introductory note to no. 74.

Henry, king not by usurpation, but by the holy ordination
of God, to Hildebrand, not pope, but false monk.

This is the salutation which you deserve, for you have
never held any office in the church without making it a
source of confusion and a curse to Christian men instead
of an honor and a blessing.   To mention only the most
obvious cases out of many, you have not only dared to touch
the Lord's anointed, the archbishops, bishops, and priests;
but you have scorned them and abused them, as if they were
ignorant servants not fit to know what their master was
doing.   This you have done to gain favor with the vulgar
crowd.   You have declared that the bishops know nothing
and that you know everything; but if you have such great
wisdom you have used it not to build but to destroy.   Therefore we believe that St. Gregory, whose name you have presumed to take, had you in mind when he said: "The heart
of the prelate is puffed up by the abundance of subjects,
and he thinks himself more powerful than all others."   All
this we have endured because of our respect for the papal
office, but you have mistaken our humility for fear, and have
dared to make an attack upon the royal and imperial authority which we received from God.   You have even threatened
to take it away, as if we had received it from you, and as
if the empire and kingdom were in your disposal and not
in the disposal of God.   Our Lord Jesus Christ has called
us to the government of the empire, but he never called you
to the rule of the church.   This is the way you have gained

advancement in the church: through craft you have obtained wealth; through wealth you have obtained favor; through favor, the power of the sword; and through the power of the sword, the papal seat, which is the seat of peace; and then from the seat of peace you have expelled peace. For you have incited subjects to rebel against their prelates by teaching them to despise the bishops, their rightful rulers. You have given to laymen the authority over priests, whereby they condemn and depose those whom the bishops have put over them to teach them. You have attacked me, who, unworthy as I am, have yet been anointed to rule among the anointed of God, and who, according to the teaching of the fathers, can be judged by no one save God alone, and can be deposed for no crime except infidelity. For the holy fathers in the time of the apostate Julian did not presume to pronounce sentence of deposition against him, but left him to be judged and condemned by God. St. Peter himself said: "Fear God, honor the king" [1 Pet. 2:17]. But you, who fear not God, have dishonored me, whom He hath established. St. Paul, who said that even an angel from heaven should be accursed who taught any other than the true doctrine, did not make an exception in your favor, to permit you to teach false doctrines. For he says: "But though we, or an angel from heaven, preach any other gospel unto you than that which we have preached unto you, let him be accursed" [Gal. 1:8]. Come down, then, from that apostolic seat which you have obtained by violence; for you have been declared accursed by St. Paul for your false doctrines and have been condemned by us and our bishops for your evil rule. Let another ascend the throne of St. Peter, one who will not use religion as a cloak of violence, but will teach the life-giving doctrine of that prince of the apostles. I, Henry, king by the grace of God, with all my bishops, say unto you: "Come down, come down, and be accursed through all the ages."

76. LETTER OF THE BISHOPS TO GREGORY VII, JANUARY 24, 1076.

Codex Udalrici, no. 162; M. G. LL. folio, II, pp. 44 ff; Doeberl, III, no. 8 a.

See introductory note to no. 74.

Siegfried, archbishop of Mainz, Udo, bishop of Trier, William, bishop of Utrecht, etc. [a list of names of bishops, twenty-six in all], to brother Hildebrand.

At first when you made yourself pope we thought it better to ignore the illegality of your action and to submit to your rule, in the hope that you would redeem your bad beginning by a just and righteous government of the church, although we realized even then the enormity of the sin which you had committed. But now the lamentable condition of the whole church shows us only too well how we were deceived in you; your violent entrance into office was but the first in a series of wicked deeds and unjust decrees. Our Lord and Redeemer has said, in more places than we can well enumerate here, that love and gentleness are the marks of his disciples, but you are known for your pride, your ambition, and your love of strife. You have introduced worldliness into the church; you have desired a great name rather than a reputation for holiness; you have made a schism in the church and offended its members, who before your time were living together in peace and charity. Your mad acts have kindled the flame of discord which now rages in the churches of Italy, Germany, France, and Spain. The bishops have been deprived of their divine authority, which rests upon the grace of the Holy Spirit received through ordination, and the whole administration of ecclesiastical matters you have given to rash and ignorant laymen. There is nowhere in the church to-day a bishop or a priest who does not hold his office through abject acquiescence in your ambitious schemes. The order of bishops, to whom the government of the church was intrusted by the Lord, you have thrown into confusion, and you have disturbed that excellent coördination of the members of Christ which Paul in so many places commends and inculcates, while the name of Christ has almost disappeared from the earth; and all this through those decrees in which you glory. Who among men is not filled with astonishment and indignation at your claims to sole authority, by which you would deprive your fellow-bishops of their coördinate rights and powers? For you assert that you have the authority to try any one of our parishioners for any sin which may have reached your ears even by chance report, and that no one of us has the power to loose or to bind such a sinner, but that it belongs to you alone or to your legate. Who that knows the scriptures does not perceive the madness of this claim? Since, therefore, it is now apparent that the church of God is in danger of destruction through your presumption, we have come to the conclusion that this state of things can no longer be endured, and we have determined to break our silence and to make public the reasons why you are unfit and have always been unfit to rule the church as pope. These are the reasons: In the first place, in the reign of emperor Henry [III] of blessed memory, you bound yourself by oath never to accept the papacy or to permit anyone else to accept it during the life of that emperor or of his son without the consent of the emperor. There are many bishops still living who can bear witness to that oath. On another occasion, when certain cardinals were aiming to secure the office, you took an oath never to accept the papacy, on condition that they should all take the same oath. You know yourself how faithfully you have kept these oaths! In the second place, it was agreed in a synod held in the time of pope Nicholas [II] and attended by 125 bishops, that no one, under penalty of excommunication, should ever accept the papacy who had not received the election of the cardinals, the approbation of the people, and the consent of the emperor. You

yourself proposed and promoted that decree and signed it
with your own hand. In the third place, you have filled
the whole church with the stench of scandal, by associating
on too intimate terms with a woman who was not a member
of your family [the countess Matilda]. We do not wish to
base any serious charge on this last accusation; we refer to
it because it outrages our sense of propriety. And yet the
complaint is very generally made that all the judgments and
acts of the papacy are passed on by the women about the
pope, and that the whole church is governed by this new
female conclave. And finally, no amount of complaint is
adequate to express the insults and outrages you have heaped
upon the bishops, calling them sons of harlots and other
vile names. Therefore, since your pontificate was begun in
perjury and crime, since your innovations have placed the
church of God in the gravest peril, since your life and conduct are stained with infamy; we now renounce our obedience, which indeed was never legally promised to you. You
have declared publicly that you do not consider us to be
bishops; we reply that no one of us shall ever hold you to
be the pope.

77. THE FIRST DEPOSITION AND EXCOMMUNICATION OF HENRY IV BY GREGORY VII, 1076.

Greg. VII. Reg., III, no. 10 a; Jaffé, II, pp. 223 ff; Doeberl, III, no. 9.

See introductory note to no. 74.

St. Peter, prince of the apostles, incline thine ear unto
me, I beseech thee, and hear me, thy servant, whom thou
hast nourished from mine infancy and hast delivered from
mine enemies that hate me for my fidelity to thee. Thou
art my witness, as are also my mistress, the mother of God,
and St. Paul thy brother, and all the other saints, that thy
holy Roman church called me to its government against my
own will, and that I did not gain thy throne by violence;

that I would rather have ended my days in exile than have obtained thy place by fraud or for worldly ambition. It is not by my efforts, but by thy grace, that I am set to rule over the Christian world which was specially intrusted to thee by Christ. It is by thy grace and as thy representative that God has given to me the power to bind and to loose in heaven and in earth. Confident of my integrity and authority, I now declare in the name of omnipotent God, the Father, Son, and Holy Spirit, that Henry, son of the emperor Henry, is deprived of his kingdom of Germany and Italy; I do this by thy authority and in defence of the honor of thy church, because he has rebelled against it. He who attempts to destroy the honor of the church should be deprived of such honor as he may have held. He has refused to obey as a Christian should, he has not returned to God from whom he had wandered, he has had dealings with excommunicated persons, he has done many iniquities, he has despised the warnings which, as thou art witness, I sent to him for his salvation, he has cut himself off from thy church, and has attempted to rend it asunder; therefore, by thy authority, I place him under the curse. It is in thy name that I curse him, that all people may know that thou art Peter, and upon thy rock the Son of the living God has built his church, and the gates of hell shall not prevail against it.

78. The Agreement at Oppenheim, October, 1076.

M. G. LL. 4to, IV, 1, nos. 64, 65; Codex Udalrici, nos. 145, 155; Doeberl, III, no. 12.

Various parts of Germany were already in revolt against Henry IV, and the immediate effect of the papal excommunication was to strengthen the rebellious party. Being almost deserted, Henry found himself unable to refuse the demands of the rebels. He agreed to submit to Gregory in all things, and rescinded the edicts by which he had deposed him. He also called on all his subjects to submit to the pope (no. 79).

Promise of king Henry to pope Hildebrand, also called Gregory.

In accordance with the advice of my subjects, I hereby promise to show henceforth fitting reverence and obedience to the apostolic office and to you, pope Gregory. I further promise to make suitable reparation for any loss of honor which you or your office may have suffered through me. And since I have been accused of certain grave crimes, I will either clear myself by presenting proof of my innocence or by undergoing the ordeal, or else I will do such penance as you may decide to be adequate for my fault.

79. EDICT ANNULLING THE DECREES AGAINST POPE GREGORY.

Cf. reference to no. 78.

Henry, by the grace of God king, to the archbishops, bishops, margraves, counts, and to his subjects of every rank and dignity, greeting and good will. Our faithful subjects have convinced us that in our recent controversy with pope Gregory we were led astray by certain evil counsellors. Therefore we now make known to all, that we have repented of our former actions and have determined henceforth to obey him in everything, as our predecessors were wont to do before us, and to make full reparation for any injury which we may have inflicted upon him or his office. We command all of you to follow our example and to offer satisfaction to St. Peter and to his vicar, pope Gregory, for any fault you may have committed, and to seek absolution from him, if any of you are under his ban.

80. LETTER OF GREGORY VII TO THE GERMAN PRINCES CONCERNING THE PENANCE OF HENRY IV AT CANOSSA, ca. JANUARY 28, 1077.

Greg. VII. Reg., IV, nos. 12, 12 a; Jaffé, II, pp. 256 ff; Doeberl, III, no. 13.

At Oppenheim Henry IV had been temporarily deposed. He sent away his counsellors who had been excommunicated, gave up all par-

ticipation in the affairs of government, laid aside all the royal insignia, and withdrew to the city of Speier, which he was not to
leave until the matter was adjusted by the pope, who was to come
to Germany and hold a diet in February, 1077. But Henry did not
keep his word. Fearing that he would be permanently deposed if the
pope should come to Germany and sit with his rebellious subjects in
judgment on him, he determined to forestall matters by going to see
the pope in Italy. So he fled from Speier and hastened as rapidly as
possible into Italy. He came to Canossa, where he humbled himself
before Gregory and received absolution. It was at least a diplomatic
triumph for Henry, because he had kept the pope from coming to
Germany and uniting with his rebellious nobles, who would have
labored hard to secure the permanent deposition of Henry. The
final decision of the matter was indeed left to the pope and the diet
which was to be held in Germany, but the pope did not go to Germany, and Henry was able to point to the fact that he had received
papal absolution. The oath which Gregory VII required of Henry
is given in no. 81.

Gregory, bishop, servant of the servants of God, to all the
archbishops, bishops, dukes, counts, and other princes of the
German kingdom, defenders of the Christian faith, greeting
and apostelic benediction.

Since you have made common cause with us and shared
our perils in the recent controversy, we have thought it only
right that you should be informed of the recent course of
events, how king Henry came to Italy to do penance, and
how we were led to grant him absolution.

According to the agreement made with your representatives we had come to Lombardy and were there awaiting
those whom you were to send to escort us into your land.
But after the time set was already passed, we received word
that it was at that time impossible to send an escort, because
of many obstacles that stood in the way, and we were greatly
exercised at this and in grave doubt as to what we ought to
do. In the meantime we learned that the king was approaching. Now before he entered Italy he had sent to us and
had offered to make complete satisfaction for his fault,

promising to reform and henceforth to obey us in all things, provided we would give him our absolution and blessing. We hesitated for some time, taking occasion in the course of the negotiations to reprove him sharply for his former sins. Finally he came in person to Canossa, where we were staying, bringing with him only a small retinue and manifesting no hostile intentions. Once arrived, he presented himself at the gate of the castle, barefoot and clad only in wretched woollen garments, beseeching us with tears to grant him absolution and forgiveness. This he continued to do for three days, until all those about us were moved to compassion at his plight and interceded for him with tears and prayers. Indeed, they marvelled at our hardness of heart, some even complaining that our action savored rather of heartless tyranny than of chastening severity. At length his persistent declarations of repentance and the supplications of all who were there with us overcame our reluctance, and we removed the excommunication from him and received him again into the bosom of the holy mother church. But first he took the oath which we have subjoined to this letter, the abbot of Cluny, the countess Matilda, the countess Adelaide, and many other ecclesiastic and secular princes going surety for him. Now that this arrangement has been reached to the common advantage of the church and the empire, we purpose coming to visit you in your own land as soon as possible. For, as you will perceive from the conditions stated in the oath, the matter is not to be regarded as settled until we have held consultation with you. Therefore we urge you to maintain that fidelity and love of justice which first prompted your action. We have not bound ourself to anything, except that we assured the king that he might depend upon us to aid him in everything that looked to his salvation and honor.

81. THE OATH OF KING HENRY.

Cf. reference to no. 80.

See introductory note to no. 80.

I, Henry, king, promise to satisfy the grievances which my archbishops, bishops, dukes, counts, and other princes of Germany or their followers may have against me, within the time set by pope Gregory and in accordance with his conditions. If I am prevented by any sufficient cause from doing this within that time, I will do it as soon after that as I may. Further, if pope Gregory shall desire to visit Germany or any other land, on his journey thither, his sojourn there, and his return thence, he shall not be molested or placed in danger of captivity by me or by anyone whom I can control. This shall apply to his escort and retinue and to all who come and go in his service. Moreover, I will never enter into any plan for hindering or molesting him, but will aid him in good faith and to the best of my ability if anyone else opposes him.

82. COUNTESS MATILDA GIVES ALL HER LANDS TO THE CHURCH, 1102.

M. G. LL. 4to, IV, 1, p. 654, no. 444.

The countess Matilda supported the papacy in its claims of temporal sovereignty, and, when she died, left it all her lands. The emperors did not recognize the validity of the legacy, and declared that she had no right to give away what belonged to the empire. The quarrel about these lands was often renewed.

In the name of the holy and undivided Trinity. . . . In the time of Gregory VII, in the Lateran palace, in the chapel of the holy cross, in the presence of [witnesses], . . . I, Matilda, by the grace of God countess, for the salvation of my soul and the souls of my parents, gave to the church of St. Peter and to Gregory VII all my possessions, present and future, by whatever title I may hold them. I

gave all my lands in Italy and Germany, and I had a document drawn up to that effect. But now the document has
disappeared, and I fear that my gift may be questioned.
Therefore, I, countess Matilda, again give to the church of
Rome, through Bernard, cardinal and legate of the same
holy church of Rome, just as I did in the time of Gregory
VII, all my possessions, present and future, in both Italy
and Germany, by whatever right I hold them, for the salvation of my soul and the souls of my parents. All these
possessions, which belong to me, with all that pertains to
them, in all their entirety, I give to the said church of Rome,
and by this deed of gift I confirm the church in the possession of them. As symbols and evidences that I have surrendered these lands I have given a knife, a knotted straw,
a glove, a piece of sod, and a twig from a tree. . . .

83. The First Privilege which Paschal II Granted to Henry V, February 12, 1111.

M. G. LL. folio, II, pp. 68 ff; Doeberl, III, no. 20 a.

In the struggle about the election and investiture of bishops,
which was begun by Gregory VII, Henry V pursued the same policy
as his father, Henry IV. He was so vigorous in pushing his claims
that Paschal II (1099-1118) yielded and in 1111 decreed that the
high clergy should give up all their fiefs and temporal offices, and
exercise only spiritual functions. But this action met with a storm
of opposition. The bishops refused to give up their temporal possessions, and resisted with such determination that Paschal was compelled to cancel his agreement with Henry V. But the king would
not be denied. He brought such pressure to bear on the pope that
he made a complete surrender and granted Henry the control of the
elections of bishops and the unconditional right to invest them with
their office (no. 84).

Paschal, bishop, servant of the servants of God, to his
beloved son Henry, and to his successors forever.

Priests are forbidden by the scriptures and by the canons
of the church to occupy themselves with secular affairs or

to attend the public courts, except in the exercise of their office, such as the saving of the souls of the condemned or the assisting of the injured. In regard to this St. Paul says: "If then ye have judgments of things pertaining to this life, set them to judge who are least esteemed in the church" [1 Cor. 6:4]. But in your kingdom bishops and abbots regularly attend the courts and perform military service, which duties necessarily bring them into contact with rapine, sacrilege, and violence. The ministers of the altar are made ministers of the royal court, and are given cities, duchies, marks, mints, and other offices to hold and to rule. As a result an unbearable custom has arisen that bishops elect cannot be consecrated until they have been invested with office by the king. Simony and worldly ambition have thereby become so prevalent that men are sometimes placed in control of the episcopal properties who have not been elected bishops; and are sometimes invested with them while the true bishops are still alive. Our predecessors, pope Gregory VII and pope Urban II, of blessed memory, were impelled by the many evils resulting from this practice to condemn lay investiture in several councils, decreeing that those who obtained ecclesiastical offices by these means should be forced to surrender them and that those who conferred the investiture should be excommunicated. This was based on the chapter of the apostolic canons which reads: "If a bishop makes use of the secular powers to obtain a diocese, he shall be deposed and those who supported him shall be cast out of the church." [See no. 33.] Following their example, we have confirmed the present decree, which has been passed by a council of bishops.

All the royal offices and benefices which belonged to the empire in the time of the emperors Karl, Ludwig, and your other predecessors, and which are now held by the church, we order to be restored to you. We forbid any bishop or abbot, under pain of anathema, to hold any of these regalia;

that is, cities, duchies, marks, counties; rights of minting, markets, or tolls; offices of advocate or hundred-man; estates which belong to the empire, with any of their appurtenances, the right to hold castles or to do military service. They shall not henceforth have anything to do with these regalia, except at the request of the king. And our successors are forbidden to disturb this arrangement or to molest you or any of your kingdom in the peaceful possession of the regalia.

On the other hand, we decree that the churches shall have absolute control of their free-will offerings and their private possessions, which is in keeping with the promise which you made in your coronation oath.

For it is necessary that the bishops be free from secular duties that they may give their time to the care of their flocks, and not be too long absent from their churches; as St. Paul says of the bishops: "They watch for your souls, as they that must give account" [Heb. 13:17].

84. The Second Privilege which Paschal II Granted to Henry V, April 12, 1111.

M. G. LL. folio, II, pp. 72 ff; Doeberl, III, no. 20 b.

See introductory note to no. 83.

Paschal, bishop, servant of the servants of God, to his beloved son, Henry, by the grace of God king of the Germans and emperor of the Romans, Augustus, greeting and apostolic benediction. It is the will of God that your kingdom should be closely bound to the holy Roman church. Your predecessors obtained the crown and empire of the Roman world because of their wisdom and virtue; you also have been exalted to that dignity by the will of God working through us. And so we confer upon you the prerogatives which our predecessors granted to former emperors. By this document we concede to you the right of investing the bishops and abbots of your kingdom with the ring and the staff, if their election has been conducted canonically and without simony or other illegality.   After their investiture they are to be consecrated in due canonical form by their bishops.   If the clergy and people elect a bishop or an abbot without first gaining your consent, he shall not be consecrated until you have invested him with his office.   The right of consecrating such bishops and abbots as have received investiture from you shall belong to the archbishops and bishops of your kingdom.   For your predecessors endowed the churches of their realm with so many benefices from their own lands and offices that it became necessary for them to control the elections of bishops and abbots, and to put down the popular disturbances that frequently arose in these elections.

As a result of this concession you ought to be the more zealous in the defence and in the enrichment of the church of Rome and the other churches of God.   If any person, ecclesiastic or layman, shall knowingly violate this decree, he shall be accursed and deprived of his office and rank.   But may God reward those who keep it, and grant that you may rule happily to his honor and glory.   Amen.

85–86.   CONCORDAT OF WORMS, 1122.
85.   THE PROMISE OF CALIXTUS II.

M. G. LL. folio, II, pp. 75 ff; Doeberl, III, no. 21 a.

The victory won by Henry V over Paschal II (no. 84) was of short duration because the Cluniac party refused to submit.   They renewed the struggle with great bitterness.   The contest lasted to 1122, when a compromise was agreed upon.   In general it may be said that the compromise was a sensible one, in that the king was recognized as having the right to invest the bishops with their fiefs and secular authority, while the pope was to invest them with their spiritual office and authority.   This settlement of the principle did not entirely end the struggle, because, in the first place, neither party observed it perfectly, and, besides, it occasionally happened that there was some doubt as to how the principle was to be applied.

Calixtus, bishop, servant of the servants of God, to his beloved son, Henry, by the grace of God emperor of the Romans, Augustus.

We hereby grant that in Germany the elections of the bishops and abbots who hold directly from the crown shall be held in your presence, such elections to be conducted canonically and without simony or other illegality. In the case of disputed elections you shall have the right to decide between the parties, after consulting with the archbishop of the province and his fellow-bishops. You shall confer the regalia of the office upon the bishop or abbot elect by giving him the sceptre, and this shall be done freely without exacting any payment from him; the bishop or abbot elect on his part shall perform all the duties that go with the holding of the regalia.

In other parts of the empire the bishops shall receive the regalia from you in the same manner within six months of their consecration, and shall in like manner perform all the duties that go with them. The undoubted rights of the Roman church, however, are not to be regarded as prejudiced by this concession. If at any time you shall have occasion to complain of the carrying out of these provisions, I will undertake to satisfy your grievances as far as shall be consistent with my office. Finally, I hereby make a true and lasting peace with you and with all of your followers, including those who supported you in the recent controversy.

86. The Promise of Henry V.

M. G. LL. folio, II, p. 76; Doeberl, III, no. 21 b.

In the name of the holy and undivided Trinity.

For the love of God and his holy church and of pope Calixtus, and for the salvation of my soul, I, Henry, by the grace of God, emperor of the Romans, Augustus, hereby surrender to God and his apostles, Sts. Peter and Paul, and to the holy Catholic church, all investiture by ring and staff. I agree that elections and consecrations shall be conducted canonically and shall be free from all interference. I surrender also the possessions and regalia of St. Peter which have been seized by me during this quarrel, or by my father in his lifetime, and which are now in my possession, and I promise to aid the church to recover such as are held by any other persons. I restore also the possessions of all other churches and princes, clerical or secular, which have been taken away during the course of this quarrel, which I have, and promise to aid them to recover such as are held by any other persons.

Finally, I make true and lasting peace with pope Calixtus and with the holy Roman church and with all who are or have ever been of his party. I will aid the Roman church whenever my help is asked, and will do justice in all matters in regard to which the church may have occasion to make complaint.

All these things have been done with the consent and advice of the princes whose names are written below: Adelbert, archbishop of Mainz; Frederick, archbishop of Cologne, etc.

87. ELECTION NOTICE, 1125.

Jaffé, V, pp. 396 ff; Doeberl, IV, no. 1.

On the death of a king of Germany, it was the duty of the archbishop of Mainz, as archchancellor of Germany, to call a diet for the purpose of electing his successor. He did this by writing a letter in practically the same terms to each of the important men of the kingdom who were members of the diet. These letters were then delivered by special messengers. The diet which met in response to this call in 1125 elected Lothar of Saxony. The tone of the letter reveals the fact that Adelbert of Mainz was inclined rather to the side of the pope. The "yoke of servitude" which was oppressing the church was the imperial control which Henry V had exercised over the ecclesiastical elections.

Adelbert, archbishop of Mainz; Frederick, archbishop of Cologne; Udalric, bishop of Constance; Buco, bishop of Worms; Arnold, bishop of Speier; Udalric, abbot of Fulda; Henry, duke of Bavaria; Frederick, duke of Suabia; Godfrey, count palatine; Berengar, count of Sulzbach, along with the other princes, ecclesiastical and secular, who were present at the funeral of the late emperor, send their greeting and most faithful services to their venerable brother, Otto, bishop of Bamberg.

After the burial of our late lord and emperor, we who were there present thought it expedient to counsel together in regard to the condition of the state. We were unwilling to make any definite plans, however, without your presence and advice, and so we determined to call a diet to meet at Mainz on St. Bartholomew's Day [August 25], hoping that this decision would meet your approval. It is our thought that the princes should meet then and take the necessary action in regard to the serious problems that confront us: the general state of the kingdom, the question of a successor, and other matters. In thus calling a diet without first gaining your approval, we have not meant to infringe in any way upon your rights or to arrogate to ourselves any peculiar authority in this matter. We ask you to bear in mind the oppression of the church in these days and to pray earnestly that in the providence of God this election may result in the freeing of the church from its yoke of servitude and in the establishing of peace for us and for our people. You are instructed to declare a special peace for your lands, to be kept during the time of the diet and four weeks thereafter, so that all may come and return in perfect security; and to come to the diet yourself in the customary manner, that is, at your own expense and without inflicting any burden upon the poor of the realm.

88. Anaclete II Gives Roger the Title of King of Sicily, 1130.

Watterich, Pont. Rom. Vitæ, II, pp. 193 ff; Doeberl, IV, no. 4.

The Norman adventurers in southern Italy were successful beyond all expectation. In 1059 Nicholas II made a duke of Roger Guiscard (see no. 58). He and his successors labored hard to advance the interests of their family, and in 1130 Roger, duke of Sicily, had the satisfaction of receiving the royal title from Anaclete II. There had been a disputed papal election that year, and Anaclete II, one of the rival claimants, needed all the help he could get. So he bought the support of Roger, giving him in return the title of king.

It is fitting that the pope should generously reward those that love the Roman church. And so, because of the labors and services of your father and mother, and because of your own efforts in behalf of the church, we have given and granted to you, Robert, by the grace of God duke of Sicily, and to your son Robert and your other children and heirs, the crown of Sicily, Apulia, and Calabria, and of all the lands given by us or our predecessors to your ancestors, Robert Guiscard and Robert his son, dukes of Apulia. You shall have and hold this kingdom, which shall take its name from the island of Sicily, with all the royal authority and dignity forever. We also grant that you and your heirs may be anointed and crowned by the archbishops of your lands whom you choose for that purpose, assisted by such bishops as you may desire. We hereby renew all gifts, concessions, and authority conferred upon you and upon your predecessors, Robert Guiscard, Robert his son, and William, dukes of Apulia, to be held and possessed by you forever. We give and grant to you and to your heirs the principality of Capua in its full extent as held now or in the past by the prince of Capua; we confer upon you the lordship over Naples and its dependencies, and the right to demand aid from the inhabitants of Benevento against your enemies. At your request we also grant to the archbishop of Palermo and to his successors the right to consecrate the three bishops of Syracuse, Girgenti, and Catania, on the condition that the authority and possessions of these churches shall not be in any way diminished by the archbishop and the church of Palermo. We reserve our decision as to the consecration of the other two bishops of Sicily for more mature deliberation. We have granted all the above concessions on the condition that you and your heirs take the oath of fidelity to us and to our successors at a place agreed upon by both parties, and that you and your heirs shall pay a tax of 600 "schifates" [a gold coin] a year to the Roman church upon demand. . . .

89. The Coronation Oath of Lothar II, June 4, 1133.

M. G. LL. folio, II, pp. 82 ff; Doeberl, IV, no. 6 a.

Every king, on his coronation as emperor, was required to take an oath to the pope, the character of which may be seen from the oath of Lothar.

This is the oath which king Lothar swore to pope Innocent in the time of the schism of the son of Pierreleone. The oath was taken by Lothar on the day of his imperial coronation before he received the crown, and was administered by Cencio Frangipani in the presence of the Roman nobles, before the basilica of the Holy Saviour, which is also called the basilica of Constantine.

I, king Lothar, promise and swear to you, pope Innocent, that I will never injure you or your successors in any way or place you in danger of captivity. I further promise to defend the honor of the papacy, and to restore the regalia of St. Peter which I may have in my possession, and to aid you in recovering such as may be held by any other persons.

90. INNOCENT II GRANTS THE LANDS OF THE COUNTESS
MATILDA AS A FIEF TO LOTHAR II, 1133.

Theiner, Cod. Dom. Temp., I, 12; Doeberl, IV, no. 6 c.

Matilda, countess of Tuscany, espoused the cause of the pope, and,
on her death, willed all her lands to him. The emperor refused to
acknowledge the validity of this will, declaring that her holdings
were feudal, and hence must revert to the crown, because they could
not be disposed of without imperial consent. [See no. 82.] Lothar
here gives up the imperial claim to them and yields them to the pope,
but receives them back as a fief. The question was not thereby
settled forever, because later emperors refused to be bound by the
action of Lothar, and renewed the imperial pretensions. These lands
were a fruitful source of contention between the popes and the
emperors. This document, as here given, is probably an abstract of
two documents, (1) the one by which the lands were conferred on
Lothar, and (2) that by which they were later transferred to Lothar's
son-in-law, Henry, duke of Bavaria.

(The document begins with a general exordium, setting forth the
common interests of papacy and empire, recalling the services of
Lothar in behalf of the church, and stating the obligation of the
pope to reward such services.)

It is on these considerations, therefore, that we now grant
you by our apostolic authority the allodial lands which the
countess Matilda formerly gave to St. Peter. In the presence of our brothers, the archbishops, bishops, and abbots,
and princes and barons, we now confer them upon you by
the investiture of the ring, on the following conditions: you
shall pay 100 pounds of silver annually to us and to our
successors; after your death the property shall revert unimpaired and without hindrance to the possession of the holy
Roman church; we and our brothers shall always have safe-
conduct and suitable entertainment whenever we pass through
or visit the land; and, finally, your representative in the
government of the land shall take an oath of fidelity to St.
Peter and to the pope.

Because of our love for you we graciously concede this
land on the same conditions to your son-in-law, Henry, duke

of Bavaria, and his wife, your daughter. It is further stipulated that the duke shall do homage to us and take an oath
of fidelity to St. Peter and to the pope; and that after their
death the land shall revert to the possession of the Roman
church, as said above. In all this there shall be no derogation of the rights and ultimate ownership of the holy Roman
church.

91. Letter of Bernard of Clairvaux to Lothar II, 1134.

Migne, 182, cols. 293 ff; Doeberl, IV, no. 7.

In 1130 there was a disputed papal election. Innocent II, on being
driven from Rome by his rival, Anaclete II, went to France, where
he enlisted Bernard of Clairvaux in his favor. Through the efforts
of Bernard the kings of France and Germany were persuaded to
support him. Lothar led an army into Italy, established Innocent
in Rome, and received the imperial crown. He failed, however, to
conquer Roger, who had been made king of Sicily by the antipope,
Anaclete II (see no. 88). Bernard wrote this letter to congratulate
Lothar on his success in Italy, to urge him to renew the war on
Roger because he was still supporting the antipope, and to rebuke
Lothar for opposing some decision of the pope in regard to a trouble
that had arisen in the church at Toul.

To Lothar, by the grace of God emperor of the Romans,
Augustus, Bernard, called abbot of Clairvaux, sends his
blessing, if the prayer of a sinner is of any avail.

Blessed be God, who has chosen you and exalted you
for a horn of salvation unto us, to the glory of his name,
the restoration of the empire, the preservation of his church
in this evil time, and the working of his salvation in the
midst of the earth. For it is by his will that you are daily
growing in strength, in honor, and in glory. And when
you recently undertook the hazardous expedition to Rome
to secure the peace of the empire and the liberty of the
church, it was by his aid that you were able to carry
it through successfully, obtaining the crown of the em-

pire without the aid of a large army. But if the earth
trembled and was silent before that little band, think what
great terror will strike the hearts of the enemy when the
king shall proceed against him in the greatness of his power.
Moreover, the justice of your cause, nay, more, a double
necessity, will inspire you. It is not my duty to incite
princes to war; but it is the duty of the defender of the
church to ward off all danger of schism; it is the duty of
the emperor to recover his crown from the Sicilian usurper.
Just as that Jew [that is, Anaclete II] rebelled against
Christ when he seized the papal chair, so anyone who would
make himself king in Sicily rebels against Cæsar.

But if we are commanded to render unto Cæsar the things
which are Cæsar's and unto God the things which are God's,
why is it that you have permitted the church of God in
Toul to be robbed, especially as Cæsar profits not thereby?
. . . For it is said that you have interfered with the pope
in his efforts to bring the oppressors of that church to justice. I beseech you to act more circumspectly and to recall
your intercession and let justice take its course, before that
church be destroyed to its foundations. I am a poor person, but a faithful subject, and if I seem importunate it is
because of my fidelity. Greet my lady the empress for me
in the love of Christ.

92. LETTER OF BERNARD TO CONRAD III, 1140.

Migne, 182, no. 183; Doeberl, IV, no. 11.

Because Roger of Sicily had supported the antipope, Bernard had
urged Lothar to make war on him. [See no. 91.] But Innocent had,
in the meantime, without consulting the emperor, made a treaty with
Roger and won his support by also granting him the royal title
(1139). Conrad III was offended by this and protested against it.
Conrad declared that the kingdom which Roger held, that is, Sicily
and southern Italy, was a part of the empire, and therefore the pope
had no right to recognize Roger as king there. Conrad regarded
Roger as a usurper. He wrote a letter to Bernard complaining of
the action of the pope. But Bernard had changed his sentiments since

Roger had espoused the cause of Innocent and had received papal confirmation. In a somewhat curt manner he tells Conrad to obey the pope.

I, unworthy person that I am, have received your letter and greeting with gratitude and devotion. The complaints of the king are ours also, especially in regard to the usurpation of the Sicilian.

I have never desired the disgrace of the king nor the diminution of his realm; my soul hates such as do desire these things. But I read: "Let every soul be subject unto the higher powers; whosoever resisteth the power, resisteth the ordinance of God" [Rom. 13:1, 2]. Hearken to this admonition, I pray you, and show such reverence to St. Peter and to his vicar as you wish to be shown to you by the whole empire. There are certain other matters which I have thought better not to put in writing; perhaps it would be better to speak of them to you personally when I see you.

93. LETTER OF CONRAD III TO THE GREEK EMPEROR, JOHN COMNENUS, 1142.

Otto Fris. Gesta Frid., I, c. 25; M. G. SS. folio, XX; Doeberl, IV, no. 12.

Although the German and Greek emperors had not adjusted their conflicting claims to southern Italy and Sicily (see no. 58, introductory note), they were agreed in regarding the Normans as usurpers and a common enemy. In order to destroy them the emperors determined to make common cause against them, as is apparent from the following letter. John Commenus, wishing to strengthen the alliance with Conrad, asked him to choose some German princess for his son, Manuel. Conrad chose his sister-in-law, Bertha von Sulzbach, who, at the time of her marriage with Manuel, assumed the name Irene.

Conrad, by the grace of God emperor of the Romans, Augustus, to John, by the same grace emperor of Constantinople, greeting and fraternal love.

As our predecessors, the Roman emperors, made friendship with your predecessors and established the honor and
glory of the kingdom of the Greeks, we desire to do the same;
and as they defended it, so we will defend it. It is known
of all men that your new Rome [Constantinople] is the
daughter of our Rome, the root from which have come your
branches and fruits. Therefore we are determined to maintain toward you the attitude of a kind mother to her daughter, all the more that we perceive in you a desire to act as
a dutiful daughter. We two should have the same interests, the same friends, and the same enemies, on land and
sea. Anyone who fails to honor the daughter shall have
occasion to know and fear the strength of the mother, be
he Norman or Sicilian, or any other. For we have not forgotten the attacks which our enemy has made upon our own
empire. With the help of God, we shall repay to every one
according to the measure of his guilt. Then the whole
world shall see how easily those who have dared to rebel
against us both are overwhelmed and cast down; for if we
cut his wings, we shall, as it were, take the enemy flying, and
cut out of his heart that arrogance which has caused him to
revolt against us. It is our firm purpose to maintain friendly
relations toward you, and we are sure you hold the same
purpose toward us, all the more now that we are bound
together by the approaching marriage of your son and the
sister of our wife, the empress. . . .

94. Letter of Wibald, Abbot of Stablo, to Eugene III, 1159.

Jaffé, I, p. 372; Doeberl, IV, no. 24 a.

The following letter shows (1) the mismanagement of the affairs
of a great monastery, (2) the troubles which might arise in connection with the election of an abbot, (3) the influence which Conrad
III exercised on such elections, and (4) the method of procedure in
elections. It will be remembered that the concordat of Worms was
now in force.

To his reverend father and lord, pope Eugene, Wibald [abbot of Stablo], sends his reverence and respect.

Our beloved brother Henry, abbot of Hersfeld, who had also been placed in charge of the abbey of Fulda, was called from this earth by God soon after our lord Conrad returned from his expedition to Jerusalem. The king was prevented from immediately settling the affairs of the monastery of Fulda by the evil state into which its affairs had fallen and by the violence of party strife within it. This delay was unfortunate, because the king was not able either to recover its possessions which had been squandered or to provide for the performance of the spiritual functions of the church, that is, the care of souls. Therefore we and our brothers, the abbot of Eberach and other clergymen, urged upon him the necessity of settling its affairs as soon as possible. Finally he came to Fulda on the 5th of April and held a diet there, which was attended by your venerable sons, the archbishop of Bremen, and the bishops of Würzburg and Halberstadt, and many secular princes and nobles. Among other things, the king sought their advice in regard to the affairs of Fulda, seeking to reach a settlement by which he might render unto God the things which are God's and unto Cæsar the things which are Cæsar's. After a long and fruitless debate . . . the king said that a certain man had been suggested to him as being of good character and holy reputation. This man, it was said, had been successful in the administration of a small monastery, which had prospered under his rule both spiritually and materially, and there was no reason for doubting that he was well fitted by his zeal and ability to govern the monastery of Fulda. If they voted to elect this man, he was sure that the monastery would recover its former honor and dignity under his wise and mild administration. All those present were delighted with this speech, as showing the interest of the king in the welfare of the church, and the matter was reported by some of us to those who had the authority to elect the abbot. They in turn were rejoiced at this turn of the affair and begged to be told the name of the man. And when it was told to them they proceeded to elect him as their abbot. This man is Mainward, abbot of Deggingen, . . . who has ruled that monastery for eight years and has been very successful in his administration. We beseech you to confirm his election, for he is recommended by those who know him best, and his election took place without his knowledge, and indeed against his will. We believe that by confirming his election and giving him your benediction you will do much to heal the wounds of the distressed congregation of Fulda. We ourselves bear witness that all the brothers of the congregation have promised obedience and devotion to their abbot elect.

May God keep you safe and unharmed to rule his holy church.

95. LETTER OF FREDERICK I TO EUGENE III, ANNOUNCING HIS ELECTION, 1152.

Jaffé, I, Wibaldi Epp., no. 372; Doeberl, IV, no. 25 a.

During the Middle Age there were many constitutional questions which had not been decided. On many points no theory had been formulated, and the practice varied. Thus it had not been clearly determined how far the pope might control the election of the German king. In 1125 Lothar had asked the pope to confirm his election; Frederick I merely informs the pope of his election and tells him the policy which he intends to pursue. Eugene III "approves" his election, but does not use the more technical word, "confirm."

To his most beloved father in Christ, Eugene, pope of the holy Roman church, Frederick, by the grace of God king of the Romans, Augustus, [sends] filial love and reverence.

. . . Following the custom of the Roman emperors, we have sent to you as ambassadors, Eberhard, venerable bishop

of Bamberg, Hillo, bishop elect of Trier, and Adam, abbot of
Eberach, to notify you of our election and of the condition
of the church and the realm.

After the death of Conrad, king of the Romans, all the
princes of the kingdom came together at Frankfurt, and on
the day of their assembling elected us king. The princes
displayed complete harmony in this election and the people
received it with the greatest approval and delight. Five days
later, just after the middle of Lent, we were anointed at
Aachen by your beloved sons, the archbishop of Cologne, and
other venerable bishops, and were raised to the throne with
their solemn benediction. And now that we have been invested with the royal authority and dignity by the homage
of the secular princes and the benediction of the bishops, we
intend to assume the royal character, as set forth in our
coronation oath; namely, to love and honor the pope, to
defend the holy Roman church and all ecclesiastical persons,
to maintain peace and order, and to protect the widows and
the fatherless and all the people committed to our care. God
has established two powers by which this world should be
ruled, the papacy and the empire; therefore we are prepared
to obey the priests of Christ, in order that, through our zeal,
the word of God may prevail during our time, and that no
one may disobey with impunity the laws of the holy fathers
or the decrees of the councils, and that the church may enjoy
her ancient honor and dignity and the empire be restored
to its former strength. We know that you were greatly distressed at the death of our uncle and predecessor Conrad,
but we assure you, beloved father, that we have succeeded
him not only in the kingdom, but also in the love which he
bore you. We undertake his work of defending the holy
Roman church, and we intend to carry on the plans which
he made for the honor and liberty of the apostolic see. Your
enemies shall be our enemies, and those that hate you shall
suffer our displeasure.

96. ANSWER OF EUGENE III, MAY 17, 1152.

Jaffé, I, Wibaldi Epp., no. 382; Doeberl, IV, no. 25 c.

See introductory note to no. 95.

Eugene, bishop, servant of the servants of God, to his beloved son in Christ, Frederick, illustrious king of the Romans, greeting and apostolic benediction.

We have received the messengers and the letter which you sent to inform us of your election by the unanimous vote of the princes. . . . We give thanks unto God, from whom cometh every good and perfect gift, for this good news, and we heartily approve your election. We are confident that you intend to take upon yourself the fulfilment of the promise which your uncle and predecessor, Conrad, gave to us and to the holy Roman church. We, on our part, shall labor for your advancement and exaltation, as is the duty of our office. We have sent you an ambassador, who will disclose to you our purpose and intention. In the meantime, we admonish you to bear in mind your oath to defend the church and the clergy of God, to keep peace and order, and to protect the widows and the fatherless, and all your people, that those who obey you and trust in you may rejoice, and that you may win glory with men and eternal life with the king of kings.

97. TREATY OF CONSTANCE, 1153.

Jaffé, I, Wibaldi Epp., no. 417; Doeberl, IV, no. 27 a.

The situation of the pope was precarious. In the first place, the Romans had rebelled against him and his rule, and had set up a government of their own. Since 1143 he had been compelled to spend most of his time outside of the city. In the second place, Roger of Sicily was in rebellion against him and threatened the papal lands with invasion from the south. And lastly, the Greek emperor was now following a vigorous policy to secure land in Italy. The pope was in sore need of help, especially against the Romans and Normans. Hence he insisted that Frederick should promise to aid

him, as well as not to make peace with his enemies without papal
consent. Frederick wished the imperial crown, and the papal blessing and support. He was planning the conquest of the Normans,
whose territory he regarded as a part of the empire. But in this
agreement it will be observed that nothing is said about who owns
Sicily and southern Italy, nor is it stipulated that the pope shall
not make terms with the Normans without the emperor's consent.
Frederick feared that the pope, who wished to gain control of the
Greek church, might make terms with the Greek emperor and help
him in his efforts to regain a foothold in Italy.

In the name of the Lord, amen. This is a copy of the
agreement and convention made between the pope, Eugene
III, and Frederick, king of the Romans, by their represen-
tatives; on the part of the pope: cardinals Gregory of Santa
Maria in Trastevere, Ubald of San Prassede, Bernard of
San Clemente, Octavian of Santa Cecilia, Roland of San
Marco, Gregory of Sant Angelo, Guido of Santa Maria in
porticu, and Bruno, abbot of Chiaravalle; on the part of the
king: Anselm, bishop of Havelberg; Hermann, bishop of
Constance; Udalrich, count of Lenzburg; Guido, count of
Guerra, and Guido, count of Bianderati.

The king will have one of his ministerials to swear for
him that he will not make a peace or a truce either with the
Romans or with Roger of Sicily without the consent of the
pope. The king will use all the power of his realm to reduce
the Romans to subjection to the pope and the Roman church.
He will protect the honor of the papacy and the regalia of
St. Peter against all men to the best of his ability, and he
will aid the church in recovering what she has lost. He will
never grant any land in Italy to the king of the Greeks, and
will use all his power in keeping him out. All these things
the king promises to observe and to do in good faith.

The pope, on his part, promises on his apostolic faith,
with the consent of the cardinals, that he will ever honor
the king as the most dearly beloved son of St. Peter, and
that he will give him the imperial crown whenever he shall

come to Italy for it. He will aid the king in maintaining and increasing the honor of his realm, as his office demands. If anyone attacks the honor or the authority of the king, the pope at the request of the king will warn him to make satisfaction, and will excommunicate him if he refuses to heed the warning. The pope will not grant any land in Italy to the king of the Greeks, and will use all the resources of St. Peter to drive him out if he invades that land. All these things shall be observed in good faith by both parties, unless they are changed by mutual consent.

98. The Stirrup Episode, 1155.

Watterich, Pont. Rom. Vitæ, II, pp. 327 ff.

This account of the stirrup episode illustrates the growing pretensions of the papacy, the temper of both Frederick I and the new pope, Adrian IV, and the importance which the Middle Age attached to matters of ceremony.

The king [Frederick] advanced with his army to the neighborhood of Sutri and encamped in Campo Grasso. The pope, however, came to Nepi, and on the day after his arrival was met there by many of the German princes and a great concourse of clergy and laymen, and conducted with his bishops and cardinals to the tent of the king. But when the cardinals who came with the pope saw that the king did not come forward to act as the esquire of the pope [i.e., to hold his stirrup while he dismounted], they were greatly disturbed and terrified, and retreated to Civita Castellana, leaving the pope before the tent of the king. And the pope, distressed and uncertain what he should do, sadly dismounted and sat down on the seat which had been prepared for him. Then the king prostrated himself before the pope, kissing his feet and presenting himself for the kiss of peace. But the pope said: "You have refused to pay me the due and accustomed honor which your predecessors, the orthodox emperors, have always paid to my predecessors, the Roman

popes, out of reverence for the apostles, Peter and Paul;
therefore I will not give you the kiss of peace until you have
made satisfaction." The king, however, replied that he was
not under obligations to perform the service. The whole of
the following day was spent in the discussion of this point,
the army in the meantime remaining there. And after the
testimony of the older princes had been taken, especially of
those who had been present at the meeting of king Lothar
and pope Innocent (II), and the ancient practice had been
determined, the princes and the royal court decided that the
king ought to act as the esquire of the pope and hold his
stirrup, out of reverence for the apostles, Peter and Paul.
On the next day the camp of the king was moved to the
territory of Nepi, on the shores of lake Janula, and there
king Frederick, in accordance with the decision of the
princes, advanced to meet the pope, who was approaching by
another way. And when the pope came within about a
stone's throw from the emperor, the emperor dismounted and
proceeded on foot to meet the pope, and there in the sight
of his army he acted as the pope's esquire, holding his stirrup for him to dismount. Then the pope gave him the kiss
of peace.

99. Treaty between Adrian IV and William of Sicily, 1156.

Watterich, Pont. Rom. Vitæ, II, pp. 352 ff; Doeberl, IV, no. 34.

By this document the long struggle between the popes and the
kings of Sicily was brought to an end. The terms of the treaty
were very favorable to the pope, but William retained as privileges
certain things which were in other countries generally regarded as
belonging to the pope. For the effects of this treaty on the relations
between Adrian IV and Frederick I, see no. 100, introductory note.

In the name of the Lord, the eternal God, and of our
Saviour, Jesus Christ, amen. To Adrian, by the grace of
God, pope of the holy Roman church, his most beloved lord

and father, and to his successors, William, by the same grace king of Sicily, duke of Apulia, and prince of Capua.

(Introduction reviewing the differences between the pope and the king of Sicily, and relating the course of the negotiations.)

We agree, therefore, to this treaty of peace as drawn up by the representatives of both of us.

1. Concerning appeals to the pope. In Apulia and its dependencies and in Calabria, appeals in ecclesiastical matters which cannot be settled by the regular ecclesiastics of those lands may be made freely to Rome. If it seems advantageous or necessary to transfer priests from one church to another, this may be done with the consent of the pope. The Roman church shall have the right to consecrate and to make visitations throughout our whole realm. The Roman church shall have the right to hold councils in any of the cities of Apulia or its dependencies or Calabria, except that a council may not be held in any city in which the king is staying, without his consent. The Roman church shall have the right to send its legates into Apulia and its dependencies and into Calabria, but those legates shall not waste the possessions of the churches to which they are sent. The Roman church shall have the same right of consecration and visitation in the island of Sicily. . . . The Roman church shall have in Sicily all the rights which it as in other parts of our kingdom, except the right of hearing appeals and sending legates, which shall be exercised only at the request of the king.

2. Concerning those churches and monasteries which have been in dispute between us. You and your successors shall have in them the rights which you exercise in other churches of our lands, which are accustomed to receive their consecration and benediction from the Roman church, and these churches shall pay the legal taxes to the Roman see.

3. Concerning elections.   The clergy shall elect a suitable person, keeping his name secret until they have notified
you.   The name shall then be reported to us, and we will
give our consent to the election, unless the person is one of
our enemies or a traitor, or for some other good reason is
displeasing to us.

4. You shall confer upon us and upon our son Roger,
and our heirs, the kingdom of Sicily, the duchy of Apulia,
and the principality of Capua, with all the lands which belong to them as follows: Naples, Salerno, and Amalfi, with
their dependencies; Marsia and all that we hold beyond
Marsia; and all the other possessions which we now hold,
or which have been held by our predecessors.   You promise,
moreover, to aid us in good faith to hold them against all
men.

5. In consideration of these concessions, we have taken
the oath of fidelity to you and to your successors and to
the Roman church, and the oath of liege homage to you.
Two copies of this oath have been made, one of which
has been signed and sealed by us and given into your keeping,
and the other sealed by you and given to us.   We agree
also to pay an annual tribute of 600 "schifates" for Apulia
and Calabria, and 500 from Marsia.   .   .   .   You agree
to grant all these things also to our heirs and successors,
on condition that they do homage to you and your successors,
and keep the promises which we have made to you.   .   .   .

100–102.   The Besançon Episode, 1157.

**100.   Letter of Adrian IV to Frederick, September
20, 1157.**

Ragewin, Gesta Friderici, III, ch. 9; M. G. SS. folio, XX; Doeberl, IV, no. 35 a.

Frederick I had been deeply offended by the treaty which Adrian
IV made with William of Sicily (no. 99), because it had been made
without his consent, and without in any way considering the claims
which the emperor laid to Sicily.   In making the treaty of Con-

stance (no. 97) Frederick had undoubtedly been outwitted by the papal diplomacy. He had been led to promise not to make peace with the Normans without the consent of the pope. He apparently took it for granted that the pope was bound in the same way not to make peace with the Normans without the imperial consent, although it was not stipulated in the agreement. While Frederick had promised certain definite things, the pope's promise was couched in general terms. He had promised to "aid the king in maintaining and increasing the honor of his realm as his office demands. If anyone attacks the honor or the authority of the king, the pope will warn him to make satisfaction," etc. The pope denied that William of Sicily was "attacking the honor or authority of the king" because the lands which William held did not belong to Frederick; they were the property of the pope himself, and therefore he might make terms with William without consulting Frederick. Frederick complained that the pope had acted in bad faith in making peace with William, and that he had broken the treaty of Constance. The pope, however, maintained that he had in no way infringed the treaty, and that Frederick had no grounds for complaint. This is the general background for the Besançon episode, the chief features of which will be clear from the following documents.

Adrian, bishop, servant of the servants of God, to his beloved son Frederick, illustrious emperor of the Romans, greeting and apostolic benediction. We wrote to you a few days ago recalling to your mind that execrable crime which was recently committed in Germany and expressing our grief that you had allowed it to go unpunished. For our venerable brother, Eskil, archbishop of Lund, on his return from the apostolic seat, was seized and made captive in your land by certain impious and wicked persons, who even threatened him and his companions with drawn swords and subjected them to dishonor and indignity.

Not only are these facts well known to you, but the report of them has spread to the most distant regions. It was your duty to avenge this wicked deed and to draw against its perpetrators the sword intrusted to you by God for the punishing of evil-doers and the protection of good men. But it is reported that you have palliated this offence and allowed it to go unpunished, so that those who committed the sacrilege are unrepentant and believe that they have done this with impunity. We are entirely at a loss to understand this negligence of yours, for our conscience does not accuse us of having offended you in any way. Indeed we have always regarded you as our most beloved son and as a Christian prince established by the grace of God upon the rock of the apostolic confession. We have loved you with sincere affection and have always treated you with the greatest kindness. You should remember, most glorious son, how graciously your mother, the holy Roman church, received you last year, how kindly she treated you, and how gladly she conferred upon you the imperial crown, the highest mark of dignity and honor; how she has always fostered you on her kindly bosom, and has always striven to do only what would be pleasing and advantageous to you. We do not regret having granted the desires of your heart; nay, we would be glad to confer even greater benefits (*beneficia*) upon you, if that were possible, because of the advantage and profit that you would be able to confer upon the church of God and upon us. But the fact that you have allowed this terrible deed, which is an offence against the church and the empire, to go unpunished has made us fear that you have been led by evil counsellors to imagine that you have some grievance against your mother, the holy Roman church, and against us. In regard to this matter and other important affairs, we have sent you these legates, two of the best and dearest of those about us, namely, our beloved sons, Bernard, cardinal priest of Santa Clara, and Roland, chancellor and cardinal priest of San Marco, men conspicuous for their piety, wisdom, and honesty. We beseech you to receive them honorably and kindly, to treat them justly, and to give full credence to the proposals which they make, as if we were speaking in person.

101. MANIFESTO OF THE EMPEROR, OCTOBER, 1157.

Ragewin, Gesta Friderici, III, ch. 11; M. G. SS. folio, xx; Doeberl, IV, no. 35 b.

God, from whom proceeds all authority in heaven and in earth, has intrusted the kingdom and the empire to us, his anointed, and has ordained that the peace of the church be preserved by the imperial arms. Therefore it is with great sorrow that we are forced to complain to you of the head of the church which Christ intended should reflect his character of charity and love of peace. For the actions of the pope threaten to produce such evils and dissensions as will corrupt the whole church and destroy its unity, and bring about strife between the empire and the papacy, unless God should intervene. These are the circumstances: We held a diet at Besançon for the purpose of considering certain matters which concerned the honor of the empire and the security of the church. At that diet legates of the pope arrived, saying that they came on a mission that would redound greatly to the honor and advantage of the empire. We gave them an honorable reception on the first day of their arrival, and on the second day, as is the custom, we called together all the princes to listen to their message. . . . Then they delivered their message in the form of a letter from the pope, of which the general tenor was as follows: the pope had conferred the imperial crown upon us and was willing to grant us even greater fiefs (*beneficia*). This was the message of fraternal love which was to further the union of the church and the empire, and bind them together in the bonds of peace, and to inspire the hearts of its hearers with love and fidelity for both rulers! Not only were we, as emperor, incensed by this false and lying statement, but all the princes who were present were so enraged that they would undoubtedly have condemned the two priests to death off-hand had they not been restrained by our presence. Moreover, we found in their possession many copies of that letter, and

blank forms sealed by the pope to be filled out at their discretion, with which they were intending to spread this venom
throughout the churches of Germany, as is their custom
from of old, and to denude the altars, rob the houses of God,
and despoil the crosses. Therefore, in order to prevent their
further progress, we compelled them to return to Rome by
the way they had come. We hold this kingdom and empire
through the election of the princes from God alone, who by
the passion of his Son placed this world under the rule of
two swords; moreover, the apostle Peter says: "Fear God,
honor the king" [1 Pet. 2:17]. Therefore, whoever says
that we hold the imperial crown as a benefice from the pope
resists the divine institution, contradicts the teaching of
Peter, and is a liar. . . .

102. LETTER OF ADRIAN IV TO THE EMPEROR, FEBRU-
ARY, 1158.

Ragewin, Gesta Friderici, III, chs. 22, 23; M. G. SS. folio, xx; Doeberl, IV, no. 35 e.

Ever since we were called by the will of God to the government of the universal church, we have tried to honor you
in every way, in order that your love and reverence for the
apostolic seat might daily increase. Therefore we were
greatly astonished to learn that you were incensed at us and
that you had treated with such scant respect the legates . . .
whom we had sent to you for the purpose of learning your
wishes. We are informed that you were enraged because
we used the word *beneficium,* at which surely the mind of
so great a person as yourself should not have been disturbed.
For although with some that word has come to have a meaning different from its original sense, yet it ought to be taken
in the sense in which we have used it and which it has had
from the beginning. For *beneficium* comes from *bonum*
and *factum,* and we used it to mean not a *feudum* (fief), but
a "good deed," in which sense it is used throughout the holy
Scriptures; as when we are said to be guided and nourished

by the *beneficium* of God, which means not the "fief," but the kindness of God. You surely admit that in placing the imperial crown upon your head we performed an act that would be regarded by all men as a "good deed." Moreover, if you misunderstood the phrase "we conferred the imperial crown upon you," and distorted it from its ordinary meaning, it could only be because you wished to misunderstand it or because you accepted the interpretation of persons who wished to disturb the peace existing between the church and the empire. For we meant by the words "we conferred" no more than "we placed," as we said above. In ordering the recall of the ecclesiastics whom we sent to make a visitation of the churches in Germany according to the right of the Roman church, you must surely recognize that you acted unwisely, for if you had any grievance you should have informed us, and we would have undertaken to satisfy your honor. Now by the advice of our beloved son Henry, duke of Bavaria and Saxony, we have sent you two legates, our brothers Henry, cardinal priest of San Nereo and Sant Achilleo, and Hyacinth, cardinal deacon of Santa Maria in Cosmedin, both wise and honorable men, and we urge you to receive them honorably and kindly, and to accept the message which they deliver as coming from the sincerity of our heart; so agreeing with them through the mediation of our son the duke, that no discord may remain between you and your holy mother, the Roman church.

103. DEFINITION OF REGALIA OR CROWN RIGHTS, GIVEN AT THE DIET HELD ON THE RONCALIAN PLAIN, 1158.

M. G. LL. folio, II, pp. 111 f; Doeberl, IV, no. 37 a.

The rights of the crown were called "regalia." When Frederick I went into Italy (1158) he found that the royal rights had been usurped by the cities and nobles. At the diet which he held on the Roncalian plain he consulted lawyers who had been trained in the law of Justinian, and asked them what the imperial rights in Italy were. Their decision, which is here given, was largely influenced by their study of the Roman law. The account which Ragewin (IV, 7) gives of this diet is as follows: "Frederick then examined into the matter of the royal jurisdiction and the regalia, which for a long time had been lost to the empire because they had been usurped and the kings had neglected to recover them. The bishops, the nobles, and the cities, since they could find no excuse for retaining these rights, resigned them to the emperor. Milan was the first to surrender them. When the emperor asked what these rights were, the decision was given that they were the right to appoint dukes, marquises, counts, and consuls [in the cities]; to coin money; to levy tolls; to collect the *fodrum* [a tax in provisions for the support of the emperor and his army when passing through the territory]; to collect customs and harbor dues; to furnish safe-conducts; to control mills, fish-ponds, bridges, and all the water-ways, and to demand an annual tax not only from the land, but also from each person."

These are the regalian rights or rights of the crown: Arimanniæ,[1] public roads, navigable rivers and those which unite to form navigable rivers, harbors, and the banks of rivers; tolls, coinage, profits from fines and penalties; ownerless and confiscated lands, and the property of those who have contracted incestuous marriages or have been outlawed for crimes mentioned in the Novellæ of Justinian; rights of conveyance on direct routes and cross-roads [2] (angariæ and parangariæ), and the prestation of ships;[3] the special taxes for the royal expedition; the appointment of officials for the administration of justice; mines; royal palaces in the customary cities; the profits of fisheries and salt-works; the property of those who are guilty of offence against the majesty of the emperor; half the treasure discovered in places belonging to the emperor or dedicated to religious purposes, and all of it if the finder was aided by the emperor.

1 Arimanniæ: Taxes paid by those who held certain lands or estates which had once been held by the *arimanni*, or free Lombards.

2 When the emperor travelled he had the right to demand conveyances of various kinds from the people of the territory through which he was passing. Angariæ were conveyances for the "direct roads"; parangariæ, conveyances for the "cross-roads." By "direct roads" are meant the chief roads; in Italy, those which led directly to Rome,

and along which the emperor must pass when going to Rome. The "cross-roads" were the less important roads, which ran at right angles to the direct roads.

3 In the same way the emperor had the right to demand ships for the transport of himself and his men.

104.　Grounds for the Quarrel between Adrian IV and Frederick I. Letter of Eberhard, Bishop of Bamberg, to Eberhard, Archbishop of Salzburg, 1159.

Ragewin, Gesta Frid., IV, c. 34; M. G. SS. folio, XX; Doeberl, IV, no. 38.

Although the stirrup episode and the Besançon episode were ended without a rupture between Frederick and Adrian, the fundamental question between them was not yet settled. Frederick continued to act in accordance with his ideas of what his office demanded, thus giving deep offence to the pope. The various matters in which the pope felt that Frederick had offended are set forth in this letter. They involve the deeper question of supremacy. The relations between the pope and emperor were becoming more and more strained. Although Frederick had previously refused to consider the propositions of the commune of Rome, he now received their ambassadors courteously. The people of the city wished to obtain his recognition of their government. Since the pope was obdurate Frederick threatened to make common cause with the rebellious city, hoping, no doubt, that Adrian would thereby be compelled to sue to him for terms.

To his reverend father and lord, Eberhard, archbishop of Salzburg, Eberhard, by the grace of God bishop of Bamberg. . . . That perilous time seems near at hand when strife shall arise between the king and the pope. The cardinals Octavianus and William, former archdeacon of Pavia, were sent by pope Adrian to the emperor with a message which began with a conciliatory introduction but which contained most vexatious matter. For instance, they said: the emperor must not send ambassadors to the city of Rome without the consent of the pope, as all the magisterial power in Rome and all the regalian rights there belong to St. Peter; the *fodrum* must not be collected from the papal estates except at the time of the imperial coronation; Italian bishops should take only the oath of fidelity to the emperor and not the oath of homage [see no. 214]; bishops shall not be required to entertain the ambassadors of the emperor in their palaces; the following possessions, belonging of right to the Roman church, must be restored: Tivoli, Ferrara, Massa, Fiscaglia, all the lands of the countess Matilda, all the land from Aquapendente to Rome, the duchy of Spoleto, and the islands of Sardinia and Corsica. The emperor was willing to do justice in these matters if the pope would give him justice in return [that is, the emperor was willing to submit each matter to trial and abide by the decision, if the pope would do the same], but the cardinals were only empowered to receive justice and not to give it, for they said that they could not bind the pope. The emperor on his part then made the following complaints: that the treaty of Constance had not been kept by the pope in the matter of his promise not to make peace with the Greeks, the Sicilians, or the Roman people without the consent of both parties [see no. 97]; that cardinals were sent through Germany without the emperor's consent, and that they entered the palaces of bishops who possessed regalian rights from the emperor; that the pope heard unjust appeals; and many similar matters. The emperor agreed that the pope should be notified of these demands by the aforesaid cardinals, but the pope refused to send other cardinals empowered to treat of these things, as the emperor had requested. In the meantime ambassadors came from the Roman people to make a treaty of peace with the emperor, and were favorably received and dismissed with honor. The emperor is about to send ambassadors both to the pope and to the city of Rome; if possible, he will make a treaty of peace with the pope, but if this fails, he will ally himself with the Romans. . . .

105–107. THE DISPUTED PAPAL ELECTION OF 1159.

105. LETTER OF ALEXANDER III ABOUT HIS ELECTION, 1159.

M. G. SS. folio, XVIII, pp, 28 f; Doeberl, IV, no. 39 a.

When Adrian IV died, 1159, the quarrel between him and the emperor had reached such a pitch of bitterness that he was about to excommunicate Frederick. But there was a party in the college of cardinals which was heartily supporting the emperor against the pope. The members of this German party, as it was called, had opposed the treaty which Adrian had made with William of Sicily (see no. 99) and had sympathized with Frederick in the Besançon episode and in his later contentions with the pope (see nos. 100–102). They believed that the pope was transcending his powers, and usurping authority which belonged to the emperor alone. But this German party, of which Octavian was the head, was hopelessly in the minority. When the cardinals met to elect a successor to Adrian IV, it was not able to secure the unanimous election of its candidate. Two popes were elected, and a schism ensued which lasted for seventeen years. Alexander III was very clever and succeeded in uniting all of Frederick's enemies against him. Under the pope's leadership and by his diplomacy, the Lombard league was formed. It completely defeated the emperor at Legnano, 1176 (see nos. 108–109). We give first a letter of Alexander III, which contains an account of his election. Then Victor's letter follows (no. 106). And finally a brief account of the election by Gerhoh of Reichersberg is given (no. 107).

Alexander, bishop, servant of the servants of God, to his venerable brothers, Syrus, archbishop of Genoa, and his suffragans, greeting and apostolic benediction.

The eternal and unchangeable will of the Creator provided that his holy and immaculate church from its very foundation should be ruled by one pastor and governor, to whom all prelates should be obedient. As members are united to one head, so they should be joined to him in perfect unity and never separate themselves from him. And Christ, who confirmed the faith of his disciples by saying: "Lo, I am with you alway, even unto the end of the world" [Matt. 28:20], will without doubt keep his promise to his church which he put under the control of his apostle [Peter]. And although his church, like the little boat of St. Peter, may sometimes be tossed about by the waves, he will preserve it in safety.

Three false brothers have gone out from us, but they were not of us, and, transforming themselves into angels of light, although they are servants of Satan, they are trying to rend and tear the church, the seamless robe of Christ, which he, in the person of the Psalmist, prayed might be delivered from the lion's mouth, and from the sword and from the power of the dog [Ps. 22:20]. Nevertheless Christ, the founder and head of the church, is carefully guarding her, his only spouse, and he will not permit the little boat of St. Peter to suffer shipwreck, although it may often be tossed about by the waves.

Our predecessor, Adrian IV, of blessed memory, died September 1, while we were at Anagni, and his body was brought to Rome and honorably buried in the customary manner in St. Peter's Church, on September 4. Nearly all the cardinals were present, and after the burial they began to take steps to elect his successor. After three days of discussion all the cardinals except three elected us, although we are not sufficient for this burden and not worthy of so high an office. The three who opposed our election were Octavian, John of St. Martin's, and Guido of Crema. God is our witness that we are telling the exact truth when we say that all the others unanimously elected us, and the other clergy and the people of Rome assented to it. But two, John and Guido, voted for Octavian and stubbornly insisted on his election. The prior of the cardinal deacons was putting the papal mantle on us in the customary manner, although we were reluctant to receive it because we saw our insufficiency for the high office. When Octavian saw this he was almost beside himself with rage, and with his own hands snatched the mantle from our neck and took it away. This caused a great tumultuous outbreak. Some of the senators were present and saw it, and one of them, inspired by the spirit of God, snatched the mantle from the hands of Octavian, who was now raging. Then Octavian, with angry face and fierce eye, turned to one of his chaplains who had come prepared for this, upbraided him, and ordered him hastily to fetch him the mantle which he had brought with him. The mantle was brought without delay, and while all the cardinals were trying to get out of the room, Octavian removed his hat, bowed his head, and received the mantle from his chaplain and another clergyman. And because there was no one else there, he had to assist them himself to put it on him. But the condemnation of God was seen in the fact that he put the mantle on with the wrong side in front. Those who were present saw it and laughed. And as he was of a crooked mind and intention, so the mantle was put on crooked as an evidence of his condemnation. When this was done, the doors of the church, which had been closed, were opened and bands of armed men with drawn swords entered and made a great noise. But they had been hired by Octavian to do this. And because that pestilential Octavian had no cardinals and bishops he surrounded himself with a band of armed knights. . . .

106.   Letter of Victor IV to the German Princes, 1159.

Ragewin, Gesta Frid., IV, ch. 60; M. G. SS. folio, XX; Doeberl, IV, no. 39 b.

See introductory note to no. 105.

Victor, bishop, servant of the servants of God, to his venerable brothers, the patriarchs, archbishops, bishops, and his dear sons, the abbots, dukes, marquises, counts, and other princes, and the imperial family who are connected with the most holy court of Frederick, the most serene and unconquered emperor of the Romans, greeting and apostolic benediction.

We believe that you cannot have forgotten how sincerely we have loved the empire and how we have labored in support of its honor and dignity. And now that we have been elevated to a higher dignity we wish to do even more for you and the empire. We therefore confidently beseech you, for the reverence which you have for St. Peter and for your love to us, to ask the emperor to take immediate steps to come to the aid and protection of the empire, which God has committed to him, and of the church of God, the bride of Christ, of which God has made him advocate and defender. If he does not, there is danger that his malicious enemies may prevail in this great struggle, and the little boat of St. Peter be overwhelmed by winds and storms, and the imperial dignity be humiliated.

We wish to inform you that under the Lord's guidance we have been elected pope. After our predecessor, Adrian IV, of blessed memory, had gone the way of all flesh and been buried in the church of St. Peter, we all came together to elect his successor. After long discussion and mature deliberation, God graciously inspired our brothers, the cardinal bishops, priests, and deacons of the holy Roman church, and the other clergy of Rome, to elect us. The people of Rome asked for our election and the senators and other nobles assented to it. We were canonically elected and then elevated to the throne of St. Peter. And on the first Sunday in October we were consecrated and received the full power of our office.

We humbly beseech you to aid us with your prayers to Him from whom come all power and dignities. Now the former chancellor, Roland, who was bound by oath in a conspiracy against the church of God and the empire in support of William of Sicily, had himself thrust into the papal office twelve days after we were elected. Such a thing had never been heard of before. If he should send you letters, you should refuse to receive them, because they are full of

lies and he is a schismatic and a heretic. Pay no attention
whatever to his letters.

107. THE ACCOUNT OF THE ELECTION AS GIVEN BY GER-
HOH OF REICHERSBERG, *ca.* 1160.

Doeberl, IV, no. 39 d.

See introductory note to no. 105.

When Adrian IV died, all the cardinal clergy of the holy
Roman church met to elect his successor. A secret ballot
was taken and the result announced. It was found that a
majority of the cardinals had voted for Roland, the chancellor of Adrian IV. A few had voted for Octavian, and
some also for *Magister* Bernard. Since there could not be
three popes, the majority tried to persuade the minority to
give up their candidates and make the election of Roland
unanimous. Those who had voted for Bernard then deserted
him and some of them joined the party of Roland. The
others said that they had no preference but would support
either Octavian or Roland, provided the election of either
were unanimous, and the church should not be divided on
account of it. The number of cardinals who supported
Octavian, or were willing to support him if elected, was seven.
But a much larger number supported Roland. The majority
then tried hard to persuade these seven to unite in electing
Roland, and won over all but three of them. Two of these,
John of Pisa, and Guido of Crema, were very contentious and
declared that they would never desert Octavian. So they with
the bishop of Tusculum made Octavian pope.

108. THE PRELIMINARY TREATY OF ANAGNI BETWEEN
ALEXANDER III AND FREDERICK I, 1176.

Kehr, Vertrag von Anagni, in Neues Archiv, XIII. pp. 109 ff; Doeberl, IV
no. 46 a.

The quarrel between the pope and emperor increased in bitterness.
At the same time the Italian cities rebelled against Frederick and
joined the pope. The Lombard league was formed and at Legnano,

1176, the emperor was utterly defeated. He then sent ambassadors to the pope at Anagni to discuss the terms of a treaty of peace. They agreed on the following articles which were afterward incorporated in the peace of Venice, 1177. The final treaty was made in 1183 and is called the treaty of Constance (see no. 109).

1. The emperor and the empress, and their son, king Henry, and all the princes promise to accept pope Alexander III as the catholic and universal pope, and to show him such reverence as their predecessors were wont to show to his predecessors.

2. The emperor promises to keep peace faithfully with pope Alexander and his successors and with the whole Roman church.

3. All the regalia and other possessions of St. Peter as held by the Roman church in the time of pope Innocent II, which have been seized by the emperor or his allies, shall be restored to pope Alexander and to the Roman church, and the emperor engages to aid the church in retaining possession of them.

4. The emperor restores to the pope and to the Roman church the control of the office of prefect of the city of Rome; the pope shall see to it that justice shall be done the emperor when he has occasion to seek his rights in the city.

5. All vassals of the church won over by the emperor to his side during the late quarrel, shall be released from their allegiance to him and restored to the pope and to the Roman church.

6. The emperor will restore to the pope and to the church the lands of the countess Matilda as they were held by the church in the time of the emperor Lothar and king Conrad and the present emperor Frederick.

7. The pope and the emperor will mutually aid one another in maintaining the honor and the rights of the empire and the church.

8. Everything unjustly taken from the churches by the

emperor or his followers during the schism shall be restored to them.

9. The emperor will make peace with the Lombards on the terms to be agreed upon by representatives appointed for this purpose by the emperor and the pope and the Lombards. In case any difficulty arises in the course of these negotiations which the representatives cannot settle, it shall be decided by the majority of the special commissioners to be appointed for this purpose by the emperor and the pope in equal numbers.

10. The emperor will make peace with the king of Sicily and with the emperor of Constantinople and with all the allies of the pope, and he will not take revenge for any wrongs which they may have committed in assisting the Roman church.

11–22. Articles referring to individuals and lesser details.

23. Pope Alexander and the cardinals on their part make peace with the emperor and the empress and their son, king Henry, and all their party. This, however, shall not prejudice those rights of controlling and judging ecclesiastical persons which are herein surrendered to the pope and to the Roman church, nor the rights of the Roman church over the lands of St. Peter now withheld by other persons, nor the special exceptions made in this document in favor of the pope and the Roman church, on one side, and the emperor and the empire, on the other.

24. The pope and the cardinals will take their oath to keep this peace, the oath to be drawn up in writing and signed by the cardinals.

25. The pope shall immediately call together as large a council as possible, and with the cardinal bishops and other clergy who may be present, shall excommunicate all who break this peace. Afterward he shall do the same in a general council.

26.   Many of the nobles of Rome and the great vassals of Campania shall also take oath to keep this peace.

27.   The emperor and the princes of the empire will also take their oaths to keep this peace, the oath to be drawn up in writing and signed by the emperor and the princes.

28.   If the pope should die first, the emperor and his son, king Henry, and the princes shall observe these terms of peace with his successors and all the cardinals and the whole Roman church, and with the Lombards and the king of Sicily and all the allies of the church.   If the emperor should die first, the pope and the cardinals and the Roman church shall observe these terms with the empress Beatrice, and her son, king Henry, and with all the German people and their allies, as written above.

29.   In the meantime the emperor shall not attack the land of St. Peter, whether held by the pope in person or by the king of Sicily or other vassals of the pope.

30.   If the negotiations for peace are broken off by either side before they are completed, which God forbid, truce shall be kept for three months after the notification of withdrawal.

109.   THE PEACE OF CONSTANCE, JANUARY 25, 1183.

Muratori, IV, pp. 307 ff; M. G. LL. folio, II, pp. 175 ff; Doeberl, IV, no. 51 c.

See introductory note to no. 108.

In the name of the holy and undivided Trinity.   Frederick, by divine mercy emperor of the Romans, Augustus, and Henry VI, his son, king of the Romans, Augustus.   . . .

1.   We, Frederick, emperor of the Romans, and our son Henry, king of the Romans, hereby grant to you, the cities, territories, and persons of the league, the regalia and other rights within and without the cities, as you have been accustomed to hold them; that is each member of the league shall have the same rights as the city of Verona has had in the past or has now.

2.   The members of the league shall exercise freely and without interference from us all the rights which they have exercised of old.

3.   These are the rights which are guaranteed to you: the *fodrum,* forests, pastures, bridges, streams, mills, fortifications of the cities, criminal and civil jurisdiction, and all other rights which concern the welfare of the city.

4.   The regalia which are not to be granted to the members of the league shall be determined in the following manner: in the case of each city, certain men shall be chosen for this purpose from both the bishopric and the city; these men shall be of good repute, capable of deciding these questions, and such as are not prejudiced against either party. Acting with the bishop of the diocese, they shall swear to inquire into the questions of the regalia and to set aside those that by right belong to us. If, however, the cities do not wish to submit to this inquisition, they shall pay to us an annual tribute of 2000 marks in silver as compensation for our regalia. If this sum seems excessive, it may be reduced.

5.   If anyone appeals to us in regard to matters which are by this treaty admitted to be under your jurisdiction, we agree not to hear such an appeal.

6.   The bishops, churches, cities, and other persons, clerical and lay, shall retain possession of the property or rights which have been granted to them before this war by us or by our predecessors, the above concessions excepted. The accustomed dues for such holdings shall be paid to us, but not the tax.

7.   Such possessions as we have granted to members of the league, inside or outside of cities, shall not be included among those regalia for which taxes are to be paid to us.

8.   All privileges, gifts, and concessions made in the time of the war by us or our representatives to the prejudice or injury of the cities, territories, or members of the league are to be null and void.

9. Consuls of cities where the bishop holds the position of count from the king or emperor shall receive their office from the bishop, if this has been the custom before. In all other cities the consuls shall receive their office from us, in the following manner: after they have been elected by the city they shall be invested with office by our representative in the city or bishopric, unless we are ourselves in Lombardy, in which case they shall be invested by us. At the end of every five years each city shall send its representative to us to receive the investiture.

10. This arrangement shall be observed by our successor, and all such investitures shall be free.

11. After our death, the cities shall receive investiture in the same way from our son and from his successors.

12. The emperor shall have the right of hearing appeals in cases involving more than 25 pounds, saving the right of the church of Brescia to hear appeals. The appellant shall not, however, be compelled to come to Germany, but he shall appeal to the representative of the emperor in the city or bishopric. This representative shall examine the case fairly and shall give judgment according to the laws and customs of that city. The decision shall be given within two months from the time of appeal, unless the case has been deferred by reason of some legal hindrance or by the consent of both parties.

13. The consuls of cities shall take the oath of allegiance to the emperor before they are invested with office.

14. Our vassals shall receive investiture from us and shall take the vassal's oath of fidelity. All other persons between the ages of 15 and 70 shall take the ordinary oath of fidelity to the emperor unless there be some good reason why this oath should be remitted.

15. Vassals who have failed to receive investiture from us or to render the services due for their fiefs, during the war or the truce, shall not on this account lose their fiefs.

16. Lands held by *libelli* and *precariæ* shall be held according to the customs of each city, the feudal law of Frederick I to the contrary notwithstanding.

17. All injuries, losses, and damages which we or our followers have sustained from the league or any of its members or allies are hereby pardoned, and all such transgressors are hereby received back into our favor.

18. We will not remain longer than is necessary in any city or bishopric.

19. It shall be permitted to the cities to erect fortifications within or without their boundaries.

20. It shall be permitted to the league to maintain its organization as it now is or to renew it as often as it desires.

110. THE FORMATION OF THE DUCHY OF AUSTRIA, 1156.

Wattenbach, Die öst. Freiheitsbriefe; Doeberl, IV, no. 31 a.

The nobles of Germany early showed the desire to free themselves from the control of the emperor and to acquire independence at the expense of the crown. The document by which Frederick I created the duchy of Austria out of the Bavarian east mark and gave it to his uncle, Henry, contains some concessions which tended to weaken the crown. Instead of binding the new duke closely to the crown and compelling him to render services commensurate with his high position, the emperor excused him from attending diets which were not held near his lands, and from military service except in the lands which adjoined his. He also gave the duke the complete administration of justice in his territory. Other princes were not slow to demand similar privileges, and the crown was gradually stripped of its powers and prerogatives. See nos. 136, 139, 153, 160. The duchy of Austria, created by this grant, came into the possession of the Hapsburg family, and formed the centre of the Hapsburg lands, the present Austro-Hungarian empire. See no. 150.

In the name of the holy and undivided Trinity. Frederick, by divine mercy emperor of the Romans, Augustus. . . . Know all our faithful subjects, present and future, that with the aid of him who sent peace on earth, we have been able to settle the long quarrel between our beloved uncle

Henry, duke of Austria, and our beloved nephew, Henry, duke of Saxony, over the possession of the duchy of Bavaria. This was accomplished at the diet of Regensburg on the day of the Nativity of the blessed Virgin Mary in the presence of many pious catholic princes. This is the way in which the settlement was reached: The duke of Austria resigned the duchy of Bavaria into our hands, and we immediately granted it in fief to the duke of Saxony. Then the duke of Bavaria [Henry of Saxony] surrendered to us the mark of Austria with all its rights and all the fiefs which the former margrave Luitpold held of the duchy of Bavaria, and we have made the mark of Austria a duchy with the consent of the princes, Wadislaus, duke of Bohemia, putting the motion and the other princes agreeing to it. This was done in order that our beloved uncle should not lose in rank by the transfer. We have now granted the duchy of Austria in fief to our uncle Henry and to his wife Theodora, decreeing by this perpetual edict that (1) they and their children after them, whether sons or daughters, shall hold and possess it by hereditary right. If our uncle and his wife should die without children, they may leave the duchy by will to whomsoever they desire. (2) We decree also that no person, great or small, shall presume to exercise any of the rights of justice within the duchy, without the consent and permission of the duke. (3) The duke of Austria does not owe any services to the empire, except to attend, when summoned, such diets as may be held in Bavaria. (4) He is not bound to join the emperor on any campaign except such as may be directed against parts of the kingdom neighboring to Austria.

111. THE BISHOP OF WÜRZBURG IS MADE A DUKE, 1168.

Bresslau, Diplomata Centum, no. 72; Doeberl, IV, no. 44.

The old duchy of Franconia disappeared with Conrad II (1024–39). The Staufer, who inherited the family lands of Conrad II, called themselves dukes of Rothenburg, and not of Franconia. A large part of the original duchy went to make up the bishoprics of Mainz, Bamberg, and Würzburg. In time the bishops of Würzburg put forth the claim that they had received the ducal office in Franconia. In a diet at Würzburg, 1168, Herold, the ambitious bishop of Würzburg, presented some forged documents to Frederick I to prove that the bishops of Würzburg were also dukes and had ducal authority in the duchy of Würzburg, which was identical with the bishopric. Frederick was deceived by these forgeries and confirmed the bishop in his usurped title and authority. The bishops of Würzburg now received the highest jurisdiction over their territory.

In the name of the holy and undivided Trinity. Frederick, by the mercy of God emperor of the Romans, Augustus. . . . Be it known to all the faithful subjects of God and of our empire, both present and future, that we held a diet at Würzburg recently, where with the aid of God we were able to reconcile the differences which had arisen among the princes of Saxony. At that diet also Herold, venerable bishop of Würzburg, attended by his whole chapter and by a large following of freemen and ministerials, besought us to confirm by our imperial authority the jurisdiction over the church and duchy of Würzburg, which has belonged to his predecessors since the time of Karl the Great. We always delight to grant the reasonable requests of suppliants, and we have no wish to disturb the arrangements made by former emperors, unless there is some need of correction. In this case it is apparent that the settlement made by the former emperors is just, and that the lands have been held unquestioned for a long time by the church and the duchy of Würzburg. Therefore, influenced by the fidelity and devotion of the bishop and by the intercessions of the chapter of · his church, whose devotion to him has touched our heart, we give and grant to the venerable bishop Herold and to his successors forever the jurisdiction and right of administering justice in the whole bishopric and duchy and all its counties; that is, the right to punish cases of rapine and incendiarism, to exercise authority over freeholds, fiefs, and vassals, and to inflict capital punishment. By our imperial authority expressed in this perpetual decree, we forbid any person, ecclesiastical or secular, to exercise any jurisdiction in these matters within the bishopric and duchy of Würzburg and its counties; except that the counts should have jurisdiction within their counties over those freemen who are known as *bargaldi.* If anyone acts contrary to this he is guilty of violating the decrees of former emperors, the rights of the church of Würzburg, and this our decree. We also forbid anyone to create hundred-courts or appoint *centgrafs* (hundred-courts) within this bishopric and duchy and its counties, except by the grant of the bishop-duke of Würzburg. Further, we have destroyed the castle of Bamberg, which has been the cause of so much trouble to the church and the whole province, and have given the hill upon which it stood to the church of Würzburg, forbidding the erection of a castle or fortification again upon it. We have destroyed also the castle of Frankenberg, which menaced the neighboring monastery of Amerbach and imperilled the peace of the church of Würzburg, and have given it under similar conditions to that church.

112. Decree of Gelnhausen, 1180.

Heinemann, Cod. Anhalt., no. 1 c; Doeberl, IV. no. 50.

As early as 953 Bruno, archbishop of Cologne, received the ducal authority over Lothringen. This gave him the power to hold local diets and to summon both the bishops and secular nobles to attend them. The Gelnhausen decree, so named because it was published in a diet held at Gelnhausen, is important because it contains an official account (1) of the trial of Henry the Lion, and (2) of the partition of the duchy of Saxony. The archbishop of Cologne now receives the ducal authority over a part of the duchy of Saxony. There is here a good illustration of the policy which Frederick I followed of weakening the great duchies by dividing them.

In the name of the holy and undivided Trinity. Frederick, by divine mercy emperor of the Romans, Augustus. . . .

Know all faithful subjects of the empire, both present and future, that Henry, former duke of Bavaria and Westphalia, has oppressed the churches of God and the nobles of the empire by seizing their lands and violating their rights, has refused to obey our summons to present himself before us and has therefore incurred the ban, and even· after that has continued to injure the churches and nobles. Now therefore on account of the injuries which he has inflicted upon these persons, and on account of the contempt which he has so often shown to us, and especially on account of his violation of feudal law, in that he refused to obey the three summonses to present himself before us, he has been judged contumacious and by the unanimous sentence of the princes in the diet held at Würzburg has been deprived of the duchies of Bavaria, Westphalia, and Engria [that is, Bavaria and Saxony] and of all the fiefs which he held of the empire, and these territories have been restored to our control.

Now by the advice of the princes we have divided the duchy of Westphalia and Engria [Saxony] into two parts and have conferred that part which is included in the dioceses of Cologne and Paderborn upon our beloved prince, Philip, archbishop of Cologne, because of his conspicuous merits, and of his labors and expenditures for the crown. We have given and granted this territory to the church of Cologne with the counties, advocates, rights of safe-conduct, domains, farms, fiefs, ministerials, serfs, and all other things which belong to that duchy; and we have solemnly invested the aforesaid Philip by the banner [flag] of the empire with that portion of the duchy which is given to his church. This was done by the decision of all the princes of the diet, and with the public consent of our relative, duke Bernard, to whom we have given the other part of the duchy of Westphalia and Engria. .   .   .

113. PAPAL ELECTION DECREE OF ALEXANDER III, 1179.

Watterich, Pont. Rom. Vitæ, II, pp. 644 f; Doeberl, IV, no. 49.

Disputed elections might easily take place, because there was no clear law governing them. It was not the majority of the cardinals who could elect, but those of the "better and wiser counsel." No matter how small the number of cardinals who might vote for a particular candidate, he could easily claim to be elected because he could say that his supporters were of the "better and wiser counsel." To prevent such occurrences, Alexander III decreed that the votes of two-thirds of the cardinals were necessary to elect.

Concerning the election of the pope. Although our predecessors have issued decrees intended to prevent disputed elections in the papacy, nevertheless, the unity of the church has frequently been imperilled by the wicked ambition of men. We have decided with the advice of our brothers and the approval of the council that something further must be done to prevent this evil. Therefore we have decreed that when the cardinals cannot come to a unanimous vote on any candidate, that person shall be regarded as pope who receives two-thirds of the votes, even if the other one-third refuse to accept him and elect a pope of their own. If anyone who has been elected by only a third of the cardinals shall presume to act as pope he and his followers shall be excommunicated and deprived of all ecclesiastical rank; they shall not be allowed to take communion, unless it be extreme unction, and unless they repent they shall have their part with Dathan and Abiram [Num. 16], whom the earth swallowed alive. No one who has been elected by less than two-thirds, shall presume to act as pope, and if he does he shall suffer the same penalty. This decree shall not be to the prejudice of the canon law or of the practice in other churches where the voice of the majority is declared to be decisive in elections, because any dispute arising in these churches can be settled by appeal to higher authority. The Roman church requires a special law, because there is in her case no higher authority to appeal to.

114–115.   Supremacy of the Papal Power.
114.   Innocent III to Acerbius, 1198.

Migne, 214, col. 377.

Innocent III here gives an interesting statement of the theory of papal supremacy and of the relations existing between papacy and empire.

Innocent III to Acerbius, prior, and to the other clergy in Tuscany.   As God, the creator of the universe, set two great lights in the firmament of heaven, the greater light to rule the day, and the lesser light to rule the night [Gen. 1:15, 16], so He set two great dignities in the firmament of the universal church,   .   .   .   the greater to rule the day, that is, souls, and the lesser to rule the night, that is, bodies. These dignities are the papal authority and the royal power. And just as the moon gets her light from the sun, and is inferior to the sun in quality, quantity, position, and effect, so the royal power gets the splendor of its dignity from the papal authority.   .   .   .

115.   The Use of the Pallium.   Innocent III to the Archbishop of Trnova (in Bulgaria), 1201.

Migne, 215, col. 294.

To the honor of omnipotent God, and of the Blessed Virgin Mary, and of the blessed apostles, Peter and Paul, and of pope Innocent and of the Roman church, as well as of the church committed to you, we give you the pallium.   It was first placed on the tomb of St. Peter, from which place we have taken it to send it to you.   It is the symbol of the full power of the bishop's office.   You shall wear the pallium only when you celebrate mass in the churches of your own diocese on the following days: Christmas, St. Stephen's, Circumcision, Epiphany, Purification of the Virgin Mary, Palm Sunday, Thursday and Saturday of Passion week, Easter Sunday, Monday after Easter, Ascension of our Lord, Pentecost, the three feasts of St. Mary, the birthday of John the Baptist, the feast days of all the apostles, All Saints' day, and when a church is to be dedicated, or bishop consecrated, or clergy ordained, on the principal feast days of your own church, and on the anniversary of your consecration.

The bishop of Rome alone always wears the pallium when celebrating mass because he has the plentitude (fullness) of ecclesiastical power, which is symbolized by the pallium. Others wear it only on certain days, and in that diocese over which they have received ecclesiastical authority, because they are called to have authority over only a part of the church, and not over all of it [as the pope is].

116–118. THE PUNISHMENT OF HERETICS.
116. INNOCENT III TO THE ARCHBISHOP OF AUCH IN GASCONY, 1198.

Migne, 214, col. 71.

Many heresies were appearing in various parts of Europe, and Innocent III made special efforts to suppress them. The three following documents illustrate the means by which he hoped to destroy them. These letters are directed to Spain and to Gascony, where the Albigensian heresy was flourishing.

The little boat of St. Peter is beaten by many storms and tossed about upon the sea, but it grieves us most of all that, against the orthodox faith, there are now arising more unrestrainedly and with more injurious results than ever before, ministers of diabolical error who are ensnaring the souls of the simple and ruining them. With their superstitions and false inventions they are perverting the meaning of the Holy Scriptures and trying to destroy the unity of the catholic church. Since we have learned from you and others that this pestilential error is growing in Gascony and in the neighboring territories, we wish you and your fellow bishops to resist it with all your might, because it is to be feared that it will spread and that by its contagion the minds of the faithful

will be corrupted. And therefore by this present apostolical
writing we give you a strict command that, by whatever
means you can, you destroy all these heresies and expel from
your diocese all who are polluted with them. You shall exercise the rigor of the ecclesiastical power against them and all
those who have made themselves suspected by associating with
them. They may not appeal from your judgments, and if
necessary, you may cause the princes and people to suppress
them with the sword.

**117. Innocent III Commands all in Authority to
aid his Legates in Destroying Heresy, 1198.**

Migne, 214, col. 142.

See introductory note to no. 116.

In order to catch the little foxes which are destroying the
vineyard of the Lord [Song of Sol. 2:15], and to separate
heretics from the society of the faithful, we have sent to you
our beloved son and brother, Rainerius, who, by the divine
aid, is powerful in both word and deed, and with him our
beloved son and brother, Guido, who fears God and is devoted
to works of love. We ask, warn, exhort, and for the forgiveness of your sins command you to receive them kindly
and render them assistance against the heretics by giving
them advice and aid. We have ordered Rainerius to go on
into Spain on certain important ecclesiastical matters, and
so we order all archbishops and bishops to use, at the command of Guido, the spiritual sword against all heretics whom
he shall name to you. And we order the laymen to confiscate
their goods and drive them out of your territories, and thus
separate the chaff from the wheat. Moreover to all who
faithfully and devoutly aid the church in preserving the faith
in this time of great danger which is threatening her, we
grant the same indulgence of sins as to those who make a
pilgrimage to the churches of St. Peter or of St. James.

118. Confiscation of the Property of Heretics. Innocent III to the King of Aragon, 1206.

Migne, 215, col. 915 f.

See introductory note to no. 116.

Since according to the gospel, the "laborer is worthy of his hire" [Luke 10:7], and in another place it is said, "Thou shalt not muzzle the mouth of the ox that treadeth out the corn" [1 Cor. 9:1], it is certainly even more fitting that a proper reward should be given those who, zealous for the divine law, labor to destroy the little foxes which are ruining the vineyard of the Lord [Song of Sol. 2:15]; we mean those who are endeavoring to pervert the Christian faith. Their reward should be all the greater, because if these foxes are killed the vineyard will be able to bear much greater fruit in works of piety. Led by such considerations, we concede to you, by this present writing, the right to reserve for your own use all the movable as well as immovable goods of heretics and of their supporters, of which you are able to get possession.

119. Innocent III Commands the French Bishops to Punish Usury, 1198.

Migne, 214, col. 376.

The code of Justinian permitted the taking of interest, but the Biblical view of the matter prevailed and in the Middle Age to accept interest in any form on loans was usury. The church often renewed her prohibitions of the custom, but was unable to abolish it. Finally in the sixteenth century the distinction was made between a reasonable and just rate of interest, which was permissible, and an excessive rate, which was declared to be usury, and therefore prohibited.

We believe that you know how pernicious the vice of usury is, since, in addition to the ecclesiastical laws which have been issued against it, the prophet says that those who put their money out at interest are to be excluded from the taber-

nacle of the Lord [Ps. 15:5]. And the New Testament, as
well as the Old, forbids the taking of interest, since the Truth
[Christ] himself says: "Lend, hoping for nothing again"
[Luke 6:35]. And the prophet says: "Thou shalt not receive usury or increase" [Ezek. 18:17]. We command you
all by this apostolical writing not to permit those who are
known as usurers to clear themselves by any subterfuge or
trick when they are charged with the crime.

120. INNOCENT III FORBIDS VIOLENCE TO THE JEWS, 1199.

Migne, 214, col. 864.

During the Middle Age the Jew received no protection from the
law. It took no account of him. He was compelled to pay for the
permission to live in a Christian state or in a Christian town. Such
a permission was often revoked at the will of the government (emperor, duke, bishop, city council, etc.), and the Jews were then
plundered by the government or the mob, and made to pay well to
have the permission renewed. Although the government often robbed
them, they had more to fear from the fanaticism and covetousness
of the mob, against which the government was generally helpless to
protect them. The more enlightened of the clergy tried to shield
them, but generally without success. This document gives an idea
of the ways in which they were commonly molested, as well as of
the enlightened humanity of Innocent III. See also nos. 299, 300.

. . . We decree that no Christian shall use violence to
compel the Jews to accept baptism. But if a Jew, of his own
accord, because of a change in his faith, shall have taken
refuge with Christians, after his wish has been made known,
he may be made a Christian without any opposition. For
anyone who has not of his own will sought Christian baptism
cannot have the true Christian faith. No Christian shall
do the Jews any personal injury, except in executing the judgments of a judge, or deprive them of their possessions, or
change the rights and privileges which they have been accustomed to have. During the celebration of their festivals, no
one shall disturb them by beating them with clubs or by throw-

ing stones at them. No one shall compel them to render any services except those which they have been accustomed to render. And to prevent the baseness and avarice of wicked men we forbid anyone to deface or damage their cemeteries or to extort money from them by threatening to exhume the bodies of their dead. . . .

121. INNOCENT III TO THE ARCHBISHOP OF ROUEN, 1198.

Migne, 214, col. 93.

It was not uncommon for clergymen to hold livings or benefices (receive an income) from different churches at the same time. In such cases, they of course found it impossible to live in all the parishes from which they received money or support. And some clergymen, although supported by some church, cared little for their clerical duties and evaded them by living in some other parish. This letter to the archbishop of Rouen represents a part of the reforming work of Innocent III. He endeavored to correct these abuses, as is apparent from this letter.

Since it is written that whoever does not work shall not eat [2 Thess. 3:10], we believe it wrong that clergymen do not serve those churches from which they have their livings. You have informed us that certain canons of the church of Rouen receive incomes and livings from the church, but do not live there, as they should, and that the church of Rouen is thereby unjustly deprived of the services of the clergy whom she supports. Therefore we grant your petition, venerable brother in Christ, and by our apostolic authority give you full power to use ecclesiastical discipline to compel them to live in their churches, as the law and custom of the church require. . . . .

122. INNOCENT III TO A BISHOP, FORBIDDING LAYMEN TO DEMAND TITHES OF THE CLERGY, 1198.

Migne, 214, col. 433 f.

This letter does not differ materially from the bull "Clericis laicos," no. 162. See the introductory note to it.

Since it is improper and contrary to reason that laymen, who are bound to pay tithes to the clergy, should presume to extort tithes from them, to the utter confusion of the established order of things, we grant your petition, and give all the monasteries, churches, and clergy of your diocese the permission to refuse to pay any tithes which may be demanded of them by laymen, no matter under what pretext such a demand may be made. And if laymen, contrary to this writing, shall attempt to collect such tithes by violence, you shall put them under ecclesiastical interdict and deprive them of the right to appeal.

123-125. THE SECULAR POWER OF INNOCENT III.
123. THE PREFECT OF ROME TAKES THE OATH OF FIDELITY TO THE POPE, 1198.

Migne, 214, cols. 18 and 529.

Innocent III attempted to build up a system of papal government in all the lands which he claimed. This document shows how his authority in Rome was recognized. No. 124 is an illustration of the oath which he required of the local princes in Italy who held lands from him. No. 125 is offered as an evidence of his government in Sicily.

The next day after the coronation of Innocent III, Peter, prefect of the city of Rome, in the consistory of the Lateran palace, publicly took the oath of fidelity to Innocent and his successors, against all men, and received from the pope a robe as the symbol of his investiture, with the prefecture. And then he did Innocent liege homage and the pope gave him a silver cup as the sign of his favor.

The oath. In the name of Christ. I, Peter, prefect of the city, swear that the land which the pope has given me to govern, I will govern to the honor and profit of the church. I will neither sell, nor hire out, nor enfeoff, nor pawn, nor aleniate in any other way, any part of it. I will carefully find out and maintain all the rights of the Roman church, and I will en-

deavor to recover those rights which she has lost; and when I
have recovered them, I will preserve and defend them as long
as I shall hold this office. I will guard the roads and administer justice. I will give diligent zeal and attention to the
guarding of the defences in order that they may be guarded
well and to the honor of the church and in accordance with her
wishes. I will neither change nor cause to be changed those
who have charge of the fortresses, nor will I introduce, or
cause to be introduced, others into the fortresses, contrary to
the command of the pope. The faithful subjects and vassals
of the pope, who live on the patrimony of the church, I will
not permit to take the oath of fidelity and homage to me
without the special command of the pope. Nor shall any of
them be required to be faithful to me except during my governorship. In the territory committed to me I will not cause
any strongholds to be built without the command of the pope.
I will give a faithful account of my governorship whenever
the pope may demand it. And I will freely resign my office
whenever the pope or the holy Roman church may command
me to do so. All these things I swear that I will faithfully
observe without fraud, to the best of my ability, the command of the pope being supreme in all things. So help me
God and these holy gospels of God.

124. John of Ceccano's Oath of Fidelity to Inno-cent III, 1201.

Migne, 217, col. 286.

See introductory note to no. 123.

In the fourth year of the pontificate of Innocent III, in the
papal palace at Anagni, a nobleman, John of Ceccano, took
an oath of fidelity to pope Innocent for Ceccano and for all
the land which he holds. The oath was taken in the presence
of cardinal bishops, priests, and deacons; there were present
also many other clergy and nobles of Anagni and of other

places, as well as the knights of John of Ceccano. And he admitted that he held Ceccano and all the rest of his land from the Roman church. And this was his oath:

I, John of Ceccano, swear that from this hour on I will be faithful to St. Peter, the Roman church, and my lord pope Innocent and his successors. I will have no share in any counsel or deed, either by word or act, to deprive them of life or limb or to capture them by fraud. Any plan which they may reveal to me either in person or by messenger or by letter I will not wittingly make known to their hurt. If I learn of an impending injury to them I will prevent it if possible; if I cannot prevent it I will inform them of it either in person or by letter or by messenger, or I will tell it to some person who, I believe, will tell them of it. I will aid them in defending Ceccano and all the land which I hold, and the other regalia of St. Peter which they hold. If they have lost any regalia, I will aid them in recovering, keeping, and defending it against all men. These things I will keep in good faith, without fraud or deceit. So help me God and these holy gospels.

After these things he put his hands into the hands of the pope and did him liege homage. And the pope graciously gave him a silver cup overlaid with gold. And afterward, in the same year, the same pope, because of his faithfulness and services of John of Ceccano and his ancestors, gave him the castle of Sitense as a fief.

125. INNOCENT III COMMANDS THE ARCHBISHOP OF MESSINA TO RECEIVE THE OATHS OF BAILIFFS IN SICILY, 1203.

Migne, 215, col. 55.

See introductory note to no. 123. This document is an evidence that the government of Sicily was administered by the pope. According to the Constitutions of Sicily, 1231, the bailiffs had jurisdiction over thefts, the use of false weights and measures, and the less important civil cases.

Knowing your orthodoxy and your faithfulness we do not hesitate to commit to your charge those things which will advance the honor of the apostolic see. Accordingly, by this apostolic writing, we command you to demand and receive, in our name, the bailiff's oath from all counts, barons, citizens, and others who have not yet taken it.

126. Innocent III Commands the English Barons to Pay their Accustomed Scutage to King John, 1206.

Migne, 217, col. 248.

Innocent III presumed to dictate to the whole Christian world in all matters, temporal as well as spiritual. The following documents, nos. 126–129, are offered merely to illustrate by a few specific cases the authority which he assumed. They explain themselves.

Innocent . . . . to his beloved sons, the great nobles, barons, and knights in England, greeting and apostolic benediction. Our most dear son, John, the illustrious king of England, has informed us that, although your ancestors were accustomed from ancient times to pay the king scutage for the baronies which they held from him, and although you yourselves have paid this scutage up to very recent times, you have now arbitrarily refused to pay scutage for the army which he led last year into Poitou. In order that your king's plans may not be interfered with by such action, we earnestly admonish and exhort you, and by this letter we command you to pay promptly and without further resistance or objection the said scutage in accordance with your obligation. For without judicial procedure he cannot be despoiled of this scutage because his ancestors and he have been accustomed to receive it, and besides, provided his right to it is admitted, he is ready to hear any just complaints that may be made to him about it.

127. Innocent III to Peter of Aragon, 1211.

Migne, 216, col. 404 f.

See introductory note to no. 126.

Since you say that while you were still a minor you did yourself great damage by making grants which now involve a large part of your income, and that, although you are very poor, you incur heavy expenses in fighting the enemies of Christianity [that is, the Mohammedans in Spain], I hereby give you the authority to revoke all the grants you made during your minority; but with this proviso, that if you wish to revoke any grants which you made to churches or to other places which are put to a religious use, such revocations shall be passed on by an ecclesiastical judge.

128. Innocent III Grants the Title of King to the Duke of Bohemia, 1204.

Migne, 215, col. 333 f.

See introductory note to no. 126 and to no. 56.

Although there have been many in Bohemia who have worn a royal crown, yet they never received the papal permission to call themselves king in their documents. Nor have we hitherto been willing to call you king, because you were crowned king by Philip, duke of Suabia, who himself had not been legally crowned, and therefore could not legally crown either you or anyone else. But since you have obeyed us, and, deserting the duke of Suabia, have gone over to the illustrious king, Otto, emperor elect, and he regards you as king, we, at his request and out of consideration of your obedience, are willing hereafter to call you king. Now that you know why this favor has been granted you, strive to shun the vice of ingratitude. And show that you have deserved our favor which we have so graciously shown you, and try also to retain it. See to it that you are solemnly crowned by Otto as soon as possible.

129. Innocent III Rebukes the English Barons for Resisting King John of England, 1216.

Migne, 217, col. 245 f.

See introductory note to no. 126.

Innocent, etc., to his beloved sons, the magnates and barons of England, greeting and apostolic benediction.

We are gravely troubled to learn that a quarrel has arisen between our most beloved son, John, king of Egland, and some of you, about certain questions that have recently been raised. Unless wise counsel prevails and diligent measures are taken to end this quarrel, it will cause injury. It is currently reported that you have rashly made conspiracies and confederacies against him, and that you have insolently, rebelliously, presumptuously, and with arms in your hands, said things to him, which, if they had to be said, should have been said humbly and submissively. We utterly condemn your conduct in these matters. You must no longer try, by such means, to hinder the king in his good plans. By our apostolic authority we hereby dissolve all conspiracies and confederacies that have been made since the quarrel between the crown and the church began, and forbid them under threat of excommunication. We order you to endeavor by clear proofs of humility and devotion to placate your king and to win his favor by rendering him those customary services which you and your ancestors have paid him and his predecessors. And in the future, if you wish to make a request of him, you shall do it, not insolently, but humbly and reverently, without offending his royal honor; and thus you will more readily obtain what you wish. We ask and beseech the king in the Lord and command him, in order to obtain forgiveness of his sins, to treat you leniently, and graciously to grant your just petitions. And thus you yourselves may rejoice to know that he has changed for the better, and on this account you and your heirs may serve him and his successors more promptly and devotedly. We ask, and, by this apostolic writing, command you to bear yourselves in such a way that England may obtain the peace she so earnestly longs for, and that you may deserve our aid and support in your times of trouble.

130. Decision of Innocent III in Regard to the Disputed Election of Frederick II, Philip of Suabia, and Otto of Brunswick, 1201.

Reg. d. Innoc. III. p. super neg. Rom. imp., no. 29; Huillard-Bréholles, I, 70–76; Böhmer-Ficker-Winkelmann, no. 5724 a; Doeberl, V, no. 8.

At the death of Henry VI, 1197, his brother, Philip of Suabia, tried to persuade the princes to elect the infant son of Henry, Frederick, as king. While some were in favor of this, others refused on the ground that it would be ruinous to elect a child king. They offered the crown to Philip, but he refused it because he was unwilling to appear to be false to his little nephew. In spite of Philip's persistent refusal a party of the princes elected him. The Guelf party elected Otto, son of Henry the Lion. Under these circumstances Innocent III declared that it was his right as pope to decide the disputed election. His reasons for deciding in favor of Otto are given in the following document.

In the name of the Father, Son, and Holy Spirit.

It is the business of the pope to look after the interests of the Roman empire, since the empire derives its origin and its final authority from the papacy; its origin, because it was originally transferred from Greece by and for the sake of the papacy, the popes making the transfer in order that the church might be better protected; its final authority, because the emperor is raised to his position by the pope who blesses him, crowns him, and invests him with the empire. Henry [VI] recognized this truth in respect to our predecessor, pope Celestine of blessed memory, for although for a little while after he had received the crown from the pope, he refused to admit this, later he came to his senses and besought the pope to invest him with the golden mantle of the empire. Therefore, since three persons have lately been elected king by diferent parties, namely, the youth [Frederick II], Philip, and Otto, so also three things must be taken into account in regard to each one, namely: the legality, the suitability, and the expediency of his election.

In respect to the youth, the son of emperor Henry, at first glance it does not seem lawful to oppose his election, because it was supported by the oaths which his father received from the princes before his death.   For although that oath may have been extorted from them by force, nevertheless it is not thereby rendered void; in the case of the oath which the children of Israel swore to Gibeon, they decided that, although it had been secured by fraud, it ought still to be kept.   Moreover, if the oath of the princes was originally extorted from them, the emperor later recognized his sin, and released them from their oath, sending back the letters in which they promised to elect his son; then the princes, in the emperor's absence, of their own accord elected his son, and almost all of them promised him fidelity and some did him homage. Therefore it does not appear that they may lawfully break that oath.   It does not seem proper for us to deprive him of his kingdom, because he has been intrusted to our guardianship and protection, and moreover it is written: "Defend the fatherless" [Ps. 82:3].   It does not seem expedient to oppose him, because, when the youth shall arrive at years of discretion and shall learn that he was deprived of his kingdom by the pope, not only will he not show us reverence, but even as far as he is able he will attack the church, and withhold from her the allegiance and dues which she should receive from the kingdom of Sicily.   On the other hand, there are good reasons why it should be lawful, fitting, and expedient to oppose his election.   It is lawful because the oaths of the princes were illegal, and the election was unwise.   For they elected as emperor a person unsuited not only to that, but to any other office, for he was then scarcely two years old and was not yet baptized.   It appears then that such illegal and unwise oaths should not be kept. The case of the oath sworn to Gibeon does not apply, for that oath could be kept without working injury to the people of Israel, while the observance of these oaths will not only injure one race, but will cause great loss and damage to the church and the whole Christian people. Nor can it be said that these oaths are legal if interpreted according to the intention of the princes who swore them. They meant that if they elected him emperor, he was not to rule immediately, but later when he came of age. But how then could they judge of his fitness to rule? Might he not turn out to be so foolish and simple as to be utterly unworthy even less honor? Suppose that they meant he should rule only when he was fitted to, and that in the meantime his father should govern the state. But later an event occurred which the princes had not thought of, and which made it neither right nor possible for the princes to keep their oaths; that is, the sudden death of the father. Now since the empire cannot be governed by a deputy, and an emperor cannot be elected for a temporary term, and since the church neither wishes nor is able to do without an emperor, it is lawful to elect some one else. It is not fitting that he should rule. For how can he rule who is himself under the rule of others? How can he protect the Christian people who is himself under the tutelage of others? It is no sufficient answer to this to say that it was to our guardianship that he was intrusted, because this was done not that we might give him the empire, but that we might hold the kingdom of Sicily for him. The Scripture says: "Woe to thee, oh land, when thy king is a child, and thy princes eat in the morning" [Eccles. 10:16]. It is not expedient that he should become emperor, because thereby the kingdom of Sicily would be united with the empire to the danger of the church; for, to say nothing of other dangers, he would, like his father before him, be unwilling to prejudice the dignity of the empire by taking the oaths of fidelity and homage to the pope for the

kingdom of Sicily.   And it is no answer to this to say that
he would later oppose the church if we deprived him of the
empire, for it is not we who are depriving him of his empire,
but his uncle [Philip] who has attempted to seize not only
the empire, but his maternal possessions as well, while we
have been defending them for him at great expense and with
great labor.

As to Philip, it does not seem lawful to oppose his election.
In deciding the legality of elections, account has to be taken
of the zeal, the rank, and the number of the electors.   It is
not easy to determine the zeal, but, in respect to the other
considerations, it is clear that Philip was elected by many
princes of high rank, and that many others have since given
him their support.   Therefore his election seems to be legal,
and not to be opposed.   It would seem also that it is not
proper for us to oppose his election, for we would appear
thereby to be taking revenge for our injuries, if, because his
father [Frederick I] and his brother [Henry VI] persecuted
the church, we should persecute him and visit upon him the
punishment incurred by the sins of others; whereas our Lord
has said: "Love your enemies, bless them that curse you, do
good to them that hate you, and pray for them which despite-
fully use you" [Matt. 5:44].   It would seem also not to be
expedient to oppose his election.   To oppose a man so strong
in wealth and supporters is like battling with the torrent with
the bare arms.   We would only make an enemy of him and
create even greater strife in the church.   We ought rather to
seek peace and pursue it, which we could do by supporting
him.   But on the other hand it seems lawful to oppose his
election, for he was excommunicated lawfully and in solemn
form by our predecessor.   Lawfully, because he had seized the
lands of St. Peter [Tuscany], and ravaged and burned them,
refusing to make satisfaction after being warned to do so
once and again by our brothers; in solemn form, for it was
done at mass in the church of St. Peter on a great feast-day,

and he himself recognized the validity of the excommunication by sending a messenger to us to beseech absolution, and by having himself absolved later after his election, by our legate, although contrary to our commands. So it is evident that he was elected while under sentence of excommunication, and some believe that he is not yet released from it. For in giving him absolution, the former bishop of Sutri did not observe the conditions laid down by us; namely, that Philip should first release the archbishop of Salerno from captivity, and should then be freed from the necessity of coming to Rome for absolution if he would take oath publicly to obey us in respect to the deeds for which he had been excommunicated, and then only should be given absolution. But the bishop of Sutri attempted to absolve him secretly while the said archbishop was still a prisoner, and without requiring any oath at all; for which disobedience he was deprived of his bishopric by us and ended his days in a monastery. Moreover, since we have frequently excommunicated Markwald and all other German and Italian supporters of Philip, Philip himself, the author of their sins, is surely subject to the same sentence. Moreover, it is notorious that he swore fidelity to the youth [Frederick], and yet has seized his kingdom and tried to seize the empire; therefore he is guilty of perjury. It is objected that we have already declared such oath to be illegal, and that he is not guilty of perjury in not keeping it, because we have said it ought not to be kept. But even if the oath was unlawful, he should not have broken it on his own authority, but should first have consulted us, after the example of the children of Israel, in the case of the oath which they swore to Gibeon; for although the oath had been won from them by fraud they did not break it of their own accord, but decided to consult the Lord. Moreover since whatever is done against the conscience leads to hell (according to the words of the apostle: "Whatsoever is not of faith is sin" [Rom. 14:23]), and since Philip excuses him-

self in this matter by saying that he would not have taken
the kingdom if he had not known that otherwise some other
persons would have seized it, it is clear that he believed he
ought to have kept the oath, and that in violating it he went
against his own conscience. So it seems that we ought to
oppose him and resist his attempt to hold the empire, since
he is legally under excommunication and is guilty of perjury.
It appears also that we may properly oppose his election, for
by his succession, brother will be succeeding brother, just as
formerly son succeeded father when Frederick handed on the
crown to his son [Henry VI] and Henry tried to do the same
for his son [Frederick II]; and thus the empire tends to
become hereditary, the abuse becoming law by long custom.
Also it appears expedient to oppose him, for he is a perse-
cutor, and of a race of persecutors, and if we do not oppose
him now we shall be arming our enemy against ourselves.

As for Otto, at first it does not seem lawful to favor him,
because he was elected by only a few electors; it does not
seem fitting, because we should have the apearance of supporting him out of hate to another; it does not seem expedient, because in comparison to the other his party is small
and weak. But there are better reasons on the other side.
In the first place, the rank of the electors and the fitness of
the candidate must be considered, as well as the number of
electors; and Otto was elected by as many or more of those
princes that have the best right to elect the emperor, and is
himself much better fitted to rule than is Philip. Then
again the Lord visits the iniquity of the fathers upon the
children unto the third and fourth generation of them that
hate him; that is, upon those that continue in the evil way
of their fathers, and Philip has certainly persisted in the
wicked persecution of the church which his father began.
Finally, although we ought not to return evil for evil, but
ought rather to bless them that curse us, yet we should not
return good for injury to those who persist in their wicked-

ness or put weapons in the hands of those who rage against us, for God himself exalted the lowly to overthrow the mighty. Therefore it is lawful, proper, and expedient for the pope to favor the election of Otto.

Far be it from us that we should defer to man rather than to God, or that we should fear the countenance of the powerful, since, according to the apostle, we should abstain not only from evil, but also from all appearance of evil [1 Thess. 5:22]. For it is written: "Cursed be the man that trusteth in man, and maketh flesh his arm" [Jer. 17:5]. On the foregoing grounds, then, we decide that the youth should not at present be given the empire; we utterly reject Philip for his manifest unfitness, and we order his usurpation to be resisted by all. As to the rest, we have commanded our legate to persuade the princes either to choose some suitable person or to refer the matter to us for final decision. If they cannot come to a decision, since we have waited long, have frequently urged them to agree, have instructed them as to our desires by letters and legates [we shall take the matter into our own hands], that we may not seem to foster discord, and that we may say with Hezekiah: "There shall be peace and truth in my days" [Is. 39:8], and that we may not be forced, like Peter, to deny the truth, which is Christ, by following afar off, to see the end [Matt. 26:58]. But since the affair will not brook delay, and since Otto is not only himself devoted to the church, but comes from devout ancestors on both sides (on his mother's side from the kings of England, and on his father's from the dukes of Saxony, all of whom were faithful servants of the holy see, especially his great-grandfather the emperor Lothar, who twice came down to Apulia on behalf of the papacy and died in the service of the Roman church), therefore we decree that he [Otto] ought to be accepted and supported as king, and ought to be given the crown of the empire, after the rights of the Roman church have been secured.

131.   TREATY BETWEEN PHILIP, KING OF GERMANY, AND PHILIP II, KING OF FRANCE, 1198.

M. G. LL. 4to, IV, 2, no. 1.

About 1200 Europe was divided into two hostile camps, as is apparent from this and the following number. They also show the parties to this struggle which culminated in the battle of Bouvines, 1214.

Philip, by the grace of God, king of the Romans, Augustus. Let all men know that because of the love which existed between our father, Frederick [I] and our brother, Henry [VI], emperors of the Romans, and Philip, king of France, and for the sake of peace, and for the public good, we have made the following peace with the said Philip, king of France.

(1)   We will aid him especially against Richard, king of England, and his nephew, Otto [IV], and Baldwin of Flanders, and Adolf, archbishop of Cologne, and against all his other enemies.   We will aid him in good faith and without treachery, whenever the opportunity is offered, if it is not against our honor.

(2)   If any of our subjects wrongs him, or his kingdom, we will warn him to make reparation within forty days after we hear of it.   If we are in Italy, the bishop of Metz shall warn him.   If he does not make good the damage which he has inflicted on the king or his realm within the forty days, the said king may take vengeance on him and we will aid him to do so.

(3)   We will not keep in our realm any vassal, whether lay or cleric, of the king of France, contrary to the will of the said king.

(4)   The said king, whenever he wishes, may take vengeance on the count of Flanders, by attacking the lands of the said count which he holds in the empire, whether they are fiefs or allodial lands.

(5)   We promise in good faith that, if we learn that anyone

is trying to injure the king of France or his realm, we will try to prevent him from doing so. If we cannot, we will inform the king of France about it. . . .

132. ALLIANCE BETWEEN OTTO IV AND JOHN OF ENGLAND, 1202.

M. G. LL. 4to, IV, 2, no. 25.

See introductory note to no. 131.

John, by the grace of God king of England, lord of Ireland, duke of Normandy and Aquitaine, count of Anjou, etc. . . . We wish all to know that, in the name of the Lord Jesus Christ, we have made a league with our beloved nephew, Otto, by the grace of God illustrious king of the Romans, Augustus, for the purpose of guarding and defending his empire and his rights, and of giving him faithful counsel and aid in maintaining his rights. By this league all quarrels and differences which existed between us have been settled and we have mutually pardoned each other. . . .

133. CONCESSIONS OF PHILIP OF SUABIA TO INNOCENT III, 1203.

Migne, 217, col. 295 ff; M. G. LL. folio, II, p. 208.

In the beginning of the war between Philip of Suabia and Otto IV, it seemed that Philip would easily be the victor. But things began to go against him and toward the end of 1202, he secretly sent messengers to the pope to see what terms he could secure. Innocent was at least willing to negotiate and sent Martin to him to discuss the situation. In the presence of Martin Philip drew up the concessions which he was willing to make. These concessions were not sufficient for Innocent, and, besides, Otto IV began to have greater success in the field against Philip. So Innocent repudiated what Martin had done and gave his support to Otto again. But the success of Otto was brief. In 1204–5, Philip began to prevail over Otto, who soon found himself without support. Then Innocent, deserting Otto for his more successful rival, renewed the negotiations with Philip. In 1208 they agreed to a treaty, but its terms were not made public, and the negotiations were not entirely completed when Philip was murdered.

I, Philip, king of the Romans, Augustus, etc. Before Martin, Camaldolensian prior, and brother Otto, monk of Salem, came to me to negotiate about making peace with the church, I had already vowed to God and to his saints to go across the sea to liberate the land of promise from the cruelty of the Gentiles [Turks]; and again after they came and told me of the peace negotiations and of the concessions which the pope was willing to make, I vowed and promised to God and to his saints and to the said prior and brother, representatives of the pope, that, at a suitable time, in good faith and without fraud, I would go on a crusade, to the support of the church and of the empire, and do all I could to liberate the said land. The following persons were witnesses of my vow: Diethelm, bishop of Constance, etc. Besides, I promised that I would do all the following things: I will restore to all churches all the possessions which my predecessors, or I, have unjustly seized or held, and I will no longer disturb them in their possessions. I will cease from all the abuses which my predecessors have practised toward the church, as for example, when a bishop or abbot dies, I will not seize his possessions [*spolia*]. I will permit the elections of bishops and other prelates to take place in a canonical way, and I surrender control in spiritual matters to the pope. With the help of the pope I will endeavor, as far as my imperial office will permit, to subject all independent monasteries to some one of the regular orders, such as the Cistercian, Camaldolensian, or Premonstratensian. And I will try to compel the clergy as well as the monks to lead a decorous life, such as is becoming to their profession. As far as I can, I will compel advocates and patrons of churches to cease from oppressing the churches with exactions, such as *angariæ* and *parangariæ*.[1] If God shall subject the empire of the Greeks to me or to my brother-in-law, I will subject the Greek church to the Roman church. I will always be a faithful and devoted son and defender of the Roman church. I will make a general law and cause it to be observed always and everywhere in my empire that whoever shall be excommunicated by the pope shall be under the ban of the empire. Furthermore, in order that this league of peace and friendship between the pope and me may be observed forever, and that all grounds for suspicion may be removed, and that he may always be to me a most gracious father and I a most faithful son to him, I will give my daughter to his nephew in marriage, and any other members of my family, male or female, I will cause to be joined in marriage to members of his family, as the pope may desire. I will make full satisfaction to God and to the church for all my offences, as the pope may command. These things were done in the presence of the bishop of Constance, etc.

¹ See no. 103, note 2.

134. Promise of Frederick II to Innocent III, 1213.

Migne, 217, cols. 301 ff.

The powerful personality of Innocent III impressed itself deeply on the young king, Frederick II. The boy was truly devoted to Innocent, who was his guardian, and was willing to do whatever the pope required of him. In 1213 he wrote the following letter to Innocent in which he concedes practically everything for which the popes had been struggling. If the emperor had kept these promises, there would have been no further contest between the papacy and the empire. But as he grew older, and became conscious of his position, and learned what the imperial claims were, he gradually reasserted them and so renewed the conflict which ended in the destruction of his family.

In the name of the holy and undivided Trinity. Frederick II, etc. . . . To you, most holy father, and to all your successors, and to the holy Roman church, who has been a true mother to us, with a humble heart and devout spirit we will always show all obedience, honor, and reverence, such as our ancestors, catholic kings and emperors, have shown your predecessors. And in order that our devotion to you may be shown to be greater than theirs we will pay you greater obedience, honor, and reverence than they did. Wishing therefore to abolish that abuse which some of our predecessors are said to have practised, we grant that the election of bishops may be free and canonical, so that he whom the whole chapter, or the majority of it, may elect may be established over the vacant church, provided there is nothing in the canon law against his election. Appeals in all ecclesiastical matters may freely be made to Rome, and no one shall attempt to interfere with them. We also will cease from that abuse which our predecessors practised, and will no longer seize the property [*spolia*] of deceased bishops or of vacant churches. Jurisdiction in all spiritual matters we yield to you and the other bishops, that those things which are Cæsar's may be rendered to Cæsar, and those which are God's to God. Moreover we will give our best help and aid in the destruction of heresy. We grant to the Roman church the free and undisturbed possession of all those lands which she has recovered from our predecessors who had despoiled her of them. If there are any such lands which she has not yet succeeded in recovering, we will, with all our strength, aid her to recover them; and if any of them shall fall into our hands we will freely restore them to her. In this we understand that the following lands are included: All the land from Radicofano to Ceperano, the march of Ancona, the duchy of Spoleto, the land of the countess Matilda, the county of Bertinoro, the exarchate of Ravenna, the Pentapolis, with the other lands lying adjacent to them, as described in many documents given by kings and emperors from the time of Ludwig, in which it is said that these lands shall belong forever to the jurisdiction and control of the Roman church. And whenever we shall be called by the pope to come and receive the imperial crown or to render any service to the church, we will receive from them *fodrum* and other entertainment only as the pope shall give his consent. As a devoted son and catholic prince we will aid the Roman Catholic church to keep and defend the kingdom of Sicily and all other rights which she possesses. . . .

135. PROMISE OF FREDERICK II TO RESIGN SICILY AFTER HIS CORONATION AS EMPEROR, 1216.

Migne, 217, cols. 305 f; M. G. LL. folio, II, pp. 228 f; Böhmer-Ficker, no. 866; Doeberl, V, no. 13 b.

The pope had with difficulty succeeded in maintaining his ownership of Sicily. Now a new danger was threatening. He feared that, if Sicily should be held by the emperor, it would lead to the revival of the imperial claims to Sicily. In order to prevent this he persuaded Frederick II to promise that as soon as he should be crowned emperor he would resign Sicily to his little son, Henry.

To his most holy father in Christ, Innocent, bishop of the holy Roman church, Frederick, by the grace of God and of Innocent king of the Romans, Augustus, and king of Sicily, offers due obedience in all things, and reverence with filial subjection.

Desiring to provide for the welfare of both the Roman church and the kingdom of Sicily, we firmly promise that as soon as we shall be crowned emperor we will release from our paternal authority our son Henry, whom we, at your command, have had crowned king [of Sicily], and we will entirely relinquish all the kingdom of Sicily on both sides of the strait [of Messina] to be held by him from the Roman church alone, just as we have held it from her. From that time we will neither regard nor call ourselves king of Sicily, but until our son becomes of age we will have the kingdom ruled by some suitable person who shall in all respects be subject to the Roman church, because the government of that kingdom is known to belong to her. We promise to do this because, if we should become emperor and at the same time

be king of Sicily, it might be inferred that the kingdom of
Sicily belonged to the empire. And such an inference would
do injury to the Roman church as well as to our heirs. In
order that this our promise may be carried into effect we have
caused a golden seal to be affixed to this document.

136. Concessions of Frederick II to the Ecclesiastical Princes of Germany, 1220.

M. G. LL. folio, II, pp. 236 f; Böhmer-Ficker, no. 114; Doeberl, V, no. 14.

Frederick II had agreed that Sicily and Germany should never be
held by the same person, but in 1220 he was scheming to have his
son Henry [VII] elected and crowned king of Germany. Now Henry
[VII] was already king of Sicily. If he were to be elected king of
Germany, he would, in accordance with his father's oath, be compelled to resign the crown of Sicily. But this Frederick did not
intend that he should do. Frederick's pretext for having his son
made king of Germany was that he could not go on a crusade without leaving his son as king to care for the government of Germany
in his absence. His real purpose was to evade his oath to the pope
and secure both crowns in the possession of his family. In spite of
the protests of the pope Frederick secured the election and coronation of his son. He bought the aid of the German clergy by granting
them large regalian rights. These concessions which he made to the
clergy bought their support for the moment and made it impossible
for the pope to proceed to extreme measures against him for having
his son crowned king of Germany, contrary to his oath. The policy
which Frederick followed here was ruinous to the German crown.
He made of each ecclesiastical prince a little king in fact, though
not in name, thus stripping the crown of its rights and powers.
For the logical and ruinous effects of this policy on the royal power,
see the Golden Bull, no. 160.

In the name of the holy and undivided Trinity. Frederick
II, by the grace of God king of the Romans, Augustus, and
king of Sicily.

We bear in grateful remembrance the fidelity of the ecclesiastical princes to us, and their help in raising us to the empire, and supporting us in that station, and in electing our
son Henry as king, and we propose to promote their interests

as they have promoted ours, and to support them as they have supported us.

Therefore since certain injurious customs, or rather abuses, have grown up during the long conflicts of the empire (which now by the favor of God have ceased), in the way of new tolls, the minting of coins which led to confusion by their similarity to existing coins, private wars of advocates, and other evils without number, we now remove these abuses by the following decrees:

1. We promise that we will never henceforth lay claim to the personal property of a prelate at his death [the right to the *spolia*], but that, if a prelate dies intestate, his possessions shall go to his successors, and that no layman shall lay claim to them on any pretext whatsoever. If the prelate made a will it shall be valid in the law.

2. We will never grant any new tolls or new mints within the territory or jurisdiction of any one of the princes except by his consent and desire. We will preserve and defend the ancient tolls and mints which have been granted to their churches, neither infringing these rights ourselves nor permitting anyone else to do so. We forbid anyone to cheapen or confuse the coinage of the princes by making coins of similar appearance.

3. We will never admit to citizenship in our cities the subjects of any of the ecclesiastical princes, who have left the services of their lord for any cause. We desire that the same consideration be shown by the ecclesiastical princes to one another, and by the lay princes to the ecclesiastics.

4. We forbid advocates to injure the property of churches committed to their care. If they do so they shall restore the damage twofold, and pay 100 marks of silver to the royal treasury as a fine.

5. If the vassal of any of the ecclesiastical princes has been convicted of offence against his lord by feudal law and has been ejected from his fief, we will protect the lord in his

retention of the fief, and if he wishes to give the fief to us we will accept it without regard to the love or hate of anyone. If the fief of an ecclesiastical lord has become vacant by the above process or by the death of the holder, we will never lay claim to it unless it is given to us by the will and desire of the lord, and we will defend him in his possession of it.

6. If any of the ecclesiastical princes has excommunicated anyone and has notified us of this by word of mouth or letter or by reliable messengers, we will refuse to have any dealings with the excommunicated person. Such a person shall be deprived of his rights before the law, this deprivation not freeing him from the obligation of answering the accusations against him, but destroying his right to bear testimony or give judgment, or to bring suit against others.

7. And since the secular sword is intended to support the spiritual sword, we declare that our ban shall follow upon the excommunication pronounced by an ecclesiastical prince, if the excommunicated person is not absolved within six weeks; the ban of the empire shall not be revoked until the excommunication is withdrawn.

8. We have promised also to support and defend the princes by our authority in all cases, and they have promised on their faith to aid us to the best of their ability against any man who resists our authority.

9. We decree also that no buildings, castles, or cities shall be erected upon ecclesiastical lands through the interests of the advocate or through any other pretext. If such are erected without the consent of those to whom the lands belong they shall be destroyed by the royal authority.

10. Following the example of our ancestor, the emperor Frederick of blessed memory, we forbid any of our officials to claim jurisdiction in the matter of tolls, mints, or other rights, in any of the cities of the ecclesiastical princes, except during the time of the public diet and eight days before and eight days after. During that time the offi-

cials of the emperor shall exercise jurisdiction in accordance with the customs of the city and the laws established by its prince. If we come into any of their cities at any other time, we will not exercise any rights in it, but the authority of the prince or the lord of the city shall continue unimpaired.

11. Finally, since the acts of men are wont to sink into oblivion through the lapse of time, we hereby decree that these benefits and privileges shall be perpetually granted to the churches, and that our successors shall preserve them and enforce them on behalf of the church. . . .

137. DECISION OF THE DIET CONCERNING THE GRANTING OF NEW TOLLS AND MINTS, 1220.

M. G. LL. folio, II, p. 237; Böhmer-Ficker, no. 1118; Doeberl, V, p. 150.

The ecclesiastical princes promptly demanded that the emperor's concessions to them (no. 136) be put into force. To illustrate the effect of his grant, we give two documents, one in response to complaints about some new tolls established by the count of Gelder, the other to the patriarch of Aquileia who had presented a long list of grievances for redress. Frederick revoked the charter which he had given the count of Gelder and gave the patriarch a charter confirming him in the possession of many regalian rights (no. 138). This latter document shows that the patriarch was in the possession of a high degree of sovereignty. It also throws light on the movement in the cities, which were throwing off the rule of their lords and establishing local self-government (see section X).

Frederick, etc. We wish all to know that while we were holding a diet at Frankfort the following decision was rendered with the consent of the princes, namely: That we have not the right to empower anyone to establish new tolls or mints to the damage or disadvantage of another. Since we have heard many complaints about the tolls and mint which the count of Gelder has established, as he says, with our permission, we inform you all that we do not grant him the permission for these tolls and this mint. We forbid him to interfere in any way with the tolls at Arnheim, or Oesterbeke, or Lobith, or in any other place on the Rhine, or with any mint. We do this regardless of the fact that he says he has our permission, and regardless of any letters, from us or any of our predecessors, which he may have.

138. FREDERICK II GIVES A CHARTER TO THE PATRIARCH OF AQUILEIA, 1220.

Böhmer-Ficker, no. 1252; Doeberl, V, pp. 150 ff.

See introduction to no. 137.

Frederick II, etc. . . . We wish all to know that in a full diet a decision was rendered by our princes that (1) the patriarch of Aquileia has the authority to take whatever action he wishes in regard to establishing a market in any of the cities, towns, villages, and in all other places, where he has jurisdiction. (2) He may put under the ban any of his subjects, and also release them from it. (3) The cities, towns, and villages, which are under his jurisdiction, have no right to elect their rulers, or consuls, or rectors, contrary to the will of the patriarch. (4) No city, commune, or organization of any kind, whether lay or cleric, over which the said patriarch has jurisdiction, has the right to interfere with the bishopric after the death of the bishop, or with any of the things which belong to the bishopric. (5) No one has the right to establish new tolls, mints, or markets, in the lands over which the patriarch has jurisdiction, without his consent. (6) No one shall build mills on any of the streams without his consent. (7) No official shall confer freedom on anyone, or sell or alienate any vineyards, fields, meadows, roads, or anything else which belongs to the regalia, without the patriarch's consent. (8) The Venetians have no right to levy a tax on the lands or anything else belonging to the patriarch, or to compel his vassals to take an oath of fidelity to them. (9) No one under the jurisdiction of the patriarch, whether free, vassal, or ministerial, has the right to make a league or alliance without the consent of the patriarch. If any such league is made, it is invalid and the parties to it shall be proscribed.   (10) No one has the right to establish new cities, towns, or markets, on land which is under the jurisdiction of the patriarch, without his consent.

139. STATUTE OF FREDERICK II IN FAVOR OF THE PRINCES, 1231-2.

M. G. LL. folio, II, pp. 291 ff; Böhmer-Ficker, no. 1965; Doeberl, V, no. 17.

Henry [VII], being a mere child when he was crowned, was under the control of regents until 1229, when he began to rule in his own name. But he fell under the influence of princes who persuaded him to grant them many regalian rights. When Frederick II came into Germany, 1231, the princes asked him to confirm the grants which his son had made them. He consented to do so and the following document was given them. Like the grant to the ecclesiastical princes in 1220, it diminished the rights of the crown and increased the independence of the princes.

In the name of the holy and undivided Trinity. Frederick II, by divine mercy emperor of the Romans, Augustus, king of Jerusalem, king of Sicily.

(Introduction stating the occasion for the statute, which confirms the grants of his son Henry.)

1.   No new castles or cities shall be erected by us or by anyone else to the prejudice of the princes.

2.   New markets shall not be allowed to interfere with the interests of former ones.

3.   No one shall be compelled to attend any market against his will.

4.   Travellers shall not be compelled to leave the old highways, unless they desire to do so.

5.   We will not exercise jurisdiction within the ban-mile of our cities.

6.   Each prince shall possess and exercise in peace according to the customs of the land the liberties, jurisdiction, and

authority over counties and hundreds which are in his own possession or are held as fiefs from him.

7.   Centgrafs shall receive their office from the prince or from the person who holds the land as a fief.

8.   The location of the hundred court shall not be changed without the consent of the lord.

9.   No nobleman shall be amenable to the hundred court.

10.   The citizens who are known as *phalburgii* [*i.e.*, persons or corporations existing outside the city, but possessing political rights within it] shall be expelled from the cities.

11.   Payments of wine, money, grain, and other rents, which free peasants have formerly agreed to pay [to the emperor], are hereby remitted, and shall not be collected henceforth.

12.   The serfs of princes, nobles, ministerials, and churches shall not be admitted to our cities.

13.   Lands and fiefs of princes, nobles, ministerials, and churches, which have been seized by our cities, shall be restored and shall never again be taken.

14.   The right of the princes to furnish safe-conduct within the lands which they hold as fiefs from us shall not be infringed by us or by anyone else.

15.   Inhabitants of our cities shall not be compelled by our judges to restore any possessions which they may have received from others before they moved there.

16.   Notorious, condemned, and proscribed persons shall not be admitted to our cities; if they have been, they shall be driven out.

17.   We will never cause any money to be coined in the land of any of the princes which shall be injurious to his coinage.

18.   The jurisdiction of our cities shall not extend beyond their boundaries, unless we possess special jurisdiction in the region.

19. In our cities the plaintiff shall bring suit in the court of the accused.

20. Lands or property which are held as fiefs shall not be pawned without the consent of the lord from whom they are held.

21. No one shall be compelled to aid in the fortifying of cities unless he is legally bound to render that service.

22. Inhabitants of our cities who hold lands outside shall pay to their lords or advocates the regular dues and services, and they shall not be burdened with unjust exactions.

23. If serfs, freemen subject to advocates, or vassals of any lord, shall dwell within any of our cities, they shall not be prevented by our officials from going to their lords.

140–142. Treaty of San Germano, 1230.
140. The Preliminary Agreement.

Huillard-Bréholles, Hist. Dipl. Fred. II, III, pp. 210 f; Böhmer-Ficker, no. 1799; Doeberl, V, no. 16 d.

The chief cause of the first quarrel between Frederick and the pope was Frederick's refusal to keep his vow to go on a crusade. In 1215, on the day he was crowned king, he vowed to make a crusade, and again in 1220, when crowned emperor, he renewed the vow. For various reasons he several times put off going. Each time the pope was deeply disappointed, but eventually accepted the emperor's excuses. Again in 1225 he renewed his vow and set the time of his departure in August, 1227. But the pope had lost confidence in Frederick, as well as his patience. He stipulated that if the emperor did not keep his word, he should be excommunicated. Frederick sailed Aug. 8, 1227, but returned to land two days later. On this account Gregory IX excommunicated him, Sept. 29, 1227. Frederick published an apology for his conduct and called a crusade to take place the following May. Without seeking to have the excommunication removed, he sailed in June, 1228. For this the pope renewed the excommunication. While Frederick was absent in Palestine, his imperial vicar in Italy came into actual conflict with the papal officials about matters of government. When Frederick returned from Palestine in 1230, the pope was hardly prepared to carry on the war. So through the intercession of various princes the peace of San Germano was brought about. The preliminary agreement is found

in no. 140. The papal stipulations are contained in no. 141. In order
to convince the pope of his good intentions and to renew friendly
relations with him, Frederick made him a visit soon after the peace
was established. The pope wrote a friend an account of this visit,
which is found in no. 142.

In the name of the Lord, amen. Bertold, patriarch of
Aquileia; Eberhard, archbishop of Salzburg; Siegfied, bishop
of Regensburg; Leopold, duke of Austria and Styria; Bernard, duke of Carinthia; Otto, duke of Meran; by the grace
of God princes of the empire. Know all people by this writing. that our mother the holy Roman church, and our lord,
Frederick, emperor of the Romans, Augustus, king of Jerusalem and Sicily, have agreed to enter into negotiations for the
purpose of discovering some means by which the cities of
Gaeta and Sant' Agatha and other cities of Sicily which have
gone over to the church may be restored to the empire without detracting from the honor of the church. The time
within which these negotiations shall be completed is limited
to one year, and the church promises to do all in her power
to discover the means of arranging the transfer within that
time. If, however, no agreement is reached within the year,
the church and the empire are to appoint each two representatives who shall try to reach a settlement. If they are unable
to agree, they shall choose a fifth person, and the majority
shall decide. The emperor has caused Thomas, count of
Acerra, to swear for him that he, the emperor, will not molest
the said lands and persons nor permit them to be molested
during the course of the negotiations, and that he will accept
the terms agreed upon by the holy Roman church and the emperor or by their respective representatives. Know also that
the emperor has pardoned the Germans, Lombards, Tuscans,
Sicilians, French, and all others who adhered to the church
party against him, and has caused the count of Acerra to swear
for him that he will never molest them nor allow them to be
molested on account of the assistance which they gave the

Roman church against him, but that he will keep true peace with them and with the church. The emperor also remits all sentences, decrees, and bans issued by him or by anyone else because of this quarrel. He promises also •that he will not invade or waste the lands of the church in the duchy [of Rome] or the march [of Ancona], as set forth in other documents under the imperial seal. We have pledged ourselves on the holy gospels to see to it that the emperor does not violate these conditions. If he does, after allowing him a certain time to make satisfaction (namely: three months in Sicily, four months in Italy, and five months outside of Italy), we will assist the church at her request against him until he shall make satisfaction. If the emperor fails to appoint representatives or prevents them from going to the conference, we will hold ourselves bound to assist the church, as said above. But if the church refuses to appoint representatives or prevents them from attending the conference we shall not be bound by this oath.

141. Papal Stipulations in the Peace of San Germano, 1230.

Huillard-Bréholles, III, pp. 218 f; Böhmer-Ficker, no. 1817; Doeberl, pp. 66 f. See introductory note to no. 140.

We, John, by the grace of God Sabine bishop, and Thomas, cardinal priest of the title of Santa Sabina, legates of the apostolic see, by the authority of the pope, make the following demands of the emperor. 1. He shall not prevent free elections and confirmations in the churches and monasteries of the kingdom. 2. He shall make satisfaction to the counts of Celano and to the sons of Rainald of Aversa, according to the terms of the agreement, in those things for which the church became security. 3. Likewise he shall make satisfaction to the Templars and Hospitallers and other ecclesiastical persons, for the property which he has taken from them, and the injuries and losses which he has inflicted upon them, and the terms of this satisfaction shall be fixed later by the church. 4. Likewise for eight months from the day of his absolution he shall furnish suitable persons under oath as security to the church. The church will name these persons from among the princes, counts, and barons of Germany, and the communes of Lombardy, Tuscany, the mark, and Romagnola, and the marquises, counts, and barons of those territories, and they shall stand as security to the church for the conduct of the emperor. If he does not obey the commands of the church, or breaks the peace, or seizes or devastates the land of the church or of her vassals, they shall aid the church against him. The church will not proceed against him at once if he commits a wrong. But if he is in the kingdom of Sicily, he may have three months; if he is in Italy, he may have four months; if he is outside of Italy, he may have five months, in which to make good any wrong he may do. Those who are security for the emperor shall give the church sealed documents containing their promise to aid her. The emperor shall, within fifteen days, send a messenger to the papal court to receive the names of those whom the church wishes as security. All the above things are stipulated. But we leave it to his honor to fulfill all that he has promised about the crusade, and to obey the church in this matter. If through preoccupation or inattention we have omitted anything which we should have included in the above stipulations, the pope shall have the right to add it.

They also declared that the pope wished to be reimbursed for all the expenses to which the church had been put outside of the kingdom in preserving her liberties and the patrimony of St. Peter.

The legates also pronounced a sentence of excommunication on the emperor which should go into effect at once if the emperor should fail to observe any of the above stipulations. . . .

142. LETTER OF GREGORY IX ABOUT THE EMPEROR'S
VISIT TO HIM AFTER THE PEACE OF SAN GERMANO, 1230.

Huillard-Bréholles, III, p. 228; Böhmer-Ficker-Winkelmann, no. 6818; Doeberl,
V, no. 16 f.

See introductory note to no. 140.

Gregory, etc. Since we know that you, as an especially
dear son, are pleased to hear good news about us, we have
determined to inform you by letter of the good fortune which
has befallen us in the last few days. The other day [Sept.
1] our most dear son in Christ, the illustrious emperor of
the Romans [Frederick II], came with great pomp and a
magnificent retinue to visit us. He manifested a devotion
which was truly filial. His humility before us and his reverence for us as the vicar of St. Peter, the prince of the apostles, were as great as any of his predecessors have shown to
any of ours. As an evidence of his favor and of his attitude
toward us, the next day after his arrival he came to see us in
our own home, not with imperial ceremony, but, as it were,
in the simplicity of a private person. He took dinner with
us and we were surprised and delighted with his kindness
and devotion. The day was rendered joyful and memorable
by the pleasure which we both received from taking dinner
together. After dinner we talked and laughed about all sorts
of matters, and we discovered that he was quite ready to
obey our wishes in all respects, in regard both to religious
matters and to the patrimony of St. Peter. By this we were
greatly comforted in the Lord, and we thought that we ought
to let you, first of all, share in our comfort and joy. We
hope you will make this known to all those about you. We
command you to make it known to our subjects in Campania
and to encourage them to remain faithful to St. Peter and
to us. Strengthen them as much as you can, and urge them
to be constant and courageous. As we have told you of the
promises of Frederick, we shall keep you informed of the way
in which he fulfils them.

143-144. The Final Struggle between Gregory IX and Frederick II.

143. Papal Charges and Imperial Defence, 1238.

Huillard-Bréholles, V, p. 249; Böhmer-Ficker, no. 2401; Doeberl, V, no. 22 e.

The peace of San Germano was not kept long. The fundamental principles of pope and emperor conflicted with each other. No peace between them could be lasting so long as the primary question of supremacy was not settled. Frederick soon began to put forth imperial claims in various matters, and the pope resisted them. The struggle grew more and more bitter and they both came into such a state of mutual exasperation and irritation that any trifle brought forth long complaints and sharp reproofs. Of the many vigorous documents which concern their final break we give only two. Gregory wrote to certain bishops ordering them to take the emperor to task on a long list of charges. They did so, and the emperor refuted them, charge by charge. These papal charges and imperial denials are given first. Gregory was not convinced by the emperor's answers. The document by which he excommunicated Frederick is given in no. 144.

To the most holy father in Christ, Gregory [IX] by the grace of God pope, his devoted bishops of Würzburg, Worms, Vercelli, and Parma, humbly commend themselves and offer due and sincere reverence.

We reverently received your letter in which you ordered us to remonstrate with our lord the Roman emperor [Frederick II] about certain matters, a list of which was enclosed in your letter. Although we hesitated to do so because we are his subjects and were not sure that he would patiently receive our remonstrances, nevertheless we reverently went to him and set forth all the things which were contained in your letter to us and also in the large number of letters which you had written to him. God who rules and directs the hearts of kings as he will brought it about that he granted us an audience and listened to our words with great readiness and humility. He also called together the venerable archbishops of Palermo and Messina, the bishops of Cremona, Lodi, Novara, and Modena, and the abbot of San Vincenzo, and a great number of friars, both Dominicans and Franciscans, and in the presence of us all he responded to each one of the charges in their order as is set forth below. And in accordance with your command, we send you a faithful statement of his answers.

1. *The papal charge.* The churches of Monreale, Cefalu, Catania, and Squillace, and the monasteries of Mileto, Santa Eufemia, Terra Maggiore, and San Giovanni in Lamæ, have been robbed of almost all of their possessions. Likewise nearly all bishoprics, churches, and monasteries have been unjustly deprived of their liberties and prerogatives. *The emperor's answer.* In regard to the complaints of the churches, which are stated in a general way, orders have been given that certain things, done in ignorance, should be corrected at once; and others have already been corrected by our faithful messenger and notary, William de Tocco. He was sent especially for this purpose and he was ordered to go first to the papal court, and, after consultation with the archbishop of Messina, to follow his counsel in revoking all the things which he found were done unjustly. He had scarcely entered the kingdom when he found certain lands in the possession of members of the imperial family [ministerials]. He dispossessed them and restored the lands to their former owners. If he should find any lands were held illegally by the emperor, he was ordered to restore them to their owners. And when the pope learned of what he had done he approved the emperor's action in sending him and the diligencce of the messenger. Since the kingdom is divided into several provinces, the messenger has not yet been able to go through them all. Hence his work is not yet done, and there are still some things to be corrected. In regard to the church of Monreale, the emperor declared that it had not suffered anything through him, unless it wished to hold him responsible for the devastations committed by the Saracens who had ravaged its lands. But they recognize neither the

emperor nor the church. Nor had they spared anyone or anything. They had devastated the land clear up to the walls of the church, and they had spared no Sicilian. In fact, they had left scarcely a Christian alive in all that territory. The emperor declares that with great difficulty and expense he has exterminated them from Sicily. If he has done the churches a wrong in this, it is at least his only one. Nor has he tried to injure them.

In regard to the church at Cefalu, the emperor said that he had done no wrong, because the kings of Sicily have always held the castle of Cefalu, which is a strong citadel in the mark of the Saracens, and commands the sea. In the days of Innocent III the bishop of Cefalu had got possession of it, not legally but through an uprising. But Innocent ordered his legate who was then in Sicily caring for the interests of Frederick, who was still a child, to take the castle from the bishop and have it kept for Frederick until he should come of age. It has not been restored to the bishop nor should it be, because he has no right to it. Even if he had a right to it, it should not be restored to him, because, according to common report, he is a forger, a homicide, a traitor, and a schismatic. Therefore even if he had a right to it, it should not be restored to him. In the same way he said he was innocent of the charges about the church of Catania, unless he were held responsible for the conduct of some of the men from the imperial domain, who, in time of war, had gone to Catania to find a place that was secure and fertile. The emperor said that he had recalled them to his domains by a general edict of the realm, by which the counts, barons, and other men of the realm recalled the men belonging to their domains, no matter where they should find them, whether on the lands of the church or in the imperial cities. Besides, in regard to these things, the statute was passed and the time set at the request of the pope, as is clear from the letters of the patriarch of Antioch and the archbishops of

Palermo and Messina. Likewise the emperor said that an
equitable trade had been made with the churches of Mileto
and Santa Eufemia, and with the abbot and monks of Terra
Maggiore. This trade had been made with the permission
of their clergy and their convents, according to the legal
form, and they to-day hold and possess the things which they
received in exchange. But the village of San Severo was
not wholly the property of the abbot of Terra Maggiore, for
another had certain rights there which he held as a fief from
the empire. It was justly condemned and destroyed, because
the men of that place in the time of an uprising had killed
Paul de Logotheta, the bailiff of the emperor, and seized
the cattle of the emperor. And yet the abbot and his monastery had received some land in exchange for their share of
this village which had been destroyed. In accordance with
a legal decision the place called Lamæ has been fortified by
the abbot of San Giovanni Rotundo, and according to both
the civil and canon law, suit about it must be brought against
him in the imperial court.

2. *The papal charge.* The possessions, both movable and
immovable, which had been taken from the Templars and
Hospitallers, have not been restored to them in accordance
with the terms of the agreement which was made. *The emperor's answer.* It is true that by a legal process and in
accordance with an ancient law of the kingdom of Sicily,
fiefs and "burgher lands" have been taken from the said
orders. But they had received those lands from those who
were invading the kingdom and waging war on the emperor.
Besides they furnished the king's enemies with horses, arms,
food, and wine, and all kinds of provisions, while refusing
to aid the emperor who was still a minor. But other fiefs
and burgher lands have been restored to them which they had
acquired before the death of William II [king of Sicily], or
for which they had a grant from some one of our predecessors.
And some burgher lands which they had bought have been

taken from them in accordance with an ancient law of Sicily, that without the king's consent no burgher lands shall be given to the said orders or left to them as a legacy; but if such lands are given them, they are bound to sell them within a year, a month, a week, and a day, to some of the citizens. This law was passed long ago, because if they were permitted to buy and accept burgher lands they would in a short time possess the whole kingdom of Sicily, which they like better than any other part of the world. And this law is valid beyond the sea.

3. *The papal charge.* He does not permit vacant bishoprics and other churches to be filled, and on this account the liberty of the church is in danger and the true faith is perishing, because there is no one to preach the word of God and care for souls. *The emperor's answer.* The emperor wishes and desires that vacant bishoprics and other churches be filled, but without infringement on the privileges and rights which his predecessors have held. He has insisted less than his predecessors on his privileges, and he has never opposed the filling of the vacant churches.

4. *The papal charge.* In regard to taxes and exactions which are extorted from churches and monasteries contrary to agreement. *The emperor's answer.* Taxes and dues are assessed on the clergy and ecclesiastical persons, not because of their ecclesiastical property, but because of their fiefs and other possessions. And this is in accordance with the common law and is practised everywhere all over the world.

5. *The papal charge.* That prelates do not dare proceed against usurers, because of an imperial edict. *The emperor's answer.* The emperor has published a new general law against usurers, in accordance with which they are condemned, and action may be brought against all their possessions. And this law is read before all prelates, and they are not prevented by it from proceeding against usurers.

6. *The papal charge.* That clergymen are seized, impris-

oned, proscribed, and killed. *The emperor's answer.* He knows nothing about any clergymen who have been seized and imprisoned, except that some have been condemned by the decision of prelates, according to their crimes. These have been surrendered to the imperial officials who have seized them. He knows nothing about clergymen who have been proscribed except that some have been charged with the crime of *lèse majesté* and have been proscribed from the kingdom. He knows nothing about any clergymen who have been slain except those who were slain by other clergymen. The church of Venusa is mourning the death of its prelate who was killed by one of his monks. In the church of San Vincenzo one monk killed another. But the monks and the clergy commit such crimes with impunity, and it is the fault of the church that they escape all canonical punishment.

7. *The papal charge.* Churches which are consecrated to the Lord are profaned and destroyed. *The emperor's answer.* He knows nothing of such churches, unless the pope means the church of Luceria; but it is said to have fallen down of itself because of its great age. And the emperor will not only permit it to be rebuilt, but he will give a good sum to the bishop for its reconstruction.

8. *The papal charge.* That he does not permit the church of Sorana to be rebuilt. *The emperor's answer.* He will permit the church of Sorana to be rebuilt, but not the town. It shall not be rebuilt as long as he lives, because it was destroyed in accordance with a legal decision.

9. *The papal charge.* That contrary to the agreement those who had supported the church in the time of struggle between the pope and emperor have been robbed of their goods and driven out of the country. *The emperor's answer.* Those who adhered to the church in the time of the struggle against the emperor are living in security in the kingdom, except those who held some office and are afraid that they will be compelled to give an account of it, and some others

who have left the kingdom to escape civil and criminal charges. The emperor will permit them to come back in safety if they will give an account of their conduct in office and respond to those who have entered suit against them. But he will do nothing against them for having adhered to the church. If the pope complains that the treaty of peace has not been kept, let him remember that contrary to its terms and to the judgment of nearly all the friars, he is holding the city of Castella. For keeping this city to the detriment of the empire he is receiving money, although the emperor has expended more than 100,000 silver marks in aiding him against the Romans. From this the church has received great advantages, for land has been taken from the Romans and restored to the church and her liberties have been recovered and reformed in Rome through the help of the emperor.

10. *The papal charge.* That he has seized and now holds imprisoned the nephew of the king of Tunis who wished to come to the pope to receive baptism. *The emperor's answer.* That the nephew of the king of Tunis was fleeing from Barbary to Sicily, not to receive baptism, but to escape his uncle who was threatening him with death. He is not held captive but is going about freely in Apulia, and although he is often urged to be baptized, he steadfastly refuses. If however he wishes to be baptized, the emperor will receive him with rejoicing. He has already expressed himself in regard to this to the archbishops of Palermo and Messina.

11. *The papal charge.* That the church is humiliated and insulted by the fact that Peter Saraceno, her faithful subject, and friar Jordan are held captive. *The emperor's answer.* Peter Saraceno has been seized because he is an enemy and detractor of the emperor. He has attacked the emperor in Rome as well as elsewhere. He did not come on the business of the king of England, but he carried a letter of the king in order that if he were arrested we might be

led to spare him. But we did not heed this letter because the king did not know what snares this man had prepared for us. In regard to the friar Jordan, although he had defamed the emperor in his sermons, the emperor neither seized him nor ordered him to be seized. But because some of the emperor's faithful subjects knew the friar's character and his trickery, and so were sure that if he stayed in the mark of Treviso and in Lombardy, he would injure the cause of the emperor, the emperor caused him to be set free and would have given him over to the archbishop of Messina, if he had been willing to submit to the said archbishop.

12. *The papal charge.* The emperor had stirred up sedition in Rome against the church with the purpose of driving out the pope and his cardinals, and, contrary to the privileges and rights of the pope, to destroy the ecclesiastical liberties. *The emperor's answer.* The emperor denies that he stirred up the sedition in Rome. But he has his faithful subjects in Rome just as his predecessors, the Roman emperors and kings of Sicily, had had. And sometimes at the election of senators, the attempt was made to injure his subjects. Under these circumstances he had assisted his subjects in their defence, and he would do so as often as it should be necessary under similar circumstances. But when the election of a senator took place harmoniously, there was no rioting, as can be proved by the testimony of the archbishops of Palermo and Messina.

13. *The papal charge.* That the emperor had ordered his subjects not to permit the papal legate, the bishop of Preneste, to pass through their territory. *The emperor's answer.* The emperor had never even dreamed of giving such an order, although he might justly have done so, because the bishop was his enemy. Although he had been sent by the pope as a religious man on a religious errand, he had nevertheless at the command of the pope, as he said, in a treacherous and wicked manner led a large part of Lombardy to revolt against

the emperor and had done all he could to incite the Lombards to rebellion.

14. *The papal charge.* The cause of the crusade is delayed by him through the quarrel which he has with certain Lombards, although the church is ready to use all her powers to secure proper satisfaction from the Lombards for what they have done against the emperor, and the Lombards themselves are ready to make satisfaction. *The emperor's answer.* He had often referred that matter to the church, but he had never received any satisfaction. For the first time, the Lombards were condemned to furnish 400 knights. But instead of sending them to aid the emperor, as they should, the pope used them to make war on the emperor. The second time, they were condemned to furnish 500 knights, but the pope declared that they should not be sent to the aid of the emperor, but that they should be sent on the crusade under the control and protection of the pope and the church. But not even this was done. The third time, at the request of the cardinals, the Sabine bishop and *Magister* Peter of Capua, the affair was again referred to the pope exactly as the pope desired. But afterward the matter was never mentioned again until the pope learned that the emperor, having been deceived so many times about it, was preparing to lead an army from Germany into Italy. And then the pope at once begged that the matter be referred to him again. And although the emperor had so often been deceived in submitting it to the pope, he nevertheless was willing to submit it to him once more, but a time limit was set and it was stipulated that it should be decided to the honor of the emperor and to the advantage of the empire. But the pope was not willing to accept these conditions, as may be proved by his letter, although he now says that he was ready to decide the case in accordance with the rights and honor of the empire. From this it is apparent that the pope's letters are contradictory to each other. And let the pope not pretend that

the emperor, in trying to restore the rights of the empire in Italy, injured the prospects of the crusade, for the letters which the emperor wrote in answer to the kings of the world and to the crusaders in France, who had chosen him as their leader, will show that he took charge of the crusade and did not neglect it. He also wrote that he wished to conduct the whole matter in accordance with the advice of the church. . . . Finally, the emperor declared that since he had been absent from the kingdom and did not know the exact condition of things, if anything had been done injurious to the church, and had not yet been corrected, he would order it to be set entirely right, and also because of the great general good which would come if there were harmony between him and the church, he would give the church any reasonable security that he would act in harmony with her, and use all his powers and means for the honor and advancement of the Christian church and for the preservation of her liberties.

144. The Excommunication of Frederick II, 1239.

Huillard-Bréholles, Hist. Dipl., I, pp. 286 ff; Böhmer-Ficker-Winkelmann, no. 7226 a; Doeberl, V, no. 22 f.

See introductory note to no. 143.

1. By the authority of the Father, Son, and Holy Spirit, and of the blessed apostles Peter and Paul, and by our own authority, we excommunicate and anathematize Frederick, the so-called emperor, because he has incited rebellion in Rome against the Roman church, for the purpose of driving the pope and his brothers [the cardinals] from the apostolic seat, thus violating the dignity and honor of the apostolic seat, the liberty of the church, and the oath which he swore to the church.

2. We excommunicate and anathematize him because he ordered his followers to prevent our brother, the venerable bishop of Preneste, the legal legate, from proceeding on his

mission to the Albigenses, upon which we had sent him for the preservation of the Catholic faith.

3. We excommunicate and anathematize him because he has not allowed the vacancies in certain bishoprics and churches to be filled, thereby imperilling the liberty of the church, and destroying the true faith, because in the absence of the pastor there is no one to declare unto the people the word of God or to care for their souls. . . .

4. We excommunicate and anathematize him because the clergy of his kingdom are imprisoned, proscribed, and slain, and because the churches of God are despoiled and profaned.

5. We excommunicate and anathematize him because he has not permitted the church of Sorana to be rebuilt.

6. We excommunicate and anathematize him because he has seized the nephew of the king of Tunis and kept him from coming to the Roman church to be baptized.

7. We excommunicate and anathematize him because he has imprisoned Peter Saraceno, a Roman noble, who was sent as a messenger to us by the king of England.

8. We excommunicate and anathematize him because he has seized the lands of the churches of Ferrara, Pigogna, and Bondenum, and the dioceses of Ferrara, Bondenum, and Lucca, and the land of Sardinia, contrary to the oath which he swore to the church.

9. We excommunicate and anathematize him because he has occupied and wasted the lands of some of the nobles of his kingdom which were held by the church.

10. We excommunicate and anathematize him because he has robbed the churches of Monreale, Cefalu, Catania, Squillace, and the monasteries of Mileto, Santa Eufemia, Terra Maggiore, and San Giovanni in Lamæ.

11. We excommunicate and anathematize him because he has robbed many bishoprics, churches, and monasteries of his kingdom of almost all their goods through his unjust trials.

12. We excommunicate and anathematize him because he

has not entirely restored to the Templars and Hospitallers the property of which he had despoiled them, as he agreed to do in the treaty of peace.

13. Because he has extorted taxes and other payments from the churches and monasteries of his kingdom contrary to the treaty of peace.

14. We excommunicate him and anathematize him because he has compelled the prelates of churches and abbots of the Cistercian and of other orders to make monthly contributions for the erection of new castles.

15. We excommunicate and anathematize him because he has treated the adherents of the papal party as if they were under the ban, confiscating their property, exiling them, and imprisoning their wives and children, contrary to the treaty of peace.

16. We excommunicate and anathematize him because he has hindered the recovery of the Holy Land and the restoration of the Roman empire.

We absolve all his subjects from their oaths of fidelity to him, forbidding them to show him fidelity as long as he is under excommunication. We shall admonish him again to give up oppressing and injuring the nobles, the poor, the widows and orphans, and others of his land, and then we shall proceed to act ourselves in the matter. For all and each of these causes, in regard to which we have frequently admonished him to no purpose, we excommunicate and anathematize him. In regard to the accusation of heresy which is made against Frederick, we shall consider and act upon this in the proper place and time.

145. Current Stories about Frederick II.

Selections from Matthew of Paris, Chronica Majora; Rolls Series, III, pp. 520 f, p. 527; IV, pp. 474, 634 f; V, pp. 99 f.

A few passages from the chronicle of Matthew of Paris are offered to illustrate the character of Frederick and to throw a little light on the great struggle between him and the pope. The last paragraph is particularly interesting because it indicates that the pope was becoming conscious that he was meeting with national opposition. But he evidently misjudged the strength of it. For after overcoming the empire, the papacy was to succumb to the French king and be subservient to him for seventy years. And the national opposition was to grow until it culminated in the great rebellion which has had many stages but has finally ended in the complete destruction of the temporal power of the pope.

It was about this time [1238] that evil reports became current, which blackened the reputation of the emperor Frederick. It was said that he questioned the catholic faith and that he had made statements that showed not only that he was weak in the faith, but that he was indeed a heretic and a blasphemer. It is not right even to repeat such things, but it is reported that he said there were three impostors who had deceived the people of their time for the purpose of gaining control of the world, Moses, Jesus, and Mohammed, and that he made certain absurd remarks about the eucharist. It is incredible that any sane man should have uttered such terrible blasphemy. His enemies also said that he believed more in the religion of Mohammed than in that of Jesus Christ, and that he kept certain Saracen women as his concubines. There was a common complaint among the people that the emperor had for a long time been allied with the Saracens, and that he was more friendly with them than with Christians. His enemies, who were always trying to blacken his character, attempted to prove these statements by many evidences; whether or not they have sinned in doing this, He alone knows who knows all things. . . . In this year [1239], while the emperor was spending the winter in Italy, he recovered certain important islands in the Mediterranean just off the shore of Pisa, the most important acquisition being the greater and more valuable part of the island of Sardinia, which belonged to the patrimony of St. Peter. The emperor, however, asserted that it belonged of old to the empire, that it had been taken from the empire illegally by occupation and other wrongful measures and that he now restored it to the empire. He said: "I have sworn, as is known to all the world, to recover the dispersed parts of my empire; and I shall give my best efforts to carrying out my oath." So he sent his son [Enzio], in spite of the prohibition of the pope, to receive in his name that portion of the island that had surrendered to him . . . [1245]. When Frederick heard that the pope had deposed him, he was terribly enraged, and could scarcely contain himself for his wrath. Looking fiercely on those who sat around him, he thundered forth: "That pope has deposed me in his synod and has taken away my crown. Was there ever such audacity; was there ever such presumption? Where are the chests that contain my treasure?" And when these were brought and opened before him at his command, he said: "See now whether my crowns are lost." Then taking one of them and putting it on his head, he stood up, with a threatening look, and spoke out in a terrible voice from the bitterness of his heart: "I have not yet lost my crown, nor shall the pope and all his synod take it from me without a bloody struggle. And has his presumption been so boundless that he has dared to depose me from the empire, me, a great prince, who have no superior, indeed no equal? So much the better for my cause; for before this I was bound to obey him, and to do him reverence, but now I am absolved from any obligation to love or reverence him or even to keep peace with him." . . . [1247]. When Frederick heard of the acts of the papal legate in Germany, he was bitterly enraged and sought everywhere for a means of wreaking vengeance upon the pope. It was feared by some wise and thoughtful men that Frederick in his wrath might turn apostate, or call in to his aid the Tartars from Russia, or give the Sultan of Babylon, with whom he was on the most friendly terms, the chance to overrun the empire with his pagan hosts, to the destruction of all Christendom. . . . [1250]. Frederick attempted to make peace with the pope, . . . but the pope replied that he would not restore the emperor to his former position on any such easy terms, since he had been deposed and condemned by the general council of Lyon.   And some asserted that the pope desired above all else utterly to crush Frederick, whom he called the great dragon, in order that he might then destroy the kings of England and of France and the other Christian kings (whom he spoke of as kinglets and little serpents), after he had overawed them by making an example of Frederick, and thus be able to rob them and their prelates at his pleasure.

IV. THE EMPIRE FROM 1250 TO 1500

146. DIET OF NÜRNBERG, 1274.

M. G. LL. folio, II, pp. 399 ff; Altmann und Bernheim, no. 12.

When Rudolf was elected king in 1273, he found that he had a crown but no income. For during the interregnum (1254–73) the German princes, both lay and clerical, had seized all the crown lands and revenues. Rudolf was glad to be king, but his private income was not sufficient to support his new dignity. Besides, he was of a miserly disposition, and was bent on getting all out of the office that he could, or at least on making the office pay for itself. So he demanded the surrender of the lands and revenues which had been seized. But no one was willing to give them up. Since Rudolf was compelled to enter suit against each one, it was necessary to have some disinterested person to act as judge in all such cases. The diet decided that this office of judge belonged to the count palatine.

As soon as the judge was decided on, Rudolf asked what he should do in regard to these lands, and he was told that he must recover them. Ottokar, king of Bohemia, had himself been a candidate for the crown, and now refused to acknowledge the election of Rudolf. The diet decided what should be done in the matter, and instructed Rudolf how he should proceed against him.

Paragraphs 5–9 reveal to a certain extent the troubled condition into which Germany had been brought by the interregnum.

1. During the meeting of the diet at Nürnberg, the princes came together as a public court of justice, in the presence of the most serene lord, Rudolf, king of the Romans, and attended by a large following of counts and barons and a great multitude of nobles and common people. And first the king asked them for a decision on the following question: who should be judge in cases which involve imperial or fiscal property, and other offences against the king or the realm,

and in which the king of the Romans makes accusation against a prince of the empire. It was decided by all the princes and barons who were present that the count palatine of the Rhine has, and has had from of old, the right to act as judge in cases where the emperor or king accuses a prince of the empire.

2. The aforesaid count palatine then took his place as judge and the king asked for a decision on this question: what might and should the king do in regard to the property, now held by others, which the former emperor Frederick [II] had held and possessed in peace and quiet before he was deposed by the princes, and in regard to other imperial property wrongfully withheld from the empire. It was decided that the king ought to lay claim to such property and recover it; and that if anyone should resist the king in his attempt to recover his own, he should use his royal power to overcome this illegal resistance to authority and to preserve the rights of the empire.

3. The king asked, in the second place, what the law was in the case of the king of Bohemia, who had wilfully allowed more than a year and a day to elapse from the day of the coronation [of Rudolf] at Aachen without seeking to be invested with his fiefs by the king of the Romans. It was decided by all the princes and barons that whenever anyone, by his own neglect or contumacy and without just excuse, failed to seek investiture of his fiefs within a year and a day, all his fiefs were forfeited by the mere lapse of time.

4. In the third place, the king asked them how he should proceed to punish the contumacy of the king of Bohemia. It was decided that the count palatine of the Rhine should send a freeman to summon the king of Bohemia to appear before the count palatine at a certain place and on a certain day, which should be six weeks and three days from the day when the decision was rendered, and to answer the accusation of contumacy brought against him by the king. If the free-

man who was chosen to carry the summons swore that he did not dare appear before the king of Bohemia or enter his lands because he had good grounds to fear personal injury, it would then be sufficient for the diet to pass an edict summoning the king of Bohemia and for the count palatine to proclaim this summons publicly in the city or town of his that was nearest to the kingdom of Bohemia. To allow this matter to be settled in an orderly way, however, eighteen days in addition to the original six weeks and three days were to be allowed for the answer to the summons, so that the king of Bohemia should appear before the count palatine at Würzburg nine weeks from the 19th of November, that is, on the 20th of January; otherwise he should be proceeded against according to the law.

5. It was decided also that the king of the Romans ought to take cognizancce of all civil and criminal cases arising on and after the day of his coronation, and of all civil cases (*i.e.*, those involving inheritances, fiefs, possessions, and property) arising even before his coronation, if they had not been settled by decision of the court, by compromise, or by some amicable agreement.

6. In regard to wrongs which date from the quarrel between the empire and the papacy in the days of the emperor Frederick (seizure of property, injuries, and damages committed by one party against the other), the king proposes to confer with the pope and to try to reach some agreement with him that shall be just to both parties.

7. The king urges and requests all those who have seized or burned or destroyed the property of others during the time from the death of emperor Frederick to the coronation of the king [*i.e.*, Rudolf], to make compensation and come to some amicable agreement with those whom they have injured; and he also requests the injured not to refuse to accept such arrangement. If the parties cannot agree, the king will himself decide the cases. This does not refer, however,

to public plunderers of churches and holy places, or to those who have made open war, all of whom are to be brought to justice immediately. Likewise all cases pending before the king or his officials ought to be settled within a reasonable time.

8. It was decided also that summonses and decrees issuing from the court or from royal officials should be written and sealed with the seal of the judges, and that such documents should be in themselves sufficient evidence of the fact of the summons without further proof, and that not more than six coins of Halle or their equivalent should be exacted for the serving of the summons.

9. The king also notified all advocates who had used their office as a pretext for oppression to come to some agreement with those whom they had injured, and not to exact or demand in the future more than is due from those for whom they act as advocates. Otherwise they will be brought to trial for their injustice.

10. He also decreed that *phalburgii* [1] should not be allowed to live in any imperial city.

[1] For the meaning of this term see no. 139, paragraph 10.

147. THE GERMAN PRINCES CONFIRM RUDOLF'S SURRENDER OF ALL IMPERIAL CLAIMS IN ITALY, 1278–79.

M. G. LL. folio, II, pp. 421 f.

Rudolf saw clearly that the policy which the German kings had followed with regard to Italy had led to their ruin. He determined to give up this fatal policy, and to devote himself to the acquisition of lands and power in Germany. Accordingly he acknowledged all the papal claims in Italy, thus surrendering all for which the emperors had fought for the last 200 years. Contenting himself with what seemed obtainable, he gracefully acknowledged the defeat and failure of his predecessors, and struck out a new policy for himself (see no. 150). The princes confirmed his agreement with the pope by this document. Notice that the princes use the figures of the two luminaries and the two swords, accepting the papal interpretation (see no. 114).

We, the princes of the empire, to all to whom these presents come. The holy Roman church has always borne a special love for Germany, and has given her a name which in secular affairs is above the name of every other power on earth [*i.e.*, the name of the empire] ; she has established the princes in Germany, like rare and beautiful trees in a garden, watering them with her special favor, and they [the princes], supported by the church, have brought forth wonderful fruit; namely, the ruler of the empire who is produced by the election of the princes. He [the emperor] is that lesser luminary in the firmament of this world which shines by the reflected light of the great luminary, the vicar of Christ. He it is who draws the material sword at the command of the pope, to support the spiritual sword which the shepherd of shepherds uses to guard his sheep, and he wields it to restrain and correct evil-doers and to aid the good and the faithful. Now we desire that all occasion of dissension and strife should be avoided, that the two swords should work together for the reformation of the whole world, and that we, the princes, who are bound to support both the church and the empire, should be recognized as lovers of peace. Therefore we approve and ratify all concessions, renewals, and new grants made by our lord Rudolf, by the grace of God king of the Romans, Augustus, to our most holy father and lord, pope Nicholas III, and to his successors, and to the Roman church; in particular, the fidelity, obedience, honor, and reverence to be paid to the popes and to the Roman church by the emperors and kings of the Romans; the possessions, honors, and dignities of the Roman church; including all the land from Radicofano to Ceperano, the march of Ancona, the duchy of Spoleto, the lands of the countess Matilda, the city of Ravenna, the Emilia, with the cities of Bobbio, Cesena, Forlimpopoli, Forli, Faenza, Imola, Bologna, Ferrara, Comacle, Adria, Gabello, Rimini, Urbino, Montefeltre, the territory of Balneum, the county of Ber-

tinoro, the exarchate of Ravenna, the Pentapolis, Massa Tra-
baria, and the adjacent lands of the church, with all the
boundaries, territories, islands, land, and water, belonging
to the aforesaid provinces, cities, territories, and places; also
the city of Rome and the kingdom of Sicily, including its
possessions on the mainland and on the island of Sicily; also
Corsica and Sardinia, and all other lands and rights belonging to the church. . . .

148. Revocation of Grants of Lands Belonging to the Imperial Domain, 1281.

M. G. LL. folio, II, p. 435; Altmann und Bernheim, no. 14.

Rudolf's efforts to secure the crown lands which had been seized
during the interregnum (see introductory note, no. 146) were not
successful. The princes often voted that he should recover them,
but each one refused to give up those which he himself held. In
spite of his continued efforts, Rudolf was unable to regain any large
part of them.

We, Rudolf, by the grace of God, etc., by this document,
declare and publicly proclaim that while we were holding
court in a regular diet at Nürnberg, a decision was rendered
and all our princes, nobles, and other faithful subjects who
were present agreed to it. This decision was that all gifts
of imperial lands and possessions confirmed or made in any
way by Richard the king, or his predecessors in the Roman
empire since the sentence of deposition was passed on Frederick II shall be invalid, and are hereby revoked, except those
that shall be approved by a majority of the electoral princes.

149. An Electoral "Letter of Consent," 1282.

Stillfried und Maerker, Monumenta Zollerana, II, p. 138; Altmann und Bernheim, no. 15.

The power of the electors as well as the weakness of the crown
after 1273 are shown by the fact that the electors compelled the
king to secure their express and written consent before taking any
important action. By this means the electors hoped to control the

policy of the king and to make their own positions secure. If what the king proposed to do was not to their interest, they made him pay well for their consent. We give here an interesting example of these "letters of consent."

Werner, by the grace of God archbishop of Mainz, etc. Desiring always to comply promptly with the wishes of our most serene lord, Rudolf, king, etc., we entirely and freely give him our permission to grant as a fief the villages of Lenkersheim, Erlebach, and Brucke, with all their belongings, to Frederick, the burggrave of Nürnberg, whenever he wishes.

150. Letter of Rudolf to Edward I, King of England, Announcing his Intention of Investing his Sons with Austria, etc., 1283.

Rymer, Fœdera, II, p. 259.

Rudolf's chief policy was the aggrandizement of his family. By all possible means he endeavored to acquire lands in such a way that they would remain in the possession of his family, no matter who should be elected as his successor. This document is interesting as throwing light on his ambitious foreign relations, but it is still more important because it speaks of a great event in the good fortunes of the Hapsburg house, namely: the acquisition of the duchies of Austria, Styria, and Carinthia, the territorial basis for its future greatness. See no. 110, for the origin of the duchy of Austria.

To the magnificent prince, Edward, by the grace of God king of England and our dearest friend, Rudolf, by the same grace king of the Romans, Augustus, a perpetual increase of love and friendship. Although the Emperor of the eternal empire, the creator of all things, has stricken our heart with an incurable wound in the death of our beloved son Hartmann, by whose marriage our two houses were to be bound together in an eternal bond of friendship, yet, for our part, his death has not put an end to our friendship for you, as we are eager to demonstrate in every way. There-

fore we have thought it right to inform you that we are pros-
pering in all things, and have been successful in securing
the consent of the electors to our plans for raising our sons
to the rank of princes and investing them with the duchies
of Austria, Styria, and Carinthia.

151. DECREE AGAINST COUNTERFEITERS, 1285.

M. G. LL. folio, II, p. 446.

Since so many individuals, cities, and monasteries had the right
to coin money, it was impossible to keep effective control of the coinage. It was inevitable that it would in the course of time be de-
based. During the interregnum this abuse seems to have grown
rapidly.

Rudolf, etc., to all the faithful subjects of the holy Roman
empire to whom these presents come, grace and every good
thing. In the court over which we presided, held at Mainz
on the day of the blessed Virgin Margaret, we asked the
princes, counts, nobles, ministerials, and other faithful subjects of our empire who were present, what should be the
penalty for coiners of false money, for those who pass false
money or knowingly have it in their possession, and for the
lords who protect such persons in their castles. It was decided that the coiner of false money should be decapitated;
that he who passed false money or knowingly had it in his
possession should lose his hand, and that the lord who protected a coiner of false money should suffer the same penalty
as the coiner.

152. THE BEGINNING OF THE SWISS CONFEDERATION, 1290.

Kopp, Urkunden zur Geschichte der eidgenössischen Bünde, no. 19.

The Swiss confederation had its beginning in the following league
which the three forest cantons, Uri, Schwyz, and Unterwalden,
made in 1290. It is in itself, however, a renewal of a still older
league, the history of which is unknown to us. This document
reveals the fact that these cantons were not entirely independent,
but were subject to some external power. For instance, they did

not choose or create their own judges, but received them from some one whom they recognized as their lord. The next document, no. 152 a, shows that unfree men, probably ministerials, had been put over them as judges.

In the name of the Lord, amen. It is a good thing for the public utility if communities agree to preserve order and peace. Therefore let all know that the men of the valley of Uri, and the community of the valley of Schwyz, and the commune of those who live within the mountains of the lower valley [Unterwalden], considering the dangers that threaten them, and in order to be better able to defend themselves and their possessions, have, in good faith, promised mutually to assist each other with aid, counsel, and support, and with their persons as well as their possessions, with all their power and with their best effort, within the valley and without, against each and all who may try to molest, harm, or injure any of us in our persons or in our possessions. Each commune promised to aid the others whenever it should be necessary, and at its own expense to assist the others in repelling the attacks of their enemies and in avenging their injuries. The three cantons took oath that they would do these things without treachery.

We hereby renew the ancient agreement which has existed among us. (1) Each man, according to his condition, shall be bound to obey his lord and to serve him in the proper manner. (2) We unanimously promise, decree, and ordain that in the aforesaid valleys we will not receive any judge who has bought his office in any way, or who is not an inhabitant of the valley. (3) If a dispute arises among us, the more prudent among us shall meet and settle it as seems best to them. If anyone refuses to accept their decision we will all assist in enforcing it. (4) Above all, we decree that whoever treacherously and without good reason kills another shall be taken and put to death, unless he can prove his own innocence and a grave offence of the other. If the murderer runs away, he shall never be permitted to return to the valley. All who receive or protect such a malefactor shall be driven out of the valley until the people agree to permit them to return. (5) If anyone, by day or night, secretly and maliciously burns the house of another, he shall never again be regarded as a citizen of the valley. And if anyone protects or defends such a malefactor within the valley, he shall make proper satisfaction to him whose house was burned. (6) If anyone seizes the property of another, his own possessions, if they are in the valley, shall be seized for the purpose of rendering just satisfaction to him whose property was taken. (7) No one shall take the property of another as a pledge [security], unless he is bondsman for him, or the latter is clearly his debtor, and then only with the special permission of the judge. (8) Each one must obey his judge, and, if necessary, must tell the name of the judge before whom he must answer. (9) If anyone resists the decision of the judge and thereby causes damage to another, we are all bound to assist in compelling him to make proper satisfaction to him whom he has injured. (10) If war [feud] or a quarrel arises between any of us, and one of the parties refuses or neglects to secure its justice or to render satisfaction, we are all bound to defend the other party.

As an evidence that these statutes shall be binding forever this present document was made at the request of the aforesaid inhabitants and sealed with the seals of the three communities.

Done in the year of our Lord 1290, at the beginning of August.

152 a. EDICT OF RUDOLF, FORBIDDING JUDGES OF SERVILE RANK TO EXERCISE AUTHORITY IN SCHWYZ, 1291.

M. G. LL. folio, II, p. 457.

The free peasants of the Swiss cantons had a serious ground of complaint in the fact that feudal lords made use of their ministerials in the administration of justice. Being themselves freemen, the peasants of Schwyz objected to being tried and judged by men of unfree rank, as the ministerials were. See nos. 296 and 297.

Rudolf, by the grace of God king of the Romans, Augustus, to all the freemen of Schwyz, his beloved subjects, grace and every good thing. We regard it as unfitting that any person of servile condition should be made a judge over you. Therefore, by our royal authority expressed in this letter, we decree that no one of servile condition shall ever in the future exercise the authority of a judge over you.

153. Concessions of Adolf, Count of Nassau, to the Archbishop of Cologne in Return for his Vote, 1292.

Ennen, Wahl des Königs Adolf von Nassau, pp. 56 ff; Altmann und Bernheim, no. 16.

Candidates for the royal crown in Germany were compelled to practise bribery in the most open and shameless manner. Each elector was determined to get as much as he could for his vote, in one way or another, and so demanded a great variety of things from the candidate. We give the agreement which Adolf, count of Nassau, was compelled to make with the archbishop of Cologne in 1292. Of course he had to pay, or at least promise to pay, something to each of the other electors. An analysis of each paragraph will make clear the advantages which the archbishop sought to obtain from Adolf in return for his vote.

The archbishop of Cologne had followed a policy of territorial expansion. The great commercial interests of his city made it desirable that it should control the water-way to the sea and, if possible, a part of the coast-line. So Siegfried attempted to get possession of the lands which lay to the north and northwest, between Cologne and the sea. This brought him into conflict with the dukes of Brabant, and led to a war. In the battle of Worringen, June 6, 1228, the archbishop was defeated, taken prisoner, and held as a captive for eleven months. During his captivity his enemies took many of his possessions from him. In addition to these misfortunes the people of Cologne rebelled against him, and seized his castles, lands, and revenues. When he was finally released from captivity, he found himself in a bad plight. He was without troops, his castles were either destroyed or in the hands of his enemies, and the gates of his city were closed against him. This explains many of the things which he demanded of Adolf.

Otto "with the arrow," the margrave of Brandenburg (d. 1309), received his title in a curious way. He made war on the archbishop of Magdeburg, and in a battle was struck on the head with an arrow. The point of the arrow could not be removed, but remained in his head for more than a year. On this account he was afterward called Otto "with the arrow."

We, Adolf, by the grace of God count of Nassau, etc. Long before the empire was made vacant by the death of Rudolf, king of the Romans, we had vowed to God to go on a crusade, if it were possible, and to render a pleasing service to God for the remission of our sins. Now we could do much more for the honor of God and the recovery of the holy land, if we, although unworthy, were elected king of the Romans. Since our reverend father, Siegfried, archbishop of Cologne, is laboring for our election and will vote for us, of our own free will and accord we promise and bind ourselves by our word of honor and by our oath to do the following things:

(1) If we are elected king of the Romans, we will protect and defend the church and all ecclesiastical persons in all their rights and liberties, and if damage is done them, we will endeavor to make it good. And we promise this especially of the church of Cologne, which has now for a long time been suffering from her heavy losses and misfortunes.

(2) Even if the other electors do not vote for us, we will accept the election at the hands of the archbishop of Cologne, and we will never give up the right to the crown which his vote gives us.

(3) And because the empire cannot prosper if the holy church of Cologne, which has suffered so many losses and misfortunes, is not first restored by the aid of the empire, we promise and of our own free will and accord bind ourselves by our word of honor and by our oath that if the archbishop votes for us, we will surrender to him and to his successors and to the church of Cologne the fortresses and

strongholds, Cochem, Wied, Landskrone, Sinzig, Duisburg, and Dortmund, in order that he may better defend and preserve the right of the realm and of the empire in those parts, and also the rights of the church of Cologne, against their enemies and opponents. We will free these places from the claims of those who now hold them, and we will give them, with all their rights, income, jurisdiction, tolls, and belongings, to be held and possessed by the said archbishop and his successors and the church of Cologne as long as we live. And we will never demand them, or any part of their income, of the archbishop as long as we live. We grant all their income, tolls, and profits during our reign to the archbishop in return for his services in holding them against our enemies and those of the empire. We reserve for ourselves only the free right to enter the said places whenever it may be necessary.

(4) The said archbishop and the church of Cologne had pawned their castles, Leggenich, Wied, Waldenburg, Rodenburg, and Aspel, to count Adolf de Monte for a certain sum of money in order to liberate the archbishop from captivity; but the Roman church had ordered the said count under threat of excommunication and interdict to restore freely and entirely the said castles to the archbishop and his church and had commissioned Rudolf, the late king of the Romans, to see that he did so. We promise therefore that we will compel count Adolf and his heirs to surrender the said castles and the village of Deutz to the archbishop and his church without any loss and without the payment of any money.

(5) We also promise to restore to the said archbishop the advocacy and jurisdiction in Essen, and the manors of Westhoven, Brakel, and Elnenhorst, and we guarantee to him the peaceable possession of them.

(6) We also promise to maintain the archbishop and his successors in the possession of the castles Wassenberg and Leidberg, and we will aid them against the duke of Brabant

and the count of Flanders and all others who may attempt to invade and seize these possessions.

(7) If the archbishop or his successors and the church of Cologne wish at their own expense to rebuild the castles, Worringen, Ysenburg, Werl, Minden, Ravensberg, Volmarstein, Hallenberg, and the other castles of the church of Cologne which were destroyed during the captivity of the archbishop, we promise to resist all violence offered them while doing so, and we will use our royal power against those who try to prevent them from rebuilding them.

(8) We also promise to confirm the archbishop in the possession of the tolls at Andernach and Rheinberg, and we will renew all the grants which have been made by emperors and kings to the said church.

(9) We also promise to restore to the archbishop and the church of Cologne the castle and possessions at Zelten, of which the archbishop was deprived during his captivity by the count of Veldenz.

(10) We also promise to compel the citizens of Cologne to make the proper satisfaction to the archbishop and the church of Cologne for their offences against the archbishop. They have now been excommunicated a year and a day and their offence is notorious, and if they do not make the proper satisfaction to the archbishop, we will, at the request of the archbishop and the church of Cologne, proscribe the citizens and confiscate their property. And we will labor with all our might and at our own expense to aid the archbishop and his successors and the church of Cologne against the citizens and all who aid them. We will not cease to make war on them nor will we make a peace, truce, or agreement with them without the consent of the archbishop, and in such matters we will follow his wishes.

(11) We also promise that if the citizens submit to the archbishop, or are subjected by him, we will not in any way interfere in the affairs of the city, nor will we require an oath

of fidelity and homage from the citizens, because the city belongs completely to the archbishop and he has jurisdiction over it in all matters both spiritual and temporal.

(12) We also promise to renew and confirm to the archbishop and the church of Cologne their protection of the monastery of Corvey, which was granted them by Rudolf, king of the Romans, and we will recover for the church of Corvey all the castles and strongholds which have been violently taken from her.

(13) We promise to give the archbishop and the church of Cologne 25,000 silver marks toward defraying the necessary expenses which he and the church of Cologne are bound to have in performing the services which they owe to the empire.

(14) In order to secure the observance of these promises, we agree to get the castles, Nassau, Dillenburg, Ginsberg, and Segen, with the full consent of count Henry, his wife, and his brother, Emicho, and also Braubach, Rheinfels, Limburg, and the castle and town of Velmar, with the consent of their lords and their heirs, and we will put all these places into the hands of the archbishop, his successors, and the church of Cologne, to be held at our expense. We will name fifty nobles and knights as good and legal security, and if the archbishop wishes, we will go into Bonn with these fifty nobles within fifteen days, and we will not leave Bonn until each and all of these promises have been fulfilled, or security given that they will be fulfilled to the satisfaction of the archbishop.

(15) We also agree that if we act contrary to these our promises, or fail to give the archbishop security, we shall thereby be deposed and we shall lose the kingdom to which we have been elected, and in that case we will renounce all claims upon the realm which we acquired by the election. And the electors shall proceed to elect another king, if the archbishop thinks it best.

(16) We will not demand the coronation, or consecration, or installation, in Aachen from the archbishop, nor in any way trouble him about it until we have given him full security that we will do all that we have promised.

(17) We likewise cancel the debt which the archbishop owes us on account of the tolls at Andernach, which he had pawned to us.

(18) We further promise to call before our court the trial which is pending between the archbishop and the count of Nassau for the recovery of losses and damages, and we will decide it according to the desire of the archbishop.

(19) We also promise to seek the favor and friendship of Otto "with the arrow," the margrave of Brandenburg, for the archbishop and the church of Cologne, as well as the favor of count Otto of Everstein.

(20) If the children of the late William, brother of Walram, who is now count of Jülich, bring suit or make war on the present count, Walram, for the possession of the county and other possessions, we will assist count Walram. And we will aid him against the duke of Brabant, the count of Flanders, and others who may make war on him.

(21) We will give the said count Walram the town of Düren as long as we live.

(22) The office of *Schultheiss* of Aachen, with all the rights of that office, we will give to whomsoever the archbishop may choose.

(23) Rudolf, king of the Romans, was in debt to the father of the said count, Walram, and had given him his note. In regard to this debt we will consult our friends and the archbishop, and we will do what is right and in some way satisfy the count.

(24) We also promise that so long as we live we will be favorable and friendly to the archbishop and the church of Cologne, and we will aid them against their enemies, and, without the consent of the archbishop and his successors,

we will never take the counts of Monte and Marka, or the duke of Brabant, or other enemies of the church of Cologne into our counsel and confidence.

(25) In testimony of this we have affixed our seal to this writing.

(26) We, John, lord of Limburg; Ulric, lord of Hagenau; Godfrey of Merenberg, and John of Rheinberg, at the command of count Adolf, have sworn and promised that we will compel the said count Adolf to fulfil each and all of these promises without treachery and fraud. And we have affixed our seals to this document.

(27) Besides we, Adolf, promise under threat of the aforesaid punishments, that we will not enfeoff anyone with the duchies of Austria and Limburg, which have reverted to the crown, nor will we make any disposition of them without the express and written consent and permission of the archbishop.

154. THE ARCHBISHOP OF MAINZ IS CONFIRMED AS ARCHCHANCELLOR OF GERMANY, 1298.

De Guden, Codex Diplom., I, pp. 904 f; Altmann und Bernheim, no. 18.

The archbishop of Mainz had long been the archchancellor of Germany, but nearly all the duties of the office were performed by others. Although his office had become a sinecure, he wished to retain it, because of the dignity which the title gave him, as well as the income of it. The archbishop of Mainz had been a determined opponent of the Hapsburg party in 1292, and again in 1298, when Adolf was deposed, he was not at first favorable to the candidacy of Albert. He may have feared that Albert, in a spirit of revenge, would attempt to deprive him of his office, or at least of some of its perquisites.

Albert, by the grace of God, king, etc. We remember with gratitude how ably and faithfully Gerhard, the venerable archbishop of Mainz, labored to elect us king and supported us after we were elected. For this we surely ought not only to protect him and his church in their liberties, rights, and prerogatives, but also to show him still greater kindness and favors. We therefore declare that the aforesaid archbishop and all his successors in the archbishopric are and ought to be archchancellors of the holy empire in Germany. And we faithfully promise and bind ourselves by this document to maintain, defend, and protect the said archbishop and his successors in the rights, honors, dignities, and liberties which belong to them because of their office as archchancellor. That is, they shall always receive a tenth of all the money which we collect from the Jews, and they shall always appoint the chancellor to take their place [and do the work of their office], and they shall have all the profits accruing from this office, whether the said archbishops are actually present at our court or not.

155. Declaration of the Election of Henry VII, 1308.

M. G. LL. folio, II, p. 491; Altmann und Bernheim, no. 19.

This document shows the last step in the election of a German king. After all the electors had discussed the candidates and expressed their choice, the count palatine of the Rhine may be said to have cast the vote of the whole body of electors for the candidate upon whom they had agreed.

In the name of the Father, Son, and Holy Spirit, amen. The kingdom and the empire of the Romans having become vacant by the death of Albert, king of the Romans, of blessed memory, notices were sent to all who have the right to vote in the election of a new king of the Romans, and on the day set all those who have any part in it were present and agreed to proceed to the election. And after each of the electors had declared his choice it appeared that all had given their votes for Henry, count of Luxemburg, agreeing upon him and naming him as king-elect, because they were confident from what they knew of his merits and his fidelity that he would defend and foster the holy Roman and universal church in her spiritual and temporal interests and would govern wisely the empire with the aid of God. Now, therefore, I, Rudolf, count palatine of the Rhine, for myself and my coelectors, by the authority which they have specially conceded to me do elect this Henry, count of Luxemburg, king of the Romans, advocate of the holy Roman and universal church, and defender of widows and orphans, and I invoke upon him the grace of the Holy Spirit.

156. The Supplying of the Office of the Archchancellor of Italy, 1310.

Lacomblet, Urkundenbuch für die Geschichte des Niederrheins, III, p. 70; Altmann und Bernheim, no. 20.

The archbishop of Cologne as archchancellor of Italy wished to enjoy the honors and revenues of his office, but the work connected with it was done by some one else. For some reason he did not wish to go into Italy with the king. So Henry VII confirmed him in his rights, and excused him from accompanying him.

Henry, by the grace of God king of the Romans, Augustus, to all present and future subjects of the holy Roman empire, grace and every good thing. . . . Henry, venerable archbishop of Cologne, archchancellor of the empire for Italy and our very dear prince, has excused himself from accompanying us across the Alps, whither, God willing, we are shortly going, because he is so occupied with our affairs here and with the interests of the empire and of his own church. Therefore, at his request, we have appointed a suitable person to accompany us in his place, and to exercise the office of chancellor in Italy for him, guarding the seals and performing such other duties as the office may require. We have also granted to the archbishop as a special grace, because of his conspicuous merits, that the honor, authority, and profits of the office shall belong entirely to him and to his church of Cologne. He whom we have put in charge of the office shall perform the duties of the chancellor in Italy in the place of the archbishop, and all persons shall obey him in all matters regarding the rights and revenues belonging to the archbishop of Cologne and shall appear before him at the accustomed place and time.

157. The Law "Licet Juris" of the Diet of Frankfort, August 8, 1338.

Altmann und Bernheim, no. 27.

John XXII had declared, in his struggle with Ludwig the Bavarian, that he had the right to confer the imperial crown, and to administer the empire during a vacancy. His broad claims offended the German people and led to a spirited but brief exhibition of national sentiment. The electors met at Rense, 1338, and emphatically declared that the imperial crown was not in any way dependent on the will of the pope, but that he whom they elected king of Germany was thereby made emperor without any action on the part of the pope. A few days later a diet was held at Frankfort, and the decision of the electors at Rense was enacted as a law. But it must be said that the electors themselves nullified it by appealing to the pope for aid when they deposed Ludwig and elected Charles IV (1346-7).

Both the canon and the civil law declare plainly that the dignity and authority of the emperor came of old directly from the Son of God, that God has appointed the emperors and kings of the world to give laws to the human race, and that the emperor obtains his office solely through his election by those who have the right to vote in imperial elections [the electors], without the confirmation and approval of anyone else. For in secular affairs he has no superior on earth, but rather is the ruler of all nations and peoples. Moreover, our Lord Jesus Christ has said: " Render unto Cæsar the things which are Cæsar's, and unto God the things which are God's." Nevertheless, certain persons, blinded by avarice and ambition, and totally ignorant of the Scriptures, have distorted the meaning of certain passages by false and wicked interpretations, and on this basis have attacked the imperial authority and the rights of the emperors, electors, and other princes and subjects of the empire. For they wrongfully assert that the emperor derives his position and authority from the pope, and that the emperor elect is not the real emperor until his election is confirmed and approved, and he is crowned by the pope. These false and dangerous assertions are clearly the work of the ancient enemy of mankind, attempting to stir up strife and discord, and to bring about confusion and dissensions among men.

In order to prevent this we now declare by the advice and with the consent of the electors and other princes of the empire, that the emperor holds his authority and position from God alone, and that it is the ancient law and custom of the empire that he who is elected emperor or king by the electors of the empire, thereby becomes true king and emperor of the Romans, and should be obeyed by all the subjects of the empire, and has full power to administer the laws of the empire and to perform all the functions of the emperor, without the approval, confirmation, authorization, or consent of the pope or any other person.

Therefore, we decree by this perpetual edict that the emperor elected by the electors or a majority of them is to be regarded and considered by all to be the true and lawful emperor, by reason of the election alone; that he is to be obeyed by all subjects of the empire; and that he has, and all must hold and assert that he has, the complete imperial power of administration and jurisdiction. If anyone contradicts these decrees and decisions or any one of them, or agrees with those who contradict them, or yields obedience to the commands, letters, or instructions of opponents of these decrees, we hereby deprive him and declare him to be deprived, by virtue of his act and of this law, of all fiefs which he holds of the empire, and of all favors, jurisdiction, privileges, and immunities which have been granted to him by us or by our predecessors. Moreover, we declare that he is guilty of offence against the majesty of the emperor, and subject to the penalties incurred by this offence.

158–159. The Diet of Coblenz, 1338.
158. Chronicle of Flanders. (French.)

Böhmer, Fontes rerum Germanicarum, I, pp. 190 f.

The name of the empire was still something to conjure with, although it was little more than a name. Not only had the emperors long since ceased to exercise any authority over the nations of Europe, but they had also become mere figure-heads in Germany and Italy. Ludwig of Bavaria was not only cowardly and ineffectual, but he was also without the means necessary to secure a vigorous forcible government in Germany. Even the thought of his disposing of the French crown, or interfering effectively in the affairs of France, was absurd. These two documents show that the idea of the world-wide empire lived on, and illustrate the way in which otherwise sensible men could make use of it when it suited their purpose. Edward III, who was just beginning the Hundred Years' War, was seeking allies against France. In securing an alliance with the emperor and the appointment as imperial vicar in the Netherlands, his purpose was to acquire the right to call on the nobles of that territory to aid him in his war.

How the emperor, wearing the imperial insignia, held a diet.

The Saturday before the Nativity of our Lady, in September of the year of grace 1338, the electoral princes of Germany came together at Coblenz, and there they held a diet, placing the emperor, Ludwig of Bavaria, upon a throne twelve feet high. The emperor wore a robe of changeable silk, and over it a mantle, and broad fanons on his arms. He wore a stole, crossed on his breast like that of a priest and richly embroidered with his arms; and on his feet he wore shoes made of the same cloth as his robe. On his head he wore a round mitre surmounted by a heavy golden crown; the crown was covered with flowers worked in gold, and in the front was a cross of gold which overtopped the flowers. He wore white silk gloves on his hands and precious rings on his fingers. In his right hand he held a golden globe surmounted by a cross, and in his left a sceptre. At the right of the emperor sat the margrave of the East Mark and of

Meissen, to whom the emperor gave the globe to hold. The king of England sat beside the emperor on a lower throne, clad in a scarlet robe, on the breast of which a castle was embroidered. At the left of the emperor sat the margrave of Jülich, to whom the emperor gave the sceptre to hold. Two steps below the emperor sat the electoral princes of the empire. Sire de Kuck, representing the duke of Brabant, stood behind the emperor, about two feet above him, holding a naked sword. And the emperor, seated on the throne and holding a diet, proclaimed to all by the words of his own mouth that he had created the king of England his vicar and lieutenant.

159. CHRONICLE OF HENRY KNYGHTON.

Böhmer, Fontes rerum Germanicarum, I, pp. 191 f.

See introductory note to no. 158.

When the emperor learned of the approach of king Edward, he set out from his place to meet him, and after travelling four days he met him near Coblenz, receiving him there with great honor. Two richly decorated thrones were set up in the market-place, and on these the emperor and the king sat. There were present in attendance four dukes, three archbishops, six bishops, and thirty-seven counts, besides a great number, estimated by the heralds at 17,000, of barons, baronets, knights, and others. The emperor held in his right hand the imperial sceptre, and in his left the golden globe as a symbol of world-wide authority. A certain knight held a drawn sword above his head. And the emperor in the presence of the people gathered there proclaimed to all the crimes, disobedience, and wickedness of the king of France. And after he had declared that the king of France had broken his faith to the emperor, he published a decree of forfeiture against him and his followers. Then the emperor made king Edward his vicar and gave him authority over the land from

Cologne to the sea, presenting him with a charter of this in the sight of all the people.

On the next day the emperor and the king of England and their nobles assembled in the cathedral, and the archbishop of Cologne said mass. And after mass the emperor and all his nobles swore to aid the king of England and to maintain his quarrel against the king of France with their lives for seven years, if the war between the said kings should last so long. They also swore that all the nobles in the territory from Cologne to the sea would come at the summons of the king of England to join him in an attack upon the king of France at any place and at any time set by him. If any one of them should fail to obey the king of England in these matters, all the other nobles of northern Germany would attack and destroy him. These affairs having been arranged and settled, the king of England received the grant of authority and returned to Brabant.

160. THE GOLDEN BULL OF CHARLES IV, 1356.

Altmann und Bernheim, no. 29.

Various things had led the emperors to follow the policy of conferring crown rights upon their princes. In order to carry out their Italian policy the Hohenstaufen had sacrificed the power of the crown in Germany (see nos. 110–112, 136, 138, 139), and after the interregnum the electors pillaged the crown at every opportunity (see nos. 149, 153). The result was that the crown was stripped of authority, while the princes had developed almost complete sovereignty in their lands. Charles IV, in the Golden Bull, attempted to fix as in a constitution the actual rights and status of the princes. He saw that Germany was no longer a monarchy, but a federation of princes.

Although from 1273 the number of electors was fixed at seven, it was not always clear who these seven were. Thus in 1313 two men claimed to possess the electoral vote of Saxony, and two others, that of Bohemia. Charles IV made provisions to prevent the recurrence of such a situation by attaching the electoral vote to the possession of certain lands (see chaps. VII, XX, and XXV),

Charles IV was himself king of Bohemia, and, knowing that it was hopeless to attempt to restore the German kingship, he exerted himself in the Golden Bull to secure for Bohemia all the advantages possible.

PART I.

(Published at Nürnberg, January 10, 1356.)

CHAPTER I.

ESCORT AND SAFE-CONDUCT FOR THE ELECTORS.

1. We decree and determine by this imperial edict that, whenever the electoral princes are summoned according to the ancient and praiseworthy custom to meet and elect a king of the Romans and future emperor, each one of them shall be bound to furnish on demand an escort and safe-conduct to his fellow electors or their representatives, within his own lands and as much farther as he can, for the journey to and from the city where the election is to be held. Any electoral prince who refuses to furnish escort and safe-conduct shall be liable to the penalties for perjury and to the loss of his electoral vote for that occasion.

2. We decree and command also that all other princes who hold fiefs from the empire by whatever title, and all counts, barons, knights, clients, nobles, commoners, citizens, and all corporations of towns, cities, and territories of the empire, shall furnish escort and safe-conduct for this occasion to every electoral prince or his representatives, on demand, within their own lands and as much farther as they can. Violators of this decree shall be punished as follows: Princes, counts, barons, knights, clients, and all others of noble rank, shall suffer the penalties of perjury, and shall lose the fiefs which they hold of the emperor or any other lord, and all their other possessions; citizens and corporations shall also suffer the penalty for perjury, shall be deprived of all the rights, liberties, privileges, and graces which they have received from the empire, and shall incur the ban of the empire against their persons and property. Those whom we deprive of their rights for this offence may be attacked by any man without appealing to a magistrate, and without danger of reprisal, for they are rebels against the state and the empire, and have attacked the honor and security of the prince, and are convicted of faithlessness and perfidy.

3. We also command that the citizens and corporations of cities shall furnish supplies to the electoral princes and their representatives on demand at the regular price and without fraud, whenever they arrive at, or depart from, the city on their way to or from the election; those who violate this decree shall suffer the penalties described in the preceding paragraph for citizens and corporations. If any prince, count, baron, knight, client, noble, commoner, citizen, or city shall attack or molest in person or goods any of the electoral princes or their representatives, on their way to or from an election, whether they have safe-conduct or not, he and his accomplices shall incur the penalties above described, according to his position and rank.

4. If there should arise any enmity or hostility between two electoral princes, it shall not be allowed to interfere with the safe-conduct which each is bound to furnish to the other on the occasion of the election, under penalty of being declared guilty of perjury, and being deprived of his vote for that occasion, as described above.

5. If any other princes, counts, barons, knights, clients, nobles, commoners, citizens, or cities are at war with any electoral prince or princes, they shall nonetheless be bound to furnish to them and their representatives escort and safe-conduct for the journey to and from the election, under the same penalties. In order to render the observance of the above demands more certain, we desire and instruct all electoral and other princes, and all counts, barons, nobles, cities, and corporations to bind themselves by oaths and written promises to observe them. If anyone refuses to do this, he

shall incur the penalties above described, according to his rank and station.

6. If any electoral prince violates any of the above or following laws of the empire, he shall be excluded by his fellow-electors from their body, and shall be deprived of his vote and his electoral dignity, and of his right to hold fiefs of the empire. If any other prince of any rank or station, or any count, baron, or noble who holds fiefs of the empire, or any of their successors to their fiefs, is guilty of a similar crime, he shall not be invested with the fiefs which he holds of the empire, nor be able to receive a fief from any other lord, and he shall incur the above penalties, according to his rank.

7. The above rules apply to escorts and safe-conduct in general, but we have thought it well to indicate also the neighboring lands which should furnish escort and safe-conduct in each separate case to each elector.

8. To the king of Bohemia, the chief cup-bearer of the empire, the following should furnish escort and safe-conduct: the archbishop of Mainz, the bishops of Bamberg and Würzburg, the burggrave of Nürnberg, etc.

9. To the archbishop of Cologne, archchancellor of the empire for Italy, the archbishops of Mainz and Trier, the count palatine of the Rhine, the landgrave of Hesse, etc.

10. To the archbishop of Trier, archchancellor of the empire for Gaul and the kingdom of Arles, the archbishop of Mainz, the count palatine of the Rhine, etc.

11. To the count palatine of the Rhine, the archbishop of Mainz.

12. To the duke of Saxony, archmarshall of the empire, the king of Bohemia, the archbishops of Mainz and Magdeburg, the bishops of Bamberg and Würzburg, the margrave of Meissen, the landgrave of Hesse, the abbots of Fulda and Hersfeld, the burggrave of Nürnberg, etc. These shall also furnish escort and safe-conduct to the margrave of Brandenburg, the archchamberlain of the empire.

13. We wish and command that each electoral prince should give due notice to those from whom he intends to require safe-conduct, of his journey and of the route by which he intends to go; and he should make a formal demand upon such persons for safe-conduct, in order that they may be able to make fitting preparations.

14. The above decrees concerning safe-conduct are to be understood to mean that any person, whether expressly named or not, from whom safe-conduct is demanded on the occasion of the election, must furnish it in good faith within his own lands, and as much farther as he can, under the penalties described above.

15. It shall be the duty of the archbishop of Mainz to send notice of the approaching election to each of the electoral princes by his messenger bearing letters patent, containing the following: first, the date on which the letter should reach the prince to whom it is directed; then the command to the electoral prince to come or send his representatives to Frankfort on the Main, three months from that date, such representatives being duly accredited by letters bearing the great seal of the prince, and giving them full power to vote for the king of the Romans and future emperor. The form of the letter of notification and of the credentials of the representatives are appended to this document, and we hereby command that these forms be used without change.

16. When the news of the death of the king of the Romans has been received at Mainz, within one month from the date of receiving it the archbishop of Mainz shall send notices of the death and of the approaching election to all the electoral princes. But if the archbishop neglects or refuses to send such notices, the electoral princes are commanded on their fidelity to assemble on their own motion and without summons at the city of Frankfort within three months from the death of the emperor, for the purpose of electing a king of the Romans and future emperor.

17. Each electoral prince or his representatives may bring with him to Frankfort at the time of the election a retinue of 200 horsemen, of whom not more than 50 shall be armed.

18. If any electoral prince, duly summoned to the election, fails to come or to send representatives with credentials containing full authority, or if he or his representatives withdraws from the place of the election before the election has been completed, without leaving behind substitutes fully accredited and empowered, he shall lose his vote in that election. . . .

CHAPTER II.

THE ELECTION OF THE KING OF THE ROMANS.

1. (Mass shall be celebrated on the day after the arrival of the electors. The archbishop of Mainz administers this oath, which the other electors repeat:)

2. "I, archbishop of Mainz, archchancellor of the empire for Germany, electoral prince, swear on the holy gospels here before me, and by the faith which I owe to God and to the holy Roman empire, that with the aid of God, and according to my best judgment and knowledge, I will cast my vote, in this election of the king of the Romans and future emperor, for a person fitted to rule the Christian people. I will give my voice and vote freely, uninfluenced by any agreement, price, bribe, promise, or anything of the sort, by whatever name it may be called. So help me God and all the saints."

3. After the electors have taken this oath, they shall proceed to the election, and shall not depart from Frankfort until the majority have elected a king of the Romans and future emperor, to be ruler of the world and of the Christian people. If they have not come to a decision within thirty days from the day on which they took the above oath, after that they shall live upon bread and water and shall not leave the city until the election has been decided.

4. Such an election shall be as valid as if all the princes

had agreed unanimously and without difference upon a candidate. If any one of the princes or his representatives has been hindered or delayed for a time, but arrives before the election is over, he shall be admitted and shall take part in the election at the stage which had been reached at the time of his arrival. According to the ancient and approved custom, the king of the Romans elect, immediately after his election and before he takes up any other business of the empire, shall confirm and approve by sealed letters for each and all of the electoral princes, ecclesiastical and secular, the privileges, charters, rights, liberties, concessions, ancient customs, and dignities, and whatever else the princes held and possessed from the empire at the time of the election; and he shall renew the confirmation and approval when he becomes emperor. The original confirmation shall be made by him as king, and the renewal as emperor. It is his duty to do this graciously and in good faith, and not to hinder the princes in the exercise of their rights.

5. In the case where three of the electors vote for a fourth electoral prince, his vote shall have the same value as that of the others to make a majority and decide the election.

CHAPTER III.

THE LOCATION OF THE SEATS OF THE ARCHBISHOPS OF TRIER, COLOGNE, AND MAINZ.

In the name of the holy and undivided Trinity, amen. Charles by the grace of God emperor of the Romans, Augustus, and king of Bohemia. . . . To prevent any dispute arising between the archbishops of Trier, Mainz, and Cologne, electoral princes of the empire, as to their priority and rank in the diet, it has been decided and is hereby decreed with the advice and consent of all the electoral princes, ecclesiastical and secular, that the archbishop of Trier shall have the seat directly opposite and facing the emperor; that the archbishop of Mainz shall have the seat at the right of the emperor when

the diet is held in the diocese or province of Mainz, or anywhere in Germany except in the diocese of Cologne; that the
archbishop of Cologne shall have the seat at the right of the
emperor when the diet is held in the diocese or province of
Cologne, or anywhere in Gaul or Italy.   This applies to all
public ceremonies: court sessions, conferring of fiefs, ban-
quets, councils, and all occasions on which the princes meet
with the emperor for the transaction of imperial business.
This order of seating shall be observed by the successors of
the present archbishops of Cologne, Trier, and Mainz, and
shall never be questioned.

CHAPTER IV.

THE LOCATION OF THE SEATS OF THE ELECTORAL PRINCES.

1.   In the imperial diet, at the council-board, table, and all
other places where the emperor or king of the Romans meets
with the electoral princes, the seats shall be arranged as follows: On the right of the emperor, first, the archbishop of
Mainz, or of Cologne, according to the province in which the
meeting is held, as arranged above; second, the king of Bohemia, because he is a crowned and anointed prince; third,
the count palatine of the Rhine; on the left of the emperor,
first, the archbishop of Cologne, or of Mainz; second, the
duke of Saxony; third, the margrave of Brandenburg.

2.   When the imperial throne becomes vacant, the archbishop of Mainz shall have the authority, which he has had
from of old, to call the other electors together for the election.   It shall be his peculiar right also, when the electors
have convened for the election, to collect the votes, asking
each of the electors separately in the following order: first,
the archbishop of Trier, who shall have the right to the first
vote, as he has had from of old; then the archbishop of
Cologne, who has the office of first placing the crown upon
the head of the king of the Romans; then the king of Bohemia, who has the priority among the secular princes, be-

cause of his royal title; fourth, the count palatine of the Rhine; fifth, the duke of Saxony; sixth, the margrave of Brandenburg. Then the princes shall ask the archbishop of Mainz in turn to declare his choice and vote. At the diet, the margrave of Brandenburg shall offer water to the emperor or king, to wash his hands; the king of Bohemia shall have the right to offer him the cup first, although, by reason of his royal dignity, he shall not be bound to do this unless he desires; the count palatine of the Rhine shall offer him food; and the duke of Saxony shall act as his marshal in the accustomed manner.

CHAPTER V.

THE RIGHTS OF THE COUNT PALATINE AND OF THE DUKE OF SAXONY.

1. During the vacancy of the empire, the count palatine of the Rhine, archseneschal of the empire, by reason of his principality and office, shall exercise the authority of the future king of the Romans in the Rhine lands, in Suabia, and in the region of the Frankish law; this includes the right to present to ecclesiastical benefices, to collect revenues and incomes, to invest with fiefs, and to receive the oath of fidelity in the name of the emperor. All of these acts, however, must be confirmed and renewed by the king of the Romans after he is elected. The count palatine shall not have the right to invest the princes of the empire with fiefs which are called *Fahnlehen*,[1] the investiture and conferring of which is reserved to the king of the Romans in person. The count palatine is expressly forbidden to alienate or mortgage the imperial lands during the period of his administration. The duke of Saxony, archmarshal of the holy empire, shall exercise the same authority during the vacancy of the empire for the region of the Saxon law, under the same conditions as expressed above.

2. The emperor or king of the Romans must appear before the count palatine of the Rhine, when he is cited by any-

one, but the count palatine shall try such cases only at the imperial diet when the emperor or king is present.

¹ In the investiture of a vassal with a fief certain symbols were used. Among other articles that were used in this way when investing the secular tenants-in-chief was the spear, to which it became customary to affix a small standard or flag, as a symbol of the regalia which were conferred with the fief. Eventually this was the only symbol used in such cases, and hence the secular fiefs which were held directly from the king came to be called "Fahnlehen," or "flag fiefs."

CHAPTER VI.

(Repeats the statements about the priority of the king of Bohemia among the secular princes.)

CHAPTER VII.

THE SUCCESSION OF THE ELECTORAL PRINCES.

1. . . . It is known and recognized throughout the world, that the king of Bohemia, the count palatine of the Rhine, the duke of Saxony, and the margrave of Brandenburg, by virtue of the principalities which they possess, have the right to vote in the election of the king of the Romans along with their coelectors, the ecclesiastical princes, and that they with the ecclesiastical princes are the true and legal electoral princes of the holy empire. In order to prevent disputes arising among the sons of these secular electoral princes in regard to the electoral authority and vote, which would be productive of delays dangerous to the state and other evils, we have fixed the succession by the present law which shall be valid forever. On the death of one of the secular electoral princes his right, voice, and vote in the election shall descend to his first-born son who is a layman; if the son has died before this, to the son's first-born son who is a layman. If the first-born lay son of the elector has died without legitimate lay sons, by virtue of the present law the succession shall go to the elector's next oldest lay son and then to his heirs, and so on according to the law of primogeniture. In case the

heir is under age the paternal uncle of the heir shall act as
guardian and administrator until the heir comes of age, which
shall be, in the case of electoral princes, at eighteen years.
Then the guardian shall immediately surrender to him the
electoral vote and authority and all the possessions of the
electorate.

2.   When any electorate falls vacant for lack of heirs, the
emperor or king of the Romans shall have the power to dispose of it, as if it reverted to the empire, saving the rights,
privileges, and customs of the kingdom of Bohemia, according to which the inhabitants of that kingdom have the right
to elect their king in case of a vacancy.

CHAPTER VIII.
THE IMMUNITY OF THE KINGDOM OF BOHEMIA AND ITS INHABITANTS.

Our predecessors, the emperors and kings of the Romans,
have conceded to our ancestors, the kings of Bohemia, and
to the kingdom and crown . . .   that no prince, baron,
noble, knight, client, citizen, or other person of the kingdom,
of any station, dignity, rank, or condition, should be cited,
haled, or summoned before any tribunal outside of the kingdom, or before any judge except the king of Bohemia and
the judges of his court.   We hereby renew and confirm this
privilege, custom, and concession by our royal authority and
power, and decree that no one of the aforesaid, prince, baron,
noble, knight, client, citizen, or peasant, or any other person,
shall be required to appear or answer before any tribunal
outside of the kingdom of Bohemia, in any case, civil, criminal, or mixed. . . .

CHAPTER IX.
MINES OF GOLD, SILVER, AND OTHER METALS.

We decree, by this present law, that our successors, the
kings of Bohemia, and all the electoral princes, ecclesiastical
and secular, shall hold and possess with full rights, all mines

of gold, silver, tin, copper, iron, lead, or other metals, and all salt works, both those already discovered and those which shall be discovered in the future, situated within their lands, domains, and dependencies. They shall also have authority to tax Jews, the right to collect tolls already in force, and all other rights which they or their predecessors have possessed to the present day.

CHAPTER X.

COINAGE.

1. We also decree that our successors, the future kings of Bohemia, shall possess and exercise in peace the rights of coinage of gold and silver, in all parts of their dominions and of the lands belonging to their subjects, in such form and manner as they may determine: a right which is known to have belonged to our predecessors, the former kings of Bohemia.

2. We also grant to the future kings of Bohemia forever the right to buy, purchase, or receive as gift or in payment, any lands, castles, possessions, or goods from any princes, magnates, counts, or other persons; such lands and property to remain, however, in their former legal status, and to pay the customary dues and services to the empire.

3. We extend this right by the present law to all the electoral princes, ecclesiastical and secular, and to their legal heirs, under the same conditions and form.

CHAPTER XI.

THE IMMUNITIES OF THE PRINCES.

1. We decree also that no count, baron, noble, vassal, burggrave, knight, client, citizen, burgher, or other subject of the churches of Cologne, Mainz, or Trier, of whatever status, condition or rank, shall be cited, haled, or summoned to any authority before any tribunal outside of the territories, boundaries, and limits of these churches and their depend-

encies, or before any judge, except the archbishops and their judges. . . . We refuse to hear appeals based upon the authority of others over the subjects of these princes; if these princes are accused by their subjects of injustice, appeal shall lie to the imperial diet, and shall be heard there and nowhere else. . . .

2. We extend this right by the present law to the secular electoral princes, the count palatine of the Rhine, the duke of Saxony, and the margrave of Brandenburg, and to their heirs, successors, and subjects forever.

CHAPTER XII.
ASSEMBLIES OF THE PRINCES.

. . . It has been decided in the general diet held at Nürnburg with the electoral princes, ecclesiastical and secular, and other princes and magnates, by their advice and with their consent, that in the future, the electoral princes shall meet every year in some city of the empire four weeks after Easter; this year they are to meet at that date in the imperial city of Metz; on that occasion, and on every meeting thereafter, the place of assembling for the following year shall be fixed by us with the advice and consent of the princes. This ordinance shall remain in force as long as it shall be pleasing to us and to the princes; and as long as it is in effect, we shall furnish the princes with safe-conduct for that assembly, going, staying, and returning. . . .

CHAPTER XIII.
THE REVOCATION OF PRIVILEGES.

We hereby decree and determine that the liberties, jurisdiction, rights, honors, and authority of the electoral princes, ecclesiastical or secular, or of any one of them, ought not to be and shall not be in any way diminished by any privileges or charters of rights, graces, immunities, customs, etc., granted or to be granted by us or our predecessors to any person of whatsoever rank, station, or dignity, or to any city, town or territory, even if it is expressly stated in such privileges and charters that they are not revocable. In so far as any such privileges do diminish the liberties, jurisdiction, rights, honors, or authority of the said electoral princes, we hereby revoke them and decree by our imperial authority that they are to be regarded as revoked and void.

CHAPTER XIV.

THE FORFEITING OF FIEFS.

In many regions it is becoming the practice for vassals and feudatories to renounce and resign verbally and without due notice the fiefs and benefices which they hold of their lords, and then to declare themselves free from their allegiance and to seize the fiefs under pretext of war. Therefore we decree hereby that such renunciation shall not be valid unless it is genuine and made with the condition that the fiefs and benefices shall revert immediately to the lords from whom they are held; those who have renounced their allegiance shall never disturb or molest their lords in the possession of these fiefs. Any subject violating this decree shall lose his fiefs and benefices, shall be branded with infamy, and placed under the imperial ban; no one shall ever give him a fief or a benefice, and any grant or investiture made to him shall be void.

CHAPTER XV.

CONSPIRACIES.

We reprobate, condemn, and declare void all detestable and illegal conspiracies, confederations, and societies, which are or shall be made by cities or by persons of any rank or station, under color of any pretext whatever, inside or outside of cities, between city and city, person and person, or city and person, without the consent of the lords of the persons or territories; for it is well known that such conspiracies are declared illegal and void by the laws of our predecessors, the august emperors. We except from this condemnation such confederations and leagues as are entered into by princes, cities, and others for the preservation of the peace of their lands; these shall remain in force until we have decreed otherwise. If any person shall violate this decree and the ancient laws against conspiracies, besides incurring the regular penalties he shall be branded with infamy and shall be fined ten pounds of gold; cities and corporations guilty of a similar crime shall be fined 100 pounds of gold, half of which shall go to the imperial treasury, and half to the lord of the district, and they shall be deprived of the liberties and privileges which they have received from the empire.

CHAPTER XVI.

PFAHLBURGHERS.

The complaint has frequently been made of late that certain citizens and subjects of princes, barons, and other lords, in order to escape from their proper subjection, have had themselves received as citizens in other cities, and thus, while dwelling in the lands, cities, towns, or regions of the lords whom they have deserted, they claim to enjoy the liberty and immunity of the other cities, and to be freed from the lord's authority, because of that citizenship; these are the persons who are called in the vulgar tongue in Germany "pfahl-burghers." Now since fraud and deceit cannot constitute a legal defense for any one, we hereby decree by our imperial authority and by the advice of the electoral princes, ecclesiastical and secular, that from this day forth within all the lands of the empire such citizens shall not enjoy the rights and liberties of the cities, unless they have actually moved into them and established their homes there, making their real residence and domicile in the cities and bearing their share of the debts, burdens, and municipal taxes. If any such persons are or shall be admitted into cities contrary to this edict, the admission shall be void of effect, and the persons shall not profit by the laws and liberties of those cities, in spite of any laws, privileges, and customs to the contrary, all of which, as far as they contradict this decree, we declare to be void; and the lords shall retain their rights over the persons and goods of their subjects who have deserted them in this manner. Those who receive the subjects of other lords on these terms contrary to our law, and who do not drive them away within one month after receiving notice of their presence, shall be fined for each such violation, 100 pounds of gold, half of which shall go to the imperial treasury and half to the lords of the deserters.

CHAPTER XVII.

RENUNCIATION OF ALLEGIANCE.

If any person renounces his allegiance or alliance without due notice and in a place where he does not have his residence, even if he thinks he has just grounds, we declare that he shall not have the right to inflict injury or violence upon those from whom he has in this manner withdrawn. And since fraud and deceit cannot constitute legal defence, we hereby declare that renunciation of this sort from the society or association of any lord or person shall not be valid, and may not be used as pretext for making war, unless the renunciation has been announced to those who are concerned personally or publicly in the place where they have their regular residence, three full days before, and the notification can be proved by good witnesses. Whoever shall make war on another without making renunciation in this form, shall be branded with infamy, just as if he had never made any renunciation, and he shall be punished as a traitor by all judges. We forbid and condemn also all unjust wars and strife, all unjust burning, wasting, and rapine, all unusual and unjust tolls and exactions for safe-conduct, under penalties fixed by the laws of the empire.

CHAPTER XVIII.

FORM OF THE LETTER OF NOTIFICATION.

"To you, the illustrious and magnificent margrave of Brandenburg, archchamberlain of the holy empire, our fellow-elector and dear friend, we give notice by these presents of the approaching election of the king of the Romans, and we summon you according to the duty of your office to come to that election at the regular place within three months from —— —— (date), or to send one or more representatives or agents with sufficient authority, in order to consider with your fellow-electors and agree upon the choice of a king of the Romans and future emperor; to remain there until the election is completed; and to do such other things as are required by the laws of the empire in this matter. Otherwise, in spite of your absence, we shall proceed with our fellow-electors to carry out the aforesaid business, as the authority of the imperial laws empowers us."

CHAPTER XIX.

FORM OF THE CREDENTIALS FOR REPRESENTATIVES OR AGENTS OF THE ELECTORAL PRINCES, SENT IN THEIR BEHALF TO THE ELECTION.

We (name), by the grace of God (title), (office) of the holy empire. Be it known to all by these presents . . . that we have constituted our faithful subjects (names) our true, legal, and special representatives and agents, to treat with our fellow-princes and electors, ecclesiastical and secular, and to agree and decide with them concerning a suitable person to be elected king of the Romans; to be present, deliberate, name, consent to, and elect the king of the Romans and future emperor in our name and for us; and to take the necessary, due, and accustomed oaths upon our soul, in regard to the aforesaid things; to appoint substitutes to do any and all things which may be necessary, useful, or convenient to the aforesaid consideration, nomination, deliberation, and election, and to do anything which we would be able to do if

we were present in person at the election, even if these things
be special and peculiar things not mentioned specifically in
the above. We will accept and ratify everything done by the
aforesaid representatives or their substitutes.

CHAPTER XX.
THE UNITY OF THE ELECTORAL PRINCIPALITIES.

It is known that the right of voting for the king of the
Romans and future emperor inheres in certain principalities,
the possessors of which have also the other offices, rights, and
dignities belonging to these principalities. We decree, therefore, by the present law that the electoral vote and other
offices, dignities, and appurtenances shall always be so united
and conjoined that the possessor of one of these principalities
shall possess and enjoy the electoral vote and all the offices,
dignities, and appurtenances belonging to it, that he shall be
regarded as electoral prince, that he and no other shall be
accepted by the other electoral princes and admitted to participation in the election and all other acts which regard the
honor and advantage of the holy empire, and that no one of
these rights, which are and ought to be inseparable, shall ever
be taken from him. And if through error or by any other
means any decision or sentence is issued by any judge against
the present law, it shall be void.

CHAPTER XXI.
THE PRECEDENCE AMONG THE ARCHBISHOPS.

We have defined above the location of the seats of the
ecclesiastical electors in the council, at the table, and on
other occasions, when the emperor meets with the electoral
princes, but we have thought it well to indicate also the order
of precedence in procession and march. Therefore we decree
by the present imperial edict that whenever the emperor or
king of the Romans meets with the electoral princes, and the
insignia are borne before him in procession, the archbishop

of Trier shall march directly before the emperor or king, no one being between them except the bearers of the insignia; and when the emperor or king marches without the insignia the archbishop shall immediately precede him. The other two archbishops [of Mainz and Cologne] shall march on either side of the archbishop of Trier, their position on the right or the left being determined by the region in which the ceremony is held, as described above.

CHAPTER XXII.

THE ORDER OF PRECEDENCE AMONG THE SECULAR ELECTORAL PRINCES, AND THE BEARERS OF THE INSIGNIA.

We also determine by the present decree the precedence among the secular electoral princes as follows: When the electoral princes march in procession with the emperor or king of the Romans in any of the ceremonies of the imperial diet and the insignia are borne before him, the duke of Saxony shall precede the emperor or king, marching between him and the archbishop of Trier, and bearing the imperial or royal sword; the count palatine of the Rhine shall march at the right of the duke of Saxony with the imperial globe, and the margrave of Brandenburg at the left with the sceptre; the king of Bohemia shall follow immediately behind the emperor or king.

CHAPTER XXIII.

BENEDICTIONS OF THE ARCHBISHOPS IN THE PRESENCE OF THE EMPEROR

When the mass is celebrated in the presence of the emperor or king, the archbishops of Mainz, Trier, and Cologne, or any two of them, being present, the archbishops shall perform the services on the different days in turn in the order of their consecration, each one on his day officiating in the confession which is said before the mass, in the presenting of the gospel to be kissed, in the giving of peace after the *Agnus Dei*, in the benedictions after the mass and before meals, and in

returning thanks after meals.   Each archbishop on his day
should invite the other archbishops to participate in the
services, to set a good example to men by honoring one
another.

PART II.

(Published at Metz. December 25, 1356.)

CHAPTER XXIV.

1.   If any person shall have joined in a conspiracy or
taken oath to join in a conspiracy with any other persons,
princes, knights, or private persons, to slay one of the
electoral princes of the holy empire, he shall be judged guilty
of offence against the majesty of the emperor, and shall be
executed, and all his goods shall be forfeited to the royal
treasury; for we regard the electoral princes as members of
our own body, and visit offences against them with the same
severity as against ourself.   [The rest of the chapter is devoted to the effects of the confiscation and attainder upon
children and heirs of criminals, etc.]

CHAPTER XXV.

If it is proper that the integrity of the ordinary principalities should be preserved, for the better securing of justice
and peace for the subjects, it is even more important that the
great principalities of the electoral princes should be kept
intact in their domains, honors, and rights.   Therefore we
determine and decree by this imperial edict that the lands,
districts, fiefs, and other possessions of the great principalities, namely, the kingdom of Bohemia, the palatinate of
the Rhine, the duchy of Saxony, and the mark of Brandenburg, should never under any circumstances be separated,
divided, or dismembered.   In order that they may be preserved in their integrity, the first-born son in each case shall
succeed to them, and shall exercise ownership and dominion

in them, unless he be incapacitated for ruling by reason of imbecility, or other notorious defect. In that case, he shall not be allowed to inherit, but the succession shall go to the nearest male lay heir on the paternal side.

CHAPTER XXVI.

1.   On the day of the imperial diet, all the electoral princes shall proceed to the imperial palace about the first hour, and shall assist the emperor or king in donning the insignia; then they shall proceed on horseback to the place of the diet with the emperor or king, preserving the order of precedence indicated above. The archchancellor of the kingdom in which the diet is held shall bear the seals of the empire or kingdom upon a silver staff; the secular princes shall bear the sceptre, globe, and sword, as indicated above; the German and Lombard crowns shall be borne, in this order, by princes of inferior rank named for this office by the emperor, immediately before the archbishop of Trier, who precedes the emperor, now wearing the imperial crown.

2.   The empress or queen, clad in her insignia, shall also proceed to the place of the diet with her officials and ladies, taking her place behind the emperor or king and behind the king of Bohemia, who follows immediately after the emperor or king.

CHAPTER XXVII.

THE OFFICES OF THE ELECTORAL PRINCES AT THE DIET.

1.   After the emperor or king is seated on his throne, the duke of Saxony shall appear before the place of the diet on horseback with a silver staff and a silver measure, each of the value of twelve marks in silver, and shall fill his measure with oats from a heap that has been placed before the building in which the diet is held. This heap of oats shall be as high as the breast of the horse on which he rides. He shall then give this measure of oats to the first servant that ap-

proaches. Then he shall thrust his staff into the heap of
oats and go away, and the vice-marshal, the count of
Pappenheim, or in his absence the marshal of the court, shall
distribute the oats. After the emperor or king has taken his
place at the table the ecclesiastical electors, supported by
other prelates, shall stand before the table and one of them
shall pronounce the blessing, according to the order of precedence established above; after the benediction the chancellor of the court shall present the seals to the archbishops,
and they shall bear them to the emperor, all three touching
with their hands the staff on which they are suspended, the
archchancellor of the kingdom in which the diet is held
marching in the middle and the other two on either side of
him. They shall lay the seals reverently before the emperor
or king, who shall immediately return them to the archbishops. The archchancellor of the kingdom in which the
diet is held shall wear the great seal of the empire about
his neck during the dinner and until he returns to his abode.
The staff, which shall be of silver of the value of twelve
marks, and the seals, shall be handed over to the chancellor
of the court. The archbishop who bears the great seal shall
return this also to the chancellor of the court by one of his
own servants, mounted on a horse which shall be presented
to the chancellor of the court as a perquisite of his office and
as a token of the love of the archchancellor.

2. The margrave of Brandenburg, the archchamberlain
of the empire, shall approach on horseback, bearing water in
silver basins of the value of twelve marks, and a beautifully
embroidered napkin, and shall dismount and offer the emperor or king water to wash his hands.

3. The count palatine of the Rhine shall approach on
horseback, bearing four silver dishes, each of the value of
three marks, filled with food, and shall dismount and carry
them in and place them on the table before the emperor or
king.

4. Then the king of Bohemia, the archcupbearer of the empire, shall ride up, bearing a silver cup or goblet, of the value of twelve marks, filled with wine and water mixed, and shall dismount and offer the goblet to the emperor or king to drink.

5. When the offices have been performed by the secular electoral princes, the vice-marshal, the count of Falkenstein, shall receive the horse and the silver basins of the margrave of Brandenburg; the master of the kitchen, the count of Nortemberg, shall receive the horse and the dishes of the count palatine of the Rhine; the vice-cupbearer, the count of Limburg, shall receive the horse and the goblet of the king of Bohemia; the vice-marshal, the count of Pappenheim, shall receive the horse, the staff, and the measure of the duke of Saxony. If these officials are not present, the ordinary officials of the court shall receive these gifts in their places.

CHAPTER XXVIII.
(Description of the banqueting table, etc.)

CHAPTER XXIX.

1. We have learned from records and traditions, that it has been the custom in the past to hold the election of the king of the Romans in Frankfort, the coronation in Aachen, and the first diet in Nürnberg; therefore we decree that in the future these ceremonies shall be held in these places, unless there shall be some legitimate obstacle. . . .

CHAPTER XXX.

THE RIGHTS OF THE OFFICIALS OF THE COURT WHEN THE PRINCES OF THE EMPIRE RECEIVE THEIR FIEFS.

(Special fees paid by the princes to these officials.)

CHAPTER XXXI.

(Requiring the secular electors to learn the Italian and Slavic languages.)

160 a AND 160 b. THE ACQUISITION OF THE MARK OF BRANDENBURG BY THE HOHENZOLLERN FAMILY, 1411.

160 a. THE CITIES OF THE MARK MAKE COMPLAINTS TO SIGISMUND, 1411. (GERMAN.)

Magdeburger Schöppenchronik, edited by Janicke, in Chroniken der deutschen Städte, VII, pp. 331 f.

The importance of the acquisition of the mark of Brandenburg by a member of the Hohenzollern family could not at that time have been foreseen. The mark, being a great sandy marsh, did not seem a valuable possession, and the nobles, especially the great von Quitzow family, were devastating it with their feuds. The cities, here as everywhere else in Germany, were for order and peace. It seems to have been due in part to their complaints and appeals to Sigismund that he chose the able and vigorous Frederick of Hohenzollern, burggrave of Nürnberg, as governor of the mark. This was an important event in the fortunes of the Hohenzollern family. Frederick and his successors managed their affairs so well that Brandenburg became the basis on which the power of the family was built up.

In the same year that Jost, the margrave, died, the king of Hungary, Sigismund, who had been elected king of the Romans, sent messengers to the cities of the old and new marks to Magdeburg and ordered them to come to Berlin on the Sunday of Midlent to hear his will concerning them. The king's representatives, John Waldaw, *præpositus* of the church at Berlin, and Wend von Eylenburg, met the aldermen of the cities at Berlin at the appointed time and asked them: "Since Jost, the margrave, is dead and the king is the hereditary lord of the land, are you willing to recognize his lordship over you and to support him?" And the aldermen answered him that they were. The cities and the nobles of the land were then ordered to come to Hungary and do homage to the king on the next St. Walpurgis day (May 1). The cities sent representatives from among their aldermen, but none of the nobles of the land came except Jaspar Gans von Putlitz. They did homage to the king and remained with him so long that they did not reach home until St. James's day

(July 25). They complained to the king about the wretched condition of the land and its troubles, and especially about the von Quitzows and certain other nobles and their supporters who controlled the land by means of the castles of which they had got possession, and who were doing great damage to the land and were carrying on war with the neighboring lords and their lands. They besought the king to take measures to prevent such war, violence, and damage. The king then said to the aldermen that he himself could not come into the mark because he had been chosen king of the Romans, and he must therefore endeavor to rule the realm and to restore unity to the church [i.e., end the schism] ; but he would send them a governor who would be able to help them. He then named the noble prince, Frederick, burggrave of Nürnberg, as the governor of the mark. This rejoiced the aldermen very much and restored their confidence. They were well pleased, and left the king and joyfully returned home.

160b. SIGISMUND ORDERS THE PEOPLE OF THE MARK TO RECEIVE FREDERICK OF HOHENZOLLERN AS THEIR GOVERNOR, 1412. (GERMAN.)

Riedel, Codex Diplomaticus Brandenburgensis, III, p. 178.

We, Sigismund, etc. Dear and faithful subjects: We hereby inform you again that we have made the noble Frederick, burggrave of Nürnberg, our dear uncle, counsellor, and prince, the head and governor of the whole mark of Brandenburg. We have given him letters to that effect. And when your representatives came to Ofen and did homage to us on behalf of the nobles and cities of the mark we orally commanded them to receive the said Frederick. Therefore we again strictly command you to receive him without any delay or opposition and to render him the homage which you owe us as your hereditary margrave, and pay homage to him according to the instructions which are contained in the letters which we have given him. He will confirm and renew all your liberties, rights, good customs, and charters, and preserve their validity just as I have done. Given at Ofen, 1412, etc.

V. THE CHURCH FROM 1250 TO 1500

161. BULL OF NICHOLAS III CONDEMNING ALL HERETICS, 1280.

Bullarium Romanum, III, ii, pp. 26 f.

In spite of the vigorous efforts of the popes to destroy heresy (see nos. 116–118) and all that the inquisitors could do, heresies increased. This bull of Nicholas III shows that more vigorous measures were being used.

Nicholas, etc. We hereby excommunicate and anathematize all heretics, the Cathari, Patareni, the Poor Men of Lyon, Passageni, Josepheni, the Arnoldists, Speronists, and all others by whatever name they may be called. (1) When condemned by the church, they shall be given over to the secular judge to be punished. Clergymen shall be degraded before being punished. (2) If any, after being seized, repent and wish to do proper penance, they shall be imprisoned for life. (3) We condemn as heretics all who believe the errors of heretics. (4) We decree that all who receive, defend, or aid heretics, shall be excommunicated. If anyone remains under excommunication a year and a day, he shall be proscribed. (5) He shall not be eligible to hold a public office, or to vote in the election of officials. (6) His word shall not be accepted. (7) He can not serve as a witness nor can he make a will. (8) He shall not succeed to an inheritance. (9) He cannot bring suit against anyone, but suit may be brought against him. (10) If he is a judge, his sentences shall be invalid, and he shall not be permitted to hear cases. (11) If he is an advocate, he shall not be permitted to perform the duties of his office. (12) If he is a notary, the documents which he draws up shall be invalid and con-

309

demned with him. (13) If he is a clergyman, he shall be deposed from his office and deprived of every benefice. (14) Those who associate with the excommunicated shall themselves be excommunicated and properly punished. (15) If those who are suspected of heresy can not prove their innocence, they shall be excommunicated. If they remain under the ban of excommunication a year, they shall be condemned as heretics. (16) They shall have no right of appeal. (17) If judges, advocates, or notaries serve them in an official way, they shall be deprived of their office. (18) The clergy shall not administer to them the sacraments, nor give them a part of the alms. If they do, they shall be deprived of their office and they can never be restored to it without the special permission of the pope. Whoever grants them Christian burial shall be excommunicated until he makes proper satisfaction. He shall not be absolved until he has with his own hands publicly dug up their bodies and cast them forth, and no one shall ever be buried in the same place. (19) We prohibit all laymen to discuss matters of the catholic faith. If anyone does so, he shall be excommunicated. (20) Whoever knows of heretics, or those who are holding secret meetings, or those who do not conform in all respects to the orthodox faith, shall make it known to his confessor, or to someone else who will bring it to the knowledge of the bishop or the inquisitor. If he does not do so, he shall be excommunicated. (21) Heretics and all who receive, support, or aid them, and all their children to the second generation, shall not be admitted to an ecclesiastical office or benefice. If any such have been admitted, their admission is illegal and invalid. For we now deprive all such of their benefices forever, and they shall never be admitted to others. If parents with their children have been freed [from excommunication], and their parents afterwards return to the heresy, their children are, by their parents' act, again brought under excommunication.

162. The Bull "Clericis Laicos" of Boniface VIII, 1298.

Tosti, Histoire de Boniface VIII, I, pp. 395 ff.

In theory all ecclesiastical persons and possessions were immune from secular taxation, but the pope frequently permitted temporal rulers to levy a tax on them for the aid of the state in times of public necessity. At the command of the pope such taxes had been assessed (1) to carry on the crusades (the Saladin tithe), (2) to make war on Frederick II, (3) to put down the heresy of the Albigenses, (4) to resist Peter of Aragon when he attacked Sicily, etc. It frequently happened that the large sums raised for the crusades went into the king's treasury, and were spent for other things. The kings, especially of England and France, found this a very convenient way of raising money. The immediate cause of the publication of this bull was the heavy assessments which the kings of England and France had just made on their clergy. Boniface recognized that the immunities and liberties of the church were thereby being destroyed. In spite of the protests of both pope and clergy, neither king restored the money or ceased to levy taxes. New names for them were so skilfully invented, and such arguments were used, that the clergy could not refuse to pay without seeming to be disloyal and unpatriotic. Boniface VIII issued this bull to put a stop to the taxation which he regarded as the pillaging of the churches. It must be observed that the pope does not prohibit such taxes altogether. He preserves his authority and the immunities of the church by retaining the right to sanction whatever taxes may be assessed on the clergy and the possessions of the church.

The kings of both England and France were engaged in policies which necessitated large expenditures, and hence they were in need of money. Besides, they were trying to centralize all authority in their hands and consequently found these ecclesiastical immunities a great obstacle in their way. We have here an evidence that the national governments had begun their long struggle against the temporal authority of the pope, for the question as to whether the king may tax the church and clergy was one phase of this struggle.

It is said that in times past laymen practiced great violence against the clergy, and our experience clearly shows that they are doing so at present, since they are not content to keep within the limits prescribed for them, but strive to do that which is prohibited and illegal. And they pay no attention to the fact that they are forbidden to exercise authority over the clergy and ecclesiastical persons and their possessions. But they are laying heavy burdens on bishops, churches, and clergy, both regular and secular, by taxing them, levying contributions on them, and extorting the half, or the tenth, or the twentieth, or some other part of their income and possessions. They are striving in many ways to reduce the clergy to servitude and to subject them to their own sway. And we grieve to say it, but some bishops and clergy, fearing where they should not, and seeking a temporary peace, and fearing more to offend man than God, submit, improvidently rather than rashly, to these abuses [and pay the sums demanded], without receiving the papal permission. Wishing to prevent these evils, with the counsel of our brethren, and by our apostolic authority, we decree that if any bishops or clergy, regular or secular, of any grade, condition, or rank, shall pay, or promise, or consent to pay to laymen any contributions, or taxes, or the tenth, or the twentieth, or the hundredth, or any other part of their income or of their possessions, or of their value, real or estimated, under the name of aid, or loan, or subvention, or subsidy, or gift, or under any other name or pretext, without the permission of the pope, they shall, by the very act, incur the sentence of excommunication. And we also decree that emperors, kings, princes, dukes, counts, barons, *podestà, capitanei,* and governors of cities, fortresses, and of all other places everywhere, by whatever names such governors may be called, and all other persons of whatever power, condition, or rank, who shall impose, demand, or receive such taxes, or shall seize, or cause to be seized, the property of churches or of the clergy, which has been deposited in sacred buildings, or shall receive such property after it has been seized, or shall give aid, counsel, or support in such things either openly or secretly, shall by that very act incur the sentence of excom-

munication. We also put under the interdict all communities
which shall be culpable in such matters. And under the
threat of deposition we strictly command all bishops and
clergy, in accordance with their oath of obedience, not to submit to such taxes without the express permission of the pope.
They shall not pay anything under the pretext that they had
already promised or agreed to do so before the prohibition
came to their knowledge. They shall not pay, nor shall the
above-named laymen receive anything in any way. And if
the ones shall pay, or the others receive anything, they shall
by that very act fall under the sentence of excommunication.
From this sentence of excommunication and interdict no one
can be absolved except in the moment of death, without the
authority and special permission of the pope. . . .

·163. BONIFACE VIII ANNOUNCES THE JUBILEE YEAR, 1300.

Tosti, Histoire de Boniface VIII, II, pp. 467 f.

Boniface, bishop, etc. We know that in times past gen-
erous indulgences and remissions of sins have been granted
those who should come to the illustrious churches of the
prince of the apostles [St. Peter's in Rome]. Our office
requires us to desire and most gladly to procure the salvation
of all, and so, regarding all such remissions and indulgences
as valid, by our apostolic authority we confirm, approve, and
renew them, and reinforce them with this present writing.
In order therefore that the most blessed apostles, Peter and
Paul, may be more highly honored in that the faithful devoutly visit their churches, and that those who do so may feel
that they are filled with spiritual gifts, we, through the mercy
of omnipotent God and trusting in the merits and authority
of his apostles [Peter and Paul], at the advice of our brethren
and in the fulness of our apostolic power, grant the fullest and
broadest forgiveness of all their sins to all who, during the
whole of this 1300th year, and to all who, in every hundredth

year to come, shall reverently come to these churches and truly repent and confess. We decree that those Romans who wish to participate in this indulgence shall visit these churches at least once a day for thirty days, either consecutively or at intervals, and all who are not Romans shall visit them in the same way for fifteen days. But the more devoutly and frequently anyone visits them, the more surely will he deserve and obtain the indulgence.

164. THE BULL "UNAM SANCTAM" OF BONIFACE VIII, 1302.

Raynaldus, anno 1302, sec. 13; Revue des Questions Historiques, vol. 46, pp. 255 f.

Boniface VIII had become involved in a bitter struggle with Philip IV of France over the question of sovereignty. Boniface went so far as to summon the French clergy to a council at Rome for the purpose of dictating a settlement of all the disorders in France. In reply to this, Philip IV assembled his states-general and assured himself of the almost unanimous support of his people against the pope, and sent him an embassy with a refusal and a warning. The pope was not disconcerted by this, but plied the ambassadors with the most extravagant statements of his secular power. On the heels of this he published this famous bull, *Unam sanctam*, which is the classic mediæval expression of the papal claims to universal temporal sovereignty. It is an excellent example of mediæval reasoning.

The true faith compels us to believe that there is one holy catholic apostolic church, and this we firmly believe and plainly confess. And outside of her there is no salvation or remission of sins, as the Bridegroom says in the Song of Solomon: "My dove, my undefiled is but one; she is the only one of her mother, she is the choice one of her that bare her" [Song of Sol. 6:9]; which represents the one mystical body, whose head is Christ, but the head of Christ is God [1 Cor. 11.3]. In this church there is "one Lord, one faith, one baptism" [Eph. 4:5]. For in the time of the flood there was only one ark, that of Noah, prefiguring the one church, and it was "finished above in one cubit" [Gen. 6:16], and had but one helmsman and master, namely, Noah. And we read that all things on the earth outside of this ark were destroyed. This church we venerate as the only one, since the Lord said by the prophet: "Deliver my soul from the sword; my darling from the power of the dog" [Ps. 22:20]. He prayed for his soul, that is, for himself, the head; and at the same time for the body; and he named his body, that is, the one church, because there is but one Bridegroom [cf. John 3:29], and because of the unity of the faith, of the sacraments, and of his love for the church. This is the seamless robe of the Lord which was not rent but parted by lot [John 19:23]. Therefore there is one body of the one and only church, and one head, not two heads, as if the church were a monster. And this head is Christ and his vicar, Peter and his successor; for the Lord himself said to Peter: "Feed my sheep" [John 21:16]. And he said "my sheep," in general, not these or those sheep in particular; from which it is clear that all were committed to him. If therefore Greeks or anyone else say that they are not subject to Peter and his successors, they thereby necessarily confess that they are not of the sheep of Christ. For the Lord says in the Gospel of John, that there is one fold and only one shepherd [John 10:16]. By the words of the gospel we are taught that the two swords, namely, the spiritual authorrity and the temporal are in the power of the church. For when the apostles said "Here are two swords" [Luke 22:38]—that is, in the church, since it was the apostles who were speaking—the Lord did not answer, "It is too much," but "It is enough." Whoever denies that the temporal sword is in the power of Peter does not properly understand the word of the Lord when he said: "Put up thy sword into the sheath" [John 18:11]. Both swords, therefore, the spiritual and the temporal, are in the power of the church. The former is to be used by the church, the latter for the church; the one by the hand of the priest, the other by the hand of kings and knights, but at the com-

mand and permission of the priest.   Moreover, it is necessary
for one sword to be under the other, and the temporal
authority to be subjected to the spiritual; for the apostle
says, "For there is no power but of God: and the powers that
are ordained of God" [Rom. 13:1]; but they would not be
ordained [*i.e.,* arranged or set in order; note the play on the
words] unless one were subjected to the other, and, as it were,
the lower made the higher by the other.   For, according to St.
Dionysius, it is a law of divinity that the lowest is made the
highest through the intermediate.   According to the law of
the universe all things are not equally and directly reduced to
order, but the lowest are fitted into their order through the
intermediate, and the lower through the higher.[1]   And we
must necessarily admit that the spiritual power surpasses any
earthly power in dignity and honor, because spiritual things
surpass temporal things.   We clearly see that this is true
from the paying of tithes, from the benediction, from the
sanctification, from the receiving of the power, and from
the governing of these things.   For the truth itself declares
that the spiritual power must establish the temporal power
and pass judgment on it if it is not good.   Thus the prophecy
of Jeremiah concerning the church and the ecclesiastical
power is fulfilled: "See, I have this day set thee over the
nations and over the kingdoms, to root out, and to pull down,
and to destroy, and to throw down, to build, and to plant"
[Jer. 1:10].   Therefore if the temporal power errs, it will be
judged by the spiritual power, and if the lower spiritual
power errs, it will be judged by its superior.   But if the
highest spiritual power errs, it can not be judged by men, but
by God alone.   For the apostle says: "But he that is spiritual
judgeth all things, yet he himself is judged of no man"
[1 Cor. 2:15].   Now this authority, although it is given to
man and exercised through man, is not human, but divine.
For it was given by the word of the Lord to Peter, and the
rock was made firm to him and his successors, in Christ him-

self, whom he had confessed. For the Lord said to Peter:
"Whatsoever thou shalt bind on earth shall be bound in
heaven: and whatsoever thou shalt loose on earth shall be
loosed in heaven" [Matt. 16:19]. Therefore whosoever
resisteth this power thus ordained of God, resisteth the ordinance of God [Rom. 13:2], unless there are two principles
(beginnings), as Manichæus pretends there are. But this we
judge to be false and heretical. For Moses says that, not in
the beginnings, but in the beginning [note the play on words],
God created the heaven and the earth [Gen. 1:1]. We therefore declare, say, and affirm that submission on the part of
every man to the bishop of Rome is altogether necessary for
his salvation.

1 This is an example of scholastic reasoning. While obscure, it
seems to be a general argument for, or explanation of, the existence
of order in the universe.

165. Conclusions Drawn by Marsilius of Padua from his "Defensor Pacis."

Marsilius of Padua, Defensor Pacis, Part III, ch. ii; Goldast, Monarchia Sancti
Romani Imperii, II, pp. 309 ff.

The *Defensor Pacis* is a treatise on politics written by Marsilius,
or Marsiglio, a canon of the church of Padua, in 1324. His authority
is the *Politics* of Aristotle, which Marsilius knew from a Latin summary current in the Middle Age. From this as a basis he constructs
a political theory and tests the existing institutions by it. The
work is divided into three parts; the first two form a diffuse essay,
and the last is a summary of his arguments in the form of forty-two
conclusiones, which are translated here, because they give in a concise
form the essential points of his theory. As regards the political
situation of his own time, the general tendency of the treatise is
imperial and anti-papal; it was used by Ludwig IV [the Bavarian]
in his conflict with the Avignon popes. Hence it was regarded by
the papal party as unorthodox and heretical. In the bull of John
XXII, 1327, five statements were selected and condemned as heresies
(see no. 166). His views on the origin and nature of the state are
Aristotelian: the state is a perfected community existing for the
good of the people; the supreme power resides in the body of the

citizens, who make the laws, and choose the form of government, etc. The prince rules by the authority of the whole body of citizens. To this body Marsilius gives the name *legislator*. The elective monarchy is the form of government preferred by Marsilius, whose ideal state thus corresponds in theory with the holy Roman empire. His views on the relation of the state and the church are very different from the views common in the Middle Age. The supreme institution is the state which has established the priesthood or the church to look after the spiritual welfare of its citizens. Hence the state has the right to control the church, but the church has not the corresponding right to control the state. The treatment of the church in itself is also interesting. Marsilius attacks the Petrine theory and the whole papal structure. All bishops are equal in religious authority, deriving their power immediately from Christ. If one priest or bishop is placed over another it is for the purpose of organization, and the authority of the superior is derived from the state. He also asserts that within the church the supreme authority is not the pope, but the general council of Christians.

Conclusion 1. The one divine canonical Scripture, the conclusions that necessarily follow from it, and the interpretation placed upon it by the common consent of Christians, are true, and belief in them is necessary to the salvation of those to whom they are made known.

2. The general council of Christians or its majority alone has the authority to define doubtful passages of the divine law, and to determine those that are to be regarded as articles of the Christian faith, belief in which is essential to salvation; and no partial council or single person of any position has the authority to decide these questions.

3. The gospels teach that no temporal punishment or penalty should be used to compel observance of divine commandments.

4. It is necessary to salvation to obey the commandments of the new divine law [the New Testament] and the conclusions that follow necessarily from it and the precepts of reason; but it is not necessary to salvation to obey all the commandments of the ancient law [the Old Testament].

5. No mortal has the right to dispense with the commands or prohibitions of the new divine law; but the general council and the Christian "legislator" [1] alone have the right to prohibit things which are permitted by the new law, under penalties in this world or the next, and no partial council or single person of any position has that right.

6. The whole body of citizens or its majority alone is the human "legislator."

7. Decretals and decrees of the bishop of Rome, or of any other bishops or body of bishops, have no power to coerce anyone by secular penalties or punishments, except by the authorization of the human "legislator."

8. The "legislator" alone or the one who rules by its authority has the power to dispense with human laws.

9. The elective principality or other office derives its authority from the election of the body having the right to elect, and not from the confirmation or approval of any other power.

10. The election of any prince or other official, especially one who has the coercive power,[2] is determined solely by the expressed will of the "legislator."

11. There can be only one supreme ruling power in a state or kingdom.

12. The number and the qualifications of persons who hold state offices and all civil matters are to be determined solely by the Christian ruler according to the law or approved custom [of the state].

13. No prince, still more, no partial council or single person of any position, has full authority and control over other persons, laymen or clergy, without the authorization of the "legislator."

14. No bishop or priest has coercive authority or jurisdiction over any layman or clergyman, even if he is a heretic.

15. The prince who rules by the authority of the "legislator" has jurisdiction over the persons and possessions of

every single mortal of every station, whether lay or clerical, and over every body of laymen or clergy.

16. No bishop or priest or body of bishops or priests has the authority to excommunicate anyone or to interdict the performance of divine services, without the authorization of the "legislator."

17. All bishops derive their authority in equal measure immediately from Christ, and it cannot be proved from the divine law that one bishop should be over or under another, in temporal or spiritual matters.

18. The other bishops, singly or in a body, have the same right by divine authority to excommunicate or otherwise exercise authority over the bishop of Rome, having obtained the consent of the "legislator," as the bishop of Rome has to excommunicate or control them.

19. No mortal has the authority to permit marriages that are prohibited by the divine law, especially by the New Testament. The right to permit marriages which are prohibited by human law belongs solely to the "legislator" or to the one who rules by its authority.

20. The right to legitimatize children born of illegitimate union so that they may receive inheritances, or other civil or ecclesiastical offices or benefits, belongs solely to the "legislator."

21. The "legislator" alone has the right to promote to ecclesiastical orders, and to judge of the qualifications of persons for these offices, by a coercive decision, and no priest or bishop has the right to promote anyone without its authority.

22. The prince who rules by the authority of the laws of Christians, has the right to determine the number of churches and temples, and the number of priests, deacons, and other clergy who shall serve in them.

23. "Separable" [3] ecclesiastical offices may be conferred or taken away only by the authority of the "legislator"; the

same is true of ecclesiastical benefices and other property devoted to pious purposes.

24. No bishop or body of bishops has the right to establish notaries or other civil officials.

25. No bishop or body of bishops may give permission to teach or practice in any profession or occupation, but this right belongs to the Christian "legislator" or to the one who rules by its authority.

26. In ecclesiastical offices and benefices those who have received consecration as deacons or priests, or have been otherwise irrevocably dedicated to God, should be preferred to those who have not been thus consecrated.

27. The human "legislator" has the right to use ecclesiastical temporalities for the common public good and defence. after the needs of the priests and clergy, the expenses of divine worship, and the necessities of the poor have been satisfied.

28. All properties established for pious purposes or for works of mercy, such as those that are left by will for the making of a crusade, the redeeming of captives, or the support of the poor, and similar purposes, may be disposed of by the prince alone according to the decision of the "legislator" and the purpose of the testator or giver.

29. The Christian "legislator" alone has the right to forbid or permit the establishment of religious orders or houses.

30. The prince alone, acting in accordance with the laws of the "legislator," has the authority to condemn heretics, delinquents, and all others who should endure temporal punishment, to inflict bodily punishment upon them, and to exact fines from them.

31. No subject who is bound to another by a legal oath may be released from his obligation by any bishop or priest, unless the "legislator" has decided by a coercive decision that there is just cause for it.

32. The general council of all Christians alone has the

authority to create a metropolitan bishop or church, and to reduce him or it from that position.

33. The Christian "legislator" or the one who rules by its authority over Christian states, alone has the right to convoke either a general or local council of priests, bishops, and other Christians, by coercive power; and no man may be compelled by threats of temporal or spiritual punishment to obey the decrees of a council convoked in any other way.

34. The general council of Christians or the Christian "legislator" alone has the authority to ordain fasts and other prohibitions of the use of food; the council or "legislator" alone may prohibit the practice of mechanical arts or teaching which divine law permits to be practiced on any day, and the "legislator" or the one who rules by its authority alone may constrain men to obey the prohibition by temporal penalties.

35. The general council of Christians alone has the authority to canonize anyone or to order anyone to be adored as a saint.

36. The general council of Christians alone has the authority to forbid the marriage of priests, bishops, and other clergy, and to make other laws concerning ecclesiastical discipline, and that council or the one to whom it delegates its authority alone may dispense with these laws.

37. It is always permitted to appeal to the "legislator" from a coercive decision rendered by a bishop or priest with the authorization of the "legislator."

38. Those who are pledged to observe complete poverty may not have in their possession any immovable property, unless it be with the fixed intention of selling it as soon as possible and giving the money to the poor; they may not have such rights in either movable or immovable property as would enable them, for example, to recover them by a coercive decision from any person who should take or try to take them away.

39.   The people as a community and as individuals, according to their several means, are required by divine law to support the bishops and other clergy authorized by the gospel, so that they may have food and clothing and the other necessaries of life; but the people are not required to pay tithes or other taxes beyond the amount necessary for such support.

40.   The Christian "legislator" or the one who rules by its authority has the right to compel bishops and other clergy who live in the province under its control and whom it supplies with the necessities of life, to perform divine services and administer the sacrament.

41.   The bishop of Rome and any other ecclesiastical or spiritual minister may be advanced to a "separable" ecclesiastical office only by the Christian "legislator" or the one who rules by its authority, or by the general council of Christians; and they may be suspended from or deprived of office by the same authority.

1 In regard to the "legislator," Marsilius cites Aristotle as follows: "The legislator or the effective cause of the law is the people, the whole body of the citizens, or the majority of that body, expressing its will and choice in a general meeting of the citizens, and commanding or deciding that certain things shall be done or left undone, under threat of temporal penalty or punishment."

2 "Coercive" or "coactive" power is the power, residing in the ruler or the officials of the state and derived from the "legislator," to compel observance of the laws or decrees of the state by force or threat of penalty.   A coercive judgment is a judgment given by an official who has the power to enforce his decisions.   Marsilius maintains that coercive power and coercive judgments are the prerogatives of the state and cannot be exercised by the church.

3 "Separable" offices of the clergy, according to Marsilius, are those functions commonly exercised by the clergy, which are not essentially bound up with their spiritual character.   The terms essential and non-essential are used as synonymous respectively with inseparable and separable.   The essential or inseparable powers of the clergy are "the power to bless the bread and wine, and turn them into the blessed body and blood of Christ, to administer the other

sacraments of the church, and to bind and to loose men from their sins." Non-essential or separable functions are the government or control of one priest over others (*i.e.*, the offices of bishop, archbishop, etc.), the administration of the sacraments, etc., in a certain place and to a certain people, and the administration of temporal possessions of the church. In respect to their separable functions the clergy are under the control of the state.

166. CONDEMNATION OF MARSILIUS OF PADUA. 1327.

Denzinger, p. 141.

The following sentences taken from Marsilius of Padua and John of Jandun were condemned by John XXII, 1327. See introductory note to no. 165.

(1) When Christ ordered the coin which was taken from the fish's mouth to be paid to the tax collector, he paid tribute to Cæsar; and he did this not out of condescension or kindness, but because he had to pay it. From this it is clear that all temporal powers and possessions of the church are subject to the emperor, and he may take them as his own.

(2) That St. Peter had no more authority than the other apostles, and was not the head over the other apostles; and that Christ left behind no head of the church, and did not appoint anyone as his vicar.

(3) That the emperor has the right to make and depose popes and to punish them.

(4) That all priests, whether pope or archbishop or simple priest, are, in accordance with the appointment of Christ, of equal authority and jurisdiction.

(6) That the whole church together can not punish any man with coactive punishment, without the permission of the emperor.

The above articles are contrary to the holy scriptures and hostile to the catholic faith and we [John XXII] declare them to be heretical and erroneous, and the aforesaid Marsilius and John [of Jandun] to be open and notorious heretics, or rather heresiarchs.

167. The Beginning of the Schism. The Manifesto
of the Revolting Cardinals. Aug. 5, 1378.

Baluzius, Vitæ Paparum Avenionensium, I, pp. 468 ff.

At the death of Gregory XI in 1378, the cardinals elected Bartholomew, archbishop of Bari, who took the title Urban VI. He soon
announced that he would not remove his court to Avignon, as many
of the cardinals wished him to do, but would remain in Rome. For
various reasons the cardinals of the French party became more and
more displeased with Urban and soon rebelled against him and
deposed him. After publishing a manifesto, in which they defended
their action, they elected Robert of Geneva, who called himself
Clement VII. The manifesto is long and full of invective and generalities, but contains very little argument and few facts. We give
only the essential part of it.

. . . After the apostolic seat was made vacant by the
death of our lord, pope Gregory XI, who died in March, we
assembled in conclave for the election of a pope, as is the
law and custom, in the papal palace, in which Gregory had
died. . . . Officials of the city with a great multitude
of the people, for the most part armed and called together
for this purpose by the ringing of bells, surrounded the
palace in a threatening manner and even entered it and almost
filled it. To the terror caused by their presence they added
threats that unless we should at once elect a Roman or an
Italian they would kill us. They gave us no time to deliberate but compelled us unwillingly, through violence and
fear, to elect an Italian without delay. In order to escape
the danger which threatened us from such a mob, we elected
Bartholomew, archbishop of Bari, thinking that he would
have enough conscience not to accept the election, since every
one knew that it was made under such wicked threats. But he
was unmindful of his own salvation and burning with ambition, and so, to the great scandal of the clergy and of the
Christian people, and contrary to the laws of the church, he
accepted this election which was offered him, although not all
the cardinals were present at the election, and it was extorted

from us by the threats and demands of the officials and
people of the city. And although such an election is null
and void, and the danger from the people still threatened us,
he was enthroned and crowned, and called himself pope and
apostolic. But according to the holy fathers and to the law
of the church, he should be called apostate, anathema,
Antichrist, and the mocker and destroyer of Christianity. . . .

168. The University of Paris and the Schism, 1393.

D'Achery, Spicilegium, I, pp. 777 f.

In 1393 the king of France asked the University of Paris to devise
a way of ending the schism. In response to this request, each member of the faculty was asked to propose in writing the way which
seemed best to him, and to advance all the possible arguments in its
favor. A commission of fifty-four professors, masters, and doctors
was then appointed to examine all the proposed ways and means.
After mature deliberation this commission proposed three possible
ways of ending the schism and drew them up in writing and forwarded
them to the king. They discussed at some length the relative advantages and disadvantages of each way. Their letter to the king is a
long one. We give only three brief extracts from it, to show the
three ways which they proposed.

The first way. Now the first way to end the schism is that
both parties should entirely renounce and resign all rights
which they may have or claim to have to the papal
office. . . .

The second way. But if both cling tenaciously to their
rights and refuse to resign, as they have done up to now, we
would propose the way of arbitration. That is, that they
should together choose worthy and suitable men, or permit
such to be chosen in a regular and canonical way, and these
shall have the full power and authority to discuss the case
and decide it, and if necessary and expedient, and approved
by those who according to the canon law have the authority
[that is, the cardinals], they may also have the right to proceed to the election of a pope.

The third way. If the rival popes, after being urged in a brotherly and friendly manner, will not accept either of the above ways, there is a third way which we propose as an excellent remedy for this sacrilegious schism. We mean that the matter shall be left to a general council. This general council might be composed, according to canon law, only of prelates, or, since many of them are very illiterate, and many of them are bitter partisans of one or the other pope, there might be joined with the prelates an equal number of masters and doctors of theology and law from the faculties of approved universities. Or if this does not seem sufficient to anyone, there might be added besides one or more representatives from cathedral chapters and the chief monastic orders, in order that all decisions might be rendered only after most careful examination and mature deliberation.

169. THE COUNCIL OF PISA DECLARES IT IS COMPETENT TO TRY THE POPES. 1409.

Raynaldus, anno 1409, sec. 71.

There was no recognized legal machinery in the church by which the schism could be ended, and there was no emperor, as in the days of Innocent II, who was willing to end it by force. It was decided to leave the matter to a general council, but there was some doubt as to (1) whether a council could be legally called by anyone except a pope, and (2) whether the council was legally empowered to cite the two papal claimants before it and decide the case between them. Finally a council was called by the cardinals; it met at Pisa and proceeded first to assert its legality and authority. The conciliar movement, begun by this council, was foreshadowed in earlier documents. See nos. 165 and 168.

This holy and general council, representing the universal church, decrees and declares that the united college of cardinals was empowered to call the council, and that the power to call such a council belongs of right to the aforesaid holy college of cardinals, especially now when there is a detestable schism. The council further declared that this holy council, representing the universal church, caused both claimants of the papal throne to be cited in the gates and doors of the churches of Pisa to come and hear the final decision [in the matter of the schism] pronounced, or to give a good and sufficient reason why such sentence should not be rendered.

170. An Oath of the Cardinals to Reform the Church. Council of Pisa, 1409.

Raynaldus, anno 1409, sec. 71.

In the great councils of Pisa and Constance there were two parties, the one in favor of reforming the church at once and ending the schism afterwards (that is, by electing another pope), and the other in favor of first electing the pope and then carrying out the reform under his direction. The latter party was victorious, but before proceeding to the election, each cardinal was compelled to take an oath that, if elected, he would not dissolve the council until a thorough reform of the church was brought about.

We, each and all, bishops, priests, and deacons of the holy Roman church, congregated in the city of Pisa for the purpose of ending the schism and of restoring the unity of the church, on our word of honor promise God, the holy Roman church, and this holy council now collected here for the aforesaid purpose, that, if any one of us is elected pope, he shall continue the present council and not dissolve it, nor, so far as is in his power, permit it to be dissolved until, through it and with its advice, a proper, reasonable, and sufficient reformation of the universal church in its head and in its members shall have been accomplished.

171. The Council of Constance Claims Supreme Authority, 1415.

V. d. Hardt, II, p. 98.

See introductory note to nos. 168, 169.

This holy synod of Constance, being a general council, and legally assembled in the Holy Spirit for the praise of God and for ending the present schism, and for the union and reformation of the church of God in its head and in its members, in order more easily, more securely, more completely, and more fully to bring about the union and reformation of the church of God, ordains, declares, and decrees as follows: And first it declares that this synod, legally assembled, is a general council, and represents the catholic church militant and has its authority directly from Christ; and everybody, of whatever rank or dignity, including also the pope, is bound to obey this council in those things which pertain to the faith, to the ending of this schism, and to a general reformation of the church in its head and members. Likewise it declares that if anyone, of whatever rank, condition, or dignity, including also the pope, shall refuse to obey the commands, statutes, ordinances, or orders of this holy council, or of any other holy council properly assembled, in regard to the ending of the schism and to the reformation of the church, he shall be subject to the proper punishment; and unless he repents, he shall be duly punished; and if necessary, recourse shall be had to other aids of justice.

172. Reforms Demanded by the Council of Constance, 1417.

V. d. Hardt, IV, p. 1452.

The reforming party in the council of Constance had been defeated in its attempt to fix the order of business which the council should follow.   As in the council at Pisa, it had been determined that the pope should be elected first and then the reform be worked out.   The leaders of the reform party were fearful that no reform would be accomplished, and so as a kind of compromise and as a last desperate effort they succeeded in having the council enact that reforms should be made in the following eighteen points.

The holy council at Constance determined and decreed that before this holy council shall be dissolved, the future pope, by the grace of God soon to be elected, with the aid of this holy council, or of men appointed by each nation, shall reform the church in its head and in the Roman curià, in conformity to the right standard and good government of the church. And reforms shall be made in the following matters: 1. In the number, character, and nationality of the cardinals. 2. In papal reservations. 3. In annates, and in common services and little services. 4. In the granting of benefices and expectancies. 5. In determining what cases may be tried in the papal court. 6. In appeals to the papal court. 7. In the offices of the *cancellaria,* and of the penitentiary. 8. In the exemptions and incorporations made during the schism. 9. In the matter of commends. 10. In the confirmation of elections. 11. In the disposition of the income of churches, monasteries, and benefices during the time when they are vacant. 12. That no ecclesiastical property be alienated. 13. It shall be determined for what causes and how a pope may be disciplined and deposed. 14. A plan shall be devised for putting an end to simony. 15. In the matter of dispensations. 16. In the provision for the pope and cardinals. 17. In indulgences. 18. In assessing tithes.

The following notes explain the various points of the reform program: 1. Various cardinals were frequently charged with luxurious living and even with grave immorality. For some time French cardinals had been in the majority. The demand was now made that all nations should have an equal representation in the college of cardinals. 2. The popes arbitrarily reserved the right to appoint to the richest livings, and their appointees had to pay well for their appointments. 3. Annates were (1) the income for a year, collected from every living or benefice when it became vacant by the death of the holder; (2) the income of a bishopric for a year, paid by the newly elected bishop. Under "common services and little services" were included various other payments, in addition to the annates, which every newly elected bishop was expected to pay the pope. 4. The pope strove to increase the number of benefices and livings to which he might appoint. It was not uncommon to sell the "expectation" to a benefice; that is, while the holder of a benefice was still alive the right or expectation of succeeding him in his benefice at his death was sold to some one. 5. The popes wished to increase the number of cases or trials that could be tried only in the papal court.

There was no clear principle to determine which cases must be tried in the papal court, and which not.   There were certain costs connected with every trial, and hence such trials were a source of income to the papal court.   6. So many appeals were made to Rome by those who had lost their cases at home or who feared they would lose them, that the papal court was overwhelmed with work and could not try them promptly.   Appeals to Rome were often made to gain time and to defeat justice.   7. The "cancellaria" was the office in which the papal secretaries wrote the bulls, letters, etc., of the pope.   The penitentiary was the office "in which are examined and delivered out the secret bulls, graces, and dispensations relating to cases of conscience, confession, and the like."   8. By exemptions is meant the freeing of a monastery from the jurisdiction of the bishop in whose diocese the monastery is situated.   "Incorporation" is the depriving a parish church of its income and giving it to another church.   9. A "commend" is the granting of a benefice temporarily on the condition that a certain sum be paid for it annually.   10. The pope must confirm the election of all bishops, abbots, etc.   11. At the death of a bishop the pope claimed the income of his bishopric until his successor was elected.   The same is true of monasteries and many ecclesiastical benefices.

173. Concerning General Councils. The Council of Constance, 39th Session, October 9, 1417.

V. d. Hardt, IV, p. 1435.

The conciliar idea was that a general council, since it represented the whole church, was the highest authority in the church, to which even the pope must submit.   The promoters of this idea planned to have a general council meet at regular intervals.

A good way to till the field of the Lord is to hold general councils frequently, because by them the briers, thorns, and thistles of heresies, errors, and schisms are rooted out, abuses reformed, and the way of the Lord made more fruitful.   But if general councils are not held, all these evils spread and flourish.   We therefore decree by this perpetual edict that general councils shall be held as follows: The first one shall be held five years after the close of this council, the second one seven years after the close of the first, and forever thereafter one shall be held every ten years.   One month before the close of each council the pope, with the approval and consent of the council, shall fix the place for holding the next council. If the pope fails to name the place the council must do so.

174. Pius II, by the Bull "Execrabilis," Condemns Appeals to a General Council, 1459.

Denzinger, p. 172.

In the great struggle with the councils the pope had come out victorious. He had successfully resisted all attempts to make any important changes in the administration of the church, or to introduce the reforms which were so loudly called for. Although the council at Basel had brought the conciliar idea into disrepute, there were many who still called for a general council as the only means of securing the reforms which were demanded. Pius II condemned and prohibited all such appeals.

The execrable and hitherto unknown abuse has grown up in our day, that certain persons, imbued with the spirit of rebellion, and not from a desire to secure a better judgment, but to escape the punishment of some offence which they have committed, presume to appeal from the pope to a future council, in spite of the fact that the pope is the vicar of Jesus Christ and to him, in the person of St. Peter, the following was said: "Feed my sheep" [John 21:16] and "Whatsoever thou shalt bind on earth shall be bound in heaven" [Matt. 16:18]. Wishing therefore to expel this pestiferous poison from the church of Christ and to care for the salvation of the flock entrusted to us, and to remove every cause of offence from the fold of our Saviour, with the advice and consent of our brothers, the cardinals of the holy Roman church, and of all the prelates, and of those who have been trained in the canon and civil law, who are at our court, and with our own sure knowledge, we condemn all such appeals and prohibit them as erroneous and detestable.

175. WILLIAM III OF SAXONY FORBIDS APPEALS TO FOREIGN COURTS, 1446.

Schilter, De libertate ecclesiarum Germaniæ, pp. 808 ff.

At this time secular rulers were everywhere growing in power, and centralizing the authority in their own hands, which led them to try to diminish the power of the clergy. This document shows the legal confusion which then existed, caused in part by the usurpations which the ecclesiastical courts practiced. Following the examples of the kings of England and France, William III, duke of Saxony, limited ecclesiastical courts to their proper jurisdiction and forbade the clergy to try secular cases. As a sovereign power he also forbade all appeals to foreign courts, which of course included the pope.

My country suffers dishonor, and great loss and injury, in that many of its inhabitants resort to foreign courts. Be it known that we have decreed that hereafter no inhabitant of our country shall summon or sue another before any foreign court, ecclesiastical or secular, for any matter whatsoever. If the case is ecclesiastical and legally comes under the jurisdiction of an ecclesiastical court, the plaintiff shall bring it before some ecclesiastical court in our country, and be content with the decision rendered there. There shall be no appeal to a foreign court. If the case is secular, it shall be brought and pleaded before the secular court where the defendant belongs. It shall be tried before that court under whose jurisdiction the case falls, and the plaintiff shall be content with the decision rendered. If any inhabitant of our land is not content with the decision, but appeals to a foreign court in any way, he shall be held to be an outlaw. He shall be banished for life and never be permitted to return to this country; and anyone may attack him and his property without any hindrance, because he is an outlaw. . . . We and our subjects have for a long time been annoyed and troubled beyond measure by the ecclesiastical judges who hear cases which do not belong under their jurisdiction. For although they are only ecclesiastical judges, they hear ecclesiastical and secular cases. And very often they render unjust decisions. The effect of this is the spread of unbelief among the people, who neglect and dishonor God and the holy church. The glory of God and the honor of the church demand that this abuse be stopped. We will therefore do all we can to have the princes and prelates who have jurisdiction in our land reform their ecclesiastical courts. For these ecclesiastical courts shall refuse to hear secular cases and try only ecclesiastical cases. We forbid all persons in our land to summon, sue, or denounce another on a secular charge before an ecclesiastical court. . . .

176. Papal Charter for the Establishment of the University of Avignon, 1303.

Bullarium Romanum, III, ii, pp. 101 f.

It was regarded as the exclusive right of the pope to establish a university, or *studium generale*, as it was called. We give the document by which he established the University of Avignon as a sample of these numerous papal establishments. It contains a clear and interesting account of the examinations and the conferring of the Master's degree.

The city of Avignon for many reasons is eminently suited and fitted to become the seat of a university. Believing that it would be for the public good if those who cultivate wisdom were introduced into the city, and that they would in time bear rich fruit, by this document we grant that a university may be established there, in which Masters [*magistri*] may teach, and scholars freely study and hear lectures, in all faculties. And when those who study in the university attain a high degree of knowledge, and ask for the permission to teach others, we grant that they may be examined in the canon and civil law, and in medicine, and in the liberal arts, and that they may be decorated with the title of Master in those faculties. All who are to be promoted to this honor shall be presented to the bishop of Avignon. He shall call together all the Masters in the faculty concerned, and without any charge he shall examine the candidates to discover their learning, eloquence, manner of reading [lecturing], and the other things which are required in those who are to be made Doctors or Masters. He shall then consult the Masters about the examination and they shall vote on the question of granting the degree [that is, decide whether the candidate passed the examination or not]. But their vote shall be kept secret, and the bishop shall never tell how they voted on the question. Those whom he finds fit, he shall approve, and grant them the permission to teach others. But those whom he finds are not fit, he shall refuse without fear or favor. If the bishopric of Avignon is vacant, the candidates shall present themselves to the *præpositus* of the church, who shall examine them and approve them in the way prescribed for the bishop.

Those who are examined and approved in Avignon and receive the license to teach, shall thereafter have the full and free right to read and teach everywhere, in that faculty in which they have been approved, without further examination or approval by anyone else.

In order that such examinations may be properly held, we command that all Masters who wish to read in the University of Avignon shall, before beginning their work there as teachers, take a public oath that they will come in person to all the examinations whenever called, and that they will, *gratis* and without fear or favor, faithfully give the bishop their judgment about the examination, in order that those who are worthy may be approved, and those who are unworthy may be rejected. Those who refuse to take this oath shall not be permitted to read in the university, or to be present at the examinations, or to share in any of the advantages or benefits of the university.

In order that the Doctors [teachers] and scholars of the university may be able to devote themselves freely to their studies, and to make good progress in them, we grant that all who are in the university, whether teachers or scholars, shall have all the privileges, liberties, and immunities which are generally granted to teachers and scholars of other universities.

177. POPULAR DISSATISFACTION THAT THE CHURCH HAD SO MUCH WEALTH, *ca.* 1480.

Goldast's Reichssatzung, p. 280.

We give a brief passage from an unknown author to illustrate the growing dissatisfaction of the common people that the church had so much wealth. It betrays a dangerous temper of mind. In the light of this the suppression of monasteries and the seizure of ecclesiastical property which was carried on on so large a scale in the sixteenth century does not seem strange.

It is as clear as day that by means of smooth and crafty words the clergy have deprived us of our rightful possessions. For they blinded the eyes of our forefathers, and persuaded them to buy the kingdom of heaven with their lands and possessions. If you priests give the poor and the chosen children of God their paternal inheritance, which before God you owe them, God will perhaps grant you such grace that you will know yourselves. But so long as you spend your money on your dear harlots and profligates, instead of upon the children of God, you may be sure that God will reward you according to your merits. For you have angered and overburdened all the people of the empire. The time is coming when your possessions will be seized and divided as if they were the possessions of an enemy. As you have oppressed the people, they will rise up against you so that you will not know where to find a place to stay.

178. COMPLAINTS OF THE GERMANS AGAINST THE POPE, 1510.

Gebhardt, Gravamina gegen den Romischen Höf, pp. 83 f.

This is a brief list of the complaints made by the Germans in 1510 and presented to Julius II. Most of them, it will be observed, are

concerned with the financial burdens with which the Germans felt
that they were overwhelmed.

(1) That popes do not feel bound to observe the bulls,
agreements, privileges, and letters which have been issued by
their predecessors, but often dispense with, suspend, and
revoke them at the request of people even of low birth. (2)
That the pope sometimes refuses to confirm the canonical
election of bishops. (3) That the pope sometimes rejects
the election of *præpositi* [provosts], although made by chapters which have paid a high price for the right to elect.
. . . (4) That the better benefices and higher offices are
reserved for the cardinals and the chief officials of the papal
court. (5) That an unlimited number of expectancies are
granted, and many are given for the same office to different
persons. And many expectancies are sold to one and the
same person. From this practice, lawsuits arise daily, which
cause all concerned to incur heavy expenses. For if a man
buys an expectancy, he will probably never get the office, but
he will surely become involved in a lawsuit about it which
will cost him a great deal of money. On this account the
proverbial saying has arisen: "If anyone obtains an expectancy from Rome, let him lay aside one or two hundred gold
coins, for he will need them in his lawsuit about it." (6)
Even when a bishopric is several times within a few years
made vacant by death, the pope without any mercy demands
the prompt and full payment of the annates. And sometimes when the pope creates new offices and enlarges his
court, more is demanded as annates than is just. . . .
(7) Churches are given to members of the papal court, some
of whom are better fitted to be mule drivers than pastors.
(8) Old indulgences are revoked and new ones sold, merely
to raise money, although the laymen are thereby made to
murmur against their clergy. (9) Tithes are collected under
the pretext that a war is to be made against the Turks, but
nothing of the kind is ever done. (10) Cases which could

easily be settled in Germany, since there are good and just
judges there, are indiscriminately called before the papal
court at Rome. St. Bernard, in writing to Eugene III,
severely criticised this practice.

179. ABUSES IN THE SALE OF INDULGENCES, 1512.

Fr. Myconius, Geschichte der Reformation.

Several references have been made to the need of a reform in the
matter of indulgences. Cardinal Raymond, papal legate in 1503,
complained that the agents who sold indulgences were actuated only
by the basest motives of gain and were thoroughly dishonest.
Myconius (his German name was Mecum) was a Franciscan monk
who became a Protestant.

We have thought it best to give first a statement of the doctrine
of indulgences in order that the abuses in their sale may be more
clearly apparent.

" It is the catholic doctrine that when a sin is forgiven its punishment is not necessarily at the same time remitted. Through the
power of the keys the eternal punishment is remitted, but generally
there remain temporal punishments which must be satisfied either
in this world by means of good works, or in the next by enduring
punishment in purgatory. The Bible, by examples as well as by
statements, teaches that with the removal of the eternal guilt and
punishment, the temporal punishment is not always remitted. Adam
and Eve, after committing sin, repented and were justified by God,
but they were driven out of Paradise and compelled to endure infinite
misfortunes, and even death itself, as a punishment of their sin. We
are taught the same by the example of the Israelites who were
pardoned for their sin of murmuring through the prayers of Moses,
but, as a punishment for their sin, were excluded from the promised
land and perished in the wilderness. . . . From this it is seen
that the Bible demands not only the conversion of the heart, but also
that we render satisfaction by enduring temporal punishment for
the sin. . . .

"This satisfaction which we must render [*i.e.*, this temporal punishment which we must endure] is a part of the sacrament of penance,
and must be imposed on us by the minister of penance [*i.e.*, the
priest]. The doctrine of indulgences is inseparably connected with
that of satisfaction. By indulgence is meant a remission of the
temporal punishment made by a priest by means of the application

of the treasure of the church. The treasure of the church is the whole sum of the merits of Jesus Christ . . . in addition to all the good works or merits of all the saints. . . . In the church, as St. Thomas Aquinas well says, some have done greater penance than the measure of their sins demanded. Others have suffered with patience many unjust tribulations, with which they would have expiated the temporal punishments of many more sins than they have committed. [All such good works in excess of what they needed to make satisfaction for their own sins are called works of supererogation, and being meritorious, their merit is added to the treasure of the church and may, at the discretion of the church, be applied to the benefit of others who are lacking in such good works.] One of the ways in which the church distributes this common possession (treasure of merits) is by means of indulgences."—From the *Theologia Dommatica* of Prof. Dati, vol. iii, Chap. XXIX, Florence, 1893.

Anno 1512. Tetzel gained by his preaching in Germany an immense sum of money which he sent to Rome. A very large sum was collected at the new mining works at St. Annaberg, where I heard him for two years. It is incredible what this ignorant and impudent monk used to say. . . . He declared that if they contributed readily and bought grace and indulgence, all the hills of St. Annaberg would become pure massive silver. Also, that, as soon as the coin clinked in the chest, the soul for whom the money was paid would go straight to heaven. . . . The indulgence was so highly prized that when the agent came to a city the bull was carried on a satin or gold cloth, and all the priests and monks, the town council, schoolmaster, scholars, men, women, girls, and children went out in procession to meet it with banners, candles, and songs. All the bells were rung and organs played. He was conducted into the church, a red cross was erected in the centre of the church, and the pope's banner displayed. . . .

Anno 1517. It is incredible what this ignorant monk said and preached. He gave sealed letters stating that even the sins which a man was intending to commit would be forgiven.

He said the pope had more power than all the apostles, all the angels and saints, even than the Virgin Mary herself. For these were all subject to Christ, but the pope was equal to Christ. After his ascension into heaven Christ had nothing more to do with the management of the church until the judgment day, but had committed all that to the pope as his vicar and vicegerent.

VI. FEUDALISM

Feudalism, as the prevailing order of society, socially, economically, and politically, makes its appearance toward the end of the tenth century. During the disorders consequent upon the disintegration of the empire of the Carolingians (see nos. 15-25) the government failed to supply protection and security, and ceased to act as a bond to hold men together. As a result, certain local, private elements of society, which were very generally diffused throughout that empire, were raised to the rank of public political institutions. It is our purpose to illustrate the origins and growth of feudalism, and the characteristic features of the feudal state. The elements which lay at the basis of the feudal system may be classified under three heads: (1) The personal dependence of one man upon another; (2) dependent tenure of land, in which the holder and user of the land was not the owner, but held it of or from another; (3) the possession by private persons or corporations of extensive sovereign rights over their lands and tenants. These elements were present in various degrees and forms in the German tribes before the migrations and in the later Roman empire, but it will be sufficient for our purpose to show the existence and the character of these elements in the tribal kingdoms and the Frankish kingdom under the Merovingians, for in these states the German and Roman people and institutions were united to form the society of the Middle Age. Then we shall attempt to illustrate the growth and development of these elements in the late Merovingian and in the Carolingian periods, and finally the characteristic features of society in the feudal age. The difficulty in illustrating the situation from public documents will be readily understood; it is due to the fact that these institutions were only partly legal or public, and to the fact that the makers of the laws took for granted a knowledge of the institutions and did not think it necessary to describe or explain them. It is hoped, however, that the notes to the passages translated will make clear their meaning and importance.

180–197. Origins.

180–183. Personal Dependence.

In the documents of the tribal kingdoms and Merovingian kingdom (*ca.* 500–700) there are many evidences of the importance for society of the dependence of one man upon another, and of the fact that this relation was superseding in importance the relation of the private man to the state. On the one hand, men became dependents and retainers of the king and the great officials and lords for mutual advantages, the superior gaining the prestige that came with the possession of a large following, and the dependents gaining employment under and connection with the great persons of the state. On the other hand, poor land-owners, or persons without lands of their own, commended themselves to landlords for the purpose of receiving protection and support. In both cases the personal dependence was connected with the holding of land, for the king or great lord frequently gave land to his followers, while the poor man who commended himself to another usually did it for the purpose of acquiring land to cultivate; this side of the relation, however, will be seen more clearly under the next section.

180. Form for the Creation of an Antrustio by the King.

Marculf's Formulæ, I, no. 18; M. G. LL. 4to, V, p. 55.

Most of the following documents are taken from books of formulæ; that is, collections of forms of documents made by various persons to serve as examples for the drawing up of charters, etc. They were probably made from actual documents by leaving out the names and inserting *ille* (such an one) or similar expressions. The formulæ of Marculf were written at the end of the seventh century. We quote them from the edition in the *Monumenta Germaniæ*, Leges, vol. v, giving only the pages in that volume after the first reference.

It is right that those who have promised us unbroken faith should be rewarded by our aid and protection. Now since our faithful subject (name) with the will of God has come to our palace with his arms and has there sworn in our hands to keep his trust and fidelity to us, therefore we decree and command by the present writing that henceforth the said (name) is to be numbered among our *antrustiones*.[1] If anyone shall presume to slay him, let him know that he shall have to pay 600 solidi as a wergeld for him.

1 The position of the *antrustio* is explained in the note to the Salic law, XLI, no. 4. See also the reference to the *leudes* in no. 189.

181. FORM FOR THE SUSPENDING OF LAWSUITS.

Marculf, I, no. 23; p. 57.

One great advantage that the dependent possessed was the support and influence of his lord in judicial trials and other matters of the sort.

Know that we have ordered the apostolic man (name) [a bishop] or the illustrious man (name) [a secular official or lord] to go to a certain place, and we now command that as long as he is away all his lawsuits, and those of his clients and dependents and people that live within his jurisdiction, are to be suspended. Therefore we decree and order by the present writing that until he returns all his cases and those of his clients, both those who go with him and those who stay on his lands, and of his people who live within his jurisdiction, shall be suspended, and afterwards he shall do justice to everyone and receive justice from everyone.

182. FORM FOR COMMENDATION. MIDDLE OF EIGHTH CENTURY.

Formulæ Turonenses, no. 43; p. 158.

Notice the reason given by the person who commends himself, the effects of commendation on both parties, and the binding nature of the agreement. The reason alleged (extreme poverty) is probably a mere form of speech, and was not present in each actual instance of commendation.

To my great lord, (name), I, (name). Since, as was well known, I had not wherewith to feed and clothe myself, I came to you and told you my wish, to commend myself to you and to put myself under your protection. I have now

done so, on the condition that you shall supply me with food
and clothing as far as I shall merit by my services, and that
as long as I live I shall perform such services for you as are
becoming to a freeman, and shall never have the right to
withdraw from your power and protection, but shall remain
under them all the days of my life. It is agreed that if either
of us shall try to break this compact he shall pay — solidi,
and the compact shall still hold. It is also agreed that two
copies of this letter shall be made and signed by us, which
also has been done.

183. Form by which the King Allows a Powerful Person to Undertake the Cases of a Poor Person.

Marculf, I, no. 21; pp. 56 f.

Our faithful subject, (name), with the will of God has
come to us and told us that he is not able on account of his
weakness to defend or to prosecute his cases before the court.
Therefore he has besought us to allow the illustrious man
(name) to take up his cases for him, both in the local court
and in the royal court, whether he prosecutes or is prosecuted,
and he has commended his affairs to him in our presence by
the staff. Therefore we command, in accordance with the
desire of both parties, that the aforesaid man (name) may
undertake the cases of the other (name), and that he shall
do justice for him and for all his possessions, and get justice
for him from others; this shall be so, as long as both desire it.

184–188. Dependent Tenure of Land.

Absolute ownership of land was giving place to possession of land
owned by others than the holder. The greater landlords (the king,
the church, and the great officials and lords) sought to acquire
cultivators for their lands, while the poorer land-owners and the
persons without lands of their own sought a means of livelihood or
protection. The usual form was the benefice or the *precarium*.
The benefice was the name applied generally in this time to land
the use of which was granted by the owner to others for a term of

years, for life, or in perpetuity. The *precarium* was a form of the benefice, the name being technically applied to lands thus granted in response to a letter of request or prayer (*litteræ precariæ*). It will be seen from the documents that the lands were usually those that had been given originally by the poor land-holder to the greater landlord and then received back as benefice or *precarium*. The reason was undoubtedly in many cases the desire of the owner to come under the protection of the greater landlord. The king also gave land to his followers and officials, either to bind them to him or to reward them for services; it is probable, although not certain, that these lands, in part at least, were held only for life or a term of years, on condition of services or faithfulness, and so were in a sense benefices.

184. Form for the Gift of Land to a Church to be Received back by the Giver as a Benefice.

Marculf, II, no. 3; pp. 74 ff.

. . . I, (name), and my wife, (name), in the name of the Lord, give by this letter of gift, and transfer from our ownership to the ownership and authority of the monastery of (name), over which the venerable abbot (name) presides, and which was founded in the honor of (name) by (name) in the county of (name), the following villas [1] (name), situated in the county of (name), with all the lands, houses, buildings, tenants, slaves, vineyards, woods, fields, pastures, meadows, streams, and all other belongings and dependencies, and all things movable and immovable which are found in the said villas now or may be added later; in order that under the protection of Christ they may be used for the support and maintenance of the monks who dwell in the aforesaid monastery. We do this on the condition that as long as either of us shall live we may possess the aforesaid villas, without prejudice to the ownership of the monastery and without diminution of the value of them, except that we shall be allowed to emancipate any of the slaves that dwell on the lands for the salvation of our souls. After the death of both of us, the aforesaid villas with any additions or improvements which may have been made, shall return immediately to the possession of the said monastery and the said abbot and his successors, without undertaking any judicial process or obtaining the consent of the heirs.

1 The term *villa*, as used in these documents, means a domain or estate with a group or village of dependent cultivators.

185. FORM FOR A PRECARIAL LETTER.

Marculf, II, no. 5; pp. 77 f.

To our lord and father in Christ, the holy and apostolic bishop (name), I (name), and my wife (name). It is well known that we have given in the name of the Lord our villa of (name), situated in the county of (name), in its entirety and with all that we possessed there, by a letter of gift to the church of (name), founded in the honor of (name), and that you have received it on behalf of the said church. And in response to our petition you have granted that as long as we or either of us shall live we shall hold the said villa as a benefice with the right of usufruct,[1] with the understanding that we shall not diminish its value in any way or alienate anything that belongs to it, but shall hold it without prejudice to the ownership of the said church or bishop. Therefore we have written this precarial letter in witness that our possession shall not work any prejudice to your ownership or any injury to the said villa; but that we only have the use of it during our lives, and that after we are dead you shall immediately recover it with all the additions and improvements which we may have made, by virtue of this precarial letter, which shall be renewed every five years, and without requiring any judicial process or obtaining the consent of the heirs; and that thereafter you shall hold it forever, or do with it whatever may seem to you to be to the best interests of the said church.

1 To hold land with the right of usufruct or to have the usufruct of land, means to hold, use, and enjoy the products of land the own-

ership of which belongs to another. Thus a benefice is a form of usufruct. It corresponds practically to modern long lease, which is sometimes expressed in our legal usage as lease for 99 years, etc.

186. FORM OF PRECARIAL LETTER.

Marculf, II, no. 39; pp. 98 f.

To our lord and father in Christ, the holy and apostolic bishop (name), I (name), and my wife (name). Since you have permitted us, as long as we or either of us shall live, to hold the land (name) belonging to your church (name), which (name) gave to the said church for the salvation of his soul, therefore for this permission and for the salvation of our souls we have given this other place (name), to belong to the said church and to you and your successors after we are both dead. This we have done on the condition that as long as we live we may possess the said places, both that which you have permitted us to use and the one which we have given you for the salvation of our souls, with the right of usufruct, without diminishing its value or prejudicing the rights of your church; and that after we are dead the said places shall immediately revert to your ownership by virtue of this precarial letter, without requiring any renewal of the letter, and in spite of any opposition from our heirs or from anyone else.

187. FORM OF PRECARIAL LETTER.

Formulæ Bituricenses, no. 2; p. 169.

To the lords (names), we (name), and (name). It is well known that our father lived on your lands and made a precarial letter to you for them, which we now renew and sign, humbly beseeching you to allow us to remain on the same lands.[1] In order that our possession of the lands may not prejudice the rights of you and your successors in them, we have deposited with you this precarial letter, agreeing that if we ever forget its terms, or ever refuse to obey you or

your agents in anything which you command, or ever assert
that this is not your land, we may be punished according to
the severity of the law as wicked violators of your rights, and
may be driven from the lands without judicial sentence.

[1] This and the following document are instances of a very common
practice; the heirs of the holder of a precarium took it over on the
same terms. The result was that the relation tended to become
permanent, and a regular class of dependent land-holders grew up.
Notice also the subjection of the holders of the precarium to the
grantors, in this case secular lords.

188. GIFT OF LAND TO BE RECEIVED BACK AND HELD IN PERPETUITY FOR A FIXED RENT.

Formulæ Augienses, B, no. 8; pp. 352 f.

The first part of the form, including the original gift of the land,
is omitted in the original, but may be supplied from a preceding
number.

I do this on the condition that as long as I live I may hold
the said lands for the said rent, and that my children and
their posterity may do the same forever.

189. TREATY OF ANDELOT, 587.

M. G. LL. 4to, II, 1, no. 6; Gregory of Tours, IX, ch. 20.

This is a treaty between two of the Merovingian kings, Gunthram
of Burgundy and Childebert II of Austrasia. It forms an incident in
the civil war begun between Sigebert and Chilperic; see no. 5, Gregory
of Tours, IV, ch. 28, and note.

It illustrates the practice of the kings of giving land to their followers and officials. This was very important in the creation of a
landed aristocracy. See the remarks above in regard to the nature
of these gifts (introductory note to nos. 184–188).

In accordance with the treaties made between Gunthram
and Sigebert of blessed memory, it is likewise agreed that
those *leudes,*[1] who after the death of Chlothar I first gave
their oaths to Gunthram and then later removed to other
parts, are to be made to return from the places where they

are now dwelling. It is also agreed that those who, after the death of Chlothar I, gave their oaths to Sigebert and then removed to other parts are in a similar manner to be made to return. Likewise whatever the aforesaid kings bestowed or with the consent of God wished to bestow upon churches or upon their faithful subjects, shall remain in the possession of the churches or subjects. And whatever shall be restored in this way to the subject of either king, legally and justly, shall be held by that person as his own. . . . And let each one possess in security whatever he has received through the munificence of preceding kings, to the time of the death of Chlothar I of blessed memory, and if anything has been taken from the faithful subjects since that time, it shall be restored to them from this moment. . . . Likewise it is agreed that neither of the kings shall entice away the *leudes* of the other or receive them; but if some of the *leudes* believe they are justified in leaving their king by reason of injuries done to them, they are to be compensated for their injuries, and made to return. . . .

1 The *leudes* are evidently the personal dependents of the king, that is, *antrustiones*. They were probably given land by the king. Notice the other references in the treaty to persons holding land from the "munificence" of the king. The same thing is referred to in nos. 190, 193, 194.

190–194. Grants of Immunity.

In the feudal age practically every landlord exercised over his lands and tenants rights and authority which are now regarded as sovereign rights belonging to the state. This was due in the main to the practice of the Merovingian and Carolingian kings of granting immunity to the churches and the great landlords, a practice which naturally grew with the increasing weakness of the monarchy and the growth of the power of the nobles. A grant of immunity operated to exclude the public officials from lands, which were then in theory under the immediate control of the king. In the late Merovingian period the weakness of the kings and the disorganization of the public administration left the control of immunity domains really in the hands of the landlords. The holder of land covered by a grant of immunity thus came to represent the state to the people on his lands. He established courts for the trial of cases arising among his tenants or represented them before the public courts; he was also frequently given the right to collect the taxes, revenues, tolls, etc., from the lands of people, which would otherwise go to the royal treasury. Most of the grants of immunity which have come down to us are in favor of church lands, but they were also granted to secular lords. The churches preserved their documents better than secular persons did.

190. Precept of Chlothar II, 584–628.

M. G. LL. 4to, II, 1, no. 8.

Notice the references to immunity, to grants of land to "churches and powerful persons" (lords and officials), and the implied right of such landlords to appoint judges for trial of cases among their tenants (private jurisdiction).

11. We grant to the churches the taxes from the fields and pastures and the tithes of swine, so that no collector or titheman shall enter the lands of a church to gather such dues for the royal treasury. Public officials shall not demand any services from the churches of clergymen who have acquired immunity from our father or grandfather.

12. Whatever has been given to churches or to clergymen or to any person through the munificence of our aforesaid predecessors of blessed memory is to belong to them in all security.

14. The property of churches, priests, and of the poor who cannot protect themselves, shall be under the protection of public officials until their cases can be brought to the king and justice be done; only in so far, however, as it shall not infringe on the rights of immunity which have been granted by former kings to any church or powerful person or to anyone else, for the keeping of peace and the preservation of discipline.

19. Bishops and powerful persons who have possessions

in various regions shall not appoint travelling judges or any judges except such as belong to the county in which they serve.

191. GRANT OF IMMUNITY TO A MONASTERY, 673.

M. G. DD. folio, I, pp. 30 f; Altmann und Bernheim, no. 112.

Childeric, king of the Franks, illustrious man. . . . We have commanded it to be made known to all that the venerable and pious abbot Berchar came to us and asked us to grant him a certain place in the forest of Vervo in Gascony, in which he might build a monastery, and to give him material and resources by which he might construct a monastery there and establish a congregation of monks. Now the request of this great man pleased us and we granted him what he asked. Then having built his monastery . . . in the honor of Sts. Peter and Paul and the other saints, he besought us, in order to make secure the whole undertaking, to bestow complete immunity upon the monastery. Therefore, we, moved to this by the kindness which Heaven has shown to us, have hearkened to the prayer of this man . . . and with the consent of our bishops and nobles do now concede entire immunity over the whole possessions of this monastery . . . for the peace of our kingdom and for the reverence which we have for this religious place. We command that no public official of any authority shall presume to enter the lands of this monastery . . . for the purpose of hearing cases, of seizing securities, of collecting taxes, of demanding entertainment, or of extorting tolls from cities or markets; nor shall he presume to exact any taxes or payments whatever, but the monks shall rule and possess, both in our time and in the future, all the property of this monastery in all places and lands, where they have possessions, as aforesaid, without being subject to the entrance of officials or to exactions on the part of the royal treasury. . . .

192. Form of a Grant of Immunity to a Monastery.

Marculf, I, no. 3; pp. 43 f.

We believe that our reign will best be rendered memorable, if we bestow suitable benefits on churches (or whatever you wish to insert here), with pious purpose, and if we secure these benefits under the protection of God by putting them in writing. Therefore, be it known to you that we have granted the request of that apostolic man, the bishop of (name), for the salvation of our souls; namely, that no public official may enter the lands which his church holds now, by our gift or by the gift of anyone else, or which his church may receive in the future, for the purpose of trying cases, or collecting taxes; but that the said bishop and his successors shall hold the said lands in the name of the Lord with full immunity. We decree therefore that neither you nor any of your subordinates or successors, nor any other public official shall presume to enter the lands of the said church for the purpose of trying cases, of collecting taxes or revenues, or receiving entertainment or seizing supplies or securities. All the taxes and other revenues which the royal treasury has a right to demand from the people on the lands of the said church, whether they be freemen or slaves, Romans or barbarians, we now bestow on the said church for our future salvation, to be used by the officials of the church forever for the best interests of the church.

193. Form by which the King Granted Lands with Immunity to Secular Persons.

Marculf, I, no. 14; pp. 52 f; Altmann und Bernheim, no. 113.

Those who from their early youth have served us or our parents faithfully are justly rewarded by the gifts of our munificence. Know therefore that we have granted to that illustrious man (name), with greatest good will, the villa called (name), situated in the county of (name), with all

its possessions and extent, in full as it was formerly held by
him *or* by our treasury. Therefore by the present charter
which we command to be observed forever, we decree that the
said (name) shall possess the villa of (name), as has been
said, in its entirety, with lands, houses, buildings, inhabitants, slaves, woods, pastures, meadows, streams, mills, and
all its appurtenances and belongings, and with all the subjects of the royal treasury who dwell on the lands, and he
shall hold it forever with full immunity from the entrance
of any public official for the purpose of exacting the royal
portion of the fines from cases arising there; to the extent
finally that he shall have, hold, and possess it in full ownership, no one having the right to expect its transfer, and
with the right of leaving it to his successors or to anyone
whom he desires, and to do with it whatever else he wishes.

194. GRANT OF IMMUNITY TO A SECULAR PERSON, 815.

Altmann und Bernheim, no. 114.

In the name of our Lord and Savior Jesus Christ. Ludwig, by divine providence emperor, Augustus. Be it known to
all our subjects, present and future, that our faithful subject,
John, has come to us and commended himself to us, and has
besought us to confirm to him the possession of lands
[described] which he and his sons and their men have cleared
and occupied. He has shown us the charter which he received
from our father Karl the Great. We have consented to do
this and have done even more; we have given him certain
villas [named] with their extent and dependencies . . .
granting that he and his sons and his posterity may hold
them in peace and security. No count, *vicarius,* or their
subordinates, or any other public official shall presume to
judge or constrain any persons living on those lands, but
John and his sons and their posterity shall judge and constrain them. . . .

195–208. Growth of the Feudal Elements During the Late Merovingian and the Carolingian Period.

The elements which we have just described and illustrated were essentially private in their nature. They assumed, however, political importance in the threatened dissolution of society, due to the failure of the public government. In a period when the state was unable to give adequate protection to the common individual, that person naturally regarded his allegiance to his real protector, his lord or landlord, as of more importance to him than his relation to the state. The natural tendency of powerful persons to increase their power over their dependents and their independence of higher authority was given its opportunity by the weakness of the monarchy and the central government. The four centuries from 550–950 were in the main a period of disorder, interrupted, of course, by the period of Carolingian strength, including the reigns of Karl Martel, Pippin, and Karl the Great. During these four centuries the existing feudal elements developed and hardened into a system of society, and two new features were added: the feudalizing of offices, and the connection of land-holding with military service. These are so characteristic of the feudal age that their origin is illustrated here.

195–196. The Feudalizing of Public Offices.

By this is meant the practice of inheritance of office and the union in one person of the characteristics of an official and a great landlord. Thereby the local officials of the king, such as the counts, tended to form an hereditary landed nobility, the office being held usually by the great landed family of the county. It is obvious that this tendency would grow in a period when the monarchy and the central government was weak, the king either being unable to restrain the powerful local officials or else granting them these privileges in order to retain their support. It is obvious also that the local officials would strive to increase their private advantages—possession of land, and personal authority over the inhabitants of their lands or districts—at the expense of their public position as representatives of the king. So in the feudal period in France, Italy, and Germany (in the last named the development was much slower), the titles duke, margrave (marquis), count, etc., ceased to have an official significance and became the titles of a landed aristocracy.

195. EDICT OF CHLOTHAR II, 614.

M. G. LL. 4to, II, 1, no. 9.

12. No one from another province or region shall be made judge [count] in any county; so that if a count has done injury to anyone he may be forced to make good the injury from his own possessions.

The count, like the *grafio* of the Salic law, was originally a servant of the king sent into the county to look after the king's interests there. It appears from this document that the counts were now appointed from among the land-owners of the county.

196. CAPITULARY OF KIERSY, 877.

* M. G. LL. 4to, II, 2, no. 282.

The capitulary of Kiersy was published by Charles the Bald, just before he left France for Italy, and was intended to regulate the affairs of the kingdom, which was entrusted to his son during his absence. It shows how completely the practice of inheritance of land and office had developed during the Carolingian period. The office, position, and lands of counts, vassals of the king, and vassals of ecclesiastical and secular lords were regarded as hereditary by this time.

3. If a count whose son accompanies us shall die during our absence, our son with the advice of our faithful subjects shall appoint one of the near relatives of the deceased count to govern the county with the aid of the officials of the county and the bishop in whose diocese it is, until we are notified of the case and have an opportunity to give the son of the count his father's honors. But if the deceased count shall leave a minor son, that son shall govern the county with the aid of the officials and the bishop in whose diocese it is, until the death of the said count has been brought to our notice and we endow the son with his father's honors. But if the count shall not leave a son, our son with the advice of our faithful subjects shall appoint someone to govern the county with the aid of the officials of the county and the bishop, until our commands in respect to it are made known.

And no one shall feel aggrieved, if we give the county to another than the one who governed it up to the time of our appointment. The same procedure shall be observed in regard to our vassals; and the bishops, abbots, and counts of our kingdom, and our other faithful subjects, shall do the same toward their men.

197–202. THE MILITARY OBLIGATION OF THE HOLDER OF LAND.

The connection of military service with the holding of land and with noble character is one of the characteristic features of the feudal system. The feudal noble was regularly the holder of a fief on terms of allegiance and military service to his superior. In the Germanic tribes military service was obligatory on every freeman, but there was also a fighting élite, or aristocracy, composed of the chiefs and their followers (see no. 1, Tacitus, chapters 13 and 14). The military obligation of the freeman remained in theory during the Merovingian and Carolingian periods, but in practice it was connected rather with the possession of land and was performed largely by the lords and their followers. Towards the end of the Merovingian period, much of the land was in the possession of the church and was escaping from public burdens because of immunity. Karl Martel found it necessary to increase the military strength of the kingdom; the particular occasion is supposed to have been the need of horsemen to meet the Arab invasion. He accordingly forced the churches to give portions of their lands to secular persons who could perform military service, and the holders of these lands were required to bring a troop of mounted warriors to the army. Such lands were held on terms of military service to the state and as *precaria* from the church. The same conditions were then attached to lands held from the king, and the term benefice—used in the earlier period of lands held from another in general—now came to be applied technically to lands held from the king or superior on condition of performing military service, usually on horseback. The number of mounted soldiers the holder of a benefice had to furnish of course varied with the size of his holding. The great lords raised the necessary troops by giving portions of their lands to their retainers on condition that the retainers should accompany them to war. So the obligation to perform military service was attached also to the small estates held not directly from the king, but from a great lord. We give here references to the appropriation of church lands, to the relation of the holder of the lands to the church and to the king, and to the extension of the name and practice to other than church lands.

197. CAPITULARY OF LESTINNES, 743.

M. G. LL. 4to, II, 1, no. 11.

This is a capitulary of Carlmann, the brother of Pippin. It is the earliest case which has come down to us of appropriation of church lands for the purpose referred to.

2. Because of the threats of war and the attacks of certain tribes on our borders, we have determined, with the consent of God and by the advice of our clergy and people, to appropriate for a time part of the ecclesiastical property for the support of our army. The lands are to be held as *precaria* for a fixed rent; one solidus, or twelve denarii, shall be paid annually to the church or monastery for each *casata* [farm]. When the holder dies the whole possession shall return to the church. If, however, the exigency of the time makes it necessary, the prince may require the *precarium* to be renewed and given out again. Care shall be taken, however, that the churches and monasteries do not incur suffering or poverty through the granting of *precaria*. If the poverty of the church makes it necessary, the whole possession shall be restored to the church.

The whole capitulary, of which paragraph 2 is translated, is concerned with ecclesiastical matters; accordingly only the interests of the church in the military benefice is explained here. The relation of the holder to the state comes out in other documents. Notice the express reason given for the appropriation, and the relation of the holder to the church from which the land was held.

198. CAPITULARY OF AQUITAINE, PIPPIN, 768.

M. G. LL. 4to, II, 1, no. 18.

5. Whoever holds a benefice from us shall be careful and diligent in its management; otherwise he shall lose the benefice, but retain his own property.

11. All secular persons who hold church lands shall hold them as *precaria*.

Paragraph 5 refers to lands held from the king. Notice the distinction made between such land and land held in full ownership. Paragraph 11 repeats the provision made in the preceding number, that lands held from the church as benefices are to be regarded as *precaria;* this is found in a number of capitularies of this period, suggesting that the holders were apt to forget their obligation to the church and to treat the land as their own property.

199. Capitulary of Heristal, 779.

M. G. LL. 4to, II, 1, no. 20.

14. (Lombard form.) Laymen who hold lands from churches as benefices by the command of the king, are to continue to hold them unless the king orders them restored to the churches.

200. General Capitulary to the Missi, 802.

M. G. LL. 4to, II, 1, no. 33.

Part of this capitulary is also translated as no. 9. This and the following document illustrate the holding of royal benefices, and the difficulty in making the holders perform their duties. It was part of the duty of the *missi* to look after the royal benefices.

6. No man shall lay waste a benefice in order to improve his own property.

201. Capitulary to the Missi, 806.

M. G. LL. 4to II, 1, no. 46.

6. We have heard that counts and other men who hold benefices from us have improved their own property at the expense of the benefices, and have made the serfs on the benefices labor on their own land, so that our benefices are waste and those dwelling on them in many places suffer great evils.

7. We have heard that some sell the benefices which they hold from us to other men in full ownership, and then, having

received the price in the public court, they buy back the lands
as allodial lands.   This must not be done, for those who do
this break the faith which they promised us.

202.   CAPITULARY CONCERNING VARIOUS MATTERS, 807.

M. G. LL. 4to, II, 1, no. 49.

3.   Concerning the Frisians, we command that our counts
and vassals who hold benefices, and all horsemen in general,
shall come to our assembly prepared for war.

203–208.   EFFECT OF THE CAROLINGIAN ORGANIZATION ON THE GROWTH OF FEUDALISM.

Karl the Great succeeded in reducing the great dukes to subjection
(see no. 7, Einhard, ch. 5 and 11, and notes), and enforcing obedience
to law in general throughout his empire, but he did not interfere
with the immunity rights of churches and lords over the inhabitants
of their lands or with dependence of vassals and tenants on the great
land-owners.   Indeed, his attempt to reduce everything to law and
system resulted in completing and fixing these relations.   The following passages illustrate the increased dependence of the lower orders
and the greater and more complete authority of the powerful persons
in the state.

203.   GENERAL CAPITULARY TO THE MISSI, 805.

M. G. LL. 4to, II, 1, no. 44.

16.   Concerning the oppression of poor freemen : that they
are not to be unjustly oppressed by more powerful persons on
any pretext, and forced to sell or give up their property.

204.   CAPITULARY OF 811.

M. G. LL. 4to, II, 1, no. 73.

This and the preceding document illustrate the attempts of the
great lords to round out their domains and increase the number of
their dependent tenants by forcing poor free land-owners to give up
their lands and become tenants.

2.   Poor men complain that they are despoiled of their
property, and they make this complaint equally against

bishops and abbots and their agents, and against counts and their subordinates.

205. Capitulary of Worms, 829.

M. G. LL. 4to, II, 2, no. 193.

6. Freemen who have no lands of their own, but live on the land of a lord, are not to be received as witnesses, because they hold land of another; but they are to be accepted as compurgators, because they are free. Those who have land of their own, and yet live on the land of a lord, are not to be rejected as witnesses because they live on the land of a lord, but their testimony shall be accepted, because they have land of their own.

Notice the effect that dependent tenure of land is having on the legal status of freemen.

206. Capitulary of Aachen, 801–813.

M. G. LL. 4to, II, 1, no. 77.

16. No one shall leave his senior, after he has received from him the value of a solidus, unless his senior attempts to kill him, to beat him with a club, to violate his wife or his daughter, or to take his hereditary possession from him.

207. Agreement of Lothar, Ludwig, and Charles, 847.

M. G. LL. 4to, II, 2, no. 204.

2. We decree that every freeman shall accept whatever senior he wishes in our kingdom, from among us and our faithful subjects.

3. We command that no man shall leave his senior without good cause, and that no lord shall receive a man who has left his senior, unless it be in accordance with the customs of our predecessors.

4. Every subject of each one of us shall go to war or

other necessary expedition with his senior, unless the kingdom is invaded and all the subjects are called out in mass to repel it, which is called *landwehr*.

208. CAPITULARY OF BOLOGNA, 811.

M. G. LL. 4to, II, 1, no. 74.

5. If any man who holds a benefice of the king shall release his subject from going to war with him or shall refuse to allow him to go and fight with him, he shall lose his benefice.

7. Concerning the vassals of the emperor who serve him in the palace, and have benefices. It is decreed that those who remain at home with the emperor shall not keep their tenants with them, but shall let them go to war with the count of the county.

The name senior is used in Carolingian documents for the lord who has authority over dependent tenants and vassals. Notice in the two documents preceding that the subjects of a lord are bound to him by law, and that they go to war, not with the general levy under command of public officials, but with their fellows of the same lands under command of the senior.

209–228. THE FEUDAL SYSTEM IN ITS DEFINITE FORM.

The elements already described became the system of society and government in the states which in the ninth and tenth centuries developed from the empire on its dissolution. The system gradually became settled and organized, the feudal kingship developed to give it a head, and it took the form recognized as the feudal system.

The features to be noticed are the relation of the vassal to his lord, the position of the king, and the economic organization of the land and the obligations of the cultivators to the landlords. The origin and growth of these features in the earlier age have been shown in nos. 180–208; it only remains to show how they were organized in the feudal age.

The vassal was bound to the lord of whom he held a benefice or fief by the oath of fidelity and homage. He also owed his lord certain services of noble character, the chief of which was military service. This was not perpetual service, but was limited by law or custom, usually consisting of 40 days' active service, and a certain amount of guard in the castle of the lord or in the castle which the vassal held as a fief of the lord. Aids or money payments were also paid by vassals on certain occasions, such as the marriage of the lord's oldest daughter, the knighting of the lord's oldest son, and the captivity of the lord. The lord had also certain rights over his vassals, which were frequently commuted for money: wardship, the right of guardianship of minor heirs, and the management and use of the fiefs during the minority; marriage, the right to choose or be consulted in the choice of a husband for female holders of fiefs; relief, the right to exact a certain payment from the heir when he succeeded to a fief; escheat, the right of taking back the fief into his own possession upon the failure of heirs, etc. These rights and payments have their origin in the personal dependence of the vassal upon the lord. They were occasional and did not form a part of the regular income of the lord, although they might be worth considerable at times. The regular income of the lord came from his domain lands, the lands which were not let out in fief, but which were cultivated by tenants or serfs, and which supplied the lord with money, resources, and services.

The authority of the king in the feudal state was very limited. This was due chiefly to the fact that each lord exercised practically sovereign rights over his lands and dependents. The feudal king was in origin one of the great feudal lords (cf. in France, Hugh Capet, duke of Francia; and in Germany, Henry I, duke of Saxony), who was chosen by the great lords and became their overlord. He had the same rights on his own domains as any feudal lord, but had only the authority of an overlord over his great vassals. He had no direct control over the vassal of his vassal, but could reach such an one only indirectly through that person's immediate superior. The holders of great domains exercised not only jurisdiction over the tenants on their lands, but possessed also other sovereign rights, such as the right of coinage, of collecting tolls and taxes, etc.

The basis of the economic life of the feudal age was the cultivation of land. Commerce, trade, and organized industry did of course exist during the Middle Age, but they were non-feudal in spirit and grew up outside of and in spite of feudalism. Land was organized in domains or estates, containing each a group of cultivators forming a community or little village. These cultivators held their land from the landlord on very complex terms of rent and services. Rents were paid in money or in a portion of the produce of the land. In each village the lord had a house, and a farm (manor-farm or head farm) which was worked by personal serfs and by the services owed by tenants. Aside from rents and services the lord possessed certain rights over his tenants, which were a source of revenue. The chief of these were: justice, the right to hold courts on his lands for the trial of cases arising among the tenants, and to levy and collect the fines; banalities (banvin, etc.); the right to sell his own wine, grain, etc., a certain number of days before the tenants could sell theirs (this he frequently released for a certain tax); the rights of market, mill, bake-oven, etc., which were owned by the lord, and from which he received tolls (these were frequently let out to other persons for an annual rent). A great lord, as a count or duke, would own a great many such domains, and would have a house or castle and farm in each one, and an agent or representative to care for his interests in the domain. Nobles of the lowest rank, as the knight or chatelain, might own only two or three, or even a single domain.

209–217. HOMAGE, INVESTITURE, AIDS, ETC.
209. HOMAGE.
Boutillier, Somme rurale, I, 18.

These documents illustrate the form of feudal practices after the system had become fairly well fixed. Most of the passages are from *Coutumiers*, codes or digests of feudal law and practice, of which there were a great many in the Middle Age. Some of the famous ones are: in England, those of Bracton and Littleton; in France, the *Établissements de St. Louis, Coutumes de Beauvaisis,* by Beaumanoir, and several provincial customs, as the *Coutumes* of Normandy, of Anjou, etc. Most of the references were taken from Du Cange, *Glossarium, Hominium.* See no. 180, for an early form of homage.

The man should put his hands together as a sign of humility, and place them between the two hands of his lord as a token that he vows everything to him and promises faith to him; and the lord should receive him and promise to keep faith with him. Then the man should say: "Sir, I enter your homage and faith and become your man by mouth and hands [*i.e.,* by taking the oath and placing his hands between those of the lord], and I swear and promise to keep faith and loyalty to you against all others, and to guard your rights with all my strength."

210. HOMAGE.

Coutume de la Marche, art. 189.

The manner of doing homage to another is as follows: The man who wishes to enter the homage and fealty of a lord should humbly request the lord to receive him into his faith; his head should be uncovered, and the lord may be seated if he wishes; the vassal should take off his belt and sword, and should kneel and say the words of homage, etc.

211. HOMAGE.

Ancienne-coutume de Normandie, art. 107.

The form of homage is as follows: The vassal who holds by noble tenure reaches out his hands and places them between the hands of his lord and says, etc.

212. HOMAGE.

Bracton, De legibus et consuetudinibus Angliæ, II, 35.

The tenant [vassal] should place his clasped hands between the hands of the lord; by this is signified, on the part of the lord, protection, defense, and guarantee; on the part of the vassal, reverence and subjection.

213. HOMAGE.

Tabularium Campaniæ, cited by Du Cange, Glossarium, *Ligius.*

I, John of Toul, make known that I am the liege man of the lady Beatrice, countess of Troyes, and of her son, Theobald, count of Champagne, against every creature, living or dead, saving my allegiance to lord Enjorand of Coucy, lord John of Arcis, and the count of Grandpré. If it should happen that the count of Grandpré should be at war with the countess and count of Champagne on his own quarrel, I will aid the count of Grandpré in my own person, and will send to the count and the countess of Champagne the knights whose service I owe to them for the fief which I hold of them.

But if the count of Grandpré shall make war on the countess
and the count of Champagne on behalf of his friends and not
in his own quarrel, I will aid in my own person the countess
and count of Champagne, and will send one knight to the
count of Grandpré for the service which I owe him for the
fief which I hold of him, but I will not go myself into the
territory of the count of Grandpré to make war on him.[1]

[1] This is a good illustration of the confusion of the feudal relation
in practice. The vassal held land in this case from four lords, to
all of whom he did homage and owed allegiance and military service.
It was the usual practice for the vassal to do *liege* homage to one
of the lords, who was his chief or liege lord, and to whom he owed
service first of all. Notice the compromise arrived at in this case.
For distinction between liege homage and simple homage see also
no. 214, and no. 218, introductory note.

214. HOMAGE OF EDWARD III OF ENGLAND TO PHILIP V
OF FRANCE, 1329.

Froissart, Chronicle, I, ch. 24. (Lettenhove's edition, II, pp. 227 ff.)

The king of England was received by the king of France
with great honor, and he and his company remained there
at Amiens fifteen days, during which many conferences were
held and many ordinances drawn up. It seems to me that on
that occasion king Edward did homage in words, but did not
place his hands in the hands of the king of France, nor did
any of his princes, prelates or representatives do so for him.
By the advice of his council king Edward refused to proceed
further until he had returned to England and had examined
the ancient charters in order to determine the manner in
which the kings of England had done homage to the kings of
France. . . . At last the king of England wrote letters
patent, sealed with his great seal, in which he acknowledged
the sort of homage that he ought to pay to the king of
France. This is the form of that letter:

Edward, by the grace of God king of England, lord of
Ireland, and duke of Aquitaine, etc. Know that when we

did homage to our beloved lord and cousin, Philip, king of France, at Amiens, he insisted that we should acknowledge that our homage was liege homage, and that in it we should expressly promise to be faithful and true to him. We would not agree to this at the time, because we did not know whether we owed him liege homage or not. Accordingly we did homage in general terms, saying that we entered into his homage in the same manner as our predecessors, the dukes of Guienne, had formerly entered into the homage of the kings of France. But now having found what that manner was, we acknowledge by the present letter that the homage which we paid to the king of France at Amiens was, is, and ought to be held to be liege homage; and that we owe him loyalty and fidelity as duke of Aquitaine, peer of France, count of Ponthieu, and count of Montreuil; and we hereby promise him such loyalty and fidelity. In order that similar disputes may not occur in the future, we promise for ourselves and for future dukes of Aquitaine that homage shall be performed in the following manner: The king of England as duke of Aquitaine shall put his hands within the hands of the king of France, and the person who speaks for the king of France shall say to the king of England as duke of Aquitaine: "You become the liege man of my lord the king of France as duke of Aquitaine, and peer of France, and you promise to keep faith and loyalty to him? Say yea." And the king of England, or the duke of Guienne, or their successor, shall say "Yea." Then the king of France shall receive the king of England, as duke of Guienne, by mouth and hands [see no. 209], saving their other rights. Moreover, when the said king of England does homage to the king of France for the counties of Ponthieu and Montreuil, he shall put his hands in the hands of the king of France for those counties, and the person who speaks for the king of France shall say, etc. . . .

215. FEUDAL AIDS.

Ancienne coutume de Normandie, I, 3, ch. 25.

The chief aids of Normandy are so called because they are rendered to chief lords [*i.e.,* to lords who receive liege homage]. It is the custom in Normandy to pay three aids . . . first, for the knighting of the lord's oldest son; second, for the marriage of the lord's oldest daughter; third, for the ransom of the lord.

216. FEUDAL AIDS.

MS. of the Chamber of Accounts, Paris; cited from **Du Cange, Glossarium,** *Hominium.*

In the chatelainerie [territory dependent on a castle] of Poitou and that region, according to the custom of the land, those who hold fiefs pay five aids to the lord: for the knighting of the lord's son, for the marriage of the lord's oldest daughter, for the rachat [1] of the lord's fief, for the crusade, and for the ransom of the lord from the hands of the Saracens.

[1] Rachat, see no. 228, Troyes, note 2.

217. FEUDAL AIDS, ETC.

From Magna Charta, 1215.

In the first part of Magna Charta, John promises to give up the abuses of feudal law which he had practiced. Thus he had exacted exorbitant payments from heirs for inheritance of fiefs (reliefs); he had forced widows and female heirs under his wardship to marry his favorites and supporters, or had exacted heavy fines if they refused; he had levied unjust aids and services, and a heavy scutage, or payment for exemption from military service.

2. If one of our knights or barons or other tenants-in-chief [*i.e.,* direct vassals] who hold by military service shall die and shall leave an heir who is of age, the heir shall receive his father's fiefs by paying only the ancient relief; namely, the heir or heirs of an earl shall pay 100 pounds for the whole earldom; the heir or heirs of a knight shall pay 100 solidi for the whole fief of the knight; and those who

inherit smaller holdings shall pay smaller reliefs according to the ancient custom.

3. But if the heir of any of our tenants-in-chief is under age and is under our ward, he shall have his fiefs when he comes of age without relief or fine.

8. No widow shall be forced to marry unless she wishes to; but she must give security that she will not marry without our consent, if she holds of us, or without the consent of her lord, if she holds of another.

12. No scutage or aid shall be exacted in our kingdom, unless by the common consent of the realm, except for the ransom of our body, the knighting of our oldest son, and the marriage of our oldest daughter; and these shall be levied at reasonable rates.

218–228. The Feudal System in Practice, Illustrated by the County of Champagne.

Actual conditions under the feudal system will, it is thought, be best illustrated by showing in some detail the workings of the system in a single important case. The following documents are taken from the great French collection of documents called "Documents inédits sur l'histoire de France"; two volumes are devoted to the county of Champagne and contain all the important documents relating to the growth and formation of the feudal territory of Champagne, the relation of the counts to their overlords on the one hand, and to their vassals on the other, and the organization of the lands retained by the counts as domain lands, *i.e.*, cultivated by tenants for the count and not let out in fief. The county of Champagne is chosen because it is one of the best examples of the formation of a great feudal territory, and because the two volumes referred to form the most complete as well as most accessible collection of illustrative material for the feudal régime in its practical working.

218–225. Homages Paid by the Count of Champagne.
218. Homage to the Duke of Burgundy, 1143.

Documents inédits, Champagne, I, p. 466.

The count of Champagne held his lands from several overlords; the ones mentioned in the following documents are: the king of

France, the duke of Burgundy, the bishops of Langres and Châlons, and the abbot of St. Denis; he also held parts of his lands from the emperor, the archbishops of Sens and Rheims, and the bishops of Auxerre and Autun. This plurality of superiors is characteristic of most of the great domains. The great fiefs came under the control of one lord by various means, inheritance, marriage, purchase, subinfeudation, etc. The great lord endeavored to complete his control of a whole region by becoming the feudal holder of all the land in the region. Since holding by feudal tenure, including homage, etc., was the regular method of acquiring land in the feudal system, it was used as a form of contract, and the personal subjection and dependence was in many cases a mere form. In cases like that of the count of Champagne the holder did homage to all the lords from whom he held lands, but could not of course observe complete allegiance to each one. So one of the superiors was recognized as his chief and liege lord, and to him the holder did *liege homage* (see no. 213, note). Notice that the count of Champagne pays *liege* homage to the king of France, who is his chief lord.

Be it known to all men, present and future, that count Theobald of Blois [1] did homage to Odo, duke of Burgundy, at Augustines, and acknowledged that he held the abbey of St. Germain at Auxerre, Chaourse, the castle of Maligny with all its dependencies, the castle of Ervy with all its dependencies, the county of Troyes, the city of Troyes, and Château-Villain, as fiefs from the duke.

[1] The territory of the count of Champagne included the counties of Blois, Troyes, Champagne, and Brie, and the holder was called by these different titles at various times.

219. HOMAGE TO PHILIP II OF FRANCE, 1198.

Documents inédits, Champagne, I, pp. 467 f.

Philip, by the grace of God king of France. Be it known to all men, present and future, that we have received our beloved nephew, Theobald, count of Troyes, as our liege man, against every creature, living or dead, for all the lands which his father, count Henry, our uncle, held from our father, and which count Henry, the brother of Theobald, held from us. Count Theobald has sworn to us on the most holy body of the Lord and on the holy gospel that he will aid us in good faith, as his liege lord, against every creature, living or dead; at his command the following persons have sworn to us that they approve of this and will support and aid him in keeping this oath: Guy of Dampierre, Gualcher of Châtillon, Geoffroy, marshal of Champagne, etc. [vassals of the count of Champagne]. If count Theobald fails in his duty to us and does not make amends within a month from the time when they learn of it, they will surrender themselves to us at Paris, to be held as prisoners until he makes amends; and this shall be done every time that he fails in his duty to us. We have sworn with our own hand that we will aid count Theobald against every creature, living or dead; at our command the following men have sworn that they approve of this and will support and aid us in keeping this oath: Pierre, count of Nevers, Drogo of Mello, William of Galande, etc. [vassals of the king]. If we fail in our duty to count Theobald, and do not make amends within a month from the time when they learn of it, they will surrender themselves to him at Troyes to be held as prisoners there until we make amends; and they shall do this every time that we fail in our duty to him. . . . We have also agreed that our beloved uncle, William, archbishop of Rheims, and the bishops of Châlons and Meaux, may place those of our lands that are in their dioceses under interdict, as often as we fail in our duty to count Theobald, unless we make amends within a month from the time when they learn of it; and count Theobald has agreed that the same archbishop and bishops may place his lands under an interdict as often as he fails in his duty to us, unless he makes amends within a month from the time when they learn of it.[1]

[1] Notice the securities given by each party; a suggestion that the oath alone was not always sufficiently binding.

220. HOMAGE TO THE DUKE OF BURGUNDY, 1200.

Documents inédits, Champagne, I, p. 468.

We, Odo, duke of Burgundy, make known to all men, present and future, that we have received our relative and faithful subject, Theobald, count of Troyes, as our man for the land which his father, count Henry, held of our father, Hugo, duke of Burgundy, just as his father, count Henry, was the man of our father. We have promised count Theobald that we and our heirs will guarantee that land to him and his heirs against every creature, living or dead, and will aid him and them in good faith with all our power to hold that land in peace and quiet.

221, 222. AGREEMENT BETWEEN BLANCHE OF CHAMPAGNE AND PHILIP II, 1201.

221. LETTER OF BLANCHE.

Documents inédits, Champagne, I, p. 469.

Notice the rights of wardship and marriage exercised by the lord in this case. The counts of Champagne claimed to be hereditary counts palatine of France (see nos. 223 and 225); notice, however, that the king of France does not use the title in speaking of the countess.

I, Blanche, countess palatine of Troyes. Be it known to all, present and future, that I have voluntarily sworn to my lord, Philip, king of France, to keep the agreements contained in this charter. . . .

I have voluntarily sworn that I will never take a husband without the advice, consent, and wish of my lord, Philip, king of France, and that I will place under his guardianship my daughter and any child of whom I may be pregnant from my late husband, count Theobald. In addition, I will turn over to him the fortresses of Bray and Montereau, and give him control of all the men who dwell there and all the knights who hold fiefs of the castles, so that if I break my promise to keep these agreements, all the aforesaid men shall hold directly of my lord, Philip, king of France; and they

shall all swear to aid him even against men and against every
other man or woman. The lord of Marolles shall put himself and his castle also under the control of the king, and simi-
larly all the knights who hold fiefs of Provins, and all the
men of Provins, and all the men of Lagny and Meaux, and
all the knights who hold fiefs of these places. . . . I
will do liege homage to my lord, Philip, king of France,
and I will keep faith with him against all creatures, living
or dead.

222. LETTER OF THE KING.

Documents inédits, Champagne, I, p. 470.

In the name of the holy and undivided Trinity, amen.
Philip, by the grace of God king of France. Be it known to
all, present and future, that we have received Blanche,
countess of Troyes, as our liege woman, for the fief which
our beloved nephew and faithful subject, Theobald, former
count of Troyes, held from us. . . . We have sworn to
her that we will keep the agreements written in this charter
in good faith, as to our liege woman; namely, that we will
protect and nourish her daughter whom she has placed in
our ward, in good faith and without deceit, and that we will
not give her in marriage until she reaches the age of twelve
years. After she has reached that age, we will provide her
with a husband in accordance with the desires and advice of
ourself, our mother, the lady Blanche, and the barons whose
names are written here, or of the persons who hold their
fiefs, if they have died. These are the barons: William,
archbishop of Rheims; Odo, duke of Burgundy; Guy of
Dampierre; Gualcher of Châtillon, etc.

223. HOMAGE TO THE BISHOP OF LANGRES, 1214.

Documents inédits, Champagne, I, p. 472.

I, Blanche, countess palatine of Troyes, make known to
all who see these presents that while my beloved lord, Wil-

liam, bishop of Langres, was at Troyes on certain business, I besought him, if he was willing, to receive there the homage of my beloved son, count Theobald. He replied that the homage ought to be made only at Langres, but that, as a favor to me and out of love to my son, he would receive it at Troyes, in order that I might be spared the journey, saving his rights and the rights of the church of Langres, and the rights of my son. Accordingly he received the homage of my son at Troyes, and I conceded and concede that this shall work no prejudice to the rights of the church of Langres, or the bishop, but that the rights of the bishop and of my son shall remain unimpaired.

224. HOMAGE TO THE BISHOP OF CHÂLONS, 1214.

Documents inédits, Champagne, I, p. 474.

Gerard, by the grace of God bishop of Châlons, to all who see these presents, greeting and sincere love in the Lord. Know that when our beloved son and faithful subject, Theobald, count of Champagne, came to us at Cherville, we were ill, and so he did homage at St. Memmie. Now in order that this may not work prejudice to future counts of Champagne, we acknowledge and bear witness that homage ought to be done at Cherville or elsewhere in the march [*i.e.,* frontier], where the bishops of Châlons and the counts of Champagne are wont to come together for conference and the transaction of business.

225. HOMAGE TO THE ABBOT OF ST. DENIS, 1226.

Documents inédits, Champagne, I, p. 476.

Peter, by the grace of God abbot of St. Denis, to all who see these presents, greeting in the Lord. Know that the noble man, Theobald, count palatine of Champagne and Blois, did homage to us for the castle of Nogent-sur-Seine and its dependencies, in the same manner as Milo of Châlons, former lord of that castle, who held it as a fief from the church of St. Denis. With the advice and consent of our chapter we have granted that the said count shall be bound to appear only in our court in matters pertaining to that fief.

226. List of the Fiefs of Champagne, about 1172.

Documents inédits, Champagne, I, pp. 22 ff.

These documents illustrate the relation of his vassals to the count of Champagne. They are taken from a register of the fiefs and vassals of the count of Champagne, drawn up about 1172. There are many instances of such registers or inventories in the feudal age; the relations of lord and vassals were apt to become confused and subject to dispute. The particular purpose of the register in this case was to determine the number of knights owing military service to the count of Champagne, and the amount of service owed by each one.

OF CHÂTILLON AND FISMES.

Count of Rethel, liege homage.

Count of Grandpré, liege homage.

Count of Roucy, liege homage.

Count of Chiny.

Roger of Rozoy, for the fief of Chaourse. Roger of Rozoy, his son [did homage].[1]

Lord of Montmort, liege homage. Guy of Montmort [did homage]. He holds in fief the rights of the forest of Vassy and many other fiefs.

Hugo of Oisy, a year's guard.

Gaulcher of Châtillon, guard and liege homage.

The sons of Guy of Châtillon, a year's guard and liege homage, etc., etc.

OF CHÂTEAU-THIERRY.

Count of Soisson. His fief is thirty pounds of the tolls and taxes of Château-Thierry.[2]

Lord of Pierrefonds.

Lord of Nesles, Fresnes, and Roiglise.

Lord of Braisne.

Lord of Bazoches is liege man of the count after the bishop of Soissons,[3] and owes three months' guard. For Coulonges and the forest as far as Ste. Gemme [his fief].

André de Ferté, liege homage and a year's guard.

Bartholomé de Thury, liege homage and a year's guard. His fief is at Thury, Coulombs, and Chacrise, etc., etc.

OF MEAUX.

Count of Vermandois.

Count of Beaumont.

Bishop of Beauvais, for the fief of Savignies.

Bochard of Montmorency. His fief is at Marly and Ferrières.

Lord of Crécy-en-Brie. For Crécy and many other fiefs.

Lord of Montjay.

Viscount of La Ferté, liege homage and guard. For his holdings at Gandelus, Fresnes, La Ferté-Gaucher, La Ferté-sous-Jouarre, and Lizy, and their dependencies, except the fief which he holds of the bishop of Meaux and the abbot of St. Faron.

Theobald of Crespy. For Bouillancy, etc., etc.

[1] This expression means apparently that the person named did the homage and performed the services for the holder of the fief, as his representative.

[2] Here is a case where the fief of a vassal is a portion of the revenues of the lord. As already noted, holding by feudal tenure was the regular form of contract in the feudal age; it was used not only in regard to the holding of land, but also for the acquisition of other possessions, as a sum of money, etc.

[3] The bishop of Soissons is the liege lord of the lord of Bazoches.

227. SUM OF THE KNIGHTS [WHO OWE SERVICE TO THE COUNT OF CHAMPAGNE].

Documents inédits, Champagne, I, pp. 73 f.

This table occurs at the end of the register of the fiefs of the count of Champagne of which the preceding number is a part. It is the sum of the knights who owe regular military service to the count, and is also therefore the number of knights whom the count should bring in answer to royal summons to war.

From La Ferté	58
Bar-sur-Aube	117
Rosnay	79
Saint-Florentin	42
Ervy	39
Villemaur	27
Vitry and dependencies	159
Bussy-le-Château	25
Mareuil-en-Brie	84
Montfélix	24
Épernay	40
Châtillon and Fismes	160
Oulchy	62
Château-Thierry	86
Meaux	149
Coulommiers	68
Montereau	29
Chantemerle	34
Bray-sur-Seine	83
Provins	265
Payns	42
Pont-sur-Seine	42
Sézanne and Lachy	85
Vertus	61
Troyes and Isle-Aumont	135
Méry-sur-Seine	21
The great fiefs	20

Whole sum of the knights.......................2,030

[Correct total ....2,036]

228. EXTENT OF THE LANDS OF THE COUNTY OF CHAM-
PAGNE AND BRIE, ABOUT 1215.

Documents inédits, Champagne, II, pp. 9 ff.

This is an inventory of the domain lands of the count of Champagne, made to determine the revenues, possessions, and rights of the
count, and the obligations and dues of the tenants and serfs. They
were determined by the examination of certain trustworthy inhabitants of each domain or village. The result was arranged according
to bailiwicks (large administrative districts), and domains or villages. Thus the cases given here are taken from the four villages
of Troyes, Nogent, Pont, and Séant, in the bailiwick of Troyes. The
student should notice the rights of the lord (justice, banvin, rachat,
mainmort, markets, tolls, etc.); the revenues from the lands; the
position of the prévôt (the lord's agent in the village), whose
services are paid by allowing him to collect and keep part of the
revenues. Note also that in this age many of the rights of the lord
are commuted for money or let out to others for an annual rent; this
was a common tendency of the later feudal age, when the lord came
more and more to appreciate the advantages of ready money over
services and rents in produce.

BAILIWICK OF TROYES.

1. Troyes.

The count has at Troyes pure and mixed justice in Troyes
and all jurisdiction over all persons,[1] except the men who
have charters of privilege and the men who live on the lands
of churches which have jurisdiction over their men by
charter or long usage.

Fines in cases coming under the high justice are levied at
the will of the count according to the character of the crimes
and the custom of the city. They are not estimated here.
Escheat and confiscation of goods for the great crimes, such
as killing, theft, rapine, heresy, etc., belong to the high
justice. The prévôt has 20 solidi of the fines which are
levied, and 60 solidi of the escheats. Besides these the
prévôt has no share in these fines, but they go to the count.

Fines for cases coming under the low justice are levied
according to the custom of Troyes. . . .

The count also has the right of mainmort by which he takes all the goods of men who die without children or heirs who should succeed, and all the goods of low-born men who die without children. . . .

The count also has within the district of Troyes the right of rachat,[2] which the widows of noble holders of fiefs must pay if they wish to marry again. The rate of the rachat has been decided to be equal to the income of the fief for a year. The prévôt has no share in the rachat.

The count also has the markets of St. John, which begin on the first Tuesday two weeks after the day of St. John the Baptist and end about the day of the Nativity of the Blessed Virgin. They are now estimated to be worth 1,000 pounds,[3] besides the fiefs of the holders of the markets which are worth 13 pounds. This market is called the "hot-weather fair" (*la foire chaude*).

He also has the markets of St. Rémy, called the "cold-weather fair" (*la foire froide*). They begin on the day after All Saints' day and last until a week before Christmas. They are estimated to be worth now about 700 pounds. . . .

The count also has the house of the German merchants where cloth is sold. . . . It is sold or rented out at the fairs of St. John and St. Rémy, and is estimated to be worth 400 pounds a year, deducting the expenses.

The count also has the stalls of the butchers . . . which are held from the count for an annual rental, paid half on the day of St. Rémy, and half on the day of the Purification of the Blessed Virgin. The count also has jurisdiction in cases arising in regard to the stalls of the butchers.

He also has the hall of the cordwainers [shoemakers], where shoes are sold on Saturday; it is situated next to the stalls of the butchers. It is held from the count for an annual rental, paid at the above-mentioned times.

The count and Nicholas of Bar-le-Duc have undivided

shares in a house back of the dwelling of the prévôt, which
contains 18 rooms, large and small. The rooms are rented
for an undivided rent of 125 solidi, of which half goes to the
said Nicholas.   . . .

The count and the said Nicholas have undivided shares in
seventeen stalls for the sale of bread and fishes. They are
now rented for 18 pounds and 18 solidi.   . . .

1 Justice was divided into high and low, or into high, middle, and
low justice. These distinctions were not everywhere the same, but
in general high justice meant jurisdiction over cases the penalty for
which was death or mutilation, and low justice, or middle and low
justice, the jurisdiction over less serious crimes. The same general
difference was understood by pure and mixed justice. When the lord
is said to have "all the justice, high and low," or "pure and mixed
justice," it is meant that he has complete jurisdiction over his subjects in all cases.

2 Rachat is the sum paid by the new holder of a fief at the time
of his entrance into the fief; it is about the same as the relief (see
no. 217, § 2, and introductory note to nos. 209-228). Here it refers
to the sum which the widow of a vassal of the count must pay when
she remarries, not for the privilege of remarrying, but for the right
to take the fief with her to her new husband.

3 Note the great value of the markets to the count. Troyes was not
a small village, but a city of some importance, and the market
rights were worth a good deal. This is a good illustration of the
seignorial or feudal control of cities, against which the citizens continually struggled. (See nos. 308, 309.)

4. Nogent-sur-Seine.

The count has a house there and the orchard that goes
with it, which the count retains for himself [*i.e.*, has not let
out in fief].

According to the statement under oath of Pierre of Pam-
peluna [etc.], the count has also all the justice, except that
which is held by others by charter or long usage.   . . .

Escheat and confiscation of goods come under the high
justice, and the prévôt has the same rights in fines and
escheats as in the case of Troyes [see above]. The smaller

fines from cases belonging to the high justice are estimated as belonging to the office of the prévôt.

The count also has the market hall and the toll from the markets and the village, every day in the week. They are estimated at 80 pounds.

He also has the banvin, which lasts a whole month, beginning on the day after Easter. It is valued at 30 pounds.

The count also has the right over the streams of Noe and Vileure. . . .

5. Extent of the domain of Pont-sur-Seine, determined by the statements of Pierre Molventre, Th. Coichard, and Robert of Besançon, who were sworn to speak the truth.

The count has a house there, and has all the justice in the village and the chatelainerie, except that which is held by others by charter or long usage. The high and low justice is exercised as described in the chapter on Troyes. The jurisdiction exercised by the prévôt is estimated to be worth 100 pounds a year, the jurisdiction over the fiefs at 14 pounds, 10 solidi, and the jurisdiction over the clergy at 26 solidi, 8 denarii.

These are the dues collected by the prévôt:

Taxes and toll from the market, and 18 solidi of the ancient small tax. Also the *lods et ventes*,[1] which are now estimated at 42 pounds.

The banvin, which lasts for 15 days, beginning about the day of St. Mary of Magdala, when the count wishes to exercise it; it is worth about 60 solidi when the count wishes to sell it. The monks of St. Étienne have the same banvin, but they are not allowed to sell it unless the count sells his.

The rents from the inhabitants of Villeneuve, now worth 60 solidi. The prévôt takes half, and the other half goes to the canons of the church of Provins. Each farm also pays 12 denarii and a measure of oats, half to the count (the prévôt does not take this) and half to the said canons. . . .

The count also has the following rents and *lods et ventes:*

Lods et ventes from the house of Robert of Besançon, and 12 solidi rent; the same from the house of Claude and 10 solidi rent; the same from the house of Ordinetus the serf, and 25 solidi rent. . . .

He also has from Saint-Martin-de-Bossenay 5 solidi of the small tax, *lods et ventes,* three hens a year, and 15 measures of oats. . . .

The count also has from Le Châtelot, near Villeneuve, seven hens a year, and five measures of oats to be paid on Christmas, and they belong to the office of the prévôt. . .

Hugo of Villeneuve, clergyman, Renerius, his brother, the prévôt of the village, Pierre Florie, Pierre Fromerit, former prévôt, and Hugo Florion, say on their oath that the count has the right of escheat from all who die in the village without heirs. . . .

1 *Lods et ventes* were payments made to the lord when the farm changed hands. The holder in these cases had the right to sell or rent his holding subject to the payment of *lods et ventes*. It may be compared to rachat or relief in the case of fiefs.

6. Extent of Séant, determined by the statements of Theobald the bailly, Ithari le Paalier, Felicité Huilliet, Guillot le Convert, and Milauti Veitu, sworn to speak the truth.

They said on their oaths that Henry, king of Navarre of blessed memory, bought the village of Séant, with its men, lands, woods, domains, and appurtenances, from the lord of Montmorency, with the dowry of lady Blanche his wife, now the wife of lord Edmund, son of the king of England, paying for it 6,500 pounds Tours.[1] The said lady Blanche has a house there and all the justice, high and low, within the boundaries of Séant. . . .

The lord of Montmorency had and the lady Blanche has 20 *journata* [2] of land in the place known as the clearing of

Forni, 10 *journata* in the clearing of John of Pont, 10 *journata* in the clearing of Pierre Courbe, and 5 *journata* in the clearing of Val de Laroi. In all, 45 journata, which are equal to about 42 arpents.

The lady also has the land tax from all the clearings; these are in meadows and contain about '250 arpents.

The lady also has the land taxes from the great field of Séant; this tax is divided into twelve parts, of which the abbeys of Valle Lucenti, Pontigny, and Dillo have five parts, and the lady the other seven. . . .

The lady also has rents, customs, and taxes from the following men:

Theobald the bailly is the man of the lady Blanche and holds of her in fief five of the eight parts of the bake-oven of Séant;[3] the other three parts are held by Adelicia and her children. The said Theobald also has a farm from the countess, for which he pays 5 solidi, 1 denarius rent, and a measure of wine, a hen, a loaf of bread, and three measures of oats.

The children of Bertelon are men of the countess and hold land of her at a rent of 11 measures of oats and the taille.[4]

The children of Baudonnet are men of the countess and hold land of her at a rent of 12 denarii and a measure of oats, and the taille. . . .

[1] An illustration of the acquisition of a fief by purchase. All the rights of the former holder went with the land to the new holder.

[2] *Journatum* is a measure of land, literally the amount which could be cultivated in a day. Probably in this case the lord had allowed some of his tenants to clear and reduce to cultivation part of his waste lands, on condition that he be given a portion of the cleared land from each tenant as payment for the permission.

[3] Note that the village bake-oven, which the lord originally erected and from which he collected tolls, has been let out as a fief and is now in the possession of two families of tenants.

[4] The *taille,* poll tax.

**229, 230.   THE ATTEMPT OF THE KING TO CONTROL THE
FEUDAL NOBLES.**

229.   THE FEUDAL LAW OF CONRAD II, 1037.

M. G. LL. 4to, IV, 1, no. 45; Doeberl, III, no. 1.

The feudal king naturally was not content with his restricted
authority under the feudal régime and attempted to assert his right
as head of the state to enforce general laws for the whole realm.
When the king was strong and able, he could do this to some extent,
but when he was weak, his commands received little attention.   In
the reigns of Conrad II and Frederick I, in Germany, the monarch
was able to control his great vassals and enforce obedience to his
laws.   But the triumph of the papacy, allied with the great nobles
of Germany, over the emperor was fatal to the development of a
strong monarchy, and after the death of Frederick II the feudal
lords became independent princes.   See the progressive concessions to
princes, nos. 136, 139, 153, 160.   In France the monarchy became
absolute by acquiring, in accordance with feudal law, actual
possession of all the great fiefs.   In England, the conflict between the
king and the feudal lords gave opportunity for the rise of a representative system of government, which was used sometimes by the
king to control the lords (as in the cases of Henry I and Henry II),
sometimes by the great lords to control the king (John and Henry
III).   Thus the feudal system, under different conditions, resulted
in France in an absolute monarchy, in England in a constitutional
monarchy, and in Germany in a weak central government and a
kingdom composed of many practically independent principalities.

In the name of the holy and undivided Trinity.   Conrad,
by the grace of God emperor of the Romans, Augustus.

(1) Know . . .   that we have ordained and established
that no knight of a bishop, abbot, margrave, count, or of anyone else, who holds a benefice from the royal or from church
lands, shall be deprived of his benefice unless he has been
convicted of a crime by his peers, according to the laws of
our ancestors.   This applies to both our great vassals and
their knights.

(2) If a conflict shall have arisen between a great vassal
and his knight, and the peers shall have judged that the knight
should lose his benefice, and if the knight alleges that he was

condemned unjustly, he shall keep his benefice until both parties have come into our presence, where the case shall be settled justly. But if the great vassal is not able to get the peers of the accused to give judgment, the accused shall hold his benefice until he and his overlord and the peers shall have come before us. In such cases, the party who appeals shall notify the other party to the suit, six weeks before he sets out to the royal court. This applies to our great vassals as well.[1]

(3) But cases between lower vassals shall be tried before their lords or before our missi.

(4) We ordain also that when any knight, either of a great vassal or of a rear-vassal, dies, his son shall have his benefice. If he does not leave a son, but a son of his son survives, this grandson shall receive his benefice, observing the custom of great vassals by giving horses and arms to his lord.[2] But if the knight leaves neither son nor grandson, but a brother or a half-brother on the father's side, that one shall have the benefice, if he is willing to become the knight of the lord of that benefice.

(5) Moreover, we forbid that any lord should trade the benefice which his knight holds, or dispose of it in any way without the knight's consent. And no one shall dare to take from his knight the lands which he holds by proprietary right or as a libellum or precarium.[3]

(6) The *fodrum* from the castles which was paid to our ancestors shall be paid to us, but we will not require any which was not paid to them.

[1] Note the right of the vassal to be tried by a court of his peers, *i.e.*, a court composed of the other vassals of the same lord; and also the right of appeal claimed for the court of the king.

[2] This is an old form of relief.

[3] Feudal tenure of land was not the only form known in the Middle Age. Other more ancient forms still existed in exceptional cases; as here: land held by proprietary right, that is, allodial possessions that had never been feudalized; land held as libellum or precarium,

which are about the same. A libellum was a piece of land held by one person from another for a term of years, for life, or with the right of inheritance, for a fixed rent, the *libellus* being the charter or grant. *Libellum, precarium*, usufruct, and *emphyteusis*, are forms of land-holding known to the later Roman law, and differing one from the other only very slightly.

230. THE FEUDAL LAW OF FREDERICK I FOR ITALY, 1158.

Ragewin, Gesta, IV, ch. 10; M. G. LL. folio, II, pp. 113 f; Doeberl, IV, no. 37 c.

Frederick, by the grace of God emperor of the Romans, Augustus, to all the faithful subjects of our empire. . . .

At the diet of Roncaglia, where we held a court of justice, as was the custom of our ancestors, the princes of Italy, the rulers of the church, and other faithful subjects made complaint that their vassals were in the habit of pawning or selling the fiefs and benefices which they held of them without their consent. Thereby the princes were deprived of the services due them from these fiefs and the dignity and the revenues of the empire were diminished. Having taken counsel with the bishops, dukes, margraves, counts, palatines, and other nobles, we therefore decree by this edict that no one henceforth shall sell or pawn or devise by will or in any way dispose of his fief or any part of it without the consent of the lord from whom he holds it. The emperor Lothar commanded under similar circumstances that such things should not be done in the future; we, however, hereby declare void not only future alienations of this sort, but also all illegal alienations that have already been made; the purchaser of the fief in such cases shall have an action at law against the seller for the recovery of the price, without regard to the length of time that has elapsed since the transaction. And as some resort to fraudulent sales and transfers under the form of free investiture after receiving the purchase price, we declare that such fictitious sales are void and condemn both seller and purchaser to the loss of the fief, which shall revert to the lord. Any lawyer who draws up such a contract knowingly shall be deprived of his office and lose his hand and be stigmatized with infamy. If any person over fourteen years of age, who has inherited a fief, fails through his own negligence to seek investiture for it from his lord within a year and a day, he shall lose the fief and it shall revert to the lord. If any vassal refuses to obey the summons of his lord to accompany him on an imperial expedition, or fails to come at the time set, or to send a suitable person in his place or to give half the revenue of the fief [as compensation for his service], he shall lose the fief and it shall revert to the lord.[1]

Duchies, marks, and counties may not be divided.[2] Any other fief may be divided if the co-heirs desire, but on the following conditions: Everyone who holds a part of the fief shall swear fidelity to the overlord; no vassal shall have more than one lord for one fief; and the lord shall not transfer the fief to another lord without the consent of the vassal. Vassals shall be responsible to the lord for the conduct of their sons; if the son of a vassal offends the lord, the father, on pain of losing his fief, shall compel him either to make satisfaction to the lord for his fault or to leave his household. If the son refuses to obey, he shall not be allowed to inherit the fief on his father's death unless he has made satisfaction. Vassals shall in a similar manner be responsible to their lord for the conduct of their vassals, and all their dependents.

In case of a controversy between two vassals of the same lord in regard to a fief, the matter shall be tried and decided by the lord. In case of a controversy between a vassal and his lord, it shall be decided by a court of peers of the vassal, sworn on their oath of fidelity to do justice in the case.

We also decree that in every oath of fidelity the fidelity to the emperor shall be excepted by name.

[1] Notice the attempt of the king to enforce his authority in military matters over the vassals of his vassals. In strict feudal law

the rear-vassal was responsible only to his immediate lord for the fulfillment of his duties, but the king generally claimed authority over them in matters in which the welfare of the state was concerned, as in the matter of military service in public wars.

2 In Germany the great lords retained for a long time in theory their character of public officials and their fiefs were regarded as administrative districts of the state. Hence the idea that they were indivisible, a character which still adhered to the lands of the electoral princes in later times (see no. 160, Golden Bull, ch. XX).

VII. COURTS, JUDICIAL PROCESSES, AND THE PEACE

I⊤ is not our purpose to give a complete account of all the mediæval courts, nor to show fully their mutual connection. Because of the great difficulties of the subject and the lack of suitable documents we name only the most important courts and offer a few passages to illustrate them. It is not that such documents are scarce that we have presented so few of them; but they contain so much that would require long explanations that they would demand far more space than we felt could properly be given to this subject. The materials which we offer illustrate the courts for the most part after 1100, but they throw light on those of the earlier period. In many other documents contained in this book there are references to courts and judicial processes which the student should carefully observe.

I. The royal court. According to mediæval theory the king was the judge in the whole realm. He had jurisdiction over all things. But because he could not be present everywhere and hear all cases, he appointed men (dukes, counts, etc.) to act as judges in his place. But they merely represented him. So whenever the king in his travels comes to a place, he at once replaces the local judge and all the machinery for the administration of justice. Since he was present in person, he needed no one to represent him. Eventually the great princes refused to receive him into their palaces because of the heavy expense in entertaining him and his numerous retinue, so his journeys as judge into their territories gradually ceased. In 1220 Frederick II agreed that he would exercise his rights as judge in the cities of the bishops only during the diets which he should hold in them and a week before and a week after. (See no. 136, par. 10.) He soon ceased to travel as judge, and after 1250 acted as judge only in and during the diets which he held.

Since in theory all judges and courts merely represented the king, he had the right to call before himself any case, no matter where it was pending. This was called the *jus evocandi*, the "right of calling." Rudolph of Hapsburg and his successors granted both princes and cities exemption from this. In the Golden Bull (no. 160, chs. VIII and XI) Charles IV renounced all right to call any of the subjects of the electoral princes before his court. These exemptions were gradually extended to all the princes, imperial cities, bishops, and other territorial lords, until in 1487 the crown completely lost its *jus evocandi.*

In the same way everyone had the right to appeal to the king, against the decision of any court. But in time the king surrendered this also in the same way to the electoral princes and agreed never to receive appeals from any of their subjects. See no. 160.

Frederick II found it impossible to attend to all the business of the royal court, and so in 1235 appointed a justiciar to represent him in all minor cases. See no. 232, par. 28. He also made provision for keeping complete records of the imperial court, and appointed a court secretary and put him under the control of the justiciar. See no. 232, par. 29.

II. The county courts. The county was composed of several districts called hundreds. Each hundred had its court, which was always held in the same place. The count received his authority as judge from the king, and with it the right to inflict the king's ban or fine of sixty shillings. The count went about from one court place to another, holding three courts a year in each place. This regular court was in session three days. If the business of the court could not be attended to in these three days, the count announced another court to be held a few weeks later. All the freemen of the hundred in which the court was held were bound to be present at it. The courts of the count were called the greater courts (*judicia majora*) and had jurisdiction over property, criminal actions of a serious character, and suits to recover serfs. The lower or hundred courts (*judicia minora,* see nos. 139, § 7; no. 231, I, 58) had jurisdiction over cases involving debts, chattels, and trespass. These lower courts were presided over by judges of inferior rank called *Schultheissen, Gografen,* or hundred-counts, who were either appointed by the count or elected by the people. They merely represented the count, and could not inflict the king's ban.

The counts were at first regarded as officials of the king, but under the influence of feudalism they became vassals and received their judgeships as fiefs.

III. Courts on the royal domain. All who lived on the crown lands, or royal domain, as they were called, were exempt from the county courts. The king appointed an official to administer justice to them. He was called an advocate and his office an advocacy. His position was similar to that of the count in the county courts. He presided over the *judicia majora,* and appointed *Schultheissen* to preside over the *judicia minora.*

IV. Courts on the lands of bishops and abbots. All those who lived on the lands of bishops and abbots who held directly from the king, were also exempt from the county courts. They were under the jurisdiction of the bishop or abbot, who appointed an advocate to preside over the higher courts, and *Schultheissen* to preside over the lower. These courts were quite like those on the royal domain.

V. The sovereign courts of the princes. The dukes received their jurisdiction with their fiefs, and in theory their courts did not differ from those of the counts. But they had a different development. For the dukes steadily developed toward sovereignty in their territories, and in 1231 many of them got complete exemption from the royal jurisdiction (see no. 139).

The duke of Austria was the first one to secure such complete exemption (1156); see no. 110. The Golden Bull (chaps. VIII and XI) shows that all the electors had acquired complete exemption and were sovereigns in their territories in the administration of justice.

VI. The courts of great landholders. Every great landholder, having a large number of vassals, held a court for the trial of all questions which arose between him and his vassals, or among his vassals. Since he also had jurisdiction over all the tenants and serfs on his lands, he of course held courts for them, which were similar to those described in III and IV. They are very similar also to the manorial courts in England.

VII. For the courts of the ministerials see nos. 297, 231, III, 42.

VIII. Ecclesiastical courts. There were also ecclesiastical courts which were presided over by clergymen, such as bishops, abbots, cathedral provosts, archbishops, etc. They tried all cases which involved offenses against the laws of the church.

IX. As the cities secured the right to govern themselves, they also in many cases got jurisdiction over themselves. In the documents in section X there are many references to courts and judicial processes in the cities. From the explanations given here the student will be able to understand at least their chief features.

X. Arbitration. Since the courts and the machinery for administering justice proved to be inefficient, it became common, especially among the cities, to create a commission of arbitration to settle all quarrels in a peaceable manner. See no. 319.

In German courts the judge was really only the presiding officer. The decision was rendered by the people who were present or by the *Schoeffen*. Generally some particular person had the right to propose the verdict (cf. no. 297, § 5). At the proper time the judge asked him what decision he wished to propose. Then the others present might agree with the proposed verdict or offer another in its stead.

In cases where there were no witnesses the accused was compelled to bring one or more of his relatives, friends, or neighbors, who swore that they believed that he was telling the truth. They were called his compurgators.

Schoeffe, pl. *Schoeffen*, were the permanent judges of the hundred court. They were instituted by Karl the Great to take the place of the temporary *rachinburgii* of the Salic law (see no. 4, title L, note 5). There were generally twelve of them in each county, and seven must be present before a court could be legally opened. They gave the decision in certain courts, and in so far they may be compared to our modern jury. They held their office for life. In the German cities the board of *Schoeffen* played a very important part in the administration of justice.

Schoeffen free, or *Schoeffenbar* free, were all the free-born. They were eligible for the office of *Schoeffe*.

The *Pfloghaften* were the free peasants who owned lands but because they did not render military service were compelled to pay an army tax. The payment of this tax was regarded as an evidence that they were not completely free, and hence their position was lower than that of the freemen who rendered military service for their lands.

The *Landsassen* were, like the *leti* (see no. 4, title L, note 1), essentially serfs, attached to the soil, and paying fixed rent and services.

The *Bauermeister* was at the head of the peasants of a village or district and acted as judge in certain cases when no other judge was at hand.

231. SACHSENSPIEGEL.

Following the revival in the study of the Roman law and the connection of Germany with Italy under the Staufer, Roman law was being introduced into Germany, where it naturally tended to replace the customary law, which was for the most part unwritten. The desire of the Saxons to preserve their own law and to prevent the uncertainty that would necessarily soon arise in it led them to attempt to codify it. Eike von Repkau, a nobleman, undertook the task of reducing their customs to writing. He called his book or code, which was written between 1215 and 1276, the *Sachsenspiegel*, that is, the mirror in which the Saxon law is seen.

I, 2. Every Christian man who has attained his majority is bound to attend the ecclesiastical court in the bishopric in which he lives three times a year. Three classes of people are exempt from this: The *Schoeffenbar* free shall attend the court of the bishop; the *Pfleghaften* shall attend the court of the *præpositus* of the cathedral, and the *Landsassen* shall attend the court of the archpriests.

They shall also all attend the civil courts. The *Schoeffenbar* free shall attend the burggrave's court [also called the advocate's court] every eighteen weeks. In it judgment is given under the king's ban. If a court is called to meet after the close of the regular court, all the *Pfleghaften* shall attend it to try all cases involving misdeeds. This attendance is all that the judge may require from them.

The *Pfleghaften* shall attend the court of the *Schultheiss* which is held every six weeks, to try cases concerning their possessions.

The *Landsassen* who have no property shall attend the court of the *Gograf* which is held every six weeks. In the courts of the *Gograf* and of the burggrave the *Bauermeister* shall make complaint of all whose duty it is to attend the court but do not do so. And he shall ask an investigation about all cases which involve bloody wounds, abusive speech, the drawing of swords in a threatening manner, and all kinds of misdeeds, provided no suit has been entered about them.

I, 53. If anyone does not attend court when it is called, or fails to prove his case when he has brought suit, or challenges a man and is defeated, or does not come promptly to court, or disturbs the court by word or deed, or fails to pay a debt when the court has given judgment against him, he

shall pay the judge his fine. In every case in which one
party secures "damages" from another, the convicted party
must also pay the judge his fine. And even in many cases
in which no damage is involved, the judge may assess his
fine. . . .

No one is fined twice for the same offence, unless he breaks
the peace on a holy day. In that case he pays two fines, one
to the ecclesiastical court and one to the civil court, and he
pays damages besides to him whom he has injured.

I, 58. If the people choose a *Gograf* for a long period, the
count or the margrave shall invest him with his office.
. . . When the count comes into the district of the
Gograf, the latter loses all his authority and cannot hold
court [because his superior, whom he merely represents, is
present]. In the same way when the king comes into the
territory which is under the jurisdiction of the count, the
count loses all his authority and cannot hold court. And
this is true of all courts. In the presence of the king all other
judges lose their authority and the king must try all cases.
A count is the same as a judge, according to old German
ideas.

II, 3. If a man is challenged to a duel who was not
warned of it before he came to court, he shall have time,
according to his rank, to prepare himself for it. The
Schoeffenbar free shall have six weeks, other freemen and
ministerials fifteen days. But for all other things that are
laid to a man's charge he shall answer at once, and either
admit or deny his guilt.

II, 12. No man may render a decision in a case to which
his lord, his vassal, or his friend is a party, if it involves
their life or honor. *Schoeffenbar* free men may render decisions in all cases, but no one may render decisions in
their cases unless he is of the same rank as they. . . .
If a man objects to a decision after it is rendered, he may
appeal to the higher judge and then to the king. In case an

appeal is made, the judge shall send his messengers who understand the case to the king. The messengers shall be freemen, and the judge shall pay all their expenses while on the journey. They shall have enough bread and beer, and three dishes for dinner and a cup of wine. Their servants shall have two dishes. He shall give five sheaves for each horse every day, and shoes for their forefeet. As soon as they learn that the king is in Saxony they shall go to him and bring back his decision within six weeks.

If the man who made the appeal loses it, he shall pay the judge his fine, and all the expenses of his messengers to the king, and damages to the man against whose decision he appealed. . . .

If a judge asks a man to render a decision, and the man is in doubt and cannot make up his mind about it, he may refuse to give a decision, and the judge shall ask someone else for a decision. . . . If a man proposes a decision and someone who is present objects to it and proposes another, the judge shall accept that decision which receives a majority of the votes of those present.

II, 13. A thief shall be hung. If a theft takes place by day in a villa [village] and the object stolen is worth less than three shillings, the *Bauermeister* may pass judgment on the thief the same day. He may punish him in his hair and skin,[1] or fine him three shillings. This is the highest sum for which the *Bauermeister* may try [*i.e.,* not more than three shillings]. But he cannot try the case the next day. But in cases involving money, or movable goods, or false weights and measures, and cheating in the sale of victuals, he may assess higher fines. Murderers, and all who steal horses from the plow, or grain from the mill, or rob churches or cemeteries, and all who are guilty of treason, or arson, or who make gain out of information entrusted to them by their lord, shall be broken on the wheel.

If anyone beats, seizes, or robs another, or burns his house,

or does violence to a woman, or breaks the peace, or is taken
in adultery, he shall have his head cut off. Whoever conceals
a thief or stolen property or aids a thief in any way, shall
be punished as a thief. Heretics, witches, and poisoners shall
be burnt.

If a judge refuses to punish a crime, he shall be punished
as if guilty of it himself. No one is bound to attend his
court or submit to his judgment if he has refused to grant
him justice.

II, 27. If a man refuses to pay bridge or ferry toll, he
shall be made to pay it fourfold. If he refuses to pay toll on
the frontier, he shall be fined thirty shillings. This is the
toll for ferries: For coming and going, four foot-passengers
shall pay a penny; a man on horseback, a half-penny; a
loaded wagon, four pence. The toll for bridges is half this.
No toll shall be collected from anyone except at bridges and
ferries. . . . An empty wagon pays half as much as a
loaded one. . . . If anyone leaves the road and drives
over cultivated land he shall pay a penny for each one of
his wheels and make good the damage he has done. If on
horseback, he shall pay half a penny besides the damage.

II, 28. If anyone cuts another's wood, or mows his grass,
or fishes in his streams, he shall pay a fine of three shillings
and make good the damage besides. If he fishes in another's
fish-pond, or cuts down trees which have been planted, or
fruit-trees, or if he takes the fruit from a tree, or cuts down
trees which mark boundaries, or removes stones which have
been set up to mark boundaries, he shall pay a fine of thirty
shillings. . . . Whoever by night steals wood that has
been cut, or grass that has been mown, shall be hung. If he
steals them by day, he shall be punished in his "hair and
skin." A fisherman may use the bank as far as he can step
from his boat.

III, 26. The king is the common judge everywhere. The
Schoeffenbar free man cannot be called before a foreign

court to fight a duel. But he must answer in the court in whose jurisdiction he is.

III, 33. Every man has the right to be tried before the king. And every man must respond if suit is brought against him before the king. . . .

III, 42. Do not be surprised that I have said nothing about the law of the ministerials. It is so varied that no one could ever come to the end of it. For under every bishop, abbot, and abbess, there are ministerials who have their special code of laws, and so I cannot set them all down here. . . .

III, 52. The king is elected as judge in all cases concerning property, fiefs, and life. But he cannot be everywhere, nor judge all cases, and so he gives *Fahnlehen* [flag-fiefs] to the princes [*i.e.*, with jurisdiction over them], and counties to counts with the power to appoint *Schultheissen,* so that they can act as judges in the king's stead.

III, 53. For every case a judge receives a fine but not damages. For no one receives damages but the man who brings the suit. And the judge cannot be both judge and a party to the suit.

III, 55. No one but the king can act as judge over the princes.

III, 60. The emperor enfeoffs all ecclesiastical princes with their fiefs using the sceptre as a symbol, and all secular princes with their *Fahnlehen* using a flag as a symbol. A *Fahnlehen* must not be vacant a year and a day. Wherever the king is, the mint and tolls of that place are surrendered to him during his stay there. And the local court is closed because he is the judge [and the local judge merely represents him]. While he is present all cases must be tried before him. The first time the king comes into the land [*i.e.,* after his election], all prisoners must be brought before him, and he shall decide whether they shall be set free or tried. . . .

III, 63. Constantine the Great gave pope Silvester the
secular fine of fifty shillings in addition to his ecclesiastical
authority, in order that he might use both secular and
ecclesiastical means to compel people to obey and do right.
So the two courts, the ecclesiastical and the secular, should
aid each other, and each should punish all who resist the
other. . . .

III, 64. If the king summons the princes to render military service to the empire, or to come to a diet, and informs
them of it by means of letters bearing his seal six weeks
before the time set, they must obey and go to the king if he
is in Germany. If they do not go, they shall pay a fine. The
princes who have *Fahnlehen* pay 100 pounds. All others pay
twelve pounds. A nobleman who does not come pays his
duke ten pounds. . . . Those who are under a count or
imperial advocate pay him sixty shillings, if he has the
king's ban. No one but the king can grant the king's
ban.

III, 69. In courts where the judge may inflict the king's
ban, neither the judge nor the *Schoeffen* shall wear caps or
hats or any covering on the head, or gloves. But they may
wear mantles on their shoulders. They shall not carry
weapons [in court]. They shall fast until they pass judgment on every man, whether he is a German or Wend. No
one except them shall pass judgment. They shall sit while
passing judgment.

III, 70. In courts where the judge has no authority to
inflict the king's ban, any man may give the decision, or be
a witness. . . .

[1] Punishment in the "hair and skin" was especially cruel. The
guilty one was flogged and his hair was wound about a stick which
was then turned around and around until the hair was all pulled out.
For some offences the hair was closely cut instead of being pulled
out, which was, of course, much more humane. Long hair was worn
by freemen as a mark of their rank.

232. FREDERIC II APPOINTS A JUSTICIAR AND A COURT SECRETARY, 1235. FROM THE PEACE OF THE LAND WHICH WAS PROCLAIMED AT MAINZ, 1235.

Altmann und Bernheim, no. 103.

(28) . . . We wish that all cases over which we cannot preside in person shall be tried by a man of approved character and good reputation, who shall be placed over the courts in our stead. And except in those cases which we reserve for our decision his judgment shall be final. We decree therefore that our court shall have as justiciar a free man, and he shall hold the office at least a year if he judges justly. He shall preside over the court every day except on Sundays and other holy days, and he shall administer justice to all litigants except to the princes and to other high persons in cases which touch their persons, rights, honor, fiefs, possessions, and inheritances, and the most important cases. All such cases we reserve for our judgment. This justiciar shall not fix the time for the more important cases which come before him without our special command. He shall not proscribe the guilty nor release from proscription. This we reserve for ourselves. He shall take oath that he will not receive anything for his decision, and that he will not be influenced by love, or hatred, or beseechings, or money, or fear, or favor, but according to his conscience, in good faith, without fraud or treachery, he will judge according to what he knows or believes to be right. We grant him all the fees which come from the absolution of those who have been proscribed, provided their cases were tried before him. We do this that he may be free to judge as he wishes, and may not find it necessary to receive gifts from anyone. He shall not remit the fine of anyone, in order that men may fear proscription.

(29) He shall have a special notary who shall keep the names of those who are proscribed, and of those who brought suit against them, an account of the case itself, and the day

on which the proscription took place; also the names of those who are absolved from proscription, and of those who brought suit against them, and the day they were freed from proscription; also the names of those who stand as security for them, and where they live, and also an account of any other security which the man to be absolved is required to furnish for the satisfaction of the one who brought suit against him. All letters and documents concerning suits shall be sent to him. He shall devote all his time to this, and shall have no other work to do at the imperial court. He shall keep a list of those who are denounced as dangerous, and when anyone is freed from suspicion, he shall take his name from the list. . . . He shall be a layman, because a clergyman is not permitted to write judgments which involve the shedding of blood, and also in order that if he does wrong in his office he may be punished properly. He shall take an oath to conduct himself faithfully and legally in his office. . . .

233. WENZEL CREATES A COMMISSION TO ARBITRATE ALL DIFFERENCES, 1389. FROM THE PEACE OF EGER, 1389. (GERMAN.)

Altmann und Bernheim, no. 107.

(2) We, king Wenzel, have made an agreement with the electors, princes, counts, lords, and the cities, and all who are parties to this league of peace, in regard to robbery, murder, arson, illegal seizure of persons, and quarrels which may arise between those who are party to this peace, that a commission shall be appointed to judge all cases of infraction of the peace, and the decision of this commission, or of a majority of it, shall be binding on all concerned. The electors, princes, counts, and lords shall name four of these commissioners, and the cities shall name four. And we will appoint a man to be president of this commission. If any member of this peace is injured by anyone, the case shall be

brought before the president of the commission. Within fourteen days he shall call the commission to meet in one of the four cities, Würzburg, Neustadt, Bamberg, or Nürnberg, as seems best to him. And the decision of this commission, or a majority of it, shall be binding, and they may call on the nearest lords, cities, officials, and judges, to aid them against the one who has broken the peace and inflicted the damage. And they shall be bound to aid them until the damage has, in the judgment of the commission, been made good.

(5) These nine men who form the commission shall swear on the holy relics that they will faithfully act as judges for rich and poor alike.

(10) If a war or quarrel arises between the lords and the cities who are in this peace, it shall be reported to the president and members of the commission. And both parties shall submit to the decision which the commission, or a majority of it, shall render in the case. If anyone refuses to submit to their decision, all the members of this league of peace shall aid the commission in enforcing it.

234–239.   Ordeals or Judgments of God.

M. G. LL. 4to, V, pp. 599 ff. Ordines judiciorum Dei.

The appeal to the judgment of God in legal cases was an old Germanic practice. There is evidence that the settlement of cases by lot, and by judicial combat or duel, was common in the earliest times. In the Salic and other laws there are references to the ordeal by hot water, etc. After the introduction of Christianity and the growth of the influence of the priest, the various ordeals were conducted by the church. The casting of lots and the judicial combat were opposed by the church, the one because it was inseparably connected with heathen rites, and the other because of its violence. Accordingly the church introduced other forms, some of which are illustrated here. The ordeal was ordinarily resorted to when the regular rules of evidence were not satisfied, as when one party could not furnish the required number of compurgators, or was accused of perjury, etc. The ordeal might be used either to determine which of two persons was in the wrong, or to test the guilt or innocence of a single accused person. The commonest forms were: (1) The ordeal of the sacrament, in which the accused took the sacrament, the expectation being that if he were guilty the consequences would be fatal; (2) the ordeal of the cross, in which the two persons stood with arms outstretched in the form of a cross, and the one whose arms fell first was regarded as guilty; (3) the ordeal by hot water; (4) the ordeal by hot iron, in which the accused either carried a piece of hot iron in his hand a certain distance or walked barefoot over pieces of hot iron; (5) the ordeal by cold water; (6) the ordeal by the bread and cheese; (7) the ordeal by the suspended bread, or psalter, in which the object suspended was expected to turn around if the accused person was guilty; (8) the judicial combat, which was not favored by the church, but which was very commonly used among the noble class.

234. Ordeal by Hot Water.
Pp. 612 ff.

(1) When men are to be tried by the ordeal of hot water, they shall first be made to come to church in all humility, and prostrate themselves, while the priest says these prayers:

First prayer. Aid, O God, those who seek thy mercy, and pardon those who confess their sins. . . .

(2) After these prayers, the priest shall rise and say the mass before all the men who are to be tried, and they shall take part in the mass. But before they take the communion, the priest shall adjure them in these words: I adjure you, by the Father, Son, and Holy Spirit, by your Christianity, by the only begotten Son of God, whom you believe to be the Redeemer of the world, by the holy Trinity, by the holy gospel, and by the relics of the saints which are kept in this church, that you do not come to the holy communion and take of it, if you have done this offence, or consented to it, or if you know who committed it, or anything else about it.

(3) If they all keep silence and no one makes any confession, the priest shall go to the altar and take communion, and then give it to the men; but before they take it he shall say: Let this body and blood of our Lord Jesus Christ be today a trial of your guilt or innocence.

(4) After the mass the priest shall go to the place where the ordeal is to be held, bearing with him the book of the gospels and a cross, and he shall say a short litany. After the litany he shall exorcise the water before it becomes hot, as follows:

(5) I exorcise thee, water, in the name of omnipotent God, and in the name of Jesus Christ, his Son, our Lord, that you may become exorcised and freed from the power of the enemy and the wiles of the devil; so that, if this man who is about to put his hand in you is innocent of the crime of which he is accused, he may escape all injury through the grace of omnipotent God. If he is guilty either in deed or knowledge of the offence of which he is accused, may the power of omnipotent God prove this upon him, so that all men may fear and tremble at the name of our Lord Jesus Christ, who lives and reigns with God.

(6) Prayer. Lord Jesus Christ, who art a just judge, strong and patient, plenteous in mercy, by whom all things are made, God of gods, Lord of lords, who didst come down from the bosom of the Father for us and our salvation, and wast born of the Virgin Mary; who by thy passion on the cross didst redeem the world; who didst descend into hell and there didst bind the devil in the outer darkness, and free by thy great power the souls of all the just who suffered there for the original sin; we beseech thee, O Lord, to send down from heaven thy Holy Spirit upon this water, which is now hot and steaming from the fire, that through it we may have a just judgment upon this man. O Lord, who didst turn the water into wine in Cana of Galilee as a sign of thy power, who didst lead the three children Meshach, Shadrach, and Abednego, through the fiery furnace without harm, who didst free Susanna from the false accusation, who didst open the eyes of the man born blind, who didst raise Lazarus after four days from the tomb, who didst reach out thy hand to Peter as he was sinking in the sea, we, thy suppliants, beseech thee

not to have regard for the errors in our prayer, but to make known to us before all men thy true and righteous judgment; so that if this man who is accused of fornication, *or* theft, *or* homicide, *or* adultery, *or* any other crime, and who is about to put his hand into the hot water, is not guilty of that crime, thou wilt so guard him that no harm or injury shall happen to that hand.

(7) Omnipotent God, we, thy unworthy and sinful servants, again beseech thee to make manifest to us thy true and righteous judgment, so that this man, who is accused and is about to undergo the ordeal, is guilty of that crime, by act or consent, because of the instigation of the devil or through his own cupidity or pride, and expects to escape or to circumvent the ordeal by some trick, his guilt may be made known upon him by thy power, and may be shown upon his hand, in order that he himself may be brought to confession and repentance, and that thy holy and righteous judgment may be made manifest to all people.

(8) [Another exorcism of the water.]

(9) Then the priest takes off the garments of each of the men and clothes them in the clean robes of an exorcist or deacon, makes them each kiss the gospel and cross of Christ, and sprinkles them with holy water. Then he makes them each take a drink of the holy water, saying to each one: I give you this water as a trial of your guilt or innocence. Then the wood is placed under the caldron and lighted, and when the water begins to get hot the priest says these prayers:

(10) In the name of the holy Trinity. God the just Judge, etc. [Similar to § 6 above.]

(11) Let us pray. God, who didst free St. Susanna from the false accusation; God, who didst rescue St. Thecla from the arena; God, who didst free St. Daniel from the lions' den, and the three children from the fiery furnace: free now the innocent, and make known the guilty.

(12) The man who is to undergo the ordeal shall say

the Lord's prayer and make the sign of the cross; then the caldron shall be taken from the fire, and the judge shall suspend a stone in the water at the prescribed depth in the regular manner, and the man shall take the stone out of the water in the name of the Lord. Then his hand shall be immediately bound up and sealed with the seal of the judge, and shall remain wrapped up for three days, when it shall be unbound and examined by suitable persons.

235. ORDEAL BY HOT IRON.

Pp. 615 f.

(1) First the priest says the prescribed mass; then he has the fire lighted, and blesses the water and sprinkles it over the fire, over the spectators, and over the place where the ordeal is to be held; then he says this prayer:

(2) O Lord, our God, the omnipotent Father, the unfailing Light, hear us, for thou art the maker of all lights. Bless, O God, the fire which we have sanctified and blessed in thy name, thou who hast illumined the whole world, that we may receive from it the light of thy glory. As thou didst illumine Moses with the fire, so illumine our hearts and minds that we may win eternal life.

(3) Then he shall say the litany. . . .

(4) The prayers. . . .

(5) Then the priest approaches the fire and blesses the pieces of iron, saying: O God, the just judge, who art the author of peace and judgest with equity, we humbly beseech thee so to bless this iron, which is to be used for the trial of this case, that if this man is innocent of the charge he may take the iron in his hand, *or* walk upon it, without receiving harm or injury; and if he is guilty this may be made manifest upon him by thy righteous power; that iniquity may not prevail over justice, nor falsehood over truth.

(6) O Lord, the holy Father, we beseech thee by the invocation of thy most holy name, by the advent of thy Son,

our Lord Jesus Christ, and by the gift of the Holy Spirit, the Comforter, to bless these pieces of iron to the manifestation of thy righteous judgment, that they may be so sanctified and dedicated that thy truth may be made known to thy faithful subjects in this trial. In the name of our Lord Jesus Christ, etc.

(7) Omnipotent God, we humbly beseech thee that in the trial which we are about to make, iniquity may not prevail over justice, nor falsehood over truth. And if anyone shall attempt to circumvent this trial by witchcraft or dealing with herbs, may it be prevented by thy power.

(8) May the blessing of God the Father, Son, and Holy Spirit descend upon these pieces of iron, that the judgment of God may be manifest in them.

(9) Then this psalm shall be said on behalf of the accused: Hear my prayer, O Lord, and give ear unto my cry. . . .

(10) Prayer: Hear, we beseech thee, O Lord, the prayer of thy suppliants, and pardon those that confess their sins, and give us pardon and peace.

(11) Then those who are to be tried shall be adjured as follows: I adjure you (name), by omnipotent God who made heaven and earth, the sea, and all that in them is, by Jesus Christ his Son, who was born and suffered for us, by the Holy Spirit, by the holy Mary, the Mother of God, and by all the holy angels, apostles, martyrs, confessors, and virgins, that you do not yield to the persuasions of the devil and presume to take the iron in your hand, if you are guilty of the crime of which you are accused, or if you know the guilty person. If you are guilty and are rash enough to take the test, may you be put to confusion and condemned, by the virtue of our Lord Jesus Christ, and by the sign of his holy cross. But if you are innocent of the crime, in the name of our Lord Jesus Christ and by the sign of his holy cross, may you have faith to take this iron in your hand; and may God, the just Judge, keep you from harm, even as he saved the three chil-

dren from the fiery furnace and freed Susanna from the false accusation; may you go through the ordeal safe and secure, and may the power of our Lord be made manifest in you this day.

(12) Then he who is about to be tried shall say: In this ordeal which I am about to undergo, I put my trust rather in the power of God the omnipotent Father to show his justice and truth in this trial, than in the power of the devil or of witchcraft to circumvent the justice and the truth of God.

(13) Then the man who is accused takes the sacrament and carries the iron to the designated place. After that the deacon shall bind up his hand and place the seal upon it. And until the hand is unwrapped [*i.e.,* at the end of three days] the man should put salt and holy water in all his food and drink.

236. ORDEAL BY COLD WATER.
Pp. 618 f.

(1) When men are to be put to the ordeal [of cold water], the process should be as follows: They shall be brought to the church, and the priest shall say the mass and the men shall take part in it. Before they take the communion, the priest shall adjure them thus:

(2) I adjure you, men, by the Father, Son, and Holy Spirit, by your Christianity, by the only begotten Son of God, by the holy Trinity, by the holy gospel, and by the relics that are kept in this church, that you do not presume to take communion, or to come to the altar if you have committed this crime, or have consented to it, or if you know the guilty person.

(3) If they all keep silence and no one confesses, the priest shall go to the altar and give them the communion. Then he shall say to them: May this body and blood of our Lord Jesus Christ be today a trial of your guilt or innocence.

(4)   After the mass, the priest shall take water that has been blessed and shall go to the place of the ordeal.   When they come there the priest shall give the men this water to drink, and shall say: May this water be a trial of your guilt or innocence.   Then he shall adjure the water in which they are to be cast, and then shall take off the clothes of the men and make each one of them kiss the holy gospel and the cross of Christ.   Then he shall sprinkle each of them with holy water and shall cast them one by one into the water.   The priest and those who are to be tried should have fasted before the trial.

(5)   Adjuration of the man who is to undergo the ordeal: I adjure you (name), by the invocation of our Lord Jesus Christ, and by the ordeal of cold water.   I adjure you by the Father, Son, and Holy Spirit, by the inseparable Trinity, by our Lord Jesus Christ, by all the angels and archangels, by the dreadful day of judgment, by the four evangelists, Matthew, Mark, Luke, and John, by the twelve apostles, by the twelve prophets, by all the saints of God, by the principalities and powers, by the dominions and virtues, by the thrones of the cherubim and seraphim, by the three children, Meshach, Shadrach, and Abednego, by the 144,000 who suffered for the name of Christ, by the baptism in which the priest gave you the new birth, that if you have seen or known anything about this theft, if you have had anything to do with it, if you have received it in your house, or consented to it, or if your heart is hardened, your heart may be melted, and the water may not receive you; may witchcraft not prevail, but may the truth be made manifest.   We beseech thee, our Lord Jesus Christ, give us a sign, so that if this man is guilty, the water may not receive him; do this to thine honor and glory, by the invocation of thy name, that all may know that thou art our Lord, who livest and reignest with the Father and the Holy Spirit, forever and ever.   Amen.

(6)   **Prayer** over the water.   We humbly beseech thee, O

Lord Jesus Christ, to give us a sign, that if this man is guilty in any way of the crime of which he is accused the water may not receive him, but he may float, and not sink in the water. Do this, O Lord Jesus Christ, to thine honor and glory by the invocation of thy holy name, that all may know that thou art the true God, and that there is no other God beside thee, who livest and reignest with God the Father in unity with the Holy Spirit forever and ever. Amen.

(7) Omnipotent God has established this ordeal, and it is righteous. Pope Eugene has ordained that it should be used throughout the whole world by all bishops, abbots, counts, and all Christians, for it is proved by many to be just and righteous. Therefore it has been decreed by them that no one may clear himself by placing his hand on the altar or on the relics, or by swearing on the bodies of the saints.

237. ORDEAL BY COLD WATER.

P. 689.

The following paragraph is taken from another ordeal by cold water which is otherwise similar to the one just given; it illustrates more minutely the way in which the accused was immersed.

(6) On the staff which is placed between the arms of the man shall be written: Behold the cross of God, let his adversaries flee. The lion of the tribe of Judah, the root of David, hath prevailed to make a righteous judgment + [sign of the cross]. May St. John the Baptist bless this water. On it shall also be written the gospel: In the beginning; and the benediction: Lord God.[1]

[1] An illustration, from an old manuscript of one of the collections of forms for ordeal, shows how the person was bound in this case. The illustration represents the ordeal as taking place from a boat. The man's knees are shown drawn up to his chin; a staff is under the bend of the knees and his arms are passed under the staff. His hands are bound at the wrist with a rope which is held by other persons in the boat. He was probably drawn out by the rope if he sank in the water.

238. ORDEAL BY THE BARLEY BREAD.

P. 691.

(1) First the priest prepares himself with the deacon, and then blesses the water; and the deacon prepares the barley flour which he mixes with the holy water and bakes, both of them saying during the process the seven penitential psalms, the litany, and the following prayers [certain prayers follow].

(2) Prayer over the bread. O God, who didst reveal the wood of the true cross on Mount Calvary, where Christ was betrayed by Judas (for God gave over his Son to be betrayed by Judas), reveal to us by the judgment of the barley bread whatever we ask in thy name.

(3) After the bread is baked the priest shall take it and place it behind the altar and shall say the mass for that day. After the mass he shall mark the bread with the sign of the cross, and shall place an iron rod in the centre of the cross, with a hook at the top to suspend it by. The priest shall keep this bread by him and use it until it spoils. When anyone is accused of theft, or fornication, or homicide, and is brought before the priest, the priest shall take the bread and give it to two Christian men, and they shall hang it by the hook between them, and the priest shall say the following adjuration. And if the man is guilty, the bread will revolve around; if he is not guilty, the bread will not move at all.

(4) Adjuration over the barley bread. I adjure thee, barley bread, by God the omnipotent Father, etc., that if this man or woman has committed, consented to, or had any part in this crime, thou shalt turn around in a circle; if he is not guilty, thou shalt not move at all. .I adjure thee, barley bread, by the Mother of God, by the prophet Hosea, and the prophet Jonah, who prophesied unto Nineveh, by Lazarus, whom God raised from the dead, by the blind man, to whom the Lord restored his sight, by all the monks and canons and all laymen, by all women, and by all the inhabitants of heaven and earth, forever and ever, amen.

239. ORDEAL BY BREAD AND CHEESE.

P. 630 f.

(1) Lord God omnipotent, holy, holy, holy. Holy Father, the invisible and eternal God, maker of all things; holy God, ruler of mortals and immortals, who dost see and know all things, who triest the hearts and the reins; O God, I beseech thee, hear the words of my prayer, that this bread and cheese may not pass the jaws and the throat of him who has committed the theft.

(2) Before the mass is begun and before the cheese is cut with the knife, while it is still whole, these words should be written round about it: "His mischief shall return upon his own head, and his violent dealing shall come down upon his own pate" [Ps. 7:16].

(3) Then bread and cheese to the weight of nine denarii shall be given to each man. The bread shall be of barley and unleavened; the cheese shall be cheese made in the month of May of the milk of ewes. While the mass is being said, those who are accused of the theft shall be in front of the altar, and one or more persons shall be appointed to watch them that they do not contrive any trick. When the communion is reached the priest shall first take the communion of the body of Christ, and then shall bless the bread and cheese, which has been carefully weighed out as above, and shall immediately give it to the men. The priest and the inspectors shall watch them carefully and see that they all swallow it. After they have swallowed it, the corners of the mouth of each shall be pressed to see that none of the bread and cheese has been kept in the mouth. Then the rest of the mass shall be said.

240–250. DOCUMENTS ON THE PEACE OF GOD, THE TRUCE OF GOD, AND THE PEACE OF THE LAND.

One of the worst features of the feudal age was the prevalence of private warfare. This was due to the warlike character of the feudal institutions, to the jealous insistence of the feudal nobles on their right to fight out their own quarrels without appeal to law, and to the weakness of the king in the feudal state. Continuous private war not only meant violence, oppression, and outrage for the weaker members of society; it also hindered or prevented any advance in civilization for the whole society. The first steps to overcome this condition were taken by the church, which was usually to be found in that age on the side of peace and order. The earliest form was the peace of God, proclaimed by provincial synods. Several of these appeared at the end of the tenth century. These forbade all violence and oppression under ecclesiastical penalty, on the ground that they were contrary to the spirit of Christianity. The peace of God did not attain any lasting success, for the turbulent nobles could not be made to give up fighting entirely. Then the church attempted to mitigate at least these evils, by means of the truce of God. In the truce of God, violence was forbidden on certain days and during certain periods. In origin the truce of God was proclaimed by the clergy of a certain diocese or archdiocese for the people of their district, but later it was sometimes adopted by the emperor or king for the whole land. The truce was to last from vespers or sunset on Wednesday to sunrise on the following Monday of every week, and also for certain whole periods. It will be seen from the documents that these days and periods had a religious significance, which is further evidence that the church regarded the keeping of the peace as a religious rather than a political duty. The means of enforcing the truce were ecclesiastical penalties, penance, anathema, excommunication, etc. The peace of the land has a different origin and character. In the empire of Karl the Great, the right to enforce the keeping of the peace belonged to the emperor, and in theory this had never been given up by the later kings and emperors. It was on this right that the emperors based their authority to proclaim the peace of the land. In appearance the great peaces of Frederick I and Frederick II were imperial edicts, but in fact they depended very largely for their authority upon the acceptance and agreement of the nobles (see nos. 245, 246). In some cases the peace of the land was proclaimed for a province (see no. 246), in others it was for the whole empire. The peace was usually proclaimed for a certain length of time. In some cases the form of the truce of God was preserved in the peace of the land, as in no. 246. The documents on the peace of the land belong in a way under section III, but it was thought better to bring them together here, because they interrupt the general historical movement of the quarrel, and because they form a subject by themselves.

240. Peace of God, Proclaimed in the Synod of Charroux, 989.

Huberti, Gottesfrieden und Landfrieden, I, p. 35.

Following the example of my predecessors, I, Gunbald, archbishop of Bordeaux, called together the bishops of my diocese in a synod at Charroux, . . . and we, assembled there in the name of God, made the following decrees:

1. Anathema against those who break into churches. If anyone breaks into or robs a church, he shall be anathema unless he makes satisfaction.

2. Anathema against those who rob the poor. If anyone robs a peasant or any other poor person of a sheep, ox, ass, cow, goat, or pig, he shall be anathema unless he makes satisfaction.

3. Anathema against those who injure clergymen. If anyone attacks, seizes, or beats a priest, deacon, or any other clergyman, who is not bearing arms (shield, sword, coat of mail, or helmet), but is going along peacefully or staying in the house, the sacrilegious person shall be excommunicated and cut off from the church, unless he makes satisfaction, or unless the bishop discovers that the clergyman brought it upon himself by his own fault.

241. Peace of God, Proclaimed by Guy of Anjou, Bishop of Puy, 990.

Huberti, Gottesfrieden, I, pp. 123 f.

In the name of the divine, supreme, and undivided Trinity. Guy of Anjou, by the grace of God bishop [of Puy], greeting and peace to all who desire the mercy of God. Be it known to all the faithful subjects of God, that because of the wickedness that daily increases among the people, we have called together certain bishops [names], and many other bishops, princes, and nobles. And since we know that only the peace-loving shall see the Lord, we urge all men, in the name of the Lord, to be sons of peace.

1.　From this hour forth, no man in the bishoprics over which these bishops rule, and in these counties, shall break into a church, . . . except that the bishop may enter a church to recover the taxes that are due him from it.[1]

2.　No man in the counties or bishoprics shall seize a horse, colt, ox, cow, ass, or the burdens which it carries, or a sheep, goat, or pig, or kill any of them, unless he requires it for a lawful expedition.[2]　On an expedition a man may take what he needs to eat, but shall carry nothing home with him; and no one shall take material for fortifying or besieging a castle except from his own lands or subjects.

3.　Clergymen shall not bear arms; no one shall injure monks or any unarmed persons who accompany them; except that the bishop or the archdeacon may use such means as are necessary to compel them to pay the taxes which they owe them.

4.　No one shall seize a peasant, man or woman, for the purpose of making him purchase his freedom, unless the peasant has forfeited his freedom.　This is not meant to restrict the rights of a lord over the peasants living on his own lands or on lands which he claims.

5.　From this hour forth no one shall seize ecclesiastical lands, whether those of a bishop, chapter, or monastery, and no one shall levy any unjust tax or toll from them; unless he holds them as *precaria* from the bishop or the brothers.

6.　No one shall seize or rob merchants.

7.　No layman shall exercise any authority in the matter of burials or ecclesiastical offerings; no priest shall take money for baptism, for it is the gift of the Holy Spirit.

8.　If anyone breaks the peace and refuses to keep it, he shall be excommunicated and anathematized and cut off from the holy mother church, until he makes satisfaction; if he refuses to make satisfaction, no priest shall say mass or perform divine services for him, no priest shall bury him or permit him to be buried in consecrated ground; no priest shall knowingly give him communion; if any priest knowingly violates this decree he shall be deposed.

¹ The meaning of this exception is not clear in the original. Apparently it is put in to preserve the right of the bishop over the churches and the clergy of his diocese, and to prevent any of the lower clergy from citing the decree in restraint of episcopal control; so also the exception in paragraph 3.

² This exception is intended to preserve the rights of the emperor and others on lawful expeditions to take what they need for the journey.

242. Truce of God, made for the Archbishopric of Arles, 1035-41.

M. G. LL. 4to, IV, 1, no. 419.

This is the earliest truce of God extant (except for the doubtful case of the council of Elne, 1027), and it is preserved only in the form of a communication recommending it to the clergy of Italy.

In the name of God, the omnipotent Father, Son, and Holy Spirit. Reginbald, archbishop of Arles, with Benedict, bishop of Avignon, Nithard, bishop of Nice, the venerable abbot Odilo [of Cluny], and all the bishops, abbots, and other clergy of Gaul, to all the archbishops, bishops, and clergy of Italy, grace and peace from God, the omnipotent Father, who is, was, and shall be.

1. For the salvation of your souls, we beseech all you who fear God and believe in him and have been redeemed by his blood, to follow the footsteps of God, and to keep peace one with another, that you may obtain eternal peace and quiet with Him.

2. This is the peace or truce of God which we have received from heaven through the inspiration of God, and we beseech you to accept it and observe it even as we have done; namely, that all Christians, friends and enemies, neighbors and strangers, should keep true and lasting peace one with another from vespers on Wednesday to sunrise on Monday, so that during these four days and five nights, all persons may

have peace, and, trusting in this peace, may go about their business without fear of their enemies.

3. All who keep the peace and truce of God shall be absolved of their sins by God, the omnipotent Father, and His Son Jesus Christ, and the Holy Spirit, and by St. Mary with the choir of virgins, and St. Michael with the choir of angels, and St. Peter with all the saints and all the faithful, now and forever.

4. Those who have promised to observe the truce and have wilfully violated it, shall be excommunicated by God the omnipotent Father, and His Son Jesus Christ, and the Holy Spirit, from the communion of all the saints of God, shall be accursed and despised here and in the future world, shall be damned with Dathan and Abiram and with Judas who betrayed his Lord, and shall be overwhelmed in the depths of hell, as was Pharaoh in the midst of the sea, unless they make such satisfaction as is described in the following:

5. If anyone has killed another on the days of the truce of God, he shall be exiled and driven from the land and shall make a pilgrimage to Jerusalem, spending his exile there. If anyone has violated the truce of God in any other way, he shall suffer the penalty prescribed by the secular laws and shall do double the penance prescribed by the canons.

6. We believe it is just that we should suffer both secular and spiritual punishment if we break the promise which we have made to keep the peace. For we believe that this peace was given to us from heaven by God; for before God gave it to his people, there was nothing good done among us. The Lord's Day was not kept, but all kinds of labor were performed on it.

7. We have vowed and dedicated these four days to God: Thursday, because it is the day of his ascension; Friday, because it is the day of his passion; Saturday, because it is the day in which he was in the tomb; and Sunday, because it is

the day of his resurrection; on that day no labor shall be done and no one shall be in fear of his enemy.

8. By the power given to us by God through the apostles, we bless and absolve all who keep the peace and truce of God; we excommunicate, curse, anathematize, and exclude from the holy mother church all who violate it.

9. If anyone shall punish violators of this decree and of the truce of God, he shall not be held guilty of a crime, but shall go and come freely with the blessing of all Christians, as a defender of the cause of God. But if anything has been stolen on other days, and the owner finds it on one of the days of the truce, he shall not be restrained from recovering it, lest thereby an advantage should be given to the thief.

10. In addition, brothers, we request that you observe the day on which the peace and truce was established by us, keeping it in the name of the holy Trinity. Drive all thieves out of your country, and curse and excommunicate them in the name of all the saints.

11. Offer your tithes and the first fruits of your labors to God, and bring offerings from your goods to the churches for the souls of the living and the dead, that God may free you from all evils in this world, and after this life bring you to the kingdom of heaven, through Him who lives and reigns with God the Father and the Holy Spirit, forever and ever. Amen.

243. TRUCE OF GOD FOR THE ARCHBISHOPRICS OF BESANCON AND VIENNE, *ca.*, 1041.

M. G. LL. 4to, IV, 1, no. 421.

1. We command all to keep the truce from sunset on Wednesday to sunrise on Monday, and from Christmas to the octave of [*i.e.*, week after] Epiphany [Jan. 6], and from Septuagesima Sunday [third Sunday before Lent] to the octave of Easter [the Sunday after Easter].

2. If anyone violates the truce and refuses to make satis-

faction, after he has been admonished three times, the bishop shall excommunicate him and shall notify the neighboring bishops of his action by letter. No bishop shall receive the excommunicated person, but shall confirm the sentence of excommunication against him in writing. If any bishop violates this decree he shall be in danger of losing his rank.

3. And since a threefold cord is stronger and harder to break than a single one, we command bishops mutually to aid one another in maintaining this peace, having regard only to God and the salvation of their people, and not to neglect this through love or fear of anyone. If any bishop is negligent in this regard, he shall be in danger of losing his rank.

244. Truce for the Bishopric of Terouanne, 1063.

M. G. LL. 4to, IV, 1, no. 422.

Drogo, bishop of Terouanne, and count Baldwin [of Hainault] have established this peace with the cooperation of the clergy and people of the land.

Dearest brothers in the Lord, these are the conditions which you must observe during the time of the peace which is commonly called the truce of God, and which begins with sunset on Wednesday and lasts until sunrise on Monday.

1. During those four days and five nights no man or woman shall assault, wound, or slay another, or attack, seize, or destroy a castle, burg, or villa, by craft or by violence.

2. If anyone violates this peace and disobeys these commands of ours, he shall be exiled for thirty years as a penance, and before he leaves the bishopric he shall make compensation for the injury which he committed. Otherwise he shall be excommunicated by the Lord God and excluded from all Christian fellowship.

3. All who associate with him in any way, who give him advice or aid, or hold converse with him, unless it be to advise him to do penance and to leave the bishopric, shall be under excommunication until they have made satisfaction.

4. If any violator of the peace shall fall sick and die before he completes his penance, no Christian shall visit him or move his body from the place where it lay, or receive any of his possessions.

5. In addition, brethren, you should observe the peace in regard to lands and animals and all things that can be possessed. If anyone takes from another an animal, a coin, or a garment, during the days of the truce, he shall be excommunicated unless he makes satisfaction. If he desires to make satisfaction for his crime he shall first restore the thing which he stole or its value in money, and shall do penance for seven years within the bishopric. If he should die before he makes satisfaction and completes his penance, his body shall not be buried or removed from the place where it lay, unless his family shall make satisfaction for him to the person whom he injured.

6. During the days of the peace, no one shall make a hostile expedition on horseback, except when summoned by the count; and all who go with the count shall take for their support only as much as is necessary for themselves and their horses.

7. All merchants and other men who pass through your territory from other lands shall have peace from you.

8. You shall also keep this peace every day of the week from the beginning of Advent to the octave of Epiphany and from the beginning of Lent to the octave of Easter, and from the feast of Rogations [the Monday before Ascension Day] to the octave of Pentecost.

9. We command all priests on feast days and Sundays to pray for all who keep the peace, and to curse all who violate it or support its violators.

10. If anyone has been accused of violating the peace and denies the charge, he shall take the communion and undergo the ordeal of hot iron. If he is found guilty, he shall do penance within the bishopric for seven years.

245. PEACE OF THE LAND ESTABLISHED BY HENRY IV, 1103.

M. G. LL. folio, II, p. 60; Doeberl, III, no. 18.

In the year of the incarnation of our Lord 1103, the emperor Henry established this peace at Mainz, and he and the archbishops and bishops signed it with their own signatures. The son of the king and the nobles of the whole kingdom, dukes, margraves, counts, and many others, swore to observe it. Duke Welf, duke Bertholf, and duke Frederick swore to keep the peace from that day to four years from the next Pentecost. They swore to keep peace with churches, clergy, monks, merchants, women, and Jews. This is the form of the oath which they swore:

No one shall attack the house of another or waste it with fire, or seize another for ransom, or strike, wound, or slay another. If anyone does any of these things he shall lose his eyes or his hand, and the one who defends him shall suffer the same penalty. If the violator flees into a castle, the castle shall be besieged for three days by those who have sworn to keep the peace, and if the violator is not given up it shall be destroyed. If the offender flees from justice out of the country, his lord shall take away his fief, if he has one, and his relatives shall take his patrimony. If anyone steals anything worth five solidi or more, he shall lose his eyes or his hand. If anyone steals anything worth less than five solidi, he shall be made to restore the theft, and shall lose his hair and be beaten with rods; if he has committed this smaller theft three times, he shall lose his eyes or his hand. If thou shalt meet thine enemy on the road and canst injure him, do so; but if he escapes to the house or castle of anyone, thou shalt let him remain there unharmed.

246. PEACE OF THE LAND FOR ELSASS, 1085–1103.

M. G. LL. 4to, IV, 1, no. 429; Doeberl, III, no. 22 b.

Be it known to all lovers of peace that the people of Elsass with their leaders have mutually sworn to maintain perpetual peace on the following terms:

1. All churches shall have peace always and everywhere. All clergy and women, merchants, hunters, pilgrims, and farmers while they work in the fields and on their way to and from their labor, shall have peace.

2. They have sworn to keep the peace especially on certain days and during certain seasons; namely, from vespers on Wednesday to sunrise on Monday of every week, on the vigils [1] and feast days of the saints, on the four times of fast,[2] from Advent to the octave of Epiphany, and from Septuagesima Sunday to the octave of Pentecost. In these times no one shall bear arms except those on journey. All public enemies of the royal majesty shall be excluded from the benefits of this peace.

3. If anyone of those who have sworn to maintain this peace shall commit any crime against one of the others, on one of these days, such as robbing, burning, seizing, or committing any other violence on his lands or in his house, or beating him so as to bring blood, he shall suffer capital punishment, if he is a freeman, and shall lose his hand, if he is a serf.

4. If anyone conceals a violator of the peace or aids him to escape, he shall suffer the penalty of the guilty person.

5. If anyone unjustly accuses one of those who have sworn to keep the peace of having violated it, or calls out the forces of the peace against him, through malice or anger, he shall suffer the penalty described above.

6. If anyone who dwells in the province has been accused of violating the peace, he shall clear himself inside of seven days by the testimony of seven of his peers, if he is a freeman or a ministerial; but if he belongs to a lower rank in the city or country, he shall clear himself by the ordeal of cold water.

7. If anyone steals anything of the value of a siclum [a coin of unknown value] or two, he shall lose his hair and his skin; if he commits the theft a second time, or steals anything

worth five sicla or more, he shall lose his hand; if he commits a theft a third time, he shall be hanged.

8.   Those who are called to attend the expedition of the emperor or one made to maintain the peace, shall go at their own expense for three days. If the expedition takes longer than that, they may levy fodder for their horses and food for themselves, but may take only grass, vegetables, apples, wood, and the implements of the hunt.

9.   Draught horses, vineyards, and crops shall always be under the peace, except that a traveler may take enough from the public road to feed his horse.

10.   Whatever anyone held by any right of ownership or possession before the peace was decreed, he shall still hold by the same right.

11.   If anyone has withdrawn from this sworn agreement to keep the peace, or confesses that he swore to it falsely, and wishes still to remain in the territory, he shall promise with seven sureties that he will keep the peace. If he refuses to promise or if he in any way opposes the peace, he shall either be subject to the penalties of this decree, or shall leave the land.

12.   All the authors of the peace should be on their guard to prevent rash or unwise action in enforcing it.

13.   The younger men should be persuaded or even forced to swear to keep the peace, for they are especially apt to neglect its provisions.

14.   Priests should watch diligently that this useful and holy peace be not disregarded by the members of their congregations, and should admonish their people every Sunday to keep it, as is decreed by pope Leo; and the beginning of the peace of God should be announced at vespers of every Wednesday with the ringing of bells.

1 The vigil is the day before the saint's day.

2 Certain days of fast in the four seasons, observed in the first week of March, the second week of June, the third week of September, and the fourth week of December.

247. DECREE OF FREDERICK I CONCERNING THE KEEPING OF PEACE, 1156.

M. G. LL. folio, II, pp. 101 ff.; Doeberl, IV, no. 32.

Frederick, by the grace of God emperor of the Romans, Augustus, to the bishops, dukes, counts, margraves, and all others to whom these presents come, his grace, peace, and love. . . . We desire that every person shall have his rights, and we command by our royal authority that peace, so long desired and so necessary to the whole land, be kept throughout all parts of our realm. The following sections show how the peace is to be kept and preserved:

1. If anyone kills a man within the territory covered by this peace, he shall suffer capital punishment, unless he can prove by judicial combat that he did it in self-defence. But if it is well known that he did it with malice and not in self-defence, he shall not be allowed to escape death, by appealing to the judicial combat, or by any other means. If a violator of the peace flees from justice, his movable property shall be confiscated by the judge and his heirs shall succeed to his patrimony, if they swear that the violator of the peace shall never with their consent receive anything from it. But if the heirs do not take this oath, they shall lose the inheritance and the count shall give it to the royal treasury and receive it back as a fief.

2. If anyone wounds another within the territory covered by the peace, he shall lose his hand and forfeit his property as above, unless he can prove by judicial combat that he did it in self-defence. The judge shall apply the law strictly against him and his property.

3. If anyone seizes another and beats him without drawing blood or pulls out his hair or beard, he shall pay ten pounds as compensation to the one whom he injured, and twenty pounds to the judge as fine. If anyone reviles another without cause, he shall pay ten pounds for the injury and ten pounds to the judge as a fine. If anyone has to give pledge to a judge for

more than twenty pounds, he shall put his property in pawn with the judge, and shall redeem it by paying the amount within four weeks; if he fails to redeem it within that time, his heirs may receive it by paying twenty pounds to the count within six weeks; otherwise the count shall give the property over to the royal treasury, and shall receive it back as a fief from the king, after paying those who have claims against it for damages.

4. If one of the clergy has been accused of violating the peace and has been convicted and proscribed, or if he has sheltered a violator of the peace, and has been convicted of these things before his bishop on sufficient testimony, he shall pay twenty pounds to the count, and make satisfaction to the bishop according to the canons. But if the clergyman refuses to obey, he shall lose his rank and his ecclesiastical benefice, and shall be placed under the ban of the empire.

5. If a judge has followed a violator of the peace with the " hue and cry " to the castle of any lord, the lord of the castle shall turn him over to justice. If the man lives in the castle and is conscious of his guilt and fears to appear before the judge, the lord of the castle shall hand over the man's movables to the judge under oath, and shall never receive the man again in his castle. If the man does not live in the castle, the lord shall send him out of his castle in security [that is, the lord is not bound to deliver him to the judge, but shall give him a chance to escape], and the judge and the people shall continue to pursue him.

6. If two men contend for the possession of a fief, and one of them presents as a witness the man who invested him with it, the count shall accept his testimony, for the giver of the fief ought to be able to recognize his own gift; and if the man can prove by trustworthy witnesses that he held the fief legally and not by violence, he shall hold it without further controversy. If it is proved that he got it by violence, he shall pay double the fine for violence and shall be deprived of the fief.

7. If three or more men contend for the possession of the same fief and each one offers as a witness the man who he asserts invested him with the fief, the judge who tries the case shall choose two men of good repute who dwell in the same province, and shall make them tell under oath which man has held the fief legally and without violence, and that man shall hold the fief in peace and security without further controversy, unless some other person can claim it justly from him.

8. If a peasant accuses a knight of violating the peace, the knight shall swear that he did it not of his own will, but in self-defence, and shall clear himself with three compurgators.

9. If a knight accuses a peasant of violating the peace, the peasant shall swear that he did it not of his own will, but in self-defence, and he shall choose whether he will clear himself by judgment either of court trial or ordeal, or by the testimony of six witnesses chosen by the judge.

10. If a knight has been accused by another knight of violating the peace, and wishes to put it to the trial by judicial combat, he shall not be allowed to fight his accuser unless he can prove that he and his ancestors were lawful knights by birth.

11. Immediately after the Nativity of the Virgin Mary, each count shall choose seven men of good repute, and shall determine with their advice and according to the character of the season the price at which grain shall be sold in each province; if any person during that year sells a measure of grain at a price higher than the one they have fixed, he shall be considered a violator of the peace, and shall pay thirty pounds for every measure that he sold above the price.

12. If a peasant bears arms, such as a spear or a sword, the judge of the district shall either confiscate the arms or fine him twenty solidi for carrying them.

13. A merchant who is travelling through the country on business may carry a sword bound to his saddle or on his

wagon, but he shall use it only to defend himself from thieves, and not against innocent persons.

14. No one shall spread nets, snares, or other traps for any animals except bears, wolves, and boars.

15. No knight shall bear arms to the count's court, unless requested to do so by the count. Public thieves when convicted shall suffer the established penalty.

16. If anyone has made illegal use of his office of advocate or any other benefice, and has been warned by his lord to desist, but has not done so, he shall be deprived of his advocacy or benefice by regular judicial procedure. If he attempts to recover his advocacy or benefice by violence he shall be regarded as a violator of the peace.

17. If anyone steals anything of the value of five solidi or more, he shall be hanged; if less than five solidi, he shall be beaten with rods and have his hair cut off with scissors.

18. If the ministerials of any lord are at war with one another, the count or the judge of the district shall enforce the law against them.

19. If a traveller wishes to feed his horse, he may take with impunity whatever he can reach by standing on the road and feed it to his horse. Anyone may take grass or green twigs for his use, if he does it without unnecessary destruction.

248. PEACE OF THE LAND DECLARED BY FREDERICK I IN ITALY, 1158.

Ragewin, Gesta, IV, ch. 10; M. G. LL. folio, II, pp. 112 f.; Doeberl, IV, no. 37 b.

Frederick, by the grace of God emperor of the Romans, Augustus, to all his subjects. We hereby command all our subjects to keep the peace, as it is decreed in this edict. The dukes, margraves, counts, and all vassals and public officials, together with the common people between the ages of 18 and 70, shall take an oath to keep the peace and to aid the officials in enforcing it. These oaths shall be renewed at the end of every five years.

1. If anyone has a grievance against another on any ground, he shall seek justice from his lawful judge.

2. Fines for the breach of peace shall be as follows: for a city, 100 pounds of gold; for a town, 20 pounds of gold; for dukes, margraves, and counts, 50 pounds of gold; for the immediate vassals of the emperor and the greater rear-vassals, 20 pounds of gold; for the other vassals and all other violators of the peace, 6 pounds of gold, and these shall also be forced to make good the injury according to the law.

3. Violence and theft shall be punished according to the law; homicide and bodily injury and all crimes shall also be punished according to law.

4. If judges and magistrates appointed by the emperor or his representative neglect to do justice or to punish violations of the peace, they shall be compelled to make good the damage and to pay the legal fine for breach of peace, and in addition they shall pay special fines to the royal treasury: the higher officials, 10 pounds of gold, and the lower officials, 3 pounds of gold. Those who are too poor to pay these fines shall be punished with blows, and shall be prohibited from dwelling within fifty miles of their former homes during a period of five years.

5. We hereby prohibit all associations and sworn leagues in city or country, whether between city and city, or between person and person, or between city and person. All such associations that now exist are hereby declared void, and every member is liable to a fine of 1 pound of gold.

6. Bishops are commanded to visit all violators of this decree in their dioceses with ecclesiastical censure, until they make satisfaction.

7. Protectors of malefactors and receivers of stolen goods shall be punished with the same fine as the criminals.

8. If anyone refuses to take the oath to keep the peace, or disobeys this decree, his goods shall be confiscated and his house destroyed.

9. We condemn and forbid all illegal exactions, especially against the church, an abuse which is of long standing. All such exactions levied in the future shall be repaid in double.

10. Contracts voluntarily made by minors on oath, which do not affect their own property, shall be valid; but all promises extorted by force or fear shall be void, especially promises not to complain of wrong or injury.

11. If anyone sells his allodial lands, he shall not sell the authority and jurisdiction of the emperor over them; sales made with these provisions are void.

249. THE PERPETUAL PEACE OF THE LAND PROCLAIMED BY MAXIMILIAN I, 1495. (GERMAN.)

Altmann und Bernheim, no. 110.

For various reasons the government had found it impossible to secure the peace of the land. One reason was that there was no effective and satisfactory machinery for punishing offenders, administering justice, and settling disputes. Maximilian not only forbade all private warfare, but also created a supreme court to try all offenders and to make it unnecessary for a man to take the law into his own hands.

We, Maximilian, etc. (1) From the time of the publication of this peace, no one, no matter of what rank or position, shall carry on a feud against another, or make war on him, or rob, seize, attack, or besiege him, or aid anyone else to do so. And no one shall attack, seize, burn, or in any other way damage any castle, city, market town, fortress, village, farmhouse, or group of houses, or in any way aid others to do such things. No one shall receive those who do such things into his house, or protect them, or give them to eat or drink. But if anyone has a ground for complaint against another, he shall summon him before the court. For the command is now given that all such matters must hereafter be tried before the supreme court.

(2) We hereby forbid all feuds and private wars throughout the whole empire.

(3) All, of whatever rank or position, who disobey this command, shall, in addition to other punishments, be put under the imperial ban, and anyone may attack their person or their property without thereby breaking the peace. All their charters and rights shall be revoked, and their fiefs shall be forfeited to their lord. And so long as the guilty one lives, the said lord shall not be bound to restore it to him or to his heirs.

(4) In case this peace is broken and violence is done to anyone, whether elector, prince, prelate, count, lord, knight, city, or anyone else, no matter of what rank or position, secular or ecclesiastical, and the guilty ones are not known, but suspicion rests on anyone, those who were injured may make complaint against the suspected ones, and summon them, and compel them to clear themselves by oath of the crimes of which they are suspected. If any of the suspected ones refuse to clear themselves in this way, or refuse to come at the appointed time, they shall be considered guilty of having broken the peace, and they shall be proceeded against in accordance with the terms of this document. But the one who summons them shall give them a safe-conduct to come and to return to their homes. If it is impossible to deliver the summons to them in person, it shall be posted in a few places which they are known to frequent. If, contrary to this peace, anyone is attacked or robbed, all those who are present and see it, or learn of it in any way, shall take action against the offender with as much earnestness and promptness as if it concerned them alone.

(5) No one shall in any way aid or protect such peace-breakers, or permit them to remain in his territory or lands, but he shall seize them and begin proceedings against them and give aid to anyone who makes complaint against them. . . .

(6) If such peace-breakers have such protection or are so strong that the state must interfere and make a campaign

against them, or if anyone who is not a member of the peace breaks the peace or aids those who have broken it, charges shall be made by the injured, or by the presiding judge of the supreme court, to us or to our representatives and to the annual diet, and aid shall be sent at once to those who have been attacked. If through war or anything else it is impossible to hold the diet, we give the presiding judge of the supreme court the authority to call us and the members of the diet together in any place where we, or our representatives, can meet and take whatever measures are necessary. But nevertheless the presiding judge and the whole court shall not cease to prosecute all such peace-breakers with all the legal means possible.

(7) There are many mercenaries in the land who are not in the service of anyone, or who do not long remain in the service of those who hire them, or their masters do not control them as they should, but they go riding about the country seeking to take advantage of people and to rob. We therefore decree that such men shall no longer be tolerated in the empire, and wherever they are found they shall be seized and examined and severely punished for their evil deeds, and all that they have shall be taken from them, and they shall give security for their good conduct by oath and bondsmen.

(8) If any clergyman breaks this peace, the bishop who has jurisdiction over him shall compel him to make good the damage which he has done, and his property shall be taken for this purpose. If the bishops are negligent in this matter, we put them as well as the peace-breakers under the ban, and deprive them of the protection of the empire, and we will in no way defend them or protect them in their evil-doing. But they may clear themselves of suspicion in the same way as laymen.

(9) During this peace no one shall make an agreement or treaty with another which shall in any way conflict with this peace. We hereby annul all the articles of such agree-

ments or treaties which are contrary to this peace, but the
rest of such agreements or treaties shall remain in force.
This peace is not intended to interfere in any way with existing treaties. Without the consent of those who have been
injured we will not free from the ban anyone who has through
an offence against the peace been proscribed, unless he clears
himself in a legal way.

(10) We command you . . . to observe this peace
in all points, and to compel all your officials and subjects to
observe it, if you wish to avoid the punishments of the imperial law and our heavy disfavor.

(11) We hereby annul all grants, privileges, etc., which
have been granted by us or our predecessors, which in any way
conflict with this peace.

(12) This peace is not intended to annul any of the laws
of the empire or commands which have already been issued,
but rather to strengthen them and to command that all men
shall hereafter observe them.

250. THE ESTABLISHMENT OF A SUPREME COURT TO TRY
PEACE-BREAKERS, 1495. (GERMAN.)

Datt, Volumen rerum Germanicarum novum, sive de pace imperii publica, p. 876.

We, Maximilian, etc., have, for good and sufficient reasons,
established a general peace of the land throughout the Roman
empire and Germany, and have ordered it to be observed. But
it cannot be enforced without the proper support and protection. Therefore at the advice of the electors, princes, and the
general diet held here at Worms, for the common good, and
for the honor of us and of the supreme court of the holy
Roman empire, we have issued the following laws and regulations in regard to it. We will appoint a presiding judge of
this court. He may be either a layman or a clergyman, a
count or a nobleman. And we will elect sixteen assistant
judges [who shall give the decision]. They shall all be
elected at this diet. They shall all be Germans of good char-

acter and of good degree of knowledge and experience, and at least half of them shall be trained in the law and the other half shall be noblemen of the rank of knight at least. The decision of the sixteen shall be final. In case of a tie the presiding judge shall have the deciding vote. Nothing shall prevent them from giving a just and legal decision. The presiding judge and the sixteen shall have no other business, but they shall devote themselves wholly to the work of this court. They shall not be absent from the sessions of the court without special permission. The sixteen shall get such permission from the presiding judge, and he from the sixteen. But never more than four of them shall be absent from the court at the same time. Neither the presiding judge nor the sixteen shall leave the city in which the court is in session except for the most weighty reasons. If the presiding judge is for a long time prevented by illness or other weighty reason from holding court, he shall, with the consent of the sixteen, give one of the sixteen, preferably a count or nobleman, the authority to represent him. And even if four or less of the sixteen are absent, the others shall have the power to try cases and render decisions as if they were all present. But in cases in which electors, princes, or those of princely rank are concerned, the presiding judge must preside in person. But if he cannot do so, he may, with the consent of the others, name a person to preside in his stead. . . . We will, with the advice of the princes and of the diet which shall meet that year, fill all vacancies which may occur in this court. If the presiding judge dies without appointing some one to preside in his stead, the sixteen shall elect some one to take his place, so that the court may not be idle until the next diet assembles. They shall elect a count or nobleman to this office; and he shall fill this office until the next diet meets, at which time we will appoint a new presiding judge.

VIII.   MONASTICISM

251.   The Rule of St. Benedict.   About 530.

Edited by E. Woelfflin.

Monasticism arose in Egypt and western Asia, where the climate was such that those who lived out-of-doors suffered very little from the inclemency of the weather. The first monks were true hermits, each one living quite alone. Very little shelter was necessary; a tree, an overhanging rock, a small cave, would offer quite enough protection against the weather. But as the movement spread to countries where there was more rain and the winters were colder their manner of life was necessarily modified. They began to live together in houses, but at the same time attempted to preserve as much of the hermit life as possible. Although under the same roof, the monks avoided life in common. Each one had his own room or cell, prepared his own food, and was as far as possible separated from his fellow monks. But the mere fact that they lived under one roof made certain rules necessary, and they had to have regulations to protect themselves against impostors. And if they had rules, there must be some one to enforce them. So in a natural way every monastery came to have an organization and certain officials. Since each monastery had its own regulations or rule, there was the widest divergence among them. By making a rule which was eventually adopted in all Greek monasteries, Basil the Great (d. 379) brought about uniformity without introducing any important changes.

Monasticism was introduced into the west toward the middle of the fourth century and spread rapidly. Here, too, each monastery made its own rule. Some of these rules achieved a local reputation and were adopted by several monasteries. But they were all eventually superseded by the rule of St. Benedict, which by fortunate circumstances came to be regarded in the west as the only proper monastic rule.

The loose organization of the monasteries had permitted many abuses to creep in (cf. ch. 1). The rule of St. Benedict was intended to correct these. Probably the worst of these abuses was the instability of the monks. This was due to the fact that they were not compelled to take a vow to remain in the monastery. Neither were their vows regarded as perpetually binding, or at least there was no means of compelling them to keep their vows, or of punishing them if they broke them. If any monk grew tired of the monastic life or found it irksome, he might leave the monastery and either enter another, or lead a vagabond sort of existence by wandering from one place to another (cf. ch. 1). In this way he could escape all the rigors of the rule and free himself from all discipline. It was not uncommon for monks to leave the monastery and go back to a life in the world. St. Benedict put an end to these abuses by requiring each monk to take a vow to remain forever in the same monastery, and by making all the vows of a monk perpetually binding: "Once a monk always a monk."

An important change was made in monasticism in the west by introducing the common life. In consequence of this all traces of the hermit life disappeared. The monks slept in a common room and ate in a common refectory. The monk spent all his time in the company of his fellow monks. Privacy was entirely unknown to him.

The rule of St. Benedict owes its popularity chiefly to the fact that Gregory I (590-604) was a Benedictine monk and gave the rule his support. St. Augustine, whom he sent as a missionary to England, was also a Benedictine, and carried the rule with him. So it was quite natural that it should have been the rule of all monasteries in England. St. Boniface, an Englishman, considered it a part of his reform to introduce the Benedictine rule into all the monasteries of Germany. Its fame and success soon led to its adoption in all the monasteries of the west.

The rule is worthy of careful study because for several centuries it governed the lives of thousands of monks who, by their piety, their works of charity in caring for the sick and giving shelter to travellers, their learning, their industry, their practice of agriculture, architecture, and other industrial and fine arts, influenced the lives of millions of laymen and advanced them in civilization. The student should note: (1) The extensive acquaintance of the monks with the Bible as shown in the large number of quotations from it and the amount of it which must be read by them in their services; (2) the character of an ideal abbot; (3) an ideal monk and the good works and virtues which he was required to practise (cf. chaps. 4, 5, and 6); (4) the administration of the monastery, which was character-

ized by a judicious mixture of democratic and monarchical principles, and a high degree of flexibility, so many things being left to
the judgment of the abbot; (5) the amount of time devoted to
work, reading, and meditation; and (6) the fact that the majority
of monks were laymen and not priests.

The first edition of the rule was written probably about 530. But
it received some additions and changes were made in it by Benedict
himself before his death, which took place in 543, or soon after.
The exact date of his death is unknown. The rule was the basis
for all the reforms in monasticism for several centuries. The new
orders which were founded for the most part merely increased its
ascetic features and made additions which were calculated to keep
the monks up to the high standard of asceticism set for them.

The great influence of the rule of St. Benedict seemed to justify us
in offering the whole of it. No other document presents so well as it
the ideals of the monkish life. The documents which follow it
illustrate some of the forms and ceremonies spoken of in the rule,
the rise of the military-monkish orders and their extensive privileges,
the founding of one of the great orders of friars, and the opposition
to them on the part of the parish or secular clergy. A few documents are also given which throw a certain side-light on the history
of the orders.

Ch. 1. *The kinds of monks.*—There are four kinds of
monks. The first kind is that of the cenobites [that is, those
living in common], those who live in a monastery according
to a rule, and under the government of an abbot. The second
is that of the anchorites, or hermits, who have learned how to
conduct the war against the devil by their long service in the
monastery and their association with many brothers, and so,
being well trained, have separated themselves from the troop,
in order to wage single combat, being able with the aid of God
to carry on the fight alone against the sins of the flesh. The
third kind (and a most abominable kind it is) is that of the
sarabites, who have not been tested and proved by obedience to
the rule and by the teaching of experience, as gold is tried in
the furnace, and so are soft and pliable like a base metal; who
in assuming the tonsure are false to God, because they still
serve the world in their lives. They do not congregate in the

Master's fold, but dwell apart without a shepherd, by twos and threes, or even alone.   Their law is their own desires, since they call that holy which they like, and that unlawful which they do not like.   The fourth kind is composed of those who are called *gyrovagi* (wanderers), who spend their whole lives wandering about through different regions and living three or four days at a time in the cells of different monks.   They are always wandering about and never remain long in one place, and they are governed by their own appetites and desires. They are in every way worse even than the sarabites.   But it is better to pass over in silence than to mention their manner of life.   Let us, therefore, leaving these aside, proceed, with the aid of God, to the consideration of the cenobites, the highest type of monks.

Ch. 2.   *The qualities necessary for an abbot.*—The abbot who is worthy to rule over a monastery ought always to bear in mind by what name he is called and to justify by his life his title of superior.   For he represents Christ in the monastery, receiving his name from the saying of the apostle: "Ye have received the Spirit of adoption, whereby we cry, Abba, Father" [Rom. 8:15].   Therefore the abbot should not teach or command anything contrary to the precepts of the Lord, but his commands and his teaching should be in accord with divine justice.   He should always bear in mind that both his teaching and the obedience of his disciples will be inquired into on the dread day of judgment.   For the abbot should know that the shepherd will have to bear the blame if the Master finds anything wrong with the flock.   Only in case the shepherd has displayed all diligence and care in correcting the fault of a restive and disobedient flock will he be freed from blame at the judgment of God, and be able to say to the Lord in the words of the prophet: "I have not hid thy righteousness within my heart; I have declared thy faithfulness and thy salvation" [Ps. 40:10]; but "they despising have scorned me" [Ezek. 20:27].   Then shall the punishment fall upon the flock who scorned his care and it shall be the punishment of death. The abbot ought to follow two methods in governing his disciples: teaching the commandments of the Lord to the apt disciples by his words, and to the obdurate and the simple by his deeds. And when he teaches his disciples that certain things are wrong, he should demonstrate it in his own life by not doing those things, lest when he has preached to others he himself should be a castaway [1 Cor. 9 :27], and lest God should sometime say to him, a sinner: "What hast thou to do to declare my statutes, or that thou shouldest take my covenant in thy mouth? Seeing that thou hatest instruction, and castest my words behind thee" [Ps. 50:16, 17], or "Why beholdest thou the mote that is in thy brother's eye, but ·considerest not the beam that is in thine own eye?" [Matt. 7:3]. Let there be no respect of persons in the monastery. Let the abbot not love one more than another, unless it be one who excels in good works and in obedience. The freeman is not to be preferred to the one who comes into the monastery out of servitude, unless there be some other good reason. But if it seems right and fitting to the abbot, let him show preference to anyone of any rank whatsoever; otherwise let them keep their own places. · For whether slave or free, we are all one in Christ [Gal. 3:28] and bear the same yoke of servitude to the one Lord, for there is no respect of persons with God [Rom. 2:11]. For we have special favor in His sight only in so far as we excel others in all good works and in humility. Therefore, the abbot should have the same love toward all and should subject all to the same discipline according to their respective merits. In his discipline the abbot should follow the rule of the apostle who says: "Reprove, rebuke, exhort" [2 Tim. 4:2]. That is, he should suit his methods to the occasion, using either threats or compliments, showing himself either a hard master or a loving father, according to the needs of the case. Thus he should reprove harshly the ob-

durate and the disobedient, but the obedient, the meek, and
the gentle he should exhort to grow in grace. We advise also
that he rebuke and punish those who neglect and scorn his
teaching. He should not disregard the transgressions of sinners, but should strive to root them out as soon as they appear,
remembering the peril of Eli, the priest of Siloam [1 Sam.
chaps. 1–4]. Let him correct the more worthy and intelligent
with words for the first or second time, but the wicked and
hardened and scornful and disobedient he should punish with
blows in the very beginning of their fault, as it is written: "A
fool is not bettered by words" [cf. Prov. 17:10]; and again
"Thou shalt beat him with the rod, and shalt deliver his soul
from hell" [Prov. 23:14].

The abbot should always remember his office and his title,
and should realize that as much is intrusted to him, so also
much will be required from him. Let him realize how difficult and arduous a task he has undertaken, to rule the hearts
and care for the morals of many persons, who require, one
encouragements, another threats, and another persuasion.
Let him so adapt his methods to the disposition and intelligence of each one that he may not only preserve the flock
committed to him entire and free from harm, but may even
rejoice in its increase.

Above all, the abbot should not be too zealous in the acquisition of earthly, transitory, mortal goods, forgetting and
neglecting the care of the souls committed to his charge, but
he should always remember that he has undertaken the government of souls of whose welfare he must render account.
Let him not be troubled about the poverty of his monastery,
since it is written: "Seek ye first the kingdom of God, and
his righteousness; and all these things shall be added unto
you" [Matt. 6:33]; and again, "For there is no want to them
that fear him" [Ps. 34:9]. Let him know that those who
undertake the care of souls must be ready to render an account
of them. So he must make a reckoning to God on the day of

judgment for all the souls according to the number of the brothers under his charge, and of his own soul as well. Therefore, while he keeps in mind the account which he must render of the sheep committed to him, and guards the interests of others, he is also solicitous for his own welfare; and while he administers correction to others by his preaching, he also frees himself from sin.

Ch. 3. *Taking counsel with the brethren.*—Whenever important matters come up in the monastery, the abbot should call together the whole congregation [that is, all the monks], and tell them what is under consideration. After hearing the advice of the brothers, he should reflect upon it and then do what seems best to him. We advise the calling of the whole congregation, because the Lord often reveals what is best to one of the younger brothers. But let the brethren give their advice with all humility, and not defend their opinions too boldly; rather let them leave it to the decision of the abbot, and all obey him. But while the disciples ought to obey the master, he on his part ought to manage all things justly and wisely. Let everyone in the monastery obey the rule in all things, and let no one depart from it to follow the desires of his own heart. Let no one of the brethren presume to dispute the authority of the abbot, either within or without the monastery; if anyone does so, let him be subjected to the discipline prescribed in the rule. But the abbot should do all things in the fear of the Lord, knowing that he must surely render account to God, the righteous judge, for all his decisions. If matters of minor importance are to be considered, concerning the welfare of the monastery, let the abbot take counsel with the older brethren, as it is written: " Do all things with counsel, and after it is done thou wilt not repent " [Ecclesiasticus 32 :24].

Ch. 4. *The instruments of good works.*—First, to love the Lord God with all the heart, and with all the soul, and with all the strength, and then his neighbor as himself. Then not to kill, not to commit adultery, not to steal, not to covet, not to bear false witness, to honor all men, and not to do to another what he would not have another do to him.   To deny himself that he may follow Christ, to chasten the body, to renounce luxuries, to love fasting.   To feed the poor, to clothe the naked, to visit the sick, to bury the dead, to offer help in trouble, to comfort the sorrowing.   To separate himself from the things of the world, to prefer nothing above the love of Christ, not to give way to anger, not to bear any grudge, not to harbor deceit in the heart, not to give false peace, not to be wanting in charity.   Not to swear, lest he perjure himself; to speak the truth from the heart.   Not to return evil for evil.   Not to injure others, but to suffer injuries patiently. To love his enemies.   Not to return curse for curse, but rather to bless; to suffer persecution for righteousness' sake.   Not to be proud, nor drunken, nor a glutton, nor given to much sleeping, nor slothful, nor complaining, nor slanderous.   To put his hope in God; when he sees anything good in himself to ascribe it to God, and when he does any evil, to ascribe it to himself.   To fear the day of judgment, to be in terror of hell, to yearn with all spiritual longing for eternal life, and to keep ever before his eyes the thought of approaching death. To guard his acts in every hour of his life, to remember that God seeth him in every place, to crush down with the aid of Christ the evil thoughts arising in his heart and to confess them to his spiritual superior.   To keep his mouth from evil and vain talk, not to love much speaking, not to speak vain and frivolous words, not to love much and loud laughter.   To listen gladly to holy reading, to pray frequently, to confess daily in prayers to God his past sins with tears and groaning, and to keep himself free from those sins afterward.   Not to yield to the desire of the flesh, to hate his own will, to obey the commands of the abbot in all things, even if the abbot (which God forbid) should himself do otherwise than he preaches, remembering the word of the Lord: "What they say, do; but what they do, do ye not." Not to wish to be called holy before he is so, but rather to strive to be holy that he may be truly so called; to obey the commandments of God in his daily life, to love chastity, to hate no one, not to be jealous or envious, not to be fond of strife, to avoid pride, to reverence his elders and cherish those younger than himself, to pray for his enemies through the love of Christ, to agree with his adversary before the going down of the sun, and never to despair of the mercy of God.

Lo, these are the implements of the spiritual profession. If they have been constantly employed by us night and day, and are reckoned up and placed to our credit at the last judgment, we shall receive that reward which the Lord himself has promised: "Eye hath not seen, nor ear heard, neither have entered into the heart of man, the things which God hath prepared for them that love him" [1 Cor. 2:9]. But these graces must be exercised in the cloister of the monastery by strict adherence to the vows and obedience to the rule.

Ch. 5. *Obedience.*—The first grade of humility is obedience without delay, which is becoming to those who hold nothing dearer than Christ. So, when one of the monks receives a command from a superior, he should obey it immediately, as if it came from God himself, being impelled thereto by the holy service he has professed and by the fear of hell and the desire of eternal life. Of such the Lord says: "As soon as he heard of me, he obeyed me" [Ps. 17:44]; and again to the apostles, "He that heareth you, heareth me" [Luke 10:16]. Such disciples, when they are commanded, immediately abandon their own business and their own plans, leaving undone what they were at work upon. With ready hands and willing feet they hasten to obey the commands of their superior, their act following on the heels of his command, and both the order and the fulfilment occurring, as it were, in the same moment of time—such promptness does the fear of the Lord inspire.

Good disciples who are inspired by the desire for eternal life gladly take up that narrow way of which the Lord said: "Narrow is the way which leadeth unto life" [Matt. 7:14]. They have no wish to control their own lives or to obey their own will and desires, but prefer to be ruled by an abbot, and to live in a monastery, accepting the guidance and control of another. Surely such disciples follow the example of the Lord who said: "I came not to do mine own will, but the will of him that sent me" [John 6:38]. But this obedience will be acceptable to God and pleasing to men only if it be not given fearfully, or half-heartedly, or slowly, or with grumbling and protests. For the obedience which is given to a superior is given to God, as he himself has said: "Who heareth you, heareth me" [Luke 10:16]. Disciples ought to obey with glad hearts, "for the Lord loveth a cheerful giver" [2 Cor. 9:7]. If the disciple obeys grudgingly and complains even within his own heart, his obedience will not be accepted by God, who sees his unwilling heart; he will gain no favor for works done in that spirit, but, unless he does penance and mends his ways, he will rather receive the punishment of those that murmur against the Lord's commands.

Ch. 6. *Silence.*—Let us do as the prophet says: "I said, I will take heed to my ways that I sin not with my tongue; I will keep my tongue with a bridle. I was dumb with silence, I held my peace even from good" [Ps. 39:1, 2]. This is the meaning of the prophet: if it is right to keep silence even from good, how much more ought we to refrain from speaking evil, because of the punishment for sin. Therefore, although it may be permitted to the tried disciples to indulge in holy and edifying discourse, even this should be done rarely, as it is written: "In a multitude of words there wanteth not sin" [Prov. 10:19], and again: "Death and life are in the power of the tongue" [Prov. 18:21]. For it is the business of the master to speak and instruct, and that of the disciples to hearken and be silent. And if the disciple must ask anything of his superior, let him ask it reverently and humbly, lest he seem to speak more than is becoming. Filthy and foolish talking and jesting we condemn utterly, and forbid the disciple ever to open his mouth to utter such words.

Ch. 7. *Humility.*—Brethren, the holy Scripture saith: "And whosoever shall exalt himself shall be abased; and he that shall humble himself shall be exalted" [Matt. 23:12]. Here we are shown that all exaltation is of a piece with pride, which the prophet tells us he avoids, saying: "Lord, my heart is not haughty nor mine eyes lofty, neither do I exercise myself in great matters, or in things too high for me. Surely I have behaved and quieted myself, as a child that is weaned of its mother; my soul is as a weaned child" [Ps. 131:1, 2]. Therefore, brethren, if we wish to attain to the highest measure of humility and to that exaltation in heaven which is only to be gained by lowliness on earth, we must raise to heaven by our deeds such a ladder as appeared to Jacob in his dream, whereon he saw angels ascending and descending. For the meaning of that figure is that we ascend by humility of heart and descend by haughtiness. And the ladder is our life here below which God raises to heaven for the lowly of heart. Our body and soul are the two sides of the ladder, in which by deeds consistent with our holy calling we insert steps whereby we may ascend to heaven.

Now the first step of humility is this, to escape destruction by keeping ever before one's eyes the fear of the Lord, to remember always the commands of the Lord, for they who scorn him are in danger of hell-fire, and to think of the eternal life that is prepared for them that fear him. So a man should keep himself in every hour from the sins of the heart, of the tongue, of the eyes, of the hands, and of the feet. He should cast aside his own will and the desires of the flesh; he should think that God is looking down on him from heaven all the time, and that his acts are seen by God and reported to him hourly by his angels. For the prophet shows that the

Lord is ever present in the midst of our thoughts, when he says: " God trieth the hearts and the reins " [Ps. 7:9], and again, " The Lord knoweth the thoughts of men " [Ps. 94:11], and again he says: " Thou hast known my thoughts from afar " [Ps. 139:2], and " The thoughts of a man are known to thee" [Ps. 76:11]. So a zealous brother will strive to keep himself from perverse thoughts by saying to himself: "Then only shall I be guiltless in his sight, if I have kept me from mine iniquity" [Ps. 18:23]. And the holy Scriptures teach us in divers places that we should not do our own will; as where it says: " Turn from thine own will " [Ecclesiasticus 18:30] ; and where we ask in the Lord's Prayer that his will be done in us ; and where it warns us : " There is a way that seemeth right unto a man, but the end thereof are the ways of death " [Prov. 14:12] ; and again, concerning the disobedient: " They are corrupt and abominable in their desires" [Ps. 14:1]. And we should always remember that God is aware of our fleshly desires ; as the prophet says, speaking to the Lord: "All my desire is before thee" [Ps. 38:9]. Therefore, we should shun evil desires, for death lieth in the way of the lusts ; as the Scripture shows, saying: "Go not after thy lusts" [Ecclesiasticus 18:30]. Therefore since the eyes of the Lord are upon the good and the wicked, and since "the Lord looked down from heaven upon the children of men to see if there were any that did understand and seek God" [Ps. 14:2], and since our deeds are daily reported to him by the angels whom he assigns to each one of us ; then, surely, brethren, we should be on our guard every hour, lest at any time, as the prophet says in the Psalms, the Lord should look down upon us as we are falling into sin, and should spare us for a space, because he is merciful and desires our conversion, but should say at the last: "These things hast thou done and I kept silence" [Ps. 50:21].

The second step of humility is this, that a man should not delight in doing his own will and desires, but should imitate the Lord who said: "I came not to do mine own will, but the will of him that sent me" [John 6:38]. And again the Scripture saith: "Lust hath its punishment, but hardship winneth a crown."

The third step of humility is this, that a man be subject to his superior in all obedience for the love of God, imitating the Lord, of whom the apostle says: "He became obedient unto death" [Phil. 2:8].

The fourth step of humility is this, that a man endure all the hard and unpleasant things and even undeserved injuries that come in the course of his service, without wearying or withdrawing his neck from the yoke, for the Scripture saith: "He that endureth to the end shall be saved" [Matt. 10:22], and again: "Comfort thy heart and endure the Lord" [Ps. 27:14]. And yet again the Scripture, showing that the faithful should endure all unpleasant things for the Lord, saith, speaking in the person of those that suffer: "Yea, for thy sake are we killed all the day long; we are counted as sheep for the slaughter" [Ps. 44:22]; and again, rejoicing in the sure hope of divine reward: "In all things we are more than conquerors through him that loved us" [Rom. 8:37]; and again in another place: "For thou, O God, hast proved us; thou hast tried us as silver is tried; thou broughtest us into the net, thou laidst affliction upon our loins" [Ps. 66:10 f]; and again to show that we should be subject to a superior: "Thou hast placed men over our heads" [Ps. 66:12]. Moreover, the Lord bids us suffer injuries patiently, saying: "Whosoever shall smite thee on the right cheek, turn to him the other also. And if any man will sue thee at the law, and take away thy coat, let him have thy cloak also. And whosoever shall compel thee to go a mile, go with him twain" [Matt. 5:39–41]. And with the apostle Paul we should suffer with false brethren, and endure persecution, and bless them that curse us.

The fifth step of humility is this, that a man should not hide the evil thoughts that arise in his heart or the sins which he has committed in secret, but should humbly confess them to his abbot; as the Scripture exhorteth us, saying: "Commit thy way unto the Lord, trust also in him" [Ps. 37:5]; and again: "O, give thanks unto the Lord, for he is good; for his mercy endureth forever" [Ps. 106:1]; and yet again the prophet saith: "I have acknowledged my sin unto thee, and mine iniquity have I not hid. I said, I will confess my transgressions unto the Lord; and thou forgavest the iniquity of my sin" [Ps. 32:5].

The sixth step of humility is this, that the monk should be contented with any lowly or hard condition in which he may be placed, and should always look upon himself as an unworthy laborer, not fitted to do what is intrusted to him; saying to himself in the words of the prophet: "I was reduced to nothing and was ignorant; I was as a beast before thee and I am always with thee" [Ps. 73:22 f].

The seventh step of humility is this, that he should not only say, but should really believe in his heart that he is the lowest and most worthless of all men, humbling himself and saying with the prophet: "I am a worm and no man; a reproach of men, and despised of all people" [Ps. 22:6]; and "I that was exhalted am humbled and confounded" [Ps. 88:15]; and again: "It is good for me that I have been afflicted, that I might learn thy statutes" [Ps. 119:71].

The eighth step of humility is this, that the monk should follow in everything the common rule of the monastery and the examples of his superiors.

The ninth step of humility is this, that the monk should restrain his tongue from speaking, and should keep silent even from questioning, as the Scripture saith: "In a multitude of words there wanteth not sin" [Prov. 10:19], and "Let not an evil speaker be established in the earth" [Ps. 140:11].

The tenth step of humility is this, that the monk should be not easily provoked to laughter, as it is written: "The fool raiseth his voice in laughter" [Ecclesiasticus 21:23].

The eleventh step of humility is this, that the monk, when he speaks, should do so slowly and without laughter, softly and gravely, using few words and reasonable, and that he should not be loud of voice; as it is written: "A wise man is known for his few words."

The twelfth step of humility is this, that the monk should always be humble and lowly, not only in his heart, but in his bearing as well. Wherever he may be, in divine service, in the oratory, in the garden, on the road, in the fields, whether sitting, walking, or standing, he should always keep his head bowed and his eyes upon the ground. He should always be meditating upon his sins and thinking of the dread day of judgment, saying to himself as did that publican of whom the gospel speaks: "Lord, I am not worthy, I a sinner, so much as to lift mine eyes up to heaven" [Luke 18:13]; and again with the prophet: "I am bowed down and humbled everywhere" [Ps. 119:107].

Now when the monk has ascended all these steps of humility, he will arrive at that perfect love of God which casteth out all fear [1 John 4:18]. By that love all those commandments which he could not formerly observe without grievous effort and struggle, he will now obey naturally and easily, as if by habit; not in the fear of hell, but in the love of Christ and by his very delight in virtue. And thus the Lord will show the working of his holy Spirit in this his servant, freed from vices and sins.

Ch. 8. *Divine worship at night* [vigils].—During the winter; that is, from the first of November to Easter, the monks should rise at the eighth hour of the night; a reasonable arrangement, since by that time the monks will have rested a little more than half the night and will have digested their food. Those brothers who failed in the psalms or the read-

ings shall spend the rest of the time after vigils (before the
beginning of matins) in pious meditation. From Easter to
the first of November matins shall begin immediately after
daybreak, allowing the brothers a little time for attending to
the necessities of nature.

Ch. 9. *The psalms to be said at night.*[1]—During the winter time, the order of service shall be as follows: first shall
be recited the verse ["Make haste, O God, to deliver me;
make haste to help me, O God," Ps. 70:1]; then this verse
three times: "O Lord, open thou my lips and my mouth
shall show forth thy praise" [Ps. 51:15]; then the third
psalm and the Gloria, the 94th Psalm responsively or in unison, a hymn, and six psalms responsively. After this the
abbot shall give the benediction with the aforesaid verse, and
the brothers shall sit down. Three lessons from the gospels
with three responses shall then be read from the lecturn by
the brothers in turn. The first two responses shall be sung
without the Gloria, but in the third response which follows the
last reading the cantor shall sing the Gloria, the monks rising from their seats at the beginning of it to show honor and
reverence to the holy Trinity. Passages are to be read from
the Old and New Testaments in the vigils, and also the exposi-
tions of these passages left by the accepted orthodox Catholic
fathers. After the three readings and the responses, six
psalms with the Halleluia shall follow, then a reading from
the epistles recited from memory, and the usual verses, the
vigils concluding with the supplication of the litany, "Kyrie
eleison."

[1] The numbering of the psalms in the authorized version differs
from their numbering in the Vulgate. We have followed the num-
berings of the latter in those passages of the Rule in which the
psalms for the services are given. But in quotations from the psalms
we have followed the translation as well as the numbering of the
authorized version, except occasionally when the translation in the
authorized version does not give the sense required by the context
of the Rule. In these cases we have translated the Latin of the

Vulgate. The following table gives the corresponding numbers **in** each version:

Authorized Version.	Vulgate.
1— 10	1— 10
11—113	10—112
114—115	113
116	114—115
117—146	116—145
147	146—147
148—150	148—150

In the Vulgate there are two psalms having the same number 10.

Ch. 10. *The order of vigils in summer.*—From Easter to the first of November the above order of worship shall be observed, except that the reading shall be shortened because of the shorter nights; that is, in place of the three lessons, one lesson from the Old Testament shall be recited from memory, with the short response. The rest of the service shall be observed as described above, so that the number of psalms read shall never be less than twelve, not counting the 3d and the 94th.

Ch. 11. *The order of vigils on Sunday.*—On Sunday the brothers shall rise earlier than on other days. The order of service in the vigils of Sunday shall be as follows: first, six psalms and the verse are to be said as described above; then the brothers, sitting down, shall read in order from their seats four lessons from the gospels, with responses, and in the fourth response the cantor shall sing the Gloria, at the beginning of which all shall rise to show reverence. After the lessons six other psalms shall be said responsively and the verse; then four more lessons shall be read with the responses as before; then three canticles chosen from the prophets by the abbot shall be sung with the Halleluia; then after the verse and the benediction of the abbot, four other lessons shall be read from the New Testament in the same order as above, and after the fourth response the abbot shall begin the hymn "We praise thee, O Lord" (Te Deum laudamus), following it with a lesson from the Gospel, during which all rise to show reverence and honor to God. After the reading all shall respond "Amen," and the abbot shall begin the hymn: "It is a good thing to praise the Lord"; then the abbot shall give the benediction, and the matins shall be begun. This order of service is to be observed on all Sundays, winter and summer, unless it should happen, which God forbid, that the brethren are late in rising, in which case the readings and responses may be shortened. But care should be taken that this does not happen, and if it does, he whose negligence caused the delay should make satisfaction to God for his fault by doing penance in the oratory.

Ch. 12. *The order of matins on Sunday.*—In the matins on the Lord's day the order of service shall be as follows: first, the 66th Psalm in unison, then the 50th Psalm with the Halleluia, then the 117th and the 62d Psalms, the *Benedictiones* [that is, Dan. 3:52–90], and the *Laudes* [that is, Pss. 148, 149, 150], a lesson from Revelation recited from memory, a response, a hymn, the usual verse, and a song from the Gospel, concluding with the litany, and the benediction.

Ch. 13. *The order of matins on week days.*—On week days the order of service in the matins shall be as follows: first, the 66th Psalm recited somewhat slowly as on Sunday, in order that all may be in their places in time to join in the 50th Psalm, which is to be recited responsively; then two psalms for the day according to this schedule: on Monday, the 5th and the 35th; on Tuesday, the 42d and the 56th; on Wednesday, the 63d and the 64th; on Thursday, the 87th and the 89th; on Friday the 75th and the 91st; and on Saturday, the 142d and the song from Deuteronomy [33:1–43], the last being divided by two Glorias. On other days, the songs from the prophets are to be sung, each on its proper day, according to the custom of the Roman church. Then shall follow the lauds, a lesson from the epistles recited from memory, the response, a hymn, the verse, and a song from the Gospel, concluding with the litany and the benediction. At the close of matins and vespers every day, the superior shall recite the Lord's prayer in the hearing of all, because of the quarrels which are apt to occur among the monks; so that the brethren, in their hearts uniting in the petition, "Forgive us our trespasses as we forgive those that trespass against us," may cleanse their hearts from sins of this sort. In other services, the last part of the prayer, "Deliver us from evil," shall be said responsively by all.

Ch. 14. *The order of vigils on Saints' days.*—On Saints' days and on all feast days, the order of service shall be the same as that for Sunday as described above, except that the psalms and responses and readings belonging to the particular day shall be used.

Ch. 15. *The occasions on which the Halleluia shall be said.*—From Easter to Pentecost the Halleluia shall be said with the psalms and responses. From Pentecost to the beginning of Lent in the vigils of the night the Halleluia shall be said only with the last six psalms; on Sundays, except in Lent, the Halleluia shall be said also with the songs at matins, prime, terce, sext, and nones, but at vespers the songs shall be said responsively. The responses shall not be said with the Halleluia except during the season from Easter to Pentecost.

Ch. 16. *The order of divine worship during the day.*— The prophet says: "Seven times a day do I praise thee" [Ps. 119:164]; and we observe this sacred number in the seven services of the day; that is, matins, prime, terce, sext, nones, vespers, and completorium; for the hours of the day-time are plainly intended here, since the same prophet provides for the nocturnal vigils, when he says in another place: "At midnight I will rise to give thanks unto thee" [Ps. 119:62]. We should therefore praise the Creator for his righteous judgments at the aforesaid times: matins, prime,

terce, sext, nones, vespers, and completorium; and at night
we should rise to give thanks unto Him.[1]

1 There were eight services to be held every day. The night service
was called vigils and was held some time between midnight and
early dawn, perhaps as early as 2 A.M. in summer, and as late as 4
or 5 in winter. The first service of the day was called matins. It
followed vigils after a short interval. It was supposed to begin
about daybreak, which is also an indefinite expression and not a
clearly fixed moment. The service of prime began with the first
period of the day, terce with the third, sext with the sixth, and
nones with the ninth. Vespers, as its name indicates, began toward
evening. Completorium, or compline, was the last service of the day
and took place just before the monks went to bed.

These designations of time are necessarily very inaccurate and
indefinite. Beginning with sunrise the day was divided into twelve
equal periods which were numbered from one to twelve. Beginning
with sunset the night was divided in the same way. The day periods
would, of course, be much longer in summer than in winter. As
their methods of measuring time were primitive and inaccurate we
must not suppose that the services took place exactly and regularly
at the same hour every day.

Ch. 17. *The number of psalms to be said at these times.*—
We have already described the order of psalms for the nocturnal vigils and for matins; let us now turn to the other
services. At prime, three psalms shall be said separately, that
is, each with a Gloria, the verse, "Make haste, O God, to
deliver me," and the hymn for the hour being said before
the psalms; then one lesson from the Epistles shall be read,
then the verse, the "Kyrie eleison," and the benediction. At
terce, sext, and nones the same order shall be observed:
first the prayer (that is, the verse, "Make haste, O God," etc.),
the hymn for the hour, the three psalms, the lesson, the verse,
the "Kyrie eleison," and the benediction. If the congregation
is large, the psalms shall be said responsively; if small, they
shall be said in unison. At vespers four psalms shall be
said responsively, then shall follow the lesson, the response,
the hymn for the hour, the Ambrosian hymn, the verse, the

song from the Gospel, the Litany, the Lord's prayer, and the benediction. At completorium, three psalms shall be said in unison, then the hymn for the hour, the lesson, the verse, the "Kyrie eleison," the benediction, and the dismissal.

Ch. 18. *The order in which these psalms shall be said.*— All the services of the daytime shall begin with the verse "Make haste, O God, to deliver me; make haste to help me, O God," followed by the Gloria and the hymn for the hour. The order in which the psalms are to be read in these services is as follows: at prime on Sunday, four sections of the 118th Psalm, and at the other services on Sunday, terce, sext, nones, three sections each of the same psalm; at prime on Monday, three psalms, the 1st, 2d, and 6th; so on through the week to Sunday again, three psalms being said at each prime in the order of arrangement to the 19th, the 9th and the 17th being divided into two readings. In this way vigils on Sunday will always begin with the 20th psalm. At terce, sext, and nones on Monday, the nine sections of the 118th psalm which remain shall be said three at each service, thus reading the whole 118th Psalm on the two days, Sunday and Monday. On Tuesday the nine psalms from the 119th to the 127th shall be read three at each of the services of terce, sext, and nones. This order of psalms, and the regular order of hymns, lessons, and verses is to be observed throughout the week, and on Sunday the reading shall begin again with the 118th psalm. At vespers four psalms are to be read daily, from the 109th to the 147th, leaving out those that are prescribed for the other services (from the 117th to the 127th, the 133d, and the 142d). As this does not make the required number of psalms, three for each day, the longer ones shall be divided, namely, the 138th, the 143d, and the 144th; and the 116th, being very short, shall be read with the 115th. The rest of the service of vespers, the lesson, the response, the hymn, the verse, and the song, shall be observed as already described. At completorium, the same psalms

shall be read each day, namely, the 4th, the 90th, and the 133d.
All the rest of the psalms, not thus arranged for, shall be
divided equally among the seven nocturnal vigils, the longer
ones being divided, making twelve readings for each night.
If this particular order of the psalms is not satisfactory, it
may be changed; but in any case, the whole psalter with its
full number of 150 psalms should be completed every week,
and should be begun again from the first at the vigils on
Sunday. Monks who read less than the whole psalter with
the customary songs during the course of the week are
assuredly lax in their devotion, since we are told that the
holy fathers were accustomed in their zeal to read in a single
day what we in our indolence can scarcely accomplish in a
whole week.

Ch. 19. *The behavior of the monks in the services.*—We
know of course that the divine presence is everywhere, and
that "the eyes of the Lord look down everywhere upon the
good and the evil," but we should realize this in its fulness,
especially when we take part in divine worship. Remember
the words of the prophet: "Serve the Lord in all fear" [Ps.
2:11], and again "Sing wisely" [Ps. 47:7], and yet again,
"In the sight of the angels I will sing unto thee" [Ps. 138:1].
Let us then consider how we should behave in the sight of
God and his angels, and let us so comport ourselves in the
service of praise that our hearts may be in harmony with
our voices.

Ch. 20. *The reverence to be shown in prayer.*—When we
have any request to make of powerful persons, we proffer
it humbly and reverently; with how much greater humility
and devotion, then, should we offer our supplications unto
God, the Lord of all. We should realize, too, that we are
not heard for our much speaking, but for the purity and the
contrition of our hearts. So when we pray, our prayer should
be simple and brief, unless we are moved to speak by the
inspiration of the spirit. The prayer offered before the con-

gregation also should be brief, and all the brothers should rise at the signal of the superior.

Ch. 21. *The deans of the monastery.*—In large congregations certain ones from among the brothers of good standing and holy lives should be chosen to act as deans and should be set to rule over certain parts under the direction of the abbot. Only persons to whom the abbot may safely intrust a share of his burdens should be selected for this office and they should be chosen not according to rank, but according to their merits and wisdom. But if any one of the deans shall be found in fault, being perhaps puffed up by his position, he should be reprimanded for his fault the second or third time, and then if he does not mend his ways he should be deposed and his place given to a worthier brother. The same treatment should be accorded the *præpositi.*

Ch. 22. *How the monks should sleep.*—The monks shall sleep separately in individual beds, and the abbot shall assign them their beds according to their conduct. If possible all the monks shall sleep in the same dormitory, but if their number is too large to admit of this, they are to be divided into tens or twenties and placed under the control of some of the older monks. A candle shall be kept burning in the dormitory all night until daybreak. The monks shall go to bed clothed and girt with girdles and cords, but shall not have their knives at their sides, lest in their dreams they injure one of the sleepers. They should be always in readiness, rising immediately upon the signal and hastening to the service, but appearing there gravely and modestly. The beds of the younger brothers should not be placed together, but should be scattered among those of the older monks. When the brothers arise they should gently exhort one another to hasten to the service, so that the sleepy ones may have no excuse for coming late.

Ch. 23. *The excommunication for lighter sins.*—If any brother shows himself stubborn, disobedient, proud, or com-

plaining, or refuses to obey the rule or to hearken to his
elders, let him be admonished in private once or twice by his
elders, as God commands. If he does not mend his ways let
him be reprimanded publicly before all. But, if, knowing
the penalty to which he is liable, he still refuses to conform,
let him be excommunicated [that is, cut off from the society
of the other monks], and if he remains incorrigible let him
suffer bodily punishment.

Ch. 24. *The forms of excommunication.*—The nature of
the excommunication and discipline should be suited to the
extent of the guilt, which is to be determined by the abbot.
If the brother is guilty of one of the lighter sins, let him be
deprived of participation in the common meal. The one
who has been thus deprived shall not lead in the psalms and
responses in the oratory or read the lessons; he shall eat
alone after the common meal; so that, for example, if the
brothers eat at the sixth hour, he shall eat at the ninth,
and if the brothers eat at the ninth hour, he shall eat at
vespers. This shall be continued until he has made suitable
satisfaction for his fault.

Ch. 25. *The excommunication for the graver sins.*—For
graver sins the brother shall be deprived of participation both
in the common meal and in the divine services. No brother
shall speak to him or have anything to do with him, but he
shall labor alone at the work assigned to him as a penance,
meditating on the meaning of that saying of the apostle: "To
deliver such an one unto Satan for the destruction of the
flesh, that the spirit may be saved in the day of the Lord
Jesus Christ" [1 Cor. 5:5]. And he shall eat alone, receiving
his food in such measure and at such time as the abbot shall
determine. No one meeting him shall bless him, and the
food which is given him shall be unblessed.

Ch. 26. *Those who consort with the excommunicated without the order of the abbot.*—If any brother shall presume to
speak to one who has been excommunicated, or shall give a

command to him, or have anything whatever to do with him, except by the order of the abbot, he shall be placed under the same sort of excommunication.

Ch. 27. *The abbot should be zealous for the correction of those who have been excommunicated.*—The abbot should exercise the greatest care over erring brothers; as it is written: "They that be whole need not a physician, but they that are sick" [Matt. 9:12]. So the abbot should use all the means that a wise physician uses: he should send secret comforters, wiser and older brothers, who will comfort the erring one, and urge him humbly to make amends, as the apostle says: "Comfort him, lest perhaps such a one should be swallowed up with too much sorrow" [2 Cor. 2:7], and again "Charity shall be confirmed in him" [2 Cor. 2:8]. Let him also be prayed for by all. It should be the greatest care of the abbot that not one of his flock should perish, using to this end all his wisdom and ability, for he is set to care for sick souls, not to rule harshly over well ones. Let him be warned in this matter by the words of God spoken to the evil shepherds of Israel through the prophet: "Ye did take that which ye saw to be strong, and that which was weak ye did cast out" [cf. Ezek. 34:3 f]. Let him rather follow the example of the good shepherd, who, leaving his ninety and nine, went out into the mountains and sought the one sheep which had gone astray; who, when he found it, had compassion on its weakness, and laid it on his own sacred shoulders and brought it back to the flock.

Ch. 28. *Those who do not mend their ways after frequent correction.*—If any brother has been frequently corrected and excommunicated, and still does not mend his ways, let the punishment be increased to the laying on of blows. But if he will not be corrected or if he attempts to defend his acts, then the abbot shall proceed to extreme measures as a wise physician will do; that is, when the poultices and ointments, as it were, of prayer, the medicines of Scripture, and

the violent remedies of excommunication and blows have all
failed, he has recourse to the last means, prayer to God, the
all-powerful, that He should work the salvation of the erring
brother. But if he still cannot be cured, then the abbot
shall proceed to the use of the knife, cutting out that evil
member from the congregation; as the apostle says: "Put
away from among yourselves that wicked person" [1 Cor.
5:13]; "If the unbelieving depart, let him depart" [1 Cor.
7:15]; that the whole flock be not contaminated by one
diseased sheep.

Ch. 29. *Shall brothers who have left the monastery be
received back?*—If a brother has left the monastery or has
been cast out for his own fault, and shall wish to be taken
back, he shall first of all promise complete reformation of
that fault, and then shall be received into the lowest grade
in the monastery to prove the sincerity of his humility. If
he again departs, he shall be received back the third time,
knowing, however, that after that he shall never again be taken
back.

Ch. 30. *The manner of correction for the young.*—The
forms of punishment should be adapted to every age and
to every order of intelligence. So if children or youths, or
those who are unable to appreciate the meaning of excommunication, are found guilty, they should be given heavy fasts
and sharp blows for their correction.

Ch. 31. *The cellarer.*—The cellarer of the monastery,
chosen from among the congregation, should be wise, sedate,
and sober; he should not be gluttonous, proud, quarrelsome,
spiteful, indolent, nor wasteful; he should fear God, since he
acts in a way as the father of the monastery. He should be
careful of everything, doing nothing except by the order of
the abbot, and observing all the commands laid upon him.
He should not rebuke the brothers roughly; if any brother is
unreasonable in his demands, he should yet treat him rea-
sonably, mildly refusing his request as being improper. He

should make his service minister to his own salvation, remembering the words of the apostle: "They that have used
the office well, purchase to themselves a good degree" [1 Tim.
3:13]. He should have special care for the sick, for children, for guests, and for the poor, seeing that he will certainly have to give a reckoning of his treatment of all these
on the day of judgment. He should look after all the utensils of the monastery as carefully as if they were the sacred
vessels of the altar, and he should be careful of the substance
of the monastery, wasting nothing. He should be neither
avaricious nor prodigal, conducting his office in moderation
under the commands of the abbot. Above all he should
conduct himself humbly; if he is not able to furnish what is
asked for, he should at least return a pleasant answer, as it
is written: "A good word is above the best gift" [Ecclesias-
ticus 18:16]. He should take charge of everything intrusted
to him by the abbot, and should not interfere in what is
prohibited to him. He should see to it that the brothers always
have the regular amount of food, and he should serve it without haughtiness or unnecessary delay, remembering the punishment which the Scripture says is meted out to those who
offend one of these little ones. In large congregations, the
cellarer should have assistants, with whose aid he may be
able to fulfil the duties committed to him without unnecessary worry. He should, moreover, so arrange the work in
his department that the distribution of food and the other
details may come at convenient hours, and may not disturb
or inconvenience anyone.

Ch. 32. *The utensils and other property of the monastery.*
—The possessions of the monastery in the way of utensils,
clothes, and other things should be intrusted by the abbot to
the charge of certain brothers whom he can safely trust, and
the various duties of caring for or collecting these things
should be divided among them. The abbot should keep a list
of these things, so that he may know what is given out or

taken back when the offices change hands. If any one of these
brothers is careless or wasteful of the goods of the monastery
which are intrusted to him, he should be reproved and if he
does not reform he should be subjected to discipline according to the rule.

Ch. 33. *Monks should not have personal property.*—The
sin of owning private property should be entirely eradicated
from the monastery. No one shall presume to give or receive anything except by the order of the abbot; no one shall
possess anything of his own, books, paper, pens, or anything
else; for monks are not to own even their own bodies and
wills to be used at their own desire, but are to look to the
father [abbot] of the monastery for everything. So they
shall have nothing that has not been given or allowed to
them by the abbot; all things are to be had in common
according to the command of the Scriptures, and no one shall
consider anything as his own property. If anyone has been
found guilty of this most grievous sin, he shall be admonished for the first and second offence, and then if he does not
mend his ways he shall be punished.

Ch. 34. *All the brothers are to be treated equally.*—It is
written: "Distribution was made unto every man as he had
need" [Acts 4:35]. This does not mean that there should
be respect of persons, but rather consideration for infirmities. The one who has less need should give thanks to God
and not be envious; the one who has greater need should be
humbled because of his infirmity, and not puffed up by the
greater consideration shown him. Thus all the members of
the congregation shall dwell together in peace. Above all
let there be no complaint about anything, either in word or
manner, and if anyone is guilty of this let him be strictly
disciplined.

Ch. 35. *The weekly service in the kitchen.*—The brothers
shall serve in their turn in the kitchen, no one being excused,
except for illness or because occupied in work of greater

importance; thus all shall learn charity and acquire the greater reward which is the recompense for service. Assistants shall be allowed to the weak, that they be not too greatly burdened in the service, and shall also be provided for all, if the size of the congregation or the conditions of the place make it necessary. In large congregations, the cellarer shall be excused from service in the kitchen, as also those who, as we have already indicated, are engaged in more important labors; but all the others shall serve in their turn. The one who goes out of office at the end of the week, should do all the cleaning on Saturday, and should wash the towels on which the monks dry their hands and their feet, and both he and the one who succeeds him shall wash the feet of all the brothers. The one who is leaving shall turn over the utensils of the service properly cleaned to the cellarer, who shall then consign them to the one who succeeds, keeping account of what he gives out and what he receives back. Those who are engaged in this service shall be allowed a piece of bread and a cup of wine an hour before the time of the common meal, so that they may serve the brethren during the meal without inconvenience or cause for complaint; but on holy days they shall fast until after the mass. On Sunday, immediately after matins, the outgoing and the incoming cooks shall kneel in the oratory and ask for the prayers of all the brothers. The one who has finished his service for the week shall say this verse three times: "Blessed art thou, O Lord God, who hast aided and consoled me," and then shall receive the benediction; the one who is entering on the service shall say: "Make haste, O God, to deliver me; make haste to help me, O God": this shall be repeated three times by all, and then he shall receive the benediction and enter upon his duties.

Ch. 36. *The care for brothers who are ill.*—Above all, care should be taken of the sick, as if they were Christ himself, as he has said: "I was sick, and ye visited me" [Matt. 25:36]; and again, "Inasmuch as ye have done it unto one

of the least of these my brethren, ye have done it unto me"
[Matt. 25:40]. But the sick should consider that the service performed for them is done to the honor of God, and
should not make it a burden for the brothers who attend them.
Those who labor in this service, on their part, should endure
it patiently, because it redounds to their greater reward. The
abbot should make it his especial care that no one suffers
neglect. A special room shall be assigned to the sick, and
they shall be given pious, diligent, and careful attendants.
The sick should also be allowed the use of baths as often as
seems expedient, a thing which is to be accorded to the young
and strong more rarely. Those who are sick or weak are,
moreover, to be permitted to eat meat to strengthen them,
but when they have recovered they shall abstain from it in
the usual manner as the others. The abbot should see to it
also that the sick are not neglected by the cellarer or the
other servants, for their negligence will be placed to his
account, if he is not diligent in correcting them.

Ch. 37. *The aged and children.*—Special regard and consideration is due to human nature in the extremes of life,
old age and childhood, and yet this must be regulated by
the rule. Their weakness shall always be taken into consideration, and the strict requirements of the rule in regard
to food may be relaxed for them, so that they may anticipate
the regular hours of eating.

Ch. 38. *The weekly reader.*—There should always be reading during the common meal, but it shall not be left to chance,
so that anyone may take up the book and read. On Sunday
one of the brothers shall be appointed to read during the
following week. He shall enter on his office after the mass
and communion, and shall ask for the prayers of all, that
God may keep him from the spirit of pride; then he shall
say this verse three times, all the brethren uniting with him:
"O Lord, open thou my lips, and my mouth shall show
forth thy praise;" then after receiving the benediction he

enters upon his office. At the common meal, the strictest silence shall be kept, that no whispering or speaking may be heard except the voice of the reader. The brethren shall mutually wait upon one another by passing the articles of food and drink, so that no one shall have to ask for anything; but if this is necessary, it shall be done by a sign rather than by words, if possible. In order to avoid too much talking no one shall interrupt the reader with a question about the reading or in any other way, unless perchance the prior may wish to say something in the way of explanation. The brother who is appointed to read shall be given the bread and wine before he begins, on account of the holy communion which he has received, and lest so long a fast should be injurious; he shall have his regular meal later with the cooks and other weekly servants. The brothers shall not be chosen to read or chant by order of rotation, but according to their ability to edify their hearers.

Ch. 39. *The amount of food.*—Two cooked dishes, served either at the sixth or the ninth hour, should be sufficient for the daily sustenance. We allow two because of differences in taste, so that those who do not eat one may satisfy their hunger with the other, but two shall suffice for all the brothers, unless it is possible to obtain fruit or fresh vegetables, which may be served as a third. One pound of bread shall suffice for the day, whether there be one meal or two. If the monks are to have supper as well as dinner, the cellarer shall cut off a third of the loaf of bread which is served at dinner and keep it for the later meal. In the case of those who engage in heavy labor, the abbot may at his discretion increase the allowance of food, but he should not allow the monks to indulge their appetites by eating or drinking too much. For no vice is more inconsistent with the Christian character; as the Master saith: "Take heed to yourselves lest at any time your hearts be overcharged with surfeiting" [Luke 21:34]. A smaller amount of food shall be given to the youths than to their elders, and in general the rule should be to eat sparingly. All shall abstain from the flesh of four-footed beasts, except the weak and the sick.

Ch. 40. *The amount of drink.*—"Each one has his own gift from God, the one in this way, the other in that" [1 Cor. 7:7], so we hesitate to determine what others shall eat or drink. But we believe that a half-measure of wine a day is enough for anyone, making due allowance, of course, for the needs of the sick. If God has given to some the strength to endure abstinence, let them use that gift, knowing that they shall have their reward. And if the climate, the nature of the labor, or the heat of summer, or other conditions make it advisable to increase this amount, the superior may do so at his own discretion, always guarding, however, against indulgence and drunkenness. Some hold, indeed, that monks should not drink wine at all. We have not been able in our day to persuade monks to agree to this; but all will admit that drink should be used sparingly, for "wine maketh even the wise to go astray" [Ecclesiasticus 19:2]. Where wine is scarce or is not found at all because of the nature of the locality, let those who live there bless God and murmur not. In any case, let there be no murmuring because of the scarcity or the lack of wine.

Ch. 41. *The time of meals.*—From Easter to Pentecost, the brethren shall dine at the sixth hour and have supper in the evening. From Pentecost on through the summer, they shall fast on Wednesday and Friday [1] until the ninth hour, unless they are laboring in the fields or find the heat of the summer too oppressive; on the other days of the week they shall dine at the sixth hour. But if the monks are working out of doors, or are oppressed with the heat, the abbot may at his discretion have dinner served every day at the sixth hour. In this, as in all matters, the abbot shall have regard for the souls of the brethren, that they be not given cause for grumbling. From the middle of September to the beginning of Lent, they shall dine at the ninth hour, and during Lent, toward evening. The time for the evening meal shall be so fixed that the brethren may eat without the aid of lamps; and indeed all the meals are to be eaten by daylight.

[1] In the early church Wednesdays and Fridays were fast-days, because Christ was believed to have been born on a Wednesday and he died on a Friday.

Ch. 42. *Silence is to be kept after completorium.*—The monks should observe the rule of silence at all times, but especially during the hours of the night. This rule shall be observed both on fast-days and on other days, as follows: on other than fast-days, as soon as the brothers rise from the table they shall sit down together, while one of them reads from the Collations or the lives of the fathers or other holy works. But the reading at this time shall not be from the Heptateuch or from the books of the Kings, which are not suitable for weak intellects to hear at this hour and may be read at other times. On fast-days the brethren shall assemble a little while after vespers, and listen to readings from the Collations. All shall be present at this reading except those who have been given other duties to be done at this time, and after the reading of four or five pages, or as much as shall occupy an hour's time, the whole congregation shall meet for completorium. After completorium no one shall be allowed to speak to another, unless some unforeseen occasion arises, as that of caring for guests, or unless the abbot has to give a command to some one; and in these cases such speaking as is necessary shall be done quietly and gravely. If anyone breaks this rule of silence he shall be severely disciplined.

Ch. 43. *Those who are late in coming to services or to meals.*—When the signal is given for the hour of worship, all should hasten to the oratory; but they shall enter gravely, so as not to give occasion for jesting. The service of God is to be placed above every other duty. At vigils, those who

do not come in until after the Gloria of the 94th Psalm
("O come, let us sing unto the Lord"), which, as we have
indicated above, is to be said slowly and solemnly, shall be
held to be tardy. Such a one shall not be allowed to take his
accustomed place in the choir, but shall be made to stand last
or in a place apart such as the abbot may have indicated for
the tardy. There he may be seen by the abbot and all the
brothers, and after the service he shall do public penance for
his fault. The purpose of placing him last or in a place apart
from the others is to make his tardiness conspicuous, so that
he may be led through very shame to correct this fault. For
if those who come late are made to stay outside of the oratory,
some of them will go back and go to bed again, or at least
sit down outside and spend the time of service in idle talk,
thus giving a chance to the evil one. Let them come inside
that they may not lose all the service, and in the future not
be tardy. At the services in the daytime, he who does not
come in until after the verse and the Gloria of the first psalm,
shall stand in the last place as already described, and shall
not be allowed to take his own place in the choir until he has
made amends, unless the abbot shall give him permission,
reserving his penance for a later time. At the common meal
all shall stand and say a verse and a prayer, and then sit
down together. He who comes in after the verse shall be
admonished for the first and second offense, and if he is again
tardy after that he shall not be allowed to share the common
meal, but shall be made to eat alone, and his portion of wine
shall be taken away until he makes satisfaction. Those who
are not present at the verse which is said at the end of the
meal shall be punished in the same way. And no one shall
eat or drink anything except at the appointed hours. If any
one refuses to eat when food is offered to him by the superior,
he shall not be allowed to do so later when he wishes it, unless
he has made satisfaction for his fault.

　Ch. 44. *The penance of the excommunicated.*—The one

who has been excommunicated for grievous sins from both
the divine services and the common meal shall do penance as
follows: During the hour of worship, he shall lie prostrate at
the door of the oratory, with his head on the ground at the
feet of all as they come out. He shall continue to do this
until the abbot has decided that he has made reparation for
his sin. Then after he has been admitted again into the oratory, he shall fall at the feet, first of the abbot and then of all
the other brothers, and shall beg them all to pray for him;
then he may be permitted to take his own place in the choir
or such other position as the abbot shall designate. But he
shall not be allowed to lead in the psalms or the reading or
any other part of the service until the abbot gives him permission. At the end of the service each day he shall prostrate
himself upon the ground in the place where he was standing,
until the abbot decides that his penance has been accomplished.
Those who for lesser faults have been excommunicated from
the table only, shall continue to do penance in the oratory
until the abbot gives them his blessing and says: "It is
enough."

Ch. 45. *The punishment of those who make mistakes in
the service.*—If anyone makes a mistake in the psalm or the
response or the antiphony or the reading, he shall make satisfaction as described. But if he is not humbled by this and
by the rebukes of his elders, and refuses to admit that he has
erred, he shall be subjected to heavier punishment for his
obstinacy. Children shall be whipped for such offences.

Ch. 46. *The punishment for other sins.*—When a brother
has committed any fault in any of his work, in doors or out,
such as losing or breaking anything, or making a mistake of
some sort, he shall go immediately to the abbot and make
satisfaction, confessing his fault before the whole congregation. If he fails to do this and leaves the mistake to be
found out and reported by another, he shall be severely punished. But if it be a secret sin, he may confess it privately

to the abbot alone or to such spiritual superiors as may be able to cure such errors without making them public.

Ch. 47.   *The manner of announcing the hour of service.*— The signal for the hour of worship both in the daytime and at night, shall be given by the abbot or by some diligent brother to whom he has intrusted that duty, so that everything may be in readiness for the service at the proper time.   The abbot shall appoint certain ones to lead in the psalms and the antiphonies after him; only those, however, shall be allowed to read or chant who are able to edify the hearers.   These shall be appointed by the abbot, and shall perform their part gravely and humbly in the fear of the Lord.

Ch. 48.   *The daily labor of the monks.*—Idleness is the great enemy of the soul, therefore the monks should always be occupied, either in manual labor or in holy reading.   The hours for these occupations should be arranged according to the seasons, as follows: From Easter to the first of October, the monks shall go to work at the first hour and labor until the fourth hour, and the time from the fourth to the sixth hour shall be spent in reading.   After dinner, which comes at the sixth hour, they shall lie down and rest in silence; but anyone who wishes may read, if he does it so as not to disturb anyone else.   Nones shall be observed a little earlier, about the middle of the eighth hour, and the monks shall go back to work, laboring until vespers.   But if the conditions of the locality or the needs of the monastery, such as may occur at harvest time, should make it necessary to labor longer hours, they shall not feel themselves ill-used, for true monks should live by the labor of their own hands, as did the apostles and the holy fathers.   But the weakness of human nature must be taken into account in making these arrangements. From the first of October to the beginning of Lent, the monks shall have until the full second hour for reading, at which hour the service of terce shall be held.   After terce, they shall work at their respective tasks until the ninth hour.

When the ninth hour sounds they shall cease from labor and be ready for the service at the second bell. After dinner they shall spend the time in reading the lessons and the psalms. During Lent the time from daybreak to the third hour shall be devoted to reading, and then they shall work at their appointed tasks until the tenth hour. At the beginning of Lent each of the monks shall be given a book from the library of the monastery which he shall read entirely through. One or two of the older monks shall be appointed to go about through the monastery during the hours set apart for reading, to see that none of the monks are idling away the time, instead of reading, and so not only wasting their own time but perhaps disturbing others as well. Anyone found doing this shall be rebuked for the first or second offence, and after that he shall be severely punished, that he may serve as a warning and an example to others. Moreover, the brothers are not to meet together at unseasonable hours. Sunday is to be spent by all the brothers in holy reading, except by such as have regular duties assigned to them for that day. And if any brother is negligent or lazy, refusing or being unable profitably to read or meditate at the time assigned for that, let him be made to work, so that he shall at any rate not be idle. The abbot shall have consideration for the weak and the sick, giving them tasks suited to their strength, so that they may neither be idle nor yet be distressed by too heavy labor.

Ch. 49. *The observance of Lent.*—Monks ought really to keep Lent all the year, but as few are able to do this, they should at least keep themselves perfectly pure during that season, and to make up for the negligence of the rest of the year by the strictest observance then. The right way to keep Lent is this: to keep oneself free from all vices and to spend the time in holy reading, in repentance, and in abstinence. During this season, therefore, we should add in some way to the weight of our regular service, by saying additional prayers or giving up some part of our food or drink, so that each one of us of his own will may offer some gift to God in addition to his usual service, to the rejoicing of the Holy Spirit. Let each one then make some sacrifice of his bodily pleasures in the way of food or drink, or the amount of sleep, or talking and jesting, thus awaiting the holy Easter with the joy of spiritual desire. But the abbot should always be consulted in regard to the sacrifice to be made, and it should be done with his consent and wish; for whatever anyone does contrary to the wish of the spiritual father will not be imputed to him for righteousness, but for presumption and vainglory. So let everything be done in accordance with the wish of the abbot.

Ch. 50. *The observance of the hours of worship by brothers who work at a distance from the monastery or are on a journey.*—Those who are at work so far from the monastery that they cannot return for service (the question of fact shall be decided by the abbot) shall nevertheless observe the regular hours, kneeling down and worshipping God in the place where they are working. So also those who are on the road shall not neglect the hour of worship, but shall keep it as best they can.

Ch. 51. *Those who are sent on short errands.*—If a brother has been sent on an errand with instructions to return the same day with an answer, he shall not presume to eat outside of the monastery unless he has been told to do so by the abbot; and if he does, he shall be excommunicated.

Ch. 52. *The oratory of the monastery.*—The oratory should be used as its name implies: that is, as a place of prayer; and for no other purpose. When the service is over, let all go out silently and reverently, so that if any brother wishes to pray there in private he may not be disturbed by others. And when anyone wishes to pray there privately let him go in quietly and pray, not noisily, but with silent tears and earnestness of heart. No one else shall be allowed to remain in the oratory after the service, lest, as we have said, they disturb those who desire to pray there.

Ch. 53. *The reception of guests.*—All guests who come to the monastery are to be received in the name of Christ, who said: "I was a stranger and ye took me in" [Matt. 25:35]. Honor and respect shall be shown to all, but especially to Christians and strangers. When a guest is announced the superior and the brothers shall hasten to meet him and shall give him the kindest welcome. At meeting, both shall say a short prayer and then they shall exchange the kiss of peace, the prayer being said first to frustrate the wiles of the devil. The manner of salutation shall be humble and devout; he who offers it to a guest shall bow his head or even prostrate his body on the ground in adoration of Christ, in whose name guests are received. The way to receive a guest is as follows: immediately on his arrival he shall be conducted to the oratory for prayer, and then the superior or some brother at his order shall sit down and read from the holy Scriptures with him for his edification. After he has been thus received, every attention shall be shown to his comfort and entertainment. The abbot may break his fast to dine with a guest, unless the day be an especially solemn fast; but the brothers shall keep the regular fasts. The abbot shall offer the guests water for their hands, and together with all the brothers shall wash their feet, all repeating this verse at the end of the ceremony: "We have thought of thy loving kindness, O Lord, in the midst of thy temple" [Ps. 48:9]. Peculiar honor shall be shown to the poor and to strangers, since it is in them that Christ is especially received; for the power of the rich in itself compels honor. The abbot shall have a special cook for himself and the guests of the monastery, so that the brothers may not be disturbed by the arrival of guests at unusual hours, a thing always liable to occur in a monastery. Two well-qualified brothers shall be appointed to this office for the year, and shall be given such help as they may need, that they may not have occasion to complain of the service. But when they have nothing to do in this service, they shall be assigned to other tasks. It shall be the rule of the monastery that those who have charge of certain offices shall have assistants when they need them, and shall themselves be assigned to other tasks when they have nothing to do in their own offices. The guest chamber, which shall contain beds with plenty of bedding, shall be placed under the charge of a God-fearing brother. No one shall venture to talk to a guest or to associate with him; and when a brother meets one, he shall greet him humbly, and ask his blessing, but shall pass on, explaining that it is not permitted to the brothers to talk with guests.

Ch. 54. *Monks are not to receive letters or anything.*—No monk shall receive letters or gifts or anything from his family or from any persons on the outside, nor shall he send anything, except by the command of the abbot. And if anything has been sent to the monastery for him he shall not receive it unless he has first shown it to the abbot and received his permission. And if the abbot orders such a thing to be received, he may yet bestow it upon anyone whom he chooses, and the brother to whom it was sent shall acquiesce without ill-will, lest he give occasion to the evil one by his discontent. If anyone breaks this rule, he shall be severely disciplined.

Ch. 55. *The vestiarius [one who has charge of the clothing] and the calciarius [one who has charge of the footwear].* —The brothers are to be provided with clothes suited to the locality and the temperature, for those in colder regions require warmer clothing than those in warmer climates. The abbot shall decide such matters. The following garments should be enough for those who live in moderate climates: A cowl and a robe apiece (the cowl to be of wool in winter and in summer light or old); a rough garment for work; and shoes and boots for the feet. The monks shall not be fastidious about the color and texture of these clothes, which are to be made of the stuff commonly used in the region where they dwell, or of the cheapest material. The abbot shall also see that the garments are of suitable length and not too short. When new garments are given out the old ones should be returned, to be kept in the wardrobe for the poor. Each monk may have two cowls and two robes to allow for change at night and for washing; anything more than this is superfluous and should be dispensed with as being a form of luxury. The old boots and shoes are also to be returned when new ones are given out. Those who are sent out on the road shall be provided with trousers, which shall be washed and restored to the vestiary when they return. There shall also be cowls and robes of slightly better material for the use of those who are sent on journeys, which also shall be given back when they return. A mattress, a blanket, a sheet, and a pillow shall be sufficient bedding. The beds are to be inspected by the abbot frequently, to see that no monk has hidden away anything of his own in them, and if anything is found there which has not been granted to that monk by the abbot, he shall be punished very severely. To avoid giving occasion to this vice, the abbot shall see that the monks are provided with everything that is necessary: cowl, robe, shoes, boots, girdle, knife, pen, needle, handkerchief, tablets, etc. For he should remember how the fathers did in this matter, as it is related in the Acts of the Apostles: "There was given unto each man according to his need" [Acts 2:45]. He should be guided in this by the requirements of the needy, rather than by the complaints of the discontented, remembering always that he shall have to give an account of all his decisions to God on the day of judgment.

Ch. 56. *The table of the abbot.*—The table of the abbot shall always be for the use of guests and pilgrims, and when there are no guests the abbot may invite some of the brothers to eat with him. But in that case, he should see that one or

two of the older brothers are always left at the common table
to preserve the discipline of the meal.

Ch. 57. *Artisans of the monastery.*—If there are any
skilled artisans in the monastery, the abbot may permit them
to work at their chosen trade, if they will do so humbly.
But if any one of them is made proud by his skill in his
particular trade or by his value to the monastery, he shall
be made to give up that work and shall not go back to it
until he has convinced the abbot of his humility. And if
the products of any of these trades are sold, those who conduct the sales shall see that no fraud is perpetrated upon the
monastery. For those who have any part in defrauding the
monastery are in danger of spiritual destruction, just as
Ananias and Sapphira for this sin suffered physical death.
Above all, avarice is to be avoided in these transactions;
rather the prices asked should be a little lower than those
current in the neighborhood, that God may be glorified in
all things.

Ch. 58. *The way in which new members are to be received.*
—Entrance into the monastery should not be made too easy,
for the apostle says: "Try the spirits, whether they are of
God" [1 John 4:1]. So when anyone applies at the monastery, asking to be accepted as a monk, he should first be
proved by every test. He shall be made to wait outside four
or five days, continually knocking at the door and begging to
be admitted; and then he shall be taken in as a guest and
allowed to stay in the guest chamber a few days. If he satis-
fies these preliminary tests, he shall then be made to serve
a novitiate of at least one year, during which he shall be
placed under the charge of one of the older and wiser brothers, who shall examine him and prove, by every possible
means, his sincerity, his zeal, his obedience, and his ability
to endure shame. And he shall be told in the plainest manner all the hardships and difficulties of the life which he has
chosen. If he promises never to leave the monastery [*sta-*

bilitas loci] the rule shall be read to him after the first two months of his novitiate, and again at the end of six more months, and finally, four months later, at the end of his year. Each time he shall be told that this is the guide which he must follow as a monk, the reader saying to him at the end of the reading: "This is the law under which you have expressed a desire to live; if you are able to obey it, enter; if not, depart in peace." Thus he shall have been given every chance for mature deliberation and every opportunity to refuse the yoke of service. But if he still persists in asserting his eagerness to enter and his willingness to obey the rule and the commands of his superiors, he shall then be received into the congregation, with the understanding that from that day forth he shall never be permitted to draw back from the service or to leave the monastery. The ceremony of receiving a new brother into the monastery shall be as follows: first he shall give a solemn pledge, in the name of God and his holy saints, of constancy, conversion of life, and obedience (*stabilitas loci, conversio morum, obedientia*); [1] this promise shall be in writing drawn up by his own hand (or, if he cannot write, it may be drawn up by another at his request, and signed with his own mark), and shall be placed by him upon the altar in the presence of the abbot, in the name of the saints whose relics are in the monastery. Then he shall say: "Receive me, O Lord, according to thy word, and I shall live; let me not be cast down from mine expectation" [Ps. 119:116]; which shall be repeated by the whole congregation three times, ending with the "Gloria Patri." Then he shall prostrate himself at the feet of all the brothers in turn, begging them to pray for him, and therewith he becomes a member of the congregation. If he has any property he shall either sell it all and give to the poor before he enters the monastery, or else he shall turn it over to the monastery in due form, reserving nothing at all for himself; for from that day forth he owns nothing, not even his own body and will.   Then he shall take off his own garments there in the oratory, and put on the garments provided by the monastery.   And those garments which he put off shall be stored away in the vestiary, so that if he should ever yield to the promptings of the devil and leave the monastery, he shall be made to put off the garments of a monk, and to put on his own worldly clothes, in which he shall be cast forth.   But the written promise which the abbbot took from the altar where he placed it shall not be given back to him, but shall be preserved in the monastery.

¹ The vows which a monk had to take are found in chap. 58 and in nos. 252–257. They are differently stated but may be summed up as follows: (1) *stabilitas loci*, stability of place, steadfastness; that is, he took a vow never to leave the monastery and give up the monastic life; (2) *conversio morum*, conversion of life; that is, to give up all secular and worldly practices and to conform to the ideals and standards of the monastic life; (3) observance of the rule; (4) obedience, that is, to the abbot and to all his superiors; (5) chastity; and (6) poverty. The last three are generally meant when "monastic vows" are spoken of.

Ch. 59.   *The presentation of children.*—If persons of noble rank wish to dedicate their son to the service of God in the monastery, they shall make the promise for him, according to the following form: they shall bind his hand and the written promise along with the consecrated host in the altar-cloth and thus offer him to God.   And in that document they shall promise under oath that their son shall never receive any of the family property, from them or any other person in any way whatsoever.   If they are unwilling to do this, and desire to make some offering to the monastery for charity and the salvation of their souls, they may make a donation from that property, reserving to themselves the usufruct during their lives, if they wish.   This shall all be done so clearly that the boy shall never have any expectations that might lead him astray, as we know to have happened.   Poor people shall do the same when they offer their sons; and if they have

no property at all they shall simply make the promise for
their son and present him to the monastery with the host
before witnesses.[1]

[1] See nos. 259, 260.

Ch. 60. *Priests who wish to live in the monastery.*—If a
priest asks to be admitted into the monastery, he shall not
be immediately accepted. But if he persists in his request,
let it be made clear to him that he shall have to obey the
whole rule, and that the regular discipline will not be relaxed
in his favor; as it is written "Friend, wherefore art thou
come?" [Matt. 26:50]. The abbot may assign him the place
nearest himself, and may give him authority to pronounce
the benediction or officiate at the mass, but the priest shall
not presume to do any of these things, except by the authority
of the abbot, for he is subject to the rule as all the others, and
should indeed set an example to them by his humility. And
when an ordination or other ceremony is held in the monastery, the priest shall occupy in the service the place which he
holds as a monk, and not that which he would have as a
priest. Members of other clerical grades [deacons, etc.] may
also be received into the monastery as ordinary monks, if they
wish to enter; but they shall be made to promise obedience
to the rule and never to leave the monastery.

Ch. 61. *The reception of strange monks.*—If a monk
from a distant region comes to the monastery and asks to be
received, accepting the conditions and the customs of the
place without fault-finding, he shall be welcomed and entertained as long as he wishes to stay. And if he humbly suggests certain faults and possible improvements in the conduct
of the monastery, the abbot shall consider his suggestions
carefully, for he may have been sent there by God for that
very purpose. If he expresses a wish to remain permanently
in that monastery, he may be admitted to membership immediately, ample opportunity having been given to discover his

real character while he was a guest. The one who has been discovered during this time, however, to be wicked or unreasonable, shall not only be refused admission to the monastery as a member, but shall be plainly told to depart, that the congregation may not be contaminated by his evil example. Those who are worthy, on the other hand, shall not only be received at their request, but may be urged to stay as a good example for the rest, since we all serve the same Lord and Master wherever we may be. The abbot may even advance such a one to a higher grade if he thinks best, for it is in his power to promote not only monks, but priests and other members of the clergy, if their character and manner of life make it expedient. But the abbot should be careful that he does not receive into his congregation monks from other monasteries who have left without the consent of their abbot, or the usual commendatory letters;[1] as it is written: "Do not unto others what ye would not that they should do unto you" [Luke 6:31].

[1] See nos. 261–264.

Ch. 62. *The ordaining of priests in the monastery.*— When the abbot wishes to ordain a priest or a deacon for the service of the monastery, he shall choose one of his own congregation who is worthy to exercise such an office. And that brother shall not be elated because of his ordination, nor presume to exercise his office except by the command of the abbot; he should rather obey the rule the more carefully because of his calling, that he may grow in grace. Except for his right to officiate at the altar, he shall occupy the same position as before his ordination, unless he is promoted to a higher grade for his merits. He shall be subject to the authority of the deans and *præpositi* of the monastery as the rest, for his priestly office ought to incline him to greater obedience, rather than to resistance to authority. But if he is rebellious and refuses to submit even after frequent admonitions from the abbot, he may be handed over to the bishop of the diocese for correction. If after that he persists in his flagrant sin, refusing utterly to obey the rule, he shall be cast out of the monastery.

Ch. 63. *Ranks among the monks.*—There shall be different ranks among the monks, the rank of each being determined by the length of his service, by the character of his life, or by the decision of the abbot. But in this matter the abbot shall be careful not to give offence to any of his congregation, nor to use his power unjustly, for God will surely demand a reckoning of all his acts and decisions. These differences in rank are to be observed by the brothers in their daily life, each one having his own position in the choir, and his own turn at the confession and communion and in leading the psalms. But these differences shall not be based solely upon age, for we are told that Samuel and Daniel while still youths were made judges over priests; but rank shall ordinarily be determined by the time of entrance upon the monastic life, except in the case of promotions and degradations which the abbot may have made for cause. Thus, for example, one who was admitted as a monk at the second hour of the day shall be the inferior of the one admitted at the first hour. But in the case of children the discipline necessary to their welfare shall not be disturbed for this consideration. The proper attributes of inferiors are honor and reverence for those above them; and of superiors, love and affectionate care for those below them. This distinction shall be observed in addressing one another; thus an inferior shall be addressed as brother, and a superior as "nonnus" [that is, tutor or elder], as a sign of paternal reverence. But the abbot, since he is the representative of Christ, shall be addressed as "lord" and "abbot" [that is, father], not for his own exaltation, but for the honor and reverence which are due to Christ; and on his part, he shall always so conduct himself as to merit the honor which is shown to him.

When two brothers meet, the inferior shall ask the other for
his blessing. The inferior shall always rise and offer his
superior his seat, and shall remain standing until the other
bids him be seated; as it is written: "In honor preferring one
another" [Rom. 12:10]. The children and youths are to be
given their own places at the table and in the oratory, for the
sake of preserving discipline, and indeed they shall be under
strict discipline in all circumstances, until they have arrived
at an age of discretion.

Ch. 64. *The ordination of the abbot.*—The election of
the abbot shall be decided by the whole congregation or by
that part of it, however small, which is of "the wiser and
better counsel." [1] And he shall be chosen for his meritorious
life and sound doctrine, even if he be the lowliest in the congregation. But if the whole congregation should agree to
choose one simply because they know that he will wink at
their vices, and the character of this abbot is discovered by
the bishop of the diocese or by the abbots and Christian men
of the neighborhood, they shall refuse their consent to the
choice and shall interfere to set a better ruler over the house
of God. If they do this with pure motives in zeal for the
service of God they shall have their reward; just as, in
neglecting to do so, they shall surely be guilty of sin. The
one who is ordained should realize that he has assumed a
heavy burden and also that he will have to render an account
of his office to God. He should understand that he is set to
rule for the profit of others and not for his own exaltation.
He must be learned in the divine law, that he may know how
and be able to bring forth things new and old [Matt. 13:52].
He shall be chaste, sober, and merciful, and always prefer
mercy to justice, as he hopes to receive the same treatment
from God. He should love the brothers, but hate their sins.
He should exercise his authority to correct with the greatest
prudence, lest, as it were, he should break the vase in his
efforts to remove the stains. Let him remember in this regard

that he himself is frail, and that "A bruised reed is not to be broken" [Is. 42:3]. We do not mean that he is to allow vices to flourish, but that he should exercise charity and care in his attempts to root them out, adapting his treatment to each case, as we said above. Let him strive to make himself loved rather than feared. He should not be violent nor easily worried, nor too obstinate in his opinions; he shall not be too jealous or suspicious of those about him, else he shall never have any peace of mind. His commands shall be given with foresight and deliberation, and he shall always examine his decisions to see whether they are made with regard for this world, or for the service of God. He shall profit by the warning of St. Jacob, where he says: "If I overdrive my flocks, they shall die all in one day" [cf. Gen. 33:13]. He should rule wisely, using discretion in all things; so that his administration may be such that the strong shall delight in it, while the weak are not offended by it. Above all, he should obey the rule in everything. Then, at the end of a good ministry, he shall receive that reward which the Lord has promised in the parable of the good servant: "Verily, I say unto you, that he shall make him ruler over all his goods" [Matt. 24:47].

1 See introductory note to no. 113.

Ch. 65. *The præpositus of the monastery.*—The ordination of *præpositi* has been a frequent source of trouble in the monastery, for some of them have acted as if they were second abbots, and by their presumption have aroused ill-feeling and dissensions in the congregation. This occurs especially where the *præpositus* is ordained by the bishops and abbots from whom his own abbot has received his ordination. Herein is found the cause of the whole trouble, for the *præpositus* is led to believe himself freed from the control of the abbot because of his equal ordination. Thence arise envying, quarrels, dissensions, and disturbances; for, the abbot and the *præpositus* being opposed to one another, the congregation is divided into

factions, to the peril of their souls. They who ordain them
in this way are responsible for these evils. Accordingly we
believe it better, for the sake of the peace of the monastery,
that the abbot rule his congregation without a *præpositus,*
intrusting the management to deans, as we have already suggested; because where several are employed with equal authority, no one can become unduly exalted. But sometimes
the circumstances seem to require the services of a *præpositus,*
or else the whole congregation humbly petitions the abbot to
appoint one. Then, if he wishes, he may, with the advice of
the brothers, choose one and ordain him himself. The *præpositus* shall have charge only of such affairs as the abbot
may intrust to him, doing nothing without his consent; for
his position calls for greater obedience because of the greater
trust committed to him. But the wicked *præpositus* who acts
presumptuously or refuses obedience to the rule shall be
admonished for his fault at least four times; after that, if
he persists in his evil ways, he shall be subjected to the discipline provided in the rule; and finally he shall be deposed
from his office, and a worthier brother put in his place. And
if he refuses to submit quietly and to take his old place in
the congregation, he shall be cast out of the monastery. But
the abbot should examine his own motives to see that he is
not actuated by envy or jealousy, for he must render account
to God for all his acts.

Ch. 66. *The doorkeeper of the monastery.*—The door of
the monastery shall be kept by an aged monk, one who is able
to perform the duties of that position wisely and whose age
will prevent him from being tempted to wander outside. He
shall have his cell near the door to be always at hand to
answer to those who knock. Everyone who knocks shall
receive a ready response, the doorkeeper welcoming him with
thanks to God for his coming and giving him his blessing.
If he needs an assistant he shall be given the services of one
of the younger brothers. If possible, the monastery should

contain within its walls everything necessary to the life and the labors of the monks, such as wells, a mill, bake-oven, gardens, etc., so that they shall have no excuse for going outside.

This rule shall be read often before the whole congregation, that no brother may be able to plead ignorance as an excuse for his sin.[1]

[1] From this last sentence it is thought that this was at one time the end of the rule, and that all the chapters which follow were added at a later date.

Ch. 67. *Brothers who are sent on errands.*—Those who are about to leave the monastery on errands, shall ask for the prayers of the abbot and the whole congregation while they are away; and this petition shall be added to the last prayer at every service during their absence. Likewise, at the end of every service on the day when they return, they shall prostrate themselves on the floor of the oratory and ask all the brothers to pray for them, because of the sins which they may have committed while out on the road, sins of seeing or of hearing or of speech. And no one of them shall venture to relate to the others anything that he saw or heard while out in the world, for herein lies the greatest danger of worldly contamination. If anyone shall do this he shall be disciplined according to the rule. Those who wander outside of the monastery without the permission of the abbot or go anywhere or do anything at all contrary to his commands shall also be punished.

Ch. 68. *Impossible commands.*—If a brother is commanded by his superior to do difficult or impossible things, he shall receive the command humbly and do his best to obey it; and if he finds it beyond human strength, he shall explain to the one in authority why it cannot be done, but he shall do this humbly and at an opportune time, not boldly as if resisting or contradicting his authority. But if after this explanation the superior still persists in his demands, he shall do his best to carry them out, believing that they are meant for his own good, and relying upon the aid of God, to whom all things are possible.

Ch. 69. *No one shall defend another in the monastery.*— No monk shall presume to come to the defence of another who has been reprimanded by his superior, even if the two are bound by the closest ties of relationship, for such actions give rise to the evils of insubordination and breach of discipline. If anyone violates this rule, he shall be severely punished.

Ch. 70. *Monks shall not strike one another.*—Monks should avoid especially the sin of presumption. Therefore, we forbid anyone to excommunicate or to strike his brother, unless by the authority directly given him by the abbot. When sinners are to be punished it shall be done before the whole congregation, for the example to the rest. Children and youths under fifteen years shall be subject to the discipline and control of all the brothers, but this, too, shall be exercised in reason and moderation. Any brother who of his own authority shall venture to strike one over that age, or who shall abuse the children unreasonably, shall be punished according to the rule; for it is written: "Do not unto others as ye would not that they should do unto you."

Ch. 71. *Monks are mutually to obey one another.*—Not only should the monks obey the abbot; they should also obey one another, for obedience is one of the chief means of grace. The commands of the abbot and of the other officials shall always have precedence over those of any persons not in authority, but next to them the younger brothers should give loving and zealous obedience to the commands of their elders. If anyone refuses to do this, resisting the commands of a superior, he shall be corrected for his fault. Whenever a brother has been reprimanded by his abbot or by any superior for a fault of any sort, or knows that he has offended such a one, he shall immediately make amends, falling at the feet of the offended, and remaining there until he has received his forgiveness and blessing. And the one who refuses to humble himself in this way shall be punished with blows, being even cast out of the monastery if he persists in his stubbornness.

Ch. 72. *The good zeal which monks should have.*—There are two kinds of zeal: one that leads away from God to destruction, and one that leads to God and eternal life. Now these are the features of that good zeal which monks should cultivate: to honor one another; to bear with one another's infirmities, whether of body or mind; to vie with one another in showing mutual obedience; to seek the good of another rather than of oneself; to show brotherly love one to another; to fear God; to love the abbot devotedly; and to prefer the love of Christ above everything else. This is the zeal that leads us to eternal life.

Ch. 73. *This rule does not contain all the measures necessary for righteousness.*—The purpose of this rule is to furnish a guide to the monastic life. Those who observe it will have at least entered on the way of salvation and will attain at least some degree of holiness. But he who aims at the perfect life must study and observe the teachings of all the holy fathers, who have pointed out in their writings the way of perfection. For every page and every word of the Bible, both the New and the Old Testament, is a perfect rule for this earthly life; and every work of the holy catholic fathers teaches us how we may direct our steps to God. The Collations, the Institutes, the Lives of the Saints, and the rule of our father, St. Basil, all serve as valuable instructions for monks who desire to live rightly and to obey the will of God. Their examples and their teachings should make us ashamed of our sloth, our evil lives, and our negligence. Thou who art striving to reach the heavenly land, first perfect thyself with the aid of Christ in this little rule, which is but the beginning of holiness, and then thou mayst under the favor of God advance to higher grades of virtue and knowledge through the teaching of these greater works.   AMEN.

252. OATH OF THE BENEDICTINES.

Jaffé, IV, p. 365.

The following documents, nos. 252-264, are examples of the various vows, letters, and other documents mentioned in the rule. As the titles explain their character, no further word of introduction seems necessary.

The promise of the monks to obey the rule of St. Benedict.

I, (name), in the holy monastery of the blessed martyr and confessor, (name), in the presence of God and his holy angels, and of our abbot, (name), promise in the name of God that I will live all the days of my life from now henceforth in this holy monastery in accordance with the rule of St. Benedict and that I will obey whatever is commanded of me. I, (name), have made this promise and written it with my own hand and signed it in the presence of witnesses.

253. MONK'S VOW.

Migne, 66, col. 820.

I, brother Gerald, in the presence of abbot Gerald and the other brothers, promise steadfastness in this monastery according to the rule of St. Benedict and the precepts of Sts. Peter and Paul; and I hereby surrender all my possessions to this monastery, built in the honor of St. Peter and governed by the abbot Gerald.

254. MONK'S VOW.

Migne, 66, col. 820.

I, brother (name), a humble monk of the monastery of St. Denis in France, in the diocese of Paris, in the name of God, the Virgin Mary, St. Denis, St. Benedict, and all the saints, and of the abbot of this monastery, do promise to keep the

vows of obedience, chastity, and poverty. I also promise, in
the presence of witnesses, steadfastness and conversion of life,
according to the rules of this monastery and the traditions
of the holy fathers.

255. Monk's Vow.

Migne, 66, col. 820.

I, brother (name), in the presence of the abbot of this
Cistercian monastery built in the honor of the ever blessed
Virgin Mary, mother of God, and in the name of God and all
his saints whose relics are kept here, do hereby promise steadfastness, conversion of life, and obedience, according to the
rule of St. Benedict.

256. Monk's Vow.

Migne, 66, col. 821.

I hereby renounce my parents, my brothers and relatives,
my friends, my possessions and my property, and the vain and
empty glory and pleasure of this world. I also renounce my
own will, for the will of God. I accept all the hardships of
the monastic life, and take the vows of purity, chastity, and
poverty, in the hope of heaven; and I promise to remain a
monk in this monastery all the days of my life.

257. The Written Profession of a Monk.

Migne, 66, col. 825.

It was my earnest desire to become a monk, but when I
applied for admission to this monastery, I was told it would
not be granted until I had been tried and proved. So I was
at first received only as a guest; after remaining in that position for several days, I was accepted as a novice to serve a
period of probation. During this period I was under the
charge of one of the older monks. He first explained to me
all the hardships and difficulties of the life of a monk, and

after I had promised steadfastness in these conditions, he said: "If you ever draw back after giving your solemn promise to obey the rule, you are not fit for the kingdom of God. You will be driven from the doors of the monastery in the old garments in which you were first admitted; for as you put off the world and your worldly garments when you became a monk, so you shall be made to put them on again to be cast out, remaining thenceforth a slave of the world to the contempt of all the righteous." But I took courage, saying with David: "By the words of thy lips, I have kept me from the paths of the destroyer" [Ps. 17:4], for I knew that if I shared the sufferings of Christ I should also share his glorious resurrection. Comforting myself with these thoughts, I promised that I would keep all these commandments, as I hoped for eternal life. Having thus convinced the father of my determination, I was accepted as a novice and made to serve a novitiate of a year, during which time the rule was read to me three times, each time with the admonition: "This is the law under which you have expressed your desire to live; if you are able to obey it, enter; if not, depart a free man." My year of novitiate being completed and my mind fully made up after this long and careful deliberation, I now earnestly pray you with tears to receive me into your congregation. Therefore I promise, as I hope for salvation, with the aid of God to observe the rule in all things, and to obey the abbot and my superiors; I become a bondsman to the rule, that I may gain eternal liberty. From this day forth I will never leave the monastery nor withdraw my neck from the yoke of this service, which I have accepted freely and of my own will after a year of deliberation. I solemnly promise steadfastness (*stabilitas loci*), conversion of life, and perfect obedience. In witness thereof I have made this promise in writing, in the name of the saints whose relics are preserved here, and in the name of the abbot, and I now present it. This document, signed with my own hand,

I now place upon the altar, whence it shall be taken and kept forever in the archives of the monastery.

258. The Ceremony of Receiving a Monk into the Monastery.

Migne, 66, cols. 829 ff.

After the novice has made his oral profession, the abbot puts on the robe in which mass is to be said. Then, after the offertory, the abbot examines the novice as follows:

The abbot asks: "Brother (name), do you renounce the world and all its vain and empty shows?" The novice replies: "I do."

The abbot: "Do you promise conversion of life?" The novice: "I do."

The abbot: "Do you promise perfect obedience to the rule of St. Benedict?" The novice: "I do."

The abbot: "And may God give you his aid."

Then the novice, or someone for him, reads his written promise, and places it first upon his head and then upon the altar. Then he prostrates himself upon the ground with his arms spread out in the form of a cross, saying the verse: "Receive me, O Lord," etc. During the "Gloria patri," the "Kyrie, eleison," the "Pater noster," and the litany, the novice remains prostrate before the altar, until the end of the service. And the brothers in the choir shall kneel while the litany is being said. Then shall be said the prayers for the occasion as commanded by the fathers. Immediately after the communion and before these prayers, the new garments, which had been folded and placed before the altar, shall be blessed, being touched with holy oil and sprinkled with water which has been blessed by the abbot. After the mass is finished, the novice, rising from the ground, puts off his old garments and puts on the robes which have just been blessed, while the abbot recites: "Exuat te Dominus," etc. Then the abbot and after him all the brothers in turn give

the new member the kiss of peace. He shall keep perfect
silence for three days after this, going about with his head
covered and receiving the communion every day.

259. OFFERING OF A CHILD TO THE MONASTERY.
Migne, 66, col. 842.

I dedicate this boy, in the name of God and his holy saints,
to serve our Lord Jesus Christ as a monk, and to remain in
this holy life all his days until his final breath.

260. OFFERING OF A CHILD TO THE MONASTERY.
Migne, 66, col. 842.

The dedication of children to the service of God is sanc-
tioned by the example of Abraham and of many other holy
men, as related in the New and Old Testaments. Therefore,
I, (name), now offer in the presence of abbot (name), this
my son, (name), to omnipotent God and to the Virgin Mary,
mother of God, for the salvation of my soul and of the souls
of my parents. I promise for him that he shall follow the
monastic life in this monastery of (name), according to the
rule of St. Benedict, and that from this day forth he shall
not withdraw his neck from the yoke of this service. I
promise also that he shall never be tempted to leave by me
or by anyone with my consent.

261. COMMENDATORY LETTER.
Migne, 66, col. 859.

To the venerable abbot (name), of the monastery of
(name), abbot (name), of the monastery of (name), sends
greeting and the holy kiss of peace. We present herewith
our brother (name), whom we have sent to you with letters of
dismissal and recommendation. We commend him to you
and beseech you to take him into your monastery, because
our monastery has become impoverished through various
reverses. (Or this) We dismiss him from his service in this

monastery and free him from his vow of obedience to us, in order that he may serve the Lord under your rule.

262. COMMENDATORY LETTER.
Migne, 66, col. 859.

To the reverend father in Christ; or:

To the pious and illustrious (name); or:

To the abbot (name), abbot (name) sends greeting in the Lord. Know that our pious brother (name), has earnestly besought us to write a commendatory letter, recommending him to your care so that he may serve the Lord under you in your monastery. We have granted his prayer and given him this letter, by which we free him from his vow of obedience to us and commend him to you, giving you the right to receive him into your monastery, if he applies within one month from this date, after which time this letter shall not be valid. This is to show that he has not been expelled from our monastery for evil conduct, but has been permitted to leave us and go to you, on account of his great desire to serve the Lord under your rule.

263. GENERAL LETTER.
Migne, 66, col. 859.

To all bishops and other ecclesiastics and to all Christian men: Know ye that I have given permission to this our brother (name), to live according to the rule wherever he shall desire, believing it to be for the advantage of the monastery and the good of his soul.

264. LETTER OF DISMISSAL.
Migne, 66, col. 859.

This our brother (name), has desired to dwell in another monastery where it seems to him he can best serve the Lord and save his own soul. Know ye, therefore, that we have given him permission by this letter of dismissal to betake himself thither.

265. THE REGULAR CLERGY. PROLOGUE OF THE RULE
OF ST. CHRODEGANG, BISHOP OF METZ, FOR HIS CLERGY,
ca. 744.

Holstenius Codex Regularum, etc., II, p. 96.

We give here only a part of the rule of St. Chrodegang, bishop of
Metz, because it makes clear the purpose for which the rule was
composed. It was for the clergy and not for the monks. The rule
itself consists of a number of paragraphs prescribing in detail the
life of the clergy who were to live together with their bishop. This
action of St. Chrodegang was not altogether new. St. Augustine,
bishop of Hippo in Africa, it is said, had all the clergy of his city
live with him in a common house very much after the fashion of
monks in a monastery. His example may have had some influence,
but it was not generally imitated. The immediate purpose of St.
Chrodegang in compelling the clergy of his diocese to live with him
was to reform them. They differed little in life and morals from
the laymen and were no doubt sadly in need of a reform. They
were now deprived of much of their independence. They ate at a
common table, slept in a common dormitory, observed common hours
of prayer and work, and in general lived a "common life." They
were clergymen, not monks, although they lived in nearly all respects
as monks, and their house, or canonry, was conducted quite like a
monastery. They were called by various names, such as regular
clergy, canons regular, regular canons, etc. Other bishops imitated
St. Chrodegang and in time it came to be regarded as the only
proper way for the clergy to live. The Cluniac reforming party supported the idea with all its power and the regular clergy was soon
organized into orders, chief of which was that of the Premonstraten-
sians, which was established about 1120.

There were of course many priests whose parishes and churches
were so far from the cathedral that they could not live with their
bishop and continue to perform their parish duties. They lived in
the world and hence were called the "secular clergy." The orders
of regular canons despised them and heaped abuse on them, chiefly
because they did not live according to a rule. The orders of regular
canons soon became rich, and tended to indolence and luxury. They
were beset by the same temptations as the monks, and their history
does not differ materially from that of the monkish orders.

If the authority of the 318 holy fathers [the council of
Nicæa, 325] and of the canons were observed, and the bishops

and their clergy were living in the proper way, it would be quite unnecessary for anyone so humble and unimportant as we to attempt to say anything about this matter [that is, the way in which the clergy should live], which has been so well treated by the holy fathers, or to add anything new to what they have said.   But since the negligence of the bishops as well as of their clergy is rapidly increasing, a further duty seems incumbent on us.   And we are certainly in great danger unless we do, if not all we should, at least all we can, to bring our clergy back to the proper way of living.

After I had been made bishop of Metz [743] and had begun to attend to the duties of my pastoral office, I discovered that my clergy as well as the people were living in a most negligent manner.   In great sorrow I began to ask what I ought to do.   Relying on divine aid and encouraged by my spiritually minded brethren, I thought it necessary to make a little rule for my clergy, by observing which they would be able to refrain from forbidden things, to put off their vices, and to cease from the evil practices which they have so long followed.   For I thought that if their minds were once cleared of their vices, it would be easy to teach them the best and holiest precepts.

265 a.   Military-monkish Orders.   The Origin of the Templars, 1119.

William of Tyre, bk. xii, chap. 7.   Bongars, Gesta Dei per Francos, p. 819 f.

The Middle Age had two ideals, the monk and the soldier.   The monk was the spiritual, the soldier the military hero.   The military-monkish orders, whose members were both monks and soldiers, represent a fusion of these two ideals.   Several other orders were formed in imitation of the Templars, such as the Hospitallers, soon after 1119; the German order, 1190; the Sword Brothers, 1202; the order of Bethlehem; the order of Calatrava, 1158; the order of Alcantara, 1156; and the Cavalleria de St. Iago de la Spada, 1161. The fact that all these orders arose on the borderland between Christians and Mohammedans, that is, in Palestine and in Spain, would indicate their close connection with the spirit of the crusades.

In the same year [1118–19] certain nobles of knightly rank, devout, religious, and God-fearing, devoting themselves to the service of Christ, made their vows to the patriarch [of Jerusalem] and declared that they wished to live forever in chastity, obedience, and poverty, according to the rule of regular canons. Chief of these were Hugo de Payens and Geoffrey of St. Omer. Since they had neither a church nor a house, the king of Jerusalem gave them a temporary residence in the palace which stands on the west side of the temple. The canons of the temple granted them, on certain conditions, the open space around the aforesaid palace for the erection of their necessary buildings, and the king, the nobles, the patriarch, and the bishops, each from his own possessions, gave them lands for their support. The patriarch and bishops ordered that for the forgiveness of their sins their first vow should be to protect the roads and especially the pilgrims against robbers and marauders. For the first nine years after their order was founded they wore the ordinary dress of a layman, making use of such clothing as the people, for the salvation of their souls, gave them. But in their ninth year a council was held at Troyes [1128] in France at which were present the archbishops of Rheims and Sens with their suffragans, the cardinal bishop of Albano, papal legate, and the abbots of Citeaux, Clairvaux, and Pontigny, and many others. At this council a rule was established for them, and, at the direction of the pope, Honorius III, and of the patriarch of Jerusalem, Stephen, white robes were appointed for their dress. Up to their ninth year they had only nine members, but then their number began to increase and their possessions to multiply. Afterward, in the time of Eugene III, in order that their appearance might be more striking, they all, knights as well as the other members of a lower grade, who were called serving men, began to sew crosses of red cloth on their robes. Their order grew with great rapidity, and now [about 1180] they have 300 knights, in their house, clothed in white mantles, besides the serving men, whose number is almost infinite. They are said to have immense possessions both here [in Palestine] and beyond the sea [in Europe]. There is not a province in the whole Christian world which has not given property to this order, so that they may be said to have possessions equal to those of kings. Since they dwelt in a palace at the side of the temple they were called "Brothers of the army of the temple." For a long time they were steadfast in their purpose and were true to their vows, but then they forgot their humility, which is the guardian of all virtues, and rebelled against the patriarch of Jerusalem who had assisted in the establishment of their order and had given them their first lands, and refused him the obedience which their predecessors had shown him. They also made themselves very obnoxious to the churches by seizing their tithes and first-fruits and plundering their possessions.

266. ANASTASIUS IV GRANTS PRIVILEGES TO THE KNIGHTS OF ST. JOHN (HOSPITALLERS), 1154.

Migne, 188, cols. 1078 ff.

. . . In accordance with your request, and following the example of our predecessors of blessed memory, Innocent [II, 1130–43], Celestine [II, 1143–44], Lucius [II, 1144–45], and Eugene [III, 1145–53], we take under the protection of St. Peter and of the apostolic see your hospital and house in Jerusalem, and all the persons and possessions belonging thereto. And we decree and command that all your goods and possessions, present and future, which are used for supplying the needs of the pilgrims and of the poor, whether in Jerusalem or in other churches or cities, from whatever source they may be acquired, shall remain unmolested in the hands of you and of your successors. You shall have the right to build houses and churches and lay out cemeteries on whatever lands may be given to your house in Jerusalem, provided that no damage is thereby done to neighboring monasteries and religious houses which already exist. And you may build chapels and lay out cemeteries for the use of pilgrims on whatever lands you may acquire. We further decree that your tax collectors shall be under the protection of St. Peter and of us, and wherever they may be no one shall dare attack them. We decree that if any member of your fraternity dies in a territory which is under the interdict, he shall not be denied a Christian burial unless he has been excommunicated by name. If any of your members, when sent out as tax collectors, come to a city, fortress, or village, which is under the interdict, they may, once a year, open the churches in such a place and hold divine services in them.

Since all your possessions should be used only to supply the needs of the pilgrims and of the poor, we decree that no one, either lay or cleric, shall presume to levy tithes on the income which you receive from lands cultivated at your own expense. No bishop shall have the right to pronounce the sentence of interdict, suspension, or excommunication in your churches. If a general interdict is put on those lands in which you are living, you shall have the right to hold divine services in your churches, provided that all those who are excommunicated by name be excluded, the doors of the churches closed, and no bells rung. In order that nothing may be lacking for the care and salvation of your souls and that you may have the advantages and blessings of the sacraments and divine services, we grant you the privilege of receiving into your mother house [at Jerusalem], as well as into all your dependent houses, all the clergy and priests who may ask for admission, provided that you first inquire into their character and ordination, and, secondly, that they are not already members of some other order. Even though their bishops do not give their consent, you have, neverthe- less, our consent to receive all such clergy, and they shall

not be subject to anyone outside of your order except the
bishop of Rome. You may receive laymen, provided that
they are freemen, into your order to assist in caring for the
poor. No man who has been received into your order, having
taken its vows and assumed its dress, shall ever be permitted
to desert and go back to the world. Nor shall any member
be permitted to lay aside the dress of the order and go into
another order or to any other place without the permission
of the brothers and of the master of the order. No person,
whether lay or cleric, shall have the right to receive and
harbor any such deserters. You shall have your altars and
churches consecrated, your clergy ordained, and your other
ecclesiastical matters attended to by the bishop of the diocese
[in which you may happen to be], provided that he is in the
favor and communion of the Roman church, and he shall
not wish to charge you anything for these services. Otherwise, you may secure the services of any catholic bishop.
When you, who are now the master of the order, die, the
brothers shall have the right to elect your successor. We
confirm all the possessions which the order has, or may acquire, on both sides of the sea [that is, in Asia and in
Europe].

In 1162, Alexander III granted the same privileges to the
Templars.

267. Innocent III Orders the Bishops of France to Guard against Simony in the Monasteries, 1211.

Migne, 217, col. 198.

In spite of numerous reforms the character of the monks had
declined. The hard and strenuous life of the early monks had given
way to one of luxury and comfort. Men were no longer impelled to
seek admission to the monasteries by the same irresistible religious
impulse which in the earlier centuries had filled the monasteries to
overflowing and made the monks models of piety. The monasteries
had become rich and offered a life of ease to all who should enter
them. The monks became aristocratic and mercenary, refusing to
receive applicants who could not pay a considerable sum of money.

In spite of the fact that monasteries were generally exempt from the control of the local bishop, and directly under the pope, Innocent III empowers the French bishops to interfere in the monasteries to correct this abuse.

Innocent . . . to his venerable brothers, the archbishops and bishops in France, greeting and apostolic benediction. We have often heard from many persons that the damnable custom, or rather abuse, which has already been condemned, has grown to such a degree in the monasteries, nunneries, and other religious houses in France that no new member is received into them except on the payment of money, so that all become guilty of simony. Lest we should seem to favor this sin by paying no heed to these complaints which have so often been made, we command you by this writing each one to visit all the monasteries in his diocese once a year and to forbid them to receive anyone on the payment of money, and we order you to repeat this prohibition in your synods. In regard to those who may disobey this prohibition, you may inflict on them whatever punishment you may think best, granting them no right of appeal.

268. Innocent III Grants the Use of the Mitre to the Abbot of Marseilles, 1204.

Migne, 217, col. 132.

The mitre was the headdress which bishops wore on important occasions. Like the pallium it was conferred on them by the pope and symbolized their high spiritual authority. Occasionally the pope granted its use to some abbot whom he wished especially to honor. Hence we have the expression, "a mitred abbot."

Innocent etc. . . . to the abbot of Marseilles. . . . Because your monastery has always kept the true faith and been ardently devoted to the Roman church we have thought that we ought to honor you personally in every way possible. In order therefore that you may be more zealously devoted to your divine duties, we have determined to grant you the use of the mitre.

269. THE FRIARS. THE RULE OF ST. FRANCIS, 1223.

Bullarium Romanum, III, i, 229 ff.

The monk deserted the world and went into a monastery to save his own soul. The world was left to look after its own salvation. St. Francis intended that the friars should save their souls by devoting themselves to the service of others. They were to spend their time in good works, caring for the sick and miserable, acting as missionaries to the heathen, preaching, comforting, and inciting to holy living. They were to be "brothers" to everybody, rendering to each one whatever service they might see to be necessary or helpful. Like Christ, they were to go about doing good (Acts 10: 38). St. Francis was possessed with the idea of imitating Christ in all things, but especially in his service to others and in his poverty. He took literally the saying of Christ: "The foxes have holes, and the birds of the air have nests; but the Son of man hath not where to lay his head" (Matt. 8: 20); and so he wished that his order should not have monasteries or houses of any kind. Poverty is holy. The brothers should spend all their time on the road, stopping only where they might find some service to be rendered. They were to be dependent on charity for everything, even for a place to sleep. The practice of poverty was in itself meritorious, and the greater the poverty of his brothers, the greater their merit. But this degree of poverty was soon found to be unattainable. Before the death of St. Francis (1226) the order had begun to amass property.

The first rule of St. Francis was written about 1210. It was probably composed chiefly of quotations from the gospels. The second rule was written perhaps about 1217, the third in 1221, and the fourth in 1223. The first two are lost. The third is preserved in three accounts, which differ slightly from each other. The fourth, which is given here, was confirmed by Honorius III in 1223. The testament of St. Francis is in many respects more important than the rule itself, because it reveals more clearly his character and ideas.

From the rule it is easy to determine the organization of the order. The general minister was the head of the whole order. The provincial ministers were each at the head of a province. In each province there were guardians who, for the most part, were at the head of a house or monastery.

About the same time, St. Dominic, a Spaniard, established the order of Preaching Friars, or Dominicans, to combat the rising heresies of the day. These two orders mutually influenced each other in many ways. They were also rivals in most things, especially in preaching and learning. The Dominicans were intrusted with the suppression of heresy. The Friars completely overshadowed all other orders during the thirteenth and fourteenth centuries.

1. This is the rule and life of the Minor Brothers, namely, to observe the holy gospel of our Lord Jesus Christ by living in obedience, in poverty, and in chastity. Brother Francis promises obedience and reverence to pope Honorius and to his successors who shall be canonically elected, and to the Roman Church. The other brothers are bound to obey brother Francis, and his successors.

2. If any, wishing to adopt this life, come to our brothers [to ask admission], they shall be sent to the provincial ministers, who alone have the right to receive others into the order. The provincial ministers shall carefully examine them in the catholic faith and the sacraments of the church. And if they believe all these and faithfully confess them and promise to observe them to the end of life, and if they have no wives, or if they have wives, and the wives have either already entered a monastery, or have received permission to do so, and they have already taken the vow of chastity with the permission of the bishop of the diocese [in which they live], and their wives are of such an age that no suspicion can rise against them, let the provincial ministers repeat to them the word of the holy gospel, to go and sell all their goods and give to the poor [Matt. 19:21]. But if they are not able to do so, their good will is sufficient for them. And the brothers and provincial ministers shall not be solicitous about the temporal possessions of those who wish to enter the order; but let them do with their possessions whatever the Lord may put into their minds to do. Nevertheless, if they ask the advice of the brothers, the provincial ministers may send them to God-fearing men, at whose advice they may give their possessions to the poor. Then the ministers shall give them the dress of a novice, namely: two robes without a hood, a girdle, trousers, a hood with a cape reaching to the girdle. But the ministers may add to these if they

think it necessary. After the year of probation is ended they shall be received into obedience [that is, into the order], by promising to observe this rule and life forever. And according to the command of the pope they shall never be permitted to leave the order and give up this life and form of religion. For according to the holy gospel no one who puts his hand to the plough and looks back is fit for the kingdom of God [Luke 9:62]. And after they have promised obedience, those who wish may have one robe with a hood and one without a hood. Those who must may wear shoes, and all the brothers shall wear common clothes, and they shall have God's blessing if they patch them with coarse cloth and pieces of other kinds of cloth. But I warn and exhort them not to despise nor judge other men who wear fine and gay clothing, and have delicious foods and drinks. But rather let each one judge and despise himself.

3. The clerical brothers shall perform the divine office according to the rite of the holy Roman church, except the psalter, from which they may have breviaries. The lay brothers shall say 24 Paternosters at matins, 5 at lauds, 7 each at primes, terces, sexts, and nones, 12 at vespers, 7 at completorium, and prayers for the dead. And they shall fast from All Saints' day [November 1] to Christmas. They may observe or not, as they choose, the holy Lent which begins at epiphany [January 6] and lasts for 40 days, and which our Lord consecrated by his holy fasts. Those who keep it shall be blessed of the Lord, but those who do not wish to keep it are not bound to do so. But they shall all observe the other Lent [that is, from Ash-Wednesday to Easter]. The rest of the time the brothers are bound to fast only on Fridays. But in times of manifest necessity they shall not fast. But I counsel, warn, and exhort my brothers in the Lord Jesus Christ that when they go out into the world they shall not be quarrelsome or contentious, nor judge others. But they shall be gentle, peaceable, and kind, mild and humble, and

virtuous in speech, as is becoming to all. They shall not ride on horseback unless compelled by manifest necessity or infirmity to do so. When they enter a house they shall say, "Peace be to this house." According to the holy gospel, they may eat of whatever food is set before them.

4. I strictly forbid all the brothers to accept money or property either in person or through another. Nevertheless, for the needs of the sick, and for clothing the other brothers, the ministers and guardians may, as they see that necessity requires, provide through spiritual friends, according to the locality, season, and the degree of cold which may be expected in the region where they live. But, as has been said, they shall never receive money or property.

5. Those brothers to whom the Lord has given the ability to work shall work faithfully and devotedly, so that idleness, which is the enemy of the soul, may be excluded and not extinguish the spirit of prayer and devotion to which all temporal things should be subservient. As the price of their labors they may receive things that are necessary for themselves and the brothers, but not money or property. And they shall humbly receive what is given them, as is becoming to the servants of God and to those who practise the most holy poverty.

6. The brothers shall have nothing of their own, neither house, nor land, nor anything, but as pilgrims and strangers in this world, serving the Lord in poverty and humility, let them confidently go asking alms. Nor let them be ashamed of this, for the Lord made himself poor for us in this world. This is that highest pitch of poverty which has made you, my dearest brothers, heirs and kings of the kingdom of heaven, which has made you poor in goods, and exalted you in virtues. Let this be your portion, which leads into the land of the living. Cling wholly to this, my most beloved brothers, and you shall wish to have in this world nothing else than the name of the Lord Jesus Christ. And wherever

they are, if they find brothers, let them show themselves to be of the same household, and each one may securely make known to the other his need. For if a mother loves and nourishes her child, how much more diligently should one nourish and love one's spiritual brother? And if any of them fall ill, the other brothers should serve them as they would wish to be served.

7. If any brother is tempted by the devil and commits a mortal sin, he should go as quickly as possible to the provincial minister, as the brothers have determined that recourse shall be had to the provincial ministers for such sins. If the provincial minister is a priest, he shall mercifully prescribe the penance for him. If he is not a priest, he shall, as may seem best to him, have some priest of the order prescribe the penance. And they shall guard against being angry or irritated about it, because anger and irritation hinder love in themselves and in others.

8. All the brothers must have one of their number as their general minister and servant of the whole brotherhood, and they must obey him. At his death the provincial ministers and guardians shall elect his successor at the chapter held at Pentecost, at which time all the provincial ministers must always come together at whatever place the general minister may order. And this chapter must be held once every three years, or more or less frequently, as the general minister may think best. And if at any time it shall be clear to the provincial ministers and guardians that the general minister is not able to perform the duties of his office and does not serve the best interests of the brothers, the aforesaid brothers, to whom the right of election is given, must, in the name of the Lord, elect another as general minister. After the chapter at Pentecost, the provincial ministers and guardians may, each in his own province, if it seems best to them, once in the same year, convoke the brothers to a provincial chapter.

9. If a bishop forbids the brothers to preach in his

diocese, they shall obey him. And no brother shall preach
to the people unless the general minister of the brotherhood
has examined and approved him and given him the right to
preach. I also warn the brothers that in their sermons their
words shall be chaste and well chosen for the profit and edification of the people. They shall speak to them of vices and
virtues, punishment and glory, with brevity of speech, because
the Lord made the word shortened over the earth [Rom.
9:28].

10. The ministers and servants shall visit and admonish
their brothers and humbly and lovingly correct them. They
shall not put any command upon them that would be against
their soul and this rule. And the brothers who are subject
must remember that for God's sake they have given up their
own wills. Wherefore I command them to obey their ministers in all the things which they have promised the Lord
to observe and which shall not be contrary to their souls and
this rule. And whenever brothers know and recognize that
they cannot observe this rule, let them go to their ministers,
and the ministers shall lovingly and kindly receive them and
treat them in such a way that the brothers may speak to them
freely and treat them as lords speak to, and treat, their
servants. For the ministers ought to be the servants of all
the brothers. I warn and exhort the brothers in the Lord
Jesus Christ to guard against all arrogance, pride, envy,
avarice, care, and solicitude for this world, detraction, and
murmuring. And those who cannot read need not be anxious
to learn. But above all things let them desire to have the
spirit of the Lord and his holy works, to pray always to God
with a pure heart, and to have humility, and patience in
persecution and in infirmity, and to love those who persecute
us and reproach us and blame us. For the Lord says, "Love
your enemies, and pray for those who persecute and speak
evil of you" [cf. Matt. 5:44]. "Blessed are they who suffer
persecution for righteousness' sake, for theirs is the kingdom

of heaven" [Matt. 5:10]. He that endureth to the end shall
be saved [Matt. 10:22].

11. I strictly forbid all the brothers to have any association or conversation with women that may cause suspicion.
And let them not enter nunneries, except those which the
pope has given them special permission to enter. Let them
not be intimate friends of men or women, lest on this account
scandal arise among the brothers or about brothers.

12. If any of the brothers shall be divinely inspired to
go among Saracens and other infidels they must get the permission to go from their provincial minister, who shall give
his consent only to those who he sees are suitable to be sent.
In addition, I command the ministers to ask the pope to
assign them a cardinal of the holy Roman church, who shall
be the guide, protector, and corrector of the brotherhood, in
order that, being always in subjection and at the feet of the
holy church, and steadfast in the catholic faith, they may
observe poverty, humility, and the holy gospel of our Lord
Jesus Christ, as we have firmly promised to do. Let no man
dare act contrary to this confirmation. If anyone should, etc.

270. The Testament of St. Francis, 1220.

Bullarium Romanum, III, i, pp. 231 ff

1. While I was still in my sins, the Lord enabled me to
begin to do penance in the following manner: It seemed to
me bitterly unpleasant to see lepers, but the Lord led me
among them and gave me pity for them. And when I left
them, that which had been bitter to me was turned into sweet-
ness of soul and body. And a short time afterward I left
the world [that is, began the religious life].

2. And the Lord gave me such faith in churches that I
knelt in simplicity and said, "We adore thee, most holy Lord
Jesus Christ, and all thy churches which are in the world,
and we bless thee because thou hast redeemed the world
through thy holy cross."

3.   Afterward the Lord gave, and still gives me, such faith in priests who live according to the form of the holy Roman church, because of their clerical character, that if they should persecute me I would still have recourse to them. And if I were as wise as Solomon and should find a poor priest in this world, I would not preach against his will in his church. And I wish to fear, love, and honor all priests as my lords. I am unwilling to think of sins in them, because I discern in them the Son of God, and they are my lords. And on this account, I wish to perceive in this world nothing of the most high Son of God except his most holy body and his most holy blood which they [the priests] receive in the sacraments, and they alone administer to others.

4.   And these most holy mysteries I wish to honor and venerate above all things, and to put them up in honorable places.

5.   And his most holy names and words, wherever I shall find them, in improper places, I wish to collect, and I ask that they be collected and put up in honorable places.

6.   We ought to honor and venerate all theologians, who minister to us the divine word, as those who minister to us the spirit of life.

7.   And afterward the Lord gave me brothers [that is, followers], and no one showed me what I ought to do, but the Lord himself revealed to me that I ought to live according to the form of the holy gospel, and I caused it to be written in a few simple words.

8.   And the pope confirmed the rule. And those who came to adopt this life gave all they had to the poor. And we were content with one robe, mended within and without, and those who wished had a girdle and trousers.

9.   We said the office as other clergymen, the laymen said Paternosters, and we gladly remained in the churches and we were simple and obedient.

10.   And I labored with my hands, and I wish to labor.

And I wish all my brothers to engage in some honest work. And those who do not know how, shall learn; not because of the desire to receive wages for their labor, but to set a good example and to escape idleness.

11. And when the wages for our labors are not given us, let us go to the table of the Lord and ask alms from door to door.

12. The Lord revealed to me this salutation that we should use it: "May the Lord give thee peace."

13. The brothers shall guard against receiving the churches and dwellings which are built for us, unless, as becomes the holy poverty which we have promised to observe in our rule, they always live there as pilgrims and strangers.

14. By their oath of obedience I firmly forbid the brothers, wherever they are, to ask for a letter from the papal court, either themselves or through another, in order to secure a church or any position, either in the hope of securing a place to preach, or because of persecution which they may suffer. But wherever they shall not be received, they shall flee to another place to do penance with the blessing of the Lord.

15. And I earnestly wish to obey the general minister of this brotherhood, and that guardian whom he may put over me. And I wish to be so entirely in his hands and so subject to his control that I cannot go, or do anything, contrary to his will, because he is my lord.

16. And although I am simple and infirm, I wish always to have a clergyman who may perform the office for me as is contained in the rule. And all other brothers are bound by their oaths to obey the guardians, and perform the office according to the rule.

17. And if any do not perform the office according to the rule, but wish to change it in some way, or if there are any who are not catholic, all the brothers are bound by their

oath of obedience to report all such, wherever they may find them, to the nearest guardian. And the guardian must watch them night and day, as a man in chains, so that they cannot escape, until he delivers them into the hands of the general minister. And the general minister shall send them with brothers who shall guard them night and day, as a man in chains, until they deliver them to the cardinal bishop of Ostia, who is the protector and corrector of this brotherhood.

18. And the brothers shall not say that this is another rule, because it is only a reminder, an admonition, an exhortation, and my testament, which I, your poor brother, Franciscus, make for you, my dear brothers, that we wholly observe the rule which we have promised to the Lord.

19. And the general minister and all the other ministers and guardians are bound by their oath of obedience not to add to, or take from, these words. But they shall always have this writing in addition to the rule, and in all the chapters when they read the rule they shall also read this. I strictly forbid all the brothers, clerical and lay, to put glosses [explanations] into the rule or this testament in order to change the simple meaning of their words. But as the Lord enabled me to say and to write the rule and these words simply and plainly, so you shall understand them simply and plainly and without gloss. And with holy works you shall observe them to the end.

20. And whoever shall observe them shall be filled in heaven with the blessing of the most high heavenly Father, and in the earth he shall be filled with the benedictions of His Son, with the most holy Spirit, the Paraclete, and with all the virtues of heaven and of all the saints. And I, your poor brother and servant, Franciscus, as far as I can, confirm to you, within and without, that most holy benediction. Amen.

271. INNOCENT IV GRANTS THE FRIARS PERMISSION TO RIDE ON HORSEBACK WHEN TRAVELLING IN THE SERVICE OF THE KING OF ENGLAND, 1250.

Migne, 217, col. 109.

Innocent [IV], servant of the servants of God, to his most beloved son in Christ [Henry III], king of England, sends greeting and apostolic benediction. Although all Dominicans and Franciscans are forbidden to ride on horseback we gladly give assent to your prayers and grant those friars, both Dominican and Franciscan, whom you may wish to take with you on your journey over sea, our full and free permission to ride on horseback whenever, on account of the exigencies of the journey, you may wish them to do so.

272. ALEXANDER IV CONDEMNS THE ATTACKS MADE ON THE FRIARS BECAUSE OF THEIR IDLENESS AND BEGGING, 1256.

Denzinger, p. 131.

The Friars soon became the favorites of the popes, who gave them almost unlimited concessions and privileges. By these privileges the authority of the Friars was made far greater than that of the parish priest. Before long the parish clergy complained that their authority was weakened and undermined by the Friars. The Friars despised the parish clergy, who in turn hated the Friars and resented their interference in the local affairs of the parish. The Friars generally were more lenient confessors and had more liberal indulgences, and hence the parish priest soon saw his parishioners deserting him and flocking to the Friars. This meant not only a diminution of his authority and influence in his own parish, but also a reduction in his income. He complained also that he could not maintain strict discipline and holy living in his parish because his people found it easy to secure light penance and large indulgences from the Friars. A long and bitter struggle ensued between them. The two following documents illustrate the criticisms which the secular clergy made on the Friars. It will be observed that in both cases the pope condemns these criticisms.

In 1256 Alexander IV condemned the following sentiments as errors: That the Friars, both Dominicans and Franciscans, are not in the way to be saved. Their begging and

poverty are neither meritorious nor able to secure their salvation, because, if they are strong, they ought to work with
their hands and not remain idle in the hope of securing aid
from others. And that they should not have the permission
of the pope or bishops to preach and to hear confession, because by this great harm is done to the parish clergy.

273. JOHN XXII CONDEMNS THE THESES OF JOHN OF
POILLY IN WHICH HE ATTACKED THE FRIARS, 1320.

Denzinger, p. 140.

John of Poilly, a professor of Theology, attacked the
Friars and set forth the following theses, which were condemned as erroneous by John XXII, 1320:

1. That all those who confess their sins to Friars who
have only a general licence to hear confession are bound to
confess the same sins again to their own priest. 2. That so
long as the edict "Omnis utriusque sexus" stands, which was
enacted in a general council, the pope himself is not able to
release parishioners from the duty of confessing their sins
once a year to their own priest, that is, their parish priest.
Nay, more, not even God himself can do this, because it
involves a contradiction. 3. That the pope has no authority
to grant a general licence to hear confession.[1]

[1] The parish priest received a licence to hear confession only in his
own parish, while the Friars received a general licence to hear confession everywhere. The decree "Omnis utriusque sexus" (All persons
of both sexes) is the twenty-first chapter of the decrees of the Lateran
council of 1215, and concerns the duty of making confession. According to its terms every Christian must confess at least once a year
to his own parish priest. If he wished to confess to some other
priest, he had first to secure the permission of his parish priest to
do so.

IX. THE CRUSADES

The following selections are meant to illustrate briefly (1) the religious value attaching to crusading, nos. 274–277; (2) the immediate origin of the crusading movement, nos. 278–280; (3) the disorders and excesses attending the first crusade, nos. 282, 283; (4) the crusade of Frederic Barbarossa, no. 285; (5) the activity of the popes in fostering the crusades, the special inducements offered by them to crusaders, etc., nos. 284, 287, 288; (6) the commercial interests of the Italian cities, nos. 286, 288.

274. THE MERITORIOUS CHARACTER OF MARTYRDOM. ORIGEN, EXHORTATION TO MARTYRDOM, 235 A.D., CHAPS. 30 AND 50. (GREEK.)

Edited by Paul Koetschau, I, pp. 26 f and 46.

The chief inducement which the church at first offered crusaders was the remission of their sins. To lose one's life in fighting against pagans and infidels, or even to wage war on them, was regarded as closely akin to martyrdom, and therefore as possessing the power to atone for sins. Cf. nos. 274–277. As the interest in the crusades declined, the church found it necessary to offer still other inducements, chiefly of a secular character. The student should compare the later documents with the earlier in order to see what new inducements were offered.

Ch. 30. But we must remember that we have sinned and that there is no forgiveness of sins without baptism, and that the gospel does not permit us to be baptized a second time with water and the spirit for the forgiveness of sins, and that therefore the baptism of martyrdom is given us. For thus it has been called, as may clearly be implied from the passage, "Can ye drink of the cup that I drink of? and be baptized with the baptism that I am baptized with?" [Mark 10:38].

And in another place it is said, "But I have a baptism to be baptized with; and how am I straitened till it be accomplished!" [Luke 12:50]. For be sure that just as the sacrifice of the Saviour was for the whole world, so the baptism by martyrdom is for the service of many who are thereby cleansed [of their sins]. For as those sitting near the altar according to the law of Moses minister forgiveness of sins to others through the blood of bulls and goats [Heb. 9:13], so the souls of those who have suffered martyrdom are now near the altar [in heaven] for a particular purpose and grant forgiveness of sins to those who pray. And at the same time we know that just as the high priest, Jesus Christ, offered himself as a sacrifice, so the priests [that is, the martyrs], of whom he is the high priest, offer themselves as a sacrifice, and on account of this sacrifice [which they make], they have a right to be at the altar [in heaven].

Ch. 50. Just as we were redeemed with the precious blood of Christ [1 Peter 1:19], who received the name which is above every name [Phil. 2:9], so by the precious blood of the martyrs will others be redeemed.

275. ORIGEN, COMMENTARY ON NUMBERS, HOMILY X, 2. (GREEK.)

I fear therefore that now since there are no more martyrs and the saints are not offered up as sacrifices [that is, as martyrs], we are not securing the remission of our sins, and that the devil, knowing that sins are forgiven by the suffering of martyrs, does not wish to stir up the heathen to persecute us.

276. FORGIVENESS OF SINS FOR THOSE WHO DIE IN BATTLE WITH THE HEATHEN. LEO IV (847–55) TO THE ARMY OF THE FRANKS.

Migne, 115, cols. 656, 657; and 161, col. 720.

Now we hope that none of you will be slain, but we wish you to know that the kingdom of heaven will be given as a reward to those who shall be killed in this war. For the Omnipotent knows that they lost their lives fighting for the truth of the faith, for the preservation of their country, and the defence of Christians. And therefore God will give them the reward which we have named.

277. Indulgence for Fighting Heathen, 878.
Migne, 126, col. 816.

John II to the bishops in the realm of Louis II [the Stammerer]. You have modestly expressed a desire to know whether those who have recently died in war, fighting in defence of the church of God and for the preservation of the Christian religion and of the state, or those who may in the future fall in the same cause, may obtain indulgence for their sins. We confidently reply that those who, out of love to the Christian religion, shall die in battle fighting bravely against pagans or unbelievers, shall receive eternal life. For the Lord has said through his prophet: "In whatever hour a sinner shall be converted, I will remember his sins no longer." By the intercession of St. Peter, who has the power of binding and loosing in heaven and on the earth, we absolve, as far as is permissible, all such and commend them by our prayers to the Lord.

278. Gregory VII Calls for a Crusade, 1074.
Migne, 148, col. 329.

Gregory VII barely missed the honor of having begun the crusading movement. His plan is clear from the following letter. The situation in 1095 was not materially different from that in 1074, and it is probable that Urban II, when he called for a crusade, had nothing more in mind than Gregory VII had when he wrote this letter. Gregory was unable to carry out his plans because ⱥe became involved in the struggle with Henry IV.

Gregory, bishop, servant of the servants of God, to all who are willing to defend the Christian faith, greeting and apostolic benediction.

We hereby inform you that the bearer of this letter, on his recent return from across the sea [from Palestine], came to Rome to visit us. He repeated what we had heard from many others, that a pagan race had overcome the Christians and with horrible cruelty had devastated everything almost to the walls of Constantinople, and were now governing the conquered lands with tyrannical violence, and that they had slain many thousands of Christians as if they were but sheep. If we love God and wish to be recognized as Christians, we should be filled with grief at the misfortune of this great empire [the Greek] and the murder of so many Christians. But simply to grieve is not our whole duty. The example of our Redeemer and the bond of fraternal love demand that we should lay down our lives to liberate them. "Because he laid down his life for us: and we ought to lay down our lives for the brethren" [1 John 3:16]. Know, therefore, that we are trusting in the mercy of God and in the power of his might and that we are striving in all possible ways and making preparations to render aid to the Christian empire [the Greek] as quickly as possible. Therefore we beseech you by the faith in which you are united through Christ in the adoption of the sons of God, and by the authority of St. Peter, prince of apostles, we admonish you that you be moved to proper compassion by the wounds and blood of your brethren and the danger of the aforesaid empire and that, for the sake of Christ, you undertake the difficult task of bearing aid to your brethren [the Greeks]. Send messengers to us at once to inform us of what God may inspire you to do in this matter.

279. The Speech of Urban II at the Council of Clermont, 1095. Fulcher of Chartres.

Bongars, Gesta Dei per Francos, I, pp. 382 f.

In 1094 or 1095, Alexius, the Greek emperor, sent to the pope, Urban II, and asked for aid from the west against the Turks, who had taken nearly all of Asia Minor from him. At the council of Clermont Urban addressed a great crowd and urged all to go to the aid of the Greeks and to recover Palestine from the rule of the Mohammedans. The acts of the council have not been preserved, but we have four accounts of the speech of Urban which were written by men who were present and heard him. We give the two most important of these accounts. The interest of the speech lies in the fact that it gave the impulse which started the crusading movement.

"Most beloved brethren: Urged by necessity, I, Urban, by the permission of God chief bishop and prelate over the whole world, have come into these parts as an ambassador with a divine admonition to you, the servants of God. I hoped to find you as faithful and as zealous in the service of God as I had supposed you to be. But if there is in you any deformity or crookedness contrary to God's law, with divine help I will do my best to remove it. For God has put you as stewards over his family to minister to it. Happy indeed will you be if he finds you faithful in your steward-ship. You are called shepherds; see that you do not act as hirelings. But be true shepherds, with your crooks always in your hands. Do not go to sleep, but guard on all sides the flock committed to you. For if through your careless-ness or negligence a wolf carries away one of your sheep, you will surely lose the reward laid up for you with God. And after you have been bitterly scourged with remorse for your faults, you will be fiercely overwhelmed in hell, the abode of death. For according to the gospel you are the salt of the earth [Matt. 5:13]. But if you fall short in your duty, how, it may be asked, can it be salted? O how great the need of salting! It is indeed necessary for you to correct with the salt of wisdom this foolish people which is so devoted to the pleasures of this world, lest the Lord, when He may wish to speak to them, find them putrefied by their sins, unsalted and stinking. For if He shall find worms, that is, sins, in them, because you have been negligent in your duty, He will command them as worthless to be thrown into the abyss of unclean things. And because you cannot restore to Him

His great loss, He will surely condemn you and drive you
from His loving presence. But the man who applies this
salt should be prudent, provident, modest, learned, peaceable,
watchful, pious, just, equitable, and pure. For how can the
ignorant teach others? How can the licentious make others
modest? And how can the impure make others pure? If
anyone hates peace, how can he make others peaceable? Or
if anyone has soiled his hands with baseness, how can he
cleanse the impurities of another? We read also that if the
blind lead the blind, both will fall into the ditch [Matt.
15:14]. But first correct yourselves, in order that, free from
blame, you may be able to correct those who are subject to
you. If you wish to be the friends of God, gladly do the
things which you know will please Him. You must especially let all matters that pertain to the church be controlled
by the law of the church. And be careful that simony does
not take root among you, lest both those who buy and those
who sell [church offices] be beaten with the scourges of the
Lord through narrow streets and driven into the place of
destruction and confusion. Keep the church and the clergy
in all its grades entirely free from the secular power. See
that the tithes that belong to God are faithfully paid from
all the produce of the land; let them not be sold or withheld. If anyone seizes a bishop let him be treated as an
outlaw. If anyone seizes or robs monks, or clergymen, or
nuns, or their servants, or pilgrims, or merchants, let him
be anathema [that is, cursed]. Let robbers and incendiaries
and all their accomplices be expelled from the church and
anathematized. If a man who does not give a part of his
goods as alms is punished with the damnation of hell, how
should he be punished who robs another of his goods? For
thus it happened to the rich man in the gospel [Luke 16:19];
for he was not punished because he had stolen the goods of
another, but because he had not used well the things which
were his.

"You have seen for a long time the great disorder in the world caused by these crimes. It is so bad in some of your provinces, I am told, and you are so weak in the administration of justice, that one can hardly go along the road by day or night without being attacked by robbers; and whether at home or abroad, one is in danger of being despoiled either by force or fraud. Therefore it is necessary to reenact the truce, as it is commonly called, which was proclaimed a long time ago by our holy fathers. I exhort and demand that you, each, try hard to have the truce kept in your diocese. And if anyone shall be led by his cupidity or arrogance to break this truce, by the authority of God and with the sanction of this council he shall be anathematized."

After these and various other matters had been attended to, all who were present, clergy and people, gave thanks to God and agreed to the pope's proposition. They all faithfully promised to keep the decrees. Then the pope said that in another part of the world Christianity was suffering from a state of affairs that was worse than the one just mentioned. He continued:

"Although, O sons of God, you have promised more firmly than ever to keep the peace among yourselves and to preserve the rights of the church, there remains still an important work for you to do. Freshly quickened by the divine correction, you must apply the strength of your righteousness to another matter which concerns you as well as God. For your brethren who live in the east are in urgent need of your help, and you must hasten to give them the aid which has often been promised them. For, as the most of you have heard, the Turks and Arabs have attacked them and have conquered the territory of Romania [the Greek empire] as far west as the shore of the Mediterranean and the Hellespont, which is called the Arm of St. George. They have occupied more and more of the lands of those Christians, and have overcome them in seven battles. They have killed and captured many, and have destroyed the churches and devastated the empire. If you permit them to continue thus for awhile with impunity, the faithful of God will be much more widely attacked by them. On this account I, or rather the Lord, beseech you as Christ's heralds to publish this everywhere and to persuade all people of whatever rank, foot-soldiers and knights, poor and rich, to carry aid promptly to those Christians and to destroy that vile race from the lands of our friends. I say this to those who are present, it is meant also for those who are absent. Moreover, Christ commands it.

"All who die by the way, whether by land or by sea, or in battle against the pagans, shall have immediate remission of sins. This I grant them through the power of God with which I am invested. O what a disgrace if such a despised and base race, which worships demons, should conquer a people which has the faith of omnipotent God and is made glorious with the name of Christ! With what reproaches will the Lord overwhelm us if you do not aid those who, with us, profess the Christian religion! Let those who have been accustomed unjustly to wage private warfare against the faithful now go against the infidels and end with victory this war which should have been begun long ago. Let those who, for a long time, have been robbers, now become knights. Let those who have been fighting against their brothers and relatives now fight in a proper way against the barbarians. Let those who have been serving as mercenaries for small pay now obtain the eternal reward. Let those who have been wearing themselves out in both body and soul now work for a double honor. Behold! on this side will be the sorrowful and poor, on that, the rich; on this side, the enemies of the Lord, on that, his friends. Let those who go not put off the journey, but rent their lands and collect money for their expenses; and as soon as winter is over and spring comes, let them eagerly set out on the way with God as their guide."

280. THE COUNCIL OF CLERMONT, 1095. ROBERT THE MONK.

Bongars, I, pp. 31 f.

In 1095 a great council was held in Auvergne, in the city of Clermont. Pope Urban II, accompanied by cardinals and bishops, presided over it. It was made famous by the presence of many bishops and princes from France and Germany. After the council had attended to ecclesiastical matters, the pope went out into a public square, because no house was able to hold the people, and addressed them in a very persuasive speech, as follows: "O race of the Franks, O people who live beyond the mountains [that is, reckoned from Rome], O people loved and chosen of God, as is clear from your many deeds, distinguished over all other nations by the situation of your land, your catholic faith, and your regard for the holy church, we have a special message and exhortation for you. For we wish you to know what a grave matter has brought us to your country. The sad news has come from Jerusalem and Constantinople that the people of Persia, an accursed and foreign race, enemies of God, 'a generation that set not their heart aright, and whose spirit was not steadfast with God' [Ps. 78:8], have invaded the lands of those Christians and devastated them with the sword, rapine, and fire. Some of the Christians they have carried away as slaves, others they have put to death. The churches they have either destroyed or turned into mosques. They desecrate and overthrow the altars. They circumcise the Christians and pour the blood from the circumcision on the altars or in the baptismal fonts. Some they kill in a horrible way by cutting open the abdomen, taking out a part of the entrails and tying them to a stake; they then beat them and compel them to walk until all their entrails are drawn out and they fall to the ground. Some they use as targets for their arrows. They compel some to stretch out their necks and then they try to see whether they can cut off their heads with one stroke of the sword. It is better to say nothing of their horrible treatment of the women. They have taken from the Greek empire a tract of land so large that it takes more than two months to walk through it. Whose duty is it to avenge this and recover that land, if not yours? For to you more than to other nations the Lord has given the military spirit, courage, agile bodies, and the bravery to strike down those who resist you. Let your minds be stirred to bravery by the deeds of your forefathers, and by the efficiency and greatness of Karl the Great, and of Ludwig his son, and of the other kings who have destroyed Turkish kingdoms, and established Christianity in their lands. You should be moved especially by the holy grave of our Lord and Saviour which is now held by unclean peoples, and by the holy places which are treated with dishonor and irreverently befouled with their uncleanness.

"O bravest of knights, descendants of unconquered ancestors, do not be weaker than they, but remember their courage. If you are kept back by your love for your children, relatives, and wives, remember what the Lord says in the Gospel: 'He that loveth father or mother more than me is not worthy of me' [Matt. 10:37]; 'and everyone that hath forsaken houses, or brothers, or sisters, or father, or mother, or wife, or children, or lands for my name's sake, shall receive a hundredfold and shall inherit everlasting life' [Matt. 19:29]. Let no possessions keep you back, no solicitude for your property. Your land is shut in on all sides by the sea and mountains, and is too thickly populated. There is not much wealth here, and the soil scarcely yields enough to support you. On this account you kill and devour each other, and carry on war and mutually destroy each other. Let your hatred and quarrels cease, your civil wars come to an end, and all your dissensions stop. Set out on the road to the holy sepulchre, take the land from that wicked people, and make it your own. That land which, as the Scripture says, is flowing with milk and honey, God gave to the children of Israel. Jerusalem is the best of all lands, more fruitful than all others, as it were a second Paradise of delights. This land our Saviour made illustrious by his birth, beautiful with his life, and sacred with his suffering; he redeemed it with his death and glorified it with his tomb. This royal city is now held captive by her enemies, and made pagan by those who know not God. She asks and longs to be liberated and does not cease to beg you to come to her aid. She asks aid especially from you because, as I have said, God has given more of the military spirit to you than to other nations. Set out on this journey and you will obtain the remission of your sins and be sure of the incorruptible glory of the kingdom of heaven."

When Pope Urban had said this and much more of the same sort, all who were present were moved to cry out with one accord, "It is the will of God, it is the will of God." When the pope heard this he raised his eyes to heaven and gave thanks to God, and, commanding silence with a gesture of his hand, he said: "My dear brethren, today there is fulfilled in you that which the Lord says in the Gospel, 'Where two or three are gathered together in my name, there am I in the midst' [Matt. 18:20]. For unless the Lord God had been in your minds you would not all have said the same thing. For although you spoke with many voices, nevertheless it was one and the same thing that made you speak. So I say unto you, God, who put those words into your hearts, has caused you to utter them. Therefore let these words be your battle cry, because God caused you to speak them. Whenever you meet the enemy in battle, you shall all cry out, 'It is the will of God, it is the will of God.' And we do not command the old or weak to go, or those who cannot bear arms. No women shall go without their husbands, or brothers, or proper companions, for such would be a hindrance rather than a help, a burden rather than an advantage. Let the rich aid the poor and equip them for fighting and take them with them. Clergymen shall not go without the consent of their bishop, for otherwise the journey would be of no value to them. Nor will this pilgrimage be of any benefit to a layman if he goes without the blessing of his priest. Whoever therefore shall determine to make this journey and shall make a vow to God and shall offer himself as a living sacrifice, holy, acceptable to God [Rom. 12:1], shall wear a cross on his brow or on his breast. And when he returns after having fulfilled his vow he shall wear the cross on his back. In this way he will obey the command of the Lord, 'Whosoever doth not bear his cross and come after me is not worthy of me'" [Luke 14:27]. When these things had been done, while all prostrated themselves on the earth and beat their breasts, one of the cardinals, named Gregory, made confession for them, and they were given absolution for all their sins. After the absolution, they received the benediction and the permission to go home.

281. The Truce of God and Indulgence for Crusaders. The Council of Clermont, 1095.

Mansi, XX, 816.

The canons of this council in their original form have not been preserved. We have translated the first two canons as Mansi has formulated them. See also nos. 240 ff. for truce of God.

1. It was decreed that monks, clergymen, women, and whatever they may have with them, shall be under the protection of the peace all the time [that is, shall never be attacked]. On three days of the week, that is, Monday, Tuesday, and Wednesday, an act of violence committed by one person against another shall not be regarded as a violation of the peace [truce]. But on the remaining four days of the week if anyone does an injury to another, he shall be held to be a violator of the holy peace [truce], and he shall be punished as has been decreed.

2. If anyone out of devotion alone and not for honor or

gain sets out for Jerusalem to free the church of God, the journey shall be regarded as the equivalent of all penance.

282. RABBLE BANDS OF CRUSADERS. EKKEHARD OF AURA, HIEROSOLIMITA.

Edited by Hagenmeyer, pp. 122 ff.

The lack of unity and organization in the first crusade gave many persons an opportunity to plunder and rob and commit all kinds of violence under the cloak of religion. Because they had taken the cross they pretended that they were privileged and might do as they pleased. They attempted to live at the expense of others. This and the following selection will give an idea of the violence and excesses committed by them. Their villainous conduct led many devout persons to criticise the crusading movement very sharply. The events described by Ekkehard occurred in 1096. He wrote the account between 1103 and 1106.

Folkmar [a priest] led his following [about 12,000] through Bohemia. When they came to Neitra, a town of Hungary, the people rose against them, took some of them prisoners and killed others. Only a very few of them escaped and they still tell how the sign of the cross appeared in the sky over them and saved them from imminent death.

Gotschalk, not a true but a false servant of God, suffered some losses while passing with his army through Austria. After entering Hungary, as a remarkable proof of their hypocrisy, they fortified a certain town on a hill and, after establishing a garrison there, the rest of them began to plunder the country round about. But the town was soon taken by the natives and many of the crusaders were killed. Gotschalk, the hireling and not a pastor, and those who were with him were driven off.

There arose also in those days a certain knight, named Emicho, a count from the Rhine region, who for a long time had been infamous because of his manner of living. Like a second Saul [1 Sam. 10 :9–13], he said that he had been called by divine revelation to engage in this sort of religious undertaking. He gathered about 12,000 crusaders, and while passing through the cities along the Rhine, Main, and Danube, led by their zeal for Christianity, they persecuted the hated race of the Jews wherever they found them, and strove either to destroy them completely or to compel them to become Christians. They were joined on the way by many men and women. When they came to the frontier of Hungary, which is protected by swamps and forests, they were prevented from entering it by guards who were stationed there for that purpose; for king Coloman had heard that the Germans made no distinction between pagans and Hungarians. The crusaders besieged Wieselburg [at the junction of the Danube and the Leitha] for six weeks, during which time they suffered a good many hardships. A foolish quarrel arose among them over the question who of them should rule as king over Hungary after they had taken it. They were about to take the city, the walls were broken down and the inhabitants were fleeing and setting fire to their own houses, when, in a miraculous manner, the victorious army of crusaders began to flee, leaving all their provisions and supplies. They escaped with nothing but their lives.

283. PETER THE HERMIT. ANONYMI GESTA FRANCORUM, 1097–99.

Edited by Hagenmeyer, pp. 106 ff.

The anonymous author of the Gesta Francorum was a knight from southern Italy who went with Boemund on the crusade. He wrote his account of the crusade at various times while on the march to Jerusalem. After the capture of the city and the battle with the Mohammedans before Ascalon, he added a chapter in which he described those events. From the passage here given it will be seen that Peter the Hermit played a very inglorious part in the first crusade. His army did not differ either in its character or in its fate from those of Folkmar, Gotschalk, and Emicho.

One of the divisions of the Franks passed through Hungary. The leaders of these were Peter the Hermit, Godfrey, his brother Baldwin, and Baldwin, count of Mt. Henno. These most powerful knights and many others, whose names I do not know, went by the road which Karl the Great, the famous king of France, had caused to be made to Constantinople. But Peter, with a large number of Germans, preceded all the others to Constantinople, which he reached August 1 [1096]. There he found some Lombards, [other] Italians, and many others assembled. The emperor had given them a market and had told them not to cross the strait until the great body of crusaders should come, because they were not numerous enough to meet the Turks in battle. But these crusaders were conducting themselves badly. They were destroying and burning palaces [in the suburbs of Constantinople], and they stole the lead with which the churches were covered, and sold it to the Greeks. At this the emperor became angry and ordered them to cross the strait. But after they crossed they continued to do all the damage possible, burning and plundering houses and churches. At length they came to Nicomedia where, because of the haughtiness of the French, the Lombards, Italians, and Germans separated from them and chose a leader named Raynald. They then marched four days into the interior. Beyond Nicæa they found a castle, named Xerigordon, which had no garrison. They took it and found in it a good deal of grain, wine, and meat, and an abundance of all kinds of provisions. The Turks, hearing that the Christians were in this castle, came to besiege it. Before the gate of the castle was a well and at the foot of the castle a spring of water. Near this spring Raynald laid an ambush to catch the Turks. But they came on St. Michael's day [September 29], and discovered the ambuscade and fell upon Raynald and those who were with him, and killed many of them. Those who escaped fled into the castle. The Turks laid close siege to the castle and cut off its supply of water. And the crusaders suffered so from thirst that they bled the horses and donkeys and drank their blood,

And some let down girdles and pieces of rags into the cistern and squeezed the water out of them into their mouths. Some even drank urine, and others, to relieve their thirst, dug holes in the ground and, lying on their backs, covered their breasts with the moist earth. The bishops and priests comforted them and urged them not to give up, saying, "Be strong in the faith of Christ, and fear not those who persecute you, as the Lord said, 'Fear not them which kill the body, but are not able to kill the soul' " [Matt. 10:28]. This continued for eight days. Finally the leader of the Germans agreed with the Turks to betray his companions to them. So, pretending to go out to fight, he fled to the Turks and many went with him. But those who would not deny their Lord were killed. The Turks took some prisoners and divided them like sheep among themselves. Some of these they put up as targets and shot arrows at them. Others they sold or gave away as if they were animals. Some took their prisoners home with them as slaves. In this way some of the Christians were taken to Chorasan, some to Antioch, some to Aleppo, and still others to other places. These were the first to suffer a glorious martyrdom for the name of the Lord Jesus.

Now the Turks, learning that Peter the Hermit and Walter the Penniless were at Civitot, which is above Nicæa, came thither with great rejoicing to kill them and those who were with them. Walter was leading his men out toward Xerigordon when the Turks met them and killed them. But Peter the Hermit had a short time before gone back to Constantinople because he could not control his people, who refused to obey him. The Turks then attacked those who were encamped near Civitot, some of whom they found asleep, others lying down, and others naked, and killed them. Among them they found a priest saying mass and killed him at the altar. Those who were able to escape fled into Civitot. Some sprang into the sea, and others hid in the woods and mountains. The Turks followed those who went into the castle, and gathered wood to burn them with the castle. But the Christians in the castle threw fire into the piles of wood, and the fire, turned against the Turks, burned some of them. But God delivered ours from the fire. But at length the Turks took them alive, divided them among themselves, as they had done before, and scattered them through all those regions. Some were sent to Chorasan and others into Persia. All this was done in the month of October [1096].

284. EUGENE III ANNOUNCES A CRUSADE, DECEMBER 1, 1145.

Migne, 180, cols. 1064 f.

Edessa was taken by Zenki, the emir of Mosul, in December, 1144. The news of this disaster was carried to the west and at the same time an appeal for help was made. For some time no response was made to this appeal, but finally Eugene III issued this call, and appointed Bernard of Clairvaux to preach the crusade. The student will observe that the pope exercises high authority in secular matters, such as the payment of interest, the pawning of fiefs, etc. Since the days of Gregory VII (1073–85), the pope acts as the supreme lawgiver in all matters, both spiritual and secular.

Eugene, bishop, servant of the servants of God, to his most beloved son, Louis, the illustrious and glorious king of the Franks, and to his beloved sons, the princes, and to all the faithful in God in Gaul, greeting and apostolic benediction.

From the history of our predecessors we learn how much they labored for the deliverance of the oriental church. For, in order to deliver it, our predecessor, Urban II, of blessed memory, sounded, as it were, a trumpet, and called together the sons of the holy Roman church from all parts of the world. At his voice, people from beyond the mountains, and especially the bravest and strongest warriors of the Franks and of Italy were inflamed with the ardor of love and came together. So a great army was collected which, with the aid of God, and not without great loss of life, freed from the filth of the pagans that city in which our Saviour died for

us and left his glorious tomb as a memorial of his suffering
for us. And they took many other cities which, for the sake
of brevity, we omit. By the grace of God and the zeal of
your fathers in defending them, these cities have, up to this
time, remained in the hands of the Christians, and Christianity has been spread in those parts, and other cities have
been valiantly taken from the infidels. But now, because
of our sins and the sins of the people in the east (we cannot
say it without great sorrow and weeping), the city of Edessa,
or Rohais, as we call it, which was the only Christian city
in those parts when the pagans held that country, has been
taken by the enemies of the cross of Christ, and many Christian fortresses have been seized by them. The archbishop of
Edessa and his clergy and many other Christians have been
killed there. The relics of the saints have been trampled
under foot by the infidels and scattered. You know as well
as we how great a danger is threatening the church and the
whole Christian world. If you bravely defend those things
which the courage of your fathers acquired, it will be the
greatest proof of your nobility and worth. But if not, it
will be shown that you have less bravery than your fathers.
Therefore we exhort, ask, command, and for the remission
of your sins, we order all of you, and especially the nobles
and the more powerful, to arm yourselves manfully to defend
the oriental church, and to attack the infidels and to liberate
the thousands of your brethren who are now their captives,
that the dignity of the Christian name may be increased, and
your reputation for courage, which is praised throughout the
world, may remain unimpaired. Take for your example
that Mattathias, who, to preserve the laws of his country,
did not hesitate to expose himself, his children, and his relatives to death, and to leave all that he possessed in this world.
And finally, by the divine aid, after many labors, he and his
family triumphed over his enemies [1 Maccabees 2:1 ff.].

Wishing, therefore, to provide for your welfare as well as

to relieve the church in the east, we grant to those who, in a spirit of devotion, shall determine to accomplish this holy and necessary work, by the authority of God conferred on us, the same remission of sins as our predecessor, Pope Urban, granted. And we decree that their wives and children, their goods and possessions, shall be under the protection of the holy church, of ourselves, and of the archbishops, bishops, and other prelates of the church of God. And until they return, or their death is known, we forbid by our apostolic authority any lawsuit to be brought against them about any of the property of which they were in peaceful possession when they took the cross. Moreover, since those who fight for the Lord should not have their minds set on fine clothing, or personal decoration, or [hunting] dogs, or falcons, or other things which savor of worldliness, we urge you to take care that those who undertake so holy a journey shall not deck themselves out with gay clothing and furs, or with gold and silver weapons, but that they shall try to supply themselves with such arms, horses, and other things as will aid them to defeat the infidels.

If any are in debt but with a pure intention set out on this holy journey, they shall not pay the interest already due; and if they or others are pledged to pay the interest, by our apostolic authority we absolve them from their oath or pledge. If their relatives or the lords on whose fiefs they live cannot or will not lend them the money [necessary for the journey], they may pawn their lands and other possessions to churches, to clergymen, or to others, without the consent of the lords of their fiefs. In accordance with the grant of our predecessor and by the authority of omnipotent God, and of St. Peter, prince of the apostles, which authority is vested in us, we grant such remission of sins and absolution that whoever shall devoutly undertake and complete so holy a journey, or shall have died while on the way, shall have absolution for all his sins which he shall have confessed with a humble and contrite heart, and he shall receive the reward of eternal life from God the rewarder of all.

285. THE THIRD CRUSADE, 1189–90. FROM THE CHRONICLE OF OTTO OF ST. BLASIEN.

M. G. SS. folio, XX, pp. 318 ff

The Greek emperor, Isaac Angelus, and Saladin had made an alliance against the sultan of Iconium, who was their common enemy. Isaac's hostility to Frederick is explained in part by the fact that he had promised Saladin to try to prevent the crusaders from reaching Palestine. It was only natural that the sultan of Iconium should try to make an alliance with Frederick, since the latter was going to attack Saladin. But before Frederick reached Iconium, the sultan had divided his government among his sons, one of whom, Kutbeddin, was governor of Iconium. Kutbeddin had made an alliance with Saladin and married one of his daughters. This explains why the treaty with Frederick was broken.

In order not to confuse the student we have corrected a few errors in Otto's account.

In the year 1187, Saladin, king of the Saracens, seeing the very base conduct of the Christians, and knowing that they were afflicted with discord, hatred, and avarice, thought the time was favorable and so planned to conquer all Syria with Palestine. He collected a very large army of Saracens from all the orient and made war on the Christians. Attacking them everywhere in Palestine with fire and sword, he took many fortresses and cities and killed or took prisoner all their Christian inhabitants, and put Saracen colonists in their place. The king of Jerusalem and the noble prince, Reinaldus [of Chatillon, governor of Kerak], and other nobles collected a large army and went out to meet Saladin. The true cross was carried at the head of the army. But they were defeated [at the battle of the Horns of Hattin, July 5, 1187] and many thousands of Christians were slain. The true cross, alas! was captured by the Saracens, and the Christians were put to flight. The king and Reinaldus and many others were taken prisoner, and carried off to Damascus, where . . . Reinaldus was beheaded, confessing the true faith. The pagans were made bold by this victory and took all the cities of the Christians except Tyre, Sidon, Tripolis, and Antioch, and a few other cities and fortresses which were the best fortified and most difficult to take. After taking Acco, where there is a port which had been the sole refuge of the Christians, they besieged Jerusalem. They destroyed all the churches about the city, among them those in Bethlehem and on the Mount of Olives. Finally the Christians surrendered, Jerusalem was taken, and the holy places were profaned and inhabited by pagans [Oct. 2, 1187].

I think that I should relate that while Jerusalem was besieged by the pagans, one of the towers of the city was taken, many of the Christians defending it were slain, and the standard of Saladin was raised over it. This caused the people to despair and they gave up the defence of the walls. And on that day the city came very nearly being taken and destroyed. But a certain German knight, seeing this, and made bold by the desperate situation, urged some of his companions to join him in making a bold attack on the enemy. They retook the tower, killed the pagans in it, tore down the standard of Saladin and threw it to the ground. By this act, he restored courage to the Christians and persuaded them to return to the defence of the walls. After the city had surrendered, as has been said, the sepulchre of the Lord was held in veneration for the sake of gain. . . .

Frederick the emperor, after ending the wars all over Germany and establishing peace, held a general diet in Mainz at mid-lent [March 27, 1188], and discussed the affairs of state. Papal delegates came to this diet and told the emperor about the destruction of the church beyond the sea [in Palestine], and, making complaint in the name of the pope and of the whole church, begged for his aid. A meeting having been held to consider the matter, Frederick offered to go to the aid of Jerusalem, and, for the remission of their sins, he and his son, Frederick, duke of Suabia, took the cross. Frederick publicly declared that he would avenge the insult which had been offered the cross, and by his example he aroused many nobles and a great multitude of various ranks and ages to take the cross. After these things were done, the cardinals preached the crusade in various parts of the country and persuaded many to leave father and mother, wife and children, and lands, for the name of Christ and to take the cross and follow him across the sea. They raised a large army. The emperor set the time of departure in May of the following year. He ordered the poor to provide themselves with at least three marks [about thirty dollars] for their expenses, and the rich to take as much money as they could. Under threat of excommunication he forbade anyone to go who did not have three marks, because he did not wish the army to be burdened with a useless crowd. After these things were done in Germany the pope sent cardinals to Philip [II], king of the Franks, and to Richard, king of the English, and persuaded them to take the cross. In England and in France he also raised a large army for the crusade.

At this time messengers of the sultan of Iconium came to Frederick and, with the intention to deceive, renewed the treaty with him. They promised him a free passage through all Cilicia if he would go peaceably. For Frederick was going to pass with his army through Cilicia, the land of the sultan, and the pagans, fearing for their land, preferred to have peace rather than war. But the outcome was not what they had expected.

At Pentecost, 1189, Frederick held a general diet at [Regensburg] . . . and had his army gather there. He gave the royal insignia to his son, king Henry. He appointed a certain income to each of his other sons, conferred titles on them, and after making all necessary arrangements, said farewell to all. His son, Frederick, duke of Suabia, the marquis of Meissen, with the Saxons, and many other princes and bishops, went with him. And so with a very large army, well equipped and organized, he set out for the orient to attack Saladin and all the enemies of the cross. While passing through Hungary its king honored him with many gifts and gave the army large supplies of flour, wine, and meat. When he entered Bulgaria the inhabitants tried to block the road. But he forced his way through, killed many of those who opposed him, took some of them prisoner, and hung them on the trees along the road. By this he showed that he was visiting the grave of the Lord not with a pilgrim's wallet, but with the sword and lance of a warrior. Thus he passed through Bulgaria and entered Greece. But the Greeks were worse than the Bulgarians. At the command of the Greek emperor they showed the army no kindness and even refused to sell them anything to eat. They shut themselves up in their fortresses, into which they had taken all their possessions. It made Frederick angry to receive such treatment from Christians, and so he permitted his army to plunder the country. He determined to treat the Greeks as pagans because, by their acts, they showed that they were aiding his enemy, Saladin. His whole army besieged Philipopolis, a very rich city, and took and plundered it. He likewise captured a very strong fortress called Demotica. By this he so frightened the Greeks that he got possession of several fortresses and cities. After devastating the country and taking much booty, he compelled the rest of the Greeks to furnish the army with provisions. These things were done about the end of August [1189]. After consulting the princes, the emperor determined to pass the winter in Greece. So he took possession of the country round about, fortified a strong mountain as a camp for his soldiers and called it Kingsmountain. Hav-

ing thus taken up a strong position against Constantinople,
he had supplies for the army brought from the neighboring
territory, and thus overcame Greek treachery with Roman
strength and German bravery. He remained there all winter to the next Easter [March 25, 1190]. The Greeks were
unable to resist his army and always fled before it.

Now the Greek emperor, not being able to withstand the
power of Frederick, made amends for what he had done, and
entered into a treaty with him. He appeased the army by
supplying them with provisions. Thus, having been reconciled with Frederick, he set him and his army across the
Propontis [March 22–28, 1190, from Gallipolis]. Frederick
now entered Asia with his army. He marched for some
time, meeting everywhere with success, and all the people
in Romania [western Asia Minor] submitted to him. As
the emperor approached Iconium, the sultan broke his treaty,
caused all the provisions to be carried into the fortresses,
and, like a barbarian and Scythian, refused to sell the army
provisions. The army suffered from hunger and were compelled to eat the flesh of mules, donkeys, and horses. Besides, the pagans attacked the rear and those who went out
foraging, and killed some of them. In this way they hindered the army. Our troops wished to meet the Saracens in
open battle and often drew themselves up in battle array,
but the Saracens always withdrew and refused to join in a
general engagement. Now although the army was annoyed
in this way and was suffering from hunger and want, the
emperor, out of regard for the treaty with the sultan, kept
his army from devastating and plundering the country, because he thought the people were attacking him without the
permission of the sultan. But when he learned from cou-
riers that the sultan had perfidiously ordered the people to
attack him, he was angry, and, declaring the sultan an
enemy, he permitted the army to take vengeance. They
devastated Cilicia, Pamphilia, and Phrygia with slaughter,

rapine, fire, and sword, while the pagan army constantly withdrew before them. The army now turned toward Iconium, which is the capital of Cilicia, and the chief residence of the sultan, and quickly took it [May 18, 1190]. It was a very populous city, well fortified with strong walls and high towers, and had in its midst an impregnable citadel. It was well supplied with victuals against a siege, while all the surrounding country was stripped of provisions, in order that when the emperor came he would not long be able to support an army there. But God overruled their efforts so that the outcome was just the opposite of what they sought. For the emperor suddenly attacked the city with great violence before the third hour of the day [9 o'clock], killed a great many of the inhabitants and took the city by storm before the ninth hour [3 o'clock P.M.]. Many people, of both sexes and of all ages, were put to the sword. The sultan with many of his nobles fled into the citadel, which the emperor began to besiege the same day. Now the sultan saw that nothing could resist the force of the Germans and that, supported by some divine power, they despised death and without hesitation attacked everything that resisted them. So, taught by dangerous experience, and thinking it necessary to demand peace from the emperor, he asked to speak with him. The emperor granted his request. The sultan then marched out of the citadel and surrendered at the discretion of the emperor, and gave hostages. After peace was made the city of Iconium and his kingdom were restored to him.

The army was thus made rich with spoil and the emperor left Iconium in triumph. The Armenian princes from all sides began to come to him, among them Leo, the noblest Christian prince of all that country. They all welcomed Frederick with joy and thanked him heartily for coming and attacking the Saracens. They were all well disposed toward him, so he set out for Tarsus, famous as the birthplace of

St. Paul. But God who is terrible in his doing toward the children of men [Ps. 66:5], showing that the time had not yet come for showing mercy on Zion [Ps. 102:13], cut the anchor of the little boat of St. Peter and permitted it to be tossed about and beaten by the storms of this world. For the great emperor, Frederick, while on the road to Tarsus, after a part of the army had crossed a certain river, went into the water to refresh himself. For it was very hot and he was a good swimmer. But the cold water overcame him and he sank. So the emperor, powerful by land and sea, met with an unfortunate death. Some say that this happened in the Cydnus river, in which Alexander the Great almost met the same fate. For the Cydnus is near Tarsus. He died in the 38th year of his reign, the 35th of his rule as emperor [June 10, 1190]. If he had lived he would have been a terror to all the orient, but by his death the army lost all its courage, and was overwhelmed with grief. His intestines and flesh were buried in Tarsus, but his bones were carried to Antioch and buried with royal ceremony.

286. Innocent III Forbids the Venetians to Traffic with the Mohammedans, 1198.

Migne, 214, col. 493.

The maritime cities of Italy took quite a part in the crusades, but their interests were largely commercial. In all the cities of the eastern Mediterranean and the Black Sea they tried to get harbor privileges, freedom from tolls or at least a reduction in them, and quarters, consisting of a few city blocks, in which their agents or colonists could reside. They carried on an extensive commerce with the Mohammedans and cleverly and selfishly made use of the crusades to increase it. While the church was glad to have their aid in the wars with the Mohammedans, it found them a disturbing element, because they were content and wished to end hostilities as soon as they had secured good commercial advantages. The popes took the position that there should be no peaceable intercourse between Christians and Mohammedans, and so tried to prevent all commerce between them. This letter of Innocent III to the people of Venice illustrates the attitude of the pope in this matter, informs us what some of the chief articles of commerce were, and shows how the pope was compelled to make concessions to the commercial spirit.

In support of the eastern province [that is, the crusading states], in addition to the forgiveness of sins which we promise those who, at their own expense, set out thither, and besides the papal protection which we give those who aid that land, we have renewed that decree of the Lateran council [held under Alexander III, 1179], which excommunicated those Christians who shall furnish the Saracens with weapons, iron, or timbers for their galleys, and those who serve the Saracens as helmsmen or in any other way on their galleys and other piratical craft, and which furthermore ordered that their property be confiscated by the secular princes and the consuls of the cities, and that, if any such persons should be taken prisoner, they should be the slaves of those who captured them. We furthermore excommunicated all those Christians who shall hereafter have anything to do with the Saracens either directly or indirectly, or shall attempt to give them aid in any way so long as the war between them and us shall last. But recently our beloved sons, Andreas Donatus and Benedict Grilion, your messengers, came and explained to us that your city was suffering great loss by this our decree, because Venice does not engage in agriculture, but in shipping and commerce. Nevertheless, we are led by the paternal love which we have for you to forbid you to aid the Saracens by selling them, giving them, or exchanging with them, iron, flax (oakum), pitch, sharp instruments, rope, weapons, galleys, ships, and timbers, whether hewn or in the rough. But for the present and until we order to the contrary, we permit those who are going to Egypt to carry other kinds of merchandise whenever it shall be necessary. In return for this favor you should be willing to go to the aid of the province of Jerusalem and you should not attempt to evade our apostolic com-

mand. For there is no doubt that he who, against his own
conscience, shall fraudulently try to evade this prohibition,
shall be under divine condemnation.

287. Papal Protection of Crusaders. Innocent III Takes the King of the Danes under his Protection, 1210.

Migne, 216, col. 258.

We commend you because, fired with zeal for the orthodox
faith and for the praise of God and for the honor of the
Christian religion, you have taken the cross and have drawn
your royal sword to repress the cruelty of an infidel people
[the Turks]. And we also give you our apostolic favor, and
take under the protection of St. Peter as well as under our
own your person and your kingdom with all your possessions, decreeing that so long as you are engaged in this work
all your possessions shall remain intact and free from all
molestation. Nevertheless we urge upon you to take all possible precautions to protect you and yours, in order that you
may not suffer any loss.[1]

1 From this sentence it may be inferred that the papal protection
was not always respected. It sometimes failed to protect the possessions of a crusader from violence and seizure.

288. Innocent III and the Lateran Council Announce a Crusade, 1215.

Bullarium Romanum (Rome, 1740), Vol. III, pars. i, pp. 173 ff.

It was the greatest ambition of Innocent III to recover Palestine
from the Mohammedans. During his pontificate he never lost sight
of this object. One of the chief purposes of the Lateran council
which he called together in 1215, was to arrange for a universal
crusade. This decree shows his earnestness in the matter, but at
the same time betrays the difficulties which were in the way. (1)
The character of the clergy was not such as to insure the best results, and their conduct was not above reproach. They were jealous
of each other, and intrigued to secure places to which much honor
and rich livings were attached (par. 2). (2) Many who took the

cross afterwards refused to go. Some had no doubt made the vow in a moment of enthusiasm; others, in a calculating spirit, hoping to gain some reputation, or secure some advantage, such as an extension of time in the payment of their debts, the cancellation of interest, the freedom from local taxation, or feudal dues, the right to raise money by pawning their fiefs, etc. (pars. 4, 10, and 11). (3) There was a general unwillingness on the part of the rich to go in person on a crusade. Nor were they all willing to equip someone to go in their place (pars. 5 and 6). (4) The commercial interests and spirit of the Italian cities were stronger than their religious sentiment, and led them to sell arms and ships to the Mohammedans, and even to serve in important positions on their boats (pars. 12, 13, and 14). (5) The warlike spirit of the west had found a new outlet in the bloody tournaments which were now much in fashion, and the feuds and private warfare offered the ambitious and adventurous knight a convenient field for the constant exercise of arms (pars. 15 and 16).

In spite of his great efforts, many things made the execution of Innocent's plan impossible. The popular days of the crusades were over. Innocent escaped a bitter disappointment only by his death, which occurred the following year, 1216.

Since we earnestly desire to liberate the holy land from the hands of the wicked, we have consulted wise men who fully understand the present situation. And at the advice of the holy council we decree that all crusaders who shall determine to go by sea shall assemble in the kingdom of Sicily a year from the first of next June. They may gather at their convenience either at Brindisi, Messina, or in any other place on either side of the strait. If the Lord permits, we shall also be there in order that the Christian army may, with our advice and aid, be well organized, and set out with the divine benediction and papal blessing.

1. Those who determine to go by land shall be ready at the same date, and they shall keep us informed of their plans in order that we may send them a suitable legate to counsel and aid them.

2. All clergymen of whatever rank, who go on the crusade, shall diligently devote themselves to prayer and exhor-

tation, by word and example teaching the crusaders always to have the fear and the love of God before their eyes and not to say or do anything to offend the divine majesty. Even if they sometimes fall into sin, they shall rise again by true penitence. They shall show humility of heart and of body, and observe moderation in their way of living and in their dress. They shall altogether avoid dissensions and rivalries, and shun hatred and envy. Thus, equipped with spiritual and material arms, they shall fight more securely against the enemies of the faith, not resting on their own power but hoping in the divine strength.

3. These clergymen shall receive all the income of their benefices for three years, just as if they were residing in them, and, if it is necessary, they may pawn their benefices for the same length of time.

4. In order that this holy undertaking may not be prevented or delayed, we earnestly command all prelates, each in his own locality, to urge and insist that all who have taken the cross fulfil their vows to the Lord. And, if necessary, they may compel them to do so, in spite of all their subterfuges, by putting their persons under excommunication and their lands under the interdict. We except, however, those who may find some real hindrance in the way, on account of which we may decide that their vow may be commuted or put off.

5. In addition to these things, that nothing relating to Christ's business may be neglected, we command patriarchs, archbishops, bishops, abbots, and all others who have the care of souls, zealously to preach the crusade to those who are under their charge, by the Father, Son, and Holy Spirit, one only true eternal God, beseeching kings, dukes, princes, marquises, counts, barons, and other magnates, as well as the communes of cities, villages, and towns, that those who do not go in person to aid the holy land may, in proportion to their wealth, furnish a suitable number of fighting men and

provide for their necessary expenses for three years. This they shall do for the remission of their sins according to the terms published in our general letter, and, for the sake of greater clearness, repeated below. Not only those who give their own ships, but also those who shall try to build ships for this purpose, shall have a share in this remission of sins.

6. If any shall be found so ungrateful to the Lord as to refuse, we warn them that they must answer for it to us before the terrible judge on the last day. Let all such consider with what conscience and what security they will be able to make their confession before the only begotten Son of God, Jesus Christ, into whose hands the Father has given all things, if, in this matter which so peculiarly concerns them, they refuse to obey him who was crucified for sinners, by whose favor and goodness they live and are sustained, nay, more, by whose blood they are redeemed.

7. Lest we should seem to put on other men's shoulders burdens so heavy that we would not so much as put a finger to them, like those who say, but do not, we give 30,000 pounds out of our savings for this work, and besides the passage-money which we give all crusaders from Rome and the surrounding country, we also give 3,000 silver marks which are left in our hands from the gifts of certain Christians, the rest having been spent for the benefit of the holy land by the patriarchs of Jerusalem and the masters of the Templars and the Hospitallers.

8. Since we wish all other prelates and clergy to have a share in this meritorious work and its reward, we, with the approval of the council, decree that all the clergy of whatever rank shall, for three years, give the twentieth of the income of their churches to the aid of the holy land, and for the collection of it we shall appoint certain persons. We except from this tax certain monks and also those who shall take the cross and go in person on the crusade.

9. Moreover, we and our brethren, the cardinals of the

holy Roman church, will pay a tenth of our incomes; and let all know that they must faithfully do this. For any cardinal who shall knowingly commit any fraud in this matter shall incur the sentence of excommunication.

10. Now, because it is only just that those who devote themselves to the service of the heavenly ruler should enjoy some special prerogative, and since it is a little more than a year until the time set for going, we decree that all who have taken the cross shall be free from all collections, taxes, and other burdens. As soon as they take the cross we receive them and their possessions under the protection of St. Peter and of ourselves, so that archbishops, bishops, and other prelates are entrusted with their defence, and besides, other protectors shall be specially appointed to defend them. And until they return or their death shall be certainly known, their possessions shall not be molested. And if anyone shall act contrary to this he shall be restrained by ecclesiastical censure.

11. If any of those who go on the crusade are bound by oath to pay interest, their creditors, under threat of ecclesiastical censure, shall be compelled to free them from their oath and from the payment of the interest. If anyone compels them to pay the interest, he shall be forced to pay it back to them. We order the secular authorities to compel the Jews to remit the interest to all crusaders, and until they do remit it they shall have no intercourse with Christians. If any are not able for the present to pay their debts to Jews, the secular authorities shall secure an extension of time for them, so that after they have set out on the journey until their return or their death is certainly known, they shall not be disturbed about the interest. The Jews shall be compelled, after deducting the necessary expenses, to apply the income which they receive in the meantime from the property which they hold in pawn, toward the payment of the debt; since a favor of this kind, which defers the

payment but does not cancel the debt, does not seem to cause much loss. Moreover, all prelates must know that they will be severely punished if they are lax in securing justice for crusaders or their families.

12. Since corsairs and pirates greatly impede the work by taking and robbing those who are going to, or returning from, the holy land, we excommunicate all who aid and protect them. Under the threat of anathema we forbid anyone knowingly to have anything to do with them in buying or selling, and we command all rulers of cities and other places to prevent them from practising this iniquity. Otherwise, since not to interfere with the wicked is the same as to aid them, and since he who does not prevent a manifest crime is suspected of having a secret share in it, we command all prelates to exercise ecclesiastical severity against their persons and lands.

13. Besides, we excommunicate and anathematize those false and impious Christians who, against Christ and the Christian people, furnish the Saracens with arms, irons, and timbers for their galleys. If any who sell galleys or ships to the Saracens, or accept positions on their piratical craft, or give them aid, counsel, or support with regard to their [war] machines to the disadvantages of the holy land, we decree that they shall be punished with the loss of all their goods, and they shall be the slaves of those who capture them. We command that this decree be published anew every Sunday and Christian feast day in all the maritime cities, and the bosom of the church shall not be opened to offenders against it unless, for the support of the holy land, they give all that they have gained from such a damnable business, and as much more from their possessions, so that they shall be justly punished for their crimes. But if they cannot pay, they shall be punished in some other way, in order that by their punishment others may be prevented from impudently attempting things of the same sort.

14. We forbid all Christians for the next four years to send their ships, or permit them to be sent, to lands inhabited by Saracens, in order that a larger supply of vessels may be on hand for those who wish to go to the aid of the holy land, and also that the Saracens may be deprived of that aid which they have been accustomed to get from this.

15. Although tournaments have been prohibited by many councils under the general threat of punishment, we forbid them for three years under the threat of excommunication, because the crusade is hindered by them.

16. Since, for the accomplishment of this work, it is necessary that Christian princes and peoples live in peace, and in order that the clergy may be able to make peace between all who are quarreling, or persuade them to make an inviolable truce, with the approval of the holy universal council we decree that a general peace shall be observed in the whole world for at least four years. And those who shall refuse to observe this peace shall be compelled to do so by excommunication of their persons and interdict on their lands, unless they have been so malicious in inflicting injuries on others that they themselves do not deserve the protection of such a peace. If they disregard the censure of the church, the ecclesiastical authorities shall invoke the secular power against them as disturbers of the business of Christ.

17. Trusting, therefore, in the mercy of omnipotent God and the authority of Saints Peter and Paul, and by the authority to bind and loose, which God has given us, to all who shall personally and at their own expense go on this crusade we grant full pardon of their sins, which they shall repent and confess, and, besides, when the just shall receive their reward we promise them eternal salvation. And to those who shall not go in person, but nevertheless at their own expense and in proportion to their wealth and rank shall send suitable men, and likewise to those who go in person

but at the expense of others, we grant the full pardon of their sins. All who shall give a fitting part of their wealth to the aid of the holy land shall, in proportion to their gifts and according to the degree of their devotion, have a share in this forgiveness. This universal council wishes to aid in the salvation of all who piously set out on this work, and therefore grants them in common the benefit of all its merits. Amen.

Given at the Lateran, 19 kal. Jan., year 18 of our pontificate.

X. SOCIAL CLASSES AND CITIES IN GERMANY

289. OTTO III FORBIDS THE UNFREE CLASSES TO AT-
TEMPT TO FREE THEMSELVES, *ca.* 1000.

Altmann und Bernheim, no. 61.

In the tenth century a large part of the peasant population of
Germany was unfree. But from this decree of Otto III it is apparent
that they were trying to escape from this condition. From various
causes they had been able to avoid rendering their servile dues, and
had, on that account, asserted their freedom.

While the number of unfree was great, they were not all equally
unfree. The lowest grade were slaves in the real sense of the word;
that is, they were chattels. But this class was not numerous and
was tending to disappear. The highest grade was composed of those
who were personally free, and who could amass property; but they
were unfree in that they had no legal status. That is, they could
not appear in court as a party to a suit, nor could they testify as
witnesses. In all legal matters they had to have some one to represent them in the court. These are the two extremes, between which
there were a great many unfree classes or groups, each differing
from the other in the degree of personal or property rights which
they possessed. An idea of some of these classes will be gained from
the following documents.

There is need of careful legislation because the princes of
the empire, both lay and clerical, rich and poor, the higher
as well as the lower, make frequent complaints that they are
not able to obtain from their unfree subjects those services
to which they have a right. For some falsely declare that
they are free because their lords, in many cases, cannot
prove the servitude which they [their unfree subjects] are
trying in a dishonest way to escape. Others are trying to
rise to the honor of freedom because their lords have, for a
long time, been hindered from knowing anything about their

545

unfree subjects, and hence the latter have not been kept in their accustomed state of servitude, nor are they forced to pay a tax as a proof of their unfree state. So on this account they declare that they are free and boast that they have lived in freedom, because for a short time they have not fulfilled their servile duties. Therefore we have issued this imperial law: (1) If a serf, led by his desire for liberty, says that he is free, his lord may settle the case by a duel with him, fighting either in person or by his champion [representative], as he may wish. The lord is given this privilege because of the great difficulty there is in proving such things in the regular way. The unfree man may secure a champion for himself if, because of age or disease, he is unable to fight. (2) In order that the unfree may not hide his real condition by avoiding his duties for a time, we decree by this our edict, which, with the help of God, shall be valid forever, that hereafter each one shall show his servile condition by paying a denar of the ordinary currency every year on the first of December to his lord or to the agent whom he shall appoint for this purpose. (3) The children of the free shall begin to pay this tax as a proof of their servile condition in their twenty-fifth year and at the appointed time. And no matter how long they may avoid paying this tax, they shall not thereby become free. (4) If any unfree man belonging to the church shall disobey this edict, he shall be fined one-half of all his goods and he shall be reduced to his former unfree condition. For an unfree man of the church may never become free. We strictly forbid the unfree of the churches to be set free, and we order all those who have, by any device, been freed to be reduced to servitude again.

290. HENRY I FREES A SERF, 926.

Bresslau, Centum Diplomata, pp. 3 f.

There were many ways in which a serf could be set free, but after 850 the form used in this document was not uncommon. A freeman was to a great extent dependent on his relatives as witnesses. He could not prove his freedom without their testimony. When a serf was set free he was without a family, because his relatives, being serfs, could not testify in court. The charter which the king gave him was the only evidence of freedom which he possessed. It took the place of the testimony of his relatives.

When a serf was freed he became a "freedman." But generally he was not entirely free, for there was still a personal bond between him and his lord, to whom he must pay a poll-tax. The coin which was knocked out of his hand symbolized this poll-tax. That is, his offer to pay the poll-tax is rejected, the coin is knocked out of his hand as a symbol that he is now entirely free, and is no longer bound to pay the poll-tax.

In the name of the holy and undivided Trinity. Henry, by the divine clemency king. Let all our faithful subjects, both present and future, know that at the request of Arnulf, our faithful and beloved duke, and also to increase our eternal reward, we have freed a certain priest, named Baldmunt, who is our serf, born on the land of the monastery of Campido. We freed him by striking a penny out of his hand in the presence of witnesses, according to the Salic law, and we have thereby released him entirely from the yoke of servitude. And by this writing we have given a sure proof of his freedom and we desire that he shall remain free forever. We ordain that the said Baldmunt, the reverend priest, shall enjoy such freedom and have such rights [that is, have the same legal status] as all those have who up to this time have been set free in this way by the kings or emperors of the Franks.

291. HENRY III FREES A FEMALE SERF, 1050.

Bresslau, Centum Diplomata, p. 49.

See introductory note to no. 290.

Henry, etc. Let all our faithful Christian subjects, both present and future, know that we, at the request of a certain nobleman, named Richolf, have freed a certain one of his female serfs, named Sigena, by striking a penny out of her hand. We have freed her from the yoke of servitude, and have decreed that the said Sigena shall in the future have the same liberty and legal status as all other female serfs have who have been freed in the same way by kings or emperors. . . .

292. THE RECOVERY OF FUGITIVE SERFS, 1224.

M. G. LL. 4to, IV, 2, no. 287.

The condition of the serfs was a hard one. They had heavy work, poor shelter, and bad food. It is not strange that they sought freedom by running away. The cities offered them a good asylum, for they regarded it as a part of their law that a serf remaining in a free city a year and a day without being reclaimed by his lord became free. The lords objected to this, but without effect. Since the cities refused to deliver serfs to their lord on demand, it was necessary for the lords to enter the city and search for them. But in doing so they ran great risk of being stoned from the house-tops. Henry [VII] prescribed that they should have protection from the king as well as from the officials of the city which they wished to search.

Henry [VII], etc. . . . When a quarrel arose between our cities of Elsass and the nobles and ministerials of the same province in regard to the serfs who had run away and gone to the cities, or might hereafter do so, . . . it was settled by the following decision: If a serf belonging to a noble or ministerial runs away and goes to one of our cities and stays there, his lord may recover him if he can bring seven persons who are of the family of the serf's mother, who will swear that he is a serf, and belongs to the said lord. If the lord cannot secure seven such witnesses, he may bring two suitable witnesses from among his neighbors, who will swear that before the serf ran away the said lord had been in peaceable possession of him, . . . and he may then recover his serf. We also decree and command that all nobles and ministerials who wish to recover their serfs may enter a city for this purpose with our permission and protection, and no one shall dare injure them. At their request

a safe-conduct shall be furnished them by the *Schultheissen*
and council of the city.

293. THE RANK OF CHILDREN BORN OF MIXED MAR-RIAGES IS FIXED, 1282.

Altmann und Bornheim, no. 76.

We, Rudolf, by the grace of God king, Augustus, wish by
this writing to inform all that while we were holding court
at Germersheim on Ash-Wednesday our faithful and beloved
subject, Adolf, count of Monte, presented the following question for an official decision: If free peasants contract marriage with unfree, or with others whether of a higher or
lower social status, what shall be the status of the children
born of such mixed marriages? And all who were present
declared that children should always have the rank of that
one of its parents who has the lower social status. And by
this writing we confirm this decision as a reasonable one.

294. FREDERICK II CONFERS NOBILITY, ABOUT 1240.

Altmann und Bernheim, no. 74.

There was a noble class among the ancient Germans. As they
established themselves on Roman soil, the nobility itself underwent
a change and it was added to in various ways. Through great possessions in land, and through appointment to office, which generally
led to the acquisition of lands, an aristocratic class was formed
which came to be regarded as noble. From the tenth century the
man who fought on horseback was a knight, and hence of the noble
class. As the class became conscious of itself and its privileges, it
tended to put up barriers and exclude from its ranks all except those
who were born into it. Thus in the days of Barbarossa if a knight
were challenged by another, he could refuse to fight him unless the
challenger could prove that his grandfather was a knight.

Frederick, etc. We wish all to know that A—— of N——
has told us that although his father was not a knight yet
he wishes to become one. He therefore besought us to make
him a knight. In order to reward the faithfulness of him
and of his family we grant his petition and, out of the ful-

ness of our power, we grant that, although his father was not a knight, and although our laws forbid anyone to be a knight who is not born of a noble family, he may nevertheless with our permission put on the military girdle, and we forbid all people to hinder or prevent him from doing this.

295. CHARLES IV CONFERS NOBILITY ON A DOCTOR OF BOTH LAWS, 1360.

Altmann und Bernheim, no. 78.

The king by virtue of his royal power could confer nobility on all whom he wished. The document of Charles IV is especially interesting as showing the degree of honor attaching to learning. The learned man was, because of his learning, the equal of the noble. He who had taken the Master's degree in both laws was thereby raised to the same social plane as the knight, but, of course, was not thereby knighted. Charles IV recognized this principle and conferred knighthood on his friend, the professor, who had received this degree.

Charles IV, by divine clemency emperor of the Romans, Augustus, and king of Bohemia, sends his favor and wishes all good to the honorable Wycker, *scholasticus* [1] of the church of St. Stephen of Mainz, his [that is, the emperor's] chaplain, intimate table companion, and devoted and beloved member of his household.

Beloved and devoted: Although, according to your birth and to the standards of the world, you were not born of a noble family and are not reckoned as a knight, nevertheless, because you are adorned with so great and remarkable knowledge of both the civil and canon law, that it supplies what you lack by birth [that is, nobility], in imitation of our predecessors, the emperors of great and renowned memory, we regard your knowledge and ability as the equivalent of nobility, and out of the fulness of our imperial power we decree that you are noble and knightly, and of the same rank, honor, and condition as any other noble and knight. Therefore we strictly command all princes, ecclesiastical and secular, counts, chiefs, nobles, and all our other faithful subjects,

to whom this letter may come, under threat of the loss of
imperial favor, to regard, hold, and treat you as such [that
is, as a knight], in all places; and out of reverence for the
holy empire to admit you to all the rights, privileges, etc.,
which noblemen are accustomed to enjoy. . . .

1 That is, he was a professor in the school connected with that
church.

296. The Law of the Family of the Bishop of Worms, 1023.

Altmann und Bernheim, no. 62; M. G. LL. 4to, I, pp. 640 ff.

The bishop of Worms was a large landholder, possessing a great
deal of the land in the city as well as in the country. This land
may be divided into two groups according to the way in which it
was held and tilled. Some of it was let out as fiefs, and from this
the bishop received only the regular feudal dues according to the
terms on which he let it out. The rest of his land was called the
domain, and was tilled by serfs who lived on it and were attached
to it. There was great variety in the condition of the serfs. Some
of them had little or no right to the products of their labors, except
to what they needed to eat and wear. It would of course be impossible
for such to acquire property. Others had a right to a greater or less
share of the products of their labors, and hence they could amass
property. Through their wealth all such could, in the course of
time, improve their condition and rise in the social scale. All those
of this servile group were unfree; they were bondmen of the church.
All of them taken together were called the family of St. Peter. They
were attached to the soil which they tilled, paid a tax in money
or in kind, or rendered services, and were under the protection of the
church and the jurisdiction of the bishop.

From paragraphs 9, 13, 16, etc., we learn that there were two
classes of these serfs, the *fisgilini*, and the *dagewardi*. Of these the
fisgilini were the higher in the social scale. According to paragraphs
9 and 29 they had a share in the *wergeld* of members of their family
and they were not compelled to render services except of a certain
kind or in certain departments of the bishop's household. The
services which they were bound to render were considered less servile,
less ignoble, than those required of the *dagewardi*. From these facts
it is inferred that their ancestors had at one time been free, but had
surrendered their lands and their freedom and become bondmen of

the church for the sake of securing protection. Bishops and abbots were generally regarded as lenient lords in comparison with secular princes, and many preferred to become bondmen of the church rather than of secular lords. The lands which they held they passed on from father to son (par. 2 and 3), and they could amass property and dispose of it (par. 1 and 4). From paragraphs 26, 27, and 28 there seems to have been some difference between the *fisgilini* who lived in the city and those who lived in the country. The former were no doubt artisans, the latter, peasants. But it is not clear what other differences existed between them.

Besides these bondmen, mention is made in the introduction and par. 14 of knights and freemen. These were the vassals of the bishop, holding the lands of the church as fiefs. They were not included in the "family of St. Peter."

Three officials are mentioned. (1) The advocate was a layman who represented the bishop and the church in all secular matters, held the three regular courts of the year, collected the fines which fell to the bishop, etc. In theory he was the protector of the church against all violence and oppression, but not infrequently he took advantage of his position, and by threats and other unjust measures oppressed the church and extorted money from it. (2) The *vidame* was the aid or representative of the advocate and assisted him in the administration of his office. (3) The "official" of the introduction is the same as the "local official" in paragraphs 2, 12, and 24. As the people on these lands lived in villages, he was probably the official whom the bishop entrusted with the government of the village. He held the local or village court. (See note to par. 13.) There were *scabini* or *Schoeffen* who assisted all these officials in administering justice (see Glossary).

In par. 29 we have the origin of a new class which came to be called ministerials. Since no. 297 treats of them especially, the student is referred to it for a discussion of this class.

Although not logically arranged, this document is in fact a little code of laws for the government of the bondmen of the church. A careful analysis of each paragraph is recommended and the student will find it profitable to attempt a classification of its provisions. The laws concerning the different classes should at least be grouped together.

This family of St. Peter may be regarded as a partial cross section of the society in and about Worms, showing many of the layers of which that society was composed. The bishop's lands were no doubt scattered about, and not in one mass. So there were other serfs, probably of different grades, as were the *fisgilini* and *dagewardi*, and other freemen, knights, etc., living as neighbors to the serfs and vassals of the bishop.

Because of the frequent lamentations of my unfortunate subjects and the great injustice done them by many who have habitually wronged the family of St. Peter, imposing different laws upon them and oppressing all the weaker ones by their unjust judgments and decisions, I, Burchard, bishop of Worms, with the advice of my clergy, knights, and of all my family, have ordered these laws to be written, in order that hereafter no advocate, nor vidame, nor official, nor any other malicious person may be able to add any new law to the detriment of the afore-mentioned family, but that the whole family, rich and poor alike, may have the same law.

1. If anyone of the family of St. Peter legally marries a woman who is also a member of the family, and gives her a dower and she has peaceable possession of it for a year and a day, then if the man dies, the wife shall hold the whole of the dower until she dies. When the woman dies, if they had no children, the dower goes to the nearest heirs of the man. If the woman dies first, the same disposition shall be made of it [that is, it reverts to the husband and his heirs]. If after marriage they acquire property, when one of them dies, the other shall have it and do what he will with it. If the wife brought any property to her husband at the time of marriage, at the death of both, their children, if they have any, shall inherit it. If they have no children, it shall return to her relatives unless she gives it away before her death. If the children die after inheriting it, it shall return to the nearest relatives of their mother.

2. If anyone has inherited a piece of land with serfs, and becomes poor and is forced to sell it, he must first, in the presence of witnesses, offer to sell it to his nearest heirs. If they will not buy it, he may sell it to any member of the family of St. Peter. If a piece of land has, by judicial proc-

ess, been declared forfeited to the bishop [because the holder has not paid the proper dues or rendered the due services], and any one of the heirs of the one who held it wishes to pay the back dues, he may do so and receive the land. But if no heir wishes to pay the back dues, the local official may let the land to any member of the family he may wish, and the one thus receiving it shall hold it. If after a few years someone comes and says: "I am the heir. I was poor, I was an orphan, I had no means of support, so I left home and have been supporting myself in another place by work," and if he tries by his own testimony alone to dispossess him who, with the consent of the bishop, received the land, and who has cultivated it well and improved it, he shall not be able to do so. For since there was no heir at the time who was willing to pay the back dues, let him to whom the local official gave it keep it. For [it may be said to the new claimant]: "If you were the heir, why did you go away? Why did you not stay at home and look after your inheritance?" No hearing shall be granted him unless he has a good and reasonable excuse [for his absence]. If anyone who has a piece of land by hereditary right dies leaving a child as heir, and this child is not able to render the service due, and there is a near relative who is willing to render the due service for this land until the heir becomes of age, he may do so. But let the heir not be disinherited because of his youth. We beg that he may be treated mercifully in this matter [that is, that he may receive his inheritance when he comes of age].

3. If anyone on our domain land dies leaving an inheritance, his heir shall receive it without being bound to give us a present, and thereafter he shall render the due service for it.

4. If any member of the family dies leaving free property, unless he has given it away, his nearest heirs shall inherit it.

5. If anyone in the presence of witnesses and with the consent of his wife parts with [alienates] any piece of property, no matter what it is, the bargain shall stand unless there is some other good reason for breaking it.

6. If anyone sells his land or his inheritance to another member of the family in the presence of one of his heirs, and that heir does not object at the time, he shall never afterwards have the right to object. If an heir were not present, but, after learning of the sale, did not object within that year, he shall afterwards not have the right to object to it.

7. If anyone is, by the judgment of his fellows, put "into the bishop's hand," he and all his possessions are in the bishop's power.

8. If anyone takes some of his fellows and does some injustice to a member of the family, he shall pay a fine for himself and for his accomplices and each one of them shall pay his own fine.

9. Five pounds of the *wergeld* of a *fisgilinus* go to the bishop's treasury and two and one-half pounds go to his friends [kin].

10. If a man and his wife die leaving a son and a daughter, the son shall receive the inheritance of the servile land [*i.e.,* the land which the father held], and the daughter shall receive the clothing of her mother and all the cash on hand. Whatever other property there is shall be divided equally between them.

11. If anyone has received a piece of land and serfs by inheritance, and takes his bed because of illness so that he cannot ride on horseback or walk alone, he shall not alienate [dispose of in any way] the land and serfs to the disadvantage of his heirs, unless he wishes to give something for the salvation of his soul. All his other property [that is, all that he has gained in addition to what he inherited] he may give to whomever he wishes.

12. In order that there may not be so many perjuries, if any member of the family has done some wrong to a fellow-member in the matter of land, or vineyards, or any other less important thing, and the case has been brought before the local official, we desire that the local official shall, with the aid of his fellows, decide the case without having anyone take an oath.

13. If any *fisgilinus* does an injustice, either great or small, he shall, like the *dagewardus,* pledge five solidi to the treasury of the bishop and pay five solidi as composition to him to whom he did the wrong, if he is of the same society. If he is outside his society he shall pledge one ounce and no oath shall be taken.

14. If anyone from the bishop's domain lands marries someone who belongs to a fief which is held from the bishop, he shall continue to be under the bishop's jurisdiction. If anyone from such a fief marries someone from the bishop's domain land, he shall continue under the jurisdiction of the lord of the fief on which he lives.

15. If anyone marries a foreign woman [that is, one who does not live on the bishop's territory], when he dies two-thirds of their possessions shall go to the bishop.

16. If a *fisgilinus* marries a *dagewarda,* their children shall be of the lower rank; and likewise if a *dagewardus* marries a *fisgilina.*

17. If anyone makes an unjust outcry in court, or becomes angry and leaves the court, or does not come in time to the court, and those sitting in the court with him do not convict him of this, he shall not take an oath about it, but the *Schoeffen* shall decide it.

18. If anyone has a suit against his fellow, he alone shall take an oath about it. But if it concerns a feud, or is against the bishop, he shall have six men [compurgators] to take an oath with him.

19. It has frequently happened that if one lent his

money to another, the borrower would repay as much as he
wished and then swear that he owed no more. In order to
prevent perjury we have decreed that the lender need not
accept the oath of the borrower but may, if he wishes,
challenge him to a duel, and so [by defeating him] prove
his indebtedness. If the lender is so important a person
that he does not wish to fight the borrower on such an
account, he may appoint someone to fight for him.

20. If anyone in the city of Worms is convicted by losing a duel, he shall pledge sixty solidi. If he is defeated by
a member of the family who lives outside of the city, he
shall pay the victor three times the amount of the fine, because he challenged him unjustly, and he shall pay the
bishop's ban, and twenty solidi to the advocate, or he shall
lose his skin and hair [that is, he shall be beaten and his head
shaved].

21. If anyone of the family of St. Peter buys a piece
of land and serfs from a free man [that is, one who is
not a member of the family], or has acquired it in any
other way, he shall not dispose of it to anyone outside
of the family, unless he exchanges it [for other land and
serfs].

22. If anyone attempts to reduce a *fisgilinus* to the rank
of a *dagewardus* and subject him to an unjust poll tax [as
a symbol of his servile rank], the *fisgilinus* shall prove his
rank by the testimony of seven of his nearest relatives, but
he shall not hire them for this purpose. If the charge is
made that his father was not a *fisgilinus,* two female witnesses shall be taken from his father's family and one from
his mother's. If it is said that his mother was not of that
rank, two shall be taken from her family and one from his
father's family, unless he can prove his rank by the testimony of the *Schoeffen* or of his relatives.

23. If any member of the family enters the house of
another with an armed force and violates his daughter, he

shall pay to her father, or to her guardian, three times the value of every piece of clothing which she had on when she was seized, and to the bishop his ban for each piece of clothing. And he shall also pay to her father a triple fine and the bishop's ban. And because the law of the church does not permit him to marry her, he shall appease her family by giving to twelve members of it twelve shields and as many lances and one pound of money.

24. If anyone confesses a debt in the presence of the local official but the said official has not the time to render a decision that day, and he who confessed the debt denies it the next day, the said official, if he had a witness to the confession, shall render the decision in accordance with the confession.

25. But if the said official had no witness to the confession, he shall render the decision according to what the man says in court and not according to his former confession.

26. If anyone in the city has inherited a building site, it cannot be declared forfeited to the bishop unless he has refused to pay the tax and all other dues for three years. After he has failed to pay these dues for three years, he shall be summoned to court three times, and if he wishes to pay all the back dues he may do so and retain the building site. If he sells the house, he forfeits the building site.

27. If anyone in the city strikes another so hard that he knocks him down, he shall pay sixty solidi to the bishop. If he strikes another with his fist or a light stick without knocking him down, he shall pay only five solidi.

28. If anyone in the city draws his sword to kill another or stretches his bow and puts an arrow on the bow-string, or tries to strike him with his lance, he shall pay sixty solidi.

29. If the bishop wishes to take a *fisgilinus* into his ser-

vice, he may put him to work under the chamberlain, or the cup-bearer, or the steward [dish-bearer], or the master of the horse, or under the official who has charge of the bishop's lands and collects the dues from them [*i.e.,* the advocate]. But if he does not wish to serve the bishop in any of these departments of the bishop's household, he may pay four denars every time the bishop is summoned by the king to call out his men for the purpose of fighting, and six when the bishop is summoned to accompany the emperor to Rome, and he must attend the three regular sessions of court which are held every year, and then he may serve whomsoever he wishes.

30. Homicides take place almost daily among the family of St. Peter, as if they were wild beasts. The members of the family rage against each other as if they were insane and kill each other for nothing. Sometimes drunkenness, sometimes wanton malice is the cause of a murder. In the course of one year thirty-five serfs of St. Peter belonging to the church of Worms have been murdered without provocation. And the murderers, instead of showing penitence, rather boast and are proud of it. Because of the great loss thus inflicted on our church, with the advice of our faithful subjects, we have made the following laws in order to put an end to such murders. If any member of the family of St. Peter kills a fellow member except in self-defence, that is, while defending either himself or his property [against the attacks of the man whom he kills], we decree that he shall be beaten and his head shaved, and he shall be branded on both jaws with a red-hot iron, made for this purpose, and he shall pay the *wergeld* and make peace in the customary way with the relatives of the man whom he killed. And those relatives shall be compelled to accept this. If the relatives of the slain man refuse to accept it and make war on the relatives of the murderer, anyone of the latter may secure himself against their violence by taking an oath that

he knew nothing of the murder and had nothing to do with
it. If the relatives of the slain man disregard such an
oath and try to injure the one who took it, even though they
do not succeed in doing so, they shall be beaten and have
their heads shaved, but they shall not be branded on the
jaws. But if they kill him or wound him, they shall be
beaten and their heads shaved, and they shall be branded
on the jaws. If a murderer escapes, all his property shall
be confiscated, but his relatives, if they are innocent, shall
not be punished for him. If the murderer does not flee,
but, in order to prove his innocence [that is, that he acted in
self-defence], wishes to fight a duel with some relative of
the slain man, and if he wins [in the duel], he shall pay the
wergeld and satisfy the relatives of the slain man. If no
relative of the slain man wishes to fight a duel with the
murderer, the murderer shall clear himself before the bishop
with the ordeal of boiling water, and pay the *wergeld*, and
make peace with the relatives of the slain man, and they
shall be compelled to accept it. If through fear of this
law the relatives of the slain man go to another family
[that is, to people who do not belong to the family of St.
Peter], and incite them to violence against the relatives of
the murderer, if they will not clear themselves by a duel
[that is, prove that they did not incite them, etc.], they shall
clear themselves before the bishop by the ordeal of boiling
water, and whoever is proven guilty by the ordeal shall be
beaten, his head shaved, and he shall be branded on the jaws.
If any member of the family who lives in the city kills
a fellow member except in self-defence, he shall be punished
in the same way, and besides he shall pay the bishop's ban,
and the *wergeld,* and make peace with the relatives of the
slain man, and they shall be compelled to accept it. If any
foreigner [that is, one who does not belong to the family
of St. Peter] who cultivates a piece of St. Peter's land

[that is, holds it as a fief from the bishop], kills a member
of the family of St. Peter except in self-defence, he shall
either be punished in the same way [that is, by beating, etc.],
or he shall lose his fief and he shall be at the mercy of the
advocate and the family of St. Peter [that is, they may
carry on a feud against him, and slay him]. If anyone who
is serving us [that is, anyone who is serving the bishop in
one of the five departments named in paragraph 29] or one
of our officials commits such a crime [that is, kills someone],
it shall be left to us to punish him as we, with the advice
of our subjects, may see fit.

31. If one member of the family has a dispute with
another about anything, such as fields, vineyards, serfs, or
money, if possible, let it be decided by witnesses without
oaths. If it cannot be decided in that way, let both parties
to the case produce their witnesses in court. After the witnesses have testified, each for his side [that is, each one says
that he believes the man whom he is supporting is telling the
truth], two men shall be chosen, one from each side, to
decide the suit by a duel. He whose champion is defeated
in the duel shall lose his suit, and his witnesses shall be
punished for bearing false witness, just as if they had taken
an oath to it.

32. If any member of the family commits a theft not
because of hunger, but from avarice and covetousness, or
habit, and the stolen object is worth five solidi or more, and
it can be proved that the thief, either in a public market or
in a meeting of his fellow members, has restored the stolen
object, or given a pledge to do so, we decree for the pre-
vention of such crimes that as a punishment of his theft the
thief shall lose his legal status—that is, if anyone accuses
him of a crime, he cannot clear himself by an oath, but must
prove his innocence by a duel or by the ordeal of boiling
water or red-hot iron. The same punishment shall be in-

flicted on one who is guilty of perjury, or of bearing false witness, and also on one who is convicted by duel of theft, and of those who plot with the bishop's enemies against the honor and safety of his lord, the bishop.

Par. 2. As a reasonable excuse, the claimant might prove that he had been serving the bishop in war, or that he had been held as a prisoner. In such cases he must have a hearing.

Par. 3. It was customary for an heir on entering into his inheritance to give his lord as a present either his best piece of furniture or clothing, or his best animal (horse, etc.). The bishop here surrenders his right to all such presents.

Par. 4. "Free property" is such as he has acquired and has the right to dispose of as he wishes.

Par. 7. "Into the bishop's hand," see especially no. 297, par. 7.

Par. 13. It is not clear what is meant by being of the same society. Probably those who lived in the same neighborhood or village were regarded as forming a society or group for administrative purposes. They were probably under the local official who has already been spoken of in the introduction.

Par. 14. Here the land which was held by the unfree or servile classes is clearly distinguished from that which was held as fiefs by freemen, knights, etc., who were the bishop's vassals.

Par. 20. The bishop's ban was sixty solidi. That is, this was a fixed sum which all who were convicted of certain offenses had to pay as a fine to the bishop.

Par. 26. In recognition of the fact that the ground or building-site originally belonged to the bishop, and that he still had a certain legal claim on it, the one who held it paid an annual tax on it. He passed it on to his heirs, but could not sell it or transfer it to anyone. For certain crimes it reverted to the bishop. It is characteristic of German mediæval law that it distinguished sharply between the building-site and the buildings on it, attaching much more importance to the building-site than to the buildings. Thus no one in the cities was entitled to citizenship who did not possess such a building-site in the city.

Par. 30. From the last three paragraphs one may gain a good idea of the amount of violence, and especially of the feuds, which raged among the serfs. The serfs of the bishop of Worms were probably no worse than those of other lords. These paragraphs also contain several indications of legal procedure which are worthy of note (see section VII).

297. THE CHARTER OF THE MINISTERIALS OF THE ARCH-BISHOP OF COLOGNE, 1154.

Altmann und Bernheim, no. 70.

It required a large number of servants to conduct the household of a great landed proprietor and prince, such as the king, a duke, count, archbishop, bishop, or abbot, was. For the household included the management of his lands, the administration of justice, etc., as well as the care of his palace, or, more likely, palaces. The household was divided into five departments, each under a head. The head of the first was the chamberlain, of the second, the cup-bearer, of the third, the steward, of the fourth, the marshal (master of the horses), and of the fifth, the advocate. The law of the bishop of Worms shows that he obtained a sufficient number of servants to man his household by calling in *fisgilini* to serve in relays. All the other great lords did the same thing. It was natural that those who had obtained some experience in this work should be called in again and again, and so it came about that those who served in this way were regarded as a class quite separate from their fellow serfs who remained in the country and did not serve in the lord's household. The position and honor became hereditary and differentiated them from all others. They gradually rose in the social scale. Every great lord, from the king down, developed such a class of servants, who were called without distinction ministerials. The kings of Germany made use of their ministerials in the administration of the government.

As soon as they became conscious of themselves as a class they began to haggle with their lords for more rights and privileges. They gradually obtained a body of rights and established a set of customs which, when written, formed a little code of laws for them. Their history shows a constant improvement in their condition and an enlargement of their rights. Every such lord needed soldiers, so he early began to arm his ministerials, to put them on horseback, and to train them to fight for him. It was soon understood that every ministerial was bound to fight for his lord. But as soon as a man began to fight on horseback, he was a knight, and the title of knight carried with it the conception of nobility. We have the strange circumstance that serfs, by fighting on horseback, partake to a certain extent of the knightly character and rank. The outcome of it was that those ministerials who fought on horseback forgot their servile origin and succeeded in attaching themselves to the nobility. They formed the lower nobility in Germany.

The ministerial knights who were developed on the lands of the Staufer served their lords in their wars and were used in the administration of the imperial government. When the Staufer family disappeared, their knights called themselves imperial knights and declared that they were attached to the crown, and owed allegiance directly to the emperor, whoever he might be.

In the name of the holy and undivided Trinity. These are the rights of the ministerials of St. Peter in Cologne, which have been decreed, fixed, and observed for a long time, and are still to be observed.

1. The ministerials of St. Peter shall take an oath of fidelity to their lord, the archbishop, without any reservation or exception, and they shall be faithful to him against every man [that is, the archbishop is their supreme lord. Their oath to him takes precedence over their oath to anyone else, even to the emperor].

2. If anyone invades the territory of Cologne and the lands of the bishopric, all the ministerials of St. Peter, both those who hold fiefs [from the archbishop] and those who do not, shall assist their lord, the archbishop, in defending his lands, and shall follow him with arms to the frontier of the bishopric. If the archbishop wishes to go beyond the limits of his bishopric, the ministerials are not bound to follow him. But they may go with him if they do so of their own accord, or if their lord can persuade them to do so [that is, by gifts, concessions, etc.]. If the lands of the archbishop, which lie outside of his bishopric, are violently invaded by anyone, the ministerials are bound to follow their lord thither for the purpose of repelling this violence.

3. If the archbishop becomes so offended by one of his ministerials that he denies him his grace and confiscates his property, that ministerial shall beg the nobles of the land, and especially those who are the highest officials of the archbishop's court, to intercede for him with the archbishop. But if he is not able to regain the archbishop's grace within a year, he may, at the end of the year, attach himself to some other lord and serve him, but he shall never assist

his new lord in plundering the lands or burning the houses on the lands of his lord, the archbishop. If the arch- bishop does not confiscate his property but merely denies him his grace, after a year he may refuse to serve the archbishop further until the archbishop again grants him his grace.

4. The ministerials of St. Peter are bound to go with their lord, the archbishop, in his expedition across the Alps for the coronation of the emperor, especially those who hold fiefs of him which have the value of five marks or more. An exception is made in favor of the advocate and treasurer. These two shall remain at home, because the advocate must collect and take care of the income from the archbishop's lands [that is, those that are not let out, but tilled by his serfs], and the treasurer must collect the money from tolls and from the mint. But all the others who hold fiefs of the archbishop, worth five marks or more, shall go if the arch- bishop wishes them to do so. To fit him for the journey and to clothe his servants the archbishop shall give each one of them ten marks and forty yards of cloth which is called "scarlet," and to every two knights he shall give a pack- horse and a saddle with all that belongs to it, and two bags with a cover for them (which is called a "dekhut"), and four horseshoes and twenty-four nails. After they reach the Alps the archbishop shall give each knight a mark a month for his expenses. If the archbishop refuses to give this mark to any knight at the proper time and place, the said knight shall inform the officials of the archbishop's court, and, if possible, by their help get his money. But if even with their aid he cannot obtain the mark, he shall, toward evening, and in the presence of a witness, place a rod which has been stripped of its bark, on the bed of the archbishop. Nor shall anyone remove this rod until the archbishop finds it on going to bed. If the archbishop asks, "Who did this?" and, on being told, gives the knight the mark due, the knight

shall proceed with him. But if the knight does not receive the mark, he shall come early the next morning to the archbishop and fall on his knees before him; and in the presence of two of his fellow ministerials he shall kiss the hem of the pallium of the archbishop. He then has the right to go back home without suffering either in his rights or honor or possessions. But if the archbishop is angry and refuses to let him kiss his pallium, the knight shall call his two fellow ministerials to witness and then he may go back home. Those who hold fiefs from the archbishop of less than five marks in value need not go on the expedition unless they wish to do so. But each one of them shall pay an army tax, that is, the half of the income of his fief. The archbishop shall announce the expedition to all his ministerials a year and a day before the time of departure.

5. Of all the ministerials of St. Peter no one shall propose a verdict [that is, render a decision in a case in court], except the advocate alone, if he is present. If he is not present, the archbishop may ask some other ministerial to propose the verdict.

6. The advocate of Cologne has the control and management [and income] of the following twelve farms: Elberfeld, Helden, Zunz, Nyle, Duze, Merreche, Pinnistorp, Lunreche, Dekstein, Blatsheim, Merzenich and Rudisheim. He may appoint and remove the overseers in them as he sees the interests of his lord the archbishop demand. Because Merzenich and Rudisheim have been given as a fief to others, Burche and Bardenbach are given the advocate in their stead. The archbishop shall have the control of all his other farms and shall appoint and remove the overseers as he pleases.

7. No ministerial of St. Peter shall fight a duel with another ministerial, no matter what the one has done to the other. If one ministerial kills another wilfully and without a good reason, the relatives of the slain man shall make

charges against the slayer before the archbishop. If the slayer confesses the deed, he shall be delivered into the power of his lord [that is, the archbishop]. If he denies the deed, the archbishop shall convict him on the testimony of seven of his ministerials who are related neither to the slayer nor to the slain. If convicted in this way he shall be delivered into the power of his lord. After he is delivered into the power of his lord he shall always follow him wherever he goes. He shall have with him three horses and two servants. But he shall never willingly let the archbishop see him, unless it happens that the archbishop unexpectedly turns and comes back by a road along which he has just passed. The archbishop shall supply him and his two servants with food and provender [for their horses]. He shall constantly follow his lord thus, and labor earnestly with the officials of the city and the lords of the land [that is, the vassals of the archbishop] and with all whom he can that they may aid him in recovering the grace of the archbishop and that he may be reconciled with the family of the man whom he has slain. If he cannot do this within a year and a day, the advocate and the treasurer shall shut him up in the room which is nearest to the chapel of St. Thomas under the palace of the archbishop. This room is so near the chapel that through its window he can daily hear the divine services. He shall be shut in the room in the following manner: A woollen thread shall be stretched from one doorpost to the other and each end fastened with a wax seal. Every day at sunrise the door of the room shall be opened and it shall remain open until sunset. He shall be under the protection of the archbishop and secure from his enemies [the family of the man whom he slew]. After sunset the door shall be closed from the inside so that he will be protected from his enemies. While he is shut up in this room he shall be at his own expense, and the archbishop shall give him nothing toward his support. Never as long as he lives shall he leave this room until he has recovered the grace of his archbishop and the friendship of the family of the man whom he has slain. The archbishop shall not grant him his grace until he has compounded with the friends of the man whom he has slain. But he may leave the room at certain times in the year, namely, at Christmas, at Easter, and on St. Peter's day [Aug. 1]. At each one of these times he may go out for three days to urge and beseech all the officials of the church, and the nobles of the land and all his friends and fellow ministerials, to intercede for him. If he fails to recover the grace of the archbishop within the three days, he shall at once return to the room and remain there as before. If he leaves the room in any other way he shall thereby lose all his rights, ecclesiastical and secular, and he shall be deprived of his honor and his Christianity [that is, he shall be excommunicated]. And if afterwards he is chased and captured and killed in the church or in sanctuary, in the city or out of it, in peace or in war, in any place and at any time, he shall not be buried in holy ground and no punishment shall be inflicted on those who have killed him. As long as he remains in the room, his friends and relatives and acquaintances may freely come to see him and stay with him, provided that in coming in or going out they do not break the thread or the seals. His wife may visit him also, but if she bears a child while he is thus imprisoned, it shall be illegitimate and shall have no secular rights [that is, it cannot inherit].

8. If a ministerial of St. Peter challenges a ministerial of the empire to a duel [to settle some suit] in the court of the archbishop, fifteen days before the duel the archbishop shall send both of them to the emperor that they may fight in his presence and the ministerial shall obtain his justice there [in the court of the emperor]. If a ministerial of the emperor challenges a ministerial of St. Peter to a duel, the emperor shall send them both to the archbishop that he may

decide the case. And if the emperor does not judge the ministerials of St. Peter but sends them to their lord the archbishop, it is evident that the nobles of the territory of Cologne who have jurisdiction on their lands, have no right to sit in judgment on the ministerials of St. Peter in matters concerning their allodial holdings and in capital charges. But if the nobles have anything against the ministerials, which concerns their persons or their allodial holdings, they shall enter suit in the archbishop's court and obtain justice there.

9. No archdeacon, no deacon, and no parish priest shall exercise ecclesiastical authority over the ministerials of St. Peter or excommunicate them for anything that they may do, unless they seize the tithes or property of the church. If they do this they must answer for it in the court of the priest in whose parish they have committed the offence. If they do anything else worthy of punishment, the chaplain of the archbishop shall punish them for it. The day after the feast of St. Peter the chaplain shall hold a synod [an ecclesiastical court] in the old house of the archbishop before the chapel of St. John, and he shall sit in the stone chair which is there. And all the ministerials of St. Peter shall be present to answer to the chaplain as to their spiritual father for all the faults which they have committed in person.

10. Every ministerial is born and appointed to service in a certain department at the court of the archbishop. There are five of these departments. In them only the ministerials of St. Peter may serve, and especially the oldest sons. They shall serve in the following manner: Each one shall serve for six weeks in that department of the household to which he was born. After one has served six weeks he shall go home and another shall take his place. If anyone wishes to go home he shall come into the presence of the archbishop and tell him that his six weeks are ended and shall ask him for permission to go home. If the arch-

bishop refuses his permission, the ministerial shall nevertheless kiss the border of the archbishop's robe and go home without offending the archbishop. But if the archbishop is not willing to be without him and can persuade him to stay [that is, by paying him in some way], the archbishop may use him in whatever honorable service he pleases, but he may not use him in any of the five departments until his turn of six weeks comes around again.

11. Every year at the three great festivals, Christmas, Easter, and St. Peter's day, the archbishop shall give new clothing to thirty of his knights. At Christmas, because it is cold, he shall give each one of the thirty a variegated fur overcoat with a collar made of marten skins and with a broad border of deerskin, and a fur coat with a broad red collar and wide sleeves. At Easter and on St. Peter's day, because it is then hot, he shall give each one a light fur mantle and a light fur coat. If he does not wish to give these clothes he shall give each one of them six marks to purchase clothing. The five officials at the head of the five departments who are then serving their six weeks at the archbishop's court shall receive clothes, and the archbishop shall distribute the others to any twenty-five knights that he may choose.

12. If a ministerial dies leaving children, his oldest son shall receive the fief which his father held [that is, if he held a fief] and the right of serving in that department to which he was born [that is, in which his father served]. If there is a second son who is a knight, but so poor that he must serve, he shall come with his war-horse, shield, and lance, to the court of the archbishop before the door of St. Peter's church, and if he has no servant, he shall dismount at the perforated stone which lies there, and run his lance through the hole in the stone, and fix his reins around the lance, and lean his shield against the stone. And all these things shall be secure and safe there under the protection of

the archbishop until he returns. Then he shall enter the church of St. Peter to pray. After his prayer he shall go into the house of the archbishop, and standing in his presence he shall declare that he is a knight and ministerial of St. Peter, and he shall offer an oath of fidelity and his services to the archbishop. If the archbishop accepts him into his court and family, he shall serve him faithfully for a whole year. Then the archbishop is bound to give him a fief and he shall serve the archbishop thereafter. But if the archbishop does not wish him and will not take him into his family, he shall kneel before those who are present and kiss the hem of the archbishop's pallium. Then he shall go back and mount his horse, and he may go wherever he wishes and serve whom he will. If his new lord makes war on the archbishop, he need not on that account refuse to serve him. If the archbishop should besiege a castle in which he [the knight] is, he [the knight] shall not desert or leave the castle, but he shall aid his new lord in defending his castle as well as he can. But he shall never ravage the territory of the archbishop or burn the houses on his lands.

Par. 3. It is characteristic of the codes for ministerials that the lord punishes them by "withdrawing his favor from them." The serious character of this punishment is seen from par. 4.

Par. 4. A white rod, *i.e.*, one stripped of its bark, had a symbolic meaning which is preserved in the German expression, "mit einem weissen Stock gehen," that is, to walk with a white cane or stick. It means that the one who carries it is helpless and without means. Thus when the Hannoverians were defeated in the battle of Langensalza in 1866, and had to surrender their arms, they cut sticks from the woods, stripped them of their bark, and went home with "white canes."

Par. 5. The archbishop presided over the court in which cases of the ministerials were tried. All the ministerials were the judges, but the advocate had the right to express his judgment first. After the advocate had said what he thought the decision or verdict should be, the others had the right to express their judgments (see section VII, introductory note).

298. The Bishop of Hamburg Grants a Charter to Colonists, 1106.

Altmann und Bernheim, no. 68.

In the time of Karl the Great the Slavs held all the territory east of the Elbe. Karl began to extend the frontiers of Germany to the east by making war on these Slavs, a policy which was continued at intervals by his successors. In this way the Slavs were slowly conquered, Christianized, and Germanized. Some of them were slain or driven out, while others remained on their lands, submitted to the Germans, and were eventually absorbed by them. The waste lands as well as those made vacant by their removal were occupied by German colonists. This charter which the bishop of Hamburg gave his colonists illustrates the terms on which such colonies were established. Since the lord of the land received many solid advantages from such colonies, it is not strange that they made great efforts to induce people to settle on their lands.

1. In the name of the holy and undivided Trinity. Frederick, by the grace of God bishop of Hamburg, to all the faithful in Christ, gives a perpetual benediction. We wish to make known to all the agreement which certain people living this side of the Rhine, who are called Hollanders, have made with us.

2. These men came to us and earnestly begged us to grant them certain lands in our bishopric, which are uncultivated, swampy, and useless to our people. We have consulted our subjects about this and, considering that this would be profitable to us and to our successors, have granted their request.

3. The agreement was made that they should pay us every year one denarius for every hide of land. We have thought it necessary to determine the dimensions of the hide, in order that no quarrel may hereafter arise about it. The hide shall be 720 royal rods long and thirty royal rods wide. We also grant them the streams which flow through this land.

4. They agreed to give the tithe according to our decree, that is, every eleventh sheaf of grain, every tenth lamb, every

tenth pig, every tenth goat, every tenth goose, and a tenth of the honey and of the flax. For every colt they shall pay a denarius on St. Martin's day [Nov. 11], and for every calf an obol [penny].

5. They promised to obey me in all ecclesiastical matters according to the decrees of the holy fathers, the canonical law, and the practice in the diocese of Utrecht.

6. They agreed to pay every year two marks for every 100 hides for the privilege of holding their own courts for the settlement of all their differences about secular matters. They did this because they feared they would suffer from the injustice of foreign judges. If they cannot settle the more important cases they shall refer them to the bishop. And if they take the bishop with them [that is, from Hamburg to the colony] for the purpose of deciding one of their trials, they shall provide for his support as long as he remains there by granting him one-third of all the fees arising from the trial; and they shall keep the other two-thirds.

7. We have given them permission to found churches wherever they may wish on these lands. For the support of the priests who shall serve God in these churches we grant a tithe of our tithes from these parish churches. They promised that the congregation of each of these churches should endow their church with a hide for the support of their priest. The names of the men who made this agreement with us are: Henry, the priest, to whom we have granted the aforesaid churches for life; and the others are laymen, Helikin, Arnold, Hiko, Fordolt, and Referic. To them and to their heirs after them we have granted the aforesaid land according to the secular laws and to the terms of this agreement.

299. THE PRIVILEGE OF FREDERICK I FOR THE JEWS, 1157.

M. G. LL. 4to, IV, 1, pp. 227 ff; Altmann und Bernheim, no. 71.

The position of the Jew in the Middle Age was a peculiar one.

The law of the state did not in any way recognize him as a citizen. But he was classed along with the right to coin money, levy tolls, appoint officials, administer justice, etc., as a *regale*, or a crown right; that is, his existence in Germany depended on the will of the king. As no mint could be established without the king's consent, so no Jews could live anywhere in the realm without the king's permission. The city which wished to permit Jews to live within its walls had first to secure the permission of the king. The Jews were made to pay well for the bare right to exist. They were subject to the king's taxation and hence were said to belong to the king's treasury. In theory they were under the king's protection, but that did not preserve them from mob violence. This document shows that while their position was anomalous, they nevertheless received liberal charters from the king.

In the name of the holy and undivided Trinity. Frederick, by the grace of God emperor of the Romans, Augustus. Be it known to all bishops, abbots, dukes, counts, and all others subject to our laws, that we have confirmed by our royal authority, expressed in the present law, the statutes in favor of the Jews of Worms and their fellow-religionists which were granted to them by our predecessor emperor Henry, in the time of Solomon, rabbi of the Jews.

1. In order that they may always look to us for justice, we command by our royal authority that no bishop or his official, and no count, *Schultheiss,* or other official except those whom they choose from among their own number, shall exercise any authority over them. The only official who may exercise such authority is the man whom the emperor puts over them in accordance with their choice, because they are entirely under the control of our treasury.

2. No one shall take from them any property which they hold by hereditary right, such as building sites, gardens, vineyards, fields, slaves, or any other movable or immovable property. No one shall interfere with their right to erect buildings against the walls of the city, on the inside or outside. If anyone molests them contrary to our edict he shall

forfeit our grace and shall restore twofold whatever he took from them.

3. They shall have free right to change money with all men anywhere in the city except at the mint or where the officials of the mint have established places for changing money.

4. They shall travel in peace and security throughout the whole kingdom for the purpose of buying and selling and carrying on trade and business. No one shall exact any toll from them or require them to pay any other public or private tax.

5. Guests may not quarter themselves on the Jews against their will. No one shall seize one of their horses for the journey of the king or the bishop, or for the royal expedition.

6. If any stolen property is found in the possession of a Jew, and he says that he bought it, he shall say under oath according to Jewish law how much he paid for it, and he shall restore it to its owner on receipt of that amount.

7. No one shall baptize the children of Jews against their will. If anyone captures or seizes a Jew and baptizes him by force, he shall pay twelve pounds of gold to the royal treasury. If a Jew expresses a wish to be baptized, he shall be made to wait three days, in order to discover whether he abandons his own law because of his belief in Christianity, or because of illegal pressure; and if he thus relinquishes his law, he shall also relinquish his right to inheritance.

8. No one shall entice away from them any of their pagan slaves under pretext of baptizing them into the Christian faith. If anyone does this, he shall pay the ban, that is, three pounds of gold, and shall restore the slave to his owner; the slave shall obey all the commands of his owner, except those that are contrary to his Christian faith.

9. Jews may have Christian maid-servants and nurses,

and may employ Christian men to work for them, except on feast days and Sundays; no bishop or other clergyman shall forbid this.

10. No Jew may own a Christian slave.

11. If a Jew brings suit against a Christian or a Christian against a Jew, each party shall follow the process of his own law as far as possible. The Jew has the same right as the Christian to prove his case and to release his sureties by his oath and the oath of another person of either law [*i.e.*, Christian or Jew].

12. No one may force a Jew to undergo the ordeal of hot iron, hot water, or cold water, or have him beaten with rods or thrown into prison, but he shall be tried according to his own law after forty days. In a case between a Christian and a Jew, the defendant cannot be convicted except by the testimony of both Christians and Jews. If a Jew appeals to the royal court in any case, he must be given time to present his case there. If anyone molests a Jew contrary to this edict, he shall pay the imperial ban of three pounds to the emperor.

13. If anyone takes part in a plan or plot to kill a Jew, both the slayer and his accomplice shall pay twelve pounds of gold to the royal treasury. If he wounds him without killing him, he shall pay one pound. If it is a serf who has wounded or slain the Jew, the lord of the serf shall either pay the fine or surrender the serf to punishment. If the serf is too poor to pay the fine, he shall suffer the penalty which was visited upon the serf who in the time of our predecessor, emperor Henry, slew the Jew named Vivus; namely, his eyes shall be torn out and his right hand cut off.

14. If the Jews have any suit or any matter to be settled among themselves, it shall be tried by their peers and by no others. If any Jew refuses to tell the truth in any case which arises among the Jews, he shall be forced to confess the truth by his own rabbi. But if a Jew has been accused

of a serious crime, he shall be allowed to appeal to the emperor, if he wishes to.

15. Besides their wine, they shall have the right to sell spices and medicines to the Christians. As we have commanded, no one may force them to furnish horses for the expedition of the emperor, or to pay any other public or private tax.

300. THE BISHOP OF SPEYER GIVES THE JEWS OF HIS CITY A CHARTER, 1084.

Altmann und Bernheim, no. 66.

As the king granted the princes the right to coin money and other regalian rights, so he also gave them the permission to establish Jews in their territories or cities. This charter which the bishop of Speyer gave the Jews of his city, presents some interesting details concerning their quarter in the city, their way of living, occupations, etc.

1. In the name of the holy and undivided Trinity. I, Rudeger, by cognomen Huozman, humble bishop of Speyer, when I wished to make a city of my village of Speyer, thought that it would greatly add to its honor if I should establish some Jews in it. I have therefore collected some Jews and located them in a place apart from the dwellings and association of the other inhabitants of the city; and that they may be protected from the attacks and violence of the mob, I have surrounded their quarter with a wall. The land for their dwellings I had acquired in a legal way; for the hill [on which they are to live] I secured partly by purchase and partly by trade, and the valley [which I have given them] I received as a gift from the heirs who possessed it. I have given them this hill and valley on condition that they pay every year three and one-half pounds of money coined in the mint of Speyer, for the use of the brothers [monks of some monastery which is not named here].

2. I have given them the free right of changing gold and silver coins and of buying and selling everything they wish

within their own walls and outside the gate clear up to the boat-landing [on the Rhine] and also on the wharf itself. And they have the same right throughout the whole city.

3. Besides, I have given them a piece of the land of the church as a burial-ground. This land they shall hold forever.

4. I have also granted that, if a Jew comes to them from some other place and is their guest for a time, he shall pay no tolls [to the city].

5. The chief priest of their synagogue shall have the same position and authority among them as the mayor of the city has among the citizens. He shall judge all the cases which arise among them or against them. If he is not able to decide any case it shall be taken before the bishop or his chamberlain.

6. They are bound to watch, guard, and defend only their own walls, in which work their servants may assist them.

7. They may hire Christian nurses and Christian servants.

8. The meats which their law forbids them to eat they may sell to Christians, and the Christians may buy them.

9. To add to my kindness to them I grant them the most favorable laws and conditions that the Jews have in any city of the German kingdom. . . .

301–325. The Cities of Germany.

In the days of Karl the Great each city with the surrounding territory formed a county which was under the jurisdiction of a count. As feudalism developed, the count became the lord of the city, and governed it in a more or less autocratic way. Besides these cities there were many villages in the time of Karl which in the course of time grew into cities. Later, still other cities, arose, some growing up around markets, or monasteries, or churches, and others developing from settlements of colonists, etc. They grew under favorable circumstances into cities, over which, however, the lord still retained his control. But in the course of time the cities freed themselves from the jurisdiction of their lord and separated themselves from the surrounding territory. They acquired a set of laws for their government, and jurisdiction over themselves. The citizens of each city became a commune possessing a number of rights, among them the right to have a market, freedom from tolls, the election of their own officials, judges, etc., the right to levy their own taxes, to coin money, to fortify their city, etc. In a word, each city freed itself from the government of its lord and got the right to govern itself.

The city charter was, in many cases at least, developed from the market charter. On this account we give a few market charters. Then a few documents are given to illustrate the rebellion of the cities against their lords, and their acquisition of municipal rights. We offer the important charter of Magdeburg, and some documents concerning the origin of the Rhine league and the early history of the Hanseatic league.

The development in the German cities was so varied that it is quite impossible in the space at our disposal to illustrate it adequately. Nearly every city offers something peculiar, interesting, and worthy of note.

301. LOTHAR II (855–69) GRANTS A MARKET TO THE MONASTERY OF PRÜM, 861.

Altmann und Bernheim, no. 150.

Markets were a part of the *regalia;* that is, no one had a right to set up a market without the king's permission. Small coins were necessary for the convenience of those who came to the market, and hence the lord of the market always received the right to establish a mint in connection with his market. In order to insure justice and fair treatment to the merchants who might bring their wares to the market, it was separated from the local jurisdiction, and the lord of the market was given jurisdiction over all crimes committed during the market and on the ground occupied by it. A further interest attaches to the charters of markets because in some cases the towns which grew up about the market-places became cities, and the market charter was developed into the city charter.

Lothar II, etc. . . . Therefore, let all our faithful subjects, both present and future, know that Ansbald, abbot of the monastery of Prüm, has told us that that place suffers great disadvantage because it is so far distant from a market and mint. On this account, he begged us to grant his monastery our permission for the establishment of a market and mint in a place which is called Romarivilla, which is not far from his monastery. Out of reverence for the Lord Jesus Christ, and for the salvation of our soul, we gladly grant his petition, and have ordered this document to be written, by which we decree and command that hereafter that monastery may have an ordinary market in the above-named place and a mint for coining denarii of the proper weight and quality. And no public official shall levy a tax of any sort on the monastery for this market and mint, but they shall be wholly for the profit of the monastery and its inmates. And that this concession may never be violated, we have ordered it to be sealed with our ring and we have signed it with our own hand. . . .

302.   Otto I Grants a Market to an Archbishop, 965.

Altmann und Bernheim, no. 154.

See introductory note to no. 301.

In the name of the undivided Trinity. Otto by the favor of God emperor, Augustus. If we grant the requests of clergymen and liberally endow the places which are dedicated to the worship of God, we believe that it will undoubtedly assist in securing for us the eternal reward. Therefore, let all know that for the love of God we have granted the petition of Adaldagus, the reverend archbishop of Hamburg, and have given him permission to establish a market in the place called Bremen. In connection with the market we grant him jurisdiction, tolls, a mint, and all other things connected therewith to which our royal treasury would have a right. We also take under our special protection all the merchants who live in that place, and grant them the same protection and rights as those merchants have who live in other royal cities. And no one shall have any jurisdiction there except the aforesaid archbishop and those to whom he may delegate it. Signed with our hand and sealed with our ring.

303. Otto III Grants a Market to Count Bertold, 999.

Altmann und Bernheim, no. 155.

See introductory note to no. 301.

In the name of the holy and undivided Trinity. Otto by the clemency of God emperor, Augustus. If we grant the petitions of our faithful subjects we shall no doubt make them more faithful to us. Therefore, we wish all our subjects, present and future, to know that, at the request of the noble duke, Hermann, we have given our count, Bertold, full authority to establish a market, with a mint, tolls, and public jurisdiction, in a certain place called Vilungen, in the county of Bara, over which count Hildibald has jurisdiction. And by royal decree we make this a legal [and regular] market, with all the functions of a market. And no one shall be permitted to interfere with it. All who wish to come to this market may come and go away in security and peace. No unjust charges shall be levied on them, but they may buy and sell and do everything else that belongs to the business of a merchant. And if anyone tries to violate or break this concession, he shall pay the same fine as one who should violate the market at Constance, or Zürich. He shall pay this fine to count Bertold, or to his representative. The aforesaid count shall have the right of holding, changing, granting, and making any arrangement in regard to this market, as he pleases. . . .

304. No One shall Compel Merchants to Come to His Market, 1236.

M. G. LL. 4to, IV, 2, no. 203.

See introductory note to no. 301.

Frederick [II], etc. . . . The venerable archbishop of Salzburg asked: When merchants are going along the public highway to a market, may anyone force them to leave the highway and go by private roads to his market? The decision of the princes was, that no one has a right to compel merchants to leave the highway, but that they may go to whatever market they wish. . . .

305.   A MARKET-COURT IS INDEPENDENT OF THE LOCAL COURT, 1218.

Altmann und Bernheim, no. 164.

See introductory note to no. 301.

Frederick II, by the grace of God king of the Romans, Augustus, and king of Sicily, etc. We wish to inform you that the following decision has been rendered in our presence by the princes and magnates of our empire. If we have granted the establishment of a market, either annual or weekly, and have given them [that is, the people to whom the market has been granted] our glove [as a symbol that they have jurisdiction over all offences committed during the market], no count nor any other judge of the province [in which the market is situated] shall exercise any jurisdiction there [that is, over crimes committed during the market], or have any power to punish crimes committed there. But if a thief, or robber, or any other criminal shall have been condemned to death there [that is, by the judge who holds the market-court] he must he handed over to the count or to the judge of the province to have the sentence executed upon him.

306.   OTTO I GRANTS JURISDICTION OVER A TOWN TO THE ABBOTS OF NEW CORVEY, 940.

Altmann und Bernheim, no. 152.

For about 300 years after the time of Karl the Great the cities of Germany did not have self-government. Under Karl they were governed by an imperial or royal official. With the appearance and growth of feudalism, the towns came into the hands of the bishops, dukes, counts, etc., and were governed by them.

Frequently new towns grew up about monasteries or the churches, especially cathedral churches. As the land on which the town was built belonged to the abbot or bishop, as the case might be, he was naturally regarded as its lord, and of course he had jurisdiction over all its inhabitants. It is apparent that such a new town had sprung up around the monastery of New Corvey, and by this document Otto I recognized that its abbot had jurisdiction over all the people who lived on the lands of the monastery.

Otto I, etc. . . . Therefore, let all our subjects, both present and future, know that, for the love of God, the salvation of our souls, and the forgiveness of our sins, at the request of our beloved wife, we have granted that all the abbots of the monastery of New Corvey,[1] beginning with Folkmar, who is now its abbot, shall have jurisdiction over all the men who live in the territory of the monastery and in the city which has been built up about it, that is, in, etc. [Here follow the names of the places over which the monastery shall have jurisdiction.] And no man and no official shall have the right of exercising over the aforesaid men that jurisdiction which is commonly called "Burgbann" [that is, the jurisdiction that goes with a town], except the abbot of the monastery and those to whom he may delegate it.

[1] New Corvey, near Paderborn, was founded in 816, for the purpose of Christianizing the newly conquered Saxons. It was named after its mother monastery, Corbie, in France. It was for a long time the most famous monastery in north Germany.

307. The Ban-mile, or the Limits of the Bishop's Authority, 1237.

M. G. LL. 4to, IV, 2, no. 205.

There was often a question as to the geographical limits of the jurisdiction of the lord of a town. In some cases his authority was bounded by the city walls. In others it extended into the country to a certain distance called a ban-league, or ban-mile.

Frederick II, etc. The archbishop of Cologne asked whether his jurisdiction extended beyond the city walls or not. The decision was that his jurisdiction extends beyond the city walls to the distance which is generally called a "ban-mile," and within that he may legally sit in judgment on all the men who are under his jurisdiction.

308. The Citizens of Cologne Expel Their Archbishop, 1074.

Sudendorf, Registrum, I, no. 3.

The chief interest in this and the following number lies in the fact that they introduce us to the beginnings of the movement in the cities toward the acquisition of self-government. As the inhabitants of the towns increased in numbers and wealth, they began to resent the manner in which they were treated by their lords. As their own interests increased in importance it became more and more annoying and exasperating when their lord interfered with their business and demanded their services or the use of articles which they were using (see the following number). A rebellion was inevitable. It began generally, if not always, with the merchant class of the population. The lords of the towns vigorously resisted, but were unable to maintain their prerogatives. The cities generally succeeded in acquiring the right to govern themselves and obtained a charter to that effect.

The citizens of Worms had been offended by their bishop, not only because of his government of them, but also because he was supporting the pope against their king, to whom they were devotedly attached.

To his beloved brother and fellow bishop, Udo, archbishop [of Trier], Anno, archbishop of Cologne, sends his love, etc. . . . You have no doubt heard about the violence and insults which I have suffered from my citizens, although I have said nothing about the matter in my letters to you. And you have also probably heard how I was restored to my place in the city by the help of others. According to the canon law, I should immediately have punished their abominable insolence with excommunication and interdict, but I restrained myself from doing so, because it might have seemed that I did it not out of zeal for the Lord, but for personal reasons. But some of the insolent ones disregarded and despised my gentle treatment of them, and at night secretly collected and threatened me with worse things than they had done before. On this account, with the advice of the bishops whom the pope sent me, I anathematized them a week after Pentecost. I beg you to publish this anathema in your diocese. Do not permit your people to be infected with the leprosy of these excommunicated persons, but keep them out of your territory, lest by their speech they excite your people to do the same things against you. I beg you to inform your bishops of this, in order that my contaminated flock may not infect theirs also.

309. THE PEOPLE OF COLOGNE REBEL AGAINST THEIR ARCHBISHOP, 1074.

Lambert of Hersfeld, Annals, M. G. SS. folio, V, 211 ff.

See introductory note to no. 308.

The archbishop spent Easter in Cologne with his friend, the bishop of Münster, whom he had invited to celebrate this festival with him. When the bishop was ready to go home, the archbishop ordered his servants to get a suitable boat ready for him. They looked all about, and finally found a good boat which belonged to a rich merchant of the city, and demanded it for the archbishop's use. They ordered it to be got ready at once and threw out all the merchandise with which it was loaded. The merchant's servants, who had charge of the boat, resisted, but the archbishop's men threatened them with violence unless they immediately obeyed. The merchant's servants hastily ran to their lord and told him what had happened to the boat, and asked him what they should do. The merchant had a son who was both bold and strong. He was related to the great families of the city, and, because of his character, very popular. He hastily collected his servants and as many of the young men of the city as he could, rushed to the boat, ordered the servants of the archbishop to get out of it, and violently ejected them from it. The advocate of the city was called in, but his arrival only increased the tumult, and the merchant's son drove him off and put him to flight. The friends of both parties seized their arms and came to their aid, and it looked as if there were going to be a great battle fought, in the city. The news of the struggle was carried to the archbishop, who immediately sent men to quell the riot, and being very angry, he threatened the rebellious young men with dire punishment in the next session of court. Now the archbishop was endowed with all virtues, and his uprightness in all matters, both of the state and of the church, had often been proved. But he had one vice. When he became angry, he could not control his tongue, but overwhelmed everybody, without distinction, with bitter upbraidings and violent vituperation. When his anger had passed, he regretted his fault and reproached himself for it. The riot in the city was finally quieted a little, but the young man, who was very angry as well as elated over his first success, kept on making all the disturbance he could. He went about the city making speeches to the people about the harsh government of the archbishop, and accused him of laying unjust burdens on the people, of depriving innocent persons of their property, and of insulting honorable citizens with his violent and offensive words. . . . It was not difficult for him to raise a mob. . . . Besides, they all regarded it as a great and glorious deed on the part of the people of Worms that they had driven out their bishop because he was governing them too rigidly. And since they were more numerous and wealthy than the people of Worms, and had arms, they disliked to have it thought that they were not equal to the people of Worms in courage, and it seemed to them a disgrace to submit like women to the rule of the archbishop, who was governing them in a tyrannical manner. . . .

310. Confirmation of the Immediateness of the Citizens of Speyer, 1267.

Altmann und Bernheim, no. 168.

Cities which were immediately subject to the king were called "imperial cities" (Reichsstädte), while those which were subject to the lord of the land in which they were situated were called "territorial cities" (Landesstädte). Many such cities rebelled against their lord, and put themselves under the king and secured his recognition of their character as imperial cities.

Philip, lord of Falkenstein, treasurer of the imperial court. By this present writing we wish to make known and publicly to declare that the citizens of the city of Speyer are joined directly to the empire so that they are in no way answerable to the bishop of Speyer [in secular matters]. This is manifest and well known to all. . . .

311. Summons Sent to an Imperial City to Attend a Diet, 1338.

Urkundenbuch der Stadt Lübeck, II, 2, p. 629 ; Altmann und Bernheim, no. 23.

An imperial city was in fact a tenant-in-chief since it held directly from the king. It therefore had a right to send its representatives to the diet.

Ludwig, etc. Because of certain important affairs of the empire, especially the controversy which has arisen between us and the pope, we have decided to summon the ecclesiastical and secular princes, the counts, barons, cities, and communities of the empire; therefore, we notify and command you, in whose fidelity, wisdom, and advice we place special confidence, to send two representatives with full credentials to Frankfort on the Tuesday before St. Laurence's day [Aug. 10], there to meet with us, and the princes, counts, and other cities. Do not seek to evade this summons, but obey it readily and willingly, if you expect to receive our grace and favor.

312. Municipal Freedom is Given to the Town Called Ebenbuchholtz, 1201.

Altmann und Bernheim, no. 163.

This is a good example of the charters by which the lord of the town surrendered his authority and granted municipal freedom to the people of the town.

In the name of the holy and undivided Trinity. Hermann,

by the grace of God bishop of Münster.   Because temporal
things imitate time and pass away with it, we have thought
it best to commit to writing those things which concern our
honor and advantage.   Let all people know, therefore, that
we have granted to our village, Ebenbuchholtz, that municipal freedom which is commonly called *"Weichbild."*   But
because that could not be done without the consent of Sueder
of Dingden, to whose county the aforesaid village belonged,
we made this agreement with him, that he should give up his
right to the *"Weichbild"* [that is, to the government of the
town, the appointment of the officials, etc.] and he should
receive in return for it civil jurisdiction over the town, such
as he has over our cities, Münster, Coesfeld, and others.
And that these agreements and arrangements may remain
unbroken forever, we have caused this document to be written
and sealed with our ring.   .   .   .

313.   The Extension of the Corporate Limits of the City of Brunswick, 1269.

Altmann und Bernheim, no. 169.

After a town had got its municipal freedom new quarters of suburbs
might easily spring up about it.   These might at first have no share
in the government of the town, but would manage their own affairs.
But in the course of time these new quarters might be incorporated
with the old town.   That is, the corporate limits of the old town
would be extended to include the new suburbs.

All the aldermen of the city of Brunswick, etc.   .   .   .
We wish it to be made known that after having taken
counsel with the older and wiser men for the best interests of
the city, we have, under oath, issued the following decree
which shall be observed forever, to the effect that hereafter
we [the aldermen from the three different parts of the city
which up to this time have had a separate organization]
shall meet in one house to take counsel together about the
affairs of the whole city.   All the income of the city, from
whatever source, shall be kept in a common fund and spent

for the common good of the whole city. In the old town
wine may be sold all the time. In that quarter of the city
called Indago [that is, the Park], however, when one vat
of wine has been sold no more shall be sold there until a
vat has been sold in the new town, and vice versa. New
aldermen shall be elected every year as follows: Seven new
aldermen shall be elected in the old town, and three of the
former aldermen from the same quarter shall be chosen to
remain in office another year. In Indago [the quarter called
the Park] four new aldermen shall be elected and two of
the former aldermen shall remain in office. In the new town
three shall be elected and one of the former shall remain in
office. Thus there shall always be twenty aldermen. They
shall take a special oath, among other things, to preserve
this union [of the three towns in one]. And that no doubt
may arise about this, we have caused this document to be
written and the seal of the city to be attached to it.
Witnesses . . .

314. The Decision of a Diet about the Establishment of City Councils in Cathedral Towns, 1218.

Altmann und Bernheim, no. 165.

The lords of the towns were generally unwilling to surrender their
authority without a struggle. They appealed to the king and to
the diet against their rebellious subjects. The decisions were almost
always in their favor, but they found it difficult to enforce them.
Neither the king nor the diet assisted them. In the struggle which
ensued between the lord and the rebellious town, the town was generally successful. It may be said that the kings seldom followed a
wise policy in this matter, but permitted themselves to be influenced
by the complaints of the lords. The German kings generally did not
understand the movement or see its importance. They did not perceive that a new order of things was arising in the cities which
was rapidly replacing the feudal system.

In the name of the holy and undivided Trinity. Frederick
II, by the favor of God king of the Romans, Augustus, and
king of Sicily. . . . Our beloved prince, Henry, bishop

of Basel, came into the presence of us and of many princes, barons, and nobles of the empire and demanded a decision about the following matter, namely: Whether we or anyone else had the right to establish a council in a city [that is, to give a city municipal freedom] which was subject to a bishop, without the bishop's consent and permission. We first asked our beloved prince, Theodoric, the venerable archbishop of Trier, about this, and he, after some deliberation, declared that we neither could nor should grant or establish a council in the city of the aforesaid bishop of Basel without the consent of him or of his successors. The question was then asked in due form of all who were present, both princes, nobles, and barons, and they confirmed the decision of the archbishop of Trier. We also, as a just judge, approve this decision, and declare it to be right. We therefore remove and depose the council which is now in Basel, and we annul the charter which we granted the people of Basel authorizing the establishment of this council, and they shall never make any further use of it. As a greater evidence of our favor and love for the aforesaid bishop of Basel, we forbid, under the threat of the loss of our favor, the people of Basel to make or set up a council or any constitution, by whatever name it may be called, without the consent and permission of their bishop. . . .

315. FREDERICK II FORBIDS THE MUNICIPAL FREEDOM OF THE TOWNS AND ANNULS ALL CITY CHARTERS, 1231-2.
Altmann und Bernheim, no. 166.

See introductory note to no. 314.

In the name of the holy and undivided Trinity. Frederick, etc. . . . (2) In various parts of Germany, through the failure to enforce the law and through neglect, certain detestable customs have become established which hide their bad character under a good appearance. By them the rights and honor of the princes of the empire are diminished and the imperial authority is weakened. It is our duty to see that these bad customs, or rather these corrupt practices, shall no longer be in force. (3) Wishing, therefore, that all the grants and concessions of liberties and privileges which we have made to the princes of the empire shall have the broadest interpretation and that the said princes may have full and undisturbed possession of them, we hereby remove and depose in every town and city of Germany all the city councils, burgomasters, mayors, aldermen, and all other officials, by whatever name they may be called, who have been established by the people of the said cities without the permission of their archbishop or bishop. (4) We also dissolve all fraternities or societies, by whatever name they may be called. (5) We also decree that, in every city or town where there is a mint, no kind of money except that which is coined in that place shall be used in the sale and purchase of all kinds of goods and provisions. (6) In times past the archbishops and bishops governed the cities and all the lands which were given them by the emperor, and we wish them to continue to do so forever, either in person or through the officials whom they may appoint for this purpose, in spite of the fact that certain abuses have crept in, and in some cities there are those who resist them. But this resistance to their lord is illegal. (7) In order that these wicked abuses may be stopped and may not have even a pretence of authority, we revoke and declare invalid and worthless all the privileges, open letters, and sealed letters, which we or our predecessors or the archbishops or bishops have given to any person, either public or private, or to any city, in favor of these societies, communes, or councils, to the disadvantage of the princes and of the empire. This document has the form of a judicial decision, being published by a decree of the princes with our full knowledge. . . .

316. BRESLAU ADOPTS THE CHARTER OF MAGDEBURG, 1261. (GERMAN.)

Altmann und Bernheim, no. 167.

Magdeburg was on the frontier between the Germans and the Slavs (Wends and Poles) of the interior. It owed its importance and growth in large part to the fact that it was the centre of the extensive trade between the two peoples. For a long time practically all the commerce between them passed through it. It had the same commercial importance for the Slavs of the interior as Lübeck did for the people along the shores of the Baltic. Because of its position it was raised to be the seat of an archbishop, and given the work of Christianizing the Slavs. Another effect of her position and commerce was seen in the organization of the Slavic cities, all of which adopted her government and laws. These so-called Slavic towns to the east of Magdeburg were established generally by German colonists who made it a condition of their going as colonists that they should have the charter of Magdeburg. And when towns were raised to the rank of cities they asked to have the charter of Magdeburg. So in 1261 when Breslau was made a city, duke Henry and his citizens of Breslau applied to Magdeburg for a copy of its charter. In response to this request the *Schoeffen* of the city drew up the following statement of the city's government. Although prolix, un-systematic, and obscure in some points, the student will be able to understand the essential features of it. Compare the legal procedure, delays, etc., with no. 4, the Salic Law.

In a city which had the charter of Magdeburg it might easily happen that a new case would arise which was not provided for in the charter. If the governing body was in doubt as to what to do, a deputation was sent to Magdeburg to ask for instructions from her board of *Schoeffen*. So in 1338 the citizens of Culm asked for in-structions on several points, and the *Schoeffen* told them what the law on these matters in Magdeburg was. We give these two docu-ments as typical, and as illustrating the government of the cities in Wendish-Polish territory.

(1) When Magdeburg was founded the inhabitants were given a charter such as they wished. They determined that they would choose aldermen every year, who, on their elec-tion, should swear that they would guard the law, honor, and interests of the city to the best of their ability and with the advice of the wisest people of the city. (2) The alder-

men have under their jurisdiction false measures, false scales, false weights, offences in the sale of all sorts of provisions, and all kinds of deception in buying and selling. If they find anyone guilty of such things, he shall pay a fine of three Wendish marks, that is, thirty-six shillings. (3) The alder-men shall take counsel with the wisest people and then ap-point their courts at whatever time they wish. Their deci-sions rendered in court are binding and must be obeyed. If anyone resists their decisions, they shall punish him. (4) If the bells are rung [to call the inhabitants to court], and anyone does not come, he shall pay a fine of six pence. If he is summoned to the court and does not come, he shall be fined five shillings. (5) If the people who are called huck-sters are convicted of cheating, they shall either be beaten and have their heads shaved, or they shall be fined three shillings, according to the choice of the aldermen. (6) If anyone is convicted of using false weights or measures, the aldermen shall punish him according to the custom of the city, or fine him thirty-six shillings. (7) The burggrave is the highest judge. He must hold three courts every year: the first one at St. Agatha's day [February 5], the second one at St. John's day [June 24], and the third one a week after St. Martin's day [November 11]. If these days fall on holy days or on "bound times" [that is, holidays on which, for some reason not here stated, no courts may be held], the court must be put off. If plaintiffs do not appear, the case must be put off. If the *Schultheiss* does not come, the case must be put off. But the *Schultheiss* who fails to come must pay the burggrave ten pounds, unless it was impossible for him to come. (8) All crimes committed 14 days before the burggrave's court meets belong solely to the jurisdiction of the burggrave. But if the burggrave is not there, the citi-zens shall choose someone else to judge in his place, if any-one has been taken in the very act of committing a crime. The fee of the burggrave is three pounds. When the burggrave rises from the judge's chair, his court is dissolved, and he then appoints the court of the *Schultheiss* to be held 14 days from the next day. (9) The *Schultheiss* holds three regular courts every year: the first one, twelve days after Christmas, the second, on the first Tuesday after Easter week, and the third, at the end of the week of Pentecost. At the close of each of these courts he shall appoint another court [if necessary], to be held fourteen days later. If these courts fall on a holy day, he may put off his court for a day or two. (10) The fee of the *Schultheiss* is eight shillings. No one shall be summoned to his court except by the *Schultheiss* himself or by his beadle. His servant shall not summon anyone. If the *Schultheiss* is not at home when a crime is committed, the people shall choose someone to judge in his place, in case they have taken some offender in the act. The *Schultheiss* shall receive his authority as a fief from the lord of the land, and he shall have a fief [besides], and he must be of legitimate birth, and born a citizen of the town. (11) If a man is wounded and cries for help, and seizes his assailant and brings him into court, and has six witnesses, the defendant is to be shown to the witnesses, so that he cannot escape. If a man inflicts a wound as deep as a nail and as long as a finger, his hand shall be cut off; for killing anyone his head shall be cut off. (12) Neither the burggrave nor the *Schultheiss* shall compel citizens to render decisions [that is, assist in holding court] at any other time than the regular sessions of the court, except when a criminal has been taken in the act. But the burggrave and the *Schultheiss* must, every day, try the cases which are brought before them. (13) If a man is wounded but puts off making complaint [to the proper official] until the next day, the accused may clear himself if he produces six witnesses. If the accused fails to appear at the next three sessions of the court, he shall, at the fourth session, be put under the ban [outlawed, proscribed]. (14) If a man dies

leaving a wife, she shall have no share in his property except
what he has given her in court, or has appointed for her
dower. She must have six witnesses, male or female, to
prove her dower. If the man made no provision for her,
her children must support her as long as she does not re-
marry. If her husband had sheep, the widow shall take them.
(15) If a man and woman have children, some of whom are
married and have received their marriage portion, and the
man dies, the children who are still at home [that is, un-
married], shall receive the inheritance. Those who have
received their marriage portion shall have no part of it [that
is, the inheritance]. Children who have received an inheritance shall not sell it without the consent of their heirs.
(16) If a man surrenders anything to another in court,
and the other holds it in peaceable possession for a year and
a day, he shall call the judge and the *Schoeffen* as witnesses
to the fact [that he has held it for a year and a day], and
thereafter no one shall bring a suit against him to recover it.
(17) If a judge or *Schoeffe* dies, he shall be declared deposed [that is, his office shall be declared vacant] by a session of court in which at least two *Schoeffen* and four free
citizens are present. Then his wife shall receive her share of
his property [that is, not until his office is declared vacant
may his widow claim her share of his property]. (18) No
one, whether man or woman, shall, on his sick-bed, give away
more than three shillings' worth of his property without the
consent of his heirs, and the woman must have the consent
of her husband. (19) If the fee or *wergeld* of the burggrave
has been adjudged to him in court, it must be paid to him
within six weeks. (20) If there are no immediate heirs
[that is, children] to an inheritance, the nearest of kin shall
share it equally. (21) If a man is wounded and cries for help
[but does not seize his assailant] and comes into court and accuses someone who was present [when he received the wound],
the accused must answer in court and defend himself. If a

man accuses more persons than he has wounds, only as many persons as he has wounds shall be prosecuted, but the defendants may clear themselves of the charges with six witnesses. (22) If an inheritance is left to a boy [that is, if his father dies], and he wishes to become a priest, he shall nevertheless receive the inheritance. But if he has an unmarried sister at home, the two shall divide it between them. (23) If a man transfers a piece of property to another in the presence of the judge and of the *Schoeffen,* the *Schoeffen* shall receive a fee of one shilling. (24) If a man brings a suit against another for a debt and gets a writ of execution against him, the defendant must, on the same day, pay the debt and also the judge's fee. (25) If a man is sued for a debt and he confesses to the debt, he must pay it within fourteen days. If he does not pay it within fourteen days, he shall pay the judge's fee, and the judge shall order him to pay it within eight days. If he does not pay it within eight days, the judge shall order him to pay it the next day. If he does not pay it, he shall pay the judge his fee for every time the judge ordered him to pay. If he does not have the money to pay, his house shall be taken in pawn for the debt. If he has no house, he shall be seized for debt wherever he may be found. Whoever gives him aid, shall pay a fine to the judge. (26) If a man's clothes are taken from him by a writ of execution, he has seventeen days in which to call a court session. (27) If a man of good reputation is accused of having caused a disturbance by day or night, he shall clear himself with six witnesses, provided he was not seen near the place where the disturbance was. (28) No widow shall use the capital of her dower or sell it. If she dies it shall go to the heirs of her husband. (29) If an inheritance is left to children, and one of them dies, the others share it equally. (30) If a man's house is taken from him as a pawn for a debt, so long as the pawn is unredeemed he shall pay the judge a fine every time he enters the house.

(31) If a man is going out of the country as a pilgrim or as a merchant, no one shall hinder him from going because of a debt, unless he brings suit against him for the debt before the judge.   (32) If anyone reviles a *Schoeffe* while he is on the bench [that is, while he is performing the duties of his office], he shall pay the *Schoeffe* the regular fine [for an offence against a *Schoeffe*], that is, thirty shillings, and he shall also pay the judge his fee.   (33) If a man reviles the *Schoeffen* after they have given a decision, he shall pay each of them the regular fine, that is, thirty shillings, and also pay the judge his regular fine.   He shall pay the judge's fine as many times as there are *Schoeffen* whom he reviled.   (34) If a man needs evidence that a quarrel or feud was legally settled in court, he shall appeal to the judge and *Schoeffen* in whose presence the feud was settled.   If they have died, he shall take the testimony of the free citizens who were in court at the time.   (35) The judge shall not reverse a decision of the *Schoeffen*.   (36) If a feud is settled out of court and one of the parties afterward renews it, the other party shall prove that it was settled by bringing six witnesses who saw and heard the settlement.   (37) If a feud is settled in court and a pledge given [that the feud shall not be renewed] and some of them [that is, one of the parties to it] renew it and they are convicted of it before the judge and the *Schoeffen*, they shall lose a hand for inflicting a wound on any of the other party, and their head if they have killed anyone.   If a man who did not agree to the settlement of the feud renews it, he shall pay the *wergeld*, that is, nine pounds for a wound and eighteen for killing anyone.   (38) If a man attacks another with intent to wound, and does wound him, he shall lose a hand for a wound, and his head if he kills him.   (39) If a man is beaten with rods on his back and abdomen so as to make black and blue spots and to cause swellings, he shall show himself to the judge and to the free citizens in court that they may see the effects of the blows,

and then he has grounds for suit against those who beat him. But if he is beaten on his head and arms and he has no other proof, the accused shall clear themselves in the regular way. If they confess [that they beat him], each one shall pay his fine and the judge's fee besides. If the man whom they beat dies, they must all answer in court for his death. If he does not die, only one of them shall answer in court, the others shall go free. (40) The burggrave and not the *Schultheiss* shall have jurisdiction over the three crimes of attacking from an ambush, violating women, and attacking with intent to kill. If the one attacked has wounds and shows them to the judge and has witnesses who heard him cry for help, the accused shall answer in court to the charges. (41) If anyone dies leaving an inheritance and no heirs appear within a year and a day to claim it, it shall go to the king. (42) If a man who has three or more children is killed, and someone is accused by one of the children of having killed his father, but is not convicted, and the court gives him a certificate that he did not commit the crime, the other children shall not renew the charge against him. (43) If a man enters suit against another, he shall make a deposit with the judge [to cover expenses?]. He shall not give this deposit to the judge, but he shall receive it back [after the suit is ended]. (44) If a man seizes a horse and declares that it was stolen or taken by force from him, he shall prove it in court. He in whose possession the horse was found, shall appeal to witnesses and name them and swear by the saints that he is not practising any deception in appealing to witnesses. After he has named his witnesses, the man who is called as a witness shall go with him a reasonable distance [that is, to meet the witnesses who have been named]. If he cannot produce the witnesses whom he boasted of having, he shall give security to the judge for the fine and the expenses to which the man who claimed the horse has been put, and he shall set a day when he shall appear in court. If he says that he bought the horse in the public market, he shall restore the horse to its owner and he shall lose the money which he paid for it. But he shall not pay a fine. The judge shall not assess a fine for the non-payment of his fine. (45) If a man claims a piece of property or an inheritance, he shall not bribe the judge in order to secure a favorable decision. If a man enters a suit against another [but in the meantime the matter is settled out of court], he shall pay nothing except the fee of the judge. (46) If a man who has been wounded does not wish to make charges against anyone, the judge cannot compel him to do so. (47) If a man is outlawed or condemned, no one but his heirs shall take his property. (48) If a man dies without having disposed of his property, it shall go to his children, if they are his equals in birth. If one of the children dies, its share goes to its mother, but she cannot dispose of it without the consent of her heirs. (49) When a child is twelve years old it may choose whom it will as guardian. The guardian must render an account to the mother and to the children of his management of the inheritance. (50) If one man says to another, " You are my property," but the man thus claimed can prove his freedom, no similar claim shall ever be made against him again. A man can prove his freedom by the testimony of three of his mother's relatives and three of his father's relatives. These witnesses may be either male or female. (51) Playing at dice is not a crime. (52) If a man is security for anything and dies, his children are not responsible for the security. If a man is security for a debt, he must pay it and make everything good. (53) If a man wounds another in the street within the corporate limits of the city [that is, on ground which is under the jurisdiction of the city] not in self-defence, wrongfully, and without provocation, and the wounded man turns and wounds him and cries for help, but because of his wounds is not able to reach the court first and make charges against his assailant, and his assailant, although he was the first to make the attack, maliciously and insolently comes into court and makes charges, the one who was first attacked shall come into court on the same day and prove by those who heard his cry for help that the other was the first to make the attack. If he can prove this he shall win his case. But he must appear the same day. (54) If two men who are from Wendish territory, even though they are not both Wends, wound each other within the corporate limits of the city, and one of them comes into court and makes charges against the other according to Wendish law, the other must answer him according to the same law. (55) When a man dies his wife shall give his sword, his horse and saddle, and his best coat of mail. She shall also give a bed, a pillow, a sheet, a table-cloth, two dishes and a towel. Some say that she should give other things also, but that is not necessary. If she does not have these things, she shall not give them, but she shall give proof for each article that she does not have it. (56) If two or more children inherit these things [named in § 55], the oldest shall take the sword and they shall share the other things equally. (57) If the children are minors, the oldest male relative on the father's side, if he is of the same rank by birth, shall receive all these things [named in § 55] and preserve them for the children. When they become of age, he shall give them to them, and in addition, all their property, unless he can prove that he has used it to their profit, or that it has been stolen or destroyed by some accident without any fault of his. He shall also be the guardian of the widow until she remarries, if he is of the same rank as she is. (58) After giving the above articles the widow shall take her dower and all that belongs to her; that is, all the sheep, geese, chests, yarn, beds, pillows, cushions, table linen, bed linen, towels, cups, candlesticks, linen, woman's clothing, finger rings, bracelets, headdress, psalters, and all prayer-books, chairs, drawers, bureaus, carpets, curtains, etc., and there are many other trinkets which belong to her, such as brushes, scissors, and mirrors, but I do not mention them. But uncut cloth, and unworked gold and silver do not belong to her. (59) All the possessions of the man except those named in § 55 belong to his inheritance. If he has given anything in pledge, he who has the right to shall redeem it if he wishes to do so. (60) If one of the children becomes a priest he shall share in the inheritance equally with his brothers, but not if he becomes a monk. (61) If a boy is put into a monastery but leaves it before he becomes of age, he retains his legal status; that is, he may inherit fiefs from his father and has all the protection of the law of the land. But if a man becomes a monk, he loses all his rights and fiefs, because he has denied his military duties. The monks of the monastery which he has entered shall be witnesses of this. (62) Cases shall be tried in the order in which they are entered. The plaintiff and the defendant have each the right to speak three times during the trial. Each one may speak until the beadle orders him to stop. (63) In all cities it is the law that the judge shall give decisions. A man who has a representative shall not speak in court. If the judge asks him whether he agrees to what his representative says, he must answer Yes or No, or he may ask for permission to speak. (64) If anyone wishes to challenge a fellow citizen to an ordeal by duel, he must ask the judge to permit him to challenge the peace-breaker in a legal manner. If this request is granted, the accuser may ask how he should challenge so as to have the support of the law. The answer is, by pulling the defendant at his collar. After the challenge, he shall tell the defendant why he challenged him. He must accuse him of having broken the peace either on the king's road, or in a village. He shall declare in which way the peace was broken. But he must accuse the defendant of having wounded him and done him violence. And this he may prove by showing his wounds or scars. Further, he shall accuse the defendant of having robbed him of his property and of having taken enough to make an ordeal necessary. He shall accuse him of all these three crimes at once. If he omits one of these he is deprived of the privilege of the ordeal.

The honorable *Schoeffen* and the aldermen of Magdeburg drew up this law of Magdeburg for the noble duke, Henry, and his citizens of Breslau, and, if necessary, will aid them in keeping it. They gave it at the request of Henry the duke and of his citizens of Breslau. In the year 1261. . . . .

317. The Schoeffen of Magdeburg give Decisions for Culm, 1338. (German.)

Altmann und Bernheim, no. 172.

See introductory note to no. 316.

1. May aldermen be deposed? To the honorable aldermen of Culm, we the *Schoeffen* of Magdeburg, your obedient servants [send greeting]. You have asked us in your letter whether aldermen may choose other aldermen, and whether they may choose from among themselves burgomasters and *Schoeffen* without the consent of the burggrave. And also whether the burggrave may depose some of the aldermen and appoint others in their place. We answer, that the aldermen may choose other aldermen for a year, and one or two burgomasters from their own number also for a year. But the burggrave has no right to depose aldermen and put others in their place.

2. Who shall choose other *Schoeffen*? The *Schoeffen* shall elect other *Schoeffen*, and those elected shall remain *Schoeffen* as long as they live. The aldermen have no right to elect *Schoeffen*. The burggrave shall confirm the *Schoeffen* who are elected.

3. May the aldermen make laws? You have also asked us whether the aldermen with the consent of their citizens may make laws among themselves and fix the penalties for

offences against them, without the consent of the burggrave, and whether the aldermen have the right to collect such penalties and retain them, or shall the burggrave and the *Schultheiss* have a share in them. And you have also asked if a man breaks the laws and refuses to pay the fine, how it is to be collected from him. We answer, that the aldermen may make laws and fix their penalties provided these laws do not conflict with the laws of the city. And they may do this without the consent of the burggrave. And they have the right to demand the payment of fines, and they may keep them for the benefit of the city; the burggrave and the *Schultheiss* shall have no part in them.

4. What if a man refuses to pay a fine? If a man refuses to pay a fine but admits that he owes it, the aldermen may seize and imprison him until he pays it. If he says he does not owe the fine, he shall prove it by taking an oath by the saints.

5. About false measures. You have further asked whether the aldermen have jurisdiction over weights and measures, false measures, and the sale of provisions, and if a man refuses to pay a fine how it shall be collected. We answer, that aldermen have jurisdiction over the said things, and that if a man refuses to pay his fine, they may seize and imprison him until he pays it, as is written above.

6. About damage done to a forest. You asked us if a man cuts wood in a forest, how he shall pay the damage. We answer, if a man cuts down trees in another's forest, or cuts his grass, or fishes in his streams, he shall pay for the damage and a fine besides.

7. How far shall a guest live from the city? You also asked us how far a man must live from the court if he wishes to have the right of a guest. We answer, if a guest is accused before the court, if he swears by the saints that he lives more than twelve miles from the court, he shall have his trial at once. If a guest enters suit against a citizen in the same

court, the citizen shall answer in court that same day if the guest demands it.

8. About attaching the property of a guest. You further asked us how you should proceed, if a man attaches the property of a guest from a far country, so that justice may be done to both. We answer, if a man attaches the property of a guest who lives so far away that you cannot get hold of him, the attachment is not to be put into execution until the guest is informed of it. If the guest does not then appear to defend his property, the attached property may be taken.

9. About taxes. You further asked us, if the citizens have property outside of the territory of the city which they hold from some lord and from which they receive an income, are they bound to pay the tax which may be assessed on property outside the city, just the same as they do on their ordinary property? We answer that, according to the law and practice of our city, every man must pay taxes on his property outside as well as inside the city, no matter where it is, and he must take an oath to its value and pay a tax accordingly.

318. THE ESTABLISHMENT OF THE RHINE LEAGUE, 1254.
M. G. LL. 4to, IV, 2, no. 428.

Commerce, the chief interest of the cities, could flourish only under peaceful conditions. But peace was a stranger to Germany toward the middle of the thirteenth century. In order to prosecute his Italian-Sicilian policy, Frederick II had left Germany to her fate. The princes were engaged in private warfare, and a large number of robber barons plied their trade and made the roads unsafe. Conrad IV was fighting for the possession of the crown and so was unable to establish peace. William of Holland was recognized in only a small territory and was practically helpless to restore order. Under these circumstances the cities of the Rhine valley determined to take matters into their own hands, and so made a league for the purpose of protecting their commerce against the robber barons and other highwaymen who infested all the roads and streams. We give the document by which the league was formed, and the one in which is embodied its first legislation.

In the name of the holy and undivided Trinity. The

judges, consuls [aldermen], and all the citizens of Mainz, Cologne, Worms, Speyer, Strassburg, Basel, and other cities which are bound together in the league of holy peace, to all the faithful of Christ, greeting in him who is the author of peace and the ground of salvation.

1. Since now for a long time many of our citizens have been completely ruined by the violence and wrongs which have been inflicted on them in the country and along the roads, and through their ruin others have also been ruined, so that innocent people, through no fault of their own, have suffered great loss, it is high time that some way be found for preventing such violence, and for restoring peace in all our lands in an equitable manner.

2. Therefore we wish to inform all that, with the aid of our Lord Jesus Christ, the author and lover of peace, and for the purpose of fostering peace and rendering justice, we have all unanimously agreed on the following terms of peace: We have mutually bound ourselves by oath to observe a general peace for ten years from St. Margaret's day [July 13, 1254]. The venerable archbishops, Gerhard of Mainz, Conrad of Cologne, Arnold of Trier, and the bishops, Richard of Worms, Henry of Strassburg, Jacob of Metz, Bertold of Basel, and many counts and nobles of the land have joined us in this oath, and they as well as we have all surrendered the unjust tolls which we have been collecting both by land and water, and we will collect them no longer.

3. This promise shall be kept in such a way that not only the greater ones among us shall have the advantage of this common protection, but all, the small with the great, the secular clergy, monks of every order, laymen, and Jews, shall enjoy this protection and live in the tranquillity of holy peace. If anyone breaks this peace, we will all go against him with all our forces, and compel him to make proper satisfaction.

4. In regard to the quarrels or differences which now

exist between members of this peace, or which may hereafter
arise, they shall be settled in the following way: Each city
and each lord, who are members of this league, shall choose
four reliable men and give them full authority to settle all
quarrels in an amicable way, or in some legal manner. . . .

319. PEACE ESTABLISHED BY THE RHINE LEAGUE, 1254.

M. G. LL. folio, II, 369 f.

See introductory note to no. 318.

In the name of the Lord, amen. In the year of our Lord
1254, on the octave of St. Michael's day [that is, a week
after Sept. 29] we, the cities of the upper and lower Rhine,
leagued together for the preservation of peace, met in the
city of Worms. We held a meeting there and carefully discussed everything pertaining to a general peace. To the honor
of God, and of the holy mother church, and of the holy empire, which is now governed by our lord, William [of Hol-
land], king of the Romans, and to the common advantage
of all, both rich and poor alike, we made the following laws.
They are for the benefit of all, both poor and great, the secular
clergy, monks, laymen, and Jews. To secure these things
which are for the public good we will spare neither ourselves
nor our possessions. The princes and lords who take the
oath are joined with us.

1. We decree that we will make no warlike expeditions
except those that are absolutely necessary and determined
on by the wise counsel of the cities and communes. We will
mutually aid each other with all our strength in securing
redress for our grievances.

2. We decree that no member of the league, whether city
or lord, Christian or Jew, shall furnish food, arms, or aid
of any kind, to anyone who opposes us or the peace.

3. And no one in our cities shall give credit, or make a
loan to them.

4. No citizen of any of the cities in the league shall

associate with such, or give them counsel, aid, or support. If anyone is convicted of doing so, he shall be ejected from the city and punished so severely in his property that he will be a warning to others not to do such things.

5. If any knight, in trying to aid his lord who is at war with us, attacks or molests us anywhere outside of the walled towns of his lord, he is breaking the peace, and we will in some way inflict due punishment on him and his possessions, no matter who he is. If he is caught in any of the cities, he shall be held as a prisoner until he makes proper satisfaction. We wish to be protectors of the peasants, and we will protect them against all violence if they will observe the peace with us. But if they make war on us, we will punish them, and if we catch them in any of the cities, we will punish them as malefactors.

6. We wish all the cities to destroy all the ferries except those in their immediate neighborhood, so that there shall be no ferries except those near the cities which are in the league. This is to be done in order that the enemies of the peace may be deprived of all means of crossing the Rhine.

7. We decree that if any lord or knight aids us in promoting the peace, we will do all we can to protect him. Whoever does not swear to keep the peace with us, shall be excluded from the general peace.

8. We decree that whoever is in our cities as a pledge [that is, as security that some contract will be kept] shall have peace from all who are in the league. We will not permit him to be molested by anyone so long as he is in one of our cities; but we will defend him, and he may enter and leave the city as he pleases.

9. But if any such man breaks his oath and flees, he shall be warned three times by the city, and if he does not return, the creditor, or the one to whom he had been security, may bring suit against him before the judges and they shall compel him to continue as security.

10. Above all we wish to affirm that we desire to live in mutual peace with the lords and all the people of the province, and we wish that each should preserve all his rights.

11. Under threat of punishment we forbid any citizen to revile the lords although they may be our enemies. For although we wish to punish them for the violence they have done us, yet before making war on them we will first warn them to cease from injuring us.

12. We decree that all correspondence about this matter with the cities of the lower Rhine shall be conducted from Mainz, and from Worms with the cities of the upper Rhine. From these two cities all our correspondence shall be carried on and all who have done us injury shall be warned. Those who have suffered injury shall send their messengers at their own expense.

13. We also promise, both lords and cities, to send four official representatives to whatever place a conference is to be held, and they shall have full authority from their cities to decide on all matters. They shall report to their cities all the decisions of the meeting. All who come with the representatives of the cities or who come to them [while in session], shall have peace, and no judgment shall be enforced against them.

14. No city shall receive non-residents, who are commonly called "pfahlburgers," as citizens.

15. We firmly promise that if any member of the league breaks the peace, we will proceed against him at once as if he were not a member, and compel him to make proper satisfaction.

16. We promise that we will faithfully keep each other informed by letter about our enemies and all others who may be able to do us damage, in order that we may take timely counsel to protect ourselves against them.

17. We decree that no one shall violently enter the house of monks or nuns, of whatever order they may be, or quarter

themselves upon them, or demand or extort food, or any kind of service, from them contrary to their will. If anyone does this he shall be held as a violator of the peace.

18. We decree that each city shall try to persuade each of its neighboring cities to swear to keep the peace. If they do not do so, they shall be entirely cut off from the peace, so that if anyone does them an injury, either in their persons or their property, he shall not thereby break the peace.

19. We wish all members of the league, cities, lords, and all others, to arm themselves properly and prepare for war, so that whenever we call upon them we shall find them ready.

20. We decree that the cities between the Mosel and Basel shall prepare 100 war boats, and the cities below the Mosel shall prepare 500, well equipped with bowmen, and each city shall prepare herself as well as she can and supply herself with arms for knights and foot-soldiers.

320. AGREEMENT BETWEEN HAMBURG AND LÜBECK, ca. 1230.

Keutgen, Urkunden zur Städtischen Verfassungsgeschichte, no. 427.

With the deposition of Henry the Lion, duke of Saxony, in 1180, and the consequent dismemberment of his duchy (see no. 112), north Germany was left without a great prince, and there was no hope that anyone would be able to unite the numerous principalities which were enjoying more or less sovereignty. The absence of any strong power gave greater opportunity for the development of the cities and made the Hanseatic league possible. This league had its origin in the league between Hamburg and Lübeck for mutual protection against robbers in 1241. But these cities had already for a long time been friendly, and had made a mutual agreement for the protection of the merchants of the one city when they went to the other. Other cities joined them in the league of 1241. The power and influence of the league grew until it was able to carry on war and to dictate in political matters to the whole north. The earliest stages of the development of the league are illustrated by nos. 320–322.

To their honorable and beloved friends, the advocate, aldermen, and other citizens of Lübeck, the advocate, aldermen, and the commune of Hamburg, greeting, etc. . . .

We wish you to know that we desire by all means to preserve the mutual love and friendship which have hitherto
existed between you and us. We desire that we shall have
the same law, so that whenever your citizens come into our
city, bringing goods that are unencumbered [that is, about
which there is no dispute or suit pending], they may possess
and enjoy them in peace and security, in the same way as
our citizens. . . .

**321. AGREEMENT FOR MUTUAL PROTECTION BETWEEN
LÜBECK AND HAMBURG, 1241.**

Keutgen, no. 428.

The advocate, council and commune of Lübeck. . . .
We have made the following agreement with our dear friends,
the citizens of Hamburg.

1. If robbers or other depredators attack citizens of either
city anywhere from the mouth of the Trave river to Hamburg, or anywhere on the Elbe river, the two cities shall bear
the expenses equally in destroying and extirpating them.

2. If anyone who lives outside the city, kills, wounds,
beats, or mishandles, without cause, a citizen of either city,
the two cities shall bear the expenses equally in punishing
the offender. We furthermore agree to share the expenses
equally in punishing those who injure their citizens in the
neighborhood of their city and those who injure our citizens
in the neighborhood of our city.

3. If any of their citizens are injured near our city [Lü-
beck], they shall ask our officials to punish the offender, and
if any of our citizens are injured near their city [Hamburg],
they shall ask their officials to punish the offender.

**322. LÜBECK, ROSTOCK, AND WISMAR PROSCRIBE
PIRATES, 1259.**

Keutgen, no. 429.

To all the faithful subjects of Christ. . . . The communes of Lübeck, Rostock, and Wismar. . . . Since most

merchants are not protected on the sea from pirates and robbers, we have, in a common council, decreed, and by this writing declare, that all who rob merchants in churches, in cemeteries, or on the water or on the land, shall be outlawed and proscribed by all cities and merchants. No matter where these robbers go with their booty, whatever city or land receives them shall be held equally guilty with them, and proscribed by all the cities and merchants. . . .

323. DECREES OF THE HANSEATIC LEAGUE, 1260–64.
Keutgen, no. 430 a.

We wish to inform you of the action taken in support of all merchants who are governed by the law of Lübeck.

(1) Each city shall, to the best of her ability, keep the sea clear of pirates, so that merchants may freely carry on their business by sea.   (2) Whoever is expelled from one city because of a crime shall not be received in another. (3) If a citizen is seized [by pirates, robbers, or bandits] he shall not be ransomed, but his sword-belt and knife shall be sent to him [as a threat to his captors].   (4) Any merchant ransoming him shall lose all his possessions in all the cities which have the law of Lübeck.   (5) Whoever is proscribed in one city for robbery or theft shall be proscribed in all. (6) If a lord besieges a city, no one shall aid him in any way to the detriment of the besieged city, unless the besieger is his lord.   (7) If there is a war in the country, no city shall on that account injure a citizen from the other cities, either in his person or goods, but shall give him protection.   (8) If any man marries a woman in one city, and another woman from some other city comes and proves that he is her lawful husband, he shall be beheaded.   (9) If a citizen gives his daughter or niece in marriage to a man [from another city], and another man comes and says that she is his lawful wife, but cannot prove it, he shall be beheaded.

This law shall be binding for a year, and after that the cities shall inform each other by letter of what decisions they make.

324. DECREES OF THE HANSEATIC LEAGUE, 1265.

Keutgen, no. 430 b.

We ought to hold a meeting once a year to legislate about the affairs of the cities.

(5) If pirates appear on the sea, all the cities must contribute their share to the work of destroying them.

325. COLOGNE MERCHANTS HAVE A GILDHALL IN LONDON, 1157.

Keutgen, no. 431.

The merchants of Cologne early had commercial dealings with London. Her commercial relations with England were more important to her than her relations with Germany, and as a result of this she generally preferred her English alliance to her less lucrative relations with other German principalities on the mainland. In international complications Cologne was apt to be found on the side of England. This document is interesting as showing the early existence of the gildhall of the merchants of Cologne, which was the starting-point of the Hanse in London.

Henry [II], by the grace of God, etc., . . . to his justiciars, sheriffs, and all his officials in England, greeting. I command you to guard, maintain, and protect all the men and citizens of Cologne as if they were my own subjects and friends, and all their goods, merchandise, and possessions. You shall not permit them to suffer any loss or damage in their house in London, which is called their gildhall, or in their goods, or merchandise, or anything else that belongs to them, because they are faithful to me, and they are in my ward and protection. They shall have complete protection, and they shall pay only their customary tolls, and you shall not exact new tolls from them. . . .

BIBLIOGRAPHY

The following list is intended to serve both as a brief bibliography of important collections of mediæval documents and as an explanation of the references. In the case of the more important collections and works a brief comment is added. Many titles are omitted where the reference in the text is clear and the work is not of general importance.

1. LARGE COLLECTIONS; NATIONAL

M. G. Monumenta Germaniæ Historica; SS., LL., DD., refer to the divisions Scriptores, Leges, Diplomata, according to which the work is arranged; folio, 4to, refer to the two forms of the collection.

Scriptores rerum Germanicarum in usum scholarum; chronicles reprinted in 8vo from M. G. SS.

Jaffé, Bibliotheca rerum Germanicarum; 6 vols.

Böhmer, Fontes rerum Germanicarum; 4 vols.

Böhmer-Ficker-Winkelmann, Regesta. Summaries of imperial documents with indications of the places where they are to be found.

Bouquet Recueil des historiens des Gaules et de la France. French collection of mediæval sources, in 23 vols.

Documents inédits sur l'histoire de France.

Muratori, Rerum Italicarum Scriptores; collection of chronicles relating chiefly to the history of Italy in the Middle Age, in 28 vols.

Rolls series, Rerum Britannicarum medii aevi scriptores, or chronicles and memorials of Great Britain and Ireland during the Middle Ages. Published under the direction of the Master of the Rolls.

Rymer, Foedera; English public documents, 20 vols.

2. LARGE COLLECTIONS; ECCLESIASTICAL AND PAPAL

Migne, Patrologia; Cursus completus patrologiæ . . . Series Latina; acts and writings of the fathers and popes, 221 vols.

Mansi, Conciliorum amplissima collectio.

Hefele, Conciliengeschichte; quotes or cites in translation many decrees of councils; 9 vols.

Baronius, Annales ecclesiastici; collection of chronicles relating to the history of the Roman Catholic church, published in 1598.

Raynaldus, Annales; continuation of Baronius.

Watterich, Pontificum Romanorum vitæ; lives of the popes, 9th to 13th centuries.

Bullarium Romanum; collection of papal bulls, 450–1550 A.D.

Corpus juris canonici; collection of decrees of councils and popes, forming the body of the canon or church law.

Liber diurnus; collection of forms of papal documents, letters, grants, bulls, etc., to serve as models for the papal secretaries.

Duchesne, Liber pontificalis.

3. SPECIAL TOPICS. SELECTED DOCUMENTS, ETC.

Die Chroniken der deutschen Städte vom 14. bis ins 16. Jahrh.; 22 vols.

Huilliard-Bréholles, Historica diplomatica Friderici secundi; 12 vols.

Doeberl, Monumenta Germaniæ Selecta; selected documents referring to the history of Germany, vols. 3–5, 1037–1250 A.D.

Altmann und Bernheim, Ausgewählte Urkunden; selected documents referring to the history of Germany in the Middle Age.

Breslau, Diplomata Centum; a collection of one hundred documents illustrating mediæval diplomatics.

GLOSSARY

This list is meant to include only technical terms which occur frequently in the text. Terms which are familiar, and those which are used only once or twice and explained in the text, are therefore not included.

abbot, head of a monastery; see no. 251, chs. 2, 64.

advocate, *advocatus*, representative of church or prelate in secular affairs; in feudal system regularly a vassal of the church, holding office and church lands as fief; see no. 296 introduction.

aids, obligations of vassal to his lord; see introductory note to nos. 209-228, and nos. 215-217.

alderman, originally head of a gild; later, regularly member of ruling council of a city.

allodial land, alod, small freehold, as distinct from tenant-farm; later in feudal **system** also applied to family possessions of a noble as distinct from lands held by title of duke, count, etc.; an instance of this latter use in no. 90.

anathema, curse, regularly associated with papal excommunication.

apostolic seat, apostolic see, the bishopric of Rome, used as a figure of speech for pope or papal office.

Augustus, from time of Otto III the title regularly assumed by emperors after imperial coronation; indicates the theory that mediæval emperors were successors to Roman emperors.

bailly, bailiff, representative of lord in the villa.

ban, (1) proscription, or outlawry, regularly that pronounced by emperor against a subject; (2) particular fine paid to emperor or king in addition to ordinary penalty, usually 60 solidi.

basilica, church, especially early church modelled on Roman public building called basilica.

Bauermeister, see introductory note to section vii.

benefice, *beneficium*, (1) a form of land-holding, practically a fief; see nos. 197-202 and introduction; (2) lands and income attached to the office of a canon.

bull, a decree or edict of the pope.

burggrave, the official representative of overlord or king in a city; later a feudal noble.

canon, (1) a decree of a council or synod; (2) one of the chapter of a bishop's church.

canon law, ecclesiastical law, the law of the church, based on the decrees of popes and councils; see no. 33, introduction, and Bibliography, Corpus juris canonici.

canonical election, election of a church official in accordance with canon law.

capitulary, decree or edict of

615

Carolingian king or emperor, drawn up with advice of Frankish assembly.

cardinal, a member of the Sacred College, the advisory body of the pope, standing next to him in Catholic hierarchy, and intrusted with duty of electing pope. Members of college have titular offices in the bishopric of Rome, as cardinal bishops (now 6 in number), cardinal presbyters (now 50), and cardinal deacons (now 14).

chamberlain, see court officials.

chancellor, official at the head of the department intrusted with drawing up and preserving documents; an important office in every royal court, frequently held by an ecclesiastic.

chaplain, priest of private church or chapel of great lord or ruler; in royal courts becomes important member of council and central administration of king.

chapter, regularly the corporation of the clergy attached to the bishop's church, including dean, præpositus, cantor, scholasticus, penitentiarius, treasurer, etc.

confession of St. Peter; see no. 45, note 1.

council, the general assembly of the church, composed of chief clergy and representatives of lower clergy, and summoned occasionally by pope or cardinals; see no. 41, note 3, and nos. 169-174.

count, comes, the chief official in a county, originally as representative of the king, later, in feudal system, as feudal lord of lesser nobles in county.

count palatine, comes palatinus, one of chief officials of royal court; in feudal system, hereditary title attached to certain possessions, as palatine county of the Rhine in Germany, and of Champagne in France.

court officials, officers of the royal courts charged with important departments of central administration: seneschal, steward, chief official in charge of royal household and domains; chamberlain, originally officer in charge of royal chamber, later practically treasurer; cupbearer, cellarer, or butler, officer in charge of vineyards; marshal or constable, officer in charge of royal stables, later of the royal army. These offices in the beginning were of private nature, were later extended to include important public functions and became hereditary in hands of great nobles, and then became merely titular and ceremonial, the real duties being performed by royal officials and servants. See no. 160, ch. 27, for this last stage, in Germany.

cupbearer, see court officials.

dean, head of a chapter of canons.

denarius, a small coin, penny, originally silver; see no. 4, I, note 2.

diet, general assembly of the empire, including in final form the great ecclesiastics and nobles, and representatives of imperial cities; see nos. 146, 158, 159, 160 for instances.

diocese, ecclesiastical district ruled over by a bishop, made up of parishes; archdiocese, ecclesiastical district of an archbishop, comprising several bishoprics.

duke, ruler of a duchy, a great feudal lord, in Germany retaining character also of a public official to time of Frederick I.

electors, electoral princes, princes of Germany who exercised the right of electing the emperor; see no. 160 for names of the electors, their prerogatives, etc.

excommunication, exclusion from the communion of the Catholic church, entailing loss of rank and privileges on part of church officials, and of allegiance of subjects on part of secular ruler; ecclesiastical outlawry.

feudal terms, see introductory note to nos. 209-228.

fief, regularly an estate or territory held from a superior on terms of personal allegiance and honorable service, usually military support.

fodrum, fodder; as an obligation, the duty of supplying provisions for the royal army.

gild, society or association of merchants of a town, or of artisans of a single trade in a town. Gild of the merchants in many cases represented the town in the struggle for a charter, and government of many towns was based on the organization of the gild.

hide, portion of a family in the lands of the village community.

hierarchy of the Catholic church, chief ecclesiastical officials; in order of authority: pope, cardinals, archbishops, bishops. For lower grades, see no. 34, note 1.

homage, ceremony of entering into personal dependence on a lord, preliminary to receiving a fief from him; see nos. 209-214, 218-225.

hundred, division of the county, mainly for judicial purposes; see no. 1, note 1, and no. 4 introduction.

hundred-court, local public court of the hundred; the regular public court in Germany; see introductory note to section vii.

hundred-man, *centenarius*, *centgraf*, presiding official of the hundred-court, usually elected by freemen of the hundred; see no. 1, note 4, and no. 4 introduction.

immunity, freedom from control of public officials; a right attached to gifts of land from king; see nos. 190-194, and introduction.

indiction, number of a year in a period of 15 years, used as a means of dating mediæval documents; established by Constantine and beginning with the year 313 A.D. To find the indiction of a year, add 3 to the number of the year and divide by 15; the remainder is the indiction of the year; if there is no remainder, the indiction is 15.

indulgence, see no. 179 introduction.

insignia, symbols of office, commonly referring to royal or imperial symbols; see nos. 158, 159, and 160, ch. 22, for insignia of emperor.

interdict, prohibition of performance of church services and sacraments, pronounced by ecclesiastical authority against a district or a country, frequently for the sins of its ruler.

investiture, the ceremony of induction into office, whether ecclesiastical or secular.

justice, in feudal system technically right of lord to try cases of inhabitants of his fief in his feudal court; see no. 228, 1, note 1; as a revenue, income from fines in feudal justice.

king of the Romans, title used by German kings from the time of Henry III before the imperial coronation; later also used by son of the emperor associated in the rule with his father.

landgrave, a feudal noble, practically the same as feudal count.

legate, special representative of the pope; see no. 66 introduction.

liege homage, see no. 218 introduction.

margrave, the official in control of a mark or frontier county; later a feudal noble.

marshal, see court officials.

metropolitan, as a noun, archbishop; as an adjective, archiepiscopal.

ministerial, servant of the king or great lord in Germany; being endowed with land and used as mounted followers in war, they become a lower nobility; see no. 297 introduction.

missi, in general, representatives of central government sent into local districts; in particular, the officials sent out annually by Karl the Great and his successors to oversee the administration of local officials, etc.; see no. 9 introduction.

notary, lower official in the department of the chancellor.

patriarch, in the west, honorary title attached to certain bishoprics, as patriarch of Aquileia; in East, bishop of highest rank, as patriarch of Constantinople.

patricius, see no. 48 introduction.

patrimony, estate or territory belonging to the pope as possession of office; Patrimony of St. Peter, land about Rome which was the basis of the states of the church.

Petrine theory, see no. 35.

pfahlburgers, phalburgii; see no. 139, sec. 10.

pontificate, papacy, period of rule of a pope.

pope, bishop of Rome and head of the church; titles: vicar of Christ, vicar of St. Peter, apostolic, universal, servant of the servants of God, etc.

præpositus, prévôt, provost, (1) member of chapter of canons, in charge of lands of the chapter; (2) a layman in charge of domain lands of a bishop; (3) the representative of great lord or king in local regions; (4) the chief of a gild, or the mayor of a city.

precarium, see introductory note to nos. 184-188.

prior, chief official under the abbot in a monastery; also ruler of a priory or small congregation of monks dependent on a monastery.

regalia, sovereign rights, or rights of the crown; see no. 83, no. 103 and introduction.

Schoeffen, scabini, originally board of judges for each hundred-court, established as a judicial reform by Karl the Great; from these develop Schoeffen of feudal domains and cities, as judges in the courts there.

Schultheiss, originally subordinate official of the count, who becomes presiding officer of lower public courts in Germany; name used also for presiding officer of court on territory of feudal lord, and in cities under jurisdiction of lord; see introductory note to section vii.

seneschal, see court officials.

senior, see no. 208, note.

serf, unfree tenant on a feudal estate, paying rent and services to the lord, bound to the soil, and subject to the jurisdiction of the lord's officials.

simony, use of money or secular influence to secure an ecclesiastical office; generally, securing of such an office by any means other than canonical election.

solidus, a gold or silver coin, shilling, containing 12 denarii; see no. 4, I, note 2.

suffragan bishop, one who has the right of voting for his archbishop.

synod, local council of bishopric or archbishopric summoned by the prelate.

vassal, one who has promised allegiance and fidelity to a superior, from whom he holds a fief.

villa, village or community of tenants and serfs on feudal domain, corresponding to English manor; the unit of organization of feudal estates.

wergeld, compensation for manslaughter, paid to the kindred of the slain man by slayer or his kindred; see no. 1, ch. 21, note 6, and no. 4, XLI, note 1.